THE
YEARBOOK OF ENGLISH STUDIES
VOLUME 28
1998

VOL. 28

1998

THE YEARBOOK

OF

ENGLISH STUDIES

*Eighteenth-Century Lexis
and Lexicography*

Editor

ANDREW GURR

Assistant Editor

PHILLIPA HARDMAN

Reviews Editor

LIONEL KELLY

Published by

W. S. Maney & Son Ltd

for the

Modern Humanities Research Association

The Yearbook of English Studies

is published by

W. S. MANEY & SON LTD

for the

MODERN HUMANITIES RESEARCH ASSOCIATION

and may be ordered from

The Honorary Treasurer, MHRA

King's College, Strand, London WC2R 2LS, England

ISSN 0306-2473

ISBN 0 901286 76 1

Printed in Great Britain by

W. S. MANEY AND SON LTD   LEEDS LS9 7DL   ENGLAND

Contents

ARTICLES (continued)

REVIEWS

REVIEWS (continued)

EDITORIAL NOTE

The special number for 1999 will be entitled 'The Text as Evidence: Revising Editorial Principles'. For 2000 the special number will be 'Time and Narrative'. The number for 2001 will be concerned with short stories and short fictions. Articles for the 2000 and 2001 issues and books for review submitted to *YES* and *MLR* should be sent to the Editor, Department of English, University of Reading, P.O. Box 218, Reading RG6 6AA, UK.

ANDREW GURR

Preface

ANDREW GURR

Viewed from the peaks of Pope's verse and Johnson's dictionary, the eighteenth century in England has a distinctly more logocentric and conservative appearance than either its predecessor or its successors. In fact it was a time of extraordinary adventurism and inventiveness in language use. The colonies flourished while the metropolis tried to stand still. The acquisition of new languages was an insidious but constant process. Alongside the inventions of Chatterton and Ossian stands Bishop Percy's scholarly assemblage of oral materials in various forms of dialect. Women's innovations in language joined the rapid spread of general readership for journals and novels. The new art of forgery developed through its cousins in pseudo-historical accounts that started with Defoe's *Journal of the Plague Year*, and made its challenges to the scholars who were working to develop editorial principles based on the antiquarian movement. Johnson's domination of the 'London' style stands against Captain Cook's quarrel with the ways in which Johnson's friend Hawksworth doctored the journal of his first round-the-world voyage for publication to an urban readership. Self-consciously radical neologizing appeared in the early Romantic poets such as Smart and in George Salmanazar's invented language. Even Johnson shifted his position over the need to fix the language against slippage between the first Preface of his *Dictionary* and the fourth in 1773.

There was more than a radical shift in concept between Johnson and the Wordsworth who wrote in the 1802 Preface to *Lyrical Ballads* that 'my language may frequently have suffered from those arbitrary connections of feelings and ideas with particular words and phrases, from which no man can altogether protect himself'. Wordsworth defended his use of language on the grounds that an author's own feelings 'are his stay and support; and, if he set them aside in one instance, he may be induced to repeat this act till his mind shall lose all confidence in itself, and become utterly debilitated'.[1] That was a positive assertion of the contrary principle to Johnson's. Johnson wrote in 1773 that

When we see men grow old and die at a certain time one after another, from century to century, we laugh at the elixir that promises to prolong life to a thousand years; and with equal justice may the lexicographer be derided, who being able to produce no example of a nation that has preserved their words and phrases from mutability, shall imagine that his dictionary can embalm his language, and secure it from

---

[1] William Wordsworth, *Lyrical Ballads*, Preface to the Second Edition.

corruption and decay, that it is in his power to change sublunary nature, and clear the world at once from folly, vanity, and affectation.[2]

This mock-modest defeatism should not be seen as a definitive statement about the processes of linguistic change that developed through the eighteenth century. Wordsworth's principles had been exercised in practice with various kinds of inventiveness throughout the preceding century.

The essays in this volume celebrate some of the different forms which that inventiveness took. Inevitably, almost half of them focus on lexicography and different features in Johnson's *Dictionary*. They range from the politics of Johnson's 'standard' English and the different preoccupations of eighteenth-century lexicography that its making generated to its role as a creator of the 'English' canon. Three of the others deal with different aspects of women's vocabulary, and two with cultural pluralism and translation. One studies the care Thomas Gray took for the presentation of his work in print, and one with Chatterton as a linguistic forger. One deals with turning oral traditions into written forms, and others assess some of the lexical inventions that Smart and Cleland introduced, using characteristic forms of camouflage in a century that followed Johnson in the suspicion that any change must be decay.

[2] Samuel Johnson, *Preface to the English Dictionary*, 4th Edn (1773).

Eighteenth-Century English Dictionaries and the Enlightenment

CAREY McINTOSH

Hofstra University, New York

In the eighteenth century lexicographers were still learning their trade, and perhaps we should not expect them to have been acutely sensitive to current intellectual trends. The commercial advantages of keeping very much abreast of new words and idioms were slight. Samuel Johnson, whose dictionary certainly dominated lexicography in the second half of the century, recommended the usage of earlier generations as a model, in preference to current usage. Nevertheless, whether they meant to or not, dictionaries seem to have 'become enlightened' during the course of the first fifty or seventy-five years of the eighteenth century. They reflected and promoted Enlightenment values. I shall present evidence here that the later eighteenth-century dictionaries not only exhibit an increasing awareness of the cultural ideals we associate with high Enlightenment but also embody those cultural ideals.

Most research on eighteenth-century English dictionaries has been concerned either with the evolution of lexicography or with Johnson's achievements in the field.[1] Thus, the two early dictionaries I quote from most frequently in this essay have been characterized as relying more on 'the subjective impressions and prejudices of the editor or his sources than [on] the objective documentation of language' that modern dictionaries aspire to.[2] Thus, more trivially and questionably, one scholar asserts that Johnson's was 'the first English dictionary that could in any way be considered as a standard, all its predecessors being mere lists of words in comparison'.[3]

My approach, while by no means incompatible with these two, is different: making common-sense allowances for idiosyncrasy and error, I take dictionaries as representative of their times. This is not an unproblematical assumption, given that every eighteenth-century dictionary drew heavily on

---

[1] For example, De Witt T. Starnes and Gertrude E. Noyes, *The English Dictionary from Cawdrey to Johnson 1604–1755* (Chapel Hill NC: University of North Carolina Press, 1946); Noel Edward Osselton, 'English Lexicography from the Beginning Up to and Including Johnson', in *Wörterbücher Dictionaries Dictionnaires*, ed. by Franz Josef Hausmann, Oskar Reichmann, Herbert Ernst Wiegand, and Ladislaw Zgusta, 3 vols (Berlin and New York: de Gruyter, 1990), II, 1943–53; James Sledd and Gwin J. Kolb, *Dr. Johnson's Dictionary: Essays in the Biography of a Book* (Chicago: University of Chicago Press, 1995); Roberta DeMaria, Jr, *Johnson's Dictionary and the Language of Learning* (Chapel Hill NC: University of North Carolina Press, 1986).

[2] John A. Simpson, 'Nathaniel Bailey and the Search for a Lexicographical Style', in *Lexicographers and their Works*, ed. by Gregory James, Exeter Linguistic Studies, 14 (Exeter: University of Exeter, 1989), pp. 181–82.

[3] H. B. Wheatley, as cited by Allen Reddick, *The Making of Johnson's Dictionary 1746–1773* (Cambridge: Cambridge University Press, 1990), p. 15.

its predecessors, sometimes lifting definitions word-for-word from books published fifty years earlier or more. Also, disconcertingly, dictionaries tended to stay in print: R. C. Alston reminds us that there were versions of Bullokar's *An English Expositor* published from 1616 to 1775 and of Nathan Bailey's *Universal Etymological English Dictionary* from 1721 to 1802. My approach relies on the likelihood that author and publisher could not afford a great number of obviously out-of-date and old-fashioned definitions in a dictionary intended for a wide current readership. The compilers of diction-aries and the booksellers who offered dictionaries to the public would not have printed one that seemed completely out of touch with current usage. When Ash (1775) copied Johnson (1755), or Johnson copied Bailey (1721), or Bailey copied Kersey (1708), most of the time they must have judged that the old definition was current enough.[4]

The 'enlightening' of eighteenth-century dictionaries can be observed within three areas: as changes in content; in style (form and content mixed); and in categories. Obviously, a number of trends that we associate with the Enlightenment do not figure in this essay, and I have not followed up all possible leads. Eighteenth-century dictionaries might also be quoted to illustrate the commercialization of culture, the new aestheticism, or evolving values such as charity, humanity, sensibility, sentiment, sympathy, socia-bility, cosmopolitanism, equality under the law, and the rights of man.

1: *Changes in Content*

1. First, and uncontroversially, later dictionaries retreated from the realms of magic and superstition. While it is true that even as up-to-date and science-minded a scholar as Ephraim Chambers accepted a large number of 'wondrous curiosities and supernatural cures' in his dictionary-like *Cyclopae-dia* of 1728, the general trend was undoubtedly away from magic and toward what we now regard as 'science'.[5]

For example, *javaris* is defined in Kersey (1708) as 'a Swine in *America* that has its Navel on the back', but in Ash (1775) simply as 'a kind of wild swine found in America'; for *Asterion*, Kersey gives 'a kind of Spider, the Bite of which is said to weaken the Knees; also an Herb call'd Cow-parsnep': Ash has the herb only. Kersey (1708) and Bailey (1721) define *witch*, *elf*, and *charm* in (almost identical) words ascribing magical powers to these beings, but in Ash (1775) a witch is '*supposed* to practice unlawful arts' (emphasis mine), and

[4] John Ash, *The New and Complete Dictionary of the English Language*, 2 vols (London 1775); Samuel Johnson, *A Dictionary of the English Language*, 2 vols (1755; repr. London: Times Books, 1979); Nathan Bailey, *An Universal Etymological English Dictionary* (1721; repr. Hildesheim and New York: Georg Olms, 1969); —— 4th edn 'with large Additions' (1728); —— 14th edn 'with considerable Improvements' (1751); John Kersey, *Dictionarium Anglo-Britannicum* (1708; repr. Menston: Scolar, 1969).
[5] Ephraim Chambers, *Cyclopaedia; or, an Universal Dictionary of Arts and Sciences*, 2 vols (1728; microfilm Woodbridge CT: Research Publications, 1991); Lael Ely Bradshaw, 'Ephraim Chambers's *Cyclopaedia*', in *Notable Encyclopedias of the Seventeenth and Eighteenth Centuries: Nine Predecessors of the Encyclopédie*, ed. by Frank A. Kafker (Oxford: Voltaire Foundation, 1981), p. 131.

the words of a charm are 'supposed to have some secret or unintelligible power'. In Sheridan (1780) an elf is 'supposed to be seen in wild places'; a charm is 'imagined to have some occult power'. It is not merely that the late-eighteenth-century world, as created or re-created in dictionaries, is less concerned with magic; we witness also a fading-out of the irrational and a foregrounding of known, knowable causes and effects. Kersey's definition of *gossamer* postulates mysterious forces and unexplained dangers: 'a kind of thin Cobweb-like Vapour that hovers in the Air, and is suppos'd to rot Sheep'; whereas Ash's definition of *gossamer* is a straightforward description of fact: 'The down of plants, the long white cobwebs which usually float in the air about the time of harvest'.

One must of course bear in mind that the 'Enlightenment' process was not homogeneous or straightforward, and eighteenth-century dictionaries provide evidence of this also. Kersey was a man of genuine learning, and though not a mathematician like his contemporary John Harris, he cannot be dismissed as a naïve or unsophisticated writer. He had drawn freely on Harris's scientific and technical knowledge in his abridgement of Edward Phillips's dictionary in 1706.[6] Where Phillips (1658) has '*Camelion*, a beast like a Lizard, that turneth himself into all colours, and lives by the aire', Kersey describes the camelion as 'a Creature like a Lizard, that frequents the Rocks; it lives upon Flies'. Kersey supplies not only the conventional meanings for *mass*, 'a huge heap, or pile [. . .]. All the Blood in a Humane Body', but also 'in *Natural Philosophy*, the quantity of Matter in any Body', a rather astute summary of what I take to be a Newtonian sense of the word. Kersey's definition of *gravity* confirms the notion that he had read Newton: 'Graveness, Soberness. In a Philosophical Sense, that Quality, by which all heavy Bodies, tend towards the Center of the Earth'.

On the other hand, there are occasional startling irrationalities in Kersey: '*Artificial Lines* [. . .] are Lines so contrived as to represent the Logarithmick Sines and Tangents, which will solve all Questions in Trigonometry, Navigation, &c'. '*Natural Magick* or *Natural Philosophy* [s.v. *magick*], a useful Science, teaching the Knowledge and mutual Application of Actives to Passives, so as to make many excellent Discoveries'. Here is the new science in older clothes.

2. The early dictionaries preserve more of feudalism than the later ones do. The definition of *benerth*, 'a Service formerly render'd by the Tenant to his Lord, with his Plough and Cart', appears in almost the same words in Kersey, in Bailey (1721), and in the fourteenth edition of Bailey (1751), but not in Johnson (1755) or Sheridan (1780).[7] (I have not found it in the *OED*. Perhaps it is a ghost, with no surviving texts to support it outside the

---

[6] Edward Phillips, *The New World of English Words* (1658; repr. Menston: Scolar, 1969). See Starnes and Noyes, p. 85.

[7] Thomas Sheridan, *A General Dictionary of the English Language*, 2 vols (1780; repr. Menston: Scolar, 1967).

dictionaries.) *Orenges*, '(in *Heraldry*) little Balls, usually represented of the Orange-Colour', appears in Kersey and Bailey, but not in Johnson, Ash, or Sheridan. Kersey lists the five *'Beasts of the Forest'*: 'The Hart, Hind, Hare, Boar, and Wolf', and the five Beasts of Chace, buck, doe, roe, fox, martern [sic]. Both Kersey and Bailey describe the *Falcon Gentle* as 'a sort of Hawk, so call'd from her familiar Courteous Disposition'.

3. The early dictionaries reflect a more rural world than the later ones do. The England of forest, farm and pasture is better represented. Kersey (1708) and Bailey (1721) give *barbes*, 'a Disease in Horses and Black Cattel, known by two Paps under the Tongue'. Until quite recently, farmers tended to spend more time with animals than with people. A *nest* in Kersey and Bailey is 'a little Lodgment, in which Birds hatch, and breed their Young'; Johnson's and Sheridan's definitions are less anthropomorphic and include a scientific term: 'The bed formed by the bird for incubation and feeding her young'. Many remnants of the games and customs of country folk are preserved in the early dictionaries and omitted from the late, for example: to *Nick the Pin*, 'to drink just to the Pin plac'd about the middle of a Wooden Bowl or Cup'; *Ascoltasmus*, 'a kind of Play, among Boys call'd, *Fox to thy Hole*'. One surprising rural custom appears in the first and survives in the fourteenth edition of Bailey (1721 and 1751):

Free Bench, the Custom of the Manors of *East* and *West Embourn* [. . .] if a customary Tenant die, the Widow shall have her *Free-Bench* in all his Copyhold Land, *Dum sola & casta fuerit*; but if she commit Incontinency, she forefeits her Estate; yet if she will come into the Court, riding backwards on a black Ram, with his Tail in her Hand, and say the Words following, the Steward is bound by the Custom to re-admit her to her *Free Bench*.

> *Here I am,*
> *Riding upon a black Ram,*
> *Like a Whore as I am;*
> *And for my* Crincum Crancum,
> *Have lost my* Bincum Bancum;
> *And for my Tail's Game,*
> *Have done this worldly Shame;*
> *Therefore, I pray you, Mr Steward, let me have my land again.*

This unattractive slice of country life does not appear in Bailey's *Dictionarium Britannicum* (1730).

4. Again, it is not surprising to discover that later dictionaries are more scientific than early. Scientific education of the general public proceeded gradually.[8] Kersey's entry for *abdomen*: 'that part of the belly which is between the Navel and the Privities; the lower Belly', may be compared with Johnson's for the same word, quoting a long and technical paragraph of descriptive anatomy from John Quincy's *Lexicon Physico-Medicum*, using

---

[8] G. S. Rousseau, 'Science Books and their Readers in the Eighteenth Century', in *Books and their Readers in Eighteenth-Century England*, ed. by Isabel Rivers (Leicester: Leicester University Press; New York: St Martin's Press, 1982), pp. 197–255.

terms such as 'peritonaeum' and 'hypogastrium'. The following sequence has interest because it incorporates research in biology, reflecting the century's gradual realization that, in spite of what Aristotle and Galen had taught, women (physiologically) are not just smaller men:[9]

1708: OVARIA (in *Anat.*) the Testicles of Females.

1721: OVARIA [in *Anatomy*] the Testicles of Females.

1751: OVARIA [in *Anat.*] the Testicles of Females, so named, because they breed a Kind of Eggs.

1755: *Ovary*, The part of the body in which impregnation is performed.

1775: *Ovary*, That part in which impregnation is performed; that part of a flower which becomes the fruit.

One consequence of the scientization of western thought was the gradual disappearance of local weights and measures. Most weights and measures began as the names of common objects: *foot, grain, yard* (in an early sense, 'branch' or 'staff'), *ton* ('barrel'). The first steps in the quantification of common object-words can be illustrated in phrases such as 'half a head taller' or 'at arm's length'. De-quantification also occurs: a *poke* was 'a large bag or sack whose size varied according to the quality and weight of the product enclosed'.[10] One *sack* was still in 1708 either 364 pounds or 350, and *sack* was also a measure of volume, three and a half bushels of apples in Kent, four in Worcestershire. The gallon measure used for beer was standardized under Queen Elizabeth; the gallon used for wine was not standardized till 1707, but by waiting a century it gained nine cubic inches. We can follow the quantification, de-quantification, and gradual disappearance of local weights and measurements in the dictionaries:

	1658	1676[11]	1708	1721	1755	1775	1780
cark	1/30 sarplar	1/30 sarplar	1/30 sarplar	1/30 sarplar	—	40 tod	—
frail	—	70lb	basket	basket	basket	basket	basket
fother	2000lb	2000lb	2000lb	2000lb*	—	a tun	—
gad	—	—	9–10ft	9–10ft	wedge	10ft	wedge
pearch	16½ft	16½ft**	16½ft	16½ft	—	5½yds	5½ yds
pipe	26gal	26gal	126gal	162gal	2hogshds	2hgs.	2hgs.
sarplar	80tod	80stone	80tod	40tod	—	½sack	—
tierce	1/3pipe	42gal	42gal	42gal	1/3pipe	1/3pipe	1/3pipe
tod	2stone	28lb	28lb	28lb	28lb***	28lb	28lb

*'2000*l.* at the Mines 2250*l.* among the *Plummers* at *London* 1950*l.*'
**or more than 20ft.
***Johnson supplies quotations for *gad, pipe* and *tod* from Shakespeare, for *tierce* from Jonson and Dorset.

[9] See Thomas W. Laqueur, *Making Sex: Body and Gender from the Greeks to Freud* (Cambridge, MA: Harvard University Press, 1990), p. 149.
[10] Ronald E. Zupko, *A Dictionary of English Weights and Measures* (Madison: University of Wisconsin Press, 1968), p. 130. Zupko is my source for the names of and information about the other non-standard units of measurement in this paragraph.
[11] Elisha Coles, *An English Dictionary* (1676; repr. Menston: Scolar, 1971).

The imprecisions in this table (e.g., more or fewer gallons in a pipe), and the disappearance of certain measures (e.g., cark, frail) are predictable from our knowledge of the history of science. Less predictable is the durability or reliability of the pearch, the tierce, and the tod. It is noteworthy that seven of these nine measures appear in Phillips (1658) and Cole (1676) in spite of how short those early word lists were (11,000 and 25,000 words respectively), and that (except in the case of *frail*) Johnson includes among his 40,000 words only those measuring terms that he found in literary texts. If we look for the words marked by Bailey with 'C.' ('Country Word') and 'N.C.' ('North Country') in Johnson, we may surmise that it was not only local weights and measurements that Johnson omitted, but local words of all kinds.

Though encyclopaedias and dictionaries are now considered to be two different genres – one organizes our knowledge; the other our lexicon — the distinction between them was not clear in the Middle Ages, in the Renaissance, or in the eighteenth century. And, of course, it is still blurry in the twentieth-century American 'college' dictionary, with its bite-size portions of general knowledge, its one-sentence biographies, its illustrations and maps.[12] Thomas Birch, Johnson's friend and grubstreet colleague, co-authored *A General Dictionary Historical and Critical* in ten volumes (1734–41), 'in which a new and accurate translation of [the encyclopaedia] of Mr Bayle is included': this was a so-called 'dictionary' that resembled an encyclopaedia; and the first edition of the *Encyclopaedia Britannica* seems very dictionary-like to a twentieth-century reader, with a great many pages devoted to brief entries for 'terms of art' in botany, religion, heraldry, 'sea-language', commerce, rhetoric, agriculture, and mythology.[13] Encyclopaedic entries became a feature of English dictionaries in the seventeenth century, when Edward Phillips (1658) added information as a help for reading the classics and literature; Elisha Coles (1676) included proper names (Osselton, p. 1946). Ephraim Chambers thought of himself as a 'lexicographer' and referred to his predecessors as 'former Dictionarists' (Preface, p. i).

An objective shared by dictionaries and encyclopaedias is pedagogical; and the audience that both genres hope to inform or teach is a (more or less) popular one. Both aim to supply a comparatively unknowing readership with as much advanced and scholarly information as it is looking for. Both undertake to survey the present state of learning: they satisfy a need to self-assess, to take stock of the world of knowledge. D'Alembert's general preface to the *Encyclopédie* of 1751 announces intentions of summarizing, clarifying, and arranging all knowledge. Cassirer observes that 'for this age, knowledge

[12] For full and enlightening information on 'encyclopedicity' in dictionaries, see Henri Béjoint, *Tradition and Innovation in Modern English Dictionaries* (Oxford: Clarendon Press, 1994), pp. 21–76.
[13] [William Smellie, Colin Macfarquhar, and Andrew Bell], *Encyclopaedia Britannica; Or, a Dictionary of Arts and Sciences*, 3 vols (1768–71; repr. Chicago: Encyclopaedia Britannica, 1968).

of its own activity, intellectual self-examination, and foresight are the proper function and essential task of thought'.[14]

I suspect that the tendency of dictionaries to take on the functions of encyclopaedias may have gathered momentum after 1751, when the first volume of the *Encyclopédie* was published, and may be related to the growth of what we now call science. Though Harris (1704) and Chambers (1728) had demonstrated that there was a good market for encyclopaedias in England, only one of the five 'rivals to Chambers' listed by Frank Kafker was published before 1751, and three of those five appeared in 1751–54 (Barrow, Owen, Crocker). George Lewis Scott's two-volume *Supplement to Mr. Chamber's Cyclopaedia* reached the reading public in 1753.[15]

A measure of the way scientism and encyclopaedism affected dictionaries is Johnson's paragraph on electricity in the first edition of his dictionary. For Kersey, electricity was simply 'the Quality that Amber, Jeat, Sealing-Wax, &c. have of drawing all sorts of very light Bodies to them, when rubbed', and Johnson's definition (attributed to Quincy) is not very different; but immediately following that definition Johnson writes:

Such was the account given a few years ago of electricity; but the industry of the present age, first excited by the experiments of *Gray*, has discovered in electricity a multitude of philosophical wonders. Bodies electrified by a sphere of glass, turned nimbly round, not only emit flame, but may be fitted with such a quantity of the electrical vapour, as, if discharged at once upon a human body, would endanger life. The force of this vapour has hitherto appeared instantaneous, persons at both ends of a long chain seeming to be struck at once. The philosophers are now endeavouring to intercept the strokes of lightning.

Surely Johnson's practice of quoting a long, technical analysis (from a recent, respected authority) of the word he is supposedly just defining (e.g., *mallows*, *plant*) is related to encyclopaedism and scientism in English dictionaries.

Though Johnson's innovations carried lexicography a giant step forward, though Johnson read widely in what we now call science (especially medicine), his *Dictionary* overall is a curious mixture of old and new. As DeMaria has shown, Johnson 'habitually compared himself' to learn scholar-poets of the Renaissance such as Joseph Scaliger;[16] his verbal universe was almost as much Latin as English, sixteenth and seventeenth as

[14] Jean Le Rond D'Alembert, *Preliminary Discourse to the Encyclopedia of Diderot*, trans. by Richard N. Schwab & Walter E. Rex (1751; repr. New York: Bobbs-Merrill, 1963); Ernst Cassirer, *The Philosophy of the Enlightenment*, trans. by Fritz C. A. Koelln and James Pettegrove (1932; repr. Boston: Beacon Press, 1955), pp. 3–4.
[15] Lael Ely Bradshaw, 'John Harris's *Lexicon technicum*', in *Notable Encyclopedias of the Seventeenth and Eighteenth Centuries: Nine Predecessors of the Encyclopédie*, ed. by Frank A. Kafker (Oxford: Voltaire Foundation, 1981), pp. 107–21; Frank A. Kafker, 'William Smellie's edition of the *Encylopaedia Brittanica*', in *Notable Encyclopedias of the Late Eighteenth Century: Eleven Successors of the Encyclopédie*, ed. by Frank A. Kafker (Oxford: Voltaire Foundation, 1994), p. 145. See also R. C. Alston, *A Bibliography of the English Language from the Invention of Printing to the Year 1800*, a corrected reprint of vols I–x (Ilkley: Janus Press, 1974).
[16] Robert De Maria, Jr, *The Life of Samuel Johnson: A Critical Biography* (Oxford: Blackwell, 1993), p. 219.

eighteenth-century. Together with modern, scientific entries like those on *electricity*, or on *misy* (illustrated from John Hill's *Materia Medica* of 1751), we find feudal terms such as *faldage* ('A privilege which anciently several lords reserved to themselves of setting up folds for sheep, in any fields within their manors') or *allodium* ('A possession held in absolute independence, without any acknowledgement of a lord paramount'), and rural words not in Bailey (1721), *nombles* ('The entrails of a deer'), *noggen* ('Hard; rough; harsh'), *ped* ('A small packsaddle').

One of the most encyclopaedic of eighteenth-century dictionaries is the final form of Bailey's 'Volume II'.[17] The first three editions of this 'bookseller's freak' (Starnes and Noyes, p. 108) were published in 1727, 1731, and 1737, ostensibly as a supplement to the dictionary of 1721, but also as an independent work and collection of odd words, including cant words and specialized or learned words not included in 1721. The 'final form' of this much-revised volume was assumed in 1756 (again, perhaps, as part of England's answer to the *Encyclopédie*) in its fourth edition, re-titled *The New Universal Etymological Dictionary*. The *New UED*, as I beg leave to call it, was re-revised in 1759 by 'Mr. [James] Buchanan' and went through six more editions or issues by 1776. This late spin-off from the Bailey industry (Bailey himself had died in 1742) makes a valiant effort to combine the genres of dictionary and encyclopaedia. It has a sprinkling of cuts, for example, to illustrate the coats of arms of the guilds. It omits a great many words (and the cognates of others) that appear in Kersey, Bailey (1721), Johnson, and Ash. It ignores the conventions that govern length of entries in medium-sized dictionaries, printing a good deal of detailed information on certain subjects, for instance, anatomy; whereas Johnson defines *nerve* in two short squibs and illustrates it with three short quotations, the *New UED* offers us twelve paragraphs, listing the different kinds of nerves in the body, cervical, intercostal, and so on. Another form of cross-dressing between these two genres is that the *New UED* reprints some of Johnson's illustrative quotations (e.g., *nestle*, *nice*; see Starnes and Noyes, p. 115).

II: *Changes in Style*

I have been discussing a few general trends in the content of eighteenth-century dictionaries. It seems to me, however, that what is new and different about the later dictionaries is not only a matter of content but also a matter of form, or rather of style, which in language is usually a mixture of form and content. The way entries were written in the second half of the century reflected changing assumptions about how language can most truly express what is true or important about the world. I shall suggest four approaches to these changes, arranged in order of increasing speculativeness.

[17] Nathaniel Bailey, *The New Universal Etymological Dictionary*, 6th edn (London, 1776).

1. The definitions or entries in later eighteenth-century dictionaries are more 'written' and less 'oral' than those in early dictionaries. I have examined elsewhere, at length, what the evolution of print culture did to English prose in the eighteenth century.[18] Here there is room only to sketch some principal features of this change: the move from colloquial language to formal and systematic; from physical to abstract; from less to more precise and differentiated; from informal to correct. My segue from science to print culture is not as abrupt as it may seem, since 'scientization' and the Enlightenment could scarcely have happened without changes in publishing, reading, and writing habits all over Europe. The standardization of weights and measures has close analogues in the standardization of languages.[19]

The earlier dictionaries are more colloquial in their use of language than the later ones: compare Kersey and Bailey, '*Plunge*, to dip over Head and Ears' with Ash on the same word: 'To put under water, to put into any state suddenly, to hurry into distress, to force in suddenly'. The later dictionaries are more systematic and abstract. Kersey writes, '*Oblong*, that is of a Figure, inclining to long'; Ash on the same word has: 'Longer than broad, having the form of a parallelogram'. A definition that Bailey adopted unquestioningly from Kersey, 'FASCIAE, [among *Astronomers*] are certain Rows of Spots in the Planet *Mars*, which appear like Swathes about his Body', is condensed, corrected, and depersonalized by Ash: 'the belts of Jupiter'.

Words and definitions in the early dictionaries reflect a world which was more obviously physical than the world of Johnson and Ash; the early dictionaries confront a 'creatural reality' (it is Auerbach's phrase) more directly than the later ones do. Compare Kersey: '*Pituita*, (*L.*) Phlegm, Snivel, Snot', with Ash: 'Phlegm, rheum'. Kersey defines *mucus* as 'Snot or Snivel'; Johnson's scientific definition takes place at a level of technicality far above such schoolyard terms: 'that which flows from the papillary processes through the os cribriforme'. Kersey includes '*Buggery*, the coupling of one Man with another, or of a Man or Woman with a brute Beast'. Johnson omits the word entirely, and Ash euphemizes it: 'An unnatural intercourse'.

Later dictionaries are more precise, make more distinctions, include more different sense of words, and discriminate more carefully among meanings. In general, Kersey (1708) recognizes homonyms but shies away from the task of distinguishing among different senses, for example: '*Bubo*, (*L.*) the Owl, a Bird: Also the Groin [. . .]: Also a kind of Boil, or Botch in the Kernelly Parts of the Body'. (It is typical of Kersey's not-always-perfectly-organized text that *kernelly* does not appear in his own dictionary, though *kernelled* walls have 'Cranies or Notches'.) Here the three different

[18] Some of what I say on this topic is drawn from *The Evolution of English Prose, 1700–1800: Style, Rhetoric, Politeness, Print Culture* (Cambridge University Press, forthcoming 1998).
[19] James and Lesley Milroy, *Authority in Language: Investigating Language Prescription and Standardization* (London: Routledge, 1985).

homographs spelled 'bubo' are listed seriatim in one entry, separated by colons; elsewhere Kersey describes homonyms in different entries (e.g., *budge*). Bailey sometimes incorporates several senses of one word in the same entry, and sometimes gives lists of synonyms that encompass more than one sense (Simpson, p. 188). Neither Kersey nor Bailey, however, seems to have appreciated that polysemy (the condition of having different senses or meanings) is a central feature of natural languages. Benjamin Martin's was the first English dictionary (1749) to number senses.

Johnson set a new standard for clarity in definitions and for sensitivity to different sense of English words. He is especially good at displaying the different meanings that a common word carries in different contexts. 'Even the simplest and the most monolithic' words, says Stephen Ullmann, 'have a number of different facets depending on the context and situation in which they are used'; '*multiplicity of aspects*' is a principal cause of the 'vagueness' of words and of polysemy.[20] A good example of Johnson's skills are the seven senses of the noun *taste*: the act of tasting; the sense of taste; sensibility, perception; the sensation itself, 'intellectual relish or discernment'; a trial (in Shakespeare but 'not in use'); a specimen. To each of these definitions are attached one or more illustrative quotations, which greatly enhance the clarity of the definitions by furnishing a context in which that particular sense makes sense. It would be hard to see a clear difference, for example, between sense #3 of *taste*, 'sensibility; perception', and sense #5, 'intellectual relish or discernment', without 'I have almost forgot the *taste* of fears' (*Macbeth*) for #3, and 'he had no *taste* of true glory' (Addison) for #5.

Not only are later eighteenth-century dictionaries more precise and abstract, they are also more correct than the early ones, in two ways: they prescribe correctness, and they are themselves more correct. People had been talking about 'correcting' the language at least since the 1660s, when the Royal Society, or at least several of its members, advocated a national academy like the Académie française. The climate of opinion in the 1750s favoured prescriptivism. Johnson's prescriptivism is not as authoritarian or forceful or consistent as it is reputed to be.[21] However, most dictionaries after 1755 were enlisted on the side of correctness of some sort. Ash, for example, takes his cue from Johnson in labelling *bang*, *belabour*, *cajole*, *conundrum*, and *doings* as '*used only in low or droll style*'.

The dictionaries themselves, the texts of their labels and definitions, also exemplify the new correctness of English prose of the later eighteenth century. In his definitions Bailey sometimes trips over pronoun reference: 'ABELINS, a sort of Christian Hereticks in *Africa*, who adopted Sons and

---

[20] Stephen Ullmann, *Semantics: An Introduction to the Science of Meaning* (1962; repr. New York: Barnes & Noble, 1979), p. 124.
[21] Carey McIntosh, *Common and Courtly Language: The Stylistics of Social Class in 18th-Century British Literature* (Philadelphia: University of Pennsylvania Press, 1986), pp. 56–59. Béjoint traces present-day anti-prescriptivism in British dictionaries back to the 'heritage' of Johnson (p. 119).

Daughters to inherit their Estates leaving their Children by their Wives, as if they were illegitimate' — does 'they' here refer to wives or children or to the Abelins themselves? Kersey, too, is sloppy with his pronouns: '*Ploce*, [. . .] a Rhetorical Figure, in which a Word is so repeated by way of *Emphasis*, that it not only expresses the thing signify'd, but also the Quality of it'. Compare the neater, more correctly written definition of *ploce* in Ash (1775): 'A mode of speech in which a word is repeated by way of illustration and emphasis'. Bailey's definitions sometimes violate rules for parallel construction. In the fourth edition (1728): 'To ABATE [in *Law*] to come to nought, abolished, quashed or rendred to no effect'. Compare Ash on to *abate*: 'to diminish [. . .] *In law*, to defeat, to overthrow'. Or compare Bailey's ungrammatical (and erroneous?) definition of *Abelins* with Ash's *Abelonians*: 'A sect of Christians whose distinguishing tenet was to marry and yet live in abstinence'.

2. The definitions and entries in later dictionaries aspire more strenuously to logical form than do those in earlier. That is, they more frequently approximate to the genus-plus-differentiae form that contemporary lexicography still depends on.[22] Kersey and Bailey are more likely to define by means of similes or comparisons than Johnson or Ash is. Kersey defines *ferret* as 'a little Creature like a Weesel'; Ash puts the same animal in a category: 'A quadruped of the weasel kind'. Where Kersey calls on two comparisons in '*Moose*, a Beast common in New England, as big as an Ox, and headed Like a Buck', Ash locates his moose in a biological genus and differentiates it from its fellow-members: 'An American beast, the largest of the deer kind'. Linnaeus's major publications were well known in Britain by the 1750s.

3. Associated with tendencies towards logical form are syntactic changes, including a tendency to nominalize the definitions of nominals. That is, in later dictionaries the definitions of nouns avoid finite verbs and verbals. Thus, *taper* in Kersey has three finite verbs: 'that is broader at the bottom, and grows less by Degrees, till it come to the top, like a Cone, or Pyramid'. *Taper* in Ash has zero finite verbs: 'Pyramidical, conical, regularly narrowed from the bottom to the top'. Thus in Kersey *owelty* or *ovealty* is 'an Equality of Services, when the Tenant Paravail owes as much to the Mesne, as the Mesne does to the Lord Paramount'; *ovelty* in Ash is 'A kind of equality of service in subordinate tenures'. I suspect that here syntax is an expression of the age's growing awareness of the importance not of particular categories but of categorization itself, as a way of 'telling the truth': Ash is not interested in what tenants may or may not *do* under ovelty but in what kind of a thing or condition ovelty *is*. There is no evidence that the English language began to dispense with finite verbs in the late eighteenth century, but

[22] J. R. Ayto, 'On Specifying Meaning', in *Lexicography: Principles and Practice*, ed. by R. R. K. Hartmann (London: Academic Press, 1983), pp. 89–98.

nominalization does seem to play a role in general stylistic/semantic trends.[23]

4. From the reader's point of view, numbering and illustrating senses in a dictionary is primarily a formal change. But polysemy in Johnson's dictionary made it possible to think about language in new ways. In effect, the acuity and many-sidedness of Johnson's definitions laid the groundwork for new approaches to language, including, of course, historical philology. Johnson's entries, taken as wholes, provide the substance on which some surprisingly modern semantic distinctions can be made. Gene Gragg traces 'the notion of a core or primary meaning which takes on an *appropriate, derived* or *related* meaning when *transferred* from its original domain to another' in Bréal (1897), Sperber (1923), Bloomfield (1933), and Ricoeur (1973), among others; this is Johnson's strategy in organizing entries for polysemous words such as *go*, more than forty senses of which derive from or are related to sense #1, 'to walk'. Eve Sweetser has legitimized a recognition of the role of metaphor in historical semantics; Johnson recognized, implicitly, that certain sense of words were figurative, for example, sense #7 of *taste*, above. Elizabeth Traugott has shown that the 'speech-act' sense of some words (e.g., *insist*) is one of the latest to develop, historically; Johnson's three senses of *insist* include one that denotes a speech act, 'Not to recede from terms or assertions; to persist in'.[24]

III: *Changes in Categories*

It has been recognized that the categories we think in terms of are not only 'natural' but also culture-bound and language-specific. Different cultures have different ideas for such seemingly fixed categories as 'green' and 'blue', not to mention 'vegetable' and 'fruit'. Categorization may depend on what we take as prototypical, not on necessary and sufficient conditions, on functional as well as on phenomenal attributes. 'Dirt' and 'chair' are 'cultural kinds'.[25] Eighteenth-century dictionaries reflected and propagated a

[23] Douglas Biber and Edward Finegan, 'Drift and the Evolution of English Style: A History of Three Genres', *Language*, 65 (1989), 487–517; Carey McIntosh, 'The Gentrification of English Prose, 1700–1800', in *Language and Civilization: In Honour of Otto Hietsch*, ed. by Claudia Blank (Frankfurt and New York: Lang, 1992), pp. 720–35.

[24] Gene B. Cragg, 'Redundancy and Polysemy: Reflections on a Point of Departure for Lexicology', in *Papers from the Parasession on the Lexicon*, ed. by Donka Farkas, W. M. Jacobsen, and K. W. Todrys (Chicago: Chicago Linguistic Society, 1978), p. 174; Eve Sweetser, *From Etymology to Pragmatics: Metaphorical and Cultural Aspects of Semantic Structure* (Cambridge: Cambridge University Press, 1990); Elizabeth Closs Traugott, 'From Propositional to Textual and Expressive Meanings; Some Semantic-Pragmatic Aspects of Grammaticalization', in *Perspectives on Historical Linguistics*, ed. by Winfred P. Lehman and Yakov Malkiel (Amsterdam and New York: Benjamins, 1982), pp. 245–71, and 'On the Rise of Epistemic Meanings in English: An Example of Subjectification in Semantic Change', *Language*, 65 (1989), 31–55.

[25] I rely here on John Lyons's wide-ranging summary of our new understanding of the cultural dimensions of categories: see *Linguistic Semantics: An Introduction* (Cambridge: Cambridge University Press, 1995), pp. 89–96. See also George Lakoff, *Women, Fire and Dangerous Things: What Categories Reveal about the Mind* (Chicago: University of Chicago Press, 1987); Béjoint, pp. 232–37.

dissolution or re-organization of some of the standard categories for words and ideas in English. Although we trace these changes in classifications for 'terms of art' and in the abbreviations and labels used by dictionaries, they seem related to the gradual metamorphosis of thinking called the Enlightenment.

Early English dictionaries routinely listed on the title page a string of fields or disciplines or areas of expertise, promising to explain the 'terms of art' belonging to these fields. Kersey's title-page specifies the following natural sciences: Anatomy, Botanicks, Chymistry, Mathematicks, Pharmacy, Physick, Philosophy [i.e., natural philosophy], and Surgery; non-scientific fields: Divinity, Grammar, Law, Logic, Music, Old Law, Rhetoric; professions or crafts: Cookery, Confectionery, Fishing, Fowling, Gardening, Handicrafts, Hawking, Heraldry, Horsemanship, Husbandry, Hunting, Maritime, Military, Traffick. Bailey's title page almost exactly duplicates Kersey's, with the addition of 'Carving'. If we go back to Phillips (1658), we pick up 'Magick', 'Curiosities', several sciences (Staticks, Dialling, Physiognomy, Chiromancy, Geometry, Astronomy, Astrology, Perspective), and three crafts (Jewelling, Painting, Graving).

Additional information about the categories for words in early dictionaries may be derived from the tables of abbreviations commonly found somewhere between the title-page and the first entry in the word list. These represent, of course, the first attempts to 'label' lexemes and to identify register, tasks that lexicographers continue to feel responsible for.[26] Besides the foreign languages from which a word may be derived (Latin, French, 'British', Chaldee, etc.), such tables tend to make rough distinctions among regions ('*N.C.* North-Country Word') and registers ('*H.T.* Hunting Term'; '*P.W.* Poetical Word'; '*C.* Country-Word'; '*Cant* Canting Word'). Again, abbreviations in Bailey (1721) follow those in Kersey (1708) very closely. Both employ several abbreviations for words no longer in use, but the only significant descriptor here is 'old': '*O.* Old Word'; '*O. P.* Old Phrase'; '*O. S.* Old Statute'.

It is as if words had been conceived of, at least through the first third of the eighteenth century, as belonging pretty securely either in the general pool of ordinary language or in the domain of a specialist, whether theologian or farrier, navigator, chemist, poet, farmer, or thief. All words were either current or 'old'. Less acceptable non-standard locutions could be safely attributed to criminals, rustics, or provincials. Categories and labels in the earlier dictionaries were static and limited in number. The assumption was, presumably, that just as an apprentice farrier gradually learned a finite number of technical terms used in caring for horses, so a student of natural philosophy gradually learned a finite number of technical terms used in

---

[26] R. R. K. Hartmann, 'Theory and Practice in Dictionary-Making', in *Lexicography: Principles and Practice*, ed. by R. R. K. Hartmann (London: Academic Press, 1983), pp. 3–11.

describing the natural world. Phillips at the head of his word list refers to the
fields his dictionary will explain as 'the Arts and Sciences, Liberal; and
Mechanick'.

The reduction or diffusion of this machinery in Johnson (1755) is quite
striking. Johnson's title-page is clean and uncluttered. The old categories
have not disappeared, since many of them crop up in square brackets and in
comments and labels attached at various places to an entry, but they are
attenuated. They seem to have lost their sharp edges. Some of them appear
in square brackets as labels: 'to *Abate* [In common law]'; 'to Abate [In
horsemanship]'; *frill* 'Used of a hawk', *saucisse* 'In gunnery'; *faldage* 'Old Law';
'To *Spoon*. In sea language, is when a ship being under sail in a storm cannot
bear it, but is obliged to put right before the wind. *Bailey*'. As this last entry
suggests, Johnson borrowed the definitions of some of his terms of art from
Bailey. He borrowed others from more up-to-date or scholarly authorities:
'*Arbuthnot on Diet*' (s.v. *Fetor*); the name and/or expertise of the authority cited
serves as label.

By transferring the traditional list of special fields to labels, by multiplying
fields, by naming an indefinite number of experts whose authority he is
drawing on, and by quoting (an indefinite number of) particular books,
Johnson in effect changes the nature of specialized knowledge, or of learning
itself: makes it more open-ended, and blurs the distinctions between fields.
By naming numerous authorities (e.g., on medicine: *Sharp's Surgery*, *Wiseman's
Surgery*, *Hill's Materia Medica*, Quincy, Arbuthnot, James), Johnson implies
that no one person or book has all the knowledge his reader needs even from
a single field. What seemed in Bailey to be a definite, limited number of
fields (e.g., Physick, Surgery) have begun to generate an indefinite number
of sub-specialties and an indefinite number of authorities interpreting them.

It is not simply knowledge that is changing in Johnson's hands; it is also
the perceived attributes of words themselves.[27] One senses that by avoiding
some of the labels that were standard in 1708 and 1721, he is trying to
modernize his dictionary. He does not mention forest law in his entry for
backcarry or *disafforest*; he omits the heraldic sense of *pile* that is prominent in
Phillips, Kersey, and Bailey; he refrains from listing the standard cant sense
of several standard cant words, *cunningman*, *mort*, *nick*. It is as if he had found
the labels in Bailey narrow and confining and decided to make up his own:
Enfeoff, 'low Latin'; *Blobber*, 'A word used in some counties for a bubble'. He
mixes diachronics with frequency in his label 'Not in use'. He mixes the
'normative' with the regional when he describes *thro'* as a 'barbarous
provincial word'. Judgements about currency, frequency, and speech

---

[27] For a general model of labelling, see Franz Josef Hausmann, 'Die Markierung im allgemeinen
einsprachigen Wörterbuch: eine Übersicht', in *Wörterbücher Dictionaries Dictionnaires*, ed. by F.J.
Hausmann, Oskar Reichmann, Herbert Ernst Wiegand, and Ladislav Zgusta, 3 vols (Berlin: de Gruyter,
1989), I, 649–57.

communities are combined in his comment on *to doff*: 'This word is in all its senses obsolete, and scarcely used except by rusticks'.

It is in labels that seem to be 'normative' that Johnson is most creative and most unpredictable. In addition to 'barbarous' (*wondrous* as adverb), 'low' (*ding*; *barley broth*; *to set by the ears*) and 'very low' (*yellowboy*), he marks some words as 'bad' (*fraughtage*), some as 'familiar' (*door* 2.), as 'ludicrous' (*deuce*, which he spells *deuse*), 'solemn' (*thyself* 2.), 'inelegant' (to *pleasure*), or 'not inelegant' (*salliance*). *Never so* is a 'solecism'. Johnson recognizes other forms of 'cant' than the argot of thieves: 'medical cant' (*nervous* 3.); 'the cant of the city' (*plum* 3.); 'Military cant' (*Fascine*). Fashionable slang terms are sometimes identified as cant: *frowzy*, *poachy*, *fun*. Many, perhaps most of these labels signify something other than just incorrectness; they express a set of attitudes that is compatible with Johnson's choice of illustrative quotations: literary, cosmopolitan, moralistic, and wary of recent innovations. Nevertheless, Donald Siebert has shown that Johnson was 'surprisingly receptive to post-Renaissance familiar language', including slang from the *Beggar's Opera* (*brimmer*, *gull*, *cully*, *peel*, *betty*), fashionable terms (*spark*, *witling*, *fribbler*, *hipps*), and London language (*bubby*, *bum*, *clapt*, *selling bargains*).[28]

Johnson's immediate influence on the way dictionaries treated categories and labels may be seen in Ash (1775). On the verso of Ash's title-page is a list of more than a hundred 'Abbreviations', totally reconceived from similar tables in Kersey and Bailey. The words that Ash uses to explain his abbreviations: Arts, Active, Addison, Adjective, Adverb, Ainsworth, Apocrypha, Arabic, Arbuthnot, Article, Ayliffe, Bailey, Baruch, Blackstone, and so on, are, with few exceptions, labels that identify languages, grammatical classes, and authors or books the word may be found in, not terms of art ('Architecture', 'Hunting Phrase') or register ('Country Phrase'). In the long run, however, labelling seems to have gravitated to a model less informal than Johnson and more systematic and discriminating than Bailey. The List of Abbreviations in Volume I of the *OED*, 2nd edn (1989), includes some of Bailey's disciplines, Astrology, Heraldry, Military, Music, Rhetoric, and Theology, plus numerous (modern) sciences; and the labels are less personal than Johnson's: catachrestical, colloquial, dialect, euphemistic, figurative, jocular, vulgar.

Surely the Enlightenment was a dominating context for the changes in categories of knowledge and in labelling in Johnson. With the development of the natural sciences, dialling, jewelling, and chiromancy, not to mention magic and 'Curiosities', either faded out or were integrated into other fields. One can imagine that the growth of a general readership, the proliferation of printed texts of all kinds, brought a number of specialized vocabularies into general circulation; they no longer seemed like terms of art (for example,

---

[28] Donald T. Siebert, '*Bubbled, Bamboozled*, and *Bit*: "Low Bad" Words in Johnson's *Dictionary*', in *Studies in English Literature* 26 (1986), 485–96.

given the new popularity of travel literature, an understanding of ordinary 'Sea terms' would no longer have been restricted to sailors). The old lists of crafts and intellectual disciplines no longer sufficed for an age that required specialized skills from the manufacturers of a pin and had done spadework for the modern disciplines of physics, economics, anthropology, mineralogy, and literary criticism. The 'mechanical' arts were gradually transforming from crafts to technologies.[29]

This sampling of these dictionaries seems to open up new perspectives on the Enlightenment. During the course of the eighteenth century in England, scholarly prose became more analytical. Not only did the new print culture nourish enlightened minds by facilitating the distribution of information and ideas, as Darnton and Eisenstein have shown,[30] it also seems to have changed the way ideas were expressed in English. The new 'writtenness' and logicality of dictionary entries reflected and promoted Enlightenment values of scientism and clarity. Secondly, the evolution of labels and 'Terms of Art' between 1658 and 1775 is an index of new attitudes towards language and towards learning. As several scholars have suggested, the later eighteenth century saw a new 'ordering of the arts', and changes in the socio-academic categories used by lexicographers answered to a new orientation of intellectual disciplines and fields of knowledge.[31]

[29] Larry Steward, *The Rise of Public Science: Rhetoric, Technology, and Natural Philosophy in Newtonian Britain, 1660–1750* (Cambridge: Cambridge University Press, 1992), pp. 3–27, 173.
[30] Robert Darnton, *The Literary Underground of the Old Regime* (Cambridge, MA: Harvard University Press, 1982; Elizabeth Eisenstein, 'On Revolution and the Printed Word', in *Revolution in History*, ed. by Roy Porter and Mikuláš Teich (Cambridge: Cambridge University Press, 1986), pp. 186–205.
[31] See Lawrence Lipking, *The Ordering of the Arts in Eighteenth-Century England* (Princeton: Princeton University Press, 1970); Michel Foucault, *Les Mots et les choses* (1966); trans. as *The Order of Things: An Archaeology of the Human Sciences* (New York: Random House, 1970); Robert Flint, *Philosophy as Scienta Scientarum and A History of Classifications of the Sciences* (Edinburgh: Blackwood, 1904).

Johnson's *Dictionary* and Dictionary Johnson*

ROBERT DEMARIA, JR AND GWIN J. KOLB

Vassar College and University of Chicago

Popular ideas about the authorship of dictionaries have a curious double life. On the one hand, any and all dictionaries of a given language are likely to be thought of under the impersonal rubric of 'the dictionary': we have often been told and often told others to 'look it up in the dictionary'. On the other hand, some particular dictionaries are closely identified with the names of their principal authors, or with the authors of the texts on which they are based. This is more true of eighteenth-century dictionaries of English than later ones; among works in English, it is pre-eminently true of Johnson's *Dictionary* and Webster's. Even the remote revisions and abridgements of these works retain the name of the author of the early editions. In fact, the later works are the ones actually entitled 'Johnson's' or Webster's', whereas the editions published within the authors' lifetimes have more conventional titles: *A Dictionary of the English Language* (1755) or *An American Dictionary of the English Language* (1828). The later, eponymous titles are justified in many ways, of course, but they tend to conceal the extent to which even the early editions of the great 'one-man' lexicons are heavily reliant on still earlier dictionaries and are, in a sense, only new editions of that ongoing impersonal work which popular speech, with some wisdom, has dubbed 'the dictionary'.

A Dictionary of the English Language (1755) became *Johnson's Dictionary* for some reasons that are only tangentially related to the fact that Johnson was the principal author, editor, and compiler. The appellation arose, in part, out of a certain phase in the construction of authorship in the late eighteenth century. Without denying that the eponymous title is in many ways apt, we wish to examine the extent to which *A Dictionary of the English Language* (1755) is really Johnson's personal creation. Such an inquiry leads us to ask a number of related questions. What kind of authorship and authority does Johnson achieve over his materials in the *Dictionary*? Is Johnson's personal life as a scholar and as a man visible in the *Dictionary*, as we expect it to be in the creations of most authors? Is the *Dictionary* the culmination of a 'declaration of independence' for authors, as Alvin Kernan has described Johnson's pre-publication letter to Chesterfield?[1] To what extent, on the other hand, is the *Dictionary* highly conventional, or merely compiled, the accretion of a

---

* Much of the research underlying this paper was done in the course of preparing the text, commentary, and introduction for *Johnson's Writings on the English Language*, our forthcoming volume in *The Yale Edition of the Works of Samuel Johnson*.

[1] *Samuel Johnson and the Impact of Print*, 2nd edn (Princeton, NJ: Princeton University Press, 1989), pp. 202–03.

tradition? How much, in short, is it the work of others? We do not think of *Webster's III* as Gove's Dictionary, *The Century Dictionary* as Whitney's, the *OED* as Murray's Dictionary, or *The Random House Dictionary* as Flexner's, although Philip Gove, Dwight Whitney, James A. H. Murray, and Stuart Flexner surely put creative energy into their respective productions. Lexicography changed, of course, from the eighteenth century to the twentieth, and Johnson's book may be more a one-man project than later dictionaries. However, ideas of authorship also change, and the title 'Johnson's Dictionary' may be partly a fiction created by a certain rather enthusiastic period in the construction of authorship.

If Johnson's authorship of the *Dictionary* is not fully personal and creative, what exactly is it? Without rejecting the creativity of Johnson's work, we want to consider at least two alternative kinds of authorship that seem to be exhibited in the *Dictionary*, one much older than the Romantic kind of authorship he is granted and one that is of about the same age but fundamentally different from the Romantic kind of authorship in being co-operative, communal, and even corporate in nature. It is at least as much true that Johnson simply followed a tradition or a recipe for lexicography in the *Dictionary* as it is that Johnson created the *Dictionary* from scratch. Only in particular and limited ways did Johnson create a modern literary product of his own fashioning and stamped with his identity; in many ways he was more like a medieval *scriptor* tracing the work of a true *auctor*. This combination of modern independence and medieval slavishness allies Johnson with a Renaissance or humanistic style of authorship. Secondly, there is a sense in which the *Dictionary* is a modern product without being highly individual, because like Reynolds's paintings, the *Dictionnaire* of the Académie Français, or the *Encyclopédie*, the work was, to a degree, manufactured through the efforts of a team of workers. Johnson's *Dictionary* is partly a machine-age production in that the work was to some extent done on a kind of assembly line in which the individual workers, the amanuenses, were set specific tasks which they could perform according to principles or instructions laid down by the 'chief engineer', who then reviewed the work and corrected it but did not alter it in fundamental ways.

I

How did *A Dictionary of the English Language* become *Johnson's Dictionary*? Suggesting that the book is a work of individual genius, as personal, idiosyncratic, as authoritative and perhaps as authoritarian as its famous author, the new title established itself along with certain conceptions of Johnson himself. Carlyle's well-known passage in *Heroes and Hero Worship* solidified one important view of the *Dictionary* with the famous remark, 'Had Johnson left us nothing but his *Dictionary*, one might have traced there a great intellect, a genuine man.'[2] By Carlyle's time a Romantic construction of the author as a rugged but expressive individual was well established, and the high Victorian describes Johnson in that vein. However, the tradition of looking at the *Dictionary* as a heroic expression of Johnson's intellectual strength is almost as old as the book itself. In the *Universal Visiter, and Monthly Memorialist* for January 1756, when the *Dictionary* was nine months old, Christopher Smart praised Johnson for his reliance on the King James Version of the Bible in setting the standard for correctness in English, and he added that the *Dictionary* is 'a work which I look upon with equal pleasure and amazement, as I do upon St Paul's Cathedral; each the work of *one* man, each the work of an *Englishman*'.[3] There were issues of national pride involved in the production and the marketing of Johnson's *Dictionary*, and nationalism always plays a part in the Romantic construction of the author as an individual. But Smart's analogy is interesting partly because it implicitly (and probably unintentionally) undermines what it asserts. The analogy and the assertion are, as it were, in different epochs: what Smart says about the *Dictionary* may be only as true as it is about St Paul's. Although he may not have meant it, Smart's language suggests that the *Dictionary* is no more, as well as no less, English than the cathedral, with its Italian Renaissance dome, and no more the work of one individual than any vast work of architecture requiring the efforts of many people over a long period of time. Christopher Wren lived and saw through the reconstruction of St Paul's more fully than any single architect had before seen through the construction of a cathedral, and, no doubt, Smart had this in mind, but other implications will out. Carlyle used a similar architectural metaphor, similarly intending to emphasize the expression of individuality in the *Dictionary*: he said, 'There is in it a kind of architectural nobleness; it stands there like a great solid square-built edifice, finished, symmetrically complete: you judge that a true Builder did it' (p. 183). Today we too acknowledge the creativity of architects, but we are more sensitive to the role of 'under-workers' in building and also to ancillary agents in literary production. Some popular theorists, such as Foucault, have gone so far as to replace authors with an 'author-function'. We do not propose to go to that length, but it seems obvious now that history has somewhat unjustly described the *Dictionary* as a purely independent and individual creation.[4]

---

[2] *On Heroes and Hero-Worship and the Heroic in History* (1841; repr. London: Chapman and Hall, 1897), p. 183.

[3] *Universal Visiter*, 1 (1756), p. 4.

[4] The present article does not provide the only evidence that the outlook may be changing. Although the *Dictionary* is barely mentioned, Johnson is a principal example of 'collective' authorship in Martha Woodmansee's article 'On the Author Effect: Recovering Collectivity', in *The Construction of Authorship: Textul Appropriation in Law and Literature*, ed. by Martha Woodmansee and Peter Jaszi (Durham, NC: Duke University Press, 1994), pp. 15–28. Frederick Bogel also 'deconstructs' some aspects of Johnson's authoritativeness and the nature of his authorship in 'Johnson and the Role of Authority', in *The New 18th Century*, ed. by Felicity Nussbaum and Laura Brown (New York: Methuen, 1987), pp. 189–209.

The image of Johnson as a rugged, struggling, independent (and therefore English) author was already well established in 1780 when Herbert Croft wrote about reading the *Dictionary* in his epistolary romance *Love and Madness*. Croft is known to Johnsonians mainly as the author who contributed the biography of Edward Young to Johnson's *Lives of the Poets*, another of Johnson's immense, and partly corporate works. Croft's protagonist in *Love and Madness*, a lover who eventually kills both himself and his married mistress, writes frequently about literary figures and current events that have some literary interest. He writes most about Chatterton. Indeed, the whole book may be largely an excuse for publishing an unauthorized biography of the recent suicide, but Croft imbues all writers with some of the proto-Romanticism that has always enveloped accounts of the 'amazing whelp', as Johnson described Chatterton. About Johnson's *Dictionary* Croft writes, 'What must have been Johnson's feelings, when, in his wonderful work, The English Dictionary, he cited the following passage from [Roger] Ascham, as an instance of the use of the word *Men*? "Wits live obscurely, men care not how; or die obscurely, men mark not when".'[5] The implication is that Johnson did the work alone and that it was symbolic of his life as a struggling, suffering, and expressive writer, something like Chatterton, who has been made out to be a quintessentially Romantic author, also somewhat unjustly.[6]

In addition to the interesting passages from Smart and Croft, there is plenty of better known evidence that the *Dictionary* was soon established in the popular mind as an individual, English, and idiosyncratic work, despite Thomas Edwards's professional, if somewhat cranky, condemnation of it in 1755 as merely a 'Booksellers' Jobb'.[7] Boswell probably did most to further the heroic image. His sentence in the *Life* (1791) is definitive: 'The Dictionary, with a Grammar and History of the English Language, being now at length published, in two volumes folio, the world contemplated with wonder so stupendous a work atchieved by one man, while other countries had thought such undertakings fit only for whole academies.'[8] Boswell was bent on making Johnson heroic in every way, starting with 'the infant Hercules of Toryism'; he also appreciated the contemporary practice of giving writers appellatives from their well-known works. He was 'Corsica Boswell', and Johnson was, of course, 'Dictionary Johnson'. We have not been able to determine the origin of this title, but the suggestion in this kind of naming is that the feat belongs to the individual alone and therefore identifies him. It surely derives from more traditionally heroic deeds done in war: some Homeric epithets, for example, celebrate martial triumphs, such

---

    [5] *Love and Madness* (London, 1780), p. 72.
    [6] For a corrective view, see Claude Rawson, 'Schoolboy Glee', *TLS*, 6 May 1994, pp. 3–4.
    [7] Thomas Edwards to Daniel Wray, Oxford, Bodleian Library, MS Bodl. 1012, p. 211; for a fuller discussion of Edwards's response, see James H. Sledd and Gwin J. Kolb, *Dr. Johnson's Dictionary: Essays in the Biography of a Book* (Chicago: University of Chicago Press, 1955), pp. 134–35.
    [8] *The Life of Samuel Johnson, LL.D.*, ed. by G. B. Hill, 2nd edn, rev. by L. F. Powell, 6 vols (Clarendon Press, 1934–64), I, 291.

as Hermes's epithet, 'the slayer of the Argus'. In literature such naming is a kind of identification better suited to the ideal world of Coleridge's criticism than to the more practical and historical assessments in Johnson's literary criticism.[9] Boswell's depiction of Johnson's *Dictionary* is consistent with his description of Johnson's meeting with the King, a signal passage of his *Life*. As 'Dictionary Johnson' and as the man admired by the King, Johnson achieves heroic stature.

The bibliographical life of the *Dictionary* precedes Boswell's *Life of Johnson* in making an apotheosis of the author. Two years after Johnson' death, an edition of the *Dictionary* called Harrison's (1786) was published with a portrait of Johnson in a frontispiece and some biographical material: this was a landmark effort to capitalize on popular appreciation of the Great Cham in marketing the *Dictionary*. The first editions of *A Dictionary of the English Language* called 'Johnson's Dictionary' were the posthumous miniature editions, which usually came with important additions, such as 'a concise epitome of the most remarkable events during the French Revolution' (7th edn (London, 1796)).[10] It is significant that Johnson's name was on the *Dictionary*, though not a part of the title, from the start because his first 'signed' work, *The Vanity of Human Wishes*, was published in 1749, only six years earlier. However, it is equally significant that it was only after his death that the book formally became 'Johnson's Dictionary'. Johnson's authorship of the *Dictionary* was acknowledged and touted from the start, but it was only after his death that more Romantic claims for the nature of this authorship were advanced and the book became truly eponymous.

II

As we hinted above, one aspect of the Romantic construction of authorship in the late eighteenth century was its association with national identity. Boswell established Johnson's heroic authorship of the *Dictionary*, as Smart had, partly by describing it as English, and he established the Englishness of Johnson's effort partly by describing it as militantly anti-French. But Johnson himself may have contributed to this part of the programme. He displays a certain amount of hostility to the French in the Preface and *Plan* of the *Dictionary*, and though Boswell printed the famous Johnsonian anecdote about the vast disproportion between the abilities of Frenchmen and Englishmen, he got it from Dr Adams, the Master of Pembroke College, who said he heard it from Johnson in 1748, when he was still in the early stages of making the *Dictionary*. It is hard to be sure about the authenticity of the

[9] In his biography of the middle years, *Dictionary Johnson* (New York: McGraw-Hill, 1979), James Clifford says only, 'so Johnson came to be called "Dictionary Johnson"' (p. 148), without citing anyone's use of the phrase.
[10] We must note, however, that the leather labels affixed to the backs of even the earliest editions of the *Dictionary* identify the work within the binding as 'Johnson's Dictionary', and such eponymous short titles had been common in binding for a long time before 1755.

account. There seem to be no extant notes or letters in the Boswell papers against which to check it, as the famous meeting with the King has been checked against the Caldwell minute (see Kernan, *Samuel Johnson*, pp. 44–45). It would not be surprising to find that Boswell doctored the account, but there is no evidence of that.[11] The story is famous, but it bears repeating partly because, like Christopher Smart's comparison of the *Dictionary* to St Paul's Cathedral, the account contains implications that run contrary to its apparent intent, and in this case the implications are not merely rhetorical in nature.

Dr Adams found him one day busy at his Dictionary, when the following dialogue ensued. Adams. 'This is a great work, Sir. How are you to get all the etymologies?' Johnson. 'Why, Sir, here is a shelf with Junius, and Skinner, and others; and there is a Welch gentleman who has published a collection of Welch proverbs, who will help me with the Welch'.[12] Adams. 'But, Sir, how can you do this in three years?' Johnson. 'Sir, I have no doubt that I can do it in three years'. Adams. 'But the French Academy, which consists of forty members, took forty years to compile their Dictionary'. Johnson. 'Sir, thus it is. This is the proportion. Let me see; forty times forty is sixteen hundred. As three to sixteen hundred, so is the proportion of an Englishman to a Frenchman'. (*Life*, 1, 186)

This account is dear to an Englishman's heart, but there is more to notice than the obvious Francophobia. While emphasizing the individuality of his effort, Johnson also acknowledges intellectual debts, particularly in the area of etymologies, and Johnson's handling of etymologies in the *Dictionary* perhaps best exemplifies the older kind of authorship that he exhibits in his book. Although the passage glorifies Johnson's single-handedness, it also opens the way to a correction of such glorification.

It is curious that Welsh is mentioned since it barely figures at all in the origin of English words. The old, 'universal' histories of language often spoke of Welsh as part of the background of English, but Johnson's etymologies and his 'History of the English Language' in the *Dictionary* very seldom follow these old histories. Johnson actually took only a few etymologies from William Baxter's *Glossarium Antiquitatem Britannicarum* (London, 1719) and none, as far as we know, from a book of Welsh proverbs. A 'true Briton' would like to find more Welsh in English because it would gratify his sense of the island's cultural independence from the continent, but Johnson knows better, in his book, if not in his conversation. This mention of Welsh casts some doubt on the veracity of Boswell's report. However, in the Preface to the *Dictionary* Johnson confirms Boswell's portrayal of his dependence upon the etymologists Stephen Skinner and Franciscus Junius. Johnson also used

[11] See *James Boswell's Life of Samuel Johnson: An Edition of the Original Manuscript*, 1, ed. by Marshall Waingrow (Edinburgh: Edinburgh University Press, 1994).
[12] The book of Welsh proverbs is a mystery. Hill notes, 'Thomas Richards (1710?–90) published in 1753 *Antiquae Linguae Britannicae Thesaurus*, to which are prefixed a Welsh Grammar and a collection of British proverbs'. However, I know of no references to this work in Johnson's *Dictionary*, and the publication date is five years later than the supposed date of the conversation with Dr Adams.

many other sources, mostly seventeenth-century writers.[13] There are relatively few etymologies that he seems to have researched or discovered independently, but some of his few speculations and several of his ill-advised borrowings unfairly earned him the reputation of an original and somewhat incompetent etymologist.

The odd thing about Johnson's etymologies is not that they are so bad, or that they are idiosyncratic, or merely charming, as many critics have complained. Johnson was mostly reflecting the state of etymological science as it stood in his time, and he did not do so uncritically. The odd thing is the extent to which Johnson criticizes his etymological sources while printing them anyway. The etymologies in the *Dictionary*, therefore, provide the simplest, most straightforward example of Johnson's humanistic style of authorship: he relies on the tradition of lexicography that he inherits and merely compiles his book, but at the same time he criticizes and glosses his authorities. In transcribing his etymologies, then irritably criticizing them, Johnson behaves like an early humanist, departing, with some hesitation from the medieval, scribal tradition of following 'mine auctor' or authority; he still copies out his authorities, but he comments upon them. He is certainly not a fully modern author, constructing his own literary property; he is repeating the work of others, but he is adding his personal comments.

In the Preface to the *Dictionary* Johnson contrasts his chief sources of etymologies, Junius and Skinner, in a passage modelled on Longinus's or Plutarch's contrast of Demosthenes and Cicero. It is an ironic version of the classical form, however, because Johnson uses it to denigrate both of his main sources of etymologies. In conclusion, Johnson says, 'Skinner is often ignorant but never ridiculous: Junius is always full of knowledge; but his variety distracts his judgement, and his learning is very frequently disgraced by his absurdities'.[14] Johnson defends his judgement by citing several of Junius's absurd etymologies in the next paragraph and in a longish footnote; we have to confess he is right when he says, 'it can be no criminal degree of censoriousness to charge that etymologist with want of judgement, who can seriously derive *dream* from *drama*, because *life is a drama*, and a *drama is a dream*' (sig. B1ʳ).[15] All the examples in Johnson's footnotes likewise display Junius's uninformed tendency to look at Saxonic words as reflexes of Greek or Hebrew words. It shows some scholarly sophistication on Johnson's part to prefer Skinner and to ridicule the old style of etymology that imagined it would be possible to locate the primitives of any language in older extant languages. But a preference for one authority over another is almost as much

---

[13] For further discussion of Johnson's sources of etymologies, see Robert DeMaria, Jr, 'Johnson's *Dictionary* and the "Teutonick" Roots of the English Language', in *Language and Civilisation*, ed. by Claudia Bank (Frankfurt a.M.: Lang, 1992), pp. 20–36.

[14] *A Dictionary of the English Language* (London, 1755), Preface, sig. B1ʳ.

[15] This appears in Junius's *Etymologicum Anglicanum* (Oxford, 1743) under 'dream' and is, in its turn largely a quotation of Meric Casaubon's *De Quatuor Linguis Commentationis* (London, 1650), but an admiring one.

authorial control as Johnson can achieve as an etymologist. Between his interview with Adams in 1748 and his Preface of 1755, Johnson's criticism of his sources became something of a philological position, but largely a negative one: 'Our knowledge of the northern literature is so scanty', he says in the Preface, 'that of words undoubtedly *Teutonick*, the original is not always to be found in any ancient language; and I have therefore inserted *Dutch* or *German* substitutes, which I consider not as radical but as parallel, not as the parents, but sisters of the English' (sig. B1ʳ). Although his awareness of their limitations grew, Johnson continued to use Junius and Skinner. By using these weak sources, Johnson is doing what *A Dictionary of the English Language*, as a derivative kind of work, must do, and the quality of the work that we call *Johnson's Dictionary* only comes out in his comments on their insufficiency. The part of the *Dictionary* that is truly Johnson's, in this case, is in his commentary on the work that he presents, rather than in the body of the work itself.

Despite Johnson's important place in the history of authorship, and his landmark letter to Chesterfield, he was often, in a sense, writing footnotes, if not to Plato, then to the great writers that he admired and the traditional themes that they established. This links him with humanistic forerunners, but also with many encyclopaedic writers of his own century. The footnote itself became in the eighteenth century a space for authorial expression both in France and in England. Pierre Bayle's footnotes gave him an opportunity to comment on the assemblages of material from others that constitute the body of his text. Gibbon likewise uses a more personal and individual voice in his footnotes, though he also takes a characteristic stance towards the history he presents in the body of his work. In his article on 'Encyclopédie' in the *Encyclopédie*, Diderot openly says he uses cross-references in the footnotes for a similarly critical purpose.[16] Johnson did not, like Bayle and Gibbon, write many actual footnotes, but he adopted the stance of the commentator or eighteenth-century footnote writer as he compiled his books out of the material of other books. He exemplifies this stance in his etymological entries within the *Dictionary*.

If we can hear Johnson's own voice in his critical commentary on the seventeenth-century etymologists, what does it sound like? For one thing, not surprisingly, Johnson's is a satirical voice. Meric Casaubon, whose *De Quatuor Linguis Commentationis* is representative of the old school of etymology, is ridiculed almost as often as he is mentioned. (Perhaps it was Johnson who gave George Eliot the idea to make Casaubon the type of the impractical scholar.) Under *to scamble* for instance, Johnson says, 'This word, which is scarcely in use, has much exercised the etymological sagacity of *Meric Casaubon*; but, as usual, to no purpose'. The ironic pomp of the phrase

---

[16] Denis Diderot, 'Encyclopédie' in *Encyclopédie, ou Dictionnaire Raisonné des Sciences, des Arts et des Métiers*, 28 vols (Paris and Neufchastel, 1751–72), v, 642a.

'etymological sagacity' is emphasized by the tailing, measured phrases, 'but, as usual, to no purpose'. On many occasions Johnson prefers the Germanistically oriented Skinner to the more universal and fantastic etymologists, but he often points to the ineptitude of his whole crew of sources. Under *wanton*, for example, Johnson rejects the work of John Minshew's polyglot lexicon, *The Guide into Tongues* (London, 1617): 'This word is derived by *Minshew* from *want one*, a man or woman that wants a companion. This etymology, however odd, *Junius* silently adopts. *Skinner*, who had more acuteness, cannot forbear to doubt it, but offers nothing better.' Johnson himself is very often in Skinner's position. He rejects the fanciful etymologies available to him in books, including those of Skinner at times, but knows not how to improve them. He is a compiler doubting the veracity of all his sources, yet only occasionally venturing to produce an explanation of his own. One of the best examples occurs under *oak*:

ac, æc, Saxon; which, says *Skinner*, to shew how easy it is to play the fool, under a shew of literature and deep researches, I will, for the diversion of my reader, derive from οἶκος, a house; the oak being the best timber for building. *Skinner* seems to have *Junius* in his thoughts, who on this very word has shown his usual fondness for Greek etymology, by a derivation more ridiculous than that by which *Skinner* had ridiculed him. *Ac* or *Oak*, says the grave critick, signified among the Saxons, like *robur* among the Latins, not only an *oak*, but *strength*, and may be well enough derived, *non incommode deduci potest*, from ἄλκη, strength; by taking the three first letters and then sinking the λ as is not uncommon.

Similar exercises occur under *to peep*, *to ferry*, *match*, and the famous *spider*, where Johnson, in a rare addition, goes on, tentatively, to offer his own explanation:

Skinner thinks this word softened from *spinder*, or *spinner*, from *spin*: *Junius*, with his usual felicity, dreams that it comes from σπιζειν, to extend; for the spider extends his web. Perhaps it comes from *spieden*, Dutch; *speyden*, Danish, to spy, to lye upon the catch. *Dor*, *Dora*, Saxon is a beetle, or properly an *humble bee*, or stingless bee. May not *spider* be *spy dor*, the insect that watches the *dor*?

This famous source of ridicule is worth quoting in full partly because in oral retelling it is often suggested that Johnson wrote, 'the insect that spies upon the door', which provokes more mirth than the erroneous but more learned remark that he really did make.[17]

Whether or not it is completely fair, when Johnson offers suggestions of his own, he is often open to the same kind of ridicule that he directs at his seventeenth-century sources. In effect, he becomes one with them by putting himself in their position, as well as by quoting them. In these instances he makes the *Dictionary* more truly his own, and he is more open to criticism. It is significant that in many of these instances Johnson uses the first person

---

[17] Like other commentators on the *Dictionary*, we have romanized Johnson's citations of Old English in deference to typographical convenience. Cited in its true form, in the distinct Anglo-Saxon typeface, with heavier lines, a curving vertical on the *d* and the right-hand branch of the *r* drooping down to the base line, 'dor' is less likely to be taken for 'door'.

singular pronoun, and, in effect, distinguishes his speculations from the rest of the book, which is, as it were, in the voices of others. To give just one example, in his etymology of *welaway* Johnson writes, 'this I once believed a corruption of *weal away*, that is, *happiness is gone*: so *Junius* explained it; but the Saxon explanation is walawa, *woe on woe*: from *welaway*, is formed by corruption *weladay*'.[18] The first person pronoun suggests that Johnson has a sense of himself standing outside the tradition he both criticizes and employs. His personal position is at the margins of the tradition, but the bulk of his book is comprised of received material.

At times Johnson comments on the etymologies and other parts of the *Dictionary* to drive home some of his principal themes. After tracing the etymology of *caitiff* to the Latin word *fur*, which has the same double meaning of 'slave and scoundrel', Johnson cites a Greek verse meaning that the loss of freedom destroys the better half of virtue. The connection between freedom of action and virtue is essential to the view of life that Johnson presents in the *Dictionary*. He uses his comment to enforce the moral implicit, for him, in the philological fact, much as he uses footnotes throughout his edition of Shakespeare to drive home morals, which the author reprehensibly left unspoken. However, Johnson's ethical as well as his etymological comments are comparatively rare in the *Dictionary*. For the most part he keeps his eye on the philological facts as they exist in the books out of which he compiled his book.

III

The same style of authorship exhibited in the etymologies is exemplified in the last parts of the book that Johnson composed: 'A History of the English Language' and 'A Grammar of the English Tongue'. In these works Johnson may be more scribe than author than in some of the other parts of the *Dictionary* but the proportions are not wildly out of agreement with those in the rest of his work.

In the Grammar Johnson's style of authorship is especially like that he employs in his etymologies. Johnson's 'Grammar of the English Tongue' is a patchwork composed of passages from earlier grammarians, with some additions and occasional comments. In these comments only does Johnson take a linguistic position in his Grammar and bring this weak section of the book into his own gravitational field. The chief English grammars to which he refers are John Wallis's *Grammaticae Linguae Anglicanae* (Oxford, 1653) and Ben Jonson's *English Grammar* (London, 1640).[19] Johnson is especially reliant on Wallis and praises him as 'the learned and sagacious Wallis, to whom

---

[18] Also see, for example, *huggermugger*.

[19] Johnson used the fourth edition of Wallis (Oxford, 1674). For an assessment of Wallis's work and an account of the editions, see E. J. Dobson, *English Pronunciation 1500–1700*, 2nd edn, 2 vols (Oxford: Clarendon Press, 1968).

every English grammarian owes a tribute of reverence' (sig. B1ʳ). Some of Johnson's more immediate predecessors had also relied heavily on Wallis, particularly James Greenwood in his *Essay towards a Practical English Grammar* (London, 1711). Like Greenwood, Johnson translates large sections of Wallis's grammar (which was written in Latin) into his Grammar, but when he looks at what he has done, on several occasions he rebels. For example, he prefaces his translation of Wallis's section on 'Etymologia' with a strong caveat; at several points he pauses in his translation to criticize Wallis's fancifulness in imagining correlations between sound and sense; and at the end of the section he makes four highly critical, numbered observations on what he has just transcribed, including the damning remark, 'Wallis's derivations are often so made, that by the same license any language may be deduced from any other' (sig. C2ʳ). These comments on Wallis juxtaposed with the large inclusions of his grammar provide another example of Johnson writing against the very dictionary that he has compiled. His treatment of the grammatical distinction between *ye* and *you* is characteristic of his behaviour in this part of the work. He prints a paradigm in which *thou* and *ye* are nominative singular and plural, whereas *thee* and *you* are oblique singular and plural. Johnson obviously does not believe in the distinction because he never observed it in his own writing;[20] but instead of changing the paradigm, he says only, '*You* is commonly used in modern writers for *ye*, particularly in the language of ceremony, where the second person plural is used for the second person singular, *You are my friend*' (sig. B1ᵛ). As in the etymological part of his *Dictionary*, in the Grammar Johnson mostly appears as a commentator, criticizing what he has included from his authorities but rarely becoming fully authoritative himself. Johnson can express personal preferences, as he does in his critique of the spelling reformers as 'ingenious men who have endeavoured to deserve well of their country by writing honor for honour' (sig. A2ᵛ). However, there are very long passages of the Grammar where Johnson simply, and almost blindly, compiles.

The principal exception to this kind of authorship in the Grammar occurs in Johnson's Prosody. Although Johnson certainly did not spend much effort on a theory or system of prosody, he produced an interesting series of examples illustrative of various metrical forms. He culled many of them from the same sources as those he used to find illustrative quotations for his definitions within the *Dictionary*: Dryden, Drayton, Milton, and Pope are prominent. However, Johnson seems also to have used his memory even more extensively in this section than in the rest of the *Dictionary*. He recalled bits of verse or song from less well-known writers such as Dr Walter Pope and David Lewis, Richard Glover, and Samuel Wesley. These authors are

---

[20] We have found one possible exception in a letter to Elizabeth Johnson, 31 January 1740 (*The Letters of Samuel Johnson*, ed. by Bruce Redford, 5 vols (Princeton, NJ: Princeton University Press, 1992–94), I, 24).

rarely or never cited in the *Dictionary* and in Johnson's selections from them we see, or hear, Johnson making the *Dictionary* a little more his own. This is especially evident in the anapaestic songs or popular poems that obviously circulated in Johnson's mind along with more serious works of English and classical literature. Surely it is Johnson the individual rather than the compiler who recalls part of a poem by Walter Pope that Ben Franklin also loved and affectionately called 'The Wishing Song':

> May I góvern my pássions with ábsolute swáy,
> And grow wíser and bétter as life wears awáy. (sig. D1ʳ)

Likewise, it is Johnson the individual who inserts the verses from the song, 'The Sailor's Rant', from a one-act play by Lewis Theobold called *Perseus and Andromeda*:

> When terrible tempests assail us,
>   And mountainous billows affright,
> Nor power nor wealth can avail us,
>   But skilful industry steers right. (sig. D1ʳ)[21]

The play was performed along with *King Lear* on 16–17 October 1752 at Covent Garden; it is not improbable that Johnson was present, and that he remembered the song when he came to the task of exemplifying this particular verse form in his Prosody (anapaestic, with a double accent on the last and a shortened first foot, over iambic tetrameter). This is fascinating in a work (the Grammar) that Johnson elsewhere made so little his own that when he copied the nicknames for Elizabeth given by Wallis he did not even add 'Tetty', the nickname he used for his wife. Most of the Grammar is simply compiled, but Johnson appears here and there at the margins, as it were, commenting, recalling childhood songs, and those he may have heard in performance in the theatre.

IV

The sort of authorship Johnson displays in his 'History of the English Language' is consistent with that in the Grammar, but it also raises some further questions about his control over the book as a whole. In the summer of 1754 Johnson spent five weeks in Oxford as the guest of Thomas Warton. His correspondence suggests that he made the trip in order to do research on his Grammer and History (*Letters*, 1, 81). He had access to manuscripts in the Bodleian Library, in some of the college libraries, and in what he later referred to as Francis Wise's 'nest of British and Saxon Antiquities' (*Letters*, 1, 109), this Bodleian librarian's private collection of coins and other materials in Elsfield, a village within walking distance of Oxford. Johnson owned a

---

[21] We wish to thank Michael Suarez and Linda Troost for help in locating this obscure reference.

copy of *Bernard's Catalogue*,[22] which listed the manuscript holdings in Oxford, so he would have been aware of what was available. But, despite the journey to Oxford and the access it provided, Johnson did not make use of manuscript materials in his History of English. In fact, it is unlikely that he used any books in Oxford which he did not have available to him in London. Most of his material comes from books that were, or at least eventually became, part of his own collection.[23] It is unclear why Johnson did not use the special resources of Oxford, but he wrote from Oxford to his publisher William Strahan in the summer of 1754, 'My journey will come to very little beyond the satisfaction of knowing that there is nothing to be done, and that I leave few advantages here to those that shall come after me' (*Letters*, 1, 82). At the end of his History, Johnson publicly states that he lacked materials: 'Thus I have deduced the English language from the age of Alfred to that of Elizabeth; in some parts for want of materials; but I hope in such a manner that its progress may be easily traced (sig. K2^r). Had he been willing or able to search manuscripts, Johnson surely could have augmented his work, but he was evidently only looking for printed material and perhaps mainly for previously excerpted material. He was only willing to compile; he was not willing to make the *Dictionary* more fully his own by doing original research.

Furthermore, careful examination of the long excerpts that comprise the overwhelming bulk of Johnson's History suggests that Johnson had the passages copied by amanuenses, either those directly in his employ or some he could have hired in Oxford, and that much of their work was not proof-read. Whoever the amanuenses were, they did not understand the English of the earliest selections because several combinations of letters are printed which are nonsense in Old English. If he read these sections over, Johnson himself could not have understood the language well. Someone did read the later selections critically. There are typographical corrections in the selections from a poor edition of *Tottel's Miscellany*, and at least one selection is evidently bowdlerized. The first selection from Sir Thomas More, the poem 'A Merry Iest', contains variants for which we cannot account on the basis of its extant publication record, and there is no manuscript record. These changes consistently eliminate the names of God and Christ from the poem, either deleting sections containing them or supplying phrases that fit

---

[22] *Catalogi Librorum Manuscriptorum Angliæ et Hiberniæ in Unum Collecti, cum Indice Alphabetico*, 2 vols (Oxford, 1697), mainly compiled by Edward Bernard; the short title by which the work came to be called offers a parallel to the title 'Johnson's Dictionary'.

[23] The principal evidence of what books Johnson owned is the catalogue to the sale of his library in 1785, and there is relatively little information on when he acquired most of his books. However, it seems likely that Johnson received several of the important, and expensive, sources of his lexicography, such as George Hickes's *Linguarum Veterum Septentrionalium Thesaurus*, 3 vols (Oxford, 1703), in the mid-1740s in payment for his work on the Harleian Catalogue.

the metrical scheme of the verses.[24] It appears that either Johnson or a scrupulous amanuensis was offended by the inclusion of the sacred names in such a frivolous poem and took it upon himself to excise them. There are slight traces of a similar scrupulousness in the transcription of some of the other sources, particularly Chaucer, in that the word *god* is consistently capitalized when the Judaeo-Christian deity is meant, even though the sources are inconsistent in doing so.

It is impossible to be sure who is responsible for these anomalies in the text, but some evidence points to V. J. Peyton, one of the seven amanuenses whom Johnson employed during the course of composing his project.[25] The evidence is not conclusive, and it is possible that Johnson himself did the bowdlerizing, but there is enough uncertainty here to raise a question about who even was compiling the *Dictionary*. If Peyton was responsible for part of the text of the History, perhaps Johnson's amanuenses have received less credit for the composition of the whole *Dictionary of the English Language* than they deserve.

The accepted theory concerning the composition of the *Dictionary* was gradually established over many years and most ably developed, detailed, and described by Allen Reddick.[26] It is well documented that Johnson did empirical research: he read English books and marked out passages that exemplify the usage of the words he includes in his *Dictionary*. He then passed the books over to his amanuenses, who copied the passages out. At first they copied them on to bound pages, which were to serve as copytext after Johnson had inserted definitions and etymologies. This method proved impractical for the compositors because they did not want double-sided copy but also because Johnson found he had more editing to do than was legibly possible on the written pages. After 1750, Johnson adopted a change in procedure whereby the illustrative quotations were copied on to slips of paper that could then be edited and pasted into place on the copytext pages. This made his procedure more modern and somewhat more mechanized: his slips of paper with isolated, individual bits of information on them resemble modern notecards. Yet, this isolation of his disparate materials also

---

[24] For example, the *Dictionary* simply omits these six lines.

> For Christes sake,
> Loke that you take,
> No thought within your brest:
> God may tourne all,
> And so he shall
> I trust unto the best.

In another place 'I wot' is substituted for 'God wot' (God knows).

[25] A manuscript copy of the *Chancellor's Court of the University of Oxford* made for Johnson by Peyton (now in the Beinecke Rare Books and Manuscript Library) shows that this amanuensis was still working for Johnson in 1755, when the *Dictionary* was finished. Perhaps his work on Johnson's History in 1754 stimulated Peyton himself to publish his small history of the English language in 1771. He did not draw much on Johnson's sources, however, and the variability of accuracy in the transcription of Johnson's History suggests that more than one amanuensis was assigned the task.

[26] *The Making of Johnson's Dictionary 1746–1773* (Cambridge: Cambridge University Press, 1990).

gave Johnson more control over the text because the space taken up by the illustrative quotations was then more fluid: he could trim the slips, edit them, or overlap them before they were pasted in. The preparation (and manipulation) of the slips, the buildings blocks of the largest part of the *Dictionary* has always been assumed to have been largely in Johnson's hands. There is good evidence of this: there are thirteen extant volumes in which Johnson has evidently marked passages for inclusion and put in the margins the initials of the words he wished them to illustrate. But at least one experienced lexicographer, Robert Burchfield, the editor of the Supplement of the *OED*, has suggested that Johnson probably had his helpers finding quotations as well as merely copying them.[27] No one knows exactly how much time Johnson's amanuenses worked; he never had all seven working for him at the same time; at least one was dismissed for cheating or stealing.[28] But even allowing for all this, Burchfield thinks there was time for them to do more than has usually been granted. One of these things may have been to copy Thomas More's poem and bowdlerize it. Since many of the amanuenses were Scottish, another of their contributions was probably to suggest some of the many Scots usages and occasional Scottish etymologies that appear in the *Dictionary*, a few of which are actually 'signed' or attributed to Alexander Macbean, the most experienced of Johnson's amanuenses. But the crucial question is whether or not the amanuenses helped with the primary research for the *Dictionary* and the formation of its building blocks, the illustrative quotations. If they did, then, to the extent that they did, Johnson's part in composing the book is that much more a matter of commentary and that much less a matter of original composition.

The extent of the amanuenses' contribution is impossible to calculate precisely, but the richest cache of manuscript materials relating to the composition of the *Dictionary*, the Sneyd-Gimbel volumes at the Beinecke Rare Books and Manuscript Library, is suggestive. At a minimum, these volumes indicate that the amanuenses made important contributions in the preparation of the fourth edition of the *Dictionary* in 1773. The three volumes of interleaved *Dictionary* pages are filled with slips of quotations pasted into place where they would go in the new edition. There are many slips from More, clearly not in Johnson's hand, and very probably from the same expensive copy of More's *Workes* (1557) which Johnson must have used as the source for passages of More included in the 'History of the English Language'. It is unlikely that Johnson marked up this fine volume; it seems more likely that he simply turned it over to V. J. Peyton and had him copy

[27] Burchfield presented this idea in a personal conversation with Robert DeMaria in 1981; he based his speculation on his extensive experience as a lexicographer who also, like Johnson, employed amanuenses.

[28] For the best accounts of the amanuenses see Allen Reddick, *The Making of Johnson's Dictionary*, and Eugene J. Thomas, 'A Bibliographical and Critical Analysis of Johnson's Dictionary with Special Reference to Twentieth-Century Scholarship' (unpublished doctoral thesis, University of Aberystwyth, 1974); we are indebted to both studies.

out passages of his choosing. Sir Thomas More is rarely or never quoted in the illustrative quotations of the first edition of the *Dictionary*, and it seems likely that Johnson had Peyton copy out slips for prospective use at the same time (1754) that he copied out the passages for the History, after the body of the *Dictionary* was finished. Perhaps Peyton worked from a borrowed volume and Johnson wanted to get all the use of it he could before it had to be returned.

It is hard to be sure, but some of the other works that are newly cited in the fourth edition or given new importance may have been read by the amanuenses alone. One such book is *The Whole Duty of Man* (Oxford, 1658), a very popular devotional book by Richard Allestree. The evidence concerning Johnson's attitude to this book is mixed. At least once he bought a copy as a gift and had it 'handsomely bound', so he evidently thought it useful reading (*Letters*, III, 158–59). On the other hand, he seems not to have read it himself, at least not until very late in life, well after the revision of the *Dictionary*. On the day after Easter 1781 in his diary Johnson reports reading 'the first Sunday in the Duty of Man, in which I had till then only looked at by compulsion or by chance'.[29] Unless he considered himself 'compelled' to read it for use in the *Dictionary*, as he had been by his mother early in life (*Life*, I, 67), it was probably a pious amanuensis, perhaps acting on Johnson's paternal instructions, who selected the quotations from this book that appear in the revised edition of the *Dictionary*. We shall never know whether or not an amanuensis also selected the many quotations in the first edition of the *Dictionary* that are taken from Allestree's other works, *The Government of the Tongue* and the *Decay of Christian Piety*. It is certainly possible that Johnson preferred assigning some such reading to others while he worked on the stylistically more attractive books, for which marked up copies survive: Shakespeare, Bacon, Burton, or Watts, for example, all writers whom Johnson liked.

When it comes to a few of the books cited on the slips of paper in the Sneyd-Gimbel volumes, it seems reasonable to entertain the further possibility that the works were actually chosen by the Scots amanuenses working on the job. Perhaps one of them decided on his own to include excerpts from the Scots poet Allan Ramsay, or from a pamphlet called *Anticrisis* (Edinburgh, 1754) in which the Edinburgh scholar and bookseller, Thomas Ruddiman, defends himself against the attacks of the pseudonymous 'James Man of Aberdeen'. It is of further interest that some of the remarks about special Scottish usages occur in comments in the margins of the Sneyd-Gimbel volumes — the space presumably left for authorial intervention, once the mechanical assemblage of materials was complete. These additions (for example, under *aleberry* and *bandog*) did not always make their

---

[29] *Diaries, Prayers and Annals*, ed. by E. L. McAdam, *The Yale Edition of the Works of Samuel Johnson*, I (New Haven, CT: Yale University Press, 1958), pp. 306–07.

way into the printed text, but they suggest a further expansion of the amanuenses' scope in the construction of the book.

We do not wish to exaggerate the argument here and press Johnson out of the picture of authorship in the *Dictionary*. There is good reason to believe that Johnson selected the passages for inclusion in the History, as well as most of those used in the rest of the *Dictionary*. He could certainly have selected Ruddiman and even Ramsay. As a whole, the texts in the History, like those in the illustrative quotations, are expressive of Johnson's intellectual interests. The selections from Chaucer and Thomas More, two of Johnson's favourites, for example, are very disproportionately large. Johnson planned at one time to write a biography of More, and he asked Thomas Warton to collect relevant manuscript material for him at the Bodleian Library (*Letters*, I, 112–13). Johnson was also very interested in Chaucer and once planned a critical edition of his works (*Life*, IV, 381). Boethius, whom Johnson loved and translated, appears in Johnson's History in three separate translations. Johnson's favourite theme, the vanity of human wishes, is the subject of several of the selections: some of More, Boethius, Lydgate, and Barclay's translation of the *Ship of Fools*. On the other hand, these are choices that locate Johnson in a fairly broad, somewhat pessimistic, branch of humanistic tradition, rather than marking him as an individual sensibility or intellect. If the selections are 'Johnsonian', then they are so in the sense that 'Johnsonian' means an attachment to a certain stream of western European thought rather than something highly individual or peculiar.

The same could be said about Johnson's illustrative quotations throughout the *Dictionary*; in them Johnson expresses his customary themes, but the majority of his choices, both of theme and of authorities, are conventional. As he suggests in the Preface, for example, Johnson was following many of the choices made in 1744 by Alexander Pope when he outlined a scheme of an English Dictionary. Pope's choices comprise a list of writers who are responsible for a majority of the illustrative quotations in the *Dictionary*: Bacon, Hooker, Clarendon, Tillotson, Dryden, Temple, Locke, Sprat, Atterbury, Addison, Swift, Ben Jonson, Roger L'Estrange, Congreve, Spenser, Shakespeare, Waller, Butler, Milton, and Prior.[30] Johnson's own, more personal choices are distinguishable in some pointed exclusions, such as Hobbes and Bolingbroke, who were on Pope's list but *personae non gratae* for Johnson.[31] Johnson's personal touch is also visible in some of the less frequently cited authors, the marginal figures. There are only a few citations of living authors, for example, and almost all of these suggest some personal

---

[30] Joseph Spence, *Observations, Anecdotes, and Characters of Books and Men*, ed. by James M. Osborn, 2 vols (Oxford: Clarendon Press, 1966), I, 170–71 and 374–75.
[31] Johnson conscientiously excluded Hobbes because he believed that his writings promoted immorality. In some of his comments in the *Dictionary* Johnson derides Bolingbroke on both religious and philological grounds (see *irony* and *owe* for examples of each), but very occasionally quotations from him creep in through citation of Pope's correspondence (e.g., *grace*, sense 8), perhaps through the agency of the amanuenses.

connection with Johnson — William Law, for example, a writer whom Johnson strongly recommended and by whom he said he was deeply influenced, David Garrick, Charlotte Lennox, Samuel Richardson, and Sir Joshua Reynolds. The citations from Richard Savage are also telling.

Richard Holmes makes much of the Savage quotations in his recent book, *Dr. Johnson and Mr Savage* (New York: Pantheon, 1993), which, like Croft's *Love and Madness*, explores the extent to which Johnson can be seen as a struggling, self-conscious writer of Chatterton's ilk. Holmes misses a couple of the Savage quotations, and he also misses what would certainly have interested him even more, Johnson's quotation of his own *Life of Savage*. When Johnson quotes himself in the *Dictionary*, as he does on several occasions, we see him simultaneously pursuing two models of authorship. I think it fair to say he is in these relatively rare moments both scribe and *auctor* or both compiler and creator, though perhaps the situation is more complex than that. Overall, an assessment of the sources for illustrative quotations in the *Dictionary* shows that Johnson acted here in a way similar to his procedure in creating the *Prefaces Critical and Biographical to the Works of the English Poets*, better known as *The Lives of the Poets*. In this massive collction of poets, running to fifty-six volumes (plus ten for the prefaces and two for the index) Johnson chose only five authors. The rest were chosen for him, though Johnson would surely have concurred in many of the choices, as he obviously concurred with Pope in choosing many of the sources of illustrative quotations for the English Dictionary.

V

It is reasonable to ask now whether the same styles of authorship evident in the etymologies, the Grammar, the History of English, and, to a degree, in the illustrative quotations, are predominant in the other parts of Johnson's *Dictionary*: the definitions, the wordlist itself, and the comments on usage. We have not done the research required to speak authoritatively on these parts of Johnson's book, but we venture a few remarks. It would be foolish to deny the originality of many of Johnson's definitions. His characteristically 'philosophic' diction is evident in many of them, as well as other aspects of his parallel and antithetical stylistic habits. On the other hand, research into some of his most famous and most tendentious sounding definitions has sometimes revealed that Johnson was being more traditional than it appears. His definitions of *oats* and of *Whig* and *Tory* are well-known examples.[32] Johnson made use of the definitions in earlier English dictionaries, such as Bailey's and Phillips's, and often cited them. He also translated parts of Robert Ainsworth's Latin–English dictionary into his definitions. He used

[32] See, for example, Lane Cooper, 'Dr. Johnson on Oats and Other Grains', *PMLA*, 52 (1937), 785–802, and James H. Sledd and Gwin J. Kolb, 'Johnson's Definitions of *Whig* and *Tory*', *PMLA*, 67 (1952), 882–85.

many glossaries to literary works, such as Hughes's glossary to Spenser and Urry's glossary to Chaucer, to find definitions. In addition, Johnson frequently used quotations from certain authors to take the place of definitions. He found Locke and Watts particularly useful in this regard, but he also used many citations from numerous technical writers, such as Edward Moxon, John Harris, and John Cowell. Although there are many characteristically Johnsonian and original definitions in the *Dictionary*, there are also a great many borrowings in this part of the book.[33]

In establishing his wordlist and commenting on usage, Johnson had an opportunity to be supremely authoritative and even authoritarian. Chesterfield certainly urged this role on Johnson, and Johnson was undoubtedly playing to his chosen patron when he rhetorically adopted a Roman role in *The Plan of a Dictionary of the English Language* (1747): 'When I survey the plan which I have laid before you, I cannot, my Lord, but confess, that I am frighted at its extent, and, like the soldiers of Cæsar, look on Britain as a new world, which it is almost madness to invade.'[34] In his advertisements for the *Dictionary* in *The World* Chesterfield returns the favour and amplifies it, declaring Johnson both his Caesar and his Pope: 'I will not only obey him, like an old Roman, as my dictator, but like a modern Roman, I will implicitly believe in him as my pope, and hold him to be infallible while in the chair.'[35] This would make Johnson's *Dictionary* precisely the kind of book that Diderot proposes to supersede in his essay on 'Encyclopédie' in the conscientiously collective and co-operative *Encyclopédie* (v, 636). But in the end Johnson moved closer to Diderot in his approach to authorship than Chesterfield would have wished. In the Preface Johnson removed all references to Caesar and adopted a more modest rhetorical role, one that is more largely in accord with his actual behaviour in the *Dictionary*. Admittedly, in the long course of this big book, Johnson does make many critical comments and peremptory judgements, but for much the most part he simply and humbly represents usage as he finds it. This means that he is largely dutifully compiling what he and his amanuenses have found in English books. Johnson's 'marginal' comments are numerous, all told, but they are scattered across a vast field (580 large folio sheets).

If we keep their relative paucity in mind, Johnson's editorial comments provide another instance, like the etymological comments, of Johnson writing against the more impersonal entity he himself has composed, *A Dictionary of the English Language*. In the Preface Johnson described his job in the *Dictionary* as 'not [to] form, but register the language' (sig. C1ᵛ), and registration is mostly what he does, though not without some rebellious and

[33] See Gwin J. Kolb and Ruth A. Kolb, 'The Selection and Use of the Illustrative Quotations in Dr. Johnson's *Dictionary*', in *New Aspects of Lexicography*, ed. by Howard Weinbrot (Carbondale, IL: University of Illinois Press, 1972), pp. 61–72.
[34] *The Works of Samuel Johnson*, 11 vols (Oxford: Oxford University Press, 1825), v, 21.
[35] *The World*, no. 100; repr. in 4 vols (London, 1755), III, 267.

acerbic commentary. A good example of Johnson's somewhat hesitant acquiescence in his more passive role occurs in his discussion of *latter*. He says, 'This is the comparative of *late*, though universally written with *tt*, contrary to analogy, and to our own practice in the superlative *latest*. When the thing of which the comparison is made is mentioned, we use *later*; as, this fruit is *later* than the rest; but *latter* when no comparison is expressed; as, those are *latter* fruits'. Dictionary Johnson, the authoritarian, prescriptive lexicographer, thinks it necessary to point out the deviation from the principle of analogy, but the humbler compiler of *A Dictionary of the English Language* must record the usage. To express his stoic acceptance despite his knowledge that there is a better way Johnson finishes the entry under *latter* with a famous quotation from Horace: 'Volet usus | Quem penes arbitrium est, et vis, et norma loquendi'.[36] Unlike a real Pope or Emperor, Johnson does not excommunicate or eliminate the offending usages. As he literally does in his edition of Shakespeare, in the *Dictionary* Johnson figuratively confines his emendations, as well as his personal, authorial voice to the 'footnotes' of his volume.

VI

Whatever is true about the rest of the *Dictionary*, that vast, still largely uncharted area, in which only the gems expressive of Johnson's personality are well known, surely the Preface and *Plan* are individual, personal, and expressive. After all, they contain some of Johnson's most famous sentences about himself. Yet even here, we find evidence of a kind of 'joint-stock' language, themes and even phrases which Johnson shares with other lexicographers and scholars. The common heritage that he expresses is transnational and owes as much to the French as to any other nation. This is ironic, of course, because Johnson's individuality and idiosyncrasy was from the start defined partly in terms of his hostility to the French.

Everyone remembers the putative 1,600 Frenchmen in the famous statement to Dr Adams reported by Boswell, but there is a commercial context for this remark that is less well known. An appeal to national pride was first printed in advertisements for the *Dictionary* in the month of its publication, April 1755, and included an epigram by David Garrick that begins,

> Talk of war with a Briton, he'll boldly advance,
> That one English soldier will beat ten of France;
> Would we alter the boast from the sword to the pen,
> Our odds are still greater, still greater our men.

---

[36] 'Ars Poetica', ll. 72–73; 'If custom will, whose arbitrary sway, | Words, and the forms of language, must obey' (*The Works of Horace*, trans. by Philip Francis (London, 1807), p. 347.

After exalting the works of other great English philosophers and poets, Garrick concludes,

> And Johnson, well arm'd like a hero of yore,
> Has beat forty French, and will beat forty more. (*Life*, I, 300–01)

This makes for good advertising, and there is some justification for it in the way Johnson behaves in the *Dictionary*, especially in the Preface of 1755. In fact, however, there are numerous ways in which Johnson is using the work of the French academicians and other lexicographers to articulate the issues he addresses and in many cases to find solutions to them. In addition, the stance of the individual against the academy was itself already conventional by 1755, so that in using it Johnson was, paradoxically, not being very individual. For these reasons, it is clear that the 'English' character of Johnson's book is partly a fabrication made by those who promoted the *Dictionary*, including Johnson himself. It is part and parcel of the same kind of characterization that dubs the book *Johnson's Dictionary*, rather than *A Dictionary of the English Language*.

A few examples should suffice to make the point. Take the famous statement of English independence in the Preface: Johnson nobly declares,

If an academy should be established for the cultivation of our stile, which I, who can never wish to see dependence multiplied, hope the spirit of *English* liberty will hinder or destroy, let them, instead of compiling grammars and dictionaries, endeavour, with all their influence, to stop the licence of translatours, whose idleness and ignorance, if it be suffered to proceed, will reduce us to babble a dialect of *France*.

(sig. C2ᵛ)

This is francophobic and xenophobic; it sounds like insular, northern, freedom-loving zeal. It makes Johnson heir to Byrhtnoth at the Battle of Maldon, but only rhetorically; in fact, it does not clearly distinguish him from many of his French intellectual counterparts. The remark echoes Boileau's complaints about French translators, which he made in a famous letter to the Académie: 'les trois quarts, tout au moins, de ceux les [anciens] ont traduit, étaient des ignorans ou des sots' ('three quarters, at least, of those who have translated the ancients are ignorant or idle').[37] In his *Plan*, which has less francophobic rhetoric, and was hailed for its good sense by a French journal,[38] Johnson specifically hopes to achieve the ends of a similar proposal by Boileau for correcting authors of received reputation:

If this part of the work can be well performed, it will be equivalent to the proposal made by Boileau to the academicians, that they should review all their polite writers, and correct such impurities as might be found in them, that their authority might not contribute, at any distant time, to the depravation of the language. (*Works*, v, 19)

---

[37] *Lives of the English Poets*, ed. by George Birkbeck Hill, 3 vols (Oxford: Clarendon Press, 1905), III, 237, n. 4; Hill cites *Œuvres de Boileau* (1747), v, 118.
[38] *Bibliotheque raisonné des ouvrages des savans* (July–September 1747).

4

In the Preface of 1755 Johnson removed the reference to Boileau and portrayed his Boileau-like concern about translation in terms of hostility to Boileau's country.

As he well knew, in distinguishing his efforts from those of academies, and academic societies, Johnson is not necessarily setting himself apart from French intellectual life or French men of letters in general. In fact, his juxtaposition between the individual lexicographer and the academy allies him with continental poets and scholars, like Boileau, whom he admired. Johnson's most famous juxtaposition occurs at the very end of the Preface:

It may gratify curiosity to inform [the world], that the *English Dictionary* was written with little assistance of the learned, and without any patronage of the great; not in the soft obscurities of retirement, or under the shelter of academick bowers, but amidst inconvenience and distraction, in sickness and in sorrow. It may repress the triumph of malignant criticism to observe, that if our language is not here fully displayed, I have only failed in an attempt which no human powers have hitherto completed. If the lexicons of ancient tongues, now immutably fixed, and comprised in a few volumes, are yet, after the toil of successive ages, inadequate and delusive; if the aggregated knowledge, and co-operating diligence of the *Italian* academicians, did not secure them from the censure of *Beni*; if the embodied criticks of *France*, when fifty years had been spent upon their work, were obliged to change its oeconomy, and give their second edition another form. I may surely be contented without the praise of perfection. (sig. C2ᵛ)

Despite the fact that it is tempting to read this passage, as Herbert Croft must have read it, as a declaration of the lonely, Romantic, original author's feelings, the passage both shows Johnson's awareness of lexicographical tradition, and is itself highly conventional. Johnson really had this opinion about academies; he expressed it clearly in *Adventurer*, no. 45 and in his 'Life' of Roscommon, but it is neither original with him nor uniquely English. Not only had his countryman, Ephraim Chambers expressed it before in similar terms,[39] it also had appeared in continental works, such as Johann Mathias Gesner's preface to the 1735 edition of Faber's *Thesaurus Eruditionis Scholasticae*. Gesner also compares his dictionary, as the work of individuals, to the dictionaries of the French and Italian academies. Like Johnson, he expresses some envy of their privileged circumstances, and he cites their failures before asking, rhetorically and pathetically, how his book could possibly achieve perfection: 'Quis deinde miretur Lexicon linguae Latinae per libros non sane nimium multos dispersae, sed eos difficultatibus magnis obsitos, ab singulis hominibus, qui quo plus ingenii adferre possent ad laborem eum, tanto sunt vel impatientiores, vel aliis in rebus occupatiores; quibus exigua lucri spes, gloria etiam minor proposita est, nondem potuisse ita expoliri, ut non relictus sit emendationi locus?' ('Then who can wonder

---

[39] In his *Considerations Preparatory to a Second Edition* (n.p., n.d. [*c.* 1730]) Ephraim Chambers hopes the new, collaborative edition of his *Cyclopedia* will 'abundantly indemnify us in the Want of what other Countries are so fond of, Royal, Imperial, Caesarian, and Ducal Academies, Palatine Societies, and the like: Splendid Names, pompous Titles, but rarely productive of Fruits answerable thereto!' (p. 4).

that a dictionary of the Latin language (which is distributed into not many books but books hedged round with great difficulties) executed by private individuals, who brought as much effort to the task as their patience or their involvement in other matters permitted, who had little hope of profit and less prospect of fame — is it surprising that the dictionary has not yet been perfected to such an extent that there remains no room for improvement?').[40]

Johnson sounds like Gesner, although he outdoes him by being only one individual, one who does not even enjoy the 'shelter of academick bowers', like Gesner's collaborators: 'illi umbratici de schola homines' (sig. b2ʳ). Yet, the similarity in the phrasing is striking, and there is some evidence that writing the *Dictionary* gave Johnson academic longings. In his letter of thanks to Oxford for granting him an honorary MA (26 February 1755) Johnson does describe himself as 'umbraticus', one who is shaded, an academic (*Letters*, 1, 99). The university degree was solicited to grace the title page of the forthcoming *Dictionary*. It was not enough for the publishers to put Johnson's name on the title page; they, and Johnson (*Letters*, 1, 88–89), wanted the academic acknowledgement for this work for commercial reasons, as they did later for Johnson's edition of Shakespeare. Just before the publication of that grand work (1765) Johnson received his LL D from Trinity College, Dublin. For Johnson's other works the title was not seen as so necessary. On the titlepage of the *Lives of the Poets*, for example, he is merely Samuel Johnson, although by this time he had received the much more highly valued Oxford LL D. On the titlepage of the *Dictionary*, Johnson is Samuel Johnson, A. M. and, in a sense, he acknowledged that writing that book made him a member of the academy, *malgre lui*.

The opposition between Johnson the individualist and the French academicians becomes most formulaic in light of the fact that such an opposition was already part of the rhetoric of French arguments about the proper construction of dictionaries. Well before its publication the *Dictionnaire de L'Académie* (Paris, 1694) was assaulted by Furetière, primarily for its plan to exclude technical terms. In 1690, two years after his death, Furetière's followers published his *Dictionnaire universel, contenant généralement tous les mots français tant vieux que modernes et les terms des sciences et des arts*. The Académie responded immediately with two supplementary volumes, edited by Pierre Corneille, *Dictionnaire des artes et des sciences* (Paris, 1694). But they did not mix this work with their principal dictionary, and the revisions of the *Dictionnaire de l'Académie* in 1718 and 1740 admit only slightly more technical terms into the main word list. The Furetière camp fought the Académie all the way, and as his survivors continued revising his work, they operated in fierce

[40] *Thesaurus Eruditionis Scholasticae* (Lipsiae, 1735), sig. b2ʳ.

opposition to it.[41] When Johnson issues his last, elegiac envoy, he sounds surprisingly like the editors of Furetière's *Dictionnaire universel* (1721). Like his French forerunners, Johnson wrote in his Preface against the possibility of achieving the praise of perfection, 'which, if I could obtain, in this gloom of solitude', he says, 'what would it avail me? I have protracted my work till most of those whom I wished to please, have sunk into the grave, and success and miscarriage are empty sounds: I therefore dismiss it with frigid tranquillity, having little to fear or hope from censure or from praise' (sig. C2ᵛ). The gloomy editors of the late Furetière had put it very much this way: 'Il peut s'assurer que nous porterons sur cela [toute l'aigreur] l'indifférence jusqu' à l'insensibilité. Sans répondre à rien, nous aban-donnerons au Public tous nos interêts et le soin de juger qui a raison, et à nos successeurs.' ('He can be sure that for these bitter disputes we bear an indifference bordering on insensibility. Without responding at all, we abandon our interest and the task of judging who is right to the Public').[42]

The tone of Furetière's legatees is grave partly because the author of their work died while working on it, but even they were being conventional because by 1721 the death of the lexicographer had already become a frequent subject in the prefaces of dictionaries.[43] Stephen Skinner's death is lamented in the preface to his *Etymologicon Linguae Anglicanae* (1671), and a lamentation over the death of Franciscus Quercus makes part of Thomas Holyoke's lugubrious history of lexicography in *A Large Dictionary* (1677). The death of Furetière before the publication of his book is described by later editors as a 'Grand example de la vanité des occupations des Savans [. . .] vanitas vanitatum, et omnia vanitas'.[44] It is likely that Johnson read such passages in earlier dictionaries, and his bosom certainly returned an echo to their treatment of the vanity of human learning. Johnson's elegiac and traditional sentiments in the Preface connect him to that lugubrious tradition of humanistic lexicography, and they set him apart from Diderot and D'Alembert, who conceived of a more corporate and collective kind of authorship for the encyclopaedists, one in which they would overcome their own death, and even the death of their civilization through their efforts (v, 644.) On the other hand, in spite of Johnson's old-world rhetoric, his *Dictionary* exhibits some of the corporate and collective features of Diderot's 'modern', impersonal book. One of these features, ironically, is the use of much material from earlier books, including, in Johnson's case, their personal sounding rhetoric, to make new books.

[41] *Dictionnaire universel* was revised and re-edited by Basnage de Bauval (1701 and 1708) and Brutel de la Rivière (1727) and augmented by the editors of the *Journal de Trévoux* in 1704 in three volumes; in 1721 in five volumes; in 1732–34 in five volumes (when it became known as the *Dictionnaire de Trévoux*); in 1743 in six volumes; and in 1752 in seven volumes plus a supplement.

[42] *Dictionnaire universel François et Latin*, 5 vols (Paris, 1721), I, xi.

[43] See the excellent article by Paul Korshin on this subject, 'Johnson and the Renaissance Dictionary', *Journal of the History of Ideas*, 35 (1974), 300–12.

[44] *Dictionnaire universel François et Latin*, 6 vols (Paris, 1743), I, xiv.

Precisely how should we think of Johnson's authorship of the *Dictionary*? Despite all we have said, it would be incorrect to dismiss the personal or even the 'Romantic' element that advertisers and glorifiers exaggerated. After all, Johnson referred to the *Dictionary* as 'his book', and his identification with the work is attested, amongst other ways, in the oft-quoted private prayer that he wrote when he set to work on the second volume (*Diaries*, p. 50). Moreover, for Johnson, his adoption of conventional sentiments about lexicography and his presentation of himself in terms inherited from his forerunners were not necessarily impersonal acts. Throughout his writing Johnson shows that he can use conventional terms to make statements that are undeniably his own. The Preface and the *Plan* are original pieces of writing even though they use conventional themes and imitations of remembered phrases. Like so many of Johnson's finest compositions, these works are fuelled by their attachment to a tradition, a transnational Latin humanist tradition that flourished in France as well as in England. The same may be said for the *Dictionary* as a whole. What should be meant by the phrase *Johnson's Dictionary* is not a one-man, individualistic, and lonely expression of philological dictates, but a redaction of long and varied traditions of lexicography. Yet, this redaction carries a kind of colouring or rubrication that is Johnson's own and a vein of commentary that inscribes his signature indelibly on the English Dictionary.

Johnson's *Dictionary* and the Canon:
Authors and Authority

ANNE McDERMOTT

University of Birmingham

Accounts of eighteenth-century literature have usually attributed the rise of literary history, and with it the inception of canon-making, to the second half of the century. Lawrence Lipking argues that there was 'no great native history of any art, no canon of what was best, no model of a standard of taste' before the middle of the eighteenth century, and he cites as key texts which contributed to the 'ordering of the arts' Warton's *History of English Poetry* (1774–81) and Johnson's *Lives of the Poets* (1779–81).[1] But this places both these developments later than they should be. Literary history, in the sense of a consciousness of English literature as a tradition which none the less changed from age to age and required interpretation within a historical context, goes back at least as far as Dryden.[2] Canon-making, as has recently been argued, has an even older history.[3] One of the issues I wish to address is the manner in which we might read Johnson's *Dictionary* as embodying a canon in its inclusion of quotations from a collection of writers from what Johnson regards as the golden age of literature, the 'wells of English

[1] Lawrence Lipking, *The Ordering of the Arts in Eighteenth-Century England* (Princeton, NJ: Princeton University Press, 1970), p. 3.

[2] Lipking argues that it was not until the period 1762–90 that histories of the various arts were written: painting by Walpole and Reynolds; music by Hawkins and Burney; poetry by Wharton and Johnson (in the *Lives of the Poets*). René Wellek had earlier argued that the rise of English literary history came only when there emerged an awareness of poems, poets, and periods; a sense of period and of development from one poet to the next; a recognition of the importance of the age in which a poet lived, a sense of historical context; see *The Rise of English Literary History* (Chapel Hill: University of North Carolina Press, 1941), p. 132. Dryden shows an awareness of these things in his 'Heads of an Answer to Rymer': 'Shakespeare and Fletcher have written to the Genius of the Age and Nation in which they liv'd: For tho' Nature, as [Rymer] objects, is the same in all Places, and Reason too the same; yet the climate, the Age, the Dispositions of the People to whom a poet writes may be so different that what pleas'd the *Greeks* would not satisfie an *English* audience', *The Works of John Dryden*, ed. by Edward Niles Hooker, H. T. Swedenborg, Jr and others, 20 vols (Berkeley and Los Angeles: University of California Press, 1956–89), XVII: *Prose 1668–1691*, ed. by Samuel Holt Monk and A. E. Wallace Maurer (1971), p. 188.

[3] See Trevor Ross, *Albion's Parnassus: The Making of the English Literary Canon* (unpublished doctoral dissertation, University of Toronto, 1988), and an article with some of the same material, 'Just When Did "British bards begin t'Immortalize"?', *Studies in Eighteenth-Century Culture*, 19 (1989), 383–98. In a more recent article, 'The Emergence of "Literature": Making and Reading the English Canon', *ELH*, 63 (1996), 397–422, Ross modifies his argument slightly by suggesting that canon-formation in the earlier period is subject to a 'restrictive presentism' (p. 403) by which works from the past were deemed canonical only if they 'could be clearly shown to contribute in some way to the productivity and stature of the present age, or to the circulation of contemporary values' (p. 401). See also Howard Felperin, *The Uses of the Canon: Elizabethan Literature and Contemporary Theory* (Oxford: Clarendon Press, 1990); Richard McKeon, 'Canonic Books and Prohibited Books: Orthodoxy and Heresy in Religion and Culture', *Critical Inquiry* (1975), 774–94; Douglas Lane Patey, 'The Eighteenth Century Invents the Canon', *Modern Language Studies*, 18 (1988), who offers the counter-argument to Ross.

undefiled', considering how this canon is constituted and what are its sources of authorization, both in selection and evaluation.

Alvin Kernan writes elegantly and persuasively of the period after the Restoration as marking the onset of a sudden rush of canon-making and he associates this with the emergence of a print culture and the professionalization of the world of letters — both developments in which Johnson was intimately involved — but, though Kernan remarks that Whiggish theories of progress have failed to satisfy in their explanation of the radical technological changes brought about by the institution of a new print-based, market-centred system, he is himself guilty of a Whiggish explanation of the ideology underlying such change. He interprets the professionalization and expansion of literature in the eighteenth century as a revolution in which the *ancien régime* of court and aristocracy was swept aside in a radical *coup d'état* and a new world of writing with distinctly democratic tendencies instituted. 'In the eighteenth century', he argues, 'the first, most radical tendency of print and its logic of multiplicity was to destroy the canon of courtly letters centered on the classics and in a revolutionary, democratic manner to level all books in a continuous surge of new, ever-accumulating print products'.[4] Kernan seems unsure whether this movement represents one of the consequences of 'capitalist tendencies' or a kind of 'literary Maoism', but he is not the first to interpret eighteenth-century, and more especially Johnson's writings in this politically proleptic manner (pp. 9, 159).[5]

The thinking that lies behind this point of view is that the expansion of literacy and of the reading public in the eighteenth century can be related to the expansion of the electorate, and both of these can be explained and causally related to developments in the primary modes of production, in print technology, and in the economic conditions that led to the demise of the patronage system and the rise of the independent professional man of letters. Kernan makes this link explicit when he writes: 'An older system of polite or courtly letters — primarily oral, aristocratic, amateur, authoritarian, court-centered — was swept away at this time and gradually replaced by a new print-based, market-centered, democratic literary system in which the major conceptions and values of literature were, while not strictly determined by print ways, still indirectly in accordance with the actualities of the print situation' (p. 4).

[4] Alvin Kernan, *Samuel Johnson & the Impact of Print* (Princeton: Princeton University Press, 1987), p. 159.
[5] Robert DeMaria also makes Johnson's *Dictionary* a monument in the progress towards democracy in his article 'The Politics of Johnson's *Dictionary*', *PMLA*, 104 (1989), 64–74, where he argues that 'the *Dictionary*, by virtue of its range of selection and presentation, belongs to the liberal tradition and fosters democracy' (p. 72). John Barrell refers to 'the general sense by which Britain is understood, in the eighteenth century, to be a democracy, a form of polity which enables and demands consideration of the whole of society, even of its unpresented, or 'virtually' represented members', in *English Language in History 1730–80: An Equal Wide Survey* (London: Hutchinson, 1983), p. 21. This causes him to allege misleadingly that Johnson refuses 'to consider the rights of the language community as an issue of any importance in the questions of how language is to be used, and on whose terms it is to be "settled"', p. 148.

On this view Johnson's *Dictionary* is a key text in the emergence of print culture, and Johnson himself, with his repudiation of patronage in his letter to Lord Chesterfield and his abjuration of critical authority in his appeal to the common reader, is a key figure in the development of the modern idea of an author. There is a parallel to be drawn, though Kernan does not do so explicitly, between the ideological changes shaping the superstructure of culture and the change in thinking which Johnson underwent while writing the *Dictionary*, as he abandoned his effort to fix the language in an authoritarian prescriptive fashion and bowed to the inexorable pressure of common usage. All this is persuasive, except for the expression of these ideas using the terminology of modern political concepts of democracy. Kernan's metaphors are thus conceptually misleading, as when he writes of Johnson's discovery while writing the *Dictionary* that 'language [. . .] has a democratic basis, existing finally only in the mouths and hands of the many who in their variety and endless change of interests make of it a "boundless chaos" ', making it sound as though the newly-literate reading public of the mid-eighteenth century had just been linguistically enfranchised in the same way that, it is assumed, they were gradually being politically enfranchised (pp. 200–01).

These metaphors are misleading because incipient democratic movements such as the Wilkite and American agitations, or the campaign for economical reform taken up by the Rockingham Whigs, did not occur until the 1770s, and incidentally caused Johnson some dismay.[6] Earlier legislation, such as the 1758 Freeholders Act and a further Act of 1760, far from extending the franchise, in fact had the effect of considerably reducing the electorate as property qualifications were increased.[7] It is this same kind of thinking which causes Robert DeMaria to give a misleading reading of the entry for 'Grubstreet' in the *Dictionary*. Under the definition of the street as a place 'inhabited by writers of small histories, dictionaries, and temporary poems; whence any mean production is called a grubstreet', Johnson appends two lines of Greek:

Χᾶιρ Ιθαχὴ μετ' ἄεθλα, μετ' ἄλγεα πιχρὰ
Ἀσπασίως τέον ὁδας ἱχάνομχι.

which DeMaria translates as:

Hail, Ithaca! after struggles and bitter hardships,
I happily arrive at your border.

DeMaria describes this as 'Johnson's oath of allegiance to his profession and perhaps also to the new, more democratic society it both depended on and

---

[6] He bemoaned the decline of authority and subordination in all areas of social and political life; see James Boswell, *Life of Samuel Johnson*, ed. by G. B. Hill, rev. by L. F. Powell, 6 vols (Oxford: Clarendon Press, 1934–50), III, 262.

[7] 31 George II c. 14 and 33 George II c. 20. See John Cannon, *Samuel Johnson and the Politics of Hanoverian England* (Oxford: Clarendon Press, 1994), p. 145.

fostered', but Johnson is making no expression of solidarity here with his hack-writing brethren, even though many of them were his friends and associates.[8] Ithaca would hardly have had connotations of democracy for Johnson; it seems far more likely that this reference to Odysseus's salute on returning home from his wanderings represents Johnson's awareness of having arrived, with the publication of his *Dictionary*, on the threshold of the world of learning after years spent in the same wretched poverty and obscurity as the Grub Street hacks. If anything, it is a renunciation of Grub Street (though Johnson never forgot his friends and never scorned their way of life). In his letter to Lord Chesterfield Johnson describes himself as 'uncourtly', but he also, significantly, describes himself as a 'scholar'.

However, Kernan is right to assert that new kinds of literary order and new sources of literary authority were being sought in the early eighteenth century as the old certainties disappeared; a small, unified, relatively cohesive, mostly aristocratic, learned group found that readership and literacy had expanded to include lower-class and unlearned readers who were ignorant of the classical languages and literature. As Howard Weinbrot has recently shown, there was a movement from the late seventeenth century onwards away from classical and towards native, British vernacular values, manifesting itself in a nationalist aesthetic in texts such as Dryden's *Essay of Dramatick Poesie* and Pope's *Rape of the Lock* and *Windsor Forest*, and later in the eighteenth century in an interest in Hebrew and Celtic languages and culture.[9] Elizabeth Elstob's *Rudiments of Grammar for the English-Saxon Tongue* was a key text in the rebirth of Saxon studies and rckindled interest in the vernacular language: as she states in her preface, her purpose was 'to shew the *polite* Men of our Age, that the Language of their Forefathers is neither so barren nor barbarous as they affirm, with equal Ignorance and Boldness'.[10] This did not mean, however, that the canon disappeared; it remained much as it had for the Restoration, but the sources of authority and the orthodoxies underlying the canon had radically changed.

Weinbrot includes numerous examples of canonical statements, ranging from the frontispiece to Matthew Pilkington's *Poems on Several Occasions* (1730), with its depiction of the major English poets, to Michael Wodhull's 'Ode to the Muses' (1760), in which a line of British worthies replace the classics. Thomas Birch's translation of Pierre Bayle's *Dictionnaire historique et critique* (1697; trans. 1734–41) adds hundreds of British biographies to the original, and these are ranged in a kind of order of merit. Part of this emerges from the century's *esprit de système*, the rage for order which took the

---

[8] DeMaria, 'The Politics of Johnson's *Dictionary*', p. 73. This interpretation was made earlier by DeMaria in *Johnson's Dictionary and the Language of Learning* (Chapel Hill and London: University of North Carolina Press, 1987) in which he refers to these lines as 'a salute to his literary homeland' and 'his own vocational identification with that locale' (pp. 26, 207).

[9] Howard D. Weinbrot, *Britannia's Issue: The Rise of British Literature from Dryden to Ossian* (Cambridge: Cambridge University Press, 1993).

[10] *Rudiments of Grammar for the English-Saxon Tongue* (1715), p. iii.

'boundless chaos' of all areas of learning from natural history to literature and went to work with a systematizing logic, subdividing and categorizing, and producing ordered descriptions ranging from Newton's division of light into the colour spectrum to Linnaeus's taxonomies. Johnson's cataloguing of the Harleian catalogue may be viewed as the quintessential taxonomic act.

This tabulating mentality was displayed in trivial games as well as in serious attempts at canon-construction. Hester Thrale had a penchant for giving her friends marks out of twenty for various qualities, while Joseph Spence constructed one of the first evaluative scales for poetry:

To distinguish ye Characters of the Poets one might use the known marks for ye different magnitudes of the Stars.

1   a great Genius, a fine writer.
2   a great Genius.
3   a fine writer.
4   a good poet in gen[era]l.
5   a tolerable Poet for ye times he lived in.
6   a middling Poet.
7   a bad Poet.
†   one never to be read.[11]

In most discussions of canon-making in the eighteenth century the *Lives of the Poets* are presented as a pivotal text. They collectively present 'Prefaces, biographical and critical, to the *most eminent* of the English poets' (my italics) and Boswell describes them as 'an elegant and accurate edition of all the English poets of reputation'.[12] But if they do represent a canon of English poetry, it is not one of Johnson's selection. He objected fiercely to the booksellers' marketing of the text: 'It is a great impudence to put *Johnson's Poets* on the back of books which Johnson neither recommended nor revised: He recommended only Blackmore on the Creation and Watts. How then are they Johnson's? This is indecent.'[13] Thomas Bonnell argues that the *Lives of the Poets* was designed as a marketing ploy to divert attention away from Bell's reprint series which was considerably cheaper and therefore available to a wider readership.[14] The deliberate presentation of the text as containing the 'most eminent' poets in an expensive edition, apparently authorized by Johnson, reinforces the impression of this text as a canon, but Johnson's critical practice within the text countervails against this impression. There seems no obvious reason why Johnson would have requested the inclusion

---

[11] *Thraliana: The Diary of Mrs. Hester Lynch Thrale (Later Mrs Piozzi) 1776–1809*, ed. by Katherine C. Balderston, 2nd edn, 2 vols (Oxford: Clarendon Press, 1951), I, 329; cited in James M. Osborn, 'Joseph Spence's Collections Relating to the Lives of the Poets', *Harvard Library Bulletin*, 16 (1968), 132. In Hester Thrale's classification Johnson receives 20 for Religion, Morality and General Knowledge, 19 for Scholarship, 0 for Person and Voice and Manner, 15 for Wit, 16 for Humour and 0 for Good Humour.

[12] *Life*, III, 110.

[13] *Life*, IV, 35, n. 3. Boswell suggests that Johnson also recommended the inclusion of Pomfret, Yalden, and Thomson (*Life*, III, 370, 109), even though he disliked Thomson's poetry.

[14] Thomas F. Bonnell, 'John Bell's *Poets of Great Britain*: The "Little Trifling Edition" Revisited', *MP*, 85 (1987), 128–52.

of a poet such as Pomfret if it were not for the consideration that 'he pleases many, and who pleases many must have some species of merit'. Johnson derives the authority for his canon from the common reader, from 'that class of readers, who without vanity or criticism seek only their own amusement'.[15]

Boswell, reading the text as Johnson's canon, was disappointed that the choice of poets was to be directed by the booksellers rather than by Johnson and asked him if he would furnish a Preface and a Life to any dunce's work, to which Johnson replied in characteristically robust fashion: 'Yes, Sir, and *say* he was a dunce'.[16] So far has criticism shed its hagiographical function that Johnson is able to say of Sheffield:

He is introduced into this collection only as a poet; and if we credit the testimony of his contemporaries, he was a poet of no vulgar rank. But favour and flattery are now at an end; criticism is no longer softened by his bounties, or awed by his splendour and, being able to take a more steady view, discovers him to be a writer that sometimes glimmers, but rarely shines, feebly laborious, and at best but pretty.[17]

These comments would seem to support the commonly held view of Johnson as the magisterial critic, dispensing judgements in a posture of unexamined authority, and riding rough-shod over the common reader.

It is certainly a view that Kernan seems to hold. He constructs a picture of Johnson's 'vigorous canon-making', not out of his encyclopaedic activities, but out of his 'dogmatic social pronouncements about literature', his rejection of the metaphysical poets and of Ossian, his preference for Richardson over Fielding, and his membership of the Club, which he calls 'an informal literary synod' of 'men who helped to determine the canon'. The self-imposed task of the Club, he supposes, was to sort out true literature from the 'literary apocrypha of ephemeral mass-cult trash the printing press spewed out daily', and he adds the finishing touch to this picture by referring to Johnson as 'the great cham of literature' (p. 159). This image of Johnson, has, however, been largely demolished by the most recent writers and scholars.

Charles Hinnant offers a slight variation on this view when he observes that Johnson's evaluative style of criticism is intrinsically canonical, that it necessarily entails the making of canonical judgements: 'The chief interest of evaluative criticism is to ascertain where renewed attention needs to be directed, or where the need to correct inflated reputations imposes a judgement counter to received or canonical ideas of the value of an author or poem.'[18] This tendency, he argues, is opposed to modern literary theory which tends to be interpretative rather than evaluative, and goes some way to explain Johnson's unpopularity, except as a straw man, with modern

---

[15] 'Life of Pomfret', *Lives of the Poets*, ed. by G. B. Hill, 3 vols (Oxford: Clarendon Press, 1905), I, 302.
[16] *Life*, III, 137.
[17] *Lives*, II, 174–75.
[18] Charles H. Hinnant, *'Steel for the Mind': Samuel Johnson and Critical Discourse* (London and Toronto: Associated University Presses, 1994), pp. 214–15.

literary theorists. Mark Booth makes much the same point when he contends that in the *Lives of the Poets* Johnson is 'occupied with the valuation of the work and not with the understanding of it', but understanding and evaluation are, for Johnson, part of the same process.[19] Evaluative criticism is not 'absolute and definite, but gradual and comparative' and depends upon successive judgements of successive generations of readers in the test of time, but Johnson is in no doubt that the common reader needs to understand the works being judged.[20] Although he acknowledges that 'approbation, though long continued, may yet be only the approbation of prejudice or fashion', yet he argues that 'what has been longest known has been most considered, and what has been most considered is best understood'.[21] Clearly, 'consideration' involves more than just the reading of texts by those 'uncorrupted with literary prejudices', and, ultimately, the effect being aimed at is understanding.[22]

Dryden would have argued that the common reader is sometimes wrong:

The liking or disliking of the people gives the Play the denomination of good or bad, but does not really make, or constitute it such. To please the people ought to be the poet's aim, because Plays are made for their delight; but it does not follow that they are always pleas'd with good Plays, or that the Plays which please them are always good.[23]

The *vox populi* does not have the last word as far as Dryden is concerned. Johnson offers similar views, though with a very different emphasis. The reading public is always 'right' in the sense that it will read what it wishes, and 'that book is good in vain which the reader throws away', but there is always room for the common reader to be instructed or educated, and it is with an eye to improving the reader's understanding of a poet that Johnson makes many of his evaluative critical comments.[24]

Johnson is well aware that other factors relating to the modes of production and publication often influence the valuation of texts, so that readers are deprived of their proper influence: 'Whoever has remarked the fate of books, must have found it governed by other causes than general consent arising from general conviction. If a new performance happens not to fall into the hands of some, who have courage to tell, and authority to propagate their opinion, it often remains long in obscurity, and perhaps

[19] Mark W. Booth, 'Johnson's Critical Judgements in the *Lives of the Poets*', *SEL*, 16 (1976), 505–15 (p. 513).
[20] See Clarence Tracy, 'Johnson and the Common Reader', *Dalhousie Review*, 57 (1977), 405–23.
[21] Preface to Shakespeare, *The Yale Edition of the Works of Samuel Johnson*, ed. by Allen T. Hazen and others (New Haven, CT, and London: Yale University Press, 1958–), VII: *Johnson on Shakespeare*, ed. by Arthur Sherbo (1968), pp. 60–61.
[22] Life of Gray, *Lives of the Poets*, III, 441–42; the full quotation is as follows: 'In the character of his *Elegy* I rejoice to concur with the common reader; for by the common sense of readers uncorrupted with literary prejudices, after all the refinements of subtilty and the dogmatism of learning, must be finally decided all claim to poetical honours.'
[23] 'A Defence of an Essay of Dramatique Poesie', *The Works of John Dryden*, IX: *Plays*, ed. by John Loftis (1966), pp. 11–12.
[24] *Lives*, I, 454.

perishes unknown and unexamined.' But in the same *Adventurer* essay Johnson proclaims that it is 'from the public, and only from the public' that an author is to 'await a confirmation of his claim'.[25]

In his discussion of the relative merits of Dryden and Pope, Johnson is aware that he might be suspected of a 'partial fondness' in his determination in favour of Dryden, and indeed this whole passage does seem to support Hinnant's and Booth's contention that Johnson is predominantly evaluative and canonical in his criticism, but at the same time Johnson asserts his confidence that 'meditation and inquiry' will cause the reader to concur with 'the reasonableness of my determination'.[26] The common reader must be a thinking reader and must be able to interpret the texts correctly before making any judgement that can be relied upon. Pomfret will appeal to those readers who lack 'criticism' and seek only their own amusement, but as understanding increases, so taste becomes more discriminating and the relative space allotted to Pomfret and to Dryden in the *Lives of the Poets* is itself indicative of the critical judgement of their merits that Johnson believes the reader will form.

Johnson had considerable faith both in the natural intelligence and in the acquired wisdom of the common reader. He can sometimes sound as though he shares the same attitudes and values as Scriblerians, as, for example, in this passage from 'A Project for the Employment of Authors':

> It is not now, as in former times, when men studied long, and passed through the severities of discipline, and the probation of publick trials, before they presumed to think themselves qualified for instructors of their countrymen; there is found a nearer way to fame and erudition, and the inclosures of literature are thrown open to every man whom idleness disposes to loiter, or whom pride inclines to set himself in view.[27]

But Johnson is here talking about the presumption of *authors*, not of readers. Johnson's confident reliance on the common reader is, in part, made possible by the spread of literacy and education in the early part of the century. Frequent comments testify to Johnson's faith in the knowledge and understanding of the common reader, such as this in *The Idler*, no. 7: 'All foreigners remark, that the knowledge of the common people of England is greater than that of any other vulgar', a knowledge he attributes to the 'universal diffusion of instruction' made possible by newspapers and periodicals, and in response to the argument that 'this teeming of the press in modern times is prejudicial to good literature', Johnson counters that 'we have now more knowledge generally diffused; all our ladies read now, which is a great extension'.[28]

[25] *The Adventurer*, no. 138, *Yale Edition*, II: *The Idler and The Adventurer*, ed. by W. J. Bate, J. M. Bullitt and L. F. Powell (1963), p. 496.
[26] *Lives*, III, 223.
[27] 'A Project for the Employment of Authors', *Universal Visiter*, April 1756, in *Works*, 11 vols (Oxford, 1825), V, 357.
[28] *The Idler*, *Yale Edition*, II, 23; *Life*, III, 333.

One thing that canons rely on is an authorizing voice or standard. Evaluative judgements must be made by somebody with acknowledged authority, or by anybody in accordance with an acknowledged principle of value. Johnson consistently repudiates that authority for himself, in spite of the impression to the contrary given by Boswell about his conversational style, and the impression gained by such readers of the *Lives of the Poets* as Percival Stockdale, who objected that prejudice and fashion 'have raised this biographer to the rank of poetical law-giver, in a free and enlightened country'.[29] Stockdale had mistaken Johnson's taste for authority in politics for a similar desire in literature.

Certainly, Johnson would not have shared Addison's half-joking desire that the critic should wield absolute power over the responses of a theatre audience in an attempt to mould and refine their taste: 'As soon as any shining Thought is expressed in the Poet, or any uncommon Grace appears in the Actor, he smites the Bench or Wainscot. If the Audience does not concur with him, he smites a second time: and if the Audience is not yet awakened, looks round him with great Wrath, and repeats the Blow a third time, which never fails to produce the Clap'.[30] Many of Addison's critical comments are of this authoritative type, as are those of contemporary editors who marked in the margins for the benefit of readers the 'beauties' of their texts. Johnson never adopted this practice in his edition of Shakespeare and is uncomfortable with the notion that the critic should adopt this magisterial role,[31] though he defends Addison's criticism on the grounds that 'his instructions were such as the characters of his readers made proper. That general knowledge which now circulates in common talk, was in his time rarely to be found. Men not professing learning were not ashamed of ignorance; and, in the female world, any acquaintance with books was distinguished only to be censured'.[32]

Johnson is more comfortable with an appeal to the common reader than many of his contemporaries perhaps because of his position within the world of letters. Not for him the apocalyptic anxieties, the self-defensive protection of a threatened world of high culture felt by the Scriblerians at the sudden upsurging flood of print production. For Pope, the new rapid growth in readers had brought about a collapse of aesthetic and moral standards — and for him the two are intimately linked — so that the lack of learning in

---

[29] *Lectures on the Truly Eminent English Poets*, 2 vols (London, 1807), I, 164, quoted in Lipking, p. 465. James Gray argues, 'No one in the history of literature can lay greater claim to being an authority than Samuel Johnson. Yet his own self-estimate was such that he would have spurned and perhaps derided such an ascription', in '*Auctor et auctoritas*: Dr. Johnson's views on the Authority of Authorship', *English Studies in Canada*, 12 (1986), 269–84 (p. 269).

[30] *The Spectator* (1711–14), ed. by Donald F. Bond, 5 vols (Oxford, 1965), no. 235, 29 November 1711.

[31] 'The poetical beauties or defects I have not been very diligent to observe. [. . .] The reader, I believe, is seldom pleased to find his opinion anticipated [. . .]. Judgement, like other faculties, is improved by practice, and its achievement is hindered by submission to dictatorial decisions, as the memory grows torpid by the use of a table book.' (Preface to Shakespeare, *Yale Edition*, VII, 104).

[32] *Lives*, II, 146.

Grub Street hacks, dunces, and lower-class readers is an index of their low moral and cultural standards.

The characteristic features of canon-making certainly apply to the Scriblerians; they felt a need to legitimate their values in the face of a number of threats to their political, cultural, social, and moral values, and they did so in the context described by Kernan: 'The official synod may be lacking, or appear only as a loose informal group like the Club, but the distinctive marks of canon-making — such as the apocrypha of Grub Street hack writing, the increase of legitimating criticism, the enormous growth in the activity of editing literary texts — all appear at this time' (p. 161). But Johnson never scorned the productions of Grub Street and never felt threatened by the 'teeming of the press'. He was more at ease than Pope in the new world of print culture, not just because he was a major exponent of the professional world of letters, nor yet because his roots were not aristocratic and he belonged to no coterie culture (though these things probably helped to form his views), but because, for him, authority lay not in the imperious views of a critic applying rigid rules or pronouncing the judgement of a refined taste and sensibility, but in the kind of knowledge of life and art which all readers could acquire. A learned author was no longer speaking to the learned reader in an enclosed, exclusive relationship; such learning as was required to appreciate the higher works of culture should not be so far beyond the reach of the ordinary reader that the effort is too great.

And so we have Johnson as early as the *Plan of an English Dictionary* (1754) considering these questions of authority and already displacing it from himself onto others. The *Plan* is dedicated to Lord Chesterfield — still at that time regarded as a patron — and Johnson dutifully repeats some of the expected tropes of a dependent author. He assigns authority to Lord Chesterfield for decisions of purity and propriety in the language and contends in his address that 'since you, whose authority in our language is so generally acknowledged, have commissioned me to declare my own opinion, I shall be considered as exercising a kind of vicarious jurisdiction'.[33] Johnson clearly feels that he lacks authority himself for this kind of linguistic pronouncement, but the location of authority in Lord Chesterfield seems like routine flattery when we know that Johnson resisted the notion of an Academy instituted to impose similar judgements by collective authority.

He seems much more convincing when he places the major source of authority for his work in other writers. Significantly, he calls these writers his 'authorities' and says that it is upon them that 'the credit of every part of this work must depend' (p. 30). He asserts that he will prefer 'writers of the first reputation to those of an inferior rank', but he is aware that such an act of selection itself requires some authority: 'It has been asked, on some

---

[33] 'The Plan of a Dictionary of the English Language' (1747), facsimile pub. with facsimile of Johnson's *Dictionary of the English Language* (Harlow: Longman, 1990), p. 30.

occasions, who shall judge the judges? And since with regard to this design a question may arise by what authority the authorities are selected, it is necessary to obviate it, by declaring that many of the writers whose testimonies will be alleged, were selected by Mr. Pope.' The authority for the usage of words is displaced on to a canon of great writers and the authority for selecting that canon is displaced on to Pope (p. 31).

All of these sources of authority will bear some examination. The dedication to Lord Chesterfield, and presumably with it the ascription to him of authority, is dismissed by Johnson in a conversation with Boswell on 22 September 1777:

Sir, the way in which the Plan of my Dictionary came to be inscribed to Lord Chesterfield, was this: I had neglected to write it by the time appointed. Dodsley suggested a desire to have it addressed to Lord Chesterfield. I laid hold of this as a pretext for delay, that it might be better done, and let Dodsley have his desire. I said to my friend, Dr. Bathurst, 'Now if any good comes of my addressing to Lord Chesterfield, it will be ascribed to deep policy, when, in fact, it was only a casual excuse for laziness.'[34]

Now the world knows that no good did come of his dedication to Lord Chesterfield, and it may be that Johnson's memory of his motives is coloured by subsequent events, but it seems clear that Johnson only ever reluctantly sought authority for matters of linguistic propriety from an aristocratic patron.[35] This is not just a matter of Johnson's famed independence and obstinacy, but a matter of principle.

His mention in the *Plan* of Pope's selection of the writers who would form his authorities is the only evidence we have of Pope's involvement, and the context of the passage implies that Pope also approved of Johnson's competence to complete the dictionary: 'Solicitous as he was for the success of this work, he would not be displeased that I have undertaken it' (p. 31). Much is being made of Pope's authority here. Johnson seems to feel the need of providing credentials in a way that Pope himself does not.

[34] *Life*, I, 185.
[35] See James H. Sledd and Gwin J. Kolb, *Dr. Johnson's Dictionary: Essays in the Biography of a Book* (Chicago: University of Chicago Press, 1955), Chapter 3. Sledd and Kolb note that Chesterfield made only eight remarks on Johnson's draft *Plan*, most of them clarifications, and of these Johnson accepts six, slightly modifies the seventh and rejects the eighth. Interestingly, the remark Johnson rejects concerns his assertion in the *Plan* that a word may have two pronunciations 'equally defensible by authority' and gives examples from Pope and Rowe of the different pronunciations of 'great' (p. 13). Chesterfield commented on the quotation from Rowe: 'This is undoubtedly a bad Rhyme, and therefore should not be quoted as an Authority, though found in a good poet', thereby setting his own authority for judging these matters higher than that of either Rowe or common usage (Sledd and Kolb, p. 93). So even at a time when Johnson was 'eager to please' his new patron, he refused to accept Chesterfield's authority. Howard Weinbrot argues that the Preface to the *Dictionary* reflects many changes from the *Plan* largely because Johnson has repudiated the authority of Chesterfield as a patron; see 'Samuel Johnson's *Plan* and Preface to the *Dictionary*: The Growth of a Lexicographer's Mind', in *New Aspects of Lexicography*, ed. by Howard D. Weinbrot (London and Amsterdam: Feffer and Simons, 1972), pp. 73–94. In the Preface, Weinbrot argues, 'authority is both respected and limited by the governing mind of Samuel Johnson' (p. 87).

The authority thus sought from Chesterfield, from Pope, and from the canon of 'the best writers' would seem at first blush to conflict with Johnson's faith in the judgement of the common reader, but it is, in fact, in the *Plan* that he first makes reference to the concept, arguing that 'since it will be required by common readers, that the explications should be sufficient for common use', he will include 'explanations real as well as verbal' (i.e. encyclopaedic as well as lexical) taken from the best writers (p. 21). Herein lies the crux of the matter: whereas most histories of lexicography introduce Johnson's *Dictionary* as an example of prescriptive practice (with an accompanying shake of the head, understanding but saddened), the implication that Johnson makes imperious, dogmatic, and sometimes prejudiced peremptory judgements, on his own authority, is not a true reflection of the text.

Allen Reddick is right to identify a tension at the heart of the work between 'its implicit claims to a unified authority and the presence of other diffuse and disparate — and sometimes competing — authorities'.[36] Johnson does impose his own authority on the text, but it is the authority of an instructor, and it is aimed at the common reader; these are not the arbitrary edicts of a linguistic dictator, but the wisdom of a common reader who has become learned by a process of education which he is opening up to others for them to follow. He exposes to common view the passages from his 'authorities' so that we may all, as readers, disagree with our instructor because he provides us with the evidence on which his judgements are based.

Johnson claims in the Preface to the *Dictionary* that he has extracted passages from the best writers in order to provide examples and authorities for his definitions, but it is clear from his practice that at least as important as these linguistic considerations is the literary desire to make the meaning of the older writers plain. These may be writers from 'the wells of English undefiled, [. . .] the pure sources of genuine diction', but many of their usages are no longer understood.[37] That this is an important concern of Johnson's seems proved by the fact that he announces in the *Plan* his decision to include some obsolete words:

Of antiquated or obsolete words, none will be included but such as are to be found in authors who wrote since the accession of Elizabeth, from which we date the golden age of our language; and of these many might be omitted, but that the reader may require, with an appearance of reason, that no difficulty should be left unresolved in books which he finds himself invited to read, as confessed and established models of stile. (p. 28)

These words are not being authorized by their occurrence in the quoted texts, since their obsolete status is unaffected by the use of them by great writers — they will still be marked by 'some note of exclusion', though not

---

[36] Allen Reddick, *The Making of Johnson's Dictionary 1746–1773*, rev. edn (Cambridge: Cambridge University Press, 1996), p. 9.
[37] Preface to *A Dictionary of the English Language*, sig. C1ʳ.

of 'disgrace'. Exemplification is also not an issue in the case of *hapax logomena*, since their single occurrence argues against their inclusion in a dictionary of common usage. The reason for including these two categories of words is simply that 'the reputation of their authors affords some extraordinary reason for their reception' and, once included, they need to be explained to enable the reader to understand and interpret correctly the quoted text (pp. 28–29). In other words, in these cases, the quotations do not exemplify and illustrate the definitions; rather, the definitions elucidate and clarify the meaning of the quoted text.[38]

This notion of authority appears to run counter to the spirit of much recent critical discourse, founded as it is on notions of epistemic uncertainty, indeterminacy, and phenomenological imprecision.[39] Text-centred and non-authorial analysis has taken precedence over homogenized, coherent accounts of fixed and determinate texts, produced by authors considered as historical personages, and collectively considered as forming a unified canon. Such exegetic and diegetic techniques as are used by Johnson run counter to the textual free-play, volatility, and temporality presupposed by a range of recent critical positions. Yet there is a tension between the overtly determined meaning of the particular word in the *Dictionary* being illustrated, exemplified, and explained by the definition and quotation, and the indeterminate intertextual meaning arising from the juxtaposition of quotations within an entry. It is much the same tension as one finds in novels of the period between diegetic authorial 'telling' and mimetic verisimilitude.[40]

There is a sense in which the concept of authority being used by Johnson in the *Dictionary* might almost be described as the medieval concept of *auctoritas*. The authors he deals with are mostly dead (literally, that is, rather than in the Barthesian sense), and the living author of the text is effaced behind an impersonality of presentation, an impersonality which is, in itself, intended to carry authority. Medieval poets invoked the name of an *auctor* to lend legitimacy to their own work, and the writings of an *auctor* possessed

---

[38] A typical instance of this practice appears in the entry for *intrenchant*. Johnson's comment is as follows: 'This word, which is, I believe, found only in *Shakespeare*, is thus explained by one of his editors: The *intrenchant* air means the air which suddenly encroaches and closes upon the space left by any body which had passed through it. *Hanmer*. I believe *Shakespeare* intended rather to express the idea of indivisibility or invulnerableness, and derived *intrenchant*, from *in* privative, and *trencher*, to cut; *intrenchant* is indeed properly *not cutting*, rather than *not to be cut*; but this is not the only instance in which *Shakespeare* confounds words of active and passive signifcation.' This is exactly the kind of editorial gloss one would expect from a scholarly editor of Shakespeare, and the quotation from *The Tempest* which follows is functioning as the passage which provoked the commentary, rather than as an illustration of the definition.

[39] See notably Stanley Fish, *Is There a Text in this Class? The Authority of Interpretative Communities* (Cambridge, MA, 1980); Roland Barthes, *The Pleasure of the Text* (New York: Hill & Wang, 1975); Michel Foucault, *Language, Counter-Memory, Practice*, ed. by D. F. Bouchard (Oxford, Blackwell, 1977) and *The Order of Things* (London: Tavistock, 1970).

[40] On this distinction, see Ian A. Bell, *Henry Fielding: Authorship and Authority* (Harlow: Longman, 1994), p. 27.

strong connotations of veracity and sagacity.[41] The concept of *auctoritas* also promotes the notion of diachronic universalism, of general and essential human nature, in a way with which Johnson would have concurred. But Johnson does not merely rest on the authority of his 'best writers'. He regularly criticizes the usage of even the greatest writers as improper. The most extended criticism of this kind is in the Preface to Shakespeare in which he castigates Shakespeare, among other things, for 'corrupt[ing] language by every mode of depravation' (p. 91).

In the *Plan* he gives warning that 'barbarous or impure words and expressions, may be branded with some note of infamy, as they are carefully to be eradicated wherever they are found; and they occur too frequently even in the best writers', and he follows up this comment with examples from Pope, Addison, and Dryden, all of which are grammatical solecisms (p. 29). Analysis of the words Johnson brands as 'barbarous' in the *Dictionary* indicates that many of them are ungrammatical in Johnson's eyes, so it is evident that Johnson is appealing to a linguistic standard independent of what is to be found in the best authors; he is, in fact, exercising that 'vicarious jurisdiction' he claimed in the *Plan* from Chesterfield and 'endeavour[ing] to support what appears to me most consonant to reason and grammar' (p. 30).[42]

Even on matters of grammar, however, Johnson resists imposing his own authority and invokes instead common usage. He argues in the *Plan* that syntax, and in particular the prepositions used in phrasal verbs, are 'originally assigned by chance' and there is no reason 'to be drawn from grammar or reason' why they should not be different (p. 19). In Johnson's view, 'speech was not formed by analogy from heaven', and he resisted the theory, promoted by the Port-Royal grammarians, that the logic of grammar could be imposed upon the language (p. 17). His attempts to impose system on the language were confined to his early intention to establish etymology as the criterion of correctness and root of meaning and to his intention with every word to

mark the progress of its meaning, and show by what gradations of intermediate sense it has passed from its primitive to its remote and accidental signification; so that every foregoing explanation should tend to that which follows, and the sense be regularly concatenated from the first notion to the last.[43]

That he abandoned both these aims in the writing of the *Dictionary*, and confesses in the Preface that he has had to yield to the overwhelming

---

[41] See Alistair Minnis, *Medieval Theory of Authorship* (London, Scolar Press, 1984).

[42] An example of the type of word Johnson labels 'barbarous' is *disannul*, to which he appends the comment: 'The word is formed contrary to analogy by those who not knowing the meaning of the word *annul*, intended to form a negative sense by the needless use of the negative article. It ought therefore to be rejected as ungrammatical and barbarous.' Examples of such expressions used by the 'best authors' include 'to set v.n. 10: it is commonly used in conversation for *sit*, which, though undoubtedly barbarous, is sometimes found in authors'.

[43] Preface to the *Dictionary*, sig. B2r.

pressure of usage, is a further measure of the resistance of his lexicographical practice to *a priori* prescriptive judgements about what is or is not 'correct'.

Alvin Kernan identifies as one of the distinctive marks of canon-making 'the enormous growth in the activity of editing literary texts', taking as a model the determination of the sacred books of the Bible and the commentaries and explications which accompany it (p. 161). The Bible is, of course, the ultimate authoritative text, endorsing and vindicating a set of religious and social values, so establishing the authenticity of the sacred books is an act of the most extreme importance. However, by Johnson's time, these were deemed to have been pretty well established by the Anglican Church and the focus was, instead, on exegesis.[44] A parallel situation may be found in literary texts;[45] the canon is more or less established, but the texts themselves are imperfect and obscure; the dull duty of an editor is to establish the text and then explain it:

In perusing a corrupted piece, [the editor] must have before him all possibilities of meaning, with all possibilities of expression. Such must be his comprehension of thought, and such his copiousness of language. Out of many readings possible, he must be able to select that which best suits with the state, opinions, and modes of language prevailing in every age, and with his author's particular cast of thought, and turn of expression.[46]

The editor must be knowledgeable about language and about meaning to perform his task adequately.

Despite Johnson's disparaging remarks about Theobald in his Preface to Shakespeare, he was clearly influenced by Theobald's innovative editorial practices, among which was his attempt to 'explain an obscure and obsolete *Term, Phrase,* or *Idea*'.[47] When Johnson expresses the hope that he has 'made my authour's meaning accessible to many who before were frightened from perusing him', and adopts as a working principle the view that 'the reading of the ancient books is probably true, and therefore is not to be disturbed for the sake of elegance, perspicuity, or mere improvement of the sense',

[44] See Marcus Walsh, 'Profession and Authority: The Interpretation of the Bible in the Seventeenth and Eighteenth Centuries', *Literature and Theology*, 19 (1995), 383–98, for a discussion of the importance attached to valid scriptural interpretation within the Anglican Church and the issues of interpretative authority this raised; see also his *Shakespeare, Milton and Eighteenth-Century Literary Editing* (Cambridge: Cambridge University Press, 1997) for a discussion of the importance of editing in the eighteenth century.

[45] Spence records Pope's assertion, 'It is easy to mark out the general course of our poetry. Chaucer, Spenser, Milton, and Dryden are the great land-marks for it', in *Anecdotes, Observations and Characters of Books and Men*, ed. by S. W. Singer (London: Centaur Press, 1964), p. 116, and Goldsmith argued that the selection of works in the canon is 'obvious, for in all languages the best productions are most easily found'; see *Collected Works*, ed. by Arthur Friedman, 5 vols (Oxford: Clarendon Press, 1966), v, 317–18.

[46] Preface to Shakespeare, *Yale Edition*, VII, 95.

[47] Preface, *The Works of Shakespeare*, ed. by Lewis Theobald, 7 vols (1733), I, xliii. Peter Seary comments: 'As an editor of Shakespeare Johnson is closer to Theobald than to any other of his predecessors' (*Lewis Theobald and the Editing of Shakespeare* (Oxford: Clarendon Press, 1990), p. 7). Theobald's copy of the second folio with his marginalia passed into Johnson's hands some time after his death in 1744. This may have been after Johnson had finished work on the *Dictionary*, but there are places where Johnson quotes Theobald's edition in preference to that of Warburton in the *Dictionary*; see Arthur M. Eastman, 'The Texts from which Johnson Printed his Shakespeare', *JEGP*, 49 (1950), 182–91.

assuming instead that his duty as an editor is to elucidate the text by trying 'if there be any interstice through which light can find its way', then he is adopting the editorial practices and principles pioneered by Theobald.[48] Theobald hoped that from his notes on the plays 'the common and learned Readers of our Author, I hope, will derive some Pleasure', and a major reason for his confidence in the pleasure of the common reader lies in his elucidation of the sense of Shakespeare's words.

Theobald saw himself as doing for Shakespeare what Pope had done for Homer, and many eighteenth-century editors saw themselves following a classical tradition.[49] George Sewell wrote in the preface to 'Volume Seven' of Pope's edition of Shakespeare: 'What then has been done by the really Learned to the dead languages, by treading backwards into the Paths of Antiquity and reviving and correcting good old Authors, we in Justice owe to our great Writers, both in Prose and Poetry. They are in some degree our *Classics*.'[50] Critical editions of Shakespeare, Milton, Spenser, Johnson, and other poets began to appear in the eighteenth century, underlining the idea that these English poets carried the same authority as the classical poets and were part of an English canon.[51]

Richard Carew had drawn an explicit parallel between the English and the classical poets in his essay 'On the Excellencie of the English Tongue':

Will you read *Virgill*? take the Earle of Surrey, *Catullus*? Shakespeare and Marlowe's fragment, *Ovid*? *Daniell*, *Lucan*? *Spencer*, *Martial*? Sir *John Davies* and others: will you have all in all for Prose and verse? take the miracle of our age Sir *Philip Sidney*.[52]

Johnson does not need to make the parallel explicit, since readers would have been familiar with Latin and Greek dictionaries in which it was common practice to include quotations from classical authors.[53] His adoption of this practice for native British writers implicitly accords them classical status and with it canonical authority.

The practice of explicating and commenting upon classical and sacred texts began in the eighteenth century to be transferred to English poetry, with all the canonical implications this carries. James Greenwood claims in his preface to *The Virgin Muse* (1717) that his book is 'a compleat Book for the *Teaching to Read Poetry*', and Ian Michael contends, 'This is the first expression in a textbook of the idea that poetry could be taught [. . .]. Only in the study

---

[48] Preface to Shakespeare, *Yale Edition*, VII, 103, 106.

[49] Seary, p. 171.

[50] Quoted in *Shakespeare: The Critical Heritage 1623–1801*, ed. by Brian W. Vickers, 6 vols (London: Routledge, 1974–81), II, 419.

[51] The copyright law of 1709, and the booksellers' need to protect their property, led to editions of authors no longer living acquiring a financial as well as an aesthetic value. A bookseller could buy the rights to an author, but he had to perpetuate that right by publishing new editions. This alone would be one factor in the rise to prominence of Shakespeare in the century, though there are many others. See, for example, Michael Dobson, *The Making of the National Poet: Shakespeare, Adaptation, and Authorship, 1660–1769* (Oxford: Clarendon Press, 1992).

[52] Printed in William Camden, *Remains Concerning Britain*, ed. by R. D. Dunn (Toronto and London: University of Toronto Press, 1984), pp. 43–44.

[53] See Sledd and Kolb, p. 42.

of foreign languages, principally Latin, Greek and Hebrew, is there evidence before now of texts being scrutinised and "taught" in order to bring out their meaning'.[54] It seems clear that the assumption underlying this practice is that the canon of English poetry is already established, has acquired the same canonical authority as classical texts and the Bible, and that what is now needed is elucidation, interpretation, and instruction for the common reader to grasp the sense of these texts.

Many anthologies of this time are aimed at school students and other groups of unlearned readers. John Clarke's *An Essay upon Poetry* (1731) for example, offers a list of 'the choicest of our English Poets' and particularly recommends Dryden and Pope's translation of the classics, which 'may be very proper to give Ladies and others unacquainted with the learned Languages, a Tast of the Poetry of the ancient Greeks and Romans'. Similarly, Ann Fisher in *The Pleasing Instructor* (1756) argues that women should try to understand 'the *Nature* and *Kinds* of Words' so that they can comprehend the sense of 'such as the Generality call *dark* and *obscure* Writers'.[55] A similar readership is clearly envisaged in the prefaces, titles and dedications to the early dictionaries, as in this example from Henry Cockeram:

The English dictionarie: or, an interpreter of hard English words. Enabling as well ladies and gentlewomen, young schollers, clarkes, merchants, as also strangers of any nation, to the understanding of the more difficult authors already printed in our language.[56]

There was already, then, a lexicographical tradition of such explication, but by the eighteenth century there develops a new emphasis on education and instruction for unlearned readers.

This same emphasis is to be found in Johnson's *Dictionary*. Though there are good linguistic reasons for including many of the quotations, others are, as Johnson announces in the Preface, included for purely pedagogical reasons: 'I was desirous that every quotation should be useful to some other end than the illustration of a word; I therefore extracted from philosophers principles of science; from historians remarkable facts; from chymists complete processes; from divines striking exhortations; and from poets beautiful descriptions'.[57] Despite his confession that he was forced to depart from his scheme, it is evident that he had as one of his primary objectives that of 'including all that was pleasing or useful in *English* literature'.

There are ideological factors governing Johnson's choice of what is 'pleasing or useful', including his religious and moral beliefs, which led to

---

[54] Ian Michael, *The Teaching of English: From the Sixteenth Century to 1870* (Cambridge: Cambridge University Press, 1987), p. 171.
[55] Michael, p. 173. These examples are taken from Trevor Thornton Ross, *Albion's Parnassus*.
[56] Henry Cockeram, *The English Dictionarie* (1623; repr. Menston: Scolar Press, 1968), title-page.
[57] Preface to the *Dictionary*, sig. B2ᵛ.

the exclusion of writers such as Hobbes, Samuel Clarke, Shaftesbury, and Thomas Chubb. To Thomas Tyers he said, 'I might have quoted *Hobbes* as an authority in language, as well as many other writers of his time: but I scorned, sir, to quote him at all; because I did not like his principles', and to Hester Thrale he said he 'never would give Shaftesbury Chubb or any wicked Writer's authority for a Word, lest it should send People to look in a Book that might injure them forever'.[58] On similar grounds he refuses to quote from Samuel Clarke, despite recommending his sermons, because of his unorthodox anti-Trinitarian beliefs.[59] We know of these exclusions because Johnson mentions them, but there are others which he does not mention. Bunyan, for example, is not quoted, though Johnson praises him highly: 'His "Pilgrim's Progress" has a great merit, both for invention, imagination, and the conduct of the story; and it has the best evidence of its merit, the general and continued approbation of mankind' (II, 238). It fulfils Johnson's criteria of pleasing the common reader and passing the test of time, yet such consensus is insufficient to gain it an entry into the *Dictionary*, perhaps because of Bunyan's Calvinist beliefs. Richard Baxter is also excluded, presumably as a Presbyterian, though his works are described by Johnson as 'all good' (IV, 226).[60] Texts which take a sectarian stance or appear to promote religious controversy (with the exception of Bramhall's treatises against Hobbes) are all excluded, and orthodox latitudinarian divines make up the body of religious writers collected in the *Dictionary*.[61] Of the moralists, Mandeville and Hume are naturally omitted, along with Shaftesbury.

Johnson does, however, seem to have been unaffected by class considerations in his selection of 'authorities'. Annette Wheeler Cafarelli is mistaken to contend that Johnson was 'contemptuous of the unearned patronage of working-class poets' and that he 'excluded upstarts in gender and class from his canon'.[62] One of the 'upstarts' in class she mentions, John Taylor 'the

---

[58] *Samuel Johnson's Early Biographers*, ed. by Robert E. Kelley and O. M. Brack, Jr (Iowa City: University of Iowa Press, 1971), p. 82; *Thraliana*, p. 34.

[59] *Life*, IV, 416, n. 2.

[60] He may be cited once in the fourth edition under *high* where the content of the quotation does not suggest William Baxter who is also cited in the *Dictionary*. Under *unconverted* in the fourth edition Johnson adds a comment to sense 2: 'Thus Baxter wrote a Call to the *Unconverted*'. Johnson's pro-Anglican views are also indicated by his inclusion of many quotations from *Eikon Basilike*, among them, as sole illustration of the word *presbyterian*: 'Chiefly was urged the abolition of episcopal, and the establishing of *presbyterian* government.' The sole quotation illustrating *protestant* is also from *Eikon Basilike*: 'This is the first example of any protestant subjects, that have taken up arms against their king, a *protestant*.' See Philip Mahone Griffiths, 'Samuel Johnson and King Charles the Martyr: Veneration in the *Dictionary*', *The Age of Johnson*, 2 (1990), 235–61.

[61] There are no quotations, for example, from Foxe's *Book of Martyrs*, while there is extensive quotation from Hooker, who is characterized by moderation and a temperate spirit. It would also be significant for Johnson, however, that Hooker defended the established church order and the system of episcopal government against attacks on it by Presbyterians.

[62] 'Johnson's *Lives of the Poets* and the Romantic Canon', *The Age of Johnson*, 1 (1989), 403–35 (p. 427). Cafarelli misreads Johnson in this way because she is trying to argue that Southey's *Lives of the Uneducated Poets* (1831) is a 'counterargument to Johnson'.

water poet', is, in fact, quoted in the *Dictionary*, where Johnson had a free choice, though he is excluded from the *Lives of the Poets* where the choice was made by the booksellers. Cafarelli's interpretation is quite different from that made by reviewers at the time. John Gilbert Cooper related to Boswell an account that 'soon after the publication of [Johnson's] Dictionary, Garrick being asked by Johnson what people thought of it, told him, that among other animadversions, it was objected that he cited authorities which were beneath the dignity of such a work, and mentioned Richardson. "Nay, (said Johnson,) I have done worse than that: I have cited *thee*, David" '.[63]

He is perhaps vulnerable to the accusation that he excluded women writers, though it is difficult to know who he could have included, since many were, at that time, unpublished, and those that were in the public print could easily have been excluded on the ground of their immorality rather than their gender. Another factor working against the inclusion of women was Johnson's avowal 'to admit no testimony of living authors, that I might not be misled by partiality, and that none of my contemporaries might have reason to complain'.[64] The fact that he breaks this rule several times in order to quote from women writers of his acquaintance, such as Elizabeth Carter and Charlotte Lennox, is testimony to the strength of his friendship with them and his respect for their learning.

One of the criteria governing his choice of writers in his lexicographical canon was the 'purity' of their English. Denham acquires a place in the canon almost exclusively on the basis of his language and is described by Johnson in the *Lives of the Poets* as 'one of the authours that improved our taste and advanced our language, and whom we ought therefore to read with gratitude' (I, 82). Johnson's limits of the 'wells of English undefiled' as extending from the age of Sidney to the Restoration are governed by a sense that the English of these writers was less corrupted by foreign importations than the contemporary language which was 'deviating towards a Gallick structure and phraseology'.[65] There are obvious nationalistic, specifically anti-French, overtones to these discussions, but there is also a sense that the language of certain authors, for example Chaucer, is too remote from current English. His verse appeared to eighteenth-century readers not to scan (often due to ignorance of the pronounced final 'e') and to lack the euphonies of Waller and Denham. But he is, none the less, regarded as 'the Father of *English* Poetry' and read with a historical relativism by such as Dryden, who remarked: 'The Verse of *Chaucer*, I confess, is not Harmonious to us; but [. . .] they who liv'd with him, and some time after him, thought it

---

[63] *Life*, IV, 4. Johnson also quotes from Samuel Boyse, a Grub-Street associate.
[64] Preface to the *Dictionary*, sig. B2ᵛ. The women Johnson quotes in the *Dictionary* are Margaret Cavendish, Jane Barker, Catherine Cockburn, Hester Mulso, Elizabeth Carter, and Charlotte Lennox.
[65] Preface to the *Dictionary*, sig. C1ʳ.

Musical. [. . .] We can only say, that he liv'd in the Infancy of our Poetry, and that nothing is brought to Perfection at the first.'[66]

At the Restoration it was widely believed that the language had reached its apogee of purity. Edward Phillips, in the dedication to his *New World of English Words* gives voice to what he calls a 'known truth, and not to be denied, that our Language hath in these latter Ages been advanced to the admiration, if not the emulation of other Nations'.[67] This linguistic vainglory may be read metonymically as a comment on broader cultural concerns related to the defining of Englishness and the disparagement of or hostility to foreign cultures. One of the defining features of Englishness is taken to be a taste for liberty (as opposed to French autocracy, for example) and this allows Shakespeare to be valued for what had previously been regarded as a weakness: his failure to conform to the rules.

Johnson clearly felt that the period up to the Restoration was a linguistic and literary golden age, but unlike Dryden and Swift, he does not believe that the purity can be restored by the authoritative determinations of a learned coterie. Dryden and fellow Royal Society intellectuals argued for a British Academy, on the model of the French, that would consist of 'gentlemen and scholars' and would not only supervise lexis and usage, but would 'pass censure and bring authors to the touch'.[68] Swift, too, argued for the establishment of an Academy made up of 'the learned and polite Persons of the Nation', but, contrary to what has been written by some commentators, Johnson did not contribute to 'the hegemonic assessment of language by characterizing the literati as a class and formulating a language that was appropriate to it'.[69] John Barrell's assertion that 'Johnson's notion of language, as of government, is quite openly and frankly one in which the majority should be idle and helpless spectators while the customs of the polite are converted into law' wrongly conflates Johnson's political views with his views on language.[70]

---

[66] Dryden, Preface to *Fables Ancient and Modern* (1700), *The Poems of John Dryden*, ed. by James Kinsley, 4 vols (Oxford: Clarendon Press, 1958), pp. 1452–53.

[67] *A New World of English Words*, sig. a3ʳ. See also Leonard Welsted, 'A Dissertation concerning the Perfection of the English Language and the State of Poetry' (1724), in which Welsted claims that the English language is not capable of a much greater perfection than it has already attained, in *The Works, In Verse and Prose, of Leonard Welsted, Esq.*, ed. by John Nichols (London, 1787), p. 122 (cited in Weinbrot, p. 97).

[68] John Evelyn, letter to Samuel Pepys, 12 August 1689, in *Diary and Correspondence*, ed. by William Bray, 2nd edn, 4 vols (1887), III, 310. See O. F. Emerson, 'John Dryden and a British Academy', *PBA*, 10 (1921), 45–58.

[69] Swift, *A Proposal for Correcting, Improving and Ascertaining the English Tongue*, ed. by Herbert Davis and Louis Landa (Oxford: Blackwell, 1957), p. 6; Olivia Smith, *The Politics of Language 1791–1819* (Oxford: Clarendon Press, 1984), p. 4.

[70] *An Equal Wide Survey*, p. 148. Olivia Smith also makes this conflation: 'The Preface and his definitions betray his political position, both his anger at corruption and his distrust of expanding political power beyond traditional boundaries' (p. 16).

Johnson's choice of language is not that of the aristocratic élite (he rejected Chesterfield's suggestions for inclusion of certain words in the *Dictionary*),[71] nor the 'learned and polite', but a common language possessed, he believed, by the best of writers:

If there be, what I believe there is, in every nation, a stile which never becomes obsolete, a certain mode of phraseology so consonant and congenial to the analogy and principles of its respective language as to remain settled and unaltered; this stile is probably to be sought in the common intercourse of life, among those who speak only to be understood, without ambition of elegance. The polite are always catching modish innovations, and the learned depart from established forms of speech, in hope of finding or making better; those who wish for distinction forsake the vulgar, when the vulgar is right.[72]

Shakespeare is an author who is to be considered 'one of the original masters of our language' precisely because his language is 'above grossness and below refinement'. It is exactly the kind of language to appeal to the common reader, and for that reason he is quoted extensively in the *Dictionary*.

There is a connection between the common reader appealed to by canonical works of literature and the common usage represented in the *Dictionary*. Canons represent the most cherished values of a community and derive their authority from the desire for permanence; in the same way, the language represented in the *Dictionary* is, in Johnson's view, the bedrock of the language, a usage that will last, and its selection is motivated by a desire for permanence. Cant words are omitted because they are 'fugitive', and unrepresentative of the core of the language: 'they cannot be regarded as any part of the durable materials of a language, and therefore must be suffered to perish with other things unworthy of preservation'.[73]

The most difficult problem facing canons is the renegotiation of values required by the addition of new works. As Johnson writes in *The Rambler*, no. 125, 'every new genius produces some innovation, which, when invented and approved, subverts the rule which the practice of foregoing authors had established'.[74] In a similar fashion, the core of the language has to accommodate neologisms and deal with obsolescence: 'As politeness increases, some expressions will be considered as too gross and vulgar for the delicate, others as too formal and ceremonious for the gay and airy; new phrases are therefore adopted, which must, for the same reasons, be in time

[71] Having ignored Johnson during production of the *Dictionary*, Chesterfield wrote two articles for Dodsley's periodical, *The World*, in which he implicitly claimed patronage of, and therefore authority over, the work as it was nearing publication. This treatment provoked Johnson's famous letter, but also his rejection of the polite usage suggested by Chesterfield. He traced the origin of *flirtation* to 'the most beautiful mouth in the world', defined the verb *to fuzz* as 'dealing twice together with the same pack of cards, for luck' and recommended restricted usage of the adjective *vastly* as in the description of a snuffbox as '*vastly* pretty, because it was *vastly* little'; see 'The Language of Ladies', *The World*, no. 101 (5 December 1754), in *Letters and Other Pieces*, ed. by R. P. Bond (New York: Doubleday, 1935), 280–85 (p. 282). See also Kernan, p. 202.
[72] Preface to Shakespeare, *Yale Edition*, VII, 68.
[73] Preface to the *Dictionary*, sig. C1ᵛ.
[74] *Yale Edition*, II: *The Rambler*, ed. by W. J. Bate and Albrecht B. Strauss (1969), p. 300.

dismissed'.[75] This continual evolution of the language, moving from neologism to obsolescence, is inevitable and describes one of those parabolas of transience associated by Johnson with all of human life: 'They rise, they shine, evaporate, and fall.'[76]

Johnson has been criticized by modern lexicographers and linguists for recording only literary usage, and this is largely true, but it is mistaken to regard this practice as élitist.[77] Johnson recorded literary usage because he thought it would last, just as the texts from which he took the words had acquired a kind of permanence from their canonical status, and this is one of the reasons he chooses to record, with some exceptions, only those texts which had passed the test of time. Pope, too, makes the connection between enduring literary fame and stability in language when he argues that both are under threat from the decay of the age:

> No longer now that Golden Age appears,
> When *Patriach-Wits* surviv'd a *thousand Years*;
> Now length of *Fame* (our *second* Life) is lost,
> And bare Threescore is all ev'n That can boast:
> Our Sons their fathers' *failing Language* see,
> And such as *Chaucer* is, shall *Dryden* be.[78]

Johnson's struggle to fix the language, to regulate and order 'the boundless chaos of a living speech' is, for him, a canonical act.

---

[75] Preface to the *Dictionary*, sig. C2^r.
[76] 'The Vanity of Human Wishes', l. 76.
[77] See, for example, Roy Harris, 'The History Men', *TLS* (3 Sepetember 1982), 935–36, cited in Kernan, pp. 197–98.
[78] 'An Essay on Criticism', ll. 478–83, *The Twickenham Edition of the Poems of Alexander Pope*, ed. by John Butt and others (London: Methuen, 1940–67).

Johnson's *Dictionary of the English Language* and its Texts: Quotation, Context, Anti-Thematics

ALLEN REDDICK

University of Zürich

Critics, users, competitors, and admirers through the centuries have attempted to make Johnson's *Dictionary* into something other than a dictionary. Some contemporary claims of the work's inadequacy as dictionary were transparently self-serving. Even the recurrent praises of Johnson's *Dictionary* as a 'monument' (to the English nation, to the English language, and so on) which is, in terms of its cultural and public function and significance largely true as a characterization, nevertheless distorted something basic about the work, especially as Johnson himself conceived of it.[1] Others more recently have called it an 'encyclopaedia', apparently in the hopes of dressing it up beyond its modest trappings as a dictionary. Robert DeMaria, Jr, in his interesting study *Johnson's 'Dictionary' and the Language of Learning*, claims liberation after reading the *Dictionary* as 'a disguised encyclopedia', citing approvingly Umberto Eco's claim that this is what all dictionaries really are: 'After spending some time reading a dictionary as a disguised encyclopedia it is possible to describe its contents.'[2] But is it really impossible to describe this dictionary without claiming that it is actually something else which is easier to describe? As well as a 'disguised encyclopedia', DeMaria has claimed the *Dictionary* as Menippean satire, that catch-all category of learned over-large didactic and ironic works stretching from Petronius to *Finnegan's Wake*. And most startling and attractive has been his case for the *Dictionary* as a collection of 'the language of learning', even a scheme for general education, with an educational curriculum whose categories include 'Ignorance', 'Knowledge', 'Truth', and so on. Such a presentation I would call attractive because it regularizes a work difficult to describe, and most of us are grateful for simplifications. It offers the book a persistent didactic character consistent with the Johnsonian moralist many find so appealing. Furthermore, it (supposedly) places Johnson into a great European humanistic tradition, which was interested in such vehicles of

---

[1] See especially James H. Sledd and Gwin J. Kolb, *Dr. Johnson's Dictionary: Essays in the Biography of a Book* (Chicago: University of Chicago Press, 1955), pp. 134–206, and Gertrude E. Noyes, 'The Critical Reception of Johnson's *Dictionary* in the Latter Eighteenth Century', *Modern Philology*, 52 (1955), 181. For the *Dictionary* as 'monument', see Allen Reddick, *The Making of Johnson's Dictionary, 1746–1773* (Cambridge: Cambridge University Press, 1990; rev. edn, 1996), pp. 176–78.

[2] Umberto Eco, *Semiotics and the Philosophy of Language* (London: Macmillan, 1984), p. 68, cited in DeMaria, *Johnson's 'Dictionary' and the Language of Learning* (Chapel Hill, NC: University of North Carolina Press, 1986), p. ix.

learning.[3] A dictionary on the other hand apparently gives such a critic, and us by implication, the impression that it is merely a functional tool, a wordlist, and we want to give Johnson's at least more credit than that. The unity which emerges when we see his *Dictionary* as a didactic encyclopaedia allows us to accept this Johnson, working helpfully in categories, finally moralistic, human, humane, wise, and so on. But a thematic reading like this provides a wisdom, to borrow from Johnson himself, that 'calms the mind, | And makes the happiness she does not find.' In other words, it is a consolatory imposition.

In the confines of this brief space, I will suggest what I think a more accurate way of seeing the text of the *Dictionary* than as a theme-bound didactic work. I will argue the following: that a dictionary necessarily tends towards the encyclopaedic, but that this tendency has little to do necessarily with theme or didacticism; that Johnson's quotations constitute separate decontextualized (and partially recontextualized) examples of uses of words in printed sources; that the partially recontextualized voices are, like Johnson's own, deflected and constrained in their illustrative function; and that the key to understanding the role of the illustrations lies in the realm of rhetoric and performance, not content and thematics. I will examine briefly the nature of the illustrative quotations and their relation to rhetoric, or voice, to the aphorism, and to content. The quotations do not function successfully as nuggets of wisdom or as parts of a thematics stretching itself throughout the text; rather their function, whatever it be, is confined almost entirely to the entry or sub-entry. The quotations comprise a series of records of printed linguistic occurrences of specific word usage in English writing which stand in some relation to the other quotations, and from which the definitions emerge to provide the gloss as well as attempt the lexical and interpretive restriction for the quotation. The rhetorical nature of the unit of the entry, or sub-entry, determines the voice, significance, the nature of the text on the page. Critical emphasis on the content of the quotations rather than context reflects a misunderstanding of what the *Dictionary* represents and indeed how one encounters it. The vehicle of the text, as arranged by Johnson, is inadequate to the preservation of a consistent didactic programme.

The insistence on the encyclopaedic is thought to allow Johnson an extra-linguistic quality and access to the conceptual content of words, apparently thought to be out of bounds for the lexicographer. Furthermore, to call Johnson's *Dictionary* something other than a dictionary may reflect a desire to pull the work out of the hands of linguists and philologists and into the discourse of literature, and literary critics. So, a critic can insist, without irony, that Johnson's *Dictionary* is not only a dictionary, but also a book (and

---

[3] DeMaria, pp. 27–32, and *passim*; for further discussion of the relation of the *Dictionary* to 'European Renaissance humanism', see DeMaria, *The Life of Samuel Johnson: A Critical Biography* (Oxford: Blackwell, 1993), pp. 110–28.

Johnson would have seen it that way); and that the *Dictionary* is related not only to dictionaries, but to other kinds of writing.[4] The insistence on such a self-evident fact seems to presuppose that dictionaries occupy separate and pristine categories devoted solely to semantic/synonymic function, when, in fact, dictionaries are always pulled out from the strictly semantic function into the larger realms of reference or signification. Such is the way of language, and books about language. And this is what Johnson's *Dictionary*, surely, is about.

Whatever validity Eco's contention that all dictionaries are 'disguised encyclopedias' has depends on the fact that the encyclopaedic tendency in lexicography is always there, whether it is exploited or resisted. It is not necessary to call a dictionary an encyclopaedia in order to allow it to provide reference to a conceptual and cultural context of words. 'In lexicography', to quote Alain Rey, 'the distinction between linguistically relevant features and descriptive features is usually blurred. The former cannot consist just of minimum features, since dictionary definitions are often linked to cultural knowledge of the world. The latter are implied in the description of cultural contents.'[5] And, indeed, to insist that a dictionary be somehow strictly 'linguistic' assumes a successful, airtight, hermetic semantic function working between *definiendum* and *definiens*. This would send us much more into the direction of a thesaurus or a wordlist, which Johnson's certainly is not. It is true that Johnson clearly exceeds his strictly semantic 'function' — the sheer number of illustrations makes this obvious. So, what is the nature of Johnson's excess?

A dictionary like Johnson's which incorporates extensive quotations from written texts necessarily exerts an unusual pressure away from the purely semantic and into the cultural realm of knowledge or reference. But there is a counter-pressure exerted in Johnson's case. The quoted passages function primarily to delimit the possibility for signification of the word. Whatever additional reasons Johnson may have had for including a passage (beauty, wisdom, for example), the first criterion is exemplification of the given sense.[6] The dynamic between quotation and definition is very close of course, since the quotation is usually not only illustrative but also generative of the given definition.[7] The partial recontextualization of the quotation in the 'free-space' of the dictionary entry breaks the pull towards the cultural

    [4] DeMaria, *Language of Learning*, pp. 3–4.

    [5] 'Definitional Semantics: Its Evolution in French Lexicography', in *Meaning and Lexicography*, ed. by Jerzy Tomaszczyk and Barbara Lewandowska-Tomaszczyk, Linguistic and Literary Studies in Eastern Europe, 28 (Amsterdam and Philadelphia: Benjamins, 1990), p. 53.

    [6] As he states in the Preface, he originally had more ambitious hopes for the illustrations: 'When first I collected these authorities, I was desirous that every quotation should be useful to some other end than the illustration of a word; I therefore extracted from philosophers principles of science; from historians remarkable facts; from chymists complete processes; from divines striking exhortations; and from poets beautiful descriptions. Such is design, while it is yet at a distance from execution' (*A Dictionary of the English Language*, (1755), sig. b2ᵛ).

    [7] Reddick, pp. 45–54.

signified; the counter-pressure pulls the rhetoric of the text, specifically the quotations, more towards the aphoristic.

The aphorism is a single utterance broken from its verbal, historical, and authorial context, removed into an artificial space of discourse, in which the emphasis is upon the linguistic performance (a linguistic construction presented unexpectedly and economically which concerns a topic usually of moral, ethical, aesthetic concern — sometimes, a 'general truth'). Allen Walker Read notes that 'under *philology* Johnson set down [as illustration] the advice from Walker, "Temper all discourses of philology with interspersions of morality". This aim connects his *Dictionary* with the collections of aphorisms and commonplaces that were very popular in the preceding centuries.'[8] The emphasis on the performance of wisdom through economical rhetoric, the essence of wit, is inherently non-encyclopaedic. The aphoristic is restrictive rather than contextual or intertextual. It is a matter of style.

Read's point is very important to understanding something crucial about Johnson's incorporation of quotations, but Johnson's illustrations are aphoristic only in certain senses. We usually understand the aphorism to be a linguistic construction detached from a wider context, containing a whole thought or expression, usually moralistic or conceptual, understandable in reference, and turned with linguistic economy. Johnson's quotations sometimes meet such a test, sometimes not. '*Hurl* ink and wit, / As madmen stones. *Ben Johnson*' under the entry *To Hurl v.a.*, or 'Corrupted light of knowledge *hurl'd*, / Sin, death, and ignorance o'er all the world. *Denham*' both, in their individual ways, represent (illustrating the definition '1. To throw with violence; to drive impetuously') an aphoristic turn, the second passage tending towards a characteristic moral emphasis. But what of 'If he thrust him of hatred, or *hurl* at him by laying of wait. *Num.* xxxv. 20' or 'She strikes the lute; but if it sound, / Threatens to *hurl* it on the ground. *Waller*'? The second is semantically useful in its illustration of the meaning given, but beyond this? And the first has some semantic relevance, though it is obscure, and its reference is virtually incoherent.

Each of these quotations is aphoristic in its brevity and its condition of being removed from its original context and put to a new function. But the new context operates primarily in relation to the definitional or exemplary function, rather than a potential extra-linguistic function. The voice of the quotation is uncertain, deracinated, decontextualized. (The Greek origin of 'aphorism' as 'definition' is relevant here, as a limiting function.) The chief difference between such a collection of quotations and a 'collection of commonplaces or aphorisms' which Read refers to is that the latter organize commentary around certain themes or topics, and announce

---

[8] 'The History of Lexicography' in *Lexicography: An Emerging International Profession*, ed. by Robert Ilson (Manchester: Manchester University Press, 1986), p. 34.

themselves as this kind of collection, with all the expectations of such a genre. With the *Dictionary*, on the other hand, the quotations are organized around specific uses of words, and their exemplary function is, explicitly, concerned primarily with a rather restricted lexical function. Certainly, Johnson hoped to intersperse his work with expressions of morality, beauty, and so on, but I would question the efficacy of the quotation to refer to external themes.[9] It is quite possible that Johnson himself would have been frustrated with such a limitation. Although the quoted authorial voice is very much circumscribed, I would argue, we may consider the probability that the contradictory dynamic introduced by the inclusion of quotations — the restrictive (the lexical) on the one hand, and the extra-referential (encyclo-paedic) on the other — is subtly at work, or at play, under each entry. The thematic problem, it seems, is that there is not (and cannot be in a dictionary) a complete recontextualization, and therefore the extra-linguistic function is restrained. It is 'unconnected' in an important sense: from original context, and here, connected only to parts of the entry, directly generating the definition, and being commented on by that definition, and affecting to some extent the etymology and orthography, and, finally, standing in some usually less certain and calculable relation to the other illustrations. Sometimes, there is a clear relation of chronology between quotations, possibly of influence, or at least of primacy. And occasionally, a juxtaposition (which may take on ironic rhetorical possibilities) between quotations which comment on one another or seem to complement one another. Though an aphorism may concern itself with a 'great truth' (that death comes to all, for instance), it is in its form inherently isolated.

Some contemporary critics of the *Dictionary* were also uncertain of the 'function' or 'voice' of the illustrations. They complained that it was not clear what the 'authorities' were 'authorizing', or the 'illustrations *illustrating*'. Specifically, several commentators complained of the lack of delineation of authority concerning proper usage among the passages quoted. For example, Andrew Kippis, the divine and biographer, complained in the 1760s that 'Johnson's Dictionary is rather a history than a standard of our language. He hath shewn by whom words have been used, and in what sense; but hath left the readers to determine what authority they have'. John Pinkerton wrote in 1785: 'The joke is, that with [Johnson] every body is an authority'.[10] In different ways, both of these commentators object to Johnson's failure to

---

[9] Johnson's comment in the Preface concerning the problem he faced in organizing and editing writing examples is relevant to this discussion: 'The examples, thus mutilated, are no longer to be considered as conveying the sentiments or doctrine of their authours; the word for the sake of which they are inserted, with all its appendant clauses, has been carefully preserved; but it may sometimes happen, by hasty detruncation, that the general tendency of the sentence may be changed: the divine may desert his tenets, or the philosopher his system' (*Dictionary*, sig. b2ᵛ).

[10] Andrew Kippis's manuscript annotations of Joseph Priestley's *A Course of Lectures on the Theory of Language and Universal Grammar* (1762), incorporated in Priestley's *Works*, ed. by J. T. Rutt, 25 vols (London, 1824), XXIII, 198; Robert Heron (John Pinkerton), *Letters of Literature* (London, 1785), p. 265; both cited in Read, pp. 38 and 47.

be prescriptive, especially in terms of word usage, and for quoting passages without making the significance (the 'authority') of the passage clear. To expand on this perception, one can say that the *Dictionary* entries are built around a collection of historical occurrences of usage whose 'voice' is equivocal, except in semantic relation to the definition. The lack of 'authority' in this sense is reflected throughout the work.

In the construction of his entries, Johnson relies on what we might call the most sceptical of empirical evidence, the recording of print performance, and transcribes it into the present text in a secondary 'performative' function, operating in relation to the other material of the entry (other quotations, definition, etymology, note on usage, and so on). If the quotation comprises a complete sentiment or idea, then its subject or content may also find a voice, but always in relation to its explicit function (as linguistic exemplification) and its subsumption under, or negotiation with, the lexicographer's voice. Its original declamatory meaning, one could argue in most cases of quotation in the *Dictionary*, is virtually held in abeyance, estranged from context and clear reference and signification. Furthermore, the quotations are not necessarily authorities for establishing proper usage, but rather for having engaged in a recordable and recorded usage.

Alvin Kernan provocatively explored the ways in which Johnson's *Dictionary* is a product of the print culture and a crucial moment of validation of and within it.[11] The connection between the print world and the *Dictionary* cannot be over-emphasized. In this sense, Johnson's entries can be seen as records of the use of words in print in contexts which offer, for the most part, an explanation or clarification of meanings of the words. Despite the perceived systematic aspect of print as opposed to the impressionistic element of oral language, reliance on the print record introduces a strong element of randomness and contingency in Johnson's selection and inclusion of examples. Not surprisingly, it depended on what he and his amanuenses happened to find in printed books, to mark, and finally to incorporate. And the evidence suggests that the selection of quotations was rather unscientific and instinctive, and that there was little way to be certain what an entry would look like until the copied manuscript material was gathered and Johnson could see what quotations he had selected (perhaps months or years earlier). A wide selection of texts was marked, and the passages eventually transcribed, but it was impossible to be sure of the make-up of the entry until late in the process. Johnson may have gone back to texts searching for passages illustrating specific letters or perhaps even missing entries, but this was the exception, and certainly came as a late measure. So, contingency was built into the process. Johnson's definitional headings are then generated out of these quotations.[12]

---

[11] Alvin Kernan, *Printing Technology, Letters, and Samuel Johnson* (Princeton, NJ: Princeton University Press, 1987), especially pp. 181–203.
[12] See Reddick, pp. 25–54, for a description and analysis of Johnson's procedure.

Elsewhere, I have argued from manuscript evidence that Johnson apparently attempted to begin to assemble (or to have his amanuenses assemble) the manuscript for the *Dictionary* at an early stage in his work, before much of the material from writers was gathered or even marked for letters which come later in the wordlist.[13] This method proved unworkable and led to a reconceptualization of the entire project. It seems very possible, although much more careful examination would need to be carried out, that Johnson's original method was in part an attempt to shape the entries in ways that DeMaria has suggested: to provide encyclopaedic reference, perhaps to include fuller quotations, and to emphasize didactic themes. One of the problems with Johnson's original attempt was that the imposition of pre-existing semantic structures on to the quotations was theoretically inadequate and inflexible, inconsistent with his philosophy of language use, and mirroring the practical problems of assembling the material. And one could add here as a hypothesis that the understandable hope for extra-linguistic message, theme, wisdom, and so on, which is suggested in the Preface, was simultaneously discovered to be impracticable in this case. Not only was all of the material to be included simply not available when these entries were being constructed, but Johnson faced a situation in which the coherence and moral didacticism he may have sought was incompatible with his desire to respond to the stricter dictates of linguistic evidence. He could, and did, choose extra-linguistically 'useful' illustrations when possible, and avoided the opposite. But any desire for consistency would be defeated by the changing exigencies of the compilation and assembly of material.

This leads us to a consideration of the ways in which Johnson's *Dictionary* records historical usage and development: is it, in fact, 'historical', as Kippis claimed? It does include quotations from earlier writers, usually those writing from the middle of the sixteenth century to the first decades of the eighteenth. And the quotations are usually ordered chronologically. But unlike the *Oxford English Dictionary*, which attempts to record the earliest usage of a word in print, and provides dates, establishing precise historical moments of usage through the centuries, Johnson collects some uses previously printed, with little concern for primacy, and arranges them as if, for the historical period which forms the limits of his canon for selection, they are under a plausible use-heading. They appear more like contemporaries, of each other and of Johnson himself. Entries in Johnson's *Dictionary* provide not histories of word use and development: rather, synchronic examples in the history of English printed texts. Notice that in Johnson's Preface to the *Dictionary* there is virtually nothing said about providing a historical record. Johnson's literary examples represent moments, which Johnson's definitions then elucidate. It has been said that Johnson so

---

[13] Reddick, pp. 37–54.

regretted language change that he insisted on a somewhat belated seven-teenth-century style of use. Though there is some truth to this observation, I believe that Johnson is simply more interested in stylistic occurrences (synchronic), but with an eye for metaphoric developments (diachronic) reflected less in the quotations than in the movement through the definitions from the root sense through the figurative senses.[14]

Johnson's dehistoricizing of the passages is another way that they are decontextualized. A quotation is usually pulled out not only from its original verbal and physical context, but also its historical context. The possibilities of its retaining something like its original voice (situated in history, reflecting its original situation of use and intention) are very slight, and again the quotation enters the 'free space' of the entry with other passages, also decontextualized. Is the 'eternal author', or the 'historical author' — the author who wrote the work from which the passage is taken — somehow incorporated unaffected into the *Dictionary* to make declamatory statements, and so on? Of course not. In fact, neither the quoted author nor Johnson himself is allowed authority or voice without a complicated negotiation of relationship and expectation within the text, and specifically under the entry.[15] It is also true that the 'authority' offered even by historical identification is for the most part denied to these authors, because the historical record is not seen to be of importance. It should be clear that these authors provide an authority which is chiefly linguistic (illustrating the existence of a particular word use), and the remainder (moral or didactic position, historical record, demonstrating proper use) is severely qualified as a result of the structure of the *Dictionary* and the way in which Johnson chooses and incorporates these passages.

Johnson's method of recording uses within a historical period as he finds them leads him often to choose a single quotation or source as illustration which may well not reflect conventional usage. One can clearly see that this accentuates the contingent quality of Johnson's dictionary, a dilemma all dictionaries, especially those which include illustrations, to some extent find themselves in.[16] Johnson's definitions function as literary criticism of the passages, to greater and lesser extent. The entire entry works as a hermetic whole, commenting within its elements on the possibilities of word usage. It is even arguable that one can view the *Dictionary*, in part, as a collection of

[14] For Johnson's establishment of definitions, see, in addition to Johnson's own Preface, Elizabeth Hedrick, 'Locke's Theory of Language and Johnson's *Dictionary*', *Eighteenth-Century Studies*, 20 (1987), 422–44; W. K. Wimsatt, *Philosophic Words: A Study of Style and Meaning in the 'Rambler' and 'Dictionary' of Samuel Johnson* (New Haven, CT: Yale University Press, 1948), especially Chapter 2; and Reddick, pp. 25–54.
[15] For a slightly different emphasis on this critical point, see Reddick, pp. 9–10.
[16] See the discussion of the necessity for lexicographers to distinguish the conventional from the unique or unusual word usage ('to typify rather than to define'), in Peter Hanks, 'Evidence and Intuition in Lexicography', in Tomaszczyk and Lewandowska-Tomaszczyk, pp. 31–41 (p. 32). He concludes that most dictionaries ('more by accident than design, I suspect') in fact frequently tend towards the unusual in word selection and definition (p. 35).

definitions which are glosses of thousands of quotations collected mainly from books by seventeenth-century authors. In this way, there is much wisdom and learning collected, but mainly rhetorical moments.

Johnson wrote that he had compiled the folio *Dictionary* 'for the use of such as aspire to exactness of criticism or elegance of style'.[17] This comment pertains specifically to the quotations and the definitions generated by the reading of them. *Criticism* implies judgement of use and *style* the active response of a writer or speaker to an act of critical judgement. Famously, Robert Browning was supposed to have qualified himself for the profession of literature 'by reading and digesting the whole of Johnson's Dictionary'.[18] He read it, it would seem, for the formation of his style: he consulted the fullest record available concerning the ability to say or write about things (situations, pleasures, feelings, phenomena). W. K. Wimsatt noted that the nineteenth-century historian Henry Thomas Buckle read the *Dictionary*, as Buckle recorded in his diary, 'to enlarge my vocabulary'.[19] For the autodidact, the *Dictionary* (to some extent itself the product of one) represents a profound beginning of that process of handing down from generation to generation the commentary on and *exempla* of word usage. Johnson is providing examples of 'doing things with words' and then describing what, in relation to a specific word, was done. W. K. Wimsatt wrote poetically, in his classic *Philosophic Words*, 'As John Ray [the seventeenth-century "physico-theologian"] had seen the Wonders of God everywhere in the Creation, Johnson's readers found the same wonders everywhere in the variegated realm of discourse of which his Dictionary was the alphabetized mirror' (p. 28). This observation is especially acute in the way that it ties the *Dictionary* to an emphasis on the world of discourse, what is and has been said about things. Johnson's *Dictionary* deals with that world, with the graphic, typographical representations of discourse. The *Dictionary* as an 'alphabetized mirror' necessarily applies its linguistic function, regardless of thematics.

Insisting that Johnson's *Dictionary* is an encyclopaedia suggests a nostalgic desire for unity and authority in a dictionary, as a reflection of a particular act of monumentalization, as determined by and reflecting authority. This desire is held, whether explicitly or otherwise, by most readers and writers. But I have suggested ways in which Johnson's accomplishment can be seen differently and be revealed as even more remarkable. Johnson's dictionary does cry out to be called something more. It is fuller than almost any other. It is inconsistent in its historical descriptions, tending the text more in the direction of an encyclopaedia than a book recording language development. It sometimes includes clearly encyclopaedic passages and quotations from

---

[17] Preface to *A Dictionary of the English Language [. . .] Abstracted from the Folio edition, by the author Samuel Johnson, A.M.* (1756).
[18] Mrs Sutherland Orr, *Life and Letters of Robert Browning* (London, 1891), p. 53.
[19] Wimsatt, p. 24, n. 10.

books of reference (indeed, encyclopaedias). But the dictionary by and large is engaged in something quite different, of which our understanding is seriously damaged by the imposition of unity, or coherence, or type. It has a field of text, and of language occurrence, and of commentary, explicit or otherwise, rather than a field of knowledge.

If the *Dictionary* consists of a scheme of general education, then it educates primarily in relation to the ability to read and to experience literature and to organize what we read into coherence and understanding. Yes, it becomes an anthology of sorts, but when the lexical purpose has primacy over the extra-lexical, the encyclopaedic, the declamatory or the expository, then the usages demonstrate, we may say, more form than content. Our emphasis in assessing the *Dictionary* needs to be on enactment, on performance, rather than on theme and message. Johnson's own words in the Preface, intended to counter prospective criticism of his illustrations, defends them not in terms of their wisdom or their truth or moral quality. He defends them on linguistic, semantic, and literary grounds:

There is more danger of censure from the multiplicity than paucity of examples; authorities will sometimes seem to have been accumulated without necessity or use, and perhaps some will be found, which might, without loss, have been omitted. But a work of this kind is not hastily to be charged with superfluities: those quotations which to careless or unskilful perusers appear only to repeat the same sense, will often exhibit, to a more accurate examiner, diversities of signification, or, at least, afford different shades of the same meaning: one will shew the word applied to persons, another to things; one will express an ill, another a good, and a third a neutral sense; one will prove the expression genuine from an ancient authour; another will shew it elegant from a modern: a doubtful authority is corroborated by another of more credit; an ambiguous sentence is ascertained by a passage clear and determinate; the word, how often soever repeated, appears with new associates and in different combinations, and every quotation contributes something to the stability or enlargement of the language. (*Dictionary*, sig. C^r)

I would argue, then, that Johnson's *Dictionary* is no more encyclopaedic than most contemporary dictionaries (in some ways less so), that it is didactic primarily in terms of style (linguistic competence) rather than content, and that it is not particularly historically concerned, despite its reliance on literary writings from the past. In fact, the quotations are virtually dehistoricized and, as such, decontextualized. It has been often and rightly remarked that Johnson was particularly preoccupied with the writing of the seventeenth century, and the fact that he incorporates quotations from this and other early periods without a clearly demonstrated concern for historical primacy is indicative of his sense that these writers write a form of modern and, needless to say, accessible English. This, I would suggest, underlies the criticisms levelled by contemporaries, Kippis and Pinkerton quoted above, as well as others, towards Johnson's incorporation of authorities. In this respect, it is true, as Pinkerton asserted, 'the joke is, that with [Johnson], every body is an authority'. But if every authority is, in most cases, equally authoritative, it is also true that each quoted voice is necessarily reoriented and constrained, as is the authorial voice of the lexicographer/poet/compiler himself, within the new and strange context of his brilliant *Dictionary*.

Johnson's *Dictionary* and the Politics of 'Standard English'

NICHOLAS HUDSON

University of British Columbia

Did Johnson's *Dictionary* support the cause of class oppression? A well-known group of studies has portrayed Johnson's work in precisely this way as an instrument for suppressing lower-class idioms and for authorizing the language of the upper classes as the only 'proper' English. According to John Barrell, whose work has strongly influenced this interpretation, there is a direct link between Johnson's allegedly authoritarian politics and his loyal support of the ruling classes in the *Dictionary*: 'Johnson's notion of language, as of government, is quite openly and frankly one in which the majority should be idle and helpless spectators, while the customs of the polite are converted into law.'[1] Citing the Preface to the *Dictionary*, Barrell points to Johnson's apparent rejection of working-class idioms, 'the fugitive cant' of the 'laborious and mercantile part of the people'.[2] Johnson embraced the language of 'gentlemen', a superficially neutral and universal standard that in fact gave full authority over English to the ruling élite. Barrell's position was later taken up by Olivia Smith, who included Johnson along with Harris and Lowth in a 'linguistic trinity' that 'contributed to the hegemony of language, justifying and perpetuating class divisions'.[3] By giving precedence to written over spoken language, Johnson divided language along 'class lines', condemning 'the language of all but the exclusively educated'.[4] Most recently, Tony Crowley has enrolled Johnson in the 'war' waged by eighteenth-century lexicographers and grammarians to crush the 'heteroglossic' vitality of English, with its many class and provincial dialects, and to create a single national idiom, 'standard English'.[5]

This interpretation of Johnson as an authoritarian Tory, dedicated to silencing the poor and uneducated, takes no account of modern scholarship by Donald Greene and others that has attempted to disabuse readers of this deceptive Victorian understanding of his politics. Yet better informed studies of the *Dictionary* have not, curiously, questioned the assumption that Johnson stigmatized vulgar language and legitimized only 'polite' idioms as proper

---

[1] *English Literature in History 1730–80: An Equal, Wide Survey* (London: Hutchinson, 1983), p. 148.
[2] Preface to the *Dictionary of the English Language*, in Johnson, *Works*, 11 vols (Oxford: Talboys and Wheeler; London: Pickering, 1825), v, 44–45.
[3] *The Politics of Language 1791–1819* (Oxford: Clarendon Press, 1984), p. 4.
[4] Smith, p. 14.
[5] See Tony Crowley, *Language in History: Theories and Text* (London and New York: Routledge, 1996), p. 94.

English.[6] My purpose here is to challenge this reading of the *Dictionary*. I will stress that Johnson by no means attempted to serve the linguistic demands of the rich and powerful, or to exclude the idiom of the poor or vulgar. So far from showing any desire to please the 'polite', Johnson regarded himself as an outsider from this class, and created a dictionary remarkable for its broad inclusiveness and, frequently, its defiance of polite standards. Johnson's major criterion for judging the propriety of English was not the 'usage' of the polite, as it was for his erstwhile patron, Lord Chesterfield. While usually seeing himself as a mere recorder of all English usage, polite or vulgar, Johnson did correct words and locutions that he considered contrary to reason and 'the genius of our tongue'.[7] These theoretically objective criteria reflect Johnson's vision of himself as an independent scholar, the servant of truth and 'science', not the upper class.

It cannot be disputed that Johnson finally attempted to authorize certain idioms and to suppress or discredit others, and that he sometimes distinguished between 'low' or 'cant' words and proper language. Yet it is significant that he initially doubted his authority to make these distinctions, donning the robes of linguistic arbiter only with the encouragement of Lord Chesterfield. In *The Plan of an English Dictionary* (1748), addressed to Chesterfield, Johnson acknowledged that 'with regard to questions of purity or propriety, I was once in doubt whether I should not attribute too much to myself, in attempting to decide them, and whether my province was to extend beyond the proposition of the question, and the display of the suffrages on each side'. It was only 'your Lordship's opinion' that finally determined him 'to interpose my own judgement'.[8] As the result of this decision, Johnson became one of the first innovators of 'usage labels' stigmatizing some eight hundred words as 'low', 'barbarous', 'vulgar', or 'cant'.[9] These include *fun* ('a low cant word'), *doodle* ('a cant word'), *bamboozle* ('a cant word not used in pure or in grave writings'), *chouse* ('a fortuitous cant word, without etymology') and *mighty* used as an intensifier ('not to be used but in very low language'). Other 'low cant words' are omitted altogether, as can be shown by glancing at the language of lower-class characters in Fanny Burney's

---

[6] Robert DeMaria has argued in 'The Politics of Johnson's *Dictionary*', *PMLA*, 104 (1989), 64–74, that a careful scrutiny of the *Dictionary* essentially confirms Donald J. Greene's repositioning of Johnson in the liberal and progressive tradition of Locke. DeMaria does not, however, consider the political implications of Johnson's excluding or stigmatizing certain kinds of words. Allen Reddick, who regards Johnson as a strong Tory, agrees that Johnson's method generally marginalized those 'less involved with the production of polite literature or printed culture' (*The Making of Johnson's Dictionary*, rev. edn, (Cambridge: Cambridge University Press, 1996), p. 35). Barrell's position is again corroborated by A. D. Horgan in *Johnson on Language* (New York: St Martin's Press, 1994), p. 84.

[7] Preface to the *Dictionary*, in *Works* (1825), v, 40.

[8] 'The Plan of an English Dictionary', in *Works* (1825), v, 19.

[9] On Johnson's importance in the development of usage labels, see Harold B. Allen, 'Samuel Johnson: Originator of Usage Labels', in M. A. Jazayery and others, *Linguistic and Literary Studies in Honor of Archibald A. Hill* (The Hague: Mouton, 1979), pp. 193–200. On the number and subdivision of these labels, see Daisuke Nagashima, *Johnson the Philologist* (Hirakata: Kansai University of Foreign Studies, 1988), pp. 128–29.

Evelina (1778), a class-conscious work that Johnson highly praised. The base social origins of Captain Mirvan and the Brangton family are marked by terms such as *grumpy*, *funny*, and *to shop*, words that ultimately found their way into standard English but into no edition of Johnson's *Dictionary*.[10]

On the other hand, 800 words is a small proportion of the 41,000-odd words in this work. And many 'low' terms do appear the *Dictionary*, most frequently without comment. Indeed, these words became ammunition for Johnson's enemies, who condemned the *Dictionary* as 'a wretched Perform-ance',[11] and its author as 'a low-bred ungenerous ruffian',[12] partly because Johnson had debased his work with vulgar language. James Thomson Callender, one of the many Scots enraged at Johnson after the Ossian affair, denounced that 'stupid affectation of completeness which descends to the definition of a f—t'.[13] *Whore*, *whoredom*, and *piss* prompted similar disgust in Callender and other authors, even into the nineteenth century. One of the many complaints made against Johnson by Noah Webster, the great American lexicographer, was that his English predecessor had defiled his *Dictionary* with 'the lowest of all vulgar words'.[14] Webster's impression that Johnson included many 'low' terms is corroborated by a second glance at Burney's *Evelina*, for we find that Johnson by no means excluded all the low expressions satirized in that work. Of the many words italicized by Burney to mark their risible vulgarity, *grudge*, *actionable*, and *fob off* all pass into Johnson's work without comment. If we consider another treasury of 'low' speech, Gay's *Beggar's Opera*, we find again that Johnson drew no consistent distinction between polite and impolite language. *To peach*, *to filch*, *slut*, and *booty* all appear in the *Dictionary* without any indication of their association with the lingo of criminals and prostitutes.

Clearly, then, Johnson made no systematic effort to exclude or even stigmatize 'low' terms. He rejected some, but as many or more are admitted: we know indeed that Johnson sought information on 'low cant phrases' from one of his amanuenses, a hard drinking card-player named Francis Stewart, whom Johnson none the less considered 'a ingenious and worthy man'.[15] We need, then, to reconsider what criteria Johnson had in mind when he excluded or warned against some low terms but included others. Did he really have in mind the need to preserve and elevate the language of the ruling classes, the polite idioms of 'gentlemen' and 'ladies'?

[10] See Frances Burney, *Evelina, or the History of a Young Lady's Entrance into the World*, ed. by Edward A. Bloom (Oxford and New York: Oxford University Press, 1968), pp. 168–69.
[11] Philip Withers, *Artistarchus; or, The Principles of Composition*, 2nd edn (London, 1787), p. 425.
[12] James Thomson Callender, *A Critical Review of the Works of Johnson* (Edinburgh, 1783; repr. New York and London: Garland, 1974), p. 34.
[13] Callender, *Critical Review*, p. v.
[14] Letter to David Ramsay, October 1807, in Harry R. Warfel, *Letters of Noah Webster* (New York: Library Publishers, 1953), p. 287.
[15] See James L. Clifford, *Dictionary Johnson* (New York: McGraw-Hill, 1979), p. 52; Reddick, *Johnson's Dictionary*, p. 62.

The attempt to denigrate a certain kind of language as too 'low' for polite discourse was not, of course, a phenomenon that began in the eighteenth century. It has a long history stretching back to classical rhetoricians such as Quintilian, who maintained that usage, 'the surest pilot in speaking', must not be understood not as the language of the majority, but as 'the agreed practice of educated men'.[16] Among Renaissance humanists who revived Quintilian's teachings, such as Bembo, Valla, and Castiglione, there was a similar contempt for 'lo volgare' and a tendency to associate proper speech with the best writing and most elegant speakers of the court.[17] The court provided the standard of 'bon usage' for many French grammarians of the seventeenth century such as Vaugelas and Bohours.[18] In eighteenth-century Britain, this tradition was carried on by courtly authors such as Lord Chesterfield, who (writing in French) warned his son to cultivate an appropriately élite standard of language:

Not to speak ill, is not sufficient; we must speak well; and the best method of attaining to that, is to read the best authors with attention; and to observe how people of fashion speak, and those who express themselves best; for shop-keepers, common-people, footmen, and maid-servants, all speak ill. They make use of low and vulgar expressions, which people of rank never use.[19]

In an age of 'upward mobility', when so many sought advice on the appropriate conduct and language, it is not surprising that grammars and conduct books urged readers to follow 'the Custom and Use of the best speakers', as James Greenwood directed in his *Essay towards a Practical English Grammar*.[20] Others looked back nostalgically to a time of greater elegance and stable aristocratic power. The elocutionist Thomas Sheridan idealized the language pronounced in the court of Queen Anne, believing that this was the mellifluous standard he heard in the voice of Jonathan Swift.[21] Sheridan's followers in the so-called 'elocution' movement denigrated working-class pronunciations and provincial dialects as 'faults' against the standard enunciation of the 'polite'.[22] A typically British version of the

---

[16] Quintilian, *Institutio Oratorio*, trans. by H. E. Butler, Loeb Classical Library, 4 vols (Cambridge, MA: Harvard University Press; London: Heinemann, 1930), I, 113, 132–33.
[17] See G. A. Padley, *Grammatical Theory in Western Europe 1500–1700*, 2 vols (Cambridge: Cambridge University Press, 1985–8), II, 5–153; Angelo Mazzocco, *Linguistic Theories in Dante and the Humanists* (Leiden, New York, and Köln: E. J. Brill, 1993), pp. 13–23 and *passim*.
[18] See Claude Favre de Vaugelas, *Remarques sur la langue française* (1647), 2 vols (Versailles: Cerg; Paris: Baudry, 1880), I, 43; Dominique Bohours, *Entretiens d'Ariste et d'Eugène*, 2nd ed. (Amsterdam, 1671), pp. 134–35.
[19] 17 October 1739, in Philip Dorner Stanhope, Lord Chesterfield, *Letters to his Son*, ed. by Oliver H. Leigh (New York: Tudor, 1937), p. 375.
[20] (London, 1711), p. 36. For a similar standard in later works, see John Fell, *An Essay towards an English Grammar* (London, 1784; repr. Menston: Scolar Press, 1967), p. 1; John Walker, *A Critical Pronouncing Dictionary* (London, 1791), p. vii.
[21] See Thomas Sheridan, *A Rhetorical Grammar of the English Language* (Dublin, 1781; repr. Menston: Scholar Press, 1969), pp. xix–xx; *A Course of Lectures on Elocution, together with two Dissertations on Language* (London, 1762), p. 30.
[22] On the elocution movement, see Wilbur Samuel Howell, *Eighteenth-Century British Logic and Rhetoric* (Princeton, NJ: Princeton University Press, 1971), pp. 143–256; Michael Shortland, 'Moving Speeches: Language and Elocution in Eighteenth-century Britain', *History of European Ideas*, 8 (1987), 639–53.

standard of 'good usage' can be found in George Campbell's *Philosophy of Rhetoric* (1776). Campbell rejected Vaugelas's standard of court usage as contrary to the 'spirit' of the British nation, which 'is more of the republican than of the monarchial'. In its place, he appealed to the usage of 'those who have had a liberal education', as supported by the consensus of 'celebrated authors'. Inspired by this desire to cleanse English of all words with a 'vile and despicable origin', Campbell condemned a long list of terms, including *fib, banter, bigot, fop, flippant, flimsy, bellytimber, thorowstitch, dumfound, transmogrify, bamboozle, topsyturvey, pellmell, helterskelter*, and *hurlyburly*.[23]

All these words, with the exception of *transmogrify*, appear in Johnson's *Dictionary*, and only *bamboozle, fib, flimsy*, and *dumfound* are singled out as either 'cant' or 'low'. The inclusion of these words suggests that Johnson by no means wished to expel 'cant' or 'low' words from use in all contexts, even among the well-bred. Johnson was concerned rather with identifying levels of usage: he meant that *bamboozle* ('a cant word not used in pure or grave writings'), like the intensifier *mighty* ('not to be used but in very low language'), were unsuitable in formal writing and conversation, though they might well be appropriate in less formal contexts. He labelled *Tory* a 'cant term', for example, yet often used it himself in conversation. Johnson's sensitivity to appropriate levels of English characterized much of his literary criticism. In an analysis of Macbeth's speech before the murder of Duncan ('Come, thick night'), he objected to Shakespeare's use of *knife, dun* and *peeping* because they were ill-suited to the language of a nobleman considering the murder of a king. *Knife*, of course, is a perfectly ordinary English word. In Johnson's assessment, however, it is unfortunately connected with 'the sordid offices' of preparing meat, and for this reason detracts from the dignity and intensity of Macbeth's soliloquy.[24] Johnson often wrote as if he regretted that such words had a distracting association with 'vulgar' or 'low' ideas. Yet as he observed in *Rambler*, no. 168, even the most enlightened and rational person had to admit that these associations were unpleasant: 'every man, however profound or abstracted, perceives himself irresistibly alienated by low terms; they who profess the most zealous adherence to truth are forced to admit that she owes part of her charms to ornaments' (p. 126).

In Johnson's view, language ideally served as the faithful medium for 'thought', which constituted the true merit of any literary work: as he wrote in his *Life of Dryden*, words should not 'draw attention to themselves which they should transmit to things'.[25] But it was vain to deny that certain kinds

[23] George Campbell, *Philosophy of Rhetoric*, ed. by Lloyd F. Bitzer (Carbondale: Southern Illinois University Press, 1963), pp. 142–45, 168–69. For an excellent overview of polite and courtly language in the eighteenth century, see Carey McIntosh, *Common and Courtly Language: The Stylistics of Social Class in 18th-Century English Literature* (Philadelphia: University of Pennsylvania Press, 1986).

[24] *Rambler*, no. 168, *The Yale Edition of the Works of Samuel Johnson*, ed. by Allen T. Hazen and others (New Haven, CT, and London: Yale University Press, 1958–), III–V: *The Rambler*, ed. by W. J. Bate and Albrecht B. Strauss (1969), V, 127–28.

[25] *Lives of the Poets*, ed. by G. B. Hill, 3 vols (Oxford: Clarendon Press, 1903), I, 420.

of words undermined our ability to appreciate the intrinsic worth of a literary work, just as shabby dress detracted from our admiration of the most worthy person. We may well think of the author himself at this point: Johnson's comments on 'low' diction correspond with prejudices that he faced in his own life, and with an important theme in his moral writings. The humiliation of poverty is an important theme of moral essays written during the time he was working on the *Dictionary*. As he observed in *Rambler*, no. 166, 'No complaint has been more frequently repeated in all ages than that of the neglect of merit associated with poverty, and the difficulty with which valuable or pleasing qualities force themselves into view, when they are obscured by indigence.'[26] This is very much the same observation that Johnson makes concerning the displeasing influence of 'low' language. In all cases, he is concerned with the fact that the external trappings of language or dress inevitably interfere with the judgement of real worth. As he insisted, 'truth [. . .] loses much of her power over the soul, when she appears disgraced by a dress uncouth and ill-adjusted' (p. 126).[27]

Johnson's observations on 'low' language were not, in short, made from Chesterfield's cool distance of elegance and rank; he wrote as a man who had personally suffered from the world's social prejudices, but who had reluctantly accepted the defects of human judgement. In the case of both words and people, he well knew that 'dress' profoundly influenced the perception of merit. This metaphor of words as the 'dress of thought' had, of course, become exceedingly hackneyed by Johnson's day. None the less, his use of this old image is distinctive for his unusually sharp separation between 'dress' and 'body' — between the arbitrary value of the term and the real intrinsic value of what the term means. Words, like people, could seem 'low' yet have inherent value. In addition, Johnson analysed the influence of 'low' language with unusual cogency. He insisted, first, that the judgement of 'lowness' was as fluctuating and artificial as any passing fashion. 'No word is naturally and intrinsically meaner than another', he wrote, evidently correcting the belief that polite people conformed to some unvarying archetype of elegant speech. On the contrary, 'words which convey ideas of dignity in one age, are banished from elegant writing or convention in another'.[28] Psychologically understood, words became 'low' through a process of merely arbitrary association, as described by Locke. 'Unpleasing images' became accidentally attached to certain terms, through their use by people in disagreeable situations, interfering with the perception of the idea that they denoted.

Hence, contrary to Barrell's reading, Johnson's warnings against 'low' terms in the *Dictionary* must be distinguished from class arrogance, or from the sturdy prejudice of an authoritarian Tory. Perhaps no British philosopher

---

[26] *The Yale Edition*, v, 116.
[27] See also *Idler*, no. 63.
[28] *Rambler*, no. 168, *The Yale Edition*, v, 126–27.

or grammarian had thought so deeply about the nature of 'low' diction, or was so sensitive to the irrationality and transience of this stigma. A similar defence of Johnson can be mounted against related charges that he supported upper-class standards of language. According to Olivia Smith, for example, Johnson upheld 'hegemonic concepts', by, among other devices, maintaining in the *Dictionary* that 'language pertains more to literary texts than to speech'.[29] Smith refers here to Johnson's assertion that he omitted many words 'of which no mention is found in books',[30] his use of illustrations from the writings of great authors, and his rejection of orthographic reform that attempted to make writing a more faithful image of speech. All these features of Johnson's *Dictionary*, Smith argues, bolstered the dominance of the literate upper-classes over the illiterate poor. Yet, as Johnson made clear in the Preface, he did not entirely restrict himself to books. In fact, he collected many words 'as industry should find, or chance should offer it, in the boundless chaos of living speech' (p. 31). Nor is it accurate to assume that he maintained an élite standard of language by relying on printed sources, for not all books draw exclusively from educated speech. In contrast with grammarians who advised readers to imitate only the 'best and most approved [. . .] Writers',[31] Johnson did not restrict himself to a canon of élite authors who purified their language of all common terms. Indeed, some delicate readers reproved his use of 'authorities [. . .] below the dignity of such a work': L'Estrange (very often), Butler's *Hudibras*, Tusser's *Husbandry*, and Howell's *Vocal Forest* all served as valuable sources of low, vulgar, or technical diction.[32] Another source of 'the diction of common life' was, as Johnson remarked, Shakespeare, whose vast range of vocabulary and 'licentious' turns of phrase (in Johnson's expression) often threatened the bounds of propriety.[33] The authority of Shakespeare, Noah Webster complained, seemed to justify the inclusion of any low or corrupt term in Johnson's work.[34]

With regard to Johnson's views on orthographic reform, it is inaccurate to assume that he subjugated vulgar speech by rejecting plans to make writing a closer image of speech. Such plans, as I have shown elsewhere, generally fell on deaf ears in Johnson's day, though they had been popular a century earlier.[35] Significantly, many dismissed orthographic reform not as

[29] *Politics of Language*, p. 16.
[30] Preface to the *Dictionary*, *Works* (1825), v, 44.
[31] Fell, *Essay towards an English Grammar*, p. 1.
[32] This criticism was conveyed to Johnson by Garrick, who mentioned Samuel Richardson. 'Nay, (said Johnson,) I have done worse than that: I have cited *thee*, David' (James Boswell, *Life of Samuel Johnson*, ed. by G. B Hill, rev. by L. F. Powell, 6 vols (Oxford: Clarendon Press, 1934–50), IV, 4). See also Noah Webster's complaint that 'no small part of his examples are taken from authors who did not write the language with purity' (*Letters*, p. 288).
[33] Preface to the *Dictionary*, *Works* (1825), v, 40. See Johnson's criticisms of Shakespeare in the definitions of 'to ake' and 'behindhand'.
[34] *Letters*, p. 287.
[35] See Nicholas Hudson, *Writing and European Thought, 1600–1830* (Cambridge: Cambridge University Press, 1984), pp. 92–118.

populist (as Smith assumes) but as élitist, for such reform assumed that the mass of writers should accept spellings devised by a small coterie of grammarians and literati.[36] On linguistic grounds, Johnson's reasoning on this issue was incisive, promoting a better understanding of the relationship between writing and speech. As he argued in the Preface, the diversity of modern spellings reflects the diversity of pronunciations that existed when 'penmen' first attempted to record speech. Only writing and print provided stability, for pronunciations still varied greatly among illiterate people, and in places where writing is rare or non-existent (pp. 24–25). In Johnson's opinion, therefore, it was more logical to make writing the standard of pronunciation than the other way round: 'For pronunciation the best general rule is, to consider those as the most elegant speakers, who deviate least from written words.'[37] This line of analysis had nothing to do with some prejudice against the lower class, or a desire to subjugate the illiterate. On the contrary, Johnson strongly and consistently defended the promotion of universal literacy, rejecting the complaint that literacy made the working class proud and unruly.[38]

An associated charge against Johnson, advanced by Tony Crowley, places him in the movement of British grammarians and lexicographers who wished to obliterate provincial dialects, along with the dialects of the poor and women.[39] In fact, Johnson was among the century's most energetic supporters of projects to preserve and protect ancient British languages. He urged Boswell to collect a whole 'folio' of 'north-country' words, encouraged William Drummond's Erse translation of the Bible, and supported William Shaw's Erse grammar; while in Wales, he showed an active concern for the preservation of Welsh, urging the republication of David ap Rhees's Welsh Grammar, and he twice wrote to the Irish antiquarian Thomas O'Connor, commending his studies of the Gaelic tongue, and lauding ancient Ireland as 'the school of the West'.[40] It is no surprise, then, that he had little sympathy for Thomas Sheridan's campaign to eliminate provincial accents and establish a uniform, courtly standard of 'pure' English. He spoke 'slightingly' of Sheridan's 'art' as both petty and futile: 'It is burning a

---

[36] As James Beattie declared in *The Theory of Language* (London, 1788), it was not 'in the power of lawgivers, much less philosophers, to make a whole people renounce the written language' (p. 45). Orthographic reform became popular in the Renaissance, when grammarians such as Thomas Smith and John Hart planned to make English writing a much more accurate image of speech. By the seventeenth century, however, authors such as Guy Miege and John Wilkins were conceding the intransigence of popular spelling, which was ultimately controlled by printers and common writers, not philosophers and grammarians. See F. H. Brengleman, 'Orthoepists, Printers, and the Rationalization of English Spelling', *Journal of English and German Philology*, 79 (1980), 332–54.

[37] Johnson, *Grammar of the English Tongue*, in *Dictionary* (1755), sig. a2ᵛ.

[38] See *Life*, II, 188. The argument that literacy would make the poor less willing to labour for the rich was the well known position of Bernard Mandeville in his *Essay on Charity and Charity-schools* (1723).

[39] See Crowley, *Language in History*, pp. 54–98.

[40] *Life*, II, 91–92; II, 28; III, 107; V, 443; I, 321–22. At least one reader criticized Johnson for not excluding certain provincial terms such as *eleot*, 'an apple used in cyder'. See Henry Croft, *An Unfinished Letter to the Right Honourable William Pitt concerning the New Dictionary of the English Language* (London, 1788), postscript, [p. 3].

farthing candle at Dover, to show light at Calais.'[41] When Boswell worried aloud about his Scottish intonation, Johnson was reassuring — 'Sir, your pronunciation is not offensive' — confessing that 'when people watch me narrowly [. .] they will find me out to be of a particular county'.[42] Indeed, it seems unlikely that Johnson made much of an effort to cleanse his speech of Lichfield intonations. Proud of his provincial and lower-middle-class roots, he praised the inhabitants of Lichfield as 'the most sober, decent people in England', even asserting that they 'spoke the purest English'. This observation bemused the more refined Boswell, who remarked that Johnson's fellow townspeople rhymed *there* with *fear* and pronounced *once* like *woonse*. Undeterred, Johnson himself aroused the amusement of Garrick and others by calling 'Who's for *poonsh*', and by insisting that *heard* should be pronounced *heerd*.[43]

At this point, let us return to the passage in the Preface to the *Dictionary* that has served as the main evidence for Johnson's supposed efforts to suppress working-class idioms and authorize the language of 'gentlemen':

Of the laborious and mercantile part of the people, the diction is in a great measure casual and mutable; many of their terms are formed for some temporary and local convenience, and though current at certain times and places, are in others utterly unknown. This fugitive cant, which is always in a state of increase or decay, cannot be regarded as any part of the durable materials of a language, and, therefore, must be suffered to perish with other things unworthy of preservation. (pp. 44–45)

Did Johnson mean here that he planned to exclude lower-class diction? We have seen that this cannot be the case, for the *Dictionary* is filled with words from across the social register. Contempt for 'the laborious and mercantile part of the people' would, indeed, be odd and inconsistent, given that Johnson ranked himself, in the first paragraph of the Preface, among those 'who toil at the lower employments of life' (p. 23). Was Johnson indicating, then, that he had excluded language connected with the specific trades of the working class and lower middle class? Such an exclusion would contradict his original plan to record 'the peculiar words of every profession', including 'those of law, merchandise, and mechanical trades, so far as they can be supposed useful to the occurrences of common life'.[44] Reviewers of the *Dictionary* agreed that Johnson's work was especially strong in precisely this area of vocabulary. As John Hawkesworth wrote in the *Gentleman's Magazine*, 'as this dictionary was not designed merely for critics, but for popular use, it comprises the peculiar words of every science, art, and profession, even to mechanical trades'.[45]

[41] *Life*, i, 453–54. See also *Life*, i, 386.
[42] *Life*, ii, 158–59.
[43] *Life*, ii, 463–64, and iii, 197.
[44] 'Plan of an English Dictionary', in *Works* (1825), v, 5.
[45] *Gentleman's Magazine*, 25 (April 1755), 147. In a review of the *Dictionary* in *Journal Britannique*, 17 (juillet et août 1755), Matthew Maty, a friend of Chesterfield, criticized Johnson's description of technical terms as 'trop étendues' (p. 225).

The key expression in the above passage seems, in fact, to be 'fugitive cant'. *Cant* is among the most characteristic and emphatic words in Johnson's observations on language. In conversation with Boswell, for example, he reproved what he called 'modern cant', such as the use of *idea* to mean 'non-visual concepts', or the use of *make money* to mean 'get money' instead of 'coin money'.[46] As these examples demonstrate, Johnson by no means equated *cant* with lower-class language, though it did originally have this association.[47] Even in the 1750s, *cant* could still mean 'a corrupt dialect used by beggars and vagabonds'. By Johnson's day, however, *cant* had widened in extension to denote 'a particular form of speaking peculiar to some certain class or body of men'. This form of speaking would certainly include the 'fugitive cant' used by 'the laborious and mercantile part of the people', that is, by those who made their money (or, rather, got their money) from the trades and from commerce. In the *Preface*, Johnson singles out commerce as a great corrupter of language. This is because 'they that have frequent intercourse with strangers, to whom they endeavour to accommodate themselves, must in time learn a mingled dialect, like the jargon which serves the traffickers on the Mediterranean and Indian coasts' (pp. 46–47). In communicating with foreigners, and even in dealing with a wide range of social groups, merchants and traders constantly innovated and transformed language with little regard for its 'purity' and 'analogy'.

By 'the laborious and mercantile part of the people', in short, Johnson clearly referred to the middle class, those involved with trade and business, and not the poor and downtrodden. The cant he meant were words such as *flimsy*, which 'crept into our language from the cant of manufacturers'. Johnson's political sympathies would have encouraged his distrust of the mercantile middle-class, the seedbed of Whiggish principles. Most important, however, this class was predominantly literate, as Johnson himself observed.[48] This factor is significant because Johnson laid most of the blame for the recent corruption of English not on speakers but on 'penmen' and those he called 'illiterate writers'.[49] Quite logically, he concluded that new words, however contrary to the general 'analogy' of English, gained authority and official currency when introduced into books and pamphlets.

---

[46] *Life*, III, 196–97.
[47] In the *Dictionary*, Johnson correctly traced *cant* to the Latin *cantus*, referring to the sing-song solicitation used by beggars even into the eighteenth century.
[48] *Life*, I, 188. Johnson's observations on the literacy of the manufacturing and commercial class have been confirmed by modern studies of literacy rates in the eighteenth century. See Roger S. Schofield, 'Dimensions of Illiteracy in England 1750–1850', in Harvey J. Graff, *Literacy and Social Development in the West: A Reader* (Cambridge: Cambridge University Press, 1981), pp. 201–13; David Vincent, *Literacy and Popular Culture, England 1750–1914* (Cambridge: Cambridge University Press, 1989).
[49] Preface to the *Dictionary*, *Works* (1825), v, 24–25, 48. The term 'illiterate writers' perhaps derives from Dryden, who is contrasting ordinary writers from those 'learn'd in schools'. See Robert De Maria, *Johnson's 'Dictionary' and the Language of Learning* (Chapel Hill and London: University of North Carolina Press, 1986), p. 54. It seems important to keep in mind that Johnson was not referring here to the lower classes, since they remained predominantly 'illiterate' in the modern sense of not knowing how to read and write. Almost half the English people were illiterate in 1755.

Johnson's views on the influence of 'print culture' were therefore more complicated and paradoxical than is sometimes assumed: he valued print as an indispensable resource to stabilize a language through dictionaries and other books, yet also saw that, by increasing the dissemination and authority of neologisms, print had accelerated linguistic disruption.[50]

Given this reasoning, cant words were not those that would normally arise in the speech of the illiterate lower-classes. Johnson insightfully pointed out that the language of 'common people' tends to be highly conservative and traditional: 'A great part of their language is proverbial. If anything rocks at all, they say *it rocks like a cradle*.'[51] Since popular speech generally resists innovation, the most stable period of any language occurs before the rise of commerce and the proliferation of books: 'The language most likely to continue long without alteration would be that of a nation raised a little, and but a little, above barbarity.'[52] The infamous 'chaos' that Johnson found in modern English, and which he set out to order and control, was most characteristic of a society that had achieved a more advanced level of cultural and economic sophistication. Linguistic disorder springs not from people at the lower end of the social spectrum, but from those who have had some education and leisure to think: 'Those who have much leisure to think will always be enlarging the stock of ideas; and every increase in knowledge, whether real or fancied, will produce new words, or combinations of words. When the mind is unchained from necessity, it will range after convenience' (p. 47).

Those with much leisure to think included, of course, the 'polite'. So far from attempting to endorse a 'polite' standard, Johnson recognized that the idle upper classes were one important source of the cant and improper innovation that he sought to correct: 'As politeness increases, some expressions will be considered as too gross and vulgar for the delicate, others as too formal and ceremonious for the gay and airy; new phrases are, therefore, adopted, which must, for the same reasons be in time dismissed' (p. 48). Fashionable society was the main conduit for the influx of French words and syntax into English, regarded by Johnson as perhaps the greatest scourge of the modern tongue. The *beau monde* also delighted in neologisms, as was brought directly to Johnson's attention by none other than Lord Chesterfield. As is well known, just before the publication of the *Dictionary* in the spring of 1755, Chesterfield wrote two papers in the *World*, apparently with the aim of resuming his authority over Johnson as patron. Johnson stiffly rebuffed Chesterfield's approaches in a letter that marks an important milestone in the rise of the professional author, free from dependence on the patronage of the great. The snub conveyed Johnson's anger at Chesterfield

---

[50] On Johnson's confidence in the stabilizing power of print, see Alvin Kernan, *Printing Technology, Letters and Samuel Johnson* (Princeton, NJ: Princeton University Press, 1987), pp. 181–205.
[51] *Life*, III, 136.
[52] Preface to the *Dictionary*, *Works* (1825), v, 47.

after years of neglect. But there was also an intellectual division between them: the fashionable earl and the proud, independent author had profoundly different understandings of the task of the lexicographer. Johnson was not about to heed this erstwhile patron's advice on how to make his work more palatable to London's genteel inhabitants.

This, indeed, was the gist of Chesterfield's papers for the *World*: Johnson should include words current in the *beau monde* in order to please people of fashion, especially fashionable ladies, to whom Chesterfield offers oily homage as the true arbiters of language. These terms included *to fuzz* (a card term meaning to deal 'twice together with the same pack of cards, for luck's sake'), *vastly* (used as an intensifier, as in 'vastly glad', 'vastly sorry' and even 'vastly little') and *flirtation* (which Chesterfield personally heard 'coined [. . .] by the most beautiful mouth in the world').[53] Of these three terms, only *flirtation* made it to Johnson's *Dictionary*, perhaps because it appears in a line by Pope. Significantly, Johnson seems also to have completely misunderstood what *flirtation* meant. Chesterfield's explanation makes it clear that this word had already gained the meaning which it retains to this day. 'Flirtation' was not exactly 'coquetry', he observed, but rather something 'short of coquetry', intimating 'only the first hints of aproximation [*sic*]' (p. 607). Johnson's definition entirely misses this new sense, though he does know that it is upper-class cant: 'FLIRTATION. A quick sprightly motion. A cant word used by women'.

Johnson's misdefinition of *flirtation* is hardly surprising. He himself was an unlikely target for this kind of attention from genteel women, as Chesterfield takes care to remind Johnson.[54] Nor was there easy access from his smoky garret to the candle-lit halls of the rich. He was, as he replied to Chesterfield, 'a retired and uncourtly scholar',[55] and the *Dictionary*, like his essays, was received by many in the *beau monde* as the work of a plodding pedant. 'Well-bred' readers widely re-echoed Thomas Edwards's criticism that Johnson had crowded his work with 'monstrous words [. . .] which never were used by any who pretended to talk or write English'.[56] Particularly ungracious were the many 'inkhorn' words such as *aedespotick, turbinated, perflation*, and so forth that, as the Marchioness Grey complained, 'really break my teeth'.[57] Johnson himself was unapologetic, even defiant, in his alleged pedantry, 'a censure which every man incurs, who has at any time the misfortune to talk

---

[53] *The World*, no. 101, 5 December 1754, pp. 604–07.

[54] Johnson's offended reaction to these papers was no doubt sparked in part by Chesterfield's oblique references to his inelegance and isolation from polite circles: 'I had a greater opinion of his impartiality and severity as judge, than of his gallantry as a fine gentleman' (p. 605).

[55] *Life*, I, 261.

[56] Letter to Daniel Wray, 23 May 1755, Oxford, Bodleian Library, Bodleian MS 1012, p. 208.

[57] Cited in Clifford, *Dictionary Johnson*, p. 80. See also James Thomson Callender's attack on Johnson's polysyllabic terms in *A Critical Review of Johnson*, pp. 27–28, and the extended attack on his diction and style in Archibald Campbell's *Lexiphanes*, discussed below. Johnson's penchant for 'inkhorn' terms reveals the influence of seventeenth-century science and philosophy on his thought, as shown by W. K. Wimsat, Jr, in *Philosophic Words: A Study of Style and Meaning in the 'Rambler' and 'Dictionary' of Samuel Johnson* (New Haven, CT: Yale University Press, 1948), pp. 1–49.

to those who cannot understand him'.[58] Nevertheless, he was quite aware that many listeners or readers in the upper class regarded difficult language and deep thoughts as a 'defect of politeness'.

The true gentleman, as John Barrell correctly points out, seemed to belong to no profession and to have no peculiar character.[59] As Johnson himself observed, 'Perfect good breeding [. . .] consists in having no particular mark of any profession, but a general elegance of manners'.[60] Yet nothing could be less true of the eccentric and outspoken Johnson. This is a man who considered scholarship a 'profession', and who displayed his erudition and force of mind with often intimidating energy and conviction. The professional writer, it is worth recalling, was conventionally associated in the eighteenth century with the squalor of Grub-Street attics, the coarse and ungracious world so mercilessly satirized by Swift and Pope. Hence, in Archibald Campbell's farcical satire of Johnson, *Lexiphanes* (1767), Johnson is portrayed lumbering through low-life London, declaiming on prostitutes, street-brawls, and tavern games in a crude parody of the *Rambler's* Latinate prose: 'It was impossible for me not to succumb under the conjunct importunities of so many illustrious associates, who all simultaneously obsecrated me to accompany them in an ambulatory project to the wakeful harbinger of the day at Chelsea, and there to recreate and invigorate our powers with buns, convivial ale, and a sober erratick game at skittles'.[61] Campbell's ostensible purpose in this satire (beyond denigrating the 'anti-Scottish' Johnson) was to halt what he considered the dangerous drift of English towards the 'absurd *Lexiphanick* style'. He contrasted Johnson's 'uncouth trash' with a style of 'true taste', associated with the genteel prose of Lord Lyttleton and other well-bred authors (pp. xxii, xxiv). Indeed, many eighteenth-century readers criticized Johnson's style as stilted and opaque, preferring the graceful style of 'gentleman-authors' such as Lyttleton, Adam Smith, Hugh Blair, and David Hume.[62]

Johnson's *Dictionary* was not, in short, a 'polite' book. The opinion that he set out to convert 'the customs of the polite' into linguistic 'law' misrepresents both the considerable inclusiveness of Johnson's lexicon, as well as his personal and intellectual isolation from the upper class. Neither Johnson's abrasive personality nor his scholarly language conformed to genteel expectations of gracious banality. But here we arrive back at our as yet

[58] *Rambler*, no. 173, *The Yale Edition*, v. 151.
[59] *English Literature in History 1730–80*, pp. 17–50.
[60] *Life*, II, 82.
[61] [Archibald Campbell], *Lexiphanes: a Dialogue* (London, 1767), p. 42.
[62] See Callender, *Critical Review of Johnson*, p. 29. In a sympathetic biography of Johnson written in 1785, William Shaw noted the prejudice faced by authors like Johnson who relied on writing for their livelihood, and were not 'independent of the Booksellers' in the manner of so-called 'gentleman authors'. Among these gentleman authors was Hume, whose gracefully written philosophy (according to Shaw) overshadowed Johnson's achievements in the 1750s. See *The Early Biographies of Samuel Johnson*, ed. by O. M. Brack, Jr and Robert E. Kelley (Iowa City: University of Iowa Press, 1974), p. 163.

unresolved question: if Johnson did not authorize polite usage, then what standard did he use in judging the propriety of language?

There were, indeed, alternatives to merely authorizing 'the Custom and Use of the best speakers'. In France, the major alternative was *raison*, to use the term commonly employed in the French tradition of 'rational grammar'. The fountain-head of this movement was the *Grammaire générale et raisonnée* (1660) by the Port-Royal authors Arnauld and Lancelot. These authors, isolated by class and theology from courtly circles, set out to overturn the criteria of 'polite' usage associated particularly with the grammar of Vaugelas.[63] The Port-Royal grammar, so influential in Enlightenment France, also made a considerable impact in Britain, though the battle-lines between 'reason' and 'usage' were somewhat less clearly marked on this side of the Channel. The conflict is detected when we compare a grammar such as James Greenwood's *Essay towards a Practical English Grammar* (1711), which defines 'right speaking' as 'the Custom and Use of the best speakers' (p. 36), with Michael Maittaire's *The English Grammar* (1712), which places the emphasis instead on the rule of 'analogy'. Maittaire borrowed this term from the tradition of classical grammar, where (as famously in the work of Varro) 'analogy' stands for the regular declension and morphology of Latin.[64] As Maittaire made clear, analogy could not be separated from an accurate record of usage: a 'word is called Analogous or Regular which followeth the general rules of the Grammar, grounded upon observations drawn from that general use'.[65] None the less, analogy could also be deployed to judge the correctness or 'purity' of even 'polite' idioms. In contrast with Greenwood's definition of grammar as polite usage, Maittaire called grammar the 'Art which teacheth the way of writing and speaking *truly* and *properly* [my italics]' (p. 1).

Did this principle of 'analogy' or 'reason' have a 'political' significance? It seems important, indeed, that this standard could be used to correct the impropriety of even upper-class language. The 'levelling' tendency of rational grammar no doubt helped to promote its immense popularity among the *lumières* of pre-Revolutionary France. In England, the correspondence between 'rational' grammar and liberal politics was less consistent: it was more common there to object to the impropriety of upper-class English without implying some defiance of the ruling order. The Tory Jonathan Swift, for example, was profoundly disillusioned with the language of the court (a feeling that he evidently failed to convey to his young friend Thomas

---

[63] On French debates pitting the standards of 'usage' and 'reason', see Padley, *Grammatical Theory*, II, 390–407. The political stakes of this debate are discussed by Ulrich Ricken in *Linguistics, Anthropology and Philosophy in the French Enlightenment*, trans. by Robert E. Norton (New York and London: Routledge, 1994), pp. 5–8.

[64] On the ancient debate concerning 'analogy' and 'anomaly' in language, see R. H. Robbins, *A Short History of Linguistics*, 2nd edn (London: Longman, 1979), pp. 20–22. For a good discussion of analogy in Varro, see Daniel J. Taylor, *Declinatio: A Study of the Linguistic Theory of Marcus Terentius Varro* (Amsterdam: Benjamins, 1974).

[65] *The English Grammar* (London, 1712; repr. Menston: Scolar Press, 1967), p. 30.

Sheridan, who later celebrated precisely this period of courtly English). Since the Restoration, Swift maintained, upper-class English had been corrupted by the wicked morals and affectation of fashionable society. As he declared in *A Proposal for Correcting [. . .] the English Tongue* (1712), 'the Court, which used to be a Standard of Propriety, and Correctness of Speech, was then [at the Restoration], and, I think, hath ever since continued the worst School in *England* for that Accomplishment'.[66] Swift's conservatism is revealed by his solution to linguistic corruption — the creation of an academy, modelled after those in France and Italy, for restoring English to the purity that he believed it once possessed in the court of Elizabeth. Although the academy would judge English according to a standard independent of current polite usage, its purpose would be to re-establish the linguistic authority of 'the learned and polite Persons of the Nation' (p. 6).

In the more liberal climate prevailing later in the century, proposals for such an academy were less likely to attract favour. Writing in 1761, Joseph Priestley maintained that 'a publick *Academy*' was 'not only unsuitable to the genius of a *free nation*, but in itself ill calculated to reform and fix a language'.[67] Priestley, a campaigner for political and religious reform, exemplifies how the use of 'analogy' could be used not to authorize upper-class idioms, but indeed to guard against the imposition of a class-bound standard. He did concede that the best writers and speakers of the language possessed 'authority'. But where these authorities differed from each other, grammarians and lexicographers should appeal to this independent principle of linguistic propriety: 'The *analogy of language* is the only thing to which we can have recourse, to adjust these differences; for language, to answer the intent of it, which is to express our thoughts with certainty in an intercourse with one another, must be fixed and consistent with itself' (p. vi). Consistent with Priestley's liberal politics, therefore, all usage, as found even in the 'best' authors and the most educated social class, was subject to a common standard adjusted by the particular 'genius' of the tongue.

Significantly, Priestley refers approvingly throughout this discussion to 'Mr. Johnson'. For, indeed, Samuel Johnson, despite his vaunted 'Toryism', held views far closer to Priestley's than to Swift's. First, Johnson objected to the creation of an academy for reasons very like those of Priestley: the 'spirit of English liberty', he declared, would surely resist this creation of such an institution, which had not, in any event, hindered the natural transformation of French or Italian.[68] Secondly, like Priestley, Johnson upheld the general 'analogy' of the language or the 'genius of the tongue' without considering whether a word belonged to a certain social class. Indeed, he never appealed to 'the Custom and Use of the best speakers'. In the *Plan of an English*

[66] *A Proposal for Correcting, Improving and Ascertaining the English Tongue*, ed. by Herbert Davis and Louis Landa (Oxford: Blackwell, 1957), p. 10.
[67] *Rudiments of English Grammar* (London, 1761; repr. Menston: Scholar Press, 1969), p. vii.
[68] Preface to the *Dictionary*, *Works* (1825), v, 49. See also v, 46.

Dictionary, he acquiesced to Chesterfield's encouragement 'to interpose my own judgment' only in the sense of preferring 'what appears to me most consonant to grammar and reason' (p. 19). At this early stage, as he later admitted, he dreamed ambitiously of making words conform to 'the nature of every substance',[69] in the manner of John Wilkins and other seventeenth-century planners of a universal language. Upon awaking as a humble lexicographer, however, Johnson confined himself to the principles of etymology and analogy. As in the work of Varro, etymology serves as the basis for analogy, for derivatives should be traceable 'by regular and constant analogy' to 'their primitives' (p. 40). Johnson certainly accepted, again like Varro, that no language follows analogy with perfect regularity, and that numerous anomalies are authorized by the intractable voice of popular usage. Yet he felt no hesitation to correct even the greatest authors cited in the *Dictionary* if they failed to conform to his independent standards for judging language. He objected, for example, to the expression 'the heart akes', though it appears in Shakespeare, and to 'most peculiar', though it appears in Dryden, whom he honoured as one of the great refiners of English.[70] Moreover, he regarded etymology as the primary test for cant, whether 'low' or 'polite'. Cant is cant not because it is used by the lower class, but because it lacks roots in the history of the language, and thus runs contrary to 'the general fabrick' of the tongue (p. 28). Hence, *higgeldy-piggeldy*, *Tory*, and *flirtation* are cant because they cannot be traced by a regular series to a genuine English source; on the other hand, *filch*, *helterskelter*, and *grudge* have roots in the Teutonic heritage of the language, and are thus accepted as legitimate English words, for all their 'lowness'. Such reasoning, we should note, is quite contrary to that followed by advocates of 'polite' usage such as George Campbell: Campbell explicitly challenged Johnson on this issue, denying that cant could be equated with 'want of etymology'. It was rather 'baseness of use' that fixed this 'disgraceful appelation' on a word.[71]

The appropriate conclusion here is not that Johnson's appeals to 'reason', 'analogy', and 'the fabrick of a language' prove that he was a liberal like Priestley. My own view, often expressed in the past, is that Johnson possessed a deeply conservative sensibility marked especially by a reverence for traditional institutions and values. This kind of conservatism is, indeed, consistent with his respect for the history and general character of the language. Moreover, while disdainful of mindless jingoism, Johnson did seek to fulfil the nationalist expectation that the *Dictionary* embody the 'genius' of

[69] Preface to the *Dictionary*, *Works* (1825), v, 42.
[70] See Nagashima, *Johnson the Philologist*, p. 129.
[71] *Philosophy of Rhetoric*, p. 168.

the English tongue.[72] This conservatism should not, however, be confused with authoritarianism, a pandering to the rich and powerful, or a contempt for the lower class and its language. Indeed, Johnson refused to regard himself as the servant of any class: he was, he always made clear, an independent man of letters, a scholar advancing general human truths, the 'slave of science, the pioneer of literature'.[73] Guided by these ideals, he created a dictionary that, while it disappointed many 'polite' people of his day, has helped to give English the lexical richness and social breadth of its first great lexicographer.

[72] Virtually every review of the *Dictionary*, laudatory or critical, stressed the importance of this project for consolidating a patriotic vision of Britain and for propogating a knowledge of English and English writers in Europe. See, for example, Sir Tanfield Leman's review in the *Monthly Review*, 12 (April 1755), 292, 322; Matthew May's review in *Journal Britannique*, 17 (1755), 218–19; the anonymous review in *London Magazine*, 24 (April 1755), 193.

[73] Preface to the *Dictionary*, *Works* (1825), v, 23.

Johnson's Revisions of his Etymologies

DAISUKE NAGASHIMA

Koshien University

It is too well known to bear repetition at any length that ever since the appearance of Johnson's *Dictionary* in 1755 its etymologies have invariably been stigmatized as the weakest part of the work.[1] We must concede that as a non-professional etymologist Johnson did very well when we consider that he lived in an age before the Copernican revolution in linguistics in the nineteenth century, and the present author elsewhere has gone so far as to claim a positive credit for Johnson by setting forth how judicious he was in etymologizing, deliberately weighing every view and opinion available and drawing a conclusion plausible enough in terms of contemporary linguistic scholarship — an attitude much in evidence not only in his major works such as his edition of Shakespeare (1765) and *Lives of the English Poets* (1779–81) but also in his minor masterpieces such as 'An Essay on the Origin and Importance of Small and Fugitive Pieces', originally written as an introduction to the *Harleian Miscellany* (8 vols, 1744–46).[2]

Soon after the completion of the *Dictionary* Johnson may be said to have been engaged in its revision, even if sporadically, throughout his life;[3] but as far as the printed text is concerned, the fourth edition (1773), set directly from the first, is the one that deserves the name of revision.[4] Johnson's

[1] I am grateful to Dr Edward M. Quackenbush for his valuable suggestions and improvements on the first draft of this essay. The first (1755) and fourth (1773) editions of Johnson's *Dictionary* used are, respectively, the one-volume quarto facsimile reprint (Tokyo: Yushodo, 1983) and the two-volume folio facsimile reprint (Beirut: Libraire du Liban, 1978).

[2] Daisuke Nagashima, *Johnson the Philologist* (Osaka, Japan: Kansai University of Foreign Studies, 1988), Chapter 4 (pp. 149–205).

[3] Important studies of Johnson's revision that have come to my notice so far are: Arthur Sherbo, 'Dr. Johnson's Revision of his *Dictionary*', *PQ*, 31 (1952), 372–82; William R. Keast, 'The Preface to *A Dictionary of the English Language*: Johnson's Revisions and the Establishment of the Text', *Studies in Bibliography*, 5 (1952–53), 129–46; James H. Sledd and Gwin J. Kolb, *Dr. Johnson's Dictionary: Essays in the Biography of a Book* (Chicago: University of Chicago Press, 1955), esp. Chapter 4 (pp. 105–33); Kolb and Sledd, 'The Reynolds Copy of Johnson's *Dictionary*', *Bulletin of the John Rylands Library*, 37 (1955), 446–75; Katharine C. Balderston, 'Dr. Johnson's Use of William Law in the Dictionary', *PQ*, 39 (1960), 379–88; Sherbo, '1773: The Year of Revision', *Eighteenth-Century Studies*, 7 (1973), 18–39; Allen Reddick, *The Making of Johnson's Dictionary 1746–1773* (Cambridge: Cambridge University Press, 1990), esp. Chapter 5 (pp. 89–169); Anne McDermott, 'The Reynolds Copy of Johnson's *Dictionary*: A Re-examination', *Bulletin of the John Rylands University Library*, 74 (1992), 29–38; Kolb and Robert DeMaria, Jr, 'The Preliminaries to Dr. Johnson's *Dictionary*: Authorial Revisions and the Establishment of the Texts', *Studies in Bibliography*, 48 (1995), 121–33.

[4] Based on a survey of the early editions of the *Dictionary* up to the seventh (1785) incorporating Johnson's revisions, and on a scrutiny of the copies bearing Johnson's notes, especially the Reynolds copy, Kolb and Sledd have come to the following verdict: 'Detailed examination of the Reynolds copy confirmed the established opinion that the fourth edition is the best printed authority for Johnson's considered judgements of English words, with the exception of somewhat more than two hundred entries in which the sixth and seventh incorporate his last revisions' ('The Reynolds Copy of Johnson's *Dictionary*', p. 456; see also Sledd and Kolb, *Dr. Johnson's Dictionary*, p. 133.)

revision has, needless to say, been intensively studied by interested scholars, but almost all those referred to in note 3 are concerned with the front matters (Preface, The History of the English Language, and A Grammar of the English Tongue) or the illustrative quotations in the body of the *Dictionary*. The sole exception is Sherbo who, on examination of Johnson's revisions of the M-words says:

I have counted slightly more than seven hundred changes under the letter M in Johnson's revision of the *Dictionary*. But this figure does not take into account one whole category of changes which are so important as to give one a false impression of the extent of Johnson's labors if they are included. I refer to the exasperating frequency with which Johnson shortens his attributions in the quotations in the revised *Dictionary*.[5]

In particular, with regard to Johnson's revisions of his etymologies, Sherbo further states:

5. Changes, additions, or omissions in etymologies: 14.

Changes occur under Macaroon, Madgehowlet, Maidenlip, Many (n. s.), Maudlin (adj.), Maundy-Thursday, Measure ([definition] 16), Mechoaclan, Methaglin, Miscreance, Mittens, Mouldwarp, Muggy, and Mum (interjection). Under Mum one finds an etymology supplied from 'Upton' and a quotation added from Spenser. It is fairly obvious that Johnson had recourse to John Upton's Spenser glossary. Muggy is described as 'a cant word' in 1755, but is freed from that odium and provided with an etymology from 'mucky' in 1773. The additional information under Maundy-Thursday can be found in Junius' *Etymologicum Anglicanum* and that under Mittens in both Junius and Skinner (*Etymologicon Linguae Latinae*). Johnson avowedly depended on both for most of his etymologies. (p. 376.)[6]

---

[5] Sherbo, 'Dr Johnson's Revision', p. 374. A new edition by Anne McDermott, integrating the first and fourth editions, facilitates study of the two editions. The CD-ROM edition was released in March 1996 by the Cambridge University Press. On its preparation, see McDermott in *Transactions of the Johnson Society for 1995* (Lichfield), pp. 29–37. Unfortunately, the transcription is not entirely reliable. To give a few instances from those examined in the present article: under Lettuce and Lorn, the opening bracket of the etymology, which is missing in the first edition, is silently supplied; Abbreuvoir, which is indicated '4 only', is registered in the first edition; in the etymology of Anomalous, the difference between the Greek words in the first and fourth editions is not represented; in the etymology in the fourth edition of To Abuse (*v.a.*), *abujus* should be *abusus* (probably the transcriber misread the long 's').

[6] In Sherbo's comments there are some apparent misunderstandings: the last word of the title of Skinner's dictionary is not *Latinae* but *Anglicanae*; Sherbo's remarks on the sources of Johnson's additional information in the etymologies of Maundy-Thursday and Mittens are puzzling, for, as is apparent in the following list, Johnson's etymologies of the two words in question have scarcely anything to do with those of Skinner and Junius:

Maundy-Thursday

Johnson (1755): [derived by *Spelman* from *mande*, a hand-basket, in which the king was accustomed to give alms to the poor.]
Johnson (1773): [. . . to the poor: by others from dies *mandati*, the day on which our Saviour gave his great *mandate*, That we should love one another.]
Skinner (1671): adopted in Junius (1743).
Junius (1743): Dies Jovis Passionis immediatè praecedens. Minshew dictum putat quasi Dies mandati, quo sc. die Christus eucharistiam institut, & magnum illud mandatum discipulis, sc. in sacramento illo commemorandi. Spelmannus longè meliùs deflectit à G. *mande*, Sportula; quia sc. illo die Rex pauperibus, quibus pedes lavat, uberiores eleemosynas distribuit. Skin.

This article is a kind of amplification of Sherbo's essay just cited; but by investigating Johnson's revisions item by item instead of presenting their broad outlines, we shall be able to reveal various facets of Johnson working at English etymologizing. Before going into detail, however, it would be profitable to see what Johnson thought of etymologizing, especially in a general dictionary. When we think of the etymology of a word today, we usually presume that it will tell us not only the ultimate source of the word in question but the historical process it has followed down to its current form, as the *OED* defines the term: '1. a. The process of tracing out and describing the elements of a word with their modifications of form and sense'. Johnson's definition is scarcely divergent, except he includes in etymology what in today's linguistics is part of word-formation: 'The descent or derivation of a word from its original; the deduction of formations from the radical word; the analysis of compound words into primitives'.

That in the collection of words Johnson was careful to include compounds is apparent in his reference to them in the *Plan*[7] and the Preface (sig. B1ᵛ), and his practice is seen under Afterages, Afterbirth, Afterclap, Aftercost, Aftercrop, and many other compounded words. His awareness of linguistic history is manifest by the fact that he added 'The History of the English Language' among the preliminaries and by the chronological arrangement of illustrative quotations in the body of the *Dictionary* (for the latter, see Johnson's remark in the Preface (sig. C1)). In practice of etymologizing, however, Johnson rejected historical exploration as too pedantic in a general dictionary:

In exhibiting the descent of our language, our etymologists seem to have been too lavish of their learning, having traced almost every word through various tongues, only to shew what was shewn sufficiently by the first derivation. This practice is of great use in synoptical lexicons, where mutilated and doubtful languages are explained by their affinity to others more certain and extensive, but is generally superfluous in English etymologies. (*Plan*, p. 15.)

We should bear in mind Johnson's notion when we examine his etymologies.

In the following pages Johnson's etymologies in the initial, medial, and final portions of his *Dictionary*, that is, of the words under A, L, and W–Y–Z (X has no headword except the letter itself), are investigated. The words newly introduced in the fourth edition (e.g. Acorned, Analogal) will as a matter of course be put outside the investigation.

Mittens

Johnson (1755): [*mitaines*, French.]
Johnson (1773): [*mitaine*, French.] It is said that *mit* is the original word; whence *mitten*, the plural, and afterwards *mittens*, as in *chicken*.
Skinner (1671): *à* Fr. G. *Mitaines*, Chirothecae crassiores hibernae, fort. q. d. Chirothecae Eremitanae, quibus sc. Eremitae utebantur, v **Hermit**.
Junius (1743): G. *mitaines*. à mitan, Medius; quod sint chirothecae veluti dimidiatae ac digitorum in apprehendendo libertatem minimè coercentes. **Mittaine** scribit Chaucerus, Pard. pr.

[7] Samuel Johnson, *The Plan of a Dictionary of the English Language* (London, 1747), pp. 13–14.

I *Minor and/or insignificant changes*

1. Punctuation, bracket, fount

Under Aisle a semicolon is changed to a comma, 'a path; and is . . .' having become 'a path, and is . . .'; under *Assiento*,[8] Wad, and Whoremaster/ Whoremonger,[9] a comma is supplied to render the sentence structure clearer, under Wild *Olive*, the final semicolon is corrected to a full stop.

Under Lettuce, Lorn, and Worst (*adj.*), the missing opening square bracket is supplied; under Abrupt and Lozenge, the closing brackets of '[*abruptus*, Lat.] Broken off.' and '[*losenge*, French.] Of unknown etymology.' are, respectively, moved after 'Broken off.' and '. . . etymology.'; under *Aborigines*, the missing brackets are furnished for 'Lat.'; under Alarum, the note 'See ALARM.', which was placed within the brackets in 1755, is now moved outside the brackets, thus causing inconsistency with Wezand and Whoop (*n.s.*) to be described in the following paragraph; under Athel/Atheling/ Adel/Æthel, probably by the compositor's error, the original brackets have disappeared.

Under Abandoning, Larch, Lives, Waped, Wex, Wezand, and Whoop (*n.s.*), 'from abandon.', 'Larix.', 'the plural of life.', 'Spenser;', 'Spenser, [. . .] Dryden.', 'see *wesand.*' (but the word cannot be found in the wordlist either of 1755 or of 1773), and 'See *hoop.*' are respectively altered to 'from *abandon.*', '*larix*, Lat.', 'the plural of *life.*', '*Spenser;*', '*Spenser*, [. . .] *Dryden.*', 'See WESAND.', and 'See Hoop.'; under Witchcraft, 'and' of '*witch* and *craft.*' of 1755 is, probably by the compositor's error, italicized.

It might be doubted whether all of these trivial alterations are authorial, or by some one of the assistants, or by the compositor or proof reader,[10] but it should be remembered that Johnson is a man of far more meticulous attention than might generally have been assumed.

2. Word (addition, deletion, correction, replacement, abbreviation and expansion)

Under Larch and Walnut, 'Lat.' is added, respectively, to '*larix*' (Larix, 1755) and '*nux juglans*'; under Laudableness, the preposition 'from' is added before '*laudable.*', probably to bring it in line with 'from *laudable.*' under the next headword Laudably; under Line (*v.a.*), 'linings being made of linen.' is

---

[8] In discussion of the necessity of collecting English words of promiscuous kinds, Johnson proposes an expedient device in the *Plan*: 'But there ought, however, to be some distinction made between the different classes of words, and therefore it will be proper to print those which are incorporated into the language in the usual character, and those which are still to be considered as foreign, in the Italick letter' (p. 7).

[9] The diagonal means that the words preceding and following it are connected by a brace in the wordlist.

[10] See Daisuke Nagashima, *Johnson's Dictionary: Its Historical Significance* [in Japanese] (Tokyo: Taishukan, 1983), pp. 303–05, where twenty-four small alterations in the Preface of the fourth edition are listed under the assumption that they are authorial. Kolb and DeMaria are not completely sure whether the alterations they have discovered are authorial or not (see 'Preliminaries', *passim*).

toned down by the addition of an adverb of frequency, '. . . often made of linen.'.

Under Affront (*v.a.*), '&' is deleted from '*ad frontem & contumelium allidere*,'; under Welk, one of the superfluous two '*welk*'s has been taken out; under Wheedle, 'and' is crossed out from 'though used by good writers, and *Locke* seems to mention it as a cant word.', the preceding comma is changed to a full stop, and '*Locke*' begins a new sentence. In the last instance, Johnson's surmise about Locke's implication doubtless comes from his considered re-reading of the Locke quotation. Moreover, what should be noted is that Johnson is ever keen to detect a 'cant' word to 'purify' his mother tongue.[11]

Under Account (*n.s.*), '*compactus*' is corrected to '*computus*'; under Affray (*v.a.*), '*frayer*' to '*fragor*'. As Amenance is now yoked with Amenage with a brace, 'It seems . . .' is by necessity remedied to 'They seem . . .'. Under Anachorete/Anachorite, 'writen' is corrected to 'written'; under Anomalous, 'ἄμαλοσ' to 'ὤμαλοσ' (rightly, 'ἀνώμαλοσ');[12] under Armigerous, 'an armour-bearer' is altered to 'an armory-bearer'; under Lean (*v.n.*), 'peter. . . . [hlinan, Sax. . . .]', to 'preter. . . . [hhlinan, Saxon . . .]',[13] introducing a correction and a new error at the same time; under Leveret, '*leivre*' is changed to '*lievret*' (not recognized in the *OED*); under Loover (Louver, 1773; both words are placed after Lover in the wordlist), '*l'ou vert*' is connected to form one word '*l'ouvert*'; under Whole (*adj.*), '*heal*, Dutch.' is corrected to '*heel*, Dutch.'; under Avenue, 'but it is generally placed on the first.' has, probably by the compositor's mistake, become 'but has it generally placed on the first.' Under Worry, 'probably' is replaced by 'perhaps'.[14]

The most frequent alteration in the category under discussion concerns the abbreviation and expansion of the names of the source languages. Here are examples in Section L: under Lactary (*adj.*), Lactation, Lacteal (*adj.*), Lucubratory, Lymphated, and Lyre, 'Latin' is shortened to 'Lat.'; under Loover (Louver, 1773), 'French' to 'Fr.'; under Lake and Lament (*v.n.*), 'French [. . .] Latin' to 'Fr. [. . .] Lat.'. These abbreviations would not seem to 'make room for more important additions', as Sherbo deplores concerning Johnson's shortenings of attributions of illustrative quotations,[15] because

---

[11] In the *Plan* (p. 16), Johnson declares: 'By tracing in this manner every word to its original, and not admitting, but with great caution, any of which no original can be found, we shall secure our language from being over-run with *cant*, from being crouded with low terms, the spawn of folly or affectation, which arise from no just principles of speech, and of which therefore no legitimate derivation can be shewn.' Johnson's first definition of Cant is: 'A corrupt dialect used by beggars and vagabonds.'

[12] For the sake of convenience, earlier Greek typefaces are replaced by those in current use (in this case the differences between -ος and its eighteenth-century ligature).

[13] There is no attempt here to reproduce earlier English typefaces (in this case the initial h).

[14] Johnson defines Probably and Perhaps as 'Likely, in likelihood' and 'Peradventure; it may be', respectively, both in 1755 and in 1773.

[15] See p. 95 above; Sherbo continues: 'A quotation under "Macebearer" in the first edition is identified as coming from "*Spectator* No. 617"; in the revised edition the number of the periodical is omitted. [. . .] I started to count these changes but soon gave them up as unimportant. I can only conjecture that they represent Johnson's attempt to make room for more important additions and yet keep the revised edition approximately the same length as the first.'

under Languet, Languid, and Languish (*v.n.*), 'Latin' and 'French' are left intact, under Longimanous and Lunisolar, 'Lat.' is expanded to 'Latin,' and under Liturgy and Loyal, 'Fr.' to 'French'. In the first ten pages of each of Sections A, L, and W, the occurrence of the spelt-out and abbreviated forms of the two source languages is as follows:

	Latin	Lat.	French	Fr.
A	4	59	5	9
L	27	31	17	19
W	5	9	1	3

Section W cannot be significant, as the initial 'w' is peculiar to the Germanic languages. Section L is somewhat noteworthy in that, compared with Section A, the number of spelt-out forms is close to that of the shortened forms. When we see, however, in the first page of Section L, that under Labent is given 'Lat.', whereas in the next line, under Labial is given 'Latin', we cannot help recalling Johnson's 'casual performances' as Keast has characterized the lexicographer's revisions (p. 145).

II   *Major or significant changes*

1. Additions

a. Etymological

Abacke, which had no etymology in 1755, is now supplied with 'from *back.*'; under Abature, the register 'a hunting term' in the brackets is replaced by 'from *abatre*, French.' (rightly, *abat[t]ure*, according to the *OED*); under *Abbreuvoir*, immediately after 'in French, a watering place.' is inserted 'Ital. *abbeverato*, dal verbo *bevere*. Lat. *bibere*. Abbeverari i cavalli.'; under Abuse (*v.a.*), the participial form '*abusus*' is added after '*abutor*', probably to show the immediate source of the English headword; under Acorn, 'the grain of the oak.' is amplified to 'the grain or fruit of the oak.', probably to prevent 'grain' from being misinterpreted; under Amulet, '*amuletum*, Lat.' is augmented to 'or *amoletum, quod malum amolitur*, Lat.'; under Argosy, to 'derived by *Pope* from *Argo*, the name of Jason's ship.' is rightly added 'supposed by others to be a vessel of *Ragusa* or *Rogosa*, a *Ragozine*, corrupted.', the original final full stop being by necessity replaced by a semicolon; under Atone, 'This derivation is much confirmed by the following passage.' is rendered clearer by amplification to '. . . the following passage of Shakespeare, and appears to be the sense still retained in Scotland.', the attribution apparently based on the quotation '*Shakes, Coriolanus* [IV, 6, 27].' under definition 1, and the following comment perhaps on information from Macbean, a Scotsman; the etymologies of La and Looby are qualified by the addition, respectively, of 'unless it be the French *la*.' and 'unless it come from *lob*.'; under Lavish (*adj.*), to 'Of this word I have been able to find no satisfactory etymology.' is added 'It may be plausibly derived from to *lave*, to *throw out*; as *profundere opes* is to be *lavish.*' [rightly, *lave* should be *lavare*, according to the *OED*]; under Ly (*v.n.*), 'when *ly* terminates the name of a place, it is derived from leag, Saxon, a field; when . . .' is modified to '. . . a field. *Gibson*. When . . .', wherein '*Gibson*' must be Edmund Gibson (1669–1748) who in 1695 published an English version of Camden's *Britannia* (1586);[16] under Warray (*v.a.*), 'from *war.*' is expanded to 'from *war*; or from *gwerroyer*, old Fr.'; to the etymology of Wearish is added 'See WEERISH.', whereby the user is referred to the headword under which a fuller etymology is furnished; under Whist, 'and *Milton* [uses it] as an adjective.' is rendered ambiguous by expansion to '. . . an adjective or a participle.', probably a result of Johnson's reconsideration of the Milton quotation under definition 2; under Wittol, to 'wittol, Sax.' is added 'from wittan, *to know.*'; under Woman, the ending 'in the plural, *wimmen, Skinner.*' is expanded to '*Skinner* and *Wallis.*', wherein Johnson apparently refers to John Wallis, *Grammatica Linguae Anglicanae* (1653);[17] under Wrought, to 'The pret. and part. pass. [. . .] of *work*; as the Dutch [. . .] *gerocht.*' is added 'or more analogically of the old word *wreak.*', whereby Johnson revealed his innocent linguistic ignorance inevitable in the eighteenth century; to Yacht, which lacked etymology in 1755, is now supplied 'a Dutch word.', but it is strange that Johnson does not give the Dutch word 'jacht' when we know that in later years he studied the language as a mental exercise or to be sure of his sanity.[18]

b. Grammatical (including morphology, phonology or prosody, and semantics)

In seventeenth- and eighteenth-century linguistics, 'morphology' of today is usually called 'etymology',[19] as is seen in the opening paragraph of Johnson's Grammar: 'Grammar, which is *the art of using words properly*, comprises four parts; Orthography, Etymology, Syntax, and Prosody.' This is not simply a matter of terminology; in Johnson as well as in linguistics in general, etymology is closely associated with phonology, morphology, and even syntax. Johnson was very well aware of this, and thought it part of the duties of a lexicographer to note grammatical peculiarities and irregularities, especially for the benefit of foreign learners of English. Hence his statements in the *Plan* and Preface:

Our inflexions therefore are by no means constant, but admit of numberless iregularities, which in this dictionary will be diligently noted. Thus *fox* makes in the plural *foxes*, but *ox* makes *oxen*. [. . .] The forms of our verbs are subject to great variety; some end their preter tense in *ed*, as I *love*, I *loved*, I have *loved*, which may be

[16] See Stuart Piggott, 'William Camden and the *Britannia*', *Proceedings of the British Academy*, 37 (1951), 199–217; later reprinted as the introduction to *Camden's Britannia 1695* (Devon: David and Charles, 1971).
[17] Johnson in his Grammar is heavily dependent on the fifth edition (1699) of Wallis's grammar (see Nagashima, *Johnson the Philologist*, pp. 61–66, 101–05, 107–15).
[18] See *Johnson the Philologist*, pp. 24–25.
[19] *OED* under Etymology 3 reads: '*Gram.* That part of grammar which treats of individual words, the parts of speech separately, their formation and inflexions.'

called the regular form [. . .]. But many depart from this rule, without agreeing in any other, as I *shake*, I *shook*, I have *shaken*, [. . .] and many others, which, as they cannot be reduced to rules, must be learned from the dictionary rather than the grammar. (*Plan*, p. 17)

Among other derivatives I have been careful to insert and elucidate the anomalous plurals of nouns and preterites of verbs, which in the *Teutonick* dialects are very frequent, and, though familiar to those who have always used them, interrput and embarrass the learners of our language. (Preface, sig. B1)

To give a few instances: under According, Johnson added to the etymology 'from *accord*.' (1755) a syntactic comment '. . ., of which it [the headword] is properly a participle, and is therefore never used but with *to*.'; under Late (*adj.*) again, he added 'in the comparative *latter* for *later*, in the superlative *latest* or *last*. *Last* is absolute and definite, more than *latest*.', a comment which falls under the category of syntactic usage; under Ambition, to the original '*ambitio*, Lat.' he in 1773 supplemented 'The desire of something higher than is possessed at present.', a semantic explication of the source word; under Latter, the original syntactic comment 'When the thing of which the comparison is made is mentioned, we use *later* [. . .]; but *latter* when no comparison is expressed' is expanded by the addition of a semantic comment '. . . but *latter* when no comparison is expressed, but the reference is merely to time'.

As for pronunciation, Johnson at first thought of indicating how each word is pronounced (see the *Plan*, pp. 12–13), but in an age when phonetics was far from a full-fledged science it is only natural that he could not do more than give occasional comments on accentuation [20] — a feature closely connected with versification and therefore a telling indication of the literary character of the *Dictionary*. And what should be noted here is the fact that the phonological comments are given within square brackets, a territory of etymology proper. Examples are seen already in 1755 under Academy, Antique, Avenue, and many others. The additions in 1773 in the scope of our examination are: under Apostolick, the added comment 'The accent is placed by Dryden on the antipenult.' apparently comes from careful re-reading of a Dryden quotation; under Low (*v.n.*), the original comment 'The adjective *low*, not high, is pronounced *lo*; the verb *low*, to *bellow*, *lou*.' is amplified to '. . . is pronounced *lo*, and would rhyme to *no*: the verb *low*, to *bellow*, *lou*; and is by *Dryden* rightly to *now*.', the second comment is again derived from Dryden's rhyme in the quotation; under Lower (*v.n.*), 'to look askance.' is expanded to 'to look askance: the *ow* sounds as *ou* in *hour*; in the word *lower*, when it means to *grow*, or *make low*, the *ow* sound [*sic*] as *o* in

---

[20] In the Preface we read: 'In settling the orthography, I have not wholly neglected the pronunciation, which I have directed, by printing an accent upon the acute or elevated syllable. It will sometimes be found, that the accent is placed by the authour quoted, on a different syllable from that marked in the alphabetical series; it is then to be understood, that custom has varied, or that the authour has, in my opinion, pronounced wrong. Short directions are sometimes given where the sound of letters is irregular, and if they are sometimes omitted, defect in such minute observation will be more easily excused, than superfluity.' (sig. A2ᵛ)

more.'; under Advertise, the original comment 'It is now spoken with the accent upon the last syllable; but appears to have been anciently accented on the second.', which was placed outside the brackets, is in 1773 moved inside; under Yux is added 'sometimes pronounced *yex*.'. But Johnson is not always consistent in practice, the phonological comments on Acceptable and Adverse, for instance, being left outside the brackets in 1773 as in 1755.

Our examination has provided two examples of alteration in morphological comment: under Anthropophagai, the original comment '*It has no singular.*', which preceded the opening bracket, is in 1773 moved to follow it; under We, the original reference '[See I.]' is altered to '[in oblique cases *us*.] See I.'

The orthographical comments in our scope are: under Leven, Lickerish/Lickerous, Wively, and Wormwood are added, respectively, 'Commonly, though less properly, written *leaven*; see LEAVEN.', 'This seems to be the proper way of spelling the word, which has no affinity with *liquour*, but with *like*.', 'It were written more analogically *wifely*, that is, *wife-like*.', and 'perhaps properly *wormwort*.'[21]

As referred to above, Johnson was considerate of foreign learners regarding the irregular conjugation of verbs, and under Lift (*v.a.*) and Light (*v.n.*), 'I *lifted*, or *lift*; I have *lifted*, or *lift*.' and 'preter. *lighted* or *light*, or *lit*.' are respectively adjoined in the brackets in 1773. But he is yet again inconsistent, for the newly supplied notes on the irregular conjugations under Load (*v.a.*). Lose (*v.a.*), Waft (*v.a.*), and Wind (*v.a.*) precede the brackets, which would seem the usual place for the information concerned.

Under Alkali, the closing bracket is now moved forward to the end of a forty-four-word encyclopedic description of the herb culled from '*Arbuthnot on Aliments.*', which indeed contains the phrase 'this they called *sal kali*, or *alkali*', but the long quotation cannot by any means be taken as etymological. Johnson's idea of etymology, at least in this case, is too broad to be accepted by any standards of today.

c. Names of animals and plants (non-etymological)

By far the most numerous additions in 1773 occur under the names of animals and plants,[22] but the words supplied in the brackets are not the source words in any sense of etymology, but just the Latin equivalents. To give an example each of animals and plants: under Larkspur and Linnet are added, respectively, '*delphinium*, and '*linaria*'. For other examples, see under Lavender, Lazarwort, Leek, Lime *tree*, or Linden, Wagtail, Wallcreeper,

---

[21] In fixing on the proper orthography, Johnson takes the etymology as the criterion: 'Some [words] still continue to be variously written, as authours differ in their care or skill: of these it was proper to enquire the true orthography, which I have always considered as depending on their derivation, and have therefore referred them to their original languages: thus I write *enchant, enchantment, enchanter*, after the *French*, and *incantation* after the *Latin*; thus *entire* is chosen rather than *intire*, because it passed to us not from the *Latin integer*, but from the *French entire*.' (Sig. A2ᵛ)

[22] On including the names of animals and plants in his wordlist, Johnson defends himself in the *Plan* (p. 8).

Wallflower,   Wallrue,   Wallwort,   Wartwort,   Watermint,   Waterrat,
Waterrocket, Waybread, Weevil, Welcome *to our House*, Whale, Wheatear,
Whitethorn, Whittentree, Witwal, Woad, Wolfsbane, Wolfsmilk, Woodbind/
Woodbine, Woodcock, Woodlark, Woodpigeon, Woodroof, Wren, Yarrow,
Yellowhammer, and Yoke-elm. The newly added *'lichen'* under Liverwort
may also be a Latin equivalent, though the name of the source language is
not given and 'Lichen' is not included in Johnson's wordlist (see *OED*).
    The same phenomenon is seen among those words which are newly added
in 1773 — words which are, as stated already, outside the scope of our
investigation: Lynden tree, Warriangle, Waterflag, Waterhen, Willoweed,
Withwind, Woodworm, Woop, and Woos.
    This feature is not new in 1773, but was already seen in 1755 under the
following words: Adder's-tongue, Alexanders, Alkanet, All-heal, Almond
tree, *Angelica*, Archangel, Arse-smart, Lady-mantle, Lady's-slipper, Lady's-
smock, Lungwort, Wallouse, Watercresses, Waterlilly, Wayfaringtree,
Weasel, Weaverfish, Wheat, Whin, Whiting, Wild *Basil*, Wild *Cucumber*, Wild
Olive, Wildservice, Willow, Wingedpea, Wintergreen, and Woodsorrel.
    Here we may note two deletions, which strictly fall under the following
category: under Lote *tree* or *nettle tree* and Lumpfish, 'Celtis.' and *'lumpus*,
Lat.', respectively, have disappeared in 1773. Has Johnson become uncertain about the etymology and the Latin equivalent that he gave in 1755?
    The source of the Latin equivalents is suggested by *'Ains.'*, *'Ainsw.'*, or
'Ainsworth.' attached in 1755 and/or 1773 to the entries of the following
words: Wallcreeper, Wallrue, Wartwort, Welcome *to our House*, Whittentree,
Witwal, Wolfsmilk, Woodroof, and Yoke-elm.
    Ainsworth, together with Bailey and Philips, is mentioned in the Preface
(sig. B1ᵛ) as one of the lexicographers Johnson drew upon for his vocabulary
and, as would easily be surmised, most of the Latin equivalents in question
are derived from him, but not all; the matter awaits further investigation.[23]

2. Deletions
    Deletions are not of so much interest as additions. To give some examples:
under *Abactor* and *Abacus*, the Latin source words 'abactor' and 'abacus' are,
respectively, deleted and 'Lat.' is spelt out as 'Latin.', whereby the awkward
tautology is remedied and the form of etymological description has come
into line with *'Acumen* [Lat.]', *'Adagio* [Italian.]', *'Adroit* [French.]', and others.
But tautology remains under such words as *Abductor, Ajutage, Axilla, Legume/*

---

[23] On Ainsworth's contributions to Johnson's *Dictionary*, see Reddick, pp. 97, 218 n. 19. A brief
consultation of Ainsworth's *Thesaurus Linguae Latinae compendiarius: Or, a compendious Dictionary of the Latin
Tongue* (London, 1736) reveals that Johnson's Latin equivalents of Adder's-tongue, Almond tree,
Archangel, Arse-smart, Yellowhammer, and Yoke-elm are identical with the Latin words given in
Ainsworth under the same headwords, but whereas Johnson under Larkspur adds *'delphinium'* in 1773,
in Ainsworth the entry reads, *'Lark's heel* [?], or *lark's spur*, Consolida [?].' Did Johnson make use of some
later edition?

Legumen, Achor, and *Lentor* (as far as the Latin word is concerned). With regard to Greek equivalents, tautology should not be blamed, because of the typographical character of the source language.

Under *Abactor, Abolish, Albugineous,* and *Articular,* the English glosses on the source words, 'a driver away', 'to blot out', 'the white of an egg', and 'belonging to the joints', respectively, are moved to follow the closing bracket, whereby the division of function between etymology and definition or semantic explanation is established, but here again Johnson is sometimes contradictory, for under Abrupt, 'Broken off.', which in 1755 was placed after the brackets, is now included within them and serves as a gloss on the preceding Latin word. To furnish fuller information about the headwords just mentioned: under *Abactor,* the definition 'Those who drive away or steal cattle in herds' is slightly altered to 'One who drives away and steals . . .'; under Abolish, 'To annul.' is amplified to 'To annul; to make void. Applied to laws or institutions.'; Albugineous, which had no definition in 1755, is now explained as 'Resembling the white of an egg.', adopting with modification the English gloss in 1755; Articular, which in 1755 served as the subject of definition beginning 'Is, in medicine, an epithet', is now defined, incorporating the original gloss, as 'Belonging to the joints. In medicine, an epithet', whereby the definition has gained due independency.

The rest of the deletions discovered follow in alphabetical order: under Accomplice, '*Complices sertae prudentius.*' is deleted, but the reason and the meaning of the Latin phrase are not clear to me; under *Acroters,* of *Acroteria,* the register label 'In architecture,' in the brackets has disappeared; under Aglet, 'A word which some derive from' is shortened to 'Some derive it from'; under Astrolabe, the Greek compound 'ἀστρογάβιον' is taken out and the etymology now consists of the compound elements 'of ἀστὴρ and λαβεῖν, to take.'; under Leer, the Latin equivalent 'facies' is eliminated from 'hleare, facies, Saxon.'; under Licorice, '*glycyrrhzza,* Lat.' is deleted, probably because Johnson has become uncertain about the Latin [the *OED* comments, 'a. Gr. γλυκύρριζα (latinized *glycyrrhiza* by Pliny)']; under Linchpin, '*linch* and *pin.*' is crossed out and the headword has now no etymology, most probably because 'Linch' has no entry in Johnson's wordlist, otherwise he usually analyses compounds to their elements, as Landholder to '*land* and *holder.*' and Landlady to '*land* and *lady.*', and so forth (see above, p. 96); under Lintel, '*linteaux,* from *linteal,* French.' is shortened to '*linteal,* French.', probably because the contemporary French form is too divergent from the English and Johnson preferred to retain the Old French form alone (see *OED*); under Loxodromick, '*loxodromus,* Lat.' following the Greek source word is eliminated; under You, 'the accusative of ȝe, ye.' is shortened to 'ȝe, ye.', probably because Johnson has come to be aware of the confusion of the case forms of the pronoun in Middle English and early Modern English; under Whomsoever, '*who* and *soever.*' is changed to 'oblique case of *whosoever.*' (Whosoever is analysed to '*who* and *ever.*').

III *Other changes*

There remain some other changes which defy classification in our scheme, and they will be presented in alphabetical sequence.

Under Abed, 'from *a*, for *at*. See (A,) and BED.' has changed to 'from *a*, for *at*, and *Bed*.'; under Angel shot, 'from *angel* and *shot*,' is thoroughly revised to 'perhaps properly *angle-shot*, being folden together with a hinge.', reflecting Johnson's reconsideration; under Apotheosis, 'from ἀπὸ and θεὸσ' is, contrary to the treatment under Astrolabe above, replaced by a compound ἀποθέωσισ, exposing Johnson's inconsistency; under Lieger, 'from *liege*.' is altered to 'more proper *legier*, or *ledger*.' (*OED*, under Legier, comments 'obs. form of LEDGER; var. LEGER *sb. Obs*.'); under Welder, which had no etymology in 1755, the original definition 'A term perhaps merely Irish; though it may be derived from *To wield*, to *turn* or *manage*: whence *wielder*, welder.' is now enclosed within the brackets, and a new definition 'Manager; actual occupier.' is supplied; under Zany, the disordered '[Probably of *zanei*] The contraction of Giovanni or sanna, or a scoff, according to *Skinner*.]' is remedied by replacing the first closing bracket with a comma and changing the initial upper case of the following 'The' to lower case.

Thus by investigating Johnson's revisions in 1773 of his etymologies, though to a very limited extent, it is possible to see various facets of Johnson's philological mind at work, and it is hoped that this essay will stimulate interested scholars to further exploration.

Some Notes on the Treatment of Dryden in Johnson's *Dictionary*

KEITH WALKER

University College, London

The first thing to say about the presence of Dryden in Johnson's *Dictionary* is that there is a lot of him. Under C, Johnson quotes Dryden 935 times: less than Shakespeare, who has 1623 quotations (that must be significant somehow), but more than double every other writer except Bacon (who has only 536 quotations, however).

Johnson went to Dryden for the most basic vocabulary. Having taken his momentous decision to read in effect the whole of English literature, I suspect Johnson went first to Dryden for what he knew Dryden would supply: illustrations of words such as As, (senses 1, 2, 8 (× 2), 11 (× 2), 14, 22, 26), AFTER, AT, (senses 3, 6 (× 3), 11, 13, 14, 16 (× 2), BE, BEAR, BREAK (21 citations), BUT, BY (15 citations), COME, DO, DRAW, GO, SEEK, SELF, SET (30 citations), SHARE; BOY, GIRL, FATHER, MOTHER; DEN, HOUSE, TABLE (but not BED).

In his wonderful Preface, Johnson complains:

My labour has likewise been much increased by a class of verbs too frequent in the *English* language, of which the signification is so loose and general, the use so vague and indeterminate, and the senses detorted so widely from the first idea, that it is hard to trace them through the maze of variation, to catch them on the brink of utter inanity, to circumscribe them by any limitations, or interpret them by words of distinct and settled meaning; such are *bear, break, come, cast, full* [did Johnson mean '*fill*'?], *get, give, do, put, set, go, run, make, take, turn, throw*. If of these the whole power is not accurately delivered, it must be remembered, that while our language is yet living, and variable by the caprice of every one that speaks it, these words are hourly shifting their relations, and can be no more be ascertained in a dictionary, than a grove, in the agitation of a storm, can be accurately delineated from its picture in the water.

After what I have already said, it will not come as a surprise that quotations from Dryden figure largely in Johnson's attempt to fix the shifting meanings of each of these words: over thirty-six quotations from Dryden among the sixty subdivisions of THROW.

The quotations from Dryden come overwhelmingly from his poetry. That is obvious to anyone who just glances at the *Dictionary*. The interesting thing is how many quotations come from Dryden's translations. Of the first hundred quotations under C, seventeen come from plays, twelve come from prose works, and a staggering sixty quotations come from Dryden's verse translations. There is one from Lucretius, two from Persius, three from

Theocritus, five from Juvenal (two from outside Dryden's stint, although *OED* quotes one of them as if it came from Dryden's), one from Homer, eleven from Ovid, twelve from Chaucer, and no less than twenty-six from Virgil. (The quotation from the end of *Aeneid*, VI under 'CANISTER' is so garbled, Johnson must have quoted it from memory.)

Of the quotations from Dryden's 'original' poems (there are only ten such), five are from *Annus Mirabilis*, one each from 'Killigrew', 'To Lady Castlemaine', 'To Etherege', and 'On the Memory of a fair Maiden Lady'. A larger sample would undoubtedly have found quotations from *Absalom and Architophel*, *The Medal*, and *The Hind and the Panther*, but I feel sure the overwhelming emphasis on the translations, especially those from Virgil and Ovid, would be maintained.

I am aware that the quotations do not need to be taken from what Johnson found central in Dryden's work, or indeed from what we find central in Dryden: but nevertheless this selection appears decidedly odd, unless we hold firmly to the fact that Johnson's purpose was simply to show that a particular word had been used by a writer of note. In other words, Johnson merely wanted to validate the word he cites by showing it has been used by an authority. And however harshly he may have written about Dryden's lapses in the *Dictionary* and elsewhere, it is indubitable that Johnson considered him an authority in matters of language and style. Perhaps *the* authority for modern English, Shakespeare's English being more or less obsolete.

The quotations come, then, overwhelmingly from the translations of the classics. Johnson leaves us in no doubt in his *Life of Dryden* that it is Dryden's Ovid, and especially Dryden's Virgil that he found particularly congenial. Besides verse quotations there is a full representation of Dryden's immense prose output. Clearly, Johnson read nearly everything: the translation of Du Fresnoy's *De arte graphica*, the preface to Dryden's 'opera' based on *Paradise Lost*, *The State of Innocence*, as well as *All for Love* and *An Essay of Dramatic Poesy*.

Of course Dryden is too various and intereting a writer to be consistently anything as staid as an authority on modern English usage, and where Johnson feels he has transgressed his comments can be quite barbed, especially in the matter of Dryden's gallicisms.

Addison seems to have popularized the notion of being beastly to the French language. He wrote in *Spectator*, 165:

I have often wished that [. . .] certain Men might be set apart, as Superintendents of our Language, to hinder any Words of a Foreign Coin from passing among us; and in particular to prohibit any *French* Phrases from becoming Current in this Kingdom, when those of our own Stamp are altogether as valuable.

So Johnson was merely following an old tradition in objecting to some gallicisms and similar innovations. He quotes Dryden's defence of his Italianism of *falsify* to mean 'to pierce, to run through' in a note of inordinate length appended to the *Aeneid* (Johnson only omits a sentence of outrageous showing-off by Dryden). Then he remarks temperately that he does not think the new meaning a good idea, especially as it has not caught on. In asserting this I am not slighting the many occasions where Johnson excoriates Dryden especially for his gallicisms: 'a word foolishly innovated by Dryden' he writes of FRAISCHEUR, 'a low word' he writes of 'To GUTTLE *v. n:* 'to gourmandise'. (Dryden's is the sole quotation under this word.) When he is confronted with a word he does not understand he does not spend long on the matter (but he makes a lucky guess, nevertheless): 'MACKEREL-GALE seems to be, in *Dryden*'s cant, a strong breeze, such, I suppose, as is desired to bring *mackerel* fish to market.' The ferocity of comments like these in what after all is a scholarly work, suggests some sort of *animus* against Dryden. But to take them in this way would be as misguided as to find that the lists of *addenda* and *corrigenda* to *OED* published regularly in *Notes and Queries* were to be thought of as a denunciation of the great dictionary. In a way it confirms Dryden's authority. And we must not get this matter out of perspective: the savage comments from Johnson form only a tiny part of his total dealings with Dryden in the *Dictionary*. Elsewhere, Johnson seems to have blamed Bolingbroke for excessive gallicisms. And he is more scathing about Prior than about Dryden: HYPER is 'a word barbarously curtailed by *Prior* from *hyper*critick [. . .] *Prior* did not know the meaning of the word'. Dryden did, and the longish quotation from him under HYPERCRITICK is the sole illustration for the word.

The remainder of my observations are very subjective, indeed impressionistic. They are that the quotations from Dryden are especially prominent in references to food and eating (see DEVOUR, FOOD, MALLOWS, METHEGLIN, MILK, MUSHROOM, NIBBLE, QUENCH, QUAFF), and in reference to the arts, especially music, painting, and literary criticism. The stress on eating words may have come about because a good deal of guzzling goes on in epic, and the stress on the arts because Dryden writes so well on these subjects, in a manner that Johnson not only approved of, but positively enjoyed.

Enjoyment, indeed, is a feature of Johnson's quoting from Dryden and *over*quotation, at any rate for the matter at hand, if it was merely to show the word had been used by a writer of note. But of course Johnson had another purpose in writing his *Dictionary*. As some celebrated remarks in his Preface make clear, he hoped to produce an anthology of (largely 'improving') passages from English literature, and in large measure succeeded in doing so. Thus once he has begun to quote a particular passage Johnson seems unable to stop himself, especially when he is quoting from Dryden. Why else would he quote, under 'LIFE *n. s.* 2', the line 'When I consider *life* 'tis all a cheat' from *Aureng-Zebe*, and then continue the quotation for a further eleven lines? Who would have expected to find this short essay in literary criticism under the word 'ABUNDANTLY'?

Heroic poetry has ever been esteemed the greatest work of human nature. In that rank has Aristotle placed it; and Longinus is so full of the like experience, that he *abundantly* confirms the other's testimony.

Under Abstemious, Johnson has:

> Clytorean streams the love of wine expel
> Such is the virtue of th'*abstemious* well,
> Whether the colder nymph that rules the flood,
> Extinguishes, and balks the drunken god;
> Or that Melampus (so have some assur'd)
> When the mad Praetides [Proetides] with charms he cur'd
> And pow'rful herbs, doth charms and simples cast
> Into the sober spring, where still their virtues last.

This is from 'Of the Pythagorean Philosophy' (ll. 485–92). Is there a covert self-reference? Boswell wrote that 'though he could be rigidly *abstemious*, [he] was not a *temperate* man'.

'The Tract and Tenor of the Sentence': Conversing, Connection, and Johnson's *Dictionary*

NIGEL WOOD

University of Birmingham

When David Hume divided 'the elegant part of mankind' into the 'learned' and the 'conversible' in 1741, he was partly defending his own choice of communicating truth in the easy (apparent) informality of the popular essay. As a 'kind of resident or ambassador from the dominions of learning to those of conversation', he perceived a necessary 'correspondence' between the two realms and, further, a dependence of one on the other: 'The materials of this commerce must chiefly be furnished by conversation and common life', even if 'the manufacturing of them alone belongs to learning'. For Hume, 'conversation' is somewhat more than a mere handmaid to learning. Those scholars 'shut up in colleges and cells, and secluded from the world and good company', cannot consult experience, the kind of education only to be found in 'common life and conversation'.[1] The exercise of conversing, for Hume, is an antidote to the 'philosophical melancholy and delirium' to which he confesses himself prone in the *Treatise of Human Nature* (1739–40):

I dine, I play a game of backgammon, I converse, and am merry with my friends; and when after three or four hour's amusement, I would return to these speculations, they appear so cold, and strained, and ridiculous, that I cannot find in my heart to enter into them any farther.[2]

Hume's wording is not casual; his enlisting of the heart and 'nature itself' in support of social intercourse is later translated into a more characteristic pitting of 'common sense and reflection' against academic scepticism.[3]

The status of conversation within eighteenth-century definitions of civility and civic humanism has been noted before. Often derived from Habermas's faith in the age's 'literary public sphere',[4] the cultivation of politeness could

---

[1] 'Of Essay Writing', *Selected Essays*, ed. by Stephen Copley and Andrew Edgar (Oxford: Oxford University Press, 1993), pp. 1–3.
[2] *A Treatise of Human Nature*, ed. by L. A. Selby-Bigge and P. H. Nidditch (Oxford: Clarendon Press, 1978), p. 269.
[3] *Enquiries concerning Human Understanding and concerning the Principles of Morals*, ed. by L. A. Selby-Bigge and P. H. Nidditch (Oxford: Clarendon Press, 1975), p. 161.
[4] The most comprehensive definition of this concept can be found in Habermas's *Strukturwandel der Öffentlichkeit* (1962), trans. by Thomas Burger in association with Frederick Lawrence as *The Structural Transformation of the Public Sphere* (Cambridge: Polity, 1989).

now be regarded as merely politics by other means:[5] a determination to cultivate what Terry Eagleton has claimed is eventually a process of 'class-consolidation [. . .] whereby the English bourgeoisie [negotiated] an historic alliance with its social superiors'.[6] Thus, the much-anthologized desire of Addison's for *The Spectator*, that, in his hands, 'Philosophy' might be dragged out of 'Closets and Libraries, Schools and Colleges, to dwell in Clubs and Assemblies, at Tea-Tables and in Coffee-Houses',[7] may appear radical in effect, even if stiflingly decorous in its means. As Stephen Copley has recently pointed out, the early periodical essayists' rhetorical ease gained energy from Shaftesbury's sunny and optimistic faith in benevolism which also supplied an apology for, or at least a comprehension of, a newly importunate commercialism in letters, in the phrase, a 'Republic of Letters', the emphasis now falling more on the first term.[8] The word *conversation* is central to this structure of civic feeling, and, although the *OED* records a potential range of available meanings prior to the century, there is also evidence to suppose that its serious and pervasive use, as opposed to 'dialogue', for example, only emerges with the movement described above. Blount's *Glossographia* (1656) does not include the word, and Elisha Coles's *An English Dictionary* (1676) is content only to gloss it (strangely) as 'a being', although *conversant* does make an appearance to signify 'keeping company'. John Kersey's project in his *Dictionarium Anglo-Britannicum* (1708), to explicate 'hard WORDS and TERMS OF ART' for the 'great Use' of *'Private Gentlemen, Young Students, Tradesmen, Shop-keepers, Artificers'* and even *'Strangers'*,[9] might account for its enlarged entry as 'familiar Discourse among several Persons; Intercourse; Demeanour', and this popular register is maintained in the noun, *Converse*, which signifies 'familiar discourse, or Correspondence'. This same formula is enlarged for Nathan Bailey, who finds it 'discourse among persons, intercourse, behaviour, society' (*Dictionarium Britannicum* (1730)). Whereas the main thrust of these attempts at definition is unsurprising to us, it may be as well to trace those marginal meanings and associations that remind us of an alternative culture. *To converse*, for Bailey and Kersey particularly, summons up a hinterland of non-verbal gestures towards society and even one's very behaviour, witnessed by one's social bearing. Expressing a thought ensures its very existence. What is moral behaviour if not made manifest?

For Johnson, especially as magnified by Boswell's lionizing, the pursuit of truth through dialogue is a prominent ingredient of how humanist thought

[5] See the discussion and review in Tony Crowley, *Language in History: Theories and Texts* (London: Routledge, 1996), pp. 73–81.
[6] *The Function of Criticism: From 'The Spectator' to Post-Structuralism* (London: Verso, 1984), p. 10.
[7] *Spectator*, no. 10 (12 March 1711), *The Spectator*, ed. by Donald F. Bond, 5 vols (Oxford: Clarendon Press, 1965), I, 44.
[8] 'Commerce, Conversation and Politeness in the Early Eighteenth-Century Periodical', *British Journal of Eighteenth-Century Studies*, 18 (1995), 63–77; see also the proto-Republican aspirations in *Spectator*, 125 (24 July 1711, I, 509–12) and 287 (29 January 1712, III, 18–22).
[9] *Dictionarium Britannicum* (London, 1730), sig. A2.

and its common pursuit might be prosecuted. This survives even when Boswell organizes his memory so as to render his converse as Socratic in method. It is usual for Johnson to treat conversation as no finishing-school delicacy, an inevitable consequence whenever one associates it with politeness. The *Life* is studded with his comments on the capacity to converse, but they rarely testify to a genteel accomplishment. On Johnson's return to Oxford in March 1773, Boswell seemed warmed by the prospect of common-room manners, only to be reminded by his companion that 'real conversation' was stifled, producing 'no fair exertion of mind' when the students were present. 'Animated conversation' entailed a 'contest for superiority', not avuncular indulgence to novices. The next day Boswell records how Johnson, feeling low in spirits, could actually avoid meeting Burke, whose conversation would so much 'call forth all [his] powers' that he would 'kill' him, if Johnson were at all under par. The test of conversation left Goldsmith at a disadvantage, even if he were 'master of a subject in his study',[10] and there is a prevalent attitude to such conviviality in the *Life* that would have it a structured event, part of a dialectic, rather than a tissue of familiar reminiscence.

This is worth stressing, as conversation for many of Johnson's contemporaries could be the attribute of the gentleman amateur. Richard Rorty, for example, finds in the century, 'witty men and learned men and pious men', but that 'there were no highbrows'.[11] This, however, is to confuse a novel rhetorical strategy with the reasons for its deployment and, in any case, registers a blindness to Hutcheson, Blair, Swift, Dennis, Burke, and Johnson himself. In Lord Chesterfield's advice to his son, alongside admonitions as to immoderate mirth, bad company, and slovenly appearance, there is a consistent concern about good conversation. When weighing book-learning and company in the balance, he claims conversation as a 'very great and rational pleasure' only if the result of forethought and the observation of social decorum, yet still laments the inevitability of encountering ignorant conversation from those who 'have not matter enough to furnish them with words to keep up a conversation' (4 October 1746).[12] The clearest description of this is in his letter of 22 February 1748:

Speak the language of the company you are in; speak it purely, and unlarded with any other. Never seem wiser, nor more learned, than the people you are with. Wear your learning, like your watch, in a private pocket: and do not merely pull it out and strike it; merely to show that you have one. (p. 67)

---

[10] James Boswell, *Life of Johnson*, ed. by R. W. Chapman, rev. edn (Oxford: Oxford University Press, 1970), pp. 693, 696, 527. See also Johnson's high regard for Burke's conversational prowess (pp. 1078–79) and Johnson's estimation of conversation as 'a trial of intellectual vigour and skill' whereby he might gain 'colloquial distinction' (pp. 1150–51).

[11] *The Consequences of Pragmatism* (Brighton: Harvester, 1982), p. 67.

[12] *Lord Chesterfield: Letters*, ed. by David Roberts (Oxford: Oxford University Press, 1992), p. 42; see also his excoriation of the 'absent man', who 'takes no part in the general conversation' (9 October 1746, p. 46), his admonition against 'vulgar conversation' (27 September 1749, pp. 162–63) and his defence of colloquial 'propriety and elegance' against 'the Vulgarism of Porters' (n.d., pp. 351–53).

Compare this with Johnson's energetic speaking for victory, which so struck Reynolds in contrast with 'his natural disposition seen in his quiet hours': 'He fought on every occasion as if his whole reputation depended upon the victory of the minute, and he fought with all the weapons.'[13] As patron of the *Dictionary*, Chesterfield's hopes that such a volume might aid 'propriety and elegancy' (letter of 1 January 1754) are of a piece with his oft-stated preference for decorum,[14] a quality that Johnson does espouse in the Preface, but, as we shall see, along with much else besides.

What differentiates these two emphases is no semantic nicety. Where Chesterfield is happy to find conversation primarily a matter of polish and skill, Johnson rarely finds decorum an aim in itself. On 21 March 1783, Boswell records Johnson's staunch enthusiasm for conversation in these terms:

There must, in the first place, be knowledge, there must be materials; in the second place, there must be a command of words; in the third place, there must be imagination, to place things in such views as they are not commonly seen in; and in the fourth place, there must be presence of mind, and a resolution that is not to be overcome by failures: this last is an essential requisite; for want of it many people do not excel in conversation.[15]

This may appear eminent common sense, but its premises are potentially more daring. One starts with cognitive certainties, yet during the cut-and-thrust of communication, the very act of pitting yourself against others takes the original thought out of the closet into the unpredictable realm of social evaluation.

For Johnson, the *Rambler* years (1750–52) were pre-eminently an exercise in reaching and moulding a reading public utilizing social and conversible skills. Its title and those of the other periodicals which he either edited or for which he supplied essays, the *Idler* (1758–60) and the *Adventurer* (1753), imply a *dégagé* urbanity that could be considered simply a commercial ploy, almost by then a generic necessity. Throughout the numbers, however, there is a recurrent theme which cannot simply be taken as opportunism: the angst of the writer imprisoned in his or her own mind-forged Cartesian cell and thus disabled for truly civilized company. *Rambler*, no. 14 (5 May 1750) examines unsparingly the life inured to the 'privacies of study', divorced quite explicitly from 'conversation', and closes the piece with a contrast between the near and far. With distance lending enchantment to the view, the cityscape of imaginative composition may appear a complex of romance associations, all spires and turrets, yet closer to it is 'perplexed with narrow passages, disgraced with despicable cottages, embarrassed with obstructions, and

---

[13] *Johnsonian Gleanings*, ed. by Aleyn Lyell Reade, 11 vols (privately printed, 1909–52), x, 55; see also the burlesques of Chesterfield's advice in *The Graces: A Poetical Epistle. From a Gentleman to his Son* (1774) and *The Fine Gentleman's Etiquette; or, Lord Chesterfield's Advice to his Son, Versified. by a Lady* (1776; repr. Augustan Reprint Society, no. 81, 1960).

[14] *Letters*, p. 297; see also undated letter, pp. 352–53.

[15] *Life*, pp. 1195–96.

clouded with smoke'.[16] *Rambler*, no. 98 (23 February 1751) details some of the substantial gains from politeness, that round of 'little civilities and ceremonious delicacies' that appear so 'inconsiderable [. . .] to the man of science' and even ignoble when formulated. Johnson, though, with conversation in mind, traces their effects in how they 'contribute to the regulation of the world, by facilitating the intercourse between one man and another' (IV, 160–61). In the very first sentence of the *Adventurer*, no. 85 (28 August 1753) he misquotes Francis Bacon's triad of 'reading makes a full man, conference a ready man and writing an exact man' from his essay 'Of Studies' to substitute 'conversation' for 'conference'.[17]

It is tempting to find in this *topos* an unexpectedly post-modernist Johnson, yet that would be as inaccurate as those verdicts pronounced by historians of language who place him exclusively as an upholder of rules and decorous regulation.[18] Conversation needs materials with which to work, yet the private notions safely contemplated in the study can form solipsistic patterns if not braced and tempered by the needs of conversation. On the one hand, there is the empty pragmatism found in *Rambler*, no. 188 (4 January 1752), where he parodies the Chesterfieldian instructions on manners to typify several typical talking heads, the 'merry fellow', 'good-natured man', the 'modest man' and the long-winded narrator, all personae that offer easy passports to a larger world but which are destined to be transient advantages, given the needs of social novelty (V, 223–24). From this vantage oral culture alone is rootless. The first illustrative quotation for *Oral* ('Delivered by mouth; not written') in the *Dictionary* is cited by Johnson as from Locke's *Some Thoughts Concerning Education* (1693): '*Oral discourse*, whose transient faults dying with the sound that gives them life, and so not subject to a strict review, most easily escapes observation.'[19] When arrived at Ostig in Skye in 1773 on his *Journey to the Western Islands* (1775), Johnson did not regret his lack of Erse, as he felt that it had never until recently been a written language, and consequently 'merely floated in the breath of the people'. It was only 'when a language begins to teem with books, [that it tended] to refinement'. 'Exactness' and 'elegance' emerge through the dissemination of expression and thought that print ensures: 'Speech becomes embodied and permanent; different modes and phrases are compared, and the best obtains

---

[16] *The Yale Edition of the Works of Samuel Johnson*, ed. by Allen T. Hazen and others (New Haven, CT and London: Yale University Press, 1958–), III–V: *The Rambler*, ed. by W. J. Bate and Albrecht B. Strauss (1969), III, 79–80.

[17] *The Yale Edition*, II: *The Idler and The Adventurer*, ed. by W. J. Bate, John M. Bullitt and C. F. Powell (1963), p. 411; see *Francis Bacon*, ed. by Brian Vickers (Oxford: Oxford University Press, 1996), p. 439.

[18] See Albert C. Baugh and Thomas Cable, *A History of the English Language*, 3rd edn (1951; repr. London: Routledge, 1978), pp. 270–79, where great weight is given to *Rambler*, no. 208 and Chesterfield's views; Crowley, pp. 54–98.

[19] Under *Orally*, a more damning association is provided by Sir Matthew Hale's comment from *The History and Analysis of the Common Law of England* (1713; 1716): 'Oral tradition were incompetent without written monuments to derive to us the original laws of a kingdom.'

an establishment.' The prospect of the furiously-travelled Erse dictionary-maker compiling his work on foot rather than in the study touches farce: 'Where the whole language is colloquial, he that has only a part, never gets the rest, as he cannot get it but by change of residence.'[20] The labour of constantly re-inventing the wheel is futility itself.

Johnson, whilst distrusting the effects of orality, still could react with alarm at the straitened way provided by books alone. For example, the second of the two quotations provided for *Oral* veers away from the educative analysis manifested by the Locke statement. In consulting Addison, Johnson acknowledged his great admiration for early Christian oratory, whereby 'St. John was appealed to as the living *oracle* of the church; [. . . in that he] personally delivered the gospel'. In the *Adventurer*, no. 85, at the same time as recognizing the fundamental part played in the transmission of culture by books, connection and thus dialectic is only permitted those who brave the perils of social discourse. The cloistered virtue 'has no facility of inculcating his speculations, of adapting himself to the various degrees of intellect which the accidents of conversation will present; but will talk to most unintelligibly, and to all unpleasantly' (p. 414). How moral can a truth be if left uncommunicated and so untried?[21]

The clubbable Johnson obeys an impulse felt no less keenly than the scholiast Johnson, and protestations that at root the two are not contradictory do not convince. Consider the cogency in Imlac's depiction of the 'dangerous prevalence of the imagination' in Chapter 44 of *Rasselas*. These 'airy notions' come to those who are usually alone, and so have 'nothing external that can divert [them]'. It is but a small step towards conceiving oneself 'what [one] is not', the melancholic situation of the Astronomer three chapters later, which in turn leads to Rasselas's own homily on 'variety' which is so 'necessary to content'. The hardship of the monks of St Anthony has its own consolation and they are, according to Imlac, less 'wretched in their silent convent than the Abyssinian princes in their prison of pleasure', yet, demonstrating conversational development, Nekayah is then distrustful of some 'monastick rule', and claims that 'future happiness' may just as easily accrue to him who 'converses openly with mankind, who succours the distressed by his charity, instructs the ignorant by his learning, and contributes by his industry to the general system of life'. It should not be forgotten that the exiled group commit themselves in the 'conclusion, in which nothing is concluded' only to return to Abyssinia, not the Happy Valley, and then only when the 'inundation' of the Nile 'should cease' and they can escape the confinement of their house.[22] More precisely placed

[20] *The Yale Edition*, IX: *A Journey to the Western Islands of Scotland*, ed. by Mary Lascelles (1971), pp. 114–16.
[21] See especially the conspectus of Johnson's work offered by Fredric V. Bogel, in his *Literature and Insubstantiality in Later Eighteenth-Century England* (Princeton, NJ: Princeton University Press, 1984), pp. 47–73.
[22] *The Yale Edition*, XVI: *Rasselas and Other Tales*, ed. by Gwin J. Kolb (1990), pp. 151–52, 164–65, 175–76.

during the compilation of the *Dictionary* are the drawn-out scenes of confinement in *Irene* (1749; though on the stocks from much earlier). In Act I, Scene 5, Aspatia is counselled to 'chase the melancholy moments' with 'converse' (l. 4), and Irene's own fatal confinement in the seraglio in Act V is prefigured by Aspatia as 'Immur'd and buried in perpetual sloth, | That gloomy slumber of the stagnant soul' (III. 8.81–82), exceptionally a self-quotation and the third illustrative quotation for *Stagnant* in the *Dictionary* ('Motionless; still; not agitated; not flowing; not running'). Indeed, the immediately preceding lines, cancelled for the printed edition and preserved in the British Museum manuscript, heaps Pelion on Ossa, having her there 'Deny'd Debar'd each privilege of human nature [*being* cancelled] | The social gayety the informing converse'. It is here that we feel the 'dull Suspence' that corrupts 'the stagnant mind' (*Vanity*, l. 344).[23]

Reaching out for others in society is less an option for Johnson than a (sometimes cruel) necessity, and, crucially, it can provide the very basis of untutored literary excellence. It should be remembered that the gloriously irregular Shakespeare provided such lucid dialogue that it appeared to 'have been gleaned by diligent selection out of common conversation, and common occurrences'. It was often the case that he consulted only those 'remarks on life or axioms of morality' that 'float in conversation', not those that emerge from 'closet' study. Rude and natural though this is, it still provides 'vigilance of observation and accuracy of distinction', pertinent reflections on humanity that could not be discovered elsewhere.[24]

If this element of Johnson's writing is admitted, then it is significant that it is specifically the word *conversation* that is so prevalent, and not some equally appropriate synonym. In the entry on *Conversation* throughout the evolution of the *Dictionary*, there is a clear division between those meanings pointing towards the mere physical act of 'familiar discourse' and 'easy talk' (meanings 1 and 2) and a more generalized term applied to social behaviour (meanings 3, 4, and, in the fourth edition, 5; see Figure 1). For meaning 3 ('Commerce; intercourse; familiarity'), Dryden's opinion of improving social knowledge comes juxtaposed with a debased alternative from *Richard III*: Richard's crocodile tears shed over Hastings's head (III.5.30–31), which also point to a purely physical extension to the term.[25] Obviously, the value of such social investment could go down as well as up. For heading 4 ('Behaviour; manner of acting in common life'), we get the tag from the first epistle general of Peter (2.12), that continues 'that, whereas they speak against you as evildoers, they may by your good works, which they shall behold, glorify God in the day of visitation'. For the fourth edition (1773), an

[23] *The Yale Edition*, VI: *Poems*, ed. by E. L. McAdam, Jr and George Milne (1964), pp. 129, 165 and n., 107.
[24] *The Yale Edition*, VII and VIII: *Johnson on Shakespeare*, ed. by Arthur Sherbo (1969), VII, 63, 85, 88.
[25] See Dryden's Preface to *Sylvae; or, The Second Part of Poetical Miscellanies* (1685), in *Essays of John Dryden*, ed. by W. P. Ker, 2 vols (Oxford: Clarendon Press, 1900), I, 253; *Richard III*, ed. by Antony Hammond (London: Methuen, 1981).

CONVERSATION.

n.s.

[*conversatio,* Latin.]

1. Familiar discourse; chat; easy talk: opposed to a formal conference.

> She went to Pamela's chamber, meaning to joy her thoughts with the sweet *conversation* of her sister.
>
> > *Sidney.*

> What I mentioned some time ago in *conversation,* was not a new thought, just then started by accident or occasion.
>
> > *Swift.*

2. A particular act of discoursing upon any subject: as. *we had a long* conversation *on that question.*

3. Commerce; intercourse; familiarity.

> The knowledge of men and manners, the freedom of habitudes, and *conversation* with the best company.
>
> > *Dryden.*

> His apparent, open guilt;
> I mean his *conversation* with Shore's wife.
>
> > *Shakes. Rich. III.*

4. Behaviour; manner of acting in common life.

> Having your *conversation* honest among the Gentiles.
>
> > Bible *1 Pet.*

5. Practical habits; knowledge by long acquaintance.

> I set down, out of long experience in business and much *conversation* in books, what I thought pertinent to this business.
>
> > *Bacon.*

> By experience and *conversation* with these bodies. a man may be enabled to give a near conjecture at the metallic ingredients of any mass.
>
> > *Woodward.*

FIGURE 1.   4th edition, *Dictionary,* 1773

extra fifth heading is given, 'practical habits; knowledge by long acquaint-ance', which incorporates a sentence from Francis Bacon that gestures to the possibility of a bridge between the world of the book and that of observation, 'I set down, out of long experience in business and much *conversation* in books, what I thought pertinent to this business'.

If this summary distinction between socializing on the one hand and overt Christian witness and/or civic duty on the other holds good, then we may sense quite why Johnson and others might have found the term useful: it promotes the social fellowship of civic humanism whilst also retaining associations of an older pattern, the public testimony of Christian uprightness that preaches its own implicit sermon. To get there one has to respond to some of the echoes from the texts and authors used as illustrative matter. For example, for meaning 3, consistency of reference is surely not the aim as the choice of Dryden's and Shakespeare's usage seems quite opposed: whilst the denotative sense is understood, the alternatives of instructive and healthy society and mere sexual congress extend its associative range. Similarly, the ideal of active Christian benevolence carried by the full context found for the quotation from 1 Peter is hardly suggested by the more neutral heading, which simply mentions any sort of public bearing. The relation of the study to a wider world is also tacit if the source for the Bacon statement is read from blind.

In the Preface to the *Dictionary* Johnson is clear that there were some words 'of which the sense [was] too subtle and evanescent to be fixed in a paraphrase'. 'Kindred senses' of a word 'may be so interwoven, that the perplexity cannot be disentangled', to such an extent that Johnson puts the pertinent question, 'When the radical idea branches out into parallel ramifications, how can a consecutive series be formed of senses in their nature collateral?' It is likely that an alternative Preface may be discovered, however, one that demonstrates a distaste at such verbal slipperiness, where Johnson quite clearly holds it a tenet of faith that in those quotations where mutilation of the original text has had to take place the integrity of the quoted statement in its original context has had to be adapted to the demands of simple demonstration. This does only 'sometimes' happen, though, and the very fact that he has to correct rash commentators could just as easily portray the quotations as more normally dealing in allusive echoes than not.[26]

This general lexicographical undertaking is probably more accurate in capturing the significant shift in meaning that makes 'conversation' so seminal at this time in accounts of civic duty and acceptable public behaviour. Although separated so as to provide a distinct account of semantic variety, the various definitions under the entry in the *Dictionary* do not stand quite so distinct in any speech-act, where the possibility for pun or fruitful ambiguity is always potentially present, even if the full textual content helps the reader in retrospect decipher a more precise shade of intended meaning. Far from 'consecutive' meanings, the term could be understood 'collaterally', where any earlier attempt at a creative quibble playing on a fusion of the physical act and the abstract ethical imperative tends to the denotative. For example, in Chapter 6 of the anonymous *The Faith and Practice of a Church of England Man*, 'Of Civil Conversation', this civility has always to be made manifest: society 'softens Mens Tempers, and makes them pliable, it reduces the Rules of Religion and Prudence into Art, it cures the Mind of that sowerness or conceitedness, to which a very retired and

---

[26] *Samuel Johnson*, ed. by Donald Greene (Oxford: Oxford University Press, 1984), pp. 315–17; for a fuller treatment of this issue, see Allen Reddick, *The Making of Johnson's Dictionary, 1746–1773*, rev. edn (Cambridge: Cambridge University Press, 1996), pp. xvii–xviii, 9–11, 33–35; Robert DeMaria, Jr, *The Life of Samuel Johnson: A Critical Biography* (Oxford: Blackwell, 1993), pp. 116–28, and *Johnson's Dictionary and the Language of Learning* (Oxford: Clarendon Press, 1986), pp. 3–60.

Monkish person is too much exposed'.[27] Richard Lucas's much-reprinted sermon, *The Influence of Conversation* (1707), moves constantly between the secular and devotional when directing his congregation to scriptural authority, which 'points out to us much nobler Purposes and Designs of Conversation, when it tells us, that our speech should be such as *may administer Grace*; that we should *build up one another in our Holy Faith*'.[28] In *Of Religious Discourse in Common Conversation* (1706) John Norris of Bemerton takes as his text Psalm 37. 30: 'The Mouth of the Righteous speaketh Wisdom, and his Tongue talketh of Judgement', to advance the need for public moral rearmament: ''Tis not the Notional, but the Practical part of Religion whose disuse in Conversation I complain of. Men do indeed talk of Religion, but not of that which is practical, nor in a practical way.' Clerics need to master 'Good Familiar Discourse', for 'Religious Thoughts when they are confined to the Mind, and transacted only in the scene of the Imagination, have not half that Influence upon the Man, as when they are cloathed with Words, and are audibly utter'd by the Tongue'.[29] A complete identification between these alternative senses of the one word can be traced in William Lupton's *Christian Conversation* (1726), where the term is defined as implying conformity: a 'metaphorical expression, taken from the State and Condition of Citizens, or Members of a Civil Community, denoting a Behaviour suitable to all the Laws and Customs of the City, or Community, to which they belong'.[30]

In these tracts polite civility is a Good Work; the demands of social intercourse prevent schismatic whimsy and prominent blasphemy. Edward Stillingfleet, the Bishop of Worcester, even nodded ruefully at the fact that 'we live in an Age, wherein the *Conversations* of the Clergy are more observed than their *Doctrine*', and concluded that 'Charity and Good Works' needed 'unblameable and holy Conversations' (note the plural) in the promotion of 'Diligence and Constancy'.[31] These have settled truths to impart, and a true dialectic is not indicated here, but we might also observe here a hybridity of sense that eventually confounds linguistic purity, where connotation leads and denotation follows.

A dichotomy does not imply contradiction and inconsistencies may, of course, be entertained where man is concerned, but Johnson's Lockean belief that words are not naturally annexed to things undermines the conception that the sudden assemblage of hitherto unconnected sentiments met in a single word may be the spark of creation or a new thought.

[27] *The Faith and Practice of a Church of England Man* (1688; 6th edn, 1703), p. 66.
[28] *The Influence of Conversation, with the Regulation thereof: A Sermon preached at St. Clement Dane, to a Religious Society* (1707), p. 20. Seven editions were printed by 1769.
[29] *Of Religious Discourse in Common Conversation. In Three Parts* (1706), pp. 6, 22–23, 20.
[30] *Christian Conversation: Dr. Lupton's Farewell Sermon* (1726), p. 3.
[31] Edward Stillingfleet, *Directions for the Conversation of the Clergy* (1710), p. 3. Compare Norris: 'Living Births of Piety that come from the Mouth in Conversation, when Hearts truly toucht with the Love of God communicate their Light and Heat' (p. 24), and Josiah Woodward, *A Serious Reflection on the Grievous Scandal of Prophane Language in Conversation*, 2nd edn (1708).

Authority has to be found, but the question should more properly be: to what end is quoted authority used? It is, therefore, a basic requirement of Johnson's lexicography that the task of fixing the language and regulating its decora of usage must confront one unnegotiable fact: that language is man-made; only thoughts have the potential to be divine. It has often been noted that Johnson's prevalent metaphors in the Preface to the *Dictionary* (1755) are often associated with pathfinding or the taking of compass-bearings. Alternatively, the *Plan* (1747), addressed to the work's would-be patron, Lord Chesterfield, before the work had commenced, betrays few doubts about the position of the lexicographer, or how relative must be her/his viewpoint: 'The chief intent [of the rule of distinction by which certain words were either chosen or excluded] was to preserve the purity and ascertain the meaning of our English idiom'. The language, he hopes, will be thus 'laid down' as in foundations,

distinct in its minutest subdivisions, and resolved into its elemental principles. And who upon this survey can forbear to wish, that these fundamental atoms of our speech might obtain the firmness and immutability of the primogenial and constituent particles of matter, that they might retain their substance while they alter their appearance, and be varied and compounded, yet not destroyed.

It is sometimes forgotten that this is a position from which Johnson almost immediately withdraws when reminding the reader that 'language is the work of man, of a being from whom permanence and stability cannot be derived'. Nevertheless, he has secure aims, looking on his task as resembling Julius Caesar's when confronted by an uncolonized Britain: whilst unable to 'complete the conquest', he may be up to discovering the coast, civilizing some of the inhabitants, and lessening the work of any future lawgiver.[32]

When in November and December 1754, Lord Chesterfield finally agreed to notice such colonial fervour in his two 'puffs' for the *Dictionary* in *The World*, he missed completely the careful (although marginal) circumspection of the *Plan* in relishing the opportunity for a 'lawful standard of our language' that at last may guide those who wish to write 'grammatically and correctly' in a time of linguistic free trade. The moment for tolerance is at an end. Johnson should benefit from 'the old roman expedient' and rest happy when elected a 'Dictator'.[33] Such conservative ideology has been analysed at some length by John Barrell. It seems clear that neither Chesterfield nor Johnson took the pains to enquire into the origin of language as did the Universal Grammarians or, indeed, into the claims of contemporary usage except to provide instances of imperfection and decay. It is symptomatic of Barrell's argument that it is the *Plan* which is more often chosen to represent this lexicographical and, by extension, political position, and not so much the Preface, for it is somewhat easier to find Johnson autocratic when he was

---

[32] *The Plan of a Dictionary of the English Language* (1747), pp. 4, 18, 33.
[33] *The World*, no. 100 (28 November 1754), repr. in 4 vols (1755), III, 267.

envisaging his task than in its more sober afterglow.[34] Constantly, the Preface derives its metaphorical interest from references to losses of context. Hence it is that lexicographers seem doomed 'only to remove rubbish and clear obstructions from the paths through which Learning and Genius press forward'. Upon first taking a 'survey' of the language, its abundance unsettles the settled view, for English speech appears 'copious without order, and energetic without rules'. Consequently, wherever he turned his view, 'there was perplexity to be disentangled'.[35] The emphasis in the Preface lies on the distracting problems that were confronted rather than the working principles that should have supplied ready solutions.

Much of this more chastened perspective emerges when outlining the need for agreed rules on semantics. Simple words function much as simple ideas in that they are rarely reducible:

Many words cannot be explained by synonyms, because the idea signified by them has not more than one appellation; nor by paraphrase, because simple ideas cannot be described. When the nature of things is unknown, or the notion unsettled and indefinite, and various in various minds, the words by which such notions are conveyed, or such things denoted, will be ambiguous and perplexed. (p. 315)

It is characteristic of Johnson that he does not have recourse at this point to the safety of an abstract grammar. What comes to his aid is, rather, the supposition of 'something intuitively known, and evident without proof' — not sense reified in formulae, but notions received from common experience.

The decision to include illustrative quotations in the *Dictionary* was not an inevitable one. Both in Thomas Blount's *Glossographia* (1656) and Nathan Bailey's *Dictionarium Brittanicum* (1730), for example, the need to show shades of meaning or usage involves a proliferation of headings, not a deeper unity. Words do not operate for Johnson according to some divine analogy, but directly from precedent, a species of case-law from the 'wells of English undefiled', namely, writing from Sidney to the Restoration. This context provides 'the pure sources of genuine diction' which pre-date deviations towards a 'Gallic structure and phraseology' (p. 319). The principle of illustrative quotations also demonstrates the desire to depart from the legacy of 'hard-word' lexicons, manuals for teaching English to the artisan or foreigner, and so contributing to the growth of a canon of acceptable usage. Robert DeMaria, Jr, has gone further than most in tracing Johnson's more immediate precursors as hailing from the encyclopaedic tradition, such as Ephraim Chambers's *Cyclopedia* (1728).[36] Johnson once asserted that he had formed his style on that of Chambers's Preface, and it should therefore come as no surprise that his passages on the making of dictionaries seem particularly apposite when representing Johnson's originality in the field.

---

[34] John Barrell, *English Literature in History, 1730–80: An Equal, Wide Survey* (London: Hutchinson, 1983), pp. 113–61.
[35] *Samuel Johnson*, p. 307.
[36] *Johnson's Dictionary*, pp. 4–8.

Chambers finds the lexicographer an 'analyst', not immediately involved in the process of improving knowledge but rather in teaching or conveying it, being led 'to unty the complexions, or bundles of ideas his predecessors had made, and reduce them to their natural simplicity'.[37] These 'bundles' are composed of ideas, not, by etymological analogy, verbal resemblances or webs of words alone. If we return to the Preface we also find that whilst there is a temporal context supplied for each word (the 'wells of English undefiled'), Johnson sees a necessary rationale in each meaning inhering in the sentence — not as atoms of single ideas, but in and during the process of signification. Here is the paragraph that immediately follows his apology for canonizing the dialect of Hooker and Bacon:

It is not sufficient that a word is found, unless it be so combined as that its meaning is apparently determined by the tract and tenor of the sentence; such passages I have therefore chosen, and when it happened that any author gave a definition of a term, or such an explanation as is equivalent to a definition, I have placed his authority as a supplement to my own. (p. 320)

A word cannot be self-evidently significant. It has to be combined with others and only then can its meaning or its background idea be traced or communicated. Well may Johnson in the Preface envisage censure from those who distrust the multiplicity of his examples.

For meaning apparently to be determined by the 'tract and tenor of the sentence' it has to be judged according to the precise circumstances of its utterance. Johnson's definition of *Tenor*, sense 3, gives: 'Sense contained; general course or drift', which, together with the first heading, 'Continuity of state; constant mode; manner of continuity; general currency', demonstrates at the very least a refusal to take up a literal perspective on linguistic use. Expression defines. *Tract* endorses this. The third definition has an illustration from William Holder's *Elements of Speech* (1669): 'As in *tract* of speech a dubious word is easily known by the coherence with the rest, and a dubious letter by the whole word: so may a deaf person, having competent knowledge of language, by an acute sagacity by some more evident word discerned by his eye, know the sense.' Individual words, as we encounter them in dictionary order and array, require a context or pattern of association. Illustration is a task also of definition.

To add to Johnson's question as to how to range semantics consecutively when any basic item of sense is known through 'parallel ramifications':whilst the work of definition must proceed by a process of disentangling, can the use of any one word derive from distinct origins, from its etymological roots? One of the most basic working principles in the *Dictionary* had thus taken Johnson far away from the *Plan*'s pious hope that words may be rendered there as 'firm and immutable' and as the 'primogenial and constituent

[37] Ephraim Chambers, *Cyclopaedia; or, A Universal Dictionary of Arts and Sciences*, 2 vols (1728; repr. 1741) I, xvi.

particles of matter'. On the contrary, language appears very much the work of man and man intent on expression. Even in the *Plan*, Johnson had noted that 'naked science is too delicate for the purposes of life' and that the 'value of a work' should be estimated by its use, not its Olympian truth (pp. 4–5).

We need to make one further very necessary distinction at this point: the separation of common usage which springs from words with an oral/aural existence from the usage of the best stylists that forms Johnson's canon of case-law. This does not leave us with a Henry Higgins Johnson, notebook in hand, spying out street English, as the *Dictionary* takes its stand on written culture, be it Milton's *Paradise Lost* or Thomas Tusser's *Guide to Animal Husbandry*. The very act of framing the words not only syntactically within the 'tract and tenor' of a sentence, but also as springing from the golden age where the language's (teutonic) structure was at its flexible zenith can be overstated.

In practice, the dictionary entries are a great deal more carefully-wrought and managed than Johnson led his first market to expect. If we look at the entry on *Conversation* again (Figure 1), we could be excused for passing over the apparently neutral opening of meaning 1. Certainly, this could be the case with the material from Sidney's *Arcadia*, II.5,[38] yet the Swift quotation is not so innocent. As the opening sentence of Swift's *A Proposal for Correcting, Improving and Ascertaining the English Tongue* (1712), its surface conversational informality is really just part of the preliminary address to Robert Harley, Earl of Oxford. The full tenor of the rest of the document is set against such a linguistic norm. In one of the very few works to which Swift actually affixed his own name there is a sustained analogy between political stability and that of a language. He sees 'no absolute Necessity why any Language should be perpetually changing', for if it were 'once refined to a certain Standard, perhaps there might be Ways to fix it for ever, or at least till we are invaded'.[39] Taken together with his *Hints towards an Essay on Conversation* (1710) and the later *A Complete Collection of Genteel and Ingenious Conversation* (1738), it is precisely the degeneracy of converse that erodes this potential bedrock.[40] In his *Life of Swift* Johnson proves no friend to this fundamentalism, claiming that it took its stand on prejudice not experience: 'The certainty and stability which, contrary to all experience, he thinks attainable, he proposes to secure by instituting an academy; the decrees of which every man would have been willing, and many would have been proud to disobey.'[41] In this instance the mutilation of the original context is not inevitable, but calculated.

[38] See *The Countess of Pembroke's Arcadia*, ed. by Maurice Evans (Harmondsworth: Penguin, 1977), p. 244.
[39] *The Prose Writings of Jonathan Swift*, ed. by Herbert Davis and others, 14 vols (Oxford: Blackwell, 1939–68), IV: *A Proposal for Correcting the ENGLISH TONGUE, Polite Conversation, etc.*, ed. by Herbert Davis and Louis Landa (1957; repr. 1973), p. 9.
[40] *Essay on Conversation*: 'Thus we see how human Nature is most debased, by the Abuse of that Faculty which is held the great Distinction between Men and Brutes' (Davis and Landa, p. 94).
[41] *Lives of the Poets*, ed. by G. B. Hill, 3 vols (Oxford: Clarendon Press, 1905), III, 16.

Johnson's debt to Locke has been widely analysed, and there is a familiar link.[42] In his *Essay Concerning Human Understanding* (1690), Locke bases language on more or less appropriate imitations of 'common sensible *ideas*' (III.1.5). In his chapter 'Of Words or Language in General', 'articulate sounds' should be '*signs of internal conceptions*' (III.1.2). General ideas are simply an adequate short-hand for otherwise complex confluences of simple ideas. Otherwise, the 'multiplication of words would have perplexed' the use of language by 'every particular thing' needing its 'distinct name' (III.1.3).[43] The analogy is thus created between primary and secondary ideas. Johnson surely follows this line of reasoning by a careful management of apparently separate meanings collected under individual words. The centrality of Locke's 'common sensible *ideas*' is evident. As Paul Fussell has exhaustively and most engagingly pointed out, the 'wardrobe' of the 'moral imagination' needed again and again a reliable relation of ideas to words in the hope of achieving a lexicon with the stability of things.[44] Note, they do not confuse words with things, but they create an analogical bridge between 'common forms' and the *sensus communis*, or 'common sense' that should be native to humanity, but rarely is.

Locke's determination to weed out error, however, is not centred on a natural history of words, for whilst stressing the arbitrariness of the words we may adopt when talking to ourselves, the communication of thought is not arbitrarily ordained. To this end, Locke distinguishes two broad classes of words and usage: Civil use and Philosophical use. Civil use upholds 'common conversation and commerce about the ordinary affairs and conveniences of civil life', whilst Philosophical use conveys a 'precise notion of things' where, by means of 'general propositions, certain and undoubted truths which the mind may rest upon and be satisfied with', are conveyed (III.9.3).[45] The usefulness of this distinction is not lost on Johnson. Whenever error is located, it is not merely usage which produces it, but rather sloppy or evasive usage. 'Philosophical' discourse, as W. K. Wimsatt has shown, meant for Johnson, the steadfast refusal to admit expressions and, by extension, notions that could not be classified.[46] This is not the same as claiming that language is modelled on a universal grammar, but it does give the lexicographer elbow-room to define even the simplest words. No word is

---

[42] See especially Robert DeMaria, Jr, 'The Theory of Language in Johnson's *Dictionary*' in *Johnson After Two Hundred Years*, ed. by Paul Korshin (Philadelphia: University of Pennsylvania Press, 1986), pp. 159–74; Elizabeth Hedrick, 'Locke's Theory of Language and Johnson's *Dictionary*', *Eighteenth-Century Studies*, 20 (1986/87), 422–44; Murray Cohen, *Sensible Words: Linguistic Practice in England, 1640–1785* (Baltimore, MD and London: Johns Hopkins University Press, 1977), especially pp. 90–95.

[43] John Locke, *An Essay Concerning Human Understanding*, ed. by John W. Yolton, 2 vols (London: Dent, 1961).

[44] *The Rhetorical World of Augustan Humanism: Ethics and Imagery from Swift to Burke* (Oxford: Oxford University Press, 1965), pp. 217–32.

[45] A wider survey of the consequences of this distinction is attempted by Nalini Jain, *The Mind's Extensive View: Samuel Johnson on Poetic Language* (Strathtay: Roland Harris Trust, 1991), pp. 38–54.

[46] *Philosophic Words: A Study of Style and Meaning in 'The Rambler' and 'Dictionary' of Samuel Johnson* (New Haven, CT: Yale University Press, 1948; repr. New York: Archon, 1968), pp. 1–19.

an island entire unto itself, for it forms synchronous associations with either civil or philosophical discourse. Yet it is authorized not by reason alone or naked science, but by Johnson's skill in finding it definable. This is no Linnaean classification, for each word must demonstrate its valency as well as its atomic structure. This is a less familiar influence.

Throughout Locke's *Essay*, 'conversation' appears to be a linch-pin. For Bacon in *The Advancement of Learning* (1605), 'civil knowledge' is that gleaned from the consideration of man in society, where individuals give themselves up to 'conversation, negotiation, and government' (Book II, 23.2).[47] For Locke, the term means rather more than demeanour, the public-spirited impulse to share insights so as to weave 'a garment of the mind' (Bacon, II.23.3). 'Common use' cannot be an arbiter of the greater accuracy called for in 'philosophical' analysis (see Locke, III.9.8, 15), yet it is a powerful antidote to the metaphysical notions much loved by schoolmen, 'whereby they had the advantage to destroy the instruments and means of discourse, conversation, instruction and society' (III.10.10) by their perplexing circumlocution. As Peter Walmsley has shown, Locke's hatred of disputations and wrangling stemmed from their egotistic investment in first thoughts.[48] Conversely, the Royal Society held the promise of conversible advancement, a genuine dialectic and open exchange. Matters of probability, rather than logical consistency, invite contest and the improvement of knowledge that emerges from the work of many minds (see III.10.6; III.6.21; III.11.24, 25; I.2.14; II.22.5).

In the first edition of the *Dictionary* Johnson included more than three thousand illustrative quotations from Locke and nearly five hundred and fifty from Isaac Watts, his close disciple. Watts, indeed, was even more explicitly wedded to the idea of clubbable discourse than his mentor, and he earned elevation to Johnson's poetic pantheon of taste in the *Lives*, apparently by the editor's own intervention: 'Few books have been perused by me with greater pleasure than his *Improvement of the Mind*, of which the radical principles may indeed be found in Locke's *Conduct of the Understanding*', which had been so 'expanded and ramified' that it demanded individual attention.[49] For Watts, 'conversation' was an essential item in spiritual as well as intellectual refinement: 'By mutual Discourse the Soul is awakened and allured to bring forth its Hoards of Knowledge, and it learns how to

[47] *The Advancement of Learning and New Atlantis*, ed. by Arthur Johnston (Oxford: Oxford University Press, 1974), pp. 171–72.
[48] See 'Civil Conversation in Locke's *Essay*', *Studies in Voltaire and the Eighteenth Century*, 303 (1992), pp. 411–13, and 'Dispute and Conversation: Probability and the Rhetoric of Natural Philosophy in Locke's *Essay*', *Journal of the History of Ideas*, 54 (1993), 381–94.
[49] *Lives*, III, 309.

DISCOU'RSE.

n.s.
[*discours*, Fr. *discursus*, Latin.]

2. Conversation; mutual intercourse of language; talk.

He waxeth wiser than himself, more by an hour's *discourse*, than by a day's meditation.

> *Bacon.*

In thy *discourse*, if thou desire to please,
All such is courteous, useful, new, or witty;
Usefulness come by labour, wit by ease,
Courtesy grows in court, news in the city.

> *Herbert.*

The vanquish'd party with the victors join'd,
Nor wanted sweet *discourse*, the banquet of the mind.

> *Dryd.*

FIGURE 2.   4th edition, *Dictionary*, 1773

render them most useful to Mankind [. . .] vast Reading without Conversation is like a *Miser* who lives only to himself.'[50] Throughout the many citations of converse and its semantic cluster in the *Dictionary*, it is rare that Johnson deploys it in an unflattering light.[51] Watts is consulted for the second quotation for *Converse* (sense 2) ('Acquaintance; cohabitation; familiarity'): 'By such a free *converse* with persons of different sects, we shall find that there are persons of good sense and virtue, persons of piety and worth'. Sense 2 of *Discourse* ('Conversation; mutual intercourse of language; talk'; see Figure 2) supplies the more consoling associations of the term. Bacon's sharp rebuke to a cloistered virtue can be found in his essay, 'Of Friendship', Herbert's unexpected praise of urbanity in 'The Church-Porch' (ll. 289–92) continues: 'Get a good stock of these, then draw the card; | That suites him best, of whom thy speech is heard', and the calming effect of speech in Dryden's Chaucerian imitation, 'The Flower and the Leaf', combines the intellectual and the convivial in 'the banquet of the mind' (l. 432).[52] In Sense 2 for *Ordinary*, Addison is found to observe that 'Method is not less

---

[50] Isaac Watts, *The Improvement of the Mind: or, a Supplement to the Art of Logick* (1741), p. 42. Compare 'A Hermit who has been shut up in his cell in a College, has contracted a sort of Mould and Rust upon his Soul' (Watts, p. 44), and Benjamin Stillingfleet, *An Essay on Conversation* (1737): 'Circulation betwixt Mind and Mind | Extends its course, and renders it refin'd' (p. 18). Johnson's annotated copy of Watts's *Logick: or, the Right Use of Reason in the Enquiry after Truth*, 8th edn (1745) can be found in the British Library (C. 28.g.9).
[51] See especially the quotations from Watts for *imbibe* (sense 2), Rogers for *set*, Dryden for *unstudied*, L'Estrange for *edifying* (sense 2), and Rogers for *accessible*.
[52] See *Francis Bacon*, p. 394; *The English Poems of George Herbert*, ed. by C. A. Patrides (London: Dent, 1974), p. 41; *The Poems of John Dryden*, ed. by James Kinsley, 4 vols (Oxford: Clarendon Press, 1958), IV, 1661.

requisite in *ordinary* conversation than in writing' (*Spectator*, no. 476), and Richard Hooker places 'virtuous conversation' as an invaluable adjunct to the clergy's 'publick readings' of canonical works in sense 2 of *Canonical* (*Of the Laws of Ecclesiastical Polity*, Book v (1597)).[53] Although ephemeral in itself, converse, as Locke more than once had cause to point out, distinguishes Mankind (III.11.5; III.6.21).

This focus on the one term, *conversation*, in relation to the *Dictionary* could be regarded as a chance reflection, and it could certainly be maintained that any number of exemplary words might have thrown light on how Johnson organized his lexicographical processes. A task so vast as the compilation of this work entails a certain humility and realism when attempting to reduce his working procedures to formulae. It is clear that there are many terms that did not require Johnson to make the careful illustrative choices I have outlined here, but by the same token it is still probable that he may have deployed many of his definitions to help interpret his stock of favoured quotations in some sort of semantic dialogue. The demands of closing down options, settling arguments, and rooting out linguistic error are only some of the impulses Dictionary Johnson obeyed. Until the complex of intertextual allusions/parodies/appropriations hidden in his illustrative work have been examined properly, the very undertaking itself has at least to be put on the agenda as a significant preliminary step.

The utility of the *Dictionary* in histories of the language as a reference-work to judge the age's decora and notions of correctness should not, however, survive without further fundamental work on the format of the book. As both Allen Reddick and Robert DeMaria, Jr (among others) have made plain, Johnson's linguistic work was always more of a creative enterprise than a dictatorial intervention, more a contribution to dialogic conversation than scholastic abstraction, and this should have us conclude that it was an even more ambitious enterprise than Chesterfield could have conceived.[54] For Henry Fielding, in his *Essay on Conversation* (1743), it epitomized social evaluation at its most elevated: 'The Primitive and literal sense of this Word is, I apprehend, to *Turn round together*; and in its more copious usage we intend by it, that reciprocal Interchange of Ideas, by which Truth is examined. Things are, in a manner, *turned round* and sifted, and all our Knowledge communicated to each other.'[55] Unlike jesting Pilate, for both ethical and personal reasons, Johnson stays for an answer.

---

[53] See *Spectator* (5 September 1712), IV, 186–87; *The Works of Mr. Richard Hooker*, ed. by John Keble, 4th edn, 3 vols (Oxford, 1863), II, 69–70 (V. 20.1).

[54] Reddick, pp. 121–40; DeMaria, *Johnson's Dictionary*, pp. 19–37.

[55] *Miscellanies by Henry Fielding, Esq.*, ed. by Henry Knight Miller and others, 2 vols (Oxford: Clarendon Press, 1972–93), I, 120.

Sir William Jones and the New Pluralism over Languages and Cultures

GARLAND CANNON

Texas A&M University

One of the brightest linguists in a century boasting scholars such as Jacob Bryant, Robert Lowth, Lord Monboddo, John Horne Tooke,[1] and Dr Johnson, Jones (1746–94) chose not to concentrate on lexicography and dictionaries in the time that he could spare from his London law practice. Otherwise, in view of the comparative, comprehensive scope of all the endeavours in his multifaceted career, his name might be enshrined today alongside that of his colleague, Dictionary Johnson. Jones viewed such work as indispensable to linguistic scholarship, but still only a tool to higher goals. In *A Grammar of the Persian Language* (London, 1771) he generalized that some scholars 'have left nothing more behind them than grammars and diction-aries; and though they deserve the praises due to unwearied pains and industry, yet they would, perhaps, have gained a more shining reputation, if they had contributed to beautify and enlighten the vast temple of learning, instead of spending their lives in adorning only its porticos and avenues'.[2] That is, the most important research should transcend the advancing of knowledge. Besides informing, research should entertain and provide moral instruction, perhaps leading to the reader's practical improvement. Let us assess Jones's writings lexicographically, concentrating on his translations and imitative works, in a roughly chronological sequence. These particularly introduced the world of Arabic, Persian, and classical Sanskrit language and culture to the West.

From the beginning of his career, within the matrix of pre-scientific linguistics characterizing the eighteenth century, Jones was somewhat innovative in his language-learning method. At Oxford he set out to learn Arabic by employing a native speaker of Arabic to help with the pronunci-ation, rather than relying on antiquated manuscripts for which there were no living speakers, as for classical Greek and Latin. Yet it was essentially a grammar-translation method, where he spent part of every morning in reading Antoine Galland's twelve-volume edition titled *Les Mille et une nuits* (Paris, 1704–17), and in transcribing and refining Mirza's Arabic version, in the prescriptive attitude of the day, meanwhile utilizing the superb Arabic

---

[1] See the assessments in Hans Aarsleff, *The Study of Language in England, 1780–1860* (Princeton, NJ: Princeton University Press, 1967).

[2] In the *Collected Works of Sir William Jones*, 13 vols (London: Stockdale and Walker, 1807; repr. Curzon Press, 1993), v, 167. Further references are given in the text.

manuscripts that Edward Pococke had brought to the Bodleian the previous century. Jones's lexicon was Meninski's vast *Thesaurus linguarum orientalium Turcicæ, Arabicæ, Persicæ* (Vienna, 1680–87). Thus he was intimately involved with Latin from the first, an experience that was useful in arriving at his famous language-family formulation in 1786 and the procedure of translating Sanskrit by first rendering it into the chronologically 'intermediate' Latin, before translating and refining the Latin version into English. This procedure was especially useful for his pioneering, polished translation of Kālidāsa's *Śakuntalā* (Calcutta, 1789). The *Thesaurus* also influenced the final form of Jones's Persian *Grammar*, for which his chief grammatical source was John Greaves's *Elementa linguæ Persicæ* (London, 1649).

His Hebrew model came from his friend Lowth, whose *De sacra poesi Hebræorum præorum prælectiones* (Oxford, 1753) inspired Jones to use Latin for his own *Poeseos Asiaticæ commentariorum* (London, 1774), and led him to include the original Oriental texts alongside his roman transliterations, translations, and even imitations. Though Jones cites Lowth's *Short Introduction to the English Language* (London, 1762) in the preface to his Persian *Grammar*, the influence of Latin is evident. A major constraint was the purpose of his long-planned book: it was to be a language-learning text for a friend who was shortly leaving for India, since it was then thought that Persian was considerably used there. While the immediately famous book should contribute to knowledge, a necessary criterion for any book concerned with language, it should mainly serve its pedagogical purpose. It was not to be a linguistic grammar like Greaves's.

As much of what became a 153-page book was to be printed in Persian, the project would be expensive. Vainly he sought financial assistance from the East India Company, which customarily bought multiple copies of new books that might be helpful to its servants in the subcontinent. Instead of advancing funds and using the book as a kind of Persian primer for the new recruits, the Company lent only its name and did not even formally promise to purchase copies when the book appeared. After five years the *Grammar* was finally published by William and John Richardson, the nephews of the novelist Samuel Richardson.

Jones's preface states that he first compared the form of his projected book 'with every composition of the same nature' that he could find, chiefly to assure originality in method, arrangement, and subject matter, but clearly also to develop a novel model for grammars of exotic languages. Thus he excluded treatment of general grammar and certain other subjects previously well done by Hermes Trismegistus ('the most judicious philosopher') and by Bishop Lowth ('the most learned divine') in *A Short Introduction*, and in the grammar that Johnson ('the most laborious scholar of the present age') prefixed to the *Dictionary* (Jones, *Works*, v, 174, 175).

Jones's preface urges readers to utilize the *Grammar* and Persian texts in conjunction with the *Thesaurus*, as the best grammar-translation method requires constant use of the most reliable dictionary. Meninski's product was not perfect but should not be condemned, because every word heard by readers could not be recorded there: 'Sounds in general are caught imperfectly by the ear, and many words are spelled and pronounced very differently.' Jones naïvely claims that his method will enable a student in less than a year 'to translate and to answer any letter [in Persian] from an Indian prince, and to converse with the natives of India, not only with fluency, but with elegance' (v, 178, 180).

The *Grammar* contains incisive grammatical and lexical materials such as his description of the word formation of compounds, where structures are grouped into 'Noun + Participle', 'Adjective + Noun', 'Noun + Noun', and some small groups (v, 256–65), in patterns to help the reader to become habituated to Persian structures. There is an index of key terms, spelled in Persian (v, 337–405), containing English definitions but no transliterations unless they are a proper noun such as *Irem* ('name of a fabulous garden in the East') or *Nadir Shah*. The book introduces various Arabic words in their first known written English form, such as *neski*, *taliq*, and the names of the alphabet letters borrowed into Persian from Arabic (*alif, bā, tā 'ain*, and so on).

Jones's Persian sources were usually literary, often from Háfiz. The most influential was a stanza in Persian, to which Jones added his prose version, 'If that lovely maid of Shiraz would accept my heart, I would give for the mole on her cheek the cities of Samarcand and Bokhara.' Thereupon he reprinted what is still his best-known poem, 'A Persian Song of Hafiz'. This creatively embroiders upon Háfiz's text, as seen in the beginning stanza (in comparison with his prose version):

> Sweet maid, if thou wouldst charm my sight,
> And bid these arms thy neck infold;
> That rosy cheek, that lily hand
> Would give thy poet more delight
> Than all Bokhára's vaunted gold,
> Than all the gems of Samarcand. (v, 315–17)

This poem effectively started the English tradition of the Oriental dreamworld of pleasure, opening the literary pluralism and showing the free reworking of the Oriental source that Edward FitzGerald, originally inspired by Jones's writings, was to do so well for Omar Khayyám.

The *Grammar* was one of Jones's most influential books. The introductory note in the Scolar Press Facsimile assesses it as 'the earliest printed grammar of Persian in English, and provided the basis for subsequent works by orientalists such as George Hadley, Robert Jones, and Francis Gladwin'. Further, it 'was quickly recognized as an important and indispensable work, and was reprinted nine times up to 1828',[3] besides a French version appearing in London in 1772, and a second French edition in 1845.

---

[3] Facsimile of the Persian *Grammar* (1771), English Linguistics 1500–1800, no 139 (Menston, Yorkshire: Scolar Press, 1969).

Jones's years of working with the Persian data for the *Grammar* had demonstrated the inadequacy of his corpus and the *Thesaurus*, and required him to engage in direct lexicography. So he drafted an elaborate revision of that dictionary in four folio volumes, for which he checked all of Meninski's Turkish, Arabic, and Persian items. In 1770–71 he placed various advertisements in the *London Chronicle* and *Gazette* for publication by subscription, proudly announcing that 'The protection of the most celebrated Universities in the world [Oxford and Cambridge], sufficiently proves its high importance to the progress of learning; and the encouragement which the Hon. East India and Turkey Companies have given it, shows, that they consider it as extremely serviceable to them in their transactions and correspondence with the powers of Asia.' But the East India Company ignored the attempted persuasion even in his third letter to them of 30 December 1770, in which Jones stated that John Uri ('who is very learned in the Eastern languages, and has been for several years employed by the University of Oxford in arranging, and examining their oriental manuscripts') was helping him by checking all the Persian data against the Bodleian's huge manuscript dictionary *Farhang-i-Jahágírí*.[4] When few subscribers appeared for the costly book, after several years Jones despairingly recommended the project to his friend John Richardson, who reworked Jones's folio volumes into *A Dictionary, Persian, Arabic, and English* (Oxford, 1777–80). The East India Company provided a subvention for the second volume, and Sir Charles Wilkins published a revision in 1829; the Company assisted Francis Johnson in publishing the dictionary in its final form of 1,420 pages (London, 1852).

The Persian *Grammar*, which was lauded in all the major periodicals, made Jones one of the most celebrated linguists in Europe. Yet, as he revised his various Oriental translations and imitations for publication but had not been questioned about the authenticity of the poetry that he was exalting in several small books in 1770–71, he was somewhat worried. The 'translation' of what James Macpherson claimed was Ossian's complete Gaelic epics *Fingal* and *Temora* (1761, 1763) had made Macpherson one of several notorious forgers of the eighteenth century. Perhaps even more strongly reflecting such an approach was Thomas Chatterton's invention of poems by a supposed fifteenth-century Bristol priest, Thomas Rowley. Jones knew Chatterton personally, hurrying to the chill room on the morning in 1772 when he heard that his young friend had just committed suicide. Jones himself had already concluded that the Rowley poems were 'a jargon of every species of dialect, ancient and modern, of every age and date'; however, they suggested a potential for a later English *Iliad* and demonstrated that 'forgeries' could be fine, exotic poetry.[5]

---

[4] Letter in Abu Taher Mojumder, 'Three New Letters by Sir William Jones', the British Library, *India Office Library and Records Report 1981*, pp. 24–35. See Cannon, *The Life and Mind of Oriental Jones* (Cambridge: Cambridge University Press, 1990), pp. 40–42.

[5] *Life and Mind of Jones*, p. 54.

So Jones's preface to his memorable *Poems, Consisting Chiefly of Translations from the Asiatick Languages* (Oxford, 1772) begins with the defensive assertion that the originals of these Eastern poems are genuine, for which he can supply the original Persian or Arabic texts. Some of his notes will reproduce passages, though 'it would be impossible to persuade some men that even *they* were not forged for the purpose'. Creatively, a few of the nine short poems are composites built from 'figures, sentiments, and descriptions' found in Arabic poetry, as in 'Solima' (*Works*, x, 199, 200). Jones urges poets who speak any European language to imitate the Oriental originals, thereby expanding his horizons from purely English poetry into a wider multiculturalism. More importantly, 'the publick would not be displeased to see the genuine compositions of *Arabia* and *Persia* in an *English* dress'. Epics such as Firdausi's *Sháhnáma* could be versified in English as easily as the *Iliad* had been rendered. These would provide 'a species of literature, which abounds with so many new expressions, new images, and new inventions', and thereby release the imagination presently constrained by neoclassicism (x, 204, 205).

Poems introduced numbers of Arabic loanwords, including *Moallakát* (now *Mu'allaqát*), *kasidah* (now *qasida*), and *Mecca* (x, 341, 346). Evidently they served their purpose of evoking the local colour, as testified by Jones's literary contemporary Elizabeth Montagu (and by posterity):

There is a gayety & splendor in the poems which is naturally derived from the happy soil & climate of the Poets & they breath Asiatick luxury, or else Mr. Jones is himself a man of a most splendid imagination. The descriptions are so fine, & all the objects so brilliant, *that the sense aches at them*, & I wish'd that Ossians poems had been laying by me, that I might sometimes have turn'd my eyes from ᵞe dazzling splendor of the Eastern noon day to the moonlight picture of a bleak mountain. Every object in these pieces is blooming & beautiful; every plant is odouriferous; the passions too are of the sort which belong in Paradise.[6]

The Oriental loanwords buttressed the pluralism that Jones was fostering. Exhibiting fascinating antique cultures, the words and their milieu are Asiatic rather than European and derive from genuine works. They are not motivated by the kind of 'political correctness' developed within twentieth-century pluralism, for Jones was like other Romantics in fervently believing in human equality of colour, religion, and all other aspects except vice. Much of Oriental literature should be known to and used by the West because it was of high quality, not because one could be a better-rounded person by knowing something about that literature. Jones was always an activist, a doer, so concerned with the rights of governed peoples that his well-deserved appointment to the Bengal Supreme Court of Judicature in 1783 was delayed for five years out of fear that his judicial rulings might (and actually did) apply his political principles to colonial Indians.

[6] In a letter of 5 September 1772 to James Beattie, partly published in *The Letters of Sir William Jones*, ed. by Garland Cannon, 2 vols (Oxford: Clarendon Press, 1970), I, 111.

His *Poems* and Francis Gladwin's two-volume collection *Asiatick Miscellany* (Calcutta, 1785–86) containing Jones's nine hymns to Hindu deities were important collections in the Western movement toward literary and linguistic pluralism. His sources are valid and verifiable, and he sensuously overlays his poems with an Oriental colouring utilizing new loanwords to help create an exotic ambience. The two anthologies introduced a genuine ethnology into British literature and initiated 'a drive for translations and imitations that were imagining themselves along anthropological lines', in an approach quite different from the inventions of Macpherson and Chatterton.[7] The two books set a model for Oriental word-borrowing as a major device to effect local colour, and speeded the addition of many more Oriental loanwords into English. Thus Romantics such as William Beckford evidently first recorded Arabic *Eblis* (1784), Robert Burns introduced *tassie* 'small cup' (1788), Robert Southey's *Curse of Kehama* added *Amrita* and other Sanskrit words (1810), and Byron introduced Turkish *tambourgi* 'drummer' (1812).

Of course, loanwords had been flooding into English since the Middle Ages.[8] During the Renaissance, translators and original writers often deliberately employed polysyllabic 'inkhorn terms' in their works, under the naïve assumption that the English lexicon lacked words and concepts which could convey the intellectual and aesthetic qualities in classical humanistic works. Books such as Sir Thomas Hoby's translation of Castiglione's *Book of the Courtier* from the Italian in 1561, Sir Thomas North's version of Plutarch's *Lives* in 1579, and John Florio's translation of Montaigne's *Essais* in 1603 are examples. The King James Version of the Bible in 1611 also introduced hundreds of new loanwords, many of which became standard English words, such as *phrases* (in Roger Ascham's *The Scholemaster*, 1570).

Middle Eastern languages like Arabic lacked such a champion for two more centuries, until Jones, reacting against the hampering effects of neoclassicism, began to make use of Middle Eastern elements so as to help rejuvenate English poetry and restore its once vibrant imagination and creativity. Though he never directly stated that English was inadequate and lacked certain 'inkhorn terms' from Arabic and Persian, his constant introduction of these words demonstrates that he considered the transfer of such items important in any serious reformation of English poesy, in anticipating the coming Romanticism, especially its Oriental aspects.[9]

The strange words clearly needed a gloss, and Jones's early translations such as his 1782 *Moallakát* (in *Works*, x, 1–196) employ subtle definitions in the text. Thus from Zuhair: 'They are mounted in carriages covered with costly awnings, and with rose-coloured veils, the linings of which have the

[7] Jerome J. McGann, *The Textual Condition* (Princeton, NJ: Princeton University Press, 1991), pp. 36–37.
[8] See Garland Cannon, *The Arabic Contributions to the English Language* (Wiesbaden: Harrassowitz, 1994), p. 71, and *Historical Change and English Word-Formation* (New York: Lang, 1987), pp. 9–13.
[9] See Garland Cannon, *A History of the English Language* (New York: Harcourt Brace Jovanovich, 1972), pp. 128–29, and *Arabic Contributions*, pp. 70–71.

hue of crimson *Anden*-wood.' Or from *Antar* (introducing the name of the poet who wrote the fine epic-like *Romance of 'Antar*): 'camels grazing on *KHIMKHIM*-berries in the midst of their tents' (i.e., simsin). Or from 'Amr: 'Our dark javelins exquisitely wrought of *KHATHAIAN* reeds'. To document the authenticity of the seven poems, Jones provides a roman transliteration for each one.

The poems name many Arab warriors, tribes, and places. The words, usually printed entirely in capitals, mainly belong in encyclopaedias and gazetteers rather than in dictionaries. But this translation, along with particularly *Śakuntalā*, did much to initiate the Romantic poetic tradition of using proper nouns for local colour, as in Byron's three Oriental tales of 1813–14 (*The Giaour, The Bride of Abydos, The Corsair*) and Thomas Moore's *Lalla Rookh* (1817), which was wildly successful and was even made into an opera. Indeed, the nineteenth century witnessed a surge in the addition of such items to English reference books. As for the words belonging to the general lexicon, a tabulation of the Arabic words that can be dated in Cannon's 1994 corpus shows that over twenty per cent of the total were recorded first in the nineteenth century. This is by far the most fruitful century, even in comparison with the twentieth, when, despite the resurgent influence from petrol wealth, the dated Arabic total is only just over sixteen per cent.[10]

Ironically, it was Jones's scholarship that often prevented his composing major poetry. When he reached India, the ancient Hindu culture fascinated him, and he was highly motivated to make it known to the West. 'The Enchanted Fruit' (1784, in *Works*, XIII, 211–33), an elegant mock-heroic verse-tale in 287 couplets, contains proportionately the largest number of would-be loanwords primarily from Sanskrit of any of his voluminous writings. This imaginative story from the *Mahābhārata* concerning the princess Draupadī and the five Pāṇḍava brothers is finely re-created across the vast cultural and chronological gulf, particularly by incorporating Indian items denoting foods, plants, geography, and Hinduism. Unfortunately, Jones decided against the internal glosses used successfully in his *Moallakát*, probably because of the metrical constraints imposed by the closed couplets. Employing italics because of the words' strangeness to English readers, he glosses each item (many lines contain two Indian terms) in a terrible cluttering of footnotes at the bottom of each page. Compounding this anti-artistic method was his decision not to number the footnotes, but instead to use symbols chiefly from the sciences. So the reader, after being startled by the italicized Indian word and its technical symbol in the text, must look back and forth in order to locate its gloss in the footnote.

'The Enchanted Fruit' might have been an outstanding verse tale; yet this artistic, scholarly failure provided another model that attracted Romantic

---

[10] *Arabic Contributions*, p. 43.

poets to this literary form.[11] In private letters Jones indicated that he thought he had accurately communicated the ancient culture, but perhaps perceived the artistic reduction occasioned by footnoted glosses. So in his hymns to Hindu deities (in *Works*, XIII, 235–333), he eschewed footnotes and returned to occasional, comparatively unobtrusive glosses in the text. Even here, scholarly zeal led him to clutter the nine hymns with all the Sanskrit epithets that he could find for the given deity. He appended brief, dense introductions to each, which, when the texts reached Europe and were immediately reprinted in British periodicals, were quietly omitted and thus no doubt left readers mystified by various undefined Indian words, both common and proper nouns.

Artistically, Jones's translation of *Śakuntalā* (1789, in *Works*, IX, 363–532) was his best, employing the most subtle, internal glossing found in any of his works. It contains 118 different transliterations, of which more than half are common nouns, few of which have been recorded in standard English dictionaries.[12] His 'inkhorn term' method is now mature and sophisticated, in comparison with his earlier transliteration of Arabic and Persian words. In numerous instances he deliberately uses a Sanskrit word for which the English lexicon already had a common word possessing a roughly equivalent meaning (but lacking the local nuances). Thus he uses *amra*, not *mango*; *kokila*, not *cuckoo*; and *madhavi*, not *jasmine*. Though the *OED* records *kokila* of this trio, crediting Jones with its first known use, few of his Sanskrit items are in the *OED*. Of those that are recorded, numbers of his usages often long predate the earliest citation: *avatar*, *Brahman*, *champac*, *lac*, *sloka*, *vedanta*, *vina* and so on. As in his Arabic and Persian translations, he further naturalizes Sanskrit words already available in English, as in *Himalaya*, *Purana*, *Veda*, and *yogi*. Overall, his procedure went beyond that of Renaissance translators such as North, who often employed the given foreign item when English had no semantic equivalent, not because they wanted to add a 'native' synonym to English. Meanwhile, like North, Jones was introducing a major literary figure to the West.

If an existing transliteration did not represent the pronunciation in his view, his own system dictated his spelling, as in 'How I wish thou hadst been seized by a tiger or an old bear, who was prowling for a *shakāl*', a spelling of *jackal* that he often employs in his version of *Hitopadeśa*. This procedure is comparable to Ascham's unsuccessful, scholarly use of the original Latin forms (*translatum*, *synonym*, *diversum*), rather than the established, anglicized forms of these Latin words. Jones, too, fails in such endeavours. Here are examples of his deft use of internal denotation in his *Śakuntalā*:

---

[11] *Life and Mind of Jones*, p. 218.

[12] *Life and Mind of Jones*, p. 311, and Cannon and Siddheshwar Pandey, 'Sir William Jones Revisited: On His Translation of the *Śakuntalā*', *Journal of the American Oriental Society*, 96 (1976), 528–35. See Edna Osborne's lengthy list of Jones's loanwords in her 'Oriental Diction and Theme in English Verse, 1740–1840', *Humanist Studies of the University of Kansas*, 2.1 (1916), 134–35.

the oily fruit of the sacred Ingudi (IX, 384)
soft as the fresh-blown Mallicà (p. 386)
this pointed blade of Cusa grass (p. 400)
her lips [. . .] surpassing the red lustre of the Carcandhu fruit (p. 495)
near the mountain Himálaya, surrounded by herds of Chamaras (p. 497)
I now see the warbling Chátacas descend from their nests (p. 513)

Besides the publication of Jones's *Śakuntalā*, 1789 saw completion of his sensual version of Jayadeva's twelfth-century lyrical drama *Gita Govinda* (*Works*, IV, 36–68). He did the original version as an exercise to help him learn Sanskrit, but its beauty led him to polish his prose. The revision is rich in Sanskrit words chiefly denoting botanical forms, as well as place-names and mythological names, which are internally defined and artistically enhance his Oriental richness of colouring. Thus Krishna praises Rādhā in seeking her forgiveness after he sported with the gopis: 'Thy lips are a *Bandhujiva*-flower; the lustre of the *Madhuca* beams on thy cheek; thine eye outshines the blue lotos; thy nose is a bud of the *Tila*; the *Cunda* blossom yields to thy teeth' (IV, 260). Such intimacy and love of nature were absorbed especially by the Romantics, as seen in Wordsworth's Lucy poems and elsewhere.

Jones's research was often brilliantly assisted by several pundits and maulvis, whom he paid from his own salary. They assisted this Western, Christian judge without reservation, even with the sacred Gāyatrī prayer from the *Rig-Veda*,[13] perceiving that his research into their ancient culture was selflessly motivated, without any colonial overtones. They wanted the culture to be as authentic as the English language could convey it. They may have been the ones to point out his original misinterpretation in thinking that in *Śakuntalā* the king (rather than the heroine) had been cursed, had lost the ring, and consequently failed to be recognized by her until the climax of the drama. Jones quietly corrected this major error in his polished translation.[14]

Jones was so selfless in such projects that he did not even include his name in the 1789 Calcutta publication of *Śakuntalā*, thereby not providing the power of his name to argue against the *Critical Review*'s cautious conclusion that this fine 'Indian' literary work might be a forgery and that 'much of the beauty depends on the peculiarities of the plants so often mentioned' (January 1791, p. 20). British friends including Sir Joseph Banks, whom Jones was assisting in transferring Indian plants to the new Kew Gardens and the St Vincent one in the West Indies, reported this disturbing review to Jones, whereupon he elaborately identified the 'literary' plants in Linnaean terms and intensified his efforts to describe all Indian plants scientifically.[15]

---

[13] See Garland Cannon, 'Sir William Jones and the Association between East and West', *Proceedings of the American Philosophical Society*, 121 (1977), 183–87.
[14] See Murray B. Emeneau, review of *Letters*, ed. by Cannon, in *Language*, 47 (1971), 959–64.
[15] See his letter to Banks of 18 October 1791, in *Letters*, II, 894; and *Life and Mind of Jones*, p. 315. Many of the plants were unknown outside India.

He never made a public defence of the play's authenticity, nor was it needed. This single translation introduced and began the transfer of the glittering Gupta culture to Europe, with movement of Kālidāsa's works soon into the ranks of what Goethe would shortly term *Weltliteratur*.

Posthumous publication of Jones's works in six volumes in 1799 further advanced his worldwide reputation, leading Lord Teignmouth and Lady Jones to add unpolished, probably unchecked manuscripts and even worksheets to their thirteen-volume edition of 1807.[16] Thus one should use caution in assessing those unrevised writings. Two examples from these will illustrate Jones's procedures in translation. In his *Hitopadeśa* he interpolates a dialectical remark into his rendering: 'In *Varanas*, replied *Caràtacà* (or *Baranasi*, not *Benares*), lived a washerman' (*Works*, XIII, 69), thereby having the *shakāl* anticipate the modern superseding of the *Benares* spelling. Secondly, when Jones is unsure of a meaning, he parenthesizes the etymon or a possible English alternative, as in 'Tales and Fables by Nizami' (*Works*, IV, 381–432): 'Bring truth (*rásti*) forward, that thou mayst be saved (*rastigàr*)'; 'An old man (*or Saint*) spoke to him in his sleep'; 'O new moon, dig up thy old rampart (or sign of the Zodiack)' (IV, 420, 421). Such an unpolished prose version of poetry can be revealing, as in it Jones advances numbers of previously borrowed Arabic words toward fuller naturalization: *caliphate, dinar, hajji, Kufic, Ramadan, Shaitan, sheik, Sufi*, and *vizier*. And he introduces *masjid* (IV, 406).

Examples of his initial linguistic doubts must not imply that he translated haphazardly or that he had no clear theory of translation. As soon as he began to study Sanskrit in the native way, in 1785, he recognized the pressing need for a consistent, possibly universal system of transliteration, since sometimes the name of a single Asian person or place was spelled so variously in roman script as to seem to be two different persons or places, or vice versa. So Jones positioned his solution, 'A Dissertation on the Orthography of Asiatick Words in Roman Letters', as the opening paper in the first volume of his Asiatic Society's *Asiatick Researches* (1788).[17] The Jonesian System, as dictionaries termed it for a century and a half, has a modern, scientific basis: Arabic, Persian, and Indic words should be spelled uniformly in English on the principle that 'each original sound may be rendered invariably by one appropriated symbol, conformably to the natural order of articulation'. This requires 'one specifick symbol for every sound used in pronouncing the language to which they belonged' (III, 253). Based on the principle of accurately representing the original sounds within a perspective of general phonetics, the system could prevent a Hindi word like *kamarband* from being spelled as divergently as *kummerbund, kemerbend*, and *Cemerbend* (now *cummerbund*, which still has the variant *kummerbund*). While impressionistic in the articulatory descriptions and naïve in the face of the

---

[16] See Garland Cannon, *Sir William Jones: A Bibliography of Primary and Secondary Sources*, Library and Information Sources in Linguistics, 7 (Amsterdam: John Benjamins, 1979), p. 26.
[17] In *Works*, III, 253–318. See *Life and Mind of Jones*, pp. 249–50.

wide dialectal variation within Arabic and Persian, the Jonesian System was soon adopted for Oriental spellings, and started scholars on the way toward what finally became the International Phonetic Alphabet, as revised at the Kiel convention in 1989.[18]

Though much of his work involved etymology, he was chary of basing substantive analysis on this, once exasperating Jacob Bryant for delicately but publicly criticizing Bryant's etymological conjecturing.[19] In his long-celebrated 'On the Gods of Greece, Italy, and India', Jones criticizes 'etymological conjectures as a weak basis for historical inquiries' (1788, *Works*, III, 349); he warily avoids using cognate 'pairs' such as *Janus–Ganesha*, *Minos–Manu*, and so on, in his provocative argument 'that a connexion subsisted between the old idolatrous nations of *Egypt*, *India*, *Greece*, and *Italy*, long before they migrated to their several settlements, and consequently before the birth of Moses' (III, 391). Thus he extended his 1786 language-family theory to religion and mythology, setting in motion violent arguments based on his too hasty comparative conclusion but ultimately pointing toward comparative religion and mythology.

Meanwhile, he was guided by the translation theory that he articulated several times. In the prefatory discourse to his *Speeches of Isæus* (1779, in *Works*, IX, 38), he had formulated his 'golden rule for good translation': 'Read the original so frequently, and study it so carefully, as to imprint on the mind a complete idea of the author's peculiar air and distinguishing features; and then to assume, as it were, his person, voice, countenance, gesture; and to represent the man himself speaking in our language instead of his own.' This distinguished translation from classical oratory introduced numbers of usually technical Latin legal terms, besides untransliterated Greek terms, which had little opportunity for assimilation into general English. It elicited an elegant letter of praise from his friend Edmund Burke (in *Letters*, I, 287).

As an M.P., Burke employed Jones to provide needed information about Muslim law in the parliamentary composing of the 1781 East India Judicature Bill, intended to help the British to judge Muslim Indian cases according to Muslim law, which was in Arabic and could not be read by British judges. This research led Jones to qualify his translation theory, which he had already done for his Isæus book and then articulated in his 1782 translation, *The Mahomedan Law of Succession*. This small book, rendering the Shafiite inheritance law that British lawyers would use in India, was the major product of his parliamentary work with Burke. In it Jones differenti-ates literary translations from the necessarily literal ones for legal texts: 'Verbal translations are generally naked and insipid, wholly destroying all the neatness and beauty of the original, yet retaining so much of the foreign

[18] See Peter Ladefoged, 'The Revised International Phonetics Alphabet, *Language*, 66 (1990), 550–52.
[19] *Life and Mind of Jones*, p. 339.

idiom and manner, as to appear always uncouth, often ridiculous.' But elegance must be sacrificed to exactness, as a legal rendering must be 'line for line, and word for word, with a fidelity almost religiously scrupulous' (*Works*, VIII, 164–65). The book contains Jones's brief preface, roman transliteration of the Arabic text, the text itself, and his unrhymed translation, so as to advance another expressed purpose, to 'habituate readers to old Arabic Manuscripts'.

When he arrived in Calcutta in 1783, he discovered that another Arabic text was inaccessible to British judges. Governor-General Warren Hastings had ordered a Persian version to be made of Siráj al-Dín's brief inheritance treatise, but the version blended a commentary and the Indian translator's notes into 600 pages that obscured the law. Jones's translation, *Al Sirájiyyah* (Calcutta, 1792), includes a fifty-page summary and his own lengthy commentary, again printing the Arabic text and again fulfilling a practical rather than artistic goal.[20] Thereby he provided two valuable texts in English to implement the principle of ruling the Muslim part of India by Muslim standards and laws. The two introduce few if any Arabic items into general English, though Jones often includes the technical term in order that the judge could consult a *maulvi* in doubtful cases. The gloss may appear in Jones's text (e.g., 'And this is the case of *mushtaraca*, or parcenary' (VIII, 191)), but is usually in a footnote. The gloss may even contain grammatical information, as for *ácdariyyah*, where he speculates as to why the Arabic term was so defined ('possibly, because the rules of succession are a little *disturbed* in favour of them' (VIII, 192)).

Jones's most important legal work was *An Essay on the Law of Bailments* (London, 1781). It drew on numerous languages from earlier centuries and cultures, for linguistics always played a fundamental role in his career. As he stated in his opening lines, a major purpose was 'to illustrate our [i.e., English] laws by a comparison of them with other nations, together with an investigation of their true spirit and reason'. His data came from a minute study of the texts of chiefly English laws and Roman laws on bailments, a foundation of civil society involving liability in lending or leasing arrangements. But Jones also compared Hindu, Mosaic, Muslim, Visigoth, and many other sets of laws, in working toward a more universal view of bailments predicated on his vision that law was actually a science. This book was the standard source for British and American lawyers for fifty years, with the third London edition being reprinted in Philadelphia in 1836. It is still cited today, particularly in American cases, including sexual harassment and motel liability.[21] It remains one of the best examples of Jones's

---

[20] *Life and Mind of Jones*, pp. 341–42.
[21] See *Jones: A Bibliography*, pp. 10–11; and *Life and Mind of Jones*, pp. 150–53. Particularly see James Oldham, 'The Survival of Sir William Jones in American Jurisprudence', in *Objects of Enquiry: The Life, Contributions, and Influences of Sir William Jones*, ed. by Garland Cannon and Kevin R. Brine (New York: New York University Press, 1995), pp. 92–101.

comparative use of antique texts, many in foreign languages and non-roman script, in collecting, interpreting, and applying bailments cases, in advancing his new pluralism over languages and cultures.

Of course his greatest direct intellectual contribution to posterity was the famous philologer's paragraph in his Third Anniversary Discourse to the Asiatic Society in 1786 (*Works*, III, 34), which has been fully analysed and praised over the past two centuries. This hypothesized the concept of language families to explain the similarities among certain languages, and sketched the framework for the Indo-European tongues, in moving philological study from an impressionistic, mythological basis toward a modern scientific comparativism.[22] When one compares the etymologies in Johnson's *Dictionary*, innovative as it was, with those in major modern collections utilizing genetic relationships such as the *OED* and *Webster's Third New International Dictionary of the English Language* (1961), the lexicographic debt ultimately owed to Jones is evident. In the philologer's paragraph he advanced his pluralism into cognate words and inflections, making it one of the major formulations in the entire history of ideas and one of the most quoted formulations of its kind.

More narrowly, his direct linguistic contribution to language change and English lexicography in the eighteenth century consisted mainly of initiating the flood of chiefly Arabic and Sanskrit loanwords into English through his translations and imitations, as well as in numbers of scholarly essays written in India. This service has not been properly recognized because no one has yet gone systematically through Jones's writings and provided the *OED* and other major dictionaries with the specific citations verifying his written introduction of the given word. And to be fair to the *OED*, some of these words occur in manuscripts not published until after the 1933 Supplement appeared, as with his use of *Sindbad*,[23] and so had no influence in the history of their usage. He used several such words in the 304 of his letters that were previously unknown until their publication among a total 596 in the 1970 *Letters*. Literarily, Jones is usually remembered as a Romantic precursor chiefly responsible for the Oriental spirit that motivated Byron, Shelley, other Romantics, Tennyson, and so on, who introduced Oriental loanwords of their own.[24]

---

[22] See Garland Cannon, 'Sir William Jones, Language Families, and Indo-European', *Word*, 43 (1992), 49–59, and 'Jones's "Sprung from Some Common Source": 1786–1986', in *Sprung from Some Common Source*, ed. by Sydney M. Lamb and E. Douglas Mitchell (Stanford, CA: Stanford University Press, 1991), pp. 23–47.

[23] In a letter to Viscount Althorp, 15 October 1775, in *Letters*, I, 206.

[24] See Garland Cannon, 'Sir William Jones and Literary Orientalism', in *Oriental Prospects: Western Literature and the Lure of the East*, ed. by Cedric Barfoot and Theo D'haen (Amsterdam: Rodopi, forthcoming). Travellers such as Sir Edwin Arnold and Lafcadio Hearn ranged widely, and it soon became common for Western residents abroad to record their travels and the customs enveloping them. For example, Mrs Isabella Bird's *Unbeaten Tracks in Japan*, 2 vols (New York: Putnam, 1881) was widely read and recorded for the first time at least twenty-two loanwords of the known 1,424 Japanese borrowings in English (see the dictionary section in Garland Cannon, *The Japanese Contributions to the English Language* (Wiesbaden: Harrassowitz, 1996)).

Nor should one forget some good earlier translators who neologized in Jones's own century, as in Christopher Smart's translation of Horace and especially of the Psalms of David (1765). But Jones far surpassed his contemporaries both in quantity of loanwords and in the varied language sources from which he may have been the first to borrow or transliterate the given item. This lexicographic contribution merits emphasis in future histories of English and places him squarely within the antiquarian movement.

Early in his spectacular career, Jones had realized the value and necessity of dictionaries. Only once had he been a pure lexicographer, in his ill-fated revision of the Meninski *Thesaurus*, though his Perisan *Grammar* and various legal translations included glossaries. He always utilized the available collections, as in the Bodleian's *Farhang-i-Jahángírí* ('which comprises the Substance of Forty Persian Lexicons', according to the title), for which he had already composed notes for an edition upon his intended return to England. He also planned to publish the *Siddhāntakaumidī* (a fairly modern recension of the Pāṇinian grammar) and a Sanskrit dictionary based on 10,000 words arranged in two alphabetical volumes that a pundit had compiled for him and for which he had prepared a Latin version.[25] Existing English dictionaries recorded almost none of these words and were generally unhelpful in his lexicographic research. He even considered assisting in the long-delayed publication of Lewis Morris's *Celtic Remains*, a historical-cultural dictionary primarily of Welsh place-names.[26] So, had Jones not had such a tragically short life, he might have left a name in pure lexicography to enhance his other linguistic accomplishments.

It should be remembered that it was difficult for one to break out of the pre-scientific linguistic matrix of the day, where speech was confused with writing, and a language could be considered to be inferior or superior to another language, so that Jones's philologer's paragraph was a truly striking advance. A modern linguist would describe a language primarily from oral data elicited from informants, whereas Jones, like Lowth and Johnson, collected data almost exclusively from written, primarily literary (usually earlier) sources. The oral materials assembled by his friend Bishop Percy, as well as oral data in the supposed Ossian manuscripts and so on, were of little or no help in his research. And they would have raised the spectre of introducing 'incorrect' forms into his prescriptively visualized corpus.

He was widely known as 'Linguist Jones' and 'Persian Jones' even in Johnson's Literary Club, but of course was never 'Dictionary Jones', comparable to 'Dictionary Johnson'. His reputation, both then and now, was enormous, but still smaller than that of Johnson in his own day. Like his old friend (and perhaps influenced by Johnson's shift from the original

[25] See *Life and Mind of Jones*, pp. 41, 353–54; and Jones, *Letters*, II, 751.
[26] See Garland Cannon and Caryl Davies, 'Sir William Jones and Lewis Morris' *Celtic Remains*, *Zeitschrift für celtische Philologie*, 48 (1996), 291–95.

premise that choosing a given spelling might fix its pronunciation and spelling forever), Jones recognized the variability of language, particularly as caused by dialects separated from others for various reasons. Though he based his transliterations on the original pronunciation, so far as could be known, and developed the Jonesian System in an effort to devise a standard transliterative guide based on theory, a close look at his writings will show that he changed his spellings with what would seem like inconsistency. In his *Hitopadeśa* a chief animal is usually a *shakal*, but is also *shakāl* or even *skakāl*, in preference to the existing English form *jackal*. His letters exhibit variant spellings such as *pundit, pandit,* and *pendit.*

In conclusion, in a larger sense, Jones helped to change the attitude of scholars and even of the ordinary person toward language study. Until deep in the nineteenth century his splendid career was held up as a model for a commoner who could attain a major place in society by studying languages and antique cultures. This kind of motivation simultaneously helped to advance his modern pluralistic view of languages and cultures. He showed that Shakespeare's name *Mahu* ('Mahound') to denote *Muhammad* as the devil was hideously biased.[27] Further, Jones's monumental translation of *Mānava-Dharmaśāstra* (Calcutta, 1794) showed an ethnocentric Europe the falsity of their view of India as a land of savages who practiced infanticide, suttee, sacrifice to divinities ringed with skulls, and deviant sexual practices. Thus in reviewing this translation, *Gentleman's Magazine* essentially retracted the bias by concluding: 'It proves, beyond all dispute, that the people of India had made great advances in civilization, at a period when the nations of Europe were in the rudest stage of social life' (71 (1801), 546).

Linguistically and culturally, Jones, like Marco Polo, served as a mine of Oriental information, which was to be exploited and extended for centuries and would be incorporated so fully into Western culture that sometimes its roots can hardly be perceived. Polo's introduction of Cathay to Europe, whether from firsthand or from hearsay and second-hand information, was crucial in Western history.[28] Jones not only presented Arabia, Persia, and especially classical India to the West, with special influences in Germany, France, and the English-speaking world. He also transferred rich, small parts of the cultures, introducing Kālidāsa and starting that Sanskrit genius on the way to an exalted status in world literature. The glories of Gupta civilization were seen to be comparable to Kubla Khan's magnificent culture as reported by Polo to a writer twenty years after his alleged sojourn in China. Jones's travels (and research based on them and his studies) were immediate, verifiable, and written by the traveller himself. But in sad contrast to Polo's

---

[27] 'The Prince of Darkness is a gentleman. Modo he's call'd, and Mahu', *King Lear*, III.4.135.
[28] Frances Wood particularly relies on omissions in Polo's *Descriptions of the World* (1298) — such as references to the Great Wall, tea, the Chinese fishing with tame cormorants, foot-binding of young girls, and so on — in challenging whether Polo ever went to China. See her *Did Marco Polo Go to China?* (London: Secker and Warburg, 1995).

international fame, Jones still remains generally unknown, even after the major bicentenary observances at New York University, the National Library of Wales, the Asiatic Society of Bengal, and elsewhere in 1994. He is barely recorded in world history and culture. However, if this modest scholar were able to know of the paradox, he would dismiss the poor recognition; his purpose of intercommunication and use of cultures and languages has been fulfilled and continues as an indirect guide for humanity.

Something Old, Something New, Something Borrowed, Something Blue: Christopher Smart and the Lexis of the Peculiar

MARCUS WALSH

University of Birmingham

It has been a truism of much recent discussion that many of the most creative poets in the mid-eighteenth century, Thomson and Collins and Gray and Smart notably, were anxious about the adequacy of the language available to them for the poetry they wished to write. As Murray Cohen, for example, has put it,

Their exquisitely developed aesthetics of failure dwells on a sense that their poetic language no longer possesses the real presence [. . .] that made the languages of Aeschylus or Spenser or Milton adequate to their meanings and feelings, [. . .] a sense [. . .] that language has been impoverished, or more extremely, that it is an enemy of poetry.[1]

That sense of inadequacy is explicit enough, and nowhere more so than in Gray's complaint, in a famous letter to Richard West, that 'our language is greatly degenerated'.[2] It is also true, however, that these poets engage in a diverse and energetic attempt to renovate language, to create the means of lively and individual expression. Collins, Gray, and Smart set out to make the language of their poetry 'peculiar', distinct from that of common life.[3] In doing so they explored new possibilities in metre, figuration, lexis, and syntax. In this paper I shall attempt to describe some aspects of Christopher Smart's lexis of the peculiar, with an emphasis on the writing of the last decade of his life.

Eighteenth-century poets of course could draw upon what came to be known as 'poetic diction'. At its worst no doubt 'poetic diction' could be little more than a kit of standard verbal parts, a set of expressions which, as William Wordsworth notoriously complained, 'have been foolishly repeated by bad Poets, till such feelings of disgust are connected with them as it is scarcely possible by any art of association to overpower'. Hogarth's

---

[1] *Sensible Words: Linguistic Practice in England 1640–1785* (Baltimore, MD, and London: Johns Hopkins University Press, 1977), pp. 77, 81.
[2] 8 April 1742, *Correspondence of Thomas Gray*, ed. by Paget Toynbee and Leonard Whibley, rev. by H. W. Starr (Oxford: Oxford University Press, 1971), p. 193.
[3] The most theoretically sophisticated modern examination of this issue is Derek Attridge, *Peculiar Language: Literature as Difference from the Renaissance to James Joyce* (London: Methuen, 1988), Chapter 3. I have considered the theory and practice of the 'peculiar' with special reference to Smart in a paper delivered at the 1995 Reading Conference on 'Early Romanticism: Later Eighteenth-Century British Poetry', which will appear in the Proceedings shortly to be published by Macmillan.

'Distressed Poet' is only the most vivid realization of the stereotype of the hackney writer in his garret, straining poetic clichés from hard-bound brains, his copy of Bysshe's *Art of English Poetry* at his elbow. Yet poetic diction was also, of course, a rich and continuous resource, 'the common inheritance of Poets', as Wordsworth himself put it, which had begun with Homer, and in English writing at least as early as Chaucer, and was drawn on by powerful poets up to and beyond Wordsworth himself.[4] Poetical dialect could be seen indeed as authorized, and comprehensible despite its separation from the real language of men, precisely because it was an inherited body of words from approved sources, as James Beattie explains in the course of an essay which is one of the century's clearest accounts of what 'poetic diction' was understood to be:

No language I am acquainted with is altogether without [poetical words and phrases]; and perhaps no language can be so, in which any number of good poems have been written. For poetry is better remembered than prose, especially by poetical authors; who will always be apt to imitate the phraseology of those they have been accustomed to read and admire; and thus, in the works of poets, down through successive generations, certain phrases may have been conveyed, which, though originally perhaps in common use, are now confined to poetical composition.[5]

Beattie provides extended lists of this inherited poetic phraseology. Some of these are 'ancient, and [. . .] once no doubt in common use in England, as many of them still are in Scotland', amongst them: *afield, amain, behest, blithe, bridal, dame, featly, gore, host, lambkin, lea, meed, lore, orisons, plod, ruth, smite, spray, strand, swain, thrall, welter, wayward*. Other words are purely poetical, and have never been in common use: *appal, attune, car, clarion, cates, courser, darkling, nightly, noiseless, pinion, slumbrous, viewless, clang, boreal, ire, lave, nymph, orient, philomel, jocund, redolent, vernal, zephyr, zone, sylvan* (pp. 220–21). Many of these words may be found in the work of Gray and Collins (as indeed in that of Keats). In these poets, of course, such words are not mechanically repeated, but often stressed into new meanings. Dryden's 'honey redolent of Spring', according to Johnson, already 'reaches the utmost limits of our language'; Gray, however, 'drove it a little more beyond common apprehension, by making "gales" to be "redolent of joy and youth"'.[6] Johnson's complaint accurately describes a vital and characteristic part of Gray's poetic method,

---

[4] Preface to the *Lyrical Ballads* (1800), in *Lyrical Ballads and other Poems, 1797–1800*, ed. by James Butler and Karen Green (Ithaca, NY, and London: Cornell University Press, 1992), p. 748. Among the important modern histories are Geoffrey Tillotson, *Augustan Poetic Diction* (London: Athlone Press, 1964); Arthur Sherbo, *English Poetic Diction from Chaucer to Wordsworth* (East Lansing: Michigan State University Press, 1975). Susie I. Tucker undertakes a more widely based analysis in *Protean Shape: A Study in Eighteenth-Century Vocabulary and Usage* (London: Athlone Press, 1967).
[5] *Essays on Poetry and Music as they Affect the Mind*, 3rd edn, corrected (London and Edinburgh, 1779), p. 213. The *Essays* were first published in 1778.
[6] *Lives of the English Poets*, ed. by George Birkbeck Hill, 3 vols (Oxford: Oxford University Press, 1905), III, 435.

the use of familiar items of poetic diction in syntactically and figuratively innovative and revivifying ways.

Very few of the words in Beattie's lists of familiar poetic diction, however, are to be found in the later poems of Christopher Smart. *Clarion*, indeed, from Beattie's list, appears in *A Song to David* (line 6). Smart celebrates the 'swans that sail and *lave*', but here a normally transitive verb is used intransitively, and the beaver who '*plods* his task', but here a normally intransitive verb is transitive.[7] Neither case resembles 'poetic diction' as it is commonly understood. Such instances of 'poetic diction' as may be found in Smart are generally more scattered than in his contemporary high lyrists, and they very often are given rather particularized senses; so 'convex', a familiar poeticism for the vault of the sky or heavens,[8] is applied by Smart to his elaborate and probably cabalistic understanding of the foundation of the world on the seven pillars.[9] Frankly poetic periphrases, such as his reference to sheep as 'the fleecy care' in the hymn 'Generosity', are relatively unusual.[10] I shall want to suggest that Smart seeks his new and answerable style, less by accepting an inheritance of poetic diction (as, with all their transforming differences of method, Gray and Collins persistently do), than by striving to create a rather more distinctive idiolect, some of whose components will seem particularly idiosyncratic.[11]

The argument about a recognizable and inherited poetic dialect is, of course, part of a larger debate about the uses of a lexis distinct from that of common life, by archaism or innovation or unfamiliarity of usage, in poetry and in other kinds of writing. In this debate the mid-century poets found themselves ranged against a formidable succession of advocates of the natural and the perspicuous. John Locke's third abuse of language is 'an *affected obscurity*; by either applying old words to new and unusual significations; or introducing new and ambiguous terms, without defining either; or else putting them so together, as may confound their ordinary meaning'.[12] In literary criticism, Johnson famously objects to Milton's 'uniform peculiarity of *Diction*', to William Collins's affectation of the obsolete 'when it was not worthy of revival', and to Gray's poetic resort to a language 'remote

---

[7] *Hymns and Spiritual Songs*, 2.31; *A Song to David*, l. 145, *The Poetical Works of Christopher Smart, II: Religious Poetry 1763–71*, ed. by Marcus Walsh and Karina Williamson (Oxford: Oxford University Press, 1983), pp. 36, 134.

[8] *OED* notes earlier instances in Milton (*Paradise Lost*, II, 434; VII, 266), and Prior (*Carmen Seculare*, l. 514). I refer throughout to the second edition of the *Oxford English Dictionary on Compact Disc*, abbreviated hereafter as *OED2*.

[9] *A Translation of the Psalms of David*, 11.24; compare 8.4, 14. I discuss Smart's exploration of this idea in my notes on these Psalms, on *A Song to David*, ll. 338–39, and in my Appendix to the *Song*, *The Poetical Works of Christopher Smart, III: A Translation of the Psalms of David*, ed. by Marcus Walsh (Oxford: Oxford University Press, 1987), pp. 394, 395; *Poetical Works, II*, pp. 148–55, 442.

[10] *Hymns for the Amusement of Children*, 21.8, *Poetical Works, II*, p. 348. Arthur Sherbo points out some of Smart's uses of poetic diction in his translation of the Psalms (*Christopher Smart: Scholar of the University* (Lansing: Michigan State University Press, 1967), p. 215).

[11] I should make clear here that I deal primarily with Smart's published verse rather than the magical and hermetic analysis of language Smart offers in *Jubilate Agno*.

[12] *Essay Concerning Human Understanding* (1690), 3.10.6.

from common use'.[13] Goldsmith, having praised Dryden, Addison, and Pope for improving and harmonizing the language, criticizes the 'misguided innovators' who succeeded them for their restoration of 'antiquated words and phrases'.[14] Of the defences of both an archaic and a new-made lexis the best known is Gray's letter to West, where he asserts that 'our poetry [. . .] has a language peculiar to itself', celebrates the use by Shakespeare and Milton of 'words of their own composition or invention' and the constant borrowing by Dryden and Pope from these great exemplars, and insists that 'our language not being a settled thing (like the French) has an undoubted right to words of an hundred years old, provided antiquity have not rendered them unintelligible'.[15] Gray was by no means alone in his defence either of the necessary peculiarity of poetic language, or of the necessity of seeking, in revived or new-made words, a lexis not deadened and familiarized by custom. In his influential Oxford lectures on the sacred Hebrew poetry, Robert Lowth repeatedly insisted that poetic language in general is necessarily peculiar, 'frequently [. . .] breaking down the boundaries by which the popular dialect is confined', and that in the ode in particular 'the diction must be choice and elegant'.[16] Edward Young, using a familiar metaphor, argued that words become 'tarnished' and thoughts 'lose their Currency' with over-use, and that hence 'we should send new Metal to the Mint, that is, new meaning to the Press'.[17] Later in the century, James Beattie restates Gray's position on verbal revivals with a somewhat different emphasis: any word which 'the majority of readers cannot understand without a glossary, may with reason be considered obsolete', but may none the less be used in poetry provided that authority may be found in the practice of Milton, Dryden, and Pope.[18]

Smart's own awareness of the theoretical debate concerning poetic language is particularly apparent throughout his extended engagement with Horace, in his prose translation published in 1756, and his verse translation of 1767, with its accompanying, and new, prose version. In the preface to the verse translation Smart discusses the nature of the Horatian *curiosa felicitas* at some length, finds it particularly prevalent in the Odes where Horace could most freely exercise 'the curiosity of choice diction', and

[13] *Lives of the English Poets*, I, 189; III, 341, 435.

[14] 'The Life of Thomas Parnell, D. D.', *Collected Works of Oliver Goldsmith*, ed. by Arthur Friedman, 5 vols (Oxford: Oxford University Press, 1966), III, 423.

[15] *Correspondence*, pp. 192–93. Much later in his life, in a letter to James Beattie, in the context of discussion of *The Minstrel*, he would warn that new words ought not to be made 'without great necessity; it is very hazardous at best', and caution against words derived from Spenser, a poet regarded throughout the eighteenth century, by most commentators, as a distinctly more dubious linguistic model (8 March 1771, *Correspondence*, pp. 1168–70).

[16] *Lectures on the Sacred Poetry of the Hebrews*, trans. by G. Gregory, 2 vols (London, 1787), I, 308; II, 198–99.

[17] *Conjectures on Original Composition* (London, 1759), pp. 13–14.

[18] *Essays on Poetry and Music as they Affect the Mind*, p. 228.

proudly claims to have achieved this quality in a number of his translations.[19] The Odes Smart nominates seem for the most part to be characterized by familiar words used in unfamiliar ways, by peculiarities of word order and syntactical construction.

For the eighteenth-century debate concerning archaism and neologism, Horace's *Ars Poetica* was the pivotal classical text. Horace tells us that individual words like all mortal things are subject to death. Old words, however, may be born again: 'multa renascentur quae iam cecidere' (l. 70).[20] This resonant line, like the rest of the passage in which it appears, gave rise to much discussion. This, for example, is part of Richard Hurd's long note in his edition of the *Art of Poetry* and the *Epistle to Augustus*, first published in 1749:

This *revival* of *old* words is one of those *niceties* in composition, not to be attempted by any but great masters. It may be done two ways, 1. by restoring such terms, as are grown entirely obsolete; or, 2. by selecting out of those, which have still a currency, and are not quite laid aside, such as are most forcible and expressive.[. . .] These *choice* words amongst such as are still in *use*, I take to be those which are employed by the old writers in some peculiarly strong and energetic sense, yet so as with good advantage, to be copied by the moderns, without seeming barbarous or affected.[. . .] The riches of a language are actually increased by retaining its old words.[21]

Hurd makes this *scholium*, composed at a particularly critical moment of the mid-century debate about poetic language, the occasion for a developed and determined statement of poetic position. The selection of the obsolete word is a task for the master poet. Verbal revivals are valued for their force, expressiveness, strength, and energy. Complaining that the resources of the language have been diminished by a false and fashionable politeness which resists 'old words, as barbarous', as well as 'many modern ones, as unpolite', Hurd goes on to declare that the time has now come 'for some master-hand to interpose and send us for supplies to our old poets'. The strength and peculiarity of poetic language is to be restored, and vindicated against modern delicacy, by the use of older words, authorized by past poetic usage.

The *Ars Poetica* also provides brief dicta on the poetic use of neologism which were at least equally open to interpretation and debate:

> In verbis etiam tenuis cautusque serendis
> dixeris egregie notum si callida verbum
> reddiderit iunctura novum.   (*Ars Poetica*, l. 46)

Some of Horace's eighteenth-century commentators did full justice to his hint of caution about the selection and use of words. In the note on this line

---

[19] *The Poetical Works of Christopher Smart, v: The Works of Horace Translated into Verse*, ed. by Karina Williamson (Oxford: Oxford University Press, 1996), p. 5.

[20] Smart's verse translation reads 'words shall revive that now are gone' (l. 130), *Poetical Works, v*, p. 357.

[21] *Q. Horatii Flacci Epistolae ad Pisones, et Augustum: With an English Commentary and Notes*, 2nd edn, 2 vols (London, 1753), I, 47–51.

in his well-known verse translation, the Reverend Philip Francis explains that Horace expects 'that a Poet who presumes to make new Words, shall have a delicate Taste, *tenuis*, and that he shall be discreet in the Use of that Indulgence which he gives him, *cautus*.[. . .] Such are the Rules which Horace and good sense establish'.[22] In his translation itself, indeed, Francis has Horace's lines speak not of frank neologism, but of inventive combination:

> Be delicate and cautious in the Use
> And Choice of Words: nor shall you fail of Praise,
> When nicely joining two new Words You raise
> A third unknown.

In his encounters with Horace, Smart negotiates some of the different possible interpretations of Horace's lines. In his literal prose translation of 1756 he follows, most closely in the offered parenthetical alternative, Francis's version: 'In the choice of his words too he must be delicate and cautious; you will express yourself admirably well, if a dextrous composition (*or combination*) should give an air of novelty to a common word'.[23] In the 1767 verse translation he makes Horace's words refer explicitly to neologism, advising the 'professor of the muse' who uses 'new words' to be 'cautious in his verse | And choice'.[24]

Scholarship to date, and particularly a brief but thorough enquiry by Susie Tucker, suggests that Smart's use of frank neologism in his published verse is significant and often characteristic, though not exceptionally extensive.[25] Amongst the examples pointed out by Tucker are the 'bees *imblossom'd* store' in the *Psalms*; *camel* as a transitive verb in the description of Jeoffry who '*camels* his back to bear the first notion of business'; the 'busy *pry*' of 'shrewd observation' in *The Hop-Garden* (given in the *Oxford English Dictionary* as the earliest nominal use); *hopland*, also in *The Hop-Garden*, and *god-childhood*, in the *Psalms*, as adjectives; and the use of *sheathe* in the sense 'cover a large surface', and of *bower* and *silver* as intransitive verbs in the *Psalms*.[26] *Silverling* was familiar as an English translation for 'shekel'; Smart uses it, neologistically and perhaps uniquely, to refer to silver fish.[27] Karina Williamson glosses *scancile*, in *The Hop-Garden* (I, 254), as a coinage from Latin *scansile*, climbable;[28] such a formation is natural in the consciously

---

[22] *A Poetical Translation of the Works of Horace: With the Original Text, and Notes Collected from the best Latin and French Commentators on that Author*, 2nd edn, 4 vols (1747), IV, 217–19 and n.

[23] *The Works of Horace, Translated Literally into English Prose*, 2 vols (London, 1756), II, 383.

[24] *Poetical Works*, V, p. 356.

[25] 'Christopher Smart and the English Language', *Notes and Queries*, 203 (1958), 468–69. A number of other instances are noted throughout the Oxford *Poetical Works*.

[26] *Psalms*, 19. 60, *Poetical Works* III, p. 44; *Jubilate Agno*, B 754, *The Poetical Works of Christopher Smart, I: Jubilate Agno*, ed. by Karina Williamson (Oxford: Oxford University Press, 1980), p. 89; *Hop-Garden*, I. 33 and II. 221, *The Poetical Works of Christopher Smart, IV: Miscellaneous Poems English and Latin*, ed. by Karina Williamson (Oxford: Oxford University Press, 1987), pp. 43, 62; *Psalms*, 119 (lamed) 31; 89.35–36; 148 (second version). 12, *Poetical Works*, III, pp. 318, 214, 5, 380.

[27] *A Song to David*, l. 341 (see my note, *Poetical Works*, II, p. 442).

[28] See *Poetical Works*, IV, p. 417.

Latinate vocabulary of this early georgic poem. Smart's use of *sultanate* as a verb is described by John Hill as 'a very pompous word, never before introduced into our own or any other language'.[29] Some of Smart's neologisms are consciously jocular; in his fable 'The English Bull Dog, Dutch Mastiff, and Quail', Smart has the bull-dog describe Italian greyhounds as 'Farinellied' (l. 40), that is, reduced to the same condition as the famous Italian castrato Carlo Farinelli.[30] Like many another poet, and according to one of the possible understandings of Horace's advice, Smart makes a number of new compounds; Tucker notes 'dumbstruck', 'fleshly-will'd', 'glass-constructed', 'heav'n-accepted', 'heav'n-arrested', 'heav'n dir-ected', and 'hope-retarded'. There are other possibilities but by no means all are decisive. It is notoriously difficult to establish that any given verbal use is the first, and Smart's use of neologism overall may have been somewhat overestimated.[31]

Smart's use of archaism is, naturally enough, more complex, more varied, and in a number of ways more idiosyncratic. One feature is a recurrent tendency to obsolete and obsolescent spellings: *grutch, rancle, querelous, destribution*.[32] There are also examples of more or less frankly archaic words and usages. Susie Tucker notes as archaisms Smart's reference to the '*baleful* eyes' of Lazarus (*Parables*, 26. 21), his description of 'the heav'n with sapphire *cield*' (*Psalms*, 89.17), and the alliterating reference to Christ's purchase of our 'ransom on the *rood*' (*Psalms*, 81. 42). When Smart has the Lord 'scoff at all [the wicked] *lease*' (*Psalms*, 37. 50), that is, 'slander' or 'lie', he uses a verbal form that seems to have been obsolete by the beginning of the seventeenth century, though the noun 'leasings' survived into the eighteenth century as a poetic archaism.[33] *Inscious*, that is, 'ignorant', not recorded later than 1652 in the *Oxford English Dictionary*, is used in Smart's verse translation of Horace (Satires, II. 3. 205), and *prescious*, an archaic form of 'prescient' which is not recorded after the end of the seventeenth century, appears both in *The Hop-Garden* (II. 129) and the *Phaedrus* (II. 9. 7). The going down of the

---

[29] *Horatian Canons of Friendship*, l. 211; 'Epithalamium', l. 53 (see Williamson's note, *Poetical Works*, IV, p. 440).

[30] See Williamson's note, *Poetical Works*, IV, p. 455.

[31] Tucker gives *mercy-gate* (which seems to be modelled on the biblical *mercy seat*, Exodus 25. 17, etc.), *taleful*, and the unpejorative use of *flighty* as innovations, but *OED2* records an example of *mercy-gate* from *c*. 1600, Thomson had written of the 'taleful [. . .] cottage hind' (*Winter*, l. 90), and Johnson gives the sense 'fleeting, swift' for *flighty* in the *Dictionary*. I refer throughout to Johnson's *Dictionary of the English Language on CD ROM*, ed. by Anne McDermott (Cambridge: Cambridge University Press, with the University of Birmingham, 1996). Williamson glosses *dulsome* (*Hop-Garden*, I. 188, *Poetical Works*, IV, p. 417) as a coinage, on the analogy of 'delightsome', but *OED2* gives an example from Lodge of 1614, and notes that the word is 'obsolete exc. dialect'.

[32] Smart uses *grutch*, or *grutching*, in *A Song to David*, l. 286; *Hop-Garden*, I. 72; *Hymns and Spiritual Songs*, 18. 28; *Horace Translated into Verse*, Odes I. 27. 20, III. 5. 52; the last example given in *OED2* is from *Robinson Crusoe*. *Rancle* (*Psalms*, 44. 98) persisted into the sixteenth century, but gave way to *ranckle* and *rankle*, which was standard by the eighteenth century. For *querelous*, see Williamson's note on *Horace Translated into Verse*, 'Ars Poetica', l. 331, *Poetical Works*, V, p. 463. Smart uses the obsolete *destribution* at *Psalms*, 25. 55, and *Hymns and Spiritual Songs*, 18. 35.

[33] Johnson's *Dictionary* gives illustrations from Spenser, Shakespeare, Prior, and Gay.

sun in Psalm 113. 3 is translated by Smart as the sun's '*department* in the WEST', an obsolete usage for 'departure'.[34] Smart regularly uses *promulge*, the older, but not by his time obsolete, form of 'promulgate'.[35] Archaisms which are more obviously poetic in derivation and character, and which might be characterized as belonging to 'poetic diction', are remarkably rare, at least in his later verse. St Stephen is referred to as the sweetest flower *gemm'd* by grace; this verbal usage, which was certainly archaic and poetic by this date, probably derives from Milton.[36] In his translation of the tenth Epistle of the first book, Smart uses *subvert* in a manner that plays on the literal sense of *subverto* in the Horatian original; too large a shoe 'will soon subvert | Your feet' (l. 78). The *Oxford English Dictionary* records no usage later than 1697, a line from Dryden's translation of the *Georgics* (IV. 312), and indeed, Smart's exploitation of the Latin sense might recall Milton's poetic methods as well as Dryden's.[37] In general, where Smart explicitly and persistently uses a recognizable 'poetic diction', it is likely to be in his earlier writings, and in such genres as the georgic, where such a lexis is deliberate and self-parodying. The clearest example perhaps is his use of Spenserian archaism (*maugre, bedight, wights, yclep'd*) in *The Hop-Garden*.[38]

Smart's poetry, and certainly his later poetry, is characterized, however, by archaisms derived from other sources than the common inheritance of poets. One pervasive and distinctive archaic element is his use of the language of the Authorized Version. In one of his essays in *The Universal Visiter* in the mid-1750s Smart himself had declared that 'as long as our admirable version of the bible continues to be read in churches, there will remain a perpetual standard for the language'.[39] But the Authorized Version was for Smart the poet more than a linguistic standard. Richard Hurd, in his commentary on Horace's *Ars Poetica*, had insisted that 'the riches of a language are [. . .] increased by retaining its old words; and besides, they have often a greater real weight and dignity'.[40] The Authorized Version, most highly authoritative of all literary exemplars, provided Smart with an older diction not only weighty and dignified, but invested too with spiritual and moral resonance. Here more than anywhere he found a language of real presence, which pervades the Christian poetry of his later years, the *Song to David*, the *Hymns and Spiritual Songs*, the *Jubilate Agno*, and his verse translation of the Psalms. Sometimes the use of a more or less archaic Authorized

---

[34] *Psalms*, 113. 12 (in my note I gloss the word, I think mistakenly, 'province', *Poetical Works*, III, p. 427). *OED2* gives no instance of *department* in the sense 'departure' later than Isaac Barrow in 1677.

[35] *Hymns and Spiritual Songs*, 9. 18; *Psalms*, 71. 61, 78. 4, 101. 6; *Parables*, 'Christ disputing amongst the doctors', l. 42.

[36] *Hymns and Spiritual Songs*, 33. 24. Compare *Paradise Lost*, VII. 324–26: 'the stately trees [. . . | . . .] gemmed | Their blossoms'. Smart uses *gem* for 'bud' in *A Song to David*, ll. 128 and 315.

[37] *Poetical Works*, V, p. 300. *OED2*, subvert v., sense 2. Compare, for example, Milton's pun on *supplant*, *Paradise Lost*, X. 513.

[38] See Williamson's note, *Poetical Works*, IV, p. 416.

[39] 'Some Thoughts on the English Language', *Universal Visiter* (January 1756), 4–9 (p. 4).

[40] *Q. Horatii Flacci Epistolae ad Pisones*, l. 49.

Version vocabulary operates at the level of quotation and near-quotation: so a line in the *Jubilate Agno*, 'bless the Lord from chambering and drunkenness' (B 34),[41] is a re-ordering of Romans 13. 13, and one of Smart's favourite phrases, 'Mammon and his leaven', takes and combines from the Bible a name for worldly wealth and a standard image for false doctrine.[42] Sometimes Smart exploits biblical meanings less directly. So David is invited to listen to Smart's *Song* from his 'blest *mansion*' (l. 16), an allusion to John 14. 2: 'In my Father's house are many mansions'. In the same poem Smart borrows the archaic *gier-eagle* (l. 454) from Leviticus 11. 18 and, taking a word used in Revelation for the gum-sandarac tree (18. 12), has '*thyine* woods' (l. 356) form part of the created world's chorus of adoration.[43] The diction of the Authorized Version provides Smart with some of his distinctive words of moral value. In *Jubilate Agno* B 149 Smart prays to God 'for all those, who have defiled themselves in matters *inconvenient*'; the word is used in the obsolete sense 'morally or ethically unsuitable, [. . .] unseemly, improper' (*OED2*, sense 3), alluding to Romans 1. 28: 'God gave them over to a reprobate mind, to do those things which are not convenient'. Smart's use of the word in his translation of the Psalms, 'stop the jesting inconvenient' (39. 35) is a more exact echo of a biblical use, in Ephesians 5. 4: 'Neither filthiness, nor foolish talking, nor jesting, which are not convenient'. One of Smart's most frequent uses in his religious verse is the verb *exact*, in the sense 'extort' or 'oppress', and the associated nouns *exactor* and *exaction*: 'shield us from the foul exactor', 'make me forgive [. . .] all that exact on me', 'exaction and excess of sin'.[44] These are words from the Authorized Version, from the Psalms for example: 'the enemy shall not exact upon him' (89. 22), or Isaiah: 'I will make [. . .] thine exactors righteousness' (60. 17), or Ezekiel: 'take away your exactions from my people, saith the Lord God' (45. 9). In many less obvious ways Smart's words and constructions echo the language of the Authorized Version. So he uses the verb *skill* with the infinitive, in the sense 'to know how to do something' (*OED2*, skill v.[1], sense 4c): 'ye that skill the flow'rs to fancy'.[45] The model is the locution used in Solomon's instructions to Hiram regarding the building of the Temple: 'There is not among us any that can skill to hew timber like unto the Sidonians.'[46]

A further significant archaic aspect of Smart's lexis is his use of dialect. In his earliest secular verse he resorts from time to time to a more or less contemporary slang or colloquialism or dialect, most commonly where considerations of genre or character require a comic effect. In 'Audivere,

---

[41] *OED2* records no non-biblical use of *chambering* in this sense later than 1613.

[42] *Song to David*, l. 286; *Psalms*, 14. 1, 118. 118; *Parables*, 18. 21. Compare Matthew 6. 24, 16. 6–12; 1 Corinthians 5. 6–8.

[43] *OED2* records this as the only non-biblical use of *thyine* later than 1571.

[44] *Hymns and Spiritual Songs*, 19. 3; *Hymns for the Amusement of Children*, 5. 7–8; *Parables*, 67. 53–54. Compare *Hymns and Spiritual Songs*, 10. 65–66, 23. 1; *Jubilate Agno*, B303–04, 472–73.

[45] *Hymns and Spiritual Songs*, 3. 49 (*Poetical Works*, II, p. 38); compare 20. 24.

[46] 1 Kings 5. 6; compare II Chronicles 2. 7.

Lyce', an early burlesque attempt at verse translation of the thirteenth Ode of Horace's Book IV, Horace's courtesan is given the name 'Mother Gunter', and, with a comic two-syllable rhyme, accused of aping 'the tricks of a bunter'.[47] *Bunter*, according to Johnson, is 'a cant word for a woman who picks up rags about the street; and used, by way of contempt, for any low vulgar woman'.[48] In 'A Description of the Vacation', Swiftian at least in its title and its rhyming quatrains, Smart uses the word *gyps* (l. 4), a Cambridge and Durham term for a college servant.[49] Even in his verse translations of Horace and Phaedrus, Smart occasionally adds raciness to a relatively neutral original by contemporary colloquialisms or dialect uses. Of one deceived in the merit of one he recommends to another, Horace uses *deceptus* (*Epistles*, I. 18. 79); the word becomes in Smart's verse translation *chous'd* ('duped, or tricked'),[50] common enough in English comic drama, but considered by Johnson to be 'perhaps a fortuitous and cant word'. Amongst the perils of the Roman street, Horace's 'ingens machina' is localized to Smart's 'timber-tug', a Kentish dialect word for a horse-drawn timber wagon (*OED2*, timber, sb.[1], sense 10).[51] The Mouse of the first Fable of Phaedrus's Book IV becomes 'a chap | That oft escap'd both snare and trap' (ll. 11–12): *chap* is familiar (in both senses) now, but was relatively recent slang when Smart wrote his translation in 1765.[52]

Such contemporary uses are deliberate, drawing attention to themselves, and effecting palpable shifts in tone and register. Arguably more significant in Smart's verse, however, than these generally rather superficial colloquial words are a number of lowland Scots and northern English dialect uses, survivals from a common language which once was spoken, as James A. H. Murray put it, 'from the Trent and Humber to the Moray Firth'.[53] These are from the point of view of the standard literary language of Smart's time not only provincial but also archaic, once in wider use but now retained only by a smaller body of regional speakers. The matter was so understood by

---

[47] 'Audivere, Lyce, Hor. Lib. 4. Ode 13', ll. 1–4, *Poetical Works*, IV, pp. 166–67. First printed in the *Magazine of Magazines* (1 August 1750), 122–23.

[48] *OED2* records the word as obsolete except in dialect use, but it was evidently current in Smart's London. Smart uses the word again in his fable 'The Pig', l. 37 (*Poetical Works*, IV, pp. 201–02), again with a two syllable rhyme ('bunter/grunter').

[49] *Poetical Works*, IV, p. 91.

[50] In Smart's translation, Epistles, I. 18. 146 (*Poetical Works*, V, p. 322).

[51] Horace, *Epistles*, II. 2. 73 (l. 138 in Smart's verse translation, *Poetical Works*, V, p. 346).

[52] *The Poetical Works of Christopher Smart, VI: A Poetical Translation of the Fables of Phaedrus*, ed. by Karina Williamson, with Anne Becher (Oxford: Oxford University Press, 1996), p. 77. See *OED2*, chap, sb. 3, sense 2. Johnson does not give this sense of the word. Further representative examples of the colloquial in Smart are *banging* and *swinging* in the sense 'thumping', 'great', 'huge'; *to bam*, 'to deceive, impose upon'; *bangs*, 'trounces' (all from the verse translation of Horace, Satires, II. 2. 73–74, II. 8. 116; Epistles, II. 2. 56, *Poetical Works*, V, pp. 220, 267, 344); *huff'd*, 'chided', 'reprimanded' (translation of Phaedrus, Fables, V. 10. 12, *Poetical Works*, VI, p. 104); and several uses of *bite* in the sense 'cheat' (including the verse translation of Horace, Epistles, I. 1. 38, I. 17. 119, *Poetical Works*, V, pp. 274, 317).

[53] *The Dialect of the Southern Counties of Scotland: Its Pronunciation, Grammar, and Historical Relations* (London: Philological Society, 1873), p. 29.

Johnson, who added this paragraph to his 'Grammar' in the fourth edition of the *Dictionary*:

The language of the northern counties retains many words now out of use, but which are commonly of the genuine Teutonick race, and is uttered with a pronunciation which now seems harsh and rough, but was probably used by our ancestors. The northern speech is therefore not barbarous but obsolete.

Smart's lowland Scottish and northern words were no doubt remembered from his schoolboy years in Durham, between 1733 (when he reached the age of eleven) and 1739. Of course it is not always possible to establish that a given word, when Smart used it, was distinctively or exclusively northern or Scots. None the less it seems to me that there is cumulatively compelling evidence for the presence in his writing of a small but recognizable body of such dialect usages. Before I present that case, it might be useful to outline a context.

The persistence of northern dialect uses in the work of James Thomson, himself a lowland Scot, is of course well known. Scotticisms are most obvious in his juvenilia. Many of Thomson's rhymes depend on a Scots pronunciation, and there is frankly Scottish diction in his burlesque 'Elegy upon James Therburn in Chatto', for instance:

> For had the carl but been aware
> That meagre death who none does spare
> T'attempt sic things should ever dare
> As stop his pipe
> He might have com'd to flee or skare
> The greedy gipe.   (l. 13)[54]

Scottish tendencies persist however in Thomson's later poetry. Many of his Latin words, of course, derive from Virgil, especially from the *Georgics*, and from Milton. Some, however, are of a more characteristically Scottish 'neo-aureate' tendency, reflecting his Scottish humanistic education: the '*cogenial* horrors' of winter, for example.[55] A number of more Teutonic and demotic uses have been pointed out by Thomson's commentators: *baffle, keen, whelms, bicker, ken, scour, flounce, clammy, lass, ravine* ('rapine'), *chapt* ('chopped', 'cut short'), *meantime, recks, friskful, aye, bootless, thronged*.[56] Such distinctively Scottish lexis in Thomson's published and widely-known verse was noted by English contemporaries, by no means always with approval. This is William Somerville's advice, in his verse epistle 'To Mr. Thomson, on the first edition of his *Seasons*':

---

[54] James Thomson, *Liberty, The Castle of Indolence, and other Poems*, ed. by James Sambrook (Oxford: Oxford University Press, 1986), p. 263.

[55] Cited by Mary Jane W. Scott in her important study, 'Scottish Language in the Poetry of James Thomson', *Neuphilologische Mitteilungen*, 82 (1981), 370–85 (p. 371).

[56] I give some of the more convincing examples from Mary Jane W. Scott's article, and from J. Logie Robertson's annotations in his edition of *The Seasons and the Castle of Indolence* (Oxford: Oxford University Press, 1891).

Read Philips much, consider Milton more;
But from their dross extract the purer ore.
To coin new words, or to restore the old
In southern bards is dangerous and bold,
But rarely, very rarely, will succeed,
When minted on the other side of Tweed.
Let perspicuity o'er all preside —
Soon shalt thou be the nation's joy and pride.   (l. 29)[57]

The advice might be Horace's, as read by a conservative eighteenth-century theorist of poetic language. Thomson is urged to study approved models, as Horace urged the Pisones to give their days and nights to the study of the Greeks (*Ars Poetica*, 268–69). In selecting diction even from those approved models, from Milton and (more surprisingly) Philips, it is none the less necessary to distinguish what belongs to the purified language. New words may be used with caution but, while Horace allows a sparing use of words from a Greek source, Somerville specifically warns against Scottish usages. Somerville makes explicit how inimical dialect is to a clear, humanistic level of style.

Such resistance to Scots usages persisted and indeed increased through the century. In the Preface to his *Dictionary* Samuel Johnson complained generally of the introduction of foreign words, 'the folly of naturalizing useless foreigners to the injury of the natives'. Though it is certainly not clear that he disapproved of Scottishness as such, in his definition of at least one word he more particularly castigated a Thomsonian introduction of a Scotticism: 'To freak: A word, I suppose, Scotch, brought into England by Thomson'.[58] Many Scots attempting to make their way in the English establishment were aware of, and often attempted to minimize, Scottish tendencies in their speech and writing.[59] Writing for Scots who aimed to master a 'correct' London English, and aiming to help them recognize what in their idiolect might expose them as Scots, Sir John Sinclair and James Beattie provided guidance which bore on literary as well as on spoken language. They rehearsed the familiar argument that languages progress

---

[57] *Poetical Works*, 2 vols (Edinburgh, 1780), ii. 33 (Vol. 75 of *Bell's Edition of the Poets of Great Britain*).
[58] The reference is to *Winter* (1746), l. 814. Johnson frequently disapproves in the *Dictionary* of Thomson's usages, but not obviously for their Scottishness: see Thomas B. Gilmore, 'Implicit Criticism of Thomson's *Seasons* in Johnson's *Dictionary*', *Modern Philology*, 86 (1989), 265–73 (pp. 266–67). James G. Basker makes the now rather problematical claim that 'a major thrust of Johnson's [. . .] *Dictionary* [. . .] was standardisation', asserts that Johnson 'systematically attempted to proscribe' Scotticisms, and frequently 'seems to have included a Scottish word or usage [. . .] simply to single it out and stigmatise it as a Scotticism' ('Scotticisms and the Problem of Cultural Identity in Eighteenth-Century Britain', *Eighteenth-Century Life*, 15 (1991), 81–95 (p. 82)). This conclusion rests on the questionable assumption that Johnson's standard usage label is also a 'warning tag'. I note something over a hundred and sixty Scots usages recorded by Johnson in the *Dictionary*: of these a clearly negative judgement is given only for *freak*, and, rather more decisively, for *scelerat*: 'a villain; a wicked wretch. A word introduced unnecessarily from the French by a Scottish author'.
[59] On James Boswell's ambivalent attitude, see Pat Rogers, 'Boswell and the Scotticism', in *New Light on Boswell: Critical and Historical Essays on the Occasion of the Bicentenary of the Life of Johnson*, ed. by Greg Clingham (Cambridge: Cambridge University Press, 1991), pp. 56–71.

toward their maturity, and that English reached its perfected state in the reign of Queen Anne, as spoken particularly in London, and as written particularly by Addison and Swift. So proper usage is defined as excluding all kinds of dialect.[60] It is incumbent on all speakers and writers of the language, not only Scots, Welsh, and Irish, but provincial English too, to put away their own peculiarities and adopt the mature and purified language. The purity of the language must not be impaired by cant and provincial words, by the foreign, the newfangled and unauthorized, or by older expressions which survive only in dialect.[61] Many words, as Horace had taught, must fall, if custom demands; yet even in these handbooks to correct English there is a recognition, which recalls Richard Hurd's note on this Horatian passage, of a central opposition between strength, distinctiveness, and peculiarity on the one hand, and purity, elegance, and correctness on the other:

many words are now condemned as Scoticisms, which were formerly admired for their strength and beauty, and may still be found in the writings of Chaucer, of Spenser, of Shakespeare, and other celebrated English authors. Indeed many words in the old English or Scottish dialects are so emphatical and significant, that [. . .] it is difficult to find words in the modern English capable of expressing their full force, and genuine meaning. But what our language has lost in strength, it has gained in elegance and correctness.[62]

Thomson would not so readily have agreed that forcibleness and peculiarity of expression might be well lost in the pursuit of the correct: 'Should I alter my Way, I would write poorly. I must chuse, what appears to me the most significant Epithet or I cannot, with any Heart, proceed'.[63] And Samuel Johnson, in his Life of Thomson, remarked that in Thomson's successive revisions of *The Seasons* there is a loss of '*race*, a word which, applied to wines, [. . .] means the flavour of the soil'.[64]

Smart's use of the northern English and Scottish dialect is certainly less characteristic, less obviously a part of his *race*. In one of the poems of the early 1760s, his translation of 'The 100th Psalm for a Scotch Tune', there is indeed to be found an overt attempt at a written version of Scots dialect:

> O gang your way and gang with glee,
> Into his courts with melody,
> And do his goodness right.

[60] An extended analysis of the larger issues of the eighteenth-century debate is provided by John Barrell in an important essay, 'The Language Properly So-called: The Authority of Common Usage', in his *English Literature in History 1730–80: An Equal, Wide Survey* (London: Hutchinson, 1983), pp. 110–75.

[61] Beattie, *The Grammarian: or, the English Writer and Speaker's Assistant: [. . .] also, Scoticisms: Designed to Correct Improprieties of Speech and Writing* (London, 1838), pp. 42–43 (Beattie's *Scoticisms* were first published in 1779); Sinclair, *Observations on the Scottish Dialect* (London and Edinburgh, 1782), pp. 1–2, 13–14.

[62] Sinclair, *Observations on the Scottish Dialect*, pp. 78–79.

[63] Letter to Mallet, 11 August 1726, *James Thomson (1700–1748) Letters and Documents*, ed. by Alan Dugald McKillop (Lawrence: University of Kansas Press, 1958), p. 46.

[64] *Lives of the English Poets*, III, 301.

His gates are not too straight nor strong
To keep out sicke a lively song,
    And sicke a menceful sight.   (l. 13)[65]

This, however, is a special case, telling us little about Smart's more general poetic methods. It first appeared in the Supplement to the *Christian's Magazine* for January to July 1761, early months of the Earl of Bute's predominance, and its choice of diction may not be without political purposes. This is evidently a language borrowed for a public occasion, a deliberate use of Scots as a literary Doric, more conventional than that of Thomson in his youth or maturity, or of Burns or Hogg in their published verse. I am concerned here, rather, with traces of a northern lexis far less densely stereotypical, scattered through his verse, which do not belong very recognizably to poetic diction (though Beattie, as we have seen, identifies a sub-set of poetic diction as words 'once no doubt in common use in England, as many of them still are in Scotland'), and which operate at a very much more internalized and integrated level of his idiolect. In some of these instances a northern dialect sense is explicit, in others the dialect sense is present as a secondary resonance. Often these words are instruments of Smart's characteristic verbal play.

I might begin by briefly developing a number of such cases which have already been pointed out by myself and by Karina Williamson, in our editorial annotations to the Oxford English Texts edition of the *Poetical Works*. In the *Jubilate*, for example, Smart tells us that 'the devil works upon damps and lowth and causes agues' (B 569). *Lowth*, used also by Smart in his *Translation of the Psalms*: 'my soul adheres to lowth and dust' (119. (daleth) 1) may well be thought a revival of an obsolete word, found in the Tyndale and Coverdale translations of Romans 8. 39 (though not in the Authorized Version). By Smart's time and before, however, the word appears to have been a northern dialect usage. Its use is evidenced at the southern limit of the old range of Northumbrian dialect. John Ray, in the expanded edition of his *Collection of English Words not Generally Used* (1691), reports this observation of Francis Brokesby, 'Rector of *Rowley* in the *East Riding* of *Yorkshire*': 'That which lies under the Hills, especially down by *Humber* and *Ouse* side [. . .] is called by the Country-people the Lowths, *i.e.* The low Country in contradiction to the *Wauds*.'[66] Considering his cat Jeoffry, Smart admiringly notes that he 'can spraggle upon waggle at the word of command' (B 748). In his translation of the fourth Satire of Horace's second book, *vagos piscis* is rendered as 'spraggling fish'.[67] *Spraggle* is a variant spelling of *sprackle*, 'to sprawl or clamber', a primarily Scots usage; the *Oxford English Dictionary*'s two examples are from passages of dialect in Burns and Walter Scott. Smart commonly uses the adjective *vague*, as in his verse translation of Psalm 106: 'idly vague | From

[65] *Poetical Works*, IV, p. 333.
[66] Sig. A5[r], and pp. 171–72.
[67] Satires, II. 4. 142, *Poetical Works*, V, p. 246.

his indulgent yoke' (l. 113).[68] The *Oxford English Dictionary* gives no instance of this adjectival use later than 1627; by Smart's time it was certainly obsolescent and probably felt as northern or Scots, like the verbal use (*OED2*, vague v.[2]). In his hymn on St Matthias's Day Smart celebrates 'the poor, alive and likely', and in his epitaph on the Reverend James Sheeles he laments that 'the likeliest are not lent to last'; *likely*, meaning 'promising', 'hopeful', as well as 'likeable', is recorded in Johnson's *Dictionary* as obsolete, and it clearly was already by Smart's time, as it still is, a distinctively northern usage.[69] In his hymn on the King's Restoration, Smart gives glory to Christ's name 'for each and all | Of Henry's gifted sword, or Edward's noble stall'.[70] *Sword* here is unusually a collective noun for a military force (compare *OED2*, sword sb.[3]); the syntactically parallel *stall*, in this context, must be read as a variant spelling of the Scots and northern dialect word *stale*, 'the main body of an army, or a body of troops'.[71] One of the examples given of strength amongst created things in *A Song to David* is 'the rapid glede, | Which makes at once his game' (l. 446). No doubt Smart's use of *glede* in this most scriptural of poems echoes the appearance of the word in the Authorized Version (Deuteronomy 14. 13), but there is also very possibly a resonance of northern dialect. The *Oxford English Dictionary* describes the word as now chiefly northern and Scots, and, from the examples given, it would seem to have been so by the end of the seventeenth century. Johnson defines *glead* as 'a buzzard hawk; a kite. It retains that name in Scotland'. *Glede* appears in John Sinclair's list of *Scotticisms* (p. 197), and John Ray's correspondent William Nicholson also includes the word in his list of northern usages, though Ray himself thought this one of a number of the words communicated to him which, in his own experience, were 'of general and common use in most Countries of England' (*Collection of English Words* (1691), sig. A6[v]). In his hymn on the New Year Smart speaks of the incarnate Christ as leaving the angels in heaven behind him in his voyage of redemption to the world, 'way from guiltless natures winning'. *Way* is probably the northern and Scots (and North American) sense 'away', and *winning* is certainly used in the Scots and northern dialect sense 'making or finding his way, proceeding'.[72] Smart's hymn for Easter Day invites the worshippers to celebration:

> Amongst the rest arouse the harp
> And with a master's nail;

---

[68] Compare *A Song to David*, l. 437; and, in his *Horace Translated into Verse*, Odes, I. 35. 9; III. 29. 24; IV. 13. 43.

[69] *Hymns and Spiritual Songs*, 8. 5, *Poetical Works*, II, p. 45; 'Epitaph on the late Mr. Sheels', l. 5, *Poetical Works*, IV, p. 333. *OED2* gives no English examples in this sense later than the seventeenth century.

[70] *Hymns and Spiritual Songs*, 17. 47–48, *Poetical Works*, II, p. 66.

[71] See *OED2*, sword sb.[3]; *OED2*, stale sb.[4], sense 3; Jamieson, *An Etymological Dictionary of the Scottish Language*. *Stale* is defined as 'a march in order of battle', noted as obsolete, and illustrated with an example dated 1513, in Rev. Oliver Heslop, *Northumberland Words: a Glossary of Words Used in the County of Northumberland and on the Tyneside*, 2 vols (London: English Dialect Society, 1892, 1893–94), p. 683.

[72] *Hymns and Spiritual Songs*, 1. 15, *Poetical Works*, II, p. 33. See *OED2*, way adv. sense 1; win v.[1] sense 12a (a); *Scottish National Dictionary*, win v.[1] sense 6.

> And from the quick vibrations carp
> The graces of the scale.[73]

The sense of *carp* is 'pluck' or 'select', from Latin *carpere*. The word was used by Virgil, Horace, and Ovid to refer to the picking of plants and flowers,[74] and Smart goes on in the next stanza to exploit this association: 'the flow'rs from every bed collect'. But perhaps there are resonances too of *carp* as a word used in earlier northern and Scottish poetry to refer to the singing of a minstrel, accompanied by the harp.[75] In his translation of Ode 25 of Horace's first book, Smart renders the lament of the younger Lydia's admirers as 'Sleep'st thou, while dying lovers winge, | O Lydia at thy door'.[76] *Winge*, a variant spelling of *whinge* (as the *Scottish National Dictionary* notes), 'to whine, to complain peevishly', originates in Scottish and northern dialect, and was apparently still chiefly confined to northern and Scottish use in Smart's time. *Whinge* is not recorded in Johnson's *Dictionary*, and the pre-1800 examples in the *Oxford English Dictionary* are mostly from Scots dialect writing. Finally, Smart's unusual spelling of *pilgramage* (*Psalms* 37. 92) may possibly be an archaic Scots form (see *OED2*, *pilgrim*, sb.), though Angus McIntosh points out to me that this spelling is also attested in fifteenth-century Middle English.

To these known instances may be added a few more possibilities and at least one certainty. In his translation of Psalm 35. 15 Smart uses the Prayer Book word *mows*: 'with distended mows censorious | Every rank offender cries' (*Psalms*, 35. 81; compare 22. 61). The word does not appear in the Authorized Version. Johnson, in the *Dictionary*, cites two Shakespearean instances, and comments: 'Wry mouth; distorted face. This word is now out of use, but retained in Scotland'. It may be thought significant that Smart here chooses the northern, and more colloquial, Prayer Book reading against the more familiar, more English, and more 'correct' *mouths*. *Wilk*, referred to in *A Song to David* (l. 249), may well have been a normal usage and a normal spelling in the eighteenth century, as the *Oxford English Dictionary* would suggest, but the usually conservative John Ray admits into the list of North Country Words in his 1691 *Collection* the '*Wilk* or *Whilk*; a Periwinkle or Sea-Snail'. Another marginal possibility is Smart's comparison of the 'archangel Liberality' to the Marquis of Granby, in 'Munificence and Modesty': 'his look like GRANBY in his geers' (l. 60).[77] *In his geers* may mean 'with his weapons' or 'in his warlike accoutrements', or, perhaps more probably, 'ready for action'. Neither the spelling nor the idiom is unexampled in the eighteenth century,[78] but John Ray's correspondent William Nicholson

[73] *Hymns and Spiritual Songs*, 11. 113–16, *Poetical Works*, II, p. 55.
[74] Virgil, *Georgics*, IV. 134; *Eclogues*, II. 47; Ovid, *Metamorphoses*, IX. 380; Horace, *Odes*, III. 27. 44.
[75] See Jamieson, *Etymological Dictionary*, carp sense 2; *OED2*, carp v.¹ sense 3.
[76] Odes I. 25. 7, *Poetical Works*, V, p. 47.
[77] *Poetical Works*, IV, p. 350.
[78] See *OED2*, gear sb. senses 2, 4.

(though not John Ray himself) thinks *gear* northern (*Collection* (1691), A7^r). There is an interesting parallel from the poetry of Thomas Tickell (who was born and brought up in Cumberland) in Johnson's quotation in the *Dictionary* (1755) under the word *dirk* (which is itself an 'Earse word'):

> In vain thy hungry mountaineers
> Come forth in all their warlike geers,
> The shield, the pistol, dirk, and dagger,
> In which they daily wont to swagger.

A rather different case is presented by a line in the *Jubilate Agno*, where a bawdy pun appears to depend on a northern pronunciation: 'Let Mnason rejoice with Vulvula a sort of fish — Good words are of God, the cant from the Devil' (B 237). The suggestion may seem neither decent nor likely, but Smart, who spent his teenage years in the north and his working life in the south, must have known how readily a flat northern short *a* may be misheard by a southern ear as a short *u*. Smart's pervasive misogyny in the *Jubilate*, as well as the way in which his wordplay in this poem is 'frequently supercharged with erotic and bodily implications', has been most recently and convincingly demonstrated by Clement Hawes, who points out a number of instances of punning not dissimilar to this one in substance and form.[79] In his translation of Ode 15 of the second book, Smart renders Horace's contrast of modern opulence and luxury with ancestral frugality and modesty:

> Their private fortunes were but small,
> But great the common fund of all.
> No grand piazzas did there then remain
> To catch the summer breezes of the northern wane.

Karina Williamson's note glosses *wane* as 'a variant spelling of *wain*, referring to the constellation Arcturus, known as the *Great* and *Lesser Wain*.'[80] This must be right: the reference to Arcturus is in the Horatian original. *Wain*, however, was the usual eighteenth-century spelling (used by Smart himself at *Epistles*, II. 1. 345), and Williamson suggests to me that by his unusual spelling Smart may intend an additional connotation, appropriately rugged in its northern flavour: *wane*, 'dwelling-place, house', a form obsolete in eighteenth-century England but surviving in Scottish and northern use.[81] Finally, what seems to me a decisive instance, a line from Smart's discussion of the English language in the *Jubilate*: 'For every word has its marrow in the

[79] Particularly at B 177, and D 236. *Mania and Literary Style: The Rhetoric of Enthusiasm from the Ranters to Christopher Smart* (Cambridge: Cambridge University Press, 1996), Chapter 7, *passim*, and especially pp. 197–98, 200, 203.
[80] *Poetical Works*, v, p. 397.
[81] See *OED2*, wane sb.^{2}. All *OED2*'s examples are pre-1600, with the exception of a poetic, archaizing instance from the *Edinburgh Magazine* (1820).

English tongue for order and for delight'.[82] There have been attempts to interpret this taking *marrow* in its anatomical sense,[83] but Smart's primary intention here is certainly the distinctive north east, and Scots, sense, 'fellow, match, partner, pair'. This whole passage of the *Jubilate* is after all explicitly concerned with the relations, specifically the pairing, of words:

> For the relations of words are in pairs first.
> For the relations of words are sometimes in oppositions. (B 598, 599).

This meaning of the word is recorded by Johnson: 'Marrow, in the Scottish dialect, to this day, denotes a fellow, companion, or associate.' *Marrow* in this sense is also noted as Scottish or northern in Ray's *Collection of English Words*, John Sinclair's *Observations on the Scottish Dialect*, and Beattie's *Scoticisms*. Both Sinclair and Beattie give the usage as obsolete.[84] Almost all of the *Oxford English Dictionary*'s citations are Scots; the remainder are Northumbrian and North East Yorkshire.[85]

These seventeen cases, even allowing that there may be others I have missed, are scarcely enough to lend any marked or consistent colouring to the voluminous body of Smart's mature verse in which they appear. None the less, they add up to a demonstration of the survival in Smart's linguistic consciousness of a small but distinct body of northern expression. They are a characteristic of his idiolect. Such expressions as *bunter, chaps*, and *chous'd* are deliberate cant uses, flagged in Smart's verse as colloquial and dialect, often chosen for comic effect. Such northern words as *likely* and *winning, stall* and *glede, mows* and *carp, marrow* and *wane*, however, form a more organic part of his own language, lexical resources on which he could draw more naturally. It is because many of these words stand between a 'standard' London dialect, or an accepted literary dialect, on the one hand, and a distinctively northern dialect on the other, so often exploiting both through primary and secondary meanings, that they are so well integrated, and often so expressive, in his verse. Less central to his poetry, no doubt, than the regular and creative use of the Authorized Version, such words none the less constitute part of the characterizing strength, the 'race', of his language. The archaic was for Smart, as for so many of his contemporaries, a vital resource for making poetic language new, but he found his older words in other places, in the Holy Book and in memories of his boyhood, as well as in the language of (to borrow Richard Hurd's expression) 'our old poets'. The

---

[82] B 595. 'Its marrow' is the reading of the editions of Bond and Williamson. William Force Stead's and Norman Callan's editions at this line (XVIII. 15 in their division of the poem), however, retain the reading of the manuscript, 'it marrow', which may not be an error: the uninflected possessive, normal in the Shakespearean Quartos, gave way only slowly to the modern *its*, and persisted especially in the north west. See *OED2*, s.v. its possessive pronoun; E. A. Abbott, *A Shakespearean Grammar*, 3rd edn, rev. (1870; repr. New York: Dover, 1966), sig. 228.

[83] For example, by Harriet Guest, *A Form of Sound Words: The Religious Poetry of Christopher Smart* (Oxford: Oxford University Press, 1989), p. 185.

[84] John Sinclair, *Observations on the Scottish Dialect*, p. 29; James Beattie, *The Grammarian [. . .]* also *Scoticisms*, p. 48.

[85] *OED2*, marrow sb. [2], senses 1a, 4.

extensive use in his verse of the vocabulary of Scripture was one of the marks which made him, for many readers in his time, not only a distinctive but also an obscure and enthusiastic voice. His more occasional resort to a northern dialect seems to have escaped the particular notice of contemporaries, but no doubt also contributed to their sense of his unusual and often difficult '*tour* of expression'.[86] Smart formed even his lexis of the peculiar with a difference.

[86] *Monthly Review*, 31 (1764), 231.

The Poet and the Publisher in Thomas Gray's Correspondence

HEIDI THOMSON

Victoria University of Wellington

'The press has in general a bad effect on the complection of one's works.'
(Thomas Gray to Horace Walpole, 28 February 1762)[1]

While recent scholarship has moved away from Thomas Gray's fame as a hypersensitive, melancholy, and proudly passive 'Poet of Sensibility' in favour of a more contextual reading of his poems, Gray's reputation for distance and alienation persists.[2] A striking example of Gray's alleged penchant for pre-Romantic retreat and élitist inertia is his supposed refusal to appear in print and his distaste for the world of print and publishing in general. Linda Zionkowski, for instance, argues in her materialist reading of Gray's relationship to his audience that 'throughout his life, Gray was notorious for shunning the press; he published much of his work anonymously and unwillingly'.[3] When Gray's involvement with publishing is mentioned at all, the emphasis is usually on his disdain for the literary marketplace and his insistence on being a gentleman as opposed to a hardworking tradesman or businessman.[4] While writers such as Samuel Johnson and Christopher Smart, Gray's contemporary at Cambridge University, openly made their living out of print, Gray did not have to resort to publication for a livelihood.[5] To some extent the distinction between professional writers and authors like Gray who did not depend on, and often despised the idea of writing for a living, has led to a notion that Gray did not

---

[1] *Correspondence of Thomas Gray*, ed. by Paget Toynbee and Leonard Whibley, cor. and add. by H. W. Starr, 3 vols (Oxford: Clarendon Press, 1971), II, 774–75. All subsequent references to Gray's *Correspondence* will be given in the text.

[2] The two recent book-length studies about Gray put him in a larger framework than has been attempted before, but they are largely confined to a study of the poetry; see Henry Weinfield, *The Poet Without a Name: Gray's Elegy and the Problem of History* (Carbondale: Southern Illinois University Press, 1991) and Suvir Kaul, *Thomas Gray and Literary Authority: A Study in Ideology and Poetics* (Stanford, CA: Stanford University Press, 1992). *Thomas Gray: Contemporary Essays*, ed. by W. B. Hutchings and William Ruddick (Liverpool: Liverpool University Press, 1993) also focuses primarily on Gray's poetry. Among the recent articles, S. H. Clark's stand out for opening up new avenues of Gray study; see ' "Pendet Homo Incertus": Gray's Response to Locke. Part One: "Dull in A New Way" ', *Eighteenth-Century Studies*, 24 (1991), 273–91, and ' "Pendet Homo Incertus": Gray's Response to Locke. Part Two: "De principiis Cogitandi" ', *Eighteenth-Century Studies*, 24 (1991), 484–503.

[3] 'Bridging the Gulf Between: The Poet and the Audience in the Work of Gray', *ELH*, 58 (1991), 333. See also, for instance, Arthur Sherbo's introduction to the facsimile edition of *Poems of Mr Gray* (Glasgow: Foulis, 1768; London: Scolar Press, 1973); Kaul, p. 200.

[4] Alvin Kernan, *Printing Technology, Letters and Samuel Johnson* (Princeton, NJ: Princeton University Press, 1987), pp. 16, 35.

[5] Johnson's immersion in the book trade dates practically from birth: see Robert DeMaria, Jr, *The Life of Samuel Johnson: A Critical Biography* (Oxford: Blackwell, 1993). See also Kernan, pp. 82–84.

wish to appear in print. Like most writers, however, and contrary to the coy pose he often struck on that account, Gray dearly loved to be read and recognized that print offered an opportunity to reach an audience. Traditionally, Horace Walpole has been held almost solely responsible for Gray's ventures into print, and while Walpole undoubtedly played a major part in publishing Gray's work, Gray controlled most publication decisions and, from the mid-1750s on, operated increasingly independently from Walpole.[6] So far no sustained discussion of Gray's relationship to print and publishing exists, and in this article I want to make a start by considering Gray's correspondence on this topic.

The correspondence vividly evokes Gray's consistent control over the publication of his own work and a striking interest in the world of print and books in general. Overall, Gray's attitude towards publishing (and life in general) is undoubtedly one of caution, but to interpret this wariness as withdrawal is probably too restrictive. His caution is triggered by the understanding that print can embellish, obscure, distort, or obliterate a message by a physical appearance over which the author no longer has any control, that print may have 'a bad effect on the complection of one's work', as Gray puts it to Walpole. Gray's perception of print is similar to what Alvin Kernan proposes as Pope's view in *The Dunciad* where print is 'a dullish, mechanical, undiscriminating, repetitive, mass medium, a true instrument of Dulness that gives extraordinary opportunities to those already inclined that way, greedy booksellers, vain, dull gentlemen, poor scribblers, pedantic schoolmasters' (p. 15). Still, Pope's view did not prevent him from seeking publication for payment, and *The Dunciad* itself, by the nature of its satire, also articulates possible standards by exposing the problems associated with printing. While Gray did not expect to earn money from publishing, he wanted to appear in print and expressed his opinions about the world of print regularly and forcefully. The relationship between Gray and Pope is not the topic of this essay, but it is worth noting that the voice in one of Gray's earliest extant English poems, 'Lines Spoken by the Ghost of John Dennis at the Devil Tavern', is not one of a melancholy poet pining away but of a recently deceased professional writer who had been satirized by Pope.[7]

At the age of twenty-four, on 21 April 1741, Gray sent a 'portrait' of himself to his friend Richard West which includes many personal characteristics which are prominent in Gray's behaviour relating to publishing. The

---

[6] Martin Price calls Walpole Gray's 'patron' in 'Sacred to Secular: Thomas Gray and the Cultivation of the Literary', in *Context, Influence, and Mid-Eighteenth-Century Poetry: Papers Presented at a Clark Library Seminar 21 March 1987 by Howard D. Weinbrot and Martin Price* (Los Angeles: William Andrews Clark Memorial Library, 1990), pp. 41–78 (p. 44); A. L. Lytton Sells, *Thomas Gray: His Life and Works* (London: Allen, 1980), pp. 68–69.

[7] *The Poems of Thomas Gray, William Collins, Oliver Goldsmith*, ed. by Robert Lonsdale (London: Longman, 1969), pp. 13–17. For the influence of Pope, see William Levine, 'From the Ridiculous to the Sublime: Gray's Transvaluation of Pope's Poetics', *PQ*, 70 (1991), 289–309.

picture contains 'a want of love for general society, indeed an inability to it' but also 'a love of truth, and detestation of every thing else' (I, 181). In addition West is to conceive of 'a little laughter, a great deal of pride, and some spirits' (I, 182). Living as he did for most of his life in the highly formalized microcosm of Cambridge University, exclusiveness rather than isolation characterized much of Gray's social life and indeed much of eighteenth-century privileged social life. The 'love of truth', the 'laughter' and 'pride' produce a cocktail which includes perfectionism, a certain arrogance, and an insistence on decorum and accuracy in the formal presentation of texts. Gray's satirical humour and pride are both triggered by the amusement, irritation, or exasperation with which he perceives any distortion of his own authorial intentions and the lack of decorum in publishing generally. Overall, I also have the impression that Gray preferred epistolary relationships to physical ones, and letter writing as a primary mode of maintaining friendships and conducting business allowed for a sense of control and perfection which no reality could match. Much of Gray's self-deprecating satire and parody is rooted in the fear of losing face and of falling short of perfection. In addition to these personal characteristics which may have influenced Gray's perspective on publishing, it should be pointed out that even though Gray's small poetic output is sometimes mentioned together with his so-called reluctance to publish, Gray did not think of himself exclusively as a poet. His correspondence and commonplace books provide ample proof of his scholarly interests, and to Walpole's repeated urging to produce more poetry he replied candidly: 'Till fourscore-and-ten, whenever the humour takes me, I will write, because I like it; and because I like myself better when I do so. If I do not write much, it is because I cannot' (III, 1018).

Gray's direct involvement with publishing started during his student days, about a decade before Robert Dodsley's publication of the Eton Ode in 1747. His hymeneal on the marriage of Frederick, Prince of Wales and Princess Augusta of Saxe-Gotha, was published in *Gratulatio Academiae Cantabrigiensis Auspicatissimas Frederici Walliae Principis & Augustae Principissae Saxo-Gothae Nuptias Celebrantis* by the Cambridge university press in 1736. At the end of the same year, on 29 December, and maybe on the basis of his acclaimed performance in the *Gratulatio*, he was also invited to write the 'Tripos-Verses', and the result was the printing of *Luna habitabilis*.[8] In addition to these publications, Gray's early letters illustrate his interest in print through parody and satire: travel writing in particular is a favourite target, as in the long parody of Addison's *Remarks on Several Parts of Italy, in the Years 1701, 1702, 1703* in the letter to Walpole of October 1735 (I, 29–33),

---

[8] See *Correspondence*, III, 1198–99, for Whibley's appendix. A printed copy of *Luna habitabilis* was part of the lot of Gray's books and manuscripts sold at Sotheby's on 4 August 1854.

and in the account of his own Grand Tour to Thomas Wharton in March 1740 (I, 138–41). The latter letter in particular illustrates Gray's humorous awareness of typographical gimmicks, the fraudulent practices of subscription, and selling points of travel writing: 'Proposals for printing by Subscription in THIS LARGE LETTER the Travels of T: G: Gent' (I, 138). To a humorous table of contents Gray adds that 'the Subscribers are to pay 20 Guineas; 19 down, & the remainder upon delivery of the book. N:B: A few are printed on the softest Royal Brown Paper for the use of the Curious' (I, 141). Gray's awareness of how both the visual impact and verbal message of a printed text are yoked into one impression surfaces in all his ventures with print. That he himself was no exception to susceptibility on the basis of appearance is illustrated by his own response to Spence's *Polymetis* when he wrote to Walpole in 1747: 'I much fear (see what it is to make a Figure) the Breadth of the Margin, & the Neatness of the Prints, which are better done that one could expect, have prevail'd upon me to like it far better, than I did in Manuscript' (I, 268).

Gray's consciousness of 'making a figure' in print and the possible threat to his 'love of truth' which accompanies it, did not, however, deter him from publishing itself. In the letter to Walpole of 8 February 1747, now primarily quoted for its reference to the 'dissolution' of literature (I, 265), Gray outlined, in considerable detail, a publication plan. Not untypically, his own suggestion in response to Walpole's idea is prefaced by a satirical point about the first edition of Spence's *Polymetis*: 'The Heads & Tails of the Dialogues, publish'd separate in 16mo, would make the sweetest Reading in Nature for young Gentlemen of Family and Fortune that are learning to dance: I am told, he has put his little Picture before it' (I, 265). Gray also throws in a rumour about his own identity as a playwright, expressing his fear of being recognized as the author of *Agrippina*, before finally taking up Walpole's suggestion for a joint publication seriously: 'But I much fear our Joynt-Stock would hardly compose a small Volume: what I have, is less considerable than you would imagine; & of that we should not be willing to publish all' (I, 266). Yet, instead of dismissing the plan altogether, Gray then sketched, in considerable detail, a proposal for a joint publication of poems by Walpole, West (who had died in 1742), and himself. The collection would consist largely of verse in Latin and translations or imitations from Latin; it would also include Gray's 'little Ode of 5 Stanza's, to the Spring' (I, 266). Gray conceived of the publication as a posthumous tribute to West's potential as a poet, thereby affirming the power of print to multiply and disseminate an author's work:

I should not care, how unwise the ordinary Sort of Readers might think my Affection for him provided those few, that ever loved any Body, or judged of any thing rightly, might from such little Remains be moved to consider, what he would have been; & to wish, that Heaven had granted him a longer Life, & a Mind more at Ease. (I, 266)

Gray's more public involvement with publishing, primarily with Robert Dodsley, the leading London bookseller, starts on 30 May 1747, with the anonymous appearance of the Eton Ode, in folio, for the price of sixpence (I, 282). Dodsley's commercial success as the publisher of the *Collection of Poems* was phenomenal, but Gray never forgot that Robert Dodsley started his career as a footman.[9] Michael Suarez has pointed out the reasons for the *Collection's* commercial success: an impressive list of contemporary authors, many of whom were associated with Pope, an image of literary taste which resisted any Grub Street connotations, and impressive aristocratic associations, often in the guise of so-called 'gentlemen editors', such as Horace Walpole, who alerted Dodsley to new poems.[10] Dodsley's enthusiasm to set a standard of literary taste by printing authors who would otherwise have been forgotten after their manuscripts had finished circulating among friends and his relentless, friendly attempts to 'charm, cajole, or reason his authors into the kind of assistance he needed' did not change Gray's opinion of him.[11] Gray's own insecurity about his origins as the son of a scrivener may have excluded any generosity of spirit towards Dodsley's attempts to reconcile gentlemanly taste and a code of aristocratic leisure with the entrepreneurial spirit of profit. More practically, Gray, accustomed to controlling every detail of his life and work, was probably not keen on Dodsley's own distinctive house style in the publication of the *Collection*.[12] Mostly, Gray avoided direct dealings with Dodsley; instead he communicated through Walpole and, later, William Mason. Only once did Gray praise Dodsley, for his ode 'Melpomene: or The Regions of Terror and Pity', but he was unaware of Dodsley's authorship ('pray who wrote it?'), and I doubt whether he would have been as charitable had he known the author's name.[13] Gray's peremptory tone extended also to Robert's successor and younger brother James, and it is to Horace Walpole's credit that he acted so patiently as Gray's go-between with the Dodsleys over a period of more than twenty years. In contrast with Gray, Walpole, secure in his aristocratic status, dealt easily with both Gray and Dodsley.

By November 1747 Walpole was acting as a 'gentleman editor' for Dodsley's *Collection of Poems, By several Hands*, and Gray wholeheartedly agreed to the inclusion of the Eton Ode, the Spring Ode, and 'Selima too, unless she be of too little importance for his patriot-collection' (I, 289–90).

---

[9] See Ralph Strauss, *Robert Dodsley: Poet, Publisher & Playwright* (London: Lane, 1910; repr. New York: Franklin, 1968). For a fine, recent introduction to Robert Dodsley's life and work, see James Tierney, *The Correspondence of Robert Dodsley 1733–1764* (Cambridge: Cambridge University Press, 1988), pp. 3–66.
[10] See Michael F. Suarez, 'Trafficking in the Muse: The Sale and Distribution of Dodsley's *Collection of Poems, 1748–1782*', *Studies on Voltaire and the Eighteenth Century*, 304 (1992), 1098–101. For Pope's central position in the *Collection*, see Suarez, 'Dodsley's *Collection of Poems* and the Ghost of Pope: The Politics of Literary Reputation', *Papers of the Bibliographical Society of America*, 88 (1994), 189–206.
[11] Richard Wendorf, 'Robert Dodsley as Editor', *Studies in Bibliography*, 31 (1978), 235–48 (p. 237). For a short account of Dodsley as editor of Gray, see Wendorf, pp. 238–41.
[12] Wendorf, p. 246.
[13] *Correspondence of Thomas Gray*, II, 530; Tierney points out that even 'the chary Thomas Gray confess[ed] a liking for it', p. 13.

The poems appeared in Volume II of Dodsley's first three-volume *Collection of Poems, By several Hands* (1748) and Gray's response to the *Collection* in a long letter to Walpole starts with his vexation over the lavish frontispiece, a lure for customers, at the expense of the paper and the appearance of the actual poems: 'He might, methinks, have spared the Graces in his frontispiece, if he chose to be oeconomical, and dressed his authors in a little more decent raiment — not in whited-brown paper and distorted characters, like an old ballad' (I, 294–95). Dodsley 'dressed his authors' for the attraction of customers and not to satisfy the ego of his authors. Gray's response affirms a sense of authorial identity which considers itself slighted by the form in which it gets presented to the world. Apparently Gray was not the only one who was unimpressed with the poor quality of Dodsley's production; the *Collection* did not sell very well, and Dodsley learnt from his mistake for the next edition:

Unlike its predecessor, this miscellany was printed on high-quality paper by John Hughes, Dodsley's favourite printer. A new engraving adorned the title-page and, while the first edition had only 11 ornaments, or one every 89 pages, the second edition sported 234 ornaments and fleurons, or one every 4.5 pages.[14]

After the complaint about the paper and the gaudy frontispiece, Gray professed to be 'ashamed to see [him]self' but he obviously took the *Collection* seriously enough to write cogently and critically about the other authors. A number of his points are implicit comments on the poetic genres which were favoured in miscellanies such as Dodsley's and the ignorance of fashionable readers. His rejection of Thomas Tickell's 'On the Prospect of Peace', for instance, was based on his abhorrence of the genre, 'a state-poem (my ancient aversion)' (I, 295), and the fact that it celebrated the Peace of Utrecht ('if Mr. Pope had wrote a panegyric on it, one could hardly have read him with patience' (I, 295)). About Walpole's satirical contribution, however, 'An Epistle from Florence to T. A. Esq., Tutor to the Earl of P', he argued that he 'was of the publishing side' (I, 296):

For though, as Mr. Chute said extremely well, the *still small voice* of Poetry was not made to be heard in a crowd; yet Satire will be heard, for all the audience are by nature her friends; especially when she appears in the spirit of Dryden, with his strength, and often with his versification. (I, 296)

While the first sentence of the above quotation has been used (out of context) to support the argument that 'to Gray, retreat from the market in letters and from the mass audience that print culture created is necessary to composition', it should be obvious that Gray is making a generic distinction, rather than a case in favour of retreat from publishing.[15] While epic or lyric poetry may not be 'heard' by all, well-expressed satire in verse, Gray suggests, appeals to all and is an appropriate genre for miscellanies. At the end of this

---

[14] Suarez, 'Trafficking in the Muse', p. 1098.
[15] Zionkowski, p. 347.

letter Gray mockingly signed himself as 'a *Miscellaneous Writer*' (I, 302), but despite his disdain for anthologies of this kind he would continue to be published in Dodsley's subsequent collections. In respect to Dodsley's collections, Gray seems to have been more worried about Dodsley's independent house style and about the mixed company he is forced to keep in the collections than about the act of publishing itself. Gray was always annoyed when the idea of a 'just volume' (as opposed to a pamphlet) took priority over a well-balanced table of contents. A loose collection of disparate material was never Gray's idea of a deserving publication. As late as 1762 he scathingly referred to Bob Lloyd's publication of a 'just quarto volume' by including, among Lloyd's own and other things, a Latin translation of the 'Elegy' and some satirical verses on Mason and Gray (II, 777–78): 'so little value have poets for themselves, especially when they would make up a just volume' (II, 778).

The publication of Gray's most famous work, the 'Elegy', was dominated by a race between two publishers, William Owen and Robert Dodsley, to be first in bringing this poem to the public, and Gray demonstrated again considerable control over the situation. Dodsley was favoured, by default, over William Owen who had intended to pirate it for publication in his *Magazine of Magazines*; Gray wrote to Walpole in February 1751:

As I am not at all disposed to be either so indulgent, or so correspondent, as they desire; I have but one bad Way left to escape the Honour they would inflict upon me. & therefore am obliged to desire you would make Dodsley print it immediately (which may be done in less than a Week's time) from your Copy, but without my Name, in what Form is most convenient for him, but in his best Paper & Character. he must correct the Press himself, & print it without any Interval between the Stanza's, because the Sense is in some Place continued beyond them; & the Title must be, Elegy, wrote in a Country Church-yard. if he would add a Line or two to say it came into his Hands by Accident, I should like it better. (I, 341–42)

Despite his low opinion of Dodsley, Gray's abhorrence at being printed in the *Magazine of Magazines* made him turn to Dodsley, request an anonymous appearance, supplemented if possible by an affirmation of the accidental acquisition of the manuscript. In addition to the clear wishes about paper and character, Gray also demanded that Dodsley correct the press (a source of particular anxiety for Gray) and gave some direction about the layout of the poem. Imperiously but obviously worried about the urgency of the matter, he added at the end of the letter: 'If Dodsley don't do this immediately, he may as well let it alone' (I, 342). Gray's letter has been read as an effort 'to make the best of what he still considered the unseemly and tasteless act of printing his poetry', but, apart from the fact that Gray had consented to appear in print before (in Dodsley's *Collection*), Gray's letters to Walpole following the publication are light-hearted and amused about the whole experience.[16] On 15 February 1751 Dodsley published the 'Elegy' as

---

[16] Kernan, p. 64.

a quarto pamphlet, price sixpence. He may have beaten the *Magazine of Magazines* which advertises that 'this Magazine will be publish'd the 16th of every successive Month' by just a day, but since the March editorial of the *Magazine* apologizes for habitual lateness of appearance, the '16th of every successive Month' may be wishful thinking rather than a reality. The 'Stanza's written in a Country Church-yard' did appear in the February issue of the *Magazine* as 'a fine copy of verses, by the very ingenious Mr. Gray, of Peter-house, Cambridge'. That Owen was peeved about the Dodsley publication is clear from the entry in the 'Books Published' section of the March issue of the *Magazine of Magazines*: 'An elegy wrote in a country church-yard. 6 d. *Dodsley*. The first edition of this was printed from a very imperfect copy, tho' a correct one was in our last Magazine, p. 160.'[17] In his thanks to Walpole for mediating, Gray jokingly resorted to publisher's jargon by referring to himself as the mother of Walpole's illegitimate child, thereby implicating Walpole in the act of authorship: 'You have indeed conducted with great decency my little *misfortune*: you have taken a paternal care of it' (I, 342).[18] Of course, Dodsley was also implicated in the production of the text, but as the nurse who 'has given it a pinch or two in the cradle, that (I doubt) it will bear the marks of as long as it lives'. Yet, the distortion of the text by Dodsley is read also to advantage: 'It will only look the more careless, and by *accident* as it were' (I, 343). While this point can be read as proof of Gray's unwillingness to publish at all, as Kernan takes it (pp. 64–65), Gray may also have wanted to obscure his own manipulation of the press to achieve publication with Dodsley as opposed to Owen.

Between September 1751 and February 1753 Gray is fully preoccupied with the plans for publication of the first volume that was to bear his own name, *Six Poems*, for which Walpole's protégé Richard Bentley was to make the illustrations and Dodsley be responsible for the publishing. The collaboration proved to be difficult and increasingly tense, culminating in Gray's angry outburst about the possibility of his portrait on the front page. As a possible result of Gray's dissatisfaction with this collaboration, Gray did entirely without Walpole's help in the preparation of the complete *Poems* publication of 1768. One obvious source of Gray's anxiety was in sharing the same page with Bentley; Loftus Jestin has demonstrated how Bentley's designs both illustrate and satirize Gray's work and character, and I would add that Gray's desire to control the editorial process of his own text is seriously limited by not being the sole provider of text, by having to acknowledge the presence of another author, not only in the same volume, as in Dodsley's collections, but on the same page.[19] Gray's outbursts to both

---

[17] *Magazine of Magazines*, Numbers 8 and 9, Volume II, 160–61, 283.
[18] When asking Shenstone for his elegies, Dodsley wrote: 'I shall loose the Fame of being the Muses' Midwife, & my hand for want of practice will forget its obstetrick faculties' (quoted by Wendorf, p. 237).
[19] Loftus Jestin, *The Answer to the Lyre: Richard Bentley's Illustrations for Thomas Gray's Poems* (Philadelphia: University of Pennsylvania Press, 1990), pp. 85, 92, 96.

Walpole and Dodsley about the relative hierarchy, order, and phrasing of the title page may well be a reflection of his uneasy relationship with the other artist. Not very surprisingly, Gray started at the outset of the project by throwing 'cold Water' on Bentley, 'which stunted his Growth' (1, 350), as he admits to Walpole, but after his initial objection, and probably to Walpole's relief, Gray seems to have been reasonably happy with Bentley's work, singling out the design of the village-funeral for the 'Elegy' for particular praise (1, 362).

In one of the letters to Walpole which dealt primarily with the preparation of *Six Poems* for the press, Gray demonstrated again his interest in publishing by introducing some plans for the 'Progress of Poesy', on which he was working at the time, carefully couching his own ambition in satirizing Dodsley's ignorance of Pindaric odes, the anticipated unenlightened audience response, and his own control over the timing of his work:

I don't know but I may send him very soon (by your hands) an ode to his own tooth, a high Pindarick upon stilts, which one must be a better scholar than he is to understand a line of, and the very best scholars will understand but a little matter here and there. It wants but seventeen lines of having an end, I don't say of being finished. As it is so unfortunate to come too late for Mr. Bentley, it may appear in the fourth volume of the Miscellanies, provided you don't think it execrable, and suppress it. (1, 364)

In the same letter Gray also insisted on revising the press of *Six Poems* himself: 'For you know you can't: and there are a few trifles I could wish altered' (1, 364). After Gray's death Walpole made a point of admitting his impatience with 'correcting the press' to Mason on 15 May 1773, thereby affirming Gray's insistence on precision and distrust of current correcting practices:

I have not the patience necessary for correcting the press. Gray was forever reproaching me with it, and in one of the letters I have just turned over, he says, 'Pray send me the proof sheets to correct, for you know you are not capable of it.' It is very true, and I hope future edition-mongers will say of those of Strawberry Hill, they have all the beautiful negligence of a gentleman.[20]

In December, Gray delayed the publication of *Six Poems* by two weeks by refusing to comply with Dodsley's request to be in town for some more alterations and expresses his dissatisfaction with the physical appearance of the text: 'I have just received the first Proofs from Dodsly. I thought it was to be Quarto, but it is a little Folio. the Stanzas are number'd, which I do not like.' (1, 367) On 12 February 1753 Gray wrote to Robert Dodsley himself; it is the one surviving letter of their correspondence, and Gray's tone is peevish

---

[20] *Horace Walpole's Correspondence with William Mason*, ed. by W. S. Lewis, Grover Cronin Jr, and Charles H. Bennett (London: Oxford University Press, 1955), p. 87. That Walpole has exaggerated the 'negligence' of the Strawberry Hill Press has been indicated by Roderick Cave, *The Private Press* (New York: Bowker, 1983), pp. 32–34.

and arrogant.[21] As it turns out, Gray was not so much disturbed by the forthcoming publication itself as by its lavish format and the association with Bentley. From this moment on, until 1768, Gray's territorial feelings about his own work prompted him to rewrite his collaboration with Bentley quite drastically: while Walpole had commissioned Bentley to design drawings for Gray's poems, Gray would argue ultimately that he incidentally supplied some poems as comments to Bentley's illustrations. In that spirit he naturally objected to a title which mentioned him first; instead he ordered the title to be:

> Designs by Mr R: Bentley
> for six Poems of
> Mr T: Gray.

Gray left no doubt as to the self-righteousness of this suggestion in an almost panicky outburst:

To have it conceived, that I publish a Collection of *Poems* (half a dozen little Matters, four of which too have already been printed again & again) thus pompously adorned would make me appear very justly ridiculous. I desire it may be understood (which is the truth) that the Verses are only subordinate, & explanatory to the Drawings & suffer'd by me to come out thus only for that reason. (1, 371)

The thought that he too would be guilty of recycling and repackaging material in 'just volume' format was too much for Gray, and his parenthetical insistence on truth seems meant to convince both Dodsley and himself of his intentions which go directly against the grain of the original plan. In terms of original timing it is nonsense to consider Gray's poems as 'subordinate' and 'explanatory' to Bentley's designs, but Gray is making it undeniably clear that for this particular edition he 'suffers' his verses to come out, in a reversal of the original plan, as explanations or illustrations to Bentley's designs. The published work, as Gray's proposed title suggests, is to focus on 'Designs by Mr R: Bentley'; the active preposition 'by' affirms the newness of Bentley's work as opposed to the long term existence of Gray's poems in the use of the possessive 'of'. In his letter of 20 February Walpole tried to argue that the drawings were made for the poems, and not the other way around, and wondered whether putting 'Designs' before 'Poems' would make the poems less Gray's (1, 374). Gray, however, stuck to his idea, convinced that while the poems would not be in any way less his, at least the publication would be more associated with Bentley than with him. Knowing very well that his name was a drawcard for potential customers because of the commercial success of the 'Elegy', Gray tried to reassure Dodsley by appealing to his aristocratic, gentlemanly aspirations; Gray argued that the

---

[21] For the letter of 12 February 1753 from Gray to Dodsley, see *Correspondence of Thomas Gray*, 1, 371 and Tierney, pp. 148–49. Tierney also lists two letters from and two letters to Thomas Gray in 1752 and 1757 as untraced (p. 549).

price would be too prohibitive to chance customers anyway, and that a discreet title-page would attract a discerning clientele:

You need not apprehend, that this change in the Title will be any prejudice to the Sale of the book. a showy title-page may serve to sell a Pamphlet of a shilling or two; but this is not of a price for chance-customers, whose eye is caught in passing by a window; & could never sell but from the notion the Town may entertain of the Merit of the Drawings, which they will be instructed in by some, that understand such things. (I, 371)

A day later, in what is possibly his most vehement letter to Walpole, Gray was outraged about the plan of having his portrait in the book: 'If you suffer my head to be printed, you infallibly will put me out of mine' (I, 372), and expected complete reassurance from Walpole about the issue: 'The thing, as it was, I know will make me ridiculous enough; but to appear in proper Person at the head of my works, consisting of half a dozen Ballads in 30 Pages, would be worse than the Pillory' (I, 372). From Walpole's reply to Gray it is clear that Dodsley, whose idea the head was, did not share Gray's low-key ideas about publishing and that he wanted to deliver a product which people would consider good value for their money:

He feared the price of half a guinea would seem too high to most purchasers; if by the expense of ten guineas more he could make the book appear so much more rich & showy (as I believe I said) as to induce people to think it cheap, the profits from selling many more copies would amply recompense him for his additional disbursement. (I, 373–74)

The plan was stopped according to Gray's wishes, even though, according to Mason's *Memoirs* the plate was already half engraved. Overall, the 1753 experience must have been too negative for Gray to want to repeat a similar collaborative venture ever again. Dodsley continued to publish his poems, but Gray's publishing relationship with Walpole became distinctly more guarded after 1753, and Gray increasingly exercised more control and initiative over publication matters, confiding also in other friends, particularly William Mason and later James Beattie. He remained friends with Walpole, however, and, in an interesting reversal of roles, encouraged him to print *The Castle of Otranto*.[22]

During 1754 and 1755 Gray steadily continued work on the two odes which became notorious for their learned obscurity, 'The Progress of Poesy' and 'The Bard'. By March 1755 his work was sufficiently advanced to write again in terms of publishing but the idea of being swallowed and controlled by a Dodsley volume irritated him, as the letter to his friend Thomas Wharton shows:

I am not so much against publishing, as against publishing *this* ['Progress of Poesy'] *alone*. I have two or three Ideas more in my head. what is to come of them? must

[22] *The Yale Edition of Horace Walpole's Correspondence*, ed. by W. S. Lewis and others, 48 vols (Oxford: Oxford University Press; New Haven, CT: Yale University Press, 1937–83), XXVIII, 6. Walpole mentioned this in a letter to Mason, on 17 April 1765.

they too come out in the shape of little six-penny flams, dropping one after another, till Mr Dodsley thinks fit to collect them with Mr this's Song and Mr tother's epigram, into a pretty volume? (I, 420)

At Christmas 1755 Walpole sent Gray some humorous verses meant to 'draw poetry' from him (I, 448–49), but Gray was less willing to disclose the progress of his work to Walpole than to his new acquaintance Edward Bedingfield who did not exhibit Walpole's high-spirited enthusiasm for copious publishing. To Bedingfield's request for a meeting, Gray humorously referred to himself as a printed author:

My wish & the only reward I ask in writing is to give some little satisfaction to a few Men of sense & character. I say a *few*, because there are but few such [. . .]. I shall by no means promise that you will like your new acquaintance, when you see him *out of print*. (I, 447)

In April 1756 Gray was reluctant to send even Bedingfield a draft of 'Progress of Poesy' because 'I can convey it to you no other way than by the Post, which is not to be depended upon, & I have been already threaten'd with publication, tho' there are no more than three copies of it in the world' (II, 462). He adds, 'you call it *celebrated*, but its celebrity is only owing to its being yet unpublish'd' (II, 462). Gray's cautious words here should not be interpreted as aversion to publication but as fear of losing control over the manuscripts himself. That he did intend the odes for publication has been confirmed, however, by the autograph signed receipt for forty guineas 'assigning Robert Dodsley copy of Gray's odes, 'Powers of Poetry' ('Progress of Poetry') and 'The Bard', and reserving Gray the right of one impression in an edition of his works. Dated 29 June 1757'.[23] Gray had not reckoned with Walpole and his newly set up Strawberry Hill Press, however, when he took his odes to London. Two years earlier Walpole had originally dreamt of another joint Gray–Bentley venture for the publication of the two odes, but Bentley, fortunately for Gray's peace of mind, had proved himself unequal to the task.[24] Undaunted by Bentley's failure and Gray's reluctance, a triumphant Walpole jubilantly announced the first project of his press to Chute on 12 July 1757:

The Stationers' Company, that is, Mr Dodsley, Mr Tonson, etc. are summoned to meet here on Sunday night. And with what do you think we open? *Cedite*, Romani *Impressores* —with nothing under Graii *Carmina*. I found him in town last week: he had brought his two odes to be printed. I snatched them out of Dodsley's hands, and they are to be the first-fruits of my press.[25]

Despite his initial grumbling in letters to Brown ('it was not in my power any how to avoid it') and Mason ('it was impossible to find a pretence for refusing

[23] Tierney, p. 516. See also Strauss, p. 164.
[24] *The Yale Edition of Horace Walpole's Correspondence*, XXXV, 251–52. On Bentley's failure to produce convincing illustrations for *The Bard*, see Jestin, p. 219.
[25] *The Yale Edition of Horace Walpole's Correspondence*, XXXV, 98–99. On Walpole's Strawberry Hill Press, see Munson Aldrich Havens, *Horace Walpole and the Strawberry Hill Press, 1757–1789* (Folcroft, PA: Folcroft Press, 1969) and A. T. Hazen, *A Bibliography of the Strawberry Hill Press* (Folkestone: Dawsons, 1973).

such a trifle'), Gray was obviously pleased with the result (II, 508, 512). The odes were published on 8 August and two days later he compliments Walpole and puts in a little barb about Walpole's lack of accuracy: 'They are very pleasant to the eye, & will do no dishonour to your Press. as you are but young in the trade, you will excuse me if I tell you that some little inaccuracies have escaped your eye' (II, 512). The public reception of the Odes as obscure, fashionable curiosities, a fascinating study in itself, is not within the scope of this article; my main point is that Gray was not reluctantly pushed into the Strawberry Hill printing venture, but that he had already initiated publication plans for the Odes himself and independently of Walpole.

Gray's last and most independent publishing venture is with the Foulis brothers of Glasgow in 1767–68. Dodsley was simultaneously preparing an edition of *Poems by Mr Gray*, and the contrast between Gray's behaviour to Foulis as opposed to Dodsley illustrates his ideas about publishing well. In his relations with Foulis, Gray was assisted by the Scottish philosopher and author of *The Minstrel*, James Beattie (1735–1803) whose own literary interests and admiration for Gray's merit as a scholar and poet were very endearing to Gray. In contrast with Walpole, Beattie never needled or teased Gray, never questioned Gray's authority. As a result, Gray, secure about his merit, could afford to relax in his response to Beattie. Finally, Gray had found a fellow gentleman poet-academic whose judgement on publishing he respected and shared, and when Beattie proposed to have Gary's complete poems printed at Glasgow, with Foulis, Gray accepted with pleasure:

The proposal you make me about printing, what little I have ever written, at Glasgow does me honour. I leave my reputation in that part of the kingdom to your care, & only desire you would not let your partiality to me & mine mislead you. if you persist in your design, Mr Foulis certainly ought to be acquainted of what I am now going to tell you. when I was in London the last spring, Dodsley the Bookseller ask'd my leave to reprint, in a smaller form all I have ever publish'd, to which I consented; & added, that I would send him a few explanatory notes, & if he would omitt entirely the *Long Story* (which was never meant for the publick, & only suffer'd to appear in that pompous edition because of Mr Bentley's designs, which were not intelligible without it) I promised to send him some thing else to print instead of it, least the bulk of so small a volume should be reduced to nothing at all. now it is very certain, that I had rather see them printed at Glasgow (especially as you will condescend to revise the press) than at London, but I know not how to retract my promise to Dodsley. (III, 982)

While Gray had to admit that he was already committed to Dodsley, his preference for Foulis as printing professionals is striking and his delight in Beattie's involvement with the project strengthened his preference for a Foulis edition of his work. To Dodsley he had already offered some new material to make up for his requested omission of the 'Long Story', a poem which had now become, at least in his eye, a mere accessory to Bentley's designs in what he now called a 'pompous edition'.

Gray's preference for Foulis over Dodsley can be attributed to the differences between the two publishing houses. Robert and Andrew Foulis of Glasgow were admired and recognized for their commitment to fine, accurate, and mostly academic printing. Elegance, accuracy, and academic interests ranked much higher with the Foulis brothers than commercial profit (and as a result Foulis died very poor while Dodsley got rich). They started out as respected University booksellers within the premises of the College of Glasgow from which they supplied the University library.[26] Their first venture in publishing was Cicero's *De natura Deorum* and their commitment to neat, correct editions of the Latin and Greek classics remained a priority throughout their printing career. Robert Foulis became University Printer in 1743 and Alexander Wilson was appointed type-founder to the University in 1748.[27] Their co-operation produced first-rate work: not only were the Foulises committed to using 'a higher proportion of fine-quality paper than did most of their contemporaries', they were also 'conscious innovators in their typography'.[28] More importantly for Gray, Robert Foulis was committed to accuracy of the press: at a time when printers were generally getting rid of correctors they employed a professional press reader.[29] Foulis's Latin and Greek classics were edited by university professors; the proof-sheets went through at least six readings and, in the unlikely event of an error in the final copy, the entire sheet was cancelled.[30] Gray's earliest reference to the Foulis brothers, or the 'Glasgow-Press' (II, 827), was in recommending them, together with John Baskerville, to William Taylor How in November 1763 for their beauty, in a letter which deplored the lack of accuracy in English printing:

The revising of the Press must be your own labour, as tedious as it is inglorious: but to this you must submit. as we improve in our types, &c: we grow daily more negligent in point of correctness, & this even in our own tongue. (II, 827)

When Gray also informed Beattie that Dodsley was not intimidated by the possibility of a Glasgow edition and that 'Mr Foulis therefore must judge for himself, whether he thinks it worth while to print, what is going to be printed at London' (III, 983), Foulis did not object and wrote to Beattie early in 1768: 'As to Mr. Dodsley's printing them at the same time, it is no disagreeable circumstance, especially as he knows they are to be printed in Scotland. This may produce emulation without envy.'[31]

Throughout 1768 Gray is steeped in publication matters. His correspondence with William Taylor How, in January, about the possible publication

---

[26] See David Murray, *Robert and Andrew Foulis and the Glasgow Press with Some Account of the Glasgow Academy of Fine Arts* (Glasgow: Maclehose, 1913), p. 7.
[27] Murray, pp. 9, 18.
[28] Philip Gaskell, *A Bibliography of the Foulis Press* (London: Hart-Davis, 1964), pp. 23, 26–29.
[29] Percy Simpson, *Proof-Reading in the Sixteenth, Seventeenth and Eighteenth Centuries* (Oxford: Oxford University Press, 1935), p. 154; Murray, p. 17.
[30] For a detailed description of the process, see Simpson, pp. 155–56.
[31] Margaret Forbes, *Beattie and his Friends* (Altricham: Stafford, 1904; repr. 1990), p. 36.

of Algarotti's works in England or Scotland prefigures his own anxiety about accuracy of the press as he warns How once more of the deficiencies of the English presses: 'as they improve in beauty, declining daily in accuracy' (III, 995). In February, Gray provides both James Dodsley (Robert's younger brother and successor) and James Beattie with the instructions for *Poems by Mr Gray*. Not surprisingly, the curt letter to Dodsley reflects Gray's main preoccupation: 'All I desire is, that the text be accurately printed, & therefore whoever corrects the press, should have some acquaintance with the Greek, latin, & Italian, as well as the English, tongues' (III, 999–1000). Yet, despite Gray's explicit desire for accuracy, one particular error must be blamed partly on Gray himself. Maybe because Gray is so anxious that the '*Long Story* must be quite omitted' (III, 1000) he is a bit less vigilant about the other poems in the collection. The instructions include an outline of the order of appearance: the ode on the Spring, 'Ode, on the death of a favourite Cat', 'Ode, on a distant prospect of Eton-College', and 'Ode, to Adversity' are all called 'Ode'; 'The progress of Poesy' and 'The Bard' both called 'Pindaric Ode'; after them come the 'The Fatal Sisters', 'The Descent of Odin', 'The Triumphs of Owen, a fragment', with 'Elegy, written in a country church-yard' as the final poem (III, 1000). Gray then continues:

You will print the four first & the last from your own large edition (first publish'd with Mr B: plates) in the 5th & 6th you will do well to follow the edition printed at St:y-hill: I mention this, because there are several little faults of the press in your Miscellanies. (III, 1000)

In the 1753 large edition, however, 'Adversity' was called a 'Hymn' and not an 'Ode', and by observation of Gray's request, 'Adversity' ended up as 'Hymn' in Dodsley's *Poems by Mr Gray*.

On 1 February 1768 Gray also wrote to James Beattie with almost identical instructions on the Glasgow edition, but his tone to Beattie differed greatly. He apologized for slowness in providing the manuscript, blaming the delay on having to make up in bulk for the omission of the 'Long Story', providing notes to the Pindarics as a concession to the stupidity of the reading public, and inserting parallel passages to give credit to the authors from whom he borrowed (III, 1002). At no point did Gray remind Foulis to be particularly careful about accuracy; instead he enthused: 'I rejoice to be in the hands of Mr Foulis, who has the laudable ambition of surpassing his Predecessors, the *Etiennes*, & the *Elzeviers* as well in literature, as in the proper art of his profession' (III, 1002). By comparing Foulis with the Etiennes and Elzeviers, noted for their scholarly interests and the beauty of their editions, Gray confirmed the Glasgow firm's reputation for fine books.[32] In the 'Instructions for Printing', however, Gray made the same mistake in advising Foulis to use the 1753 Folio edition as his model (III, 1004), but the fact that

[32] James Maclehose praises Foulis in similar terms in *The Glasgow University Press* (Glasgow: Glasgow University Press, 1931). 'Few men, since the days of Caxton, have done more than Robert Foulis to raise the standard of printing and to inspire a love for fine books' (p. 194).

Beattie did not have access to a 1753 edition may account for the 'Ode (not 'Hymn') to Adversity' in the Foulis edition. Beattie had to rely on a copy of Dodsley's *Collection* to transcribe the first four odes and the 'Elegy'. Because he was forced to use a Dodsley product, which Gray would definitely consider a dubious source, Beattie made sure that he gave priority to Gray's 'Instructions' for his own transcription ('in order, and with the titles and mottos and notes, you desired'). Eager to distance himself from the authority of Dodsley he also wrote:

Such of the typographical errors as were obvious I have avoided; and I flatter myself that my Manuscript is pretty correct, for Your poems have been deeply imprinted on my memory for many years; however I shall recommend it to Foulis to compare the Manuscript with the folio Edition, if it can be got. (III, 1010)

Beattie's enthusiasm about his job as editor is palpable throughout: 'I shall spare no pains to render our Scotch Edition in some measure worthy of the work, and of the Author' (III, 1011). He advised the printer to the 'size of paper, page, and type' and recommended end notes as opposed to footnotes. Two thirds of the letter is taken up with observations on the poems themselves with Beattie presenting himself as a knowing, enlightened, inspired reader, a reader who is very different from a Dodsley *Collection* reader in other words. 'The Bard', for instance, contrary to most opinions, is praised for its clarity and strength, 'but readers now-a-days have nothing in view but amusement; and have little relish for a book that requires any degree of attention' (III, 1011). At the end of his letter Beattie expresses his gratitude for Gray's gift of a copy on publication, and adds:

But you owe me no thanks for what I have done in preparing this Edition; it was a most agreable amusement to me; and I think I have done my country a service and even an honour in being the first projector of so good a work.

I write by this post to Mr Foulis to let him know that the Manuscript is ready and will be sent by the first sure hand. None of Your instructions will be forgotten. (III, 1012)

In contrast with Walpole, Beattie managed to reassure Gray about accuracy and timing. Neither a dilettante nor a professional publisher, he presented his own role of editor and go-between, however meticulously performed, as an exercise of leisure and voluntary service, as opposed to mercantile profit.

The finished product, a handsome large quarto, pleased both Beattie and Gray. Beattie called it 'one of the most elegant pieces of printing that the Glasgow press, or any other press, has ever produced. It does honour to every person concerned in it; to Mr Foulis the printer, and even to me the publisher, as well as to the author.[33] Gray considered it a 'most beautiful edition', but regrets that Foulis will not get much advantage out of it 'as Dodsley has contrived to glut the Town already with two editions before-hand, one of 1500, & the other of 750, both indeed far inferior to that of

---

[33] William Forbes, *An Account of the Life and Writings of James Beattie*, 2 vols (Edinburgh, 1806), I, 115.

Glasgow, but sold at half the price' (III, 1048). He also asked Beattie to convey his 'acknowledgements to Mr. Foulis, for the pains and expence he has been at in this publication' (III, 1048). The Advertisement to the Foulis edition offers another insight into the relationship between Gray and this highly favoured printer:

Some Gentlemen may be surprized to see an edition of Mr. Gray's Poems printed at Glasgow, at the same time that they are printed for Mr. Dodsley at London. For their satisfaction the printers mention what follows.

The property belongs to the Author, and this edition is by his permission. As an expression of their high esteem and gratitude, they have endeavoured to print it in the best manner.

Mr. Beattie, Professor of Philosophy in the University of Aberdeen, first proposed this undertaking. When he found that it was most agreeable to the printers, he procured Mr. Gray's consent, and transcribed the whole with accuracy. His transcription is followed in this Edition.

This is the first work in the Roman character which they have printed with so large a type; and they are obliged to Doctor Wilson for preparing so expeditiously, and with so much attention, characters of so beautiful a form.[34]

Beattie's authority as Professor, the emphasis on the accuracy of the transcription, Wilson's type, Gray's explicit consent all contribute to the superior status of this edition to the Dodsley one. Robert Foulis knew exactly how to approach Gray on the sensitive issue of profit:

As we had more at heart doing justice to the merits of the poems, than procuring profit, we printed no more copies than what we thought we could be able to sell in our own shop [. . .] we can, however, from the agreeable reception they met with in Glasgow, afford a little present for Mr. Gray, which shall be either a copy of our folio edition of Homer or a set of our new edition of the Greek Historians, in twenty-nine volumes. (III, 1071)

The exclusive sale of a limited number of copies, the emphasis on the intrinsic value of the poems as opposed to commercial profit, the lavishness of the 'little present' all emphasize the priority of the author over the volume and contrast sharply with the overtly commercial Dodsley approach. Beattie and Gray remained respectful friends until Gray's death, and in Beattie's defence of Gray's 'Installation Ode' in November 1769 we can see them bonding one more time against careless readers and printers alike.

I have heard some people object to its obscurity; but sure their attention must be very superficial, or their apprehension very weak, who do so. I understood every word of it at the first reading, except one passage (which however I made out at the second) where the printer had made nonsense, by placing a full point at the end of a line where there ought to have been no point at all. (III, 1083)

Not surprisingly, Walpole felt 'extremely out of humour' (III, 1013) at having been left in the dark about Gray's writing and publishing activities. Gray's unrepentant reply of 25 February made it clear that he had extricated

---

[34] Thomas Gray, *Poems by Mr. Gray* (Glasgow: Foulis, 1768).

himself from the Walpole–Bentley ties entirely, and that his poems, unadorned, would stand by themselves:

Dodsley told me in the spring that the plates from Mr. Bentley's designs were worn out, and he wanted to have them copied and reduced to a small scale for a new edition. I dissuaded him from so silly an expense, and desired he would put in no ornaments at all. The *Long Story* was to be totally omitted, as its only use (that of explaining the prints) was gone. (III, 1017)

To make up for the omission of the 'Long Story' and possibly also Bentley's lavish illustrations, Gray argued 'lest *my works* should be mistaken for the works of a flea, or a pismire, I promised to send him an equal weight of poetry or prose; so, since my return hither, I put up about two ounces of stuff' (III, 1017–18). However deprecating Gray may have sounded about his addition of 'two ounces', it is obvious that he preferred his poems to stand by themselves than in the company of Bentley's drawings.

Gray may have been difficult and at times reluctant in his interaction with publishers, but his continuous, determined involvement with the publication of his own work proves convincingly that he did not 'shun' the press. His perfectionism, his sense of authorial individuality, his distaste for print as a means of making a living, and his desire to control the production process are all part of Gray's relationship to print. Recognition of Gray's enjoyment at seeing himself in print may open new perspectives on the various connections between eighteenth-century authors and print, and, more specifically, it may also clarify Gray's involvement with the world in which he lived.

The Voice of the 'Translatress': From Aphra Behn to Elizabeth Carter

MIRELLA AGORNI

University of Warwick

Eighteenth-century women's writing activities have recently attracted a certain degree of critical interest, but attention has generally been focused on specific literary genres, such as autobiography, the novel, drama, and, more recently, poetry. Other genres, such as historical writing, reviewing, and above all translation have often been neglected or given only marginal consideration. Yet translation represented one of the very few cultural activities open to women in the early modern period.[1] The main reason for this neglect seems to be the derivative nature of translation, which has always been perceived as marginal *vis-à-vis* original production. Furthermore, the notion of authorship is put in jeopardy by any act of translation, since the relationship between original author and translator can never be taken for granted.

Douglas Robinson has recently emphasized the emergence of a phenomenon he defines as the 'feminization' of translation in sixteenth-century England. At that time women started to exploit the discourse of translation in order to find a public voice and at the same time to counter the widespread belief which equated publication with sexual licentiousness.[2] According to Tina Krontikis, a woman translator 'could hide behind another author (usually male) and protect herself against accusations pertaining to ideas and content'.[3] During the Reformation period women were encouraged to undertake translation of religious works, and this helped to create a greater flexibility in the field of female publication. However, the same religious motivations which allowed women to work on translation can be perceived as a means to prevent their venture into original literary production. As Sherry Simon points out: 'We are led to wonder whether translation condemned women to the margins of discourse or, on the contrary, rescued them from imposed silence.'[4] Like any other literary activity, translation is the product of complex cultural and historical constraints and therefore it

---

[1] As Margaret Patterson Hannay points out, women could also occasionally subvert the original, and insert their personal or political statements. See *Silent but for the Word: Tudor Women as Patrons, Translators and Writers of Religious Works*, ed. by Margaret Patterson Hannay (Kent, OH: Kent State University Press, 1986), p. 4.

[2] Douglas Robinson, 'Theorizing Translation in a Woman's Voice: Subverting the Rhetoric of Patronage, Courtly Love and Morality', *The Translator*, 1 (1995), 153–75 (p. 153).

[3] *Oppositional Voices: Women as Writers and Translators of Literature in the English Renaissance* (London: Routledge, 1992), p. 21.

[4] *Gender in Translation: Cultural Identity and the Politics of Transmission* (London: Routledge, 1996), p. 46.

can be argued that while it had an emancipating effect on women's writing in certain historical periods, on other occasions it worked in the service of conservative and restrictive forces with an inhibiting influence on female literary expression. It is hardly useful to look for some sort of historical progression in women's use of translation. Any translation project must be considered *per se*, being the product of a number of heterogeneous constraints such as the role played by patronage, the prestige of the original text, the influence of ideological and cultural pressures, and so on, but over and above all it should be emphasized, in Janet Todd's words, that 'literature is not progressive'.[5] For instance, Todd points out that some sophisticated narrative techniques of late-seventeenth-century women writers, such as the use of an independent narrative voice, will be heard again only a hundred years later.[6] Hence, it does not seem useful to look for linear developments in literature as has often been the case, for example, with the accounts of the birth of the novel. Attempts at reading literary history in this way have often proved teleologically biased, as Ros Ballaster demonstrates in her analysis of existing critical literature on the rise of the novel:

The rise in prestige of the novel form through the century does not necessarily betoken increasing sophistication in narrative technique, nor should we allow our analysis of eighteenth-century fiction to be overly determined by the realist aesthetics that came to dominate in the century that followed.[7]

The purpose of this paper is to demonstrate the impact of the complex ideological process defined as 'feminization' of early-eighteenth-century literature on the activity of women translators. The distinctive outspokenness of sixteenth- and seventeenth-century women translators was not going to be matched by their eighteenth-century successors. Paradoxically, Aphra Behn's translation of a scientific treatise by the French philosopher Fontenelle offered her a better opportunity to voice her experience as a woman and a writer than a similar translation would do for Elizabeth Carter fifty years later, in spite of the fact that Carter's work was specifically addressed to a female readership. And yet, according to a seemingly compensatory logic, Behn's translation works were almost immediately forgotten, whereas Carter's fame as the celebrated translator of Epictetus continued to circulate well into the nineteenth century.

Prefaces to translations offered a space for women to find their public voices and develop new means of self-expression in the early modern period. The best example is probably Margaret Tyler's preface to her translation from the Spanish of a romance by Diego Ortuñez de Calahorra, entitled *A*

---

[5] Janet Todd, *The Sign of Angellica: Women, Writing and Fiction 1660–1800* (London: Virago, 1989), p. 2.
[6] Todd is referring to the experiments in the use of narrative voices by women writers such as Behn and Delarivier Manley, which will be repeated by Fanny Burney and Ann Radcliffe only in the late eighteenth century. Todd, p. 2.
[7] *Seductive Forms: Women's Amatory Fiction from 1684 to 1740* (Oxford: Clarendon Press, 1992), p. 23. See especially her discussion of Ian Watt's seminal work on the birth of the novel (pp. 7–12).

Mirrour of Princely Deeds and Knighthood (1578).[8] This work is remarkable for being one of the earliest feminist manifestos in England. Krontikis points out that Tyler was probably the first woman writer to denounce the inhibiting effects of the patriarchal divisions of genre and gender on female literary expression (p. 45). At the time her own explicit transgression of the unspoken rule which allowed women to translate only works of a religious nature was perceived as a sheer innovation.

In her preface Tyler sets out to justify women's right to deal with secular literature. Although the battle scenes and the violence described by chivalric romances were arguably outside feminine experience, Tyler claims that women were nevertheless familiar with these motives, at least on a purely literary level. In fact they were often designated as the addressees of courtly romances, which were usually dedicated to them by male authors. Hence, Tyler reasonably concludes, if women were allowed to read these kind of texts, then they should also be permitted to translate them:

And if men may and do bestow such of their travailes upon Gentlewomen, then may we women read such of their workes as they dedicate unto us, and if we may read them, why not farther wade in them to search of a truth. And then much more why not deale by translation in such arguments, especially this kind of exercise, being a matter of more heede then of deep invention or exquisite learning.[9]

Tyler's stress on the secondary nature of translation *vis-à-vis* original writing is especially significant in her attempt at claiming such activity as a safe territory for women.

A century later another 'translatress', Aphra Behn (1640–89), no longer felt compelled to emphasize the marginal status of translation.[10] On the contrary, the preface to her version from the French of Bernard le Bovier de Fontenelle's *Entretiens Sur La Pluralité des Mondes* is confidently entitled 'Essay on Translated Prose', and boldly compared to the essay by the Earl of Roscommon on the translation of poetry.[11]

In the seventeenth century translation was a prestigious activity in England: this is confirmed by the fact that leading literary figures of the time,

---

[8] As Krontikis points out, Tyler's work helped to establish the practice of translating romance directly from the original language and made this genre popular in England (p. 45).

[9] *First Feminists: British Women Writers 1578–1799*, ed. by Moira Ferguson (Bloomington: Indiana University Press, 1985), p. 56.

[10] Behn wanted to make explicit the gender of the translator by defining herself as 'translatress'. In her translation of Abraham Cowley's *Six Books of Plants* (1689), Book VI, she inserted a passage, marked by an annotation on the margin: 'the translatress in her own person speaks'. The passage refers to the subject of female authorship: Behn addresses the laurel with the following words:

> I by a double right thy Bounties claim,
> Both from my Sex, and in *Apollo*'s Name:
> Let me with *Sappho* and *Orinda* be
> Oh ever sacred Nymph, adorn'd by thee;
> And give my Verses Immortality.

See Elizabeth Spearing, 'Aphra Behn: the Politics of Translation', in *Aphra Behn Studies*, ed. by Janet Todd (Cambridge, Cambridge University Press, 1996), pp. 154–77 (p. 174).

[11] *The Discovery of New Worlds* (1688), repr. in *Histories, Novels and Translations, Written by the most Ingenious Mrs BEHN* (1700).

such as John Dryden, devoted a large part of their time to this activity. Furthermore, this period saw the publication of influential commentaries on the theoretical aspects of translation: Dryden's preface to *Ovid's Epistles* appeared in 1680 and the Earl of Roscommon's *Essay on Translated Verse* in 1685. As Simon points out, the translation of texts from antiquity was considered as a necessary complement to original literary production: 'The overlapping literary functions of translation and creative writing result from the neo-classical valorization of the arts of imitation' (p. 53). However, women did not derive much benefit from such an improved consideration of translation: the prestigious versions from Latin and Greek were still a male-dominated area because women did not usually have access to classical languages. In fact women's efforts were confined to translation from contemporary European languages, especially French, German, and Italian. Therefore, female translation was still held captive by the laws of genre and gender in the late seventeenth century.

Aphra Behn's translation of Fontenelle is unusual for her time because it deals with the subject of empirical science, or natural philosophy as it was known at the time, which was still taboo for the female sex.[12] The French original presented itself as a simplified version of the Copernican system, consisting of dialogues between a male philosopher and a marchioness.

Unaccustomed as she was to the conventional topos of modesty frequently used by women writers, Behn does apologize for her scant familiarity with scientific subjects in this case. In her dedication to the Earl of Drumlangrig she begs pardon for her work's lack of accuracy: 'If it is not done with that exactness it merits, I hope your Lordship will pardon it in a *Woman*, who is not supposed to be well versed in the Terms of Philosophy, being but a new beginner in that Science.'[13]

In her preface, Behn explains the reasons which brought her to select Fontenelle's text for translation. Market considerations are given a primary role: *Entretiens* had been successfully received both in its country of origin and in England in the original version and furthermore the reputation of the author was perceived as a guarantee for this literary enterprise. Yet other aspects of the French text which had attracted her interest are especially significant, as they allow us a glimpse into Behn's early feminist view of literature. She points out that Fontenelle's use of French in his treatise was a daring novelty at a time when Latin was still the dominant language for science. Obviously French was more accessible than Latin to female readers. Moreover, and even more unusually, Fontenelle had introduced a woman as one of the central characters of his dialogues. As Simon points out, Behn

[12] The Duchess of Newcastle, one of the few women amateurs who dared to publish her poems on scientific subjects, was ridiculed for her unusual interest in science in Thomas Wright's play *Female Vertuoso's* (1693). See Todd, *Angellica*, pp. 24–25.
[13] Aphra Behn, 'Essay on Translated Prose', *A Discovery of New Worlds*, in *The Works of Aphra Behn*, ed. by Janet Todd, 6 vols (London: Pickering and Chatto, 1993), IV, 73–86 (p. 72).

seems to be echoing the argument of her predecessor Tyler when she claims that 'an English Woman might adventure to translate any thing, a French Woman may be supposed to have spoken' (p. 73). The fact that a female character had been introduced into a male writer's text seems to become an invitation for Behn to voice her identity as a woman translator.

By stressing the novelty factor in Fontenelle's text, Behn manages to draw attention to the stumbling blocks against women's involvement in literature, either as consumers or producers. Not only does translation offer her the opportunity to contribute to the dissemination of progressive ideas, but it also helps her to participate in the discussion on subjects such as science and philosophy to which she was denied access as a female writer. For example, Fontenelle's translation gave Behn the chance to comment upon the theoretical aspects of translation and enter into the seventeenth-century debate on the nature of language.

She argues that French and English are extremely different languages and therefore it is particularly difficult to translate from one into the other. This was not the case with English and Italian, for example, because she claims that both of them were directly derived from Latin. Nowadays it seems hardly possible to draw a distinction of this kind between two Romance languages such as Italian and French; Behn was probably influenced on this issue by the strong anti-French prejudices of her age. In spite of the fact that some of her linguistic notions are evidently inaccurate, the translator's interest in the non-symmetrical nature of languages seems to provide a scholarly basis for the discussion of her work.[14] Her main insight concerns the 'Genius' of the Nation, a concept to be developed by Romantic aesthetics more than a century later. Behn points out that 'the nearer the Genious and Humour of two Nations agree, the Idioms of their Speech are the nearer' (p. 74), thus revealing a precocious perception of the phenomena of translation as culturally-determined, rather than purely linguistic.

Behn's understanding of the complex cultural aspect of translation is manifested also by her attention to the different rhetorical conventions in English and French. She claims that French, unlike English, is characterized by a large use of 'Repetitions and Tautologies' (p. 76), whose main effect is that of generating confusion. Yet she does not advocate a strategy of naturalization which would obliterate the peculiar nature of the text. Instead, she suggests a way between the two extremes of literal and free translation, a practice similar to Dryden's balanced 'paraphrase', which aims at the faithful reproduction of the sense and 'character' of the original.[15] However, unlike Dryden, whose translation thinking was mainly grounded

---

[14] On this subject, see Simon, p. 57.
[15] In his preface to *Ovid's Epistles* (1680) Dryden had described the activity of translation by using three well-known categories: metaphrase (word for word translation), paraphrase (sense for sense translation), and imitation (the translator could alter the original to make it conform to the target-culture conventions). Extracts of Dryden's preface have been reprinted in André Lefevere, *Translation/History/Culture: A Sourcebook* (London, Routledge, 1992), pp. 102–05.

on purely linguistic notions, Behn's strategies were based upon an early perception of cultural identity, as clearly appears from her statements concerning the translation of the peculiarly elaborate French style:

If one endeavours to make it *English* Standard, it is no Translation. If one follows their Flourishes and Embroideries, it is worse than *French* Tinsel. But these defects are only comparatively, in respect of *English*: and I do not say this so much, to condemn the *French*, as to praise our own Mother-Tongue, for what we think a Deformity, they may think a Perfection. (p. 76)

In the final part of her essay, Behn concentrates on a detailed criticism of Fontenelle's text. The main objection she raises to the French work is that it lacks coherence. She acknowledges the importance of Fontenelle's efforts to make scientific subjects more accessible to a wide readership by using a familiar language in his treatise. The French author is in fact addressing an audience which would not otherwise have partaken of the recent scientific developments. It is precisely for this purpose that the marchioness is introduced as one of the central characters: the French text is addressed to a category of readers traditionally deprived of the benefits of education, who could be properly represented by the metaphor of women's cultural exclusion. The marchioness herself embodies the ideal readers of the text: like them, she lacks even the basic notions of science.

Reflecting upon the impact his text was going to have on female readers, Fontenelle asked himself whether his portrait of a fictitious female character could encourage real women to undertake the study of philosophy:

In this Discourse I have introduced a fair Lady to be instructed in Philosophy, which, till now, never heard any speak of it; imagining, by this Fiction, I shall render my Work more agreeable, and to encourage the fair Sex [. . .] by the Example of a Lady who had no supernatural Character, and who never goes beyond the Bounds of a Person who has no Tincture of Learning, and yet understands all that is told her, and retains all the notions of *Tourbillions* and Worlds, without Confusion: And why should this imaginary Lady have the Precedency of all the rest of her delicate Sex? Or do they believe they are not as capable as conceiving that which she learned with so much Facility?[16]

However, the exploitative use of the image of woman, who is merely a symbol of the wider dissemination of science advocated by the author, is clearly perceived by Behn. She points out that Fontenelle is pushing his argument too far: by aiming to entertain his readers as well as to instruct them, he creates an excessively colloquial style which threatens to make his subject sound ridiculous. Furthermore, the character of his marchioness is not convincing: 'He makes her say a great many very silly things, tho' sometimes she makes Observations so learned, that the greatest Philosophers in Europe could make no better' (p. 77).

---

[16] 'The Author's Preface', in Todd, *Works of Aphra Behn*, pp. 87–91 (pp. 88–89).

Behn's translation of Fontenelle is extremely literal, as Behn herself makes clear in her preface.[17] She limits her interventions into the text to the few announced in her preface. The most significant is the correction of a mistake made by the author, who had pronounced the depth of the atmosphere of the Earth to be twenty or thirty leagues, rather than two or three, as the translator points out on the basis of authority of philosophers such as Descartes and Rohalt. The intention to respect the character of the original is reaffirmed in the very last lines of her preface, in which she points out the difference between the art of imitation and that of translation, which were often treated as interchangeable in the seventeenth century. Behn announces to her readers that what she is providing them with is a translation: 'And I resolv'd either to give you the *French* Book into *English*, or to give you the subject quite changed and made my own; but having neither health nor leisure for the last I offer you the first such as it is' (p. 86).

Behn's success as the first professional woman writer marked a significant stage in the development of a female literary tradition. Her desire for a large readership and her reflections on the position of women in her society were bound to exert a strong influence on her successors. From the late seventeenth century onwards women began to acquire a commercial as well as a literary role, and consequently gained a new visibility. Yet Jeslyn Medoff speaks of an 'Inglorious Revolution' for women writers in her analysis of the complex changes affecting their works between the end of the seventeenth century and the beginning of the eighteenth.[18] Such a definition applies to the complex transformations occurring after Behn's death. Medoff highlights the consequences of this event on other female writers:

Women writers who followed in her wake would have to make conscious decisions about accepting, rejecting or refashioning her precedents, not only in style and subject matter but in the personae of their writings, in the personae they, as authors, would assume in public (in formal letters, prefaces, dedications and the like), and in the way they tried to control their reputations as women, which were essentially inseparable from their reputations as writers. (pp. 34–35)

The process of reassessment of Behn's literary legacy started as early as the beginning of the eighteenth century. After her death in 1689 her reputation declined rapidly and at the turn of the century her career was a notorious example used in order to intimidate, rather than encourage prospective women writers. The most evident case was that of Dryden, who, after having praised Behn's translation of Ovid's 'Oenone to Paris' in 1680, turned abruptly against her, defining both her conduct and her writing as immoral twenty years later.[19]

---

[17] She points out that she has 'translated the Book near the Words of the Author' (p. 86).
[18] 'The Daughters of Behn', in *Women, Writing, History*, ed. by Isobel Grundy and Susan Wiseman (London: Batsford, 1992), pp. 33–54 (p. 33).
[19] Medoff quotes Dryden's letter to the young poet Elizabeth Thomas, written shortly before his death in 1700. He writes: 'Avoid [. . .] the Licenses which Mrs Behn allowed her self, of writing loosely, and giving (if I may have leave to say so) some Scandal to the Modesty of her Sex' (p. 33).

Such a rapid decline in the reputation of Behn was the effect of a complex redefinition of writing which was taking place at various levels in the post-Restoration period. Jane Spencer has called attention to the new emphasis on three terms in early-eighteenth-century literature, 'nature, morality and modesty', a concern which will increase later on in the century, during the 'age of sensibility'.[20] A parallel between literature and femininity started to emerge soon after Behn's death. The notion of woman's special nature gradually took over from the Aristotelian hierarchical vision (which saw women as similar in kind but inferior in degree to men) by positing an essential difference between the two sexes. The nineteenth century was to conceive the theory of the two separate spheres, the public and the private domains respectively, for the two sexes. In the meantime, in the eighteenth century the already mentioned conflation between literature and femininity helped to define the former as separated from the public, political field. Spencer points out that consequently literature was supposed to exert only an indirect influence on the world, in much the same way as women were assumed to do (p. xi). Literature became gradually detached from social life and transformed into a kind of fetish, in a process which appeared to match the deep transformation of women's status. Terry Eagleton argues that the emergence of individualism and the growth of Protestant ideology — the hallmarks of an unfolding middle class — encouraged a new 'turn to the subject' and an introspective attitude which appeared to resemble traditional feminine qualities.[21] As a result, women acquired a more prominent position in the literary field in the course of the eighteenth century. However, female ventures into the public sphere had to be negotiated on new and more restrictive terms. Women's writing was gradually confined to the representation of certain themes, which were essentially restricted to the realm of privacy. As Spencer points out, women's literary success went hand in hand with the suppression of many forms of feminist opposition (p. xi).

According to Ballaster, two diametrically opposed feminine traditions were confronting each other at the beginning of the eighteenth century:

The early eighteenth century, then, saw a split between female-authored pious and didactic love fiction, stressing the virtues of chastity and sentimental marriage, and erotic fiction by women, with its voyeuristic attention to the combined pleasures and ravages of seduction. (p. 33)

Ballaster argues that the new moral tone in literature is best represented by the fiction of women writers such as Elizabeth Rowe (1674–1737), Penelope Aubin (1679–1731), and Jane Barker (1688–1726). At first sight arranging these writers into a unique and homogeneous tradition might appear problematic, as they were neither strictly contemporary nor did they produce works belonging to the same genres. Yet the thin but concrete thread which

---

[20] *The Rise of the Woman Novelist: From Aphra Behn to Jane Austen* (Oxford: Blackwell, 1986), p. 77.
[21] Terry Eagleton, *The Rape of Clarissa: Writing, Sexuality and Class Struggle in Samuel Richardson* (Oxford: Blackwell, 1982), pp. 13–17.

unites them is clearly visible in both the overly didactic tone of their prose and the care they took in maintaining an unblemished reputation. In the early eighteenth century women writers turned definitely away from the discredited image of Behn and took inspiration from the life and work of Elizabeth Rowe.[22]

The poet and translator Elizabeth Carter (1717–1806) was one of Rowe's symbolic daughters. A revised version of her poem 'On the Death of Mrs Rowe' (1737) was prefixed to the edition of the *Miscellaneous Works* of Rowe.[23] Carter celebrates her as a champion of her sex, the moral woman poet whose works and reputation eventually came to rescue women's poetical efforts from the dominating influence of her unprincipled predecessors. Women writing before Rowe had misused the gifts they had received from their Muse by producing a corrupted kind of art. Female poetry finds its true vocation only after the appearance of Rowe on the literary scene:

> The Muse, for vices not her own accus'd,
> With blushes view'd her sacred gifts abus'd;
> Those gifts for nobler purposes assign'd,
> To raise the thoughts, and moralize the mind[24].

With her emphasis on religious experience, Rowe represented a kind of role-model for the younger Carter, who was ready to accept the restrictive principles of modest femininity embodied by her predecessor. In the final lines of her poem, Carter expresses her desire to follow Rowe in developing an unfolding tradition of 'moral' poetry by women:

> Fixt on my soul shall thy example grow,
> And be my genius and my guide below;
> To this I'll point my first, my noblest views,
> Thy spotless verse shall regulate my Muse. (p. 152)

In 1738 Edward Cave, publisher of the well-known periodical the *Gentleman's Magazine*, commissioned Carter to translate a text by Francesco Algarotti, which appeared in Italian in 1737 under the title *Il Newtonianismo per le dame: ovvero Dialoghi sopra la luce e il colore*.[25] This text had met with an enormous success in Italy, where it was printed in four editions and translated into three languages during the author's lifetime. According to Rupert Hall, *Il Newtonianismo* eventually went through thirty-one editions

---

[22] Rowe seems best to represent the eighteenth-century ideals of feminine and literary virtue. After the untimely death of her husband, she retired to a life of perfect solitude. Her literary production is characterized by a strong religious vein, particularly her epistolary work *Friendship in Death, or Letters from the Dead to the Living* (1728).

[23] The earliest version of this poem had appeared in the pages of the *Gentleman's Magazine*, 8 (April 1737). The revised version was also printed in the same periodical two years later.

[24] Elizabeth Carter, 'On the Death of Mrs Rowe', *Gentleman's Magazine*, 8 (March 1739), 152.

[25] Algarotti was a member of the Venetian nobility and his interest in Newton's philosophy had brought him in touch with fellows of the Royal Society in Rome, such as Martin Folkes who had encouraged him to complete his work. In 1734, during the first of his visits to London, he was himself elected member of the Royal Society, and it was probably on that occasion that he met Thomas Birch, one of the commissioners of Carter's translation.

and was translated into English, French, German, Dutch, Swedish, and Portuguese.[26] The first edition was dedicated to Fontenelle, from whom the Italian author had borrowed the structure of the text, which consisted of a series of dialogues between a male philosopher and a lady. In this case the purpose of the text was to popularize Newton's scientific discoveries, particularly in the field of optics.

Between 1738 and 1739 Carter worked on the translation of the Italian text, which was published in May 1739. The name of the translator was not printed in the frontispiece, and she did not write any preface to her work. However, she was widely known to have been responsible for the English text. In June the *Gentleman's Magazine* published a poem dedicated to 'Miss Carter', praising her translation of Algarotti. The work was acclaimed as a significant novelty, a simplified version of Newton's philosophy which offered women a palatable version of science:

> Now may the *British* fair, with *Newton*, soar
> To worlds remote, and range all nature o'er;
> Of motion learn the late discover'd cause,
> and beauteous fitness of its settled laws.[27]

The role of the translator was emphasized as she was considered responsible for making science accessible to her countrywomen. In a way, translator and original author were seen as one and the same person, joined by their common intention of furthering women's education.

Thomas Birch, a friend of Carter and one of the principal patrons of the work, also drew attention to the combination of two elements: the essay's targeting of a female public and the fact that the translation had been produced by a woman. In his long review of the translation published in the *History of the Works of the Learned* he wrote:

The *English* Translation has this remarkable Circumstance to recommend it to the Curiosity of the Public, as the Excellence of it will to the Approbation of all good Judges, that as the Work itself is design'd for the Use of the Ladies, it is now render'd into our Language, and illustrated with several curious Notes, by a young Lady, Daughter of Dr *Nicholas Carter*, of *Deal* in Kent.[28]

A few months after the publication of the translation, Carter sent a copy of it to Mrs Rowe's brother, Theophilus Rowe.[29] In a letter to the translator,

---

[26] Rupert Hall, 'La matematica, Newton, e la letteratura' in *Scienza e letteratura nella cultura italiana del Settecento*, ed by Renzo Cremante and Walter Tega (Bologna: Mulino, 1984), pp. 29–46 (p. 37). The remarkable fame of this work is linked with the peculiar circumstances of its reception in Italy: it was included in the *Index librorum prohibitorum* by the ecclesiastical authorities in Rome in 1739. It is reasonable to assume that news about this ban would have aroused the curiosity of the English public, generally hostile to Catholic opinion in that period. Yet no mention of this fact has been found in any of the responses to Carter's translation, including reviews in the literary periodicals of the time.
[27] J. Swan, 'To Miss Carter: On her translation of Sir ISAAC NEWTON'S Philosophy Explain'd for the Use of the Ladies, from the Italian of SIG. ALGAROTTI', *Gentleman's Magazine*, 9 (June 1739), 322.
[28] Thomas Birch, 'Article XXXI', *The History of the Works of the Learned*, (June 1739), pp. 391–408 (pp. 393–94).
[29] For an account of this circumstance see Montagu Pennington's *Memoirs of the Life of Mrs Elizabeth Carter* (London, 1807), pp. 46–47.

Rowe praised her work and highlighted the bond uniting translator and reader when they are of the same sex. Rowe considered this as a sure basis for a powerful and beneficial influence on female readers. Moreover, the translator was admired not only for the accuracy of her work, but also for her personal qualities: her grace and lightness of touch made her a model women should follow in order to achieve moral and intellectual improvement:

The public, and particularly the fair sex, are inexpressibly indebted to the translator, and will, I am persuaded, be sensible of their obligations. [. . .] I hope, Madam, the example you give, with how much grace and ease, wisdom and philosophy sit on a Lady, even in the bloom of youth and beauty, will allow your own charming part of the creation to imitate, as well as to admire you. (pp. 46–47)

The reasons inducing Cave to commission the translation of *Il Newtonianismo* are not immediately clear. Although scientific subjects were in great demand in the early popular press, translating a simplified version of Newton's *Optics*, which had already attracted a great deal of comment in England, might at first sight appear strange. Algarotti's appeal to a female audience and his apparent resolution to improve women's education seem to be the most plausible explanations for Cave's interest. However, a careful reading of *Il Newtonianismo* reveals that its appeal to ladies was in fact only a formal, decorative element in the structure of the work. It is not clear whether Cave (or Birch, who was in touch with the original author) clearly understood the extent of Algarotti's actual commitment to the improvement of female education. But even more intriguing questions are raised by the exceptional success of Carter's translation, which was published in four editions in the eighteenth century.[30]

In spite of the fact that handbooks for women touched upon many subjects in this period, from health to literature and from art to economics, they carefully avoided scientific areas. Thus, an introduction to the system of thought of the most celebrated among English philosophers, in a text specifically addressed to a female readership, was bound to be perceived as a radical novelty in England in the mid-eighteenth century.

To return to the Italian original, it would be simplistic to present the strong impact of *Il Newtonianismo* on Italian culture, confirmed by its many reprints, as the mere effect of a successful popularization of scientific discoveries. Over and above this, the dissemination of scientific ideas became a pretext for the author to denounce the stagnant nature of the Italian society of the period. The experimental method perfected by Newton was, according to Algarotti, the final result of a socio-cultural revolution set in motion by the English school of philosophy, which he considered highly innovative in comparison with the scholastic, authoritative tradition still reigning in Italy at the time. The liberating effects of the empirical tradition, which had

---

[30] Carter's translation was reprinted in 1742, 1765, and 1772 with the following titles respectively: *Sir Isaac Newton's Theory of Light and Colours*, 2 vols (London, 1742), *The Philosophy of Sir Isaac Newton.* (Glasgow, 1765), and *The Lady's Philosophy: or Sir Isaac Newton's Theory of Light and Colours* (London, 1772).

bestowed on the individual the key to knowledge, was readily acknowledged by Algarotti, who aimed at transposing the scientific revolution brought about by Newton's theories to the social field. Algarotti points out that the most radical effect of the new English epistemology could be observed in its application to the field of politics: the extraordinary result of this was a form of government which was not the product of abstract speculation, but rather a combination between the material needs of the people and the authority of the ruling classes.[31]

The style and language of Algarotti's essay cannot be considered in isolation from its reformist purpose. The author's resolution to write a scientific treatise in Italian (or, rather, in what was still in the process of becoming a national language) must have been perceived as a daring innovation. Such an undertaking was also a precise indication of the fact that the author was trying to appeal to a readership far wider than the circle of cultivated readers who could read Newton's work in its original language. Algarotti was in fact addressing an extended audience, which was not supposed to be familiar even with the basic notions of science. The function of his appeal to a female public was precisely the same as Fontelle's some fifty years before: women were used as a kind of rhetorical device to represent the cultural exclusion of the ideal readers. And the style of the essay had to be adapted to their needs: a female readership could justify the elaborate literary style employed by the author, who aims at entertaining his readers as well as instructing them. To this end, Algarotti had to make the language of science less abstract by inserting images and 'figures of speech':

The abstruse Points, upon which I have been obliged to treat, were only such as are absolutely necessary, and always interspersed with something that may relieve the Mind from that Attention which they require. In the most delightful Walk we are sometimes glad to find a verdant Turf to repose ourselves upon. Lines and mathematical Figures are entirely excluded, as they would have given these Discourses too scientific an Air. (p. vi)

Il Newtonianismo was in fact far from recommended to a female readership. Algarotti's gallant style becomes at times rich in erotic allusions, which appear to create a masculine discourse relegating woman to her traditional position as object.

Carter's translation was to smooth down precisely these sexist ambiguities. If the appeal to female readers had to be taken literally, then a faithful translation of Algarotti's erotic language became impossible. The two principal strategies employed by the translator will be broadly defined as gender-induced and culture-induced manipulations. In order to transform *Il*

[31] See this example taken from Carter's translation of Algarotti: 'Not to say any Thing further of Natural Philosophy, which seems a Province the most adapted to the Discoveries of Observations, is not Politics indebted to these for that wise and real Government, which renders the Southern Suns less pleasing than the Cloudy Regions of the North, where the Liberty of the People is made compatible with the Superiority of the Nobles, and the Authority of the Sovereign?' (Francesco Algarotti, *Sir Isaac Newton's Philosophy Explain'd for the Use of the Ladies*, 2 vols (London, 1739), II, 17).

Newtonianismo into a handbook for women, radical changes had to be made: not only had Algarotti's peculiar misogynist traits to be omitted, but also his social reforming purpose had to be revised.

Carter's principal strategy was to modify the original author's representation of the female body. Eighteenth-century translation norms were of substantial aid to her in this case, as they prescribed that the notions of grace and delicacy must always prevail, even at the cost of betraying the original text.[32] Therefore, the translator did not have to worry if her compliance with the rigid codes of femininity of her time compelled her to neglect some aspects of the original. On the contrary, her strategy had the convenient effect of rendering the appeal to a female public more plausible than it was in Algarotti's text. Thus, Carter systematically omitted all the libertine images employed by the Italian author, the best example of this being Algarotti's description of semen in a passage referring to the minute worlds discovered after the invention of the microscope, which is simply eliminated in the translation.

Carter also avoided translating those gallantries of Algarotti's which, exceeding their limits, became eroticism of a clearly misogynist nature. For example, she left out the original author's *double entendre* in the passage in which he explains the phenomenon of the refraction of light by using the image of the Marchioness in her bathroom. Paradoxically, her version seems to acquire greater scientific rigour when set against the original:

Ecco una cosa, m'interrupp'ella, che io non a molto, essendo nel bagno, osservai attentamente, che mi sorprese, e di cui m'inquietava la ragione. Altro ella non è, soggiuns'io, che la rifrazione che soffrono i raggi passando dall'acqua nell'aria. Egli sarebbe una buona cosa lo spiegarvene minutamente gli effetti, e gli scherzi sul margine del vostro bagno. Sapete voi quanti curiosi d'Ottica fareste?[33]

This is the very Thing, said she, interrupting me, that I lately observed when I was in the Bath, and I was extremely surprised and puzzled to find out the Reason of it. It is nothing else, answered I, but the Refraction which the Rays suffer in passing from Air into Water.[34]

Another kind of textual intervention was also necessary, in order to turn a radically political text into a popularization of scientific topics specifically addressed to women: the original text's longings for socio-political change

---

[32] This practice was justified by Alexander Fraser Tytler in his *Essays on the Principles of Translation* (1791), when he claimed that suppression was allowed when the original text displayed concepts or images which went against contemporary notions of decorum. For example see the following passage: 'If a translator is bound, in general, to adhere with fidelity to the matters of the age and country to which his original belongs, there are some instances in which he will find it necessary to make a slight sacrifice to the manners of his modern readers. The ancients, in the expression of resentment or contempt, made use of many epithets and appellations which sound extremely shocking to our more polished ears' *Essays on the Principles of Translation*, ed. by J. F. Huntsman (Amsterdam: Benjamins, 1978), p. 271.

[33] Algarotti, *Il Newtonianismo*, p. 118.

[34] Algarotti, *Sir Isaac Newton's*, I, 119. Carter eliminates the following statements: "Twere a good thing to explain to you all the effects minutely on the rim of your bath. Do you know how much curiosity about Optics this would arouse?' [my translation].

were systematically eliminated in the English translation. Unlike gender-induced manipulation, the translator's alterations of the socio-cultural aspects of Algarotti's text do not seem to be the result of a deliberate strategy. Some of them appear rather to be the effect of Carter's lack of familiarity with the socio-historical conditions of the geographical area known as 'Italy' in those days. This becomes especially clear when Carter translates a passage in which Algarotti denounces the backward state of Italian culture in comparison with contemporary European dynamism. The intellectual ferment of the age of Enlightenment had not reached his country yet, but the author was looking forward to a more widespread circulation of ideas, which would soon put an end to this state of affairs. He hoped that the new knowledge of the 'Age of Realities' would eventually come to improve the social condition of Italian people. When Carter translates Algarotti's wish that the Enlightenment will eventually arrive 'una volta anco per noi' (literally meaning 'for us too, at last) as 'once more', she certainly demonstrates scant familiarity with the Italian language, but what is especially interesting here is that her version is diametrically opposed to Algarotti's principal argument, according to which the new ideas had not reached Italy yet. Here is the passage in Italian and then in translation:

Il Secolo delle cose vegna una volta anco per noi, e il sapere non ad irruvidir l'animo, o a piatire sopra una vecchia e disusata frase, ma a pulir serva, se è possibile, e ad abbellir la Società (p. xi)

Let the Age of Realities once more arise among us, and Knowledge instead of giving a rude and savage Turn to the Mind, and exciting endless Disputes and wrangling upon some obsolete Phrase, serve to polish and adorn Society. (1, xvi)

Although on a purely linguistic level Carter's version looks extremely literal, her translation strategies deeply altered the principal characteristics of the Italian text and deprived it of its reforming tension, which belonged with its socio-cultural setting. As a result, the translation became extremely different from its original.

Unlike Behn's translation at the end of the seventeenth century, Carter's work did not offer her any opportunity to express her gendered voice, nor did it appear to help her to develop a deep awareness of the theoretical aspects of translation. Rather, the English version of *Il Newtonianismo* seems to be primarily the product of commercial interests, which effectively transformed a radically political treatise into a manual for the education of women, one of the many handbooks which reached great popularity at the beginning of the eighteenth century. In order to ensure the success of the text, the image of the female translator was exploited by reviewers and critics. Carter was made to represent the readership to which the target text was addressed: in the eyes of the public she was the first woman to experience those benefits which Algarotti's text had made available to the female sex.

However, in the long run such a manipulative use of the female image paradoxically helped Carter to develop her own means of self-expression. Thanks to her friendship with other women, Carter established connections with influential public figures, who in turn helped her to publish her translation from the Greek of *All the Works of Epictetus* in 1758.[35] This time Carter not only put her name to her work, but also wrote a long introduction, in which she described her difficult task in giving new life to a culture which no longer existed. This work brought her extraordinary fame and social prestige, and as a celebrated learned woman she provided a role model for many young women in the eighteenth century.

These few examples of women's translation activity should serve to illustrate that the history of translation, like literary history, is not progressive. Behn's outspoken voice as a woman translator remained a solitary example for many years. Yet, even when historical circumstances and ideologies appeared to be particularly unpropitious for female self-expression, women's voices were not totally suppressed. As we have seen, even Carter's apparent compliance with the new ideology of femininity of the eighteenth century bore its fruits for the unfolding of a tradition of women translators. The linear development of history often gives place to the discontinuous but vibrant thread of genealogy when women's production is taken into account.

[35] In the 1740s Carter started a lifelong correspondence with her friend Catherine Talbot, who lived with the family of the Bishop of Oxford, Thomas Secker. In 1748 Talbot asked Carter to translate Epictetus's works for her personal use. Talbot soon decided to inform the Bishop of this project and he began to read and comment on the translation, which was eventually published in 1758. See Pennington, especially pp. 108–43.

The 'Words I in fancy say for you': Sarah Fielding's Letters and Epistolary Method

MIKA SUZUKI

Nihon University, Japan

As letter writing became increasingly fashionable, an awareness of literary values in letters cultivated suspicion about sincerity in epistolary discourse in the eighteenth century.[1] Samuel Johnson (1709–84), while emphasizing that 'in a Man's Letters [. . .] his soul lies naked', cast doubt on the sincerity of other people's letters.[2] He shrewdly detects the manipulative powers of published 'genuine' letters which take advantage of the reader's supposition that private letters reveal 'true' aspects of the self otherwise unknown. He maintains that 'there is, indeed, no transaction which offers stronger temptations to fallacy and sophistication than epistolary intercourse' and reads Pope's letters cautiously:

it must be remembered that he had the power of favouring himself: he might have originally had publication in his mind, and have written with care, or have afterwards selected those which he had most happily conceived, or most diligently laboured.[3]

Johnson's suspicion is placed on Pope's use of letters as a means of manipulating his self-image. He perceives letters not so much as a firsthand straightforward revelation of a private self as a representation of it, the degree of sincerity or manipulation of which depends on the writer's personality.

Johnson's insight about the potential gap between the assumption of undisguised self and the constructed self in letters can be extended and applied to 'femininity' in epistolary discourse. The eminent success of *Pamela*, *Clarissa*, and the subsequent vogue of the epistolary novel emphasizes the epistolary form as a quintessentially feminine genre in the eighteenth century, not least because Samuel Richardson's (1689–1761) virtuous

I wish to thank the Japan Society for the Promotion of Sciences for providing funding (1995–97) to undertake the research upon which this paper is based. Grant-in-Aid for Scientific Research by the Ministry of Education has facilitated the research. I am grateful to Isobel Grundy, Chris Read, Warren Chernaik, and the members of Women's Studies Group, London, for their comments and suggestions.

[1] For the vogue of letter writing see, for example, John Butt and Geoffrey Carnall, *The Age of Johnson: 1740–1789* (Oxford: Clarendon Press, 1979), pp. 326–45; *The Familiar Letter in the Eighteenth Century*, ed. by Howard Anderson and others (Lawrence: University of Kansas Press, 1966), pp. 269–82; Bruce Redford, *The Converse of the Pen: Acts of Intimacy in the Eighteenth-Century Familiar Letter* (Chicago and London: University of Chicago Press, 1986).

[2] *The Letters of Samuel Johnson*, ed. by Bruce Redford, 5 vols (Oxford: Clarendon Press, 1992), III, 89.

[3] Samuel Johnson, *Lives of the English Poets*, ed. by George Birkbeck Hill, 3 vols (Oxford: Clarendon Press, 1905), III, 207, 159.

heroines scribble privately and he was welcomed by enthusiastic responses especially from women. In this context, this form is regarded as a very important medium in which women could express themselves, and writers exploited this convenience of a supposedly private and feminine vehicle for entry to the public sphere of publication.[4] In this progress of the epistolary form, women's affinity for an emotional and seemingly artless kind of epistolary writing became a stereotype.[5]

Importantly, epistolary writing is not only the literary form through which the female voice can find a means of expression, but also it can be a particularly convenient instrument for the construction of femininity, as the male-authored examples of Pamela and Clarissa suggest.[6] Recently the 'temptations to fallacy' in epistolary writing have been discussed and reconsidered in terms of women and the representation of women in it.[7]

Linda S. Kauffman proposes a scrutiny of these presuppositions in examining epistolary discourses by focusing on amorous epistles. Underscoring that epistolary texts subvert conventional dichotomies by combining apparent opposites: for example, discourse and narrative, spontaneity and calculation, or feminine and masculine, she maintains that the writing women in her analysis perform a challenge to the traditional concepts of representation of women (pp. 20–27). As a result, she throws doubt on various dichotomized assumptions about women and 'feminine' writing, for example, the concept of women's writing as 'natural' and 'spontaneous'. As she points out, a danger in examining women's epistolary writing is 'reducing the art to the life, as if women were incapable of writing about anything but

---

[4] See Christine Mary Salmon, 'Representations of the Female Self in Familiar Letters 1650–1780' (unpublished doctoral thesis, University of London, 1991), p. 7; introduction to *Writing the Female Voice: Essays on Epistolary Literature*, ed. by Elizabeth C. Goldsmith (London: Pinter, 1989), p. vii; Mary A. Favret, *Romantic Correspondence: Women, Politics and Fiction of Letters* (Cambridge: Cambridge University Press, 1993), pp. 1–7, 12–13. Favret starts her argument on how women writers used the letter form to acquire a public voice by analysing the ambivalent forces of epistles in terms of individualism: the epistolary writing offers a space to express the individual's intimate self while it allows the expressed privacy to become the property of public debate.

[5] See, for example, Elizabeth C. Goldsmith, 'Authority, Authenticity, and the Publication of Letters by Women', in *Writing the Female Voice*, pp. 46–59 (p. 46); Elizabeth J. MacArthur, 'Devious Narratives: Refusal of Closure in Two Eighteenth-Century Epistolary Novels', *Eighteenth-Century Studies*, 21 (1987–88), 1–20; Ruth Perry, *Women, Letters, and the Novel* (New York: AMS Press, 1980), pp. ix, x, 68–70.

[6] Among others, a display of femininity in *The Portuguese Letters* has become a major focus in discussion of the construction of 'feminine' voice in epistolary writing. See Linda S. Kauffman, *Discourses of Desire: Gender, Genre, and Epistolary Fictions* (Ithaca, NY, and London: Cornell University Press, 1986), pp. 91–118; Katharine A. Jensen, 'Male Models of Feminine Epistolarity; or, How to Write Like a Woman in Seventeenth-Century France', in *Writing the Female Voice*, pp. 25–45; Goldsmith, 'Authority, Authenticity, and the Publication of Letters by Women'. The authorship of *Les lettres Portugaises* is not certain, but there is a provisional agreement that it was written not by a woman but by a Frenchman, Gabriel-Joseph de Lavergne de Guilleragues. See the introduction to *Les lettres Portugaises* in *The Novel in Letters: Epistolary Fiction in the Early English Novel*, ed. by Natascha Würzbach (London: Routledge, 1969), pp. 3–4; Kauffman, pp. 46, 85, 92–93; Jensen, p. 27. Elizabeth J. MacArthur brings into focus the assumptions in dealing with epistles when she examines the way the critics have handled *Les lettres Portugaises* in *Extravagant Narratives: Closure and Dynamics in the Epistolary Form* (Princeton, NJ: Princeton University Press, 1990), pp. 99–116.

[7] Goldsmith, introduction to *Writing the Female Voice*, pp. vii–xiii.

themselves, and lacked aesthetic control and imagination' (p. 21). Katharine A. Jensen also explores the presupposition of the epistolary genre's being 'feminine'. She shows that in seventeenth-century France the representative natural and spontaneous 'feminine' writings were in fact written by male authors and purported to be written by women. She maintains that by emphasizing women's emotional power and social skilfulness as exercised in the salon, men in effect styled women's textual patterns. An oral and ephemeral social art is ascribed to women; the written and especially the printed world is allotted to men. Once this boundary of separate realms was drawn, men invented 'feminine' literary styles and imposed them on women. Her argument is that through this prescription women were excluded from literary art, stylistic and rhetorical dexterity, and that men controlled and narrowed the scope of women's writings, confining them in effect to love letters.[8] In this way the mechanism of construction of 'feminine' letters has been analysed. If the tradition of 'feminine' epistles was thus contrived, works inconsistent with the tradition and the struggles of women against its current are worth reconsideration and reinterpretation.

In fact, the 'feminie' tendencies are more frequently found in epistolary novels than in 'genuine' letters. 'Feminine' fictional epistolary writing must have influenced letter-writing patterns, but other models and values than those found in epistolary fiction were working in women's patterns of letter-writing. There were women such as Elizabeth Carter (1717–1806) and Lady Mary Wortley Montagu (1689–1762), whose engagingly interesting epistolary styles have been distinguished from such constructed 'feminine' manners. As for Elizabeth Carter, C. M. Salmon points out that her image as a virtuous domestic exemplary woman was determined by an early-nineteenth-century publication of *Sketch of the Character of Mrs. Elizabeth Carter*. Instead of the saintly restraints of a dutiful woman, she finds in Carter's letters a more vivacious, comic, and wild spirit.[9] Concerning Lady Mary, Cynthia Lowenthal underscores the theatrically performed 'artistic power of her "textual tapestry"' in her letters.[10] She points out that because of her aristocratic status, Lady Mary's letters present a conflict of public and private life, rather than the typically 'feminine' emotional private experience (pp. 2–4). Interestingly, she is 'almost altogether resistant both to the standards of female behavior [the novels] advocate and to the values they articulate' (p. 155).

As a well-informed scholarly person, Sarah Fielding (1710–68) had much in common with Lady Mary and Carter. She knew how women were expected to behave and express themselves and did not openly deviate from

---

[8] Jensen, pp. 25–45. Patricia Meyer Spacks argues that Jane Austen's *Lady Susan* is a notable exception, free from the restriction and claiming female mastery of language ('Female Resources: Epistles, Plot, and Power', in *Writing the Female Voice*, pp. 63–76).

[9] Salmon, pp. 60, 182, 262, 267, 269.

[10] Cynthia Lowenthal, *Lady Mary Wortley Montagu and the Eighteenth-Century Familiar Letter* (Athens, GA and London: University of Georgia Press, 1994), p. 1.

such expectations.[11] But still, her epistolary discourse is different from what is understood as a typically 'feminine' outflow of emotions. Like Lady Mary and Carter, her viewpoint is disengaged and analytical. Furthering the reconsideration of the presupposition of 'feminine' familiar letters, I shall examine what she attempts to present in her epistolary discourse, referring to her fictional letters as well as her 'genuine' ones.

Critics have found little to praise in Sarah Fielding's 'genuine' letters. The extant letters are not many in number and they are letters of greeting and gratitude, rather than of intimacy.[12] A letter to Elizabeth Montague (1720–1800) has been referred to as one 'not of sufficient interest for quotation'.[13] Montagu's attention to Sarah Fielding was always very practical, not out of friendly intimacy, but more in the form of charitable benevolence towards an impoverished woman whose literary activities had not brought her sufficient reward.[14] This distance was intensified by Sarah Fielding's reserve. In a letter to Montagu she wrote in justification of her reticence: 'True Love ever hesitates, and is bashful, whilst Hypocrisy steps forward with an assured air, and from its intrepid boldness doubts not the obtaining belief' (*Correspondence*, p. 175). This represents not only her ethical belief but her mode of expression. She resorts to this kind of generalized objective discourse rather than to subjective sentences of personal sentiment.

An overall characteristic of her letters is the absence of a conscious display of personal sentiments. She does not show a willingness to participate in the exchange of private feelings. Rather, intellectual analysis and the discourse of reason keep the letters from being emotional and intimate. She was as deferential in her letters to James Harris (1709–80) as she was to Elizabeth Montagu. When Sarah Fielding wrote with Jane Collier to Harris, the tone of the letter is cautious, dry, and rational. It conveys their thanks to Harris, who sent them a copy of his learned book, *Hermes*. They modestly abstain from commenting on it directly, quoting 'Mr. Pope's observation that "a little Learning is a dang'rous thing" '. Instead they express their gratitude for its helpful effect on them:

turning our studies from the barren Desarts of arbitrary words, into cultivated Plains where amidst the greatest variety we may in every part trace the footsteps of

[11] See Jane Spencer, *The Rise of the Woman Novelist: From Aphra Behn to Jane Austen* (Oxford: Blackwell, 1986), pp. 75–103.
[12] *The Correspondence of Henry and Sarah Fielding*, ed. by Martin C. Battestin and Clive T. Probyn (Oxford: Clarendon Press, 1993), pp. 123–76. An exceptional agitated letter can be found among the letters to Richardson (p. 175). She feels invited to write down the emotional agitation she experienced as a result of reading his work and expresses her reaction in shorter simple clauses. Her expressions fall into the stereotypical 'natural' and 'spontaneous' patterns of women's epistolary style. Richardson offered a fictional model to follow and Sarah Fielding was one who gave him a response complying with his prescription. This is probably an instance of a woman imitating a fictional construction of a supposedly feminine style.
[13] *Mrs. Montagu, 'Queen of the Blues': Her Letters and Friendships from 1762 to 1800*, ed. by Reginald Blunt, 2 vols (London: Constable, [n.d.]), I, 158.
[14] Montagu's care for Sarah Fielding is recorded in the letters between her and Sarah Scott: MO 5292, MO 5821, MO 5829, MO 5832, MO 5834, MO 5319, MO 5856, MO 5872, MO 5879, and MO 5881 (The Montagu Collection, The Huntington Library, San Marino, California).

Reason, and where how much soever we wander, yet with such a guide we may still avoid confusion. (p. 125)[15]

They fashion themselves as students who have acquired discipline by the help of 'kind Instructor' Harris. This modesty seems to consolidate female submission. Not only do they style themselves as students, but also this letter places themselves in the disorder of language, while the role of Harris is to regulate and organize language. They put Harris and themselves in the stereotypical moulds of the male in charge of order and the female as embodiment of disorder.[16]

Nevertheless, this letter underscores a positive characteristic of her epistles behind the humble manner. A significant point here is that Sarah Fielding and Jane Collier do not remain in the region of disorder. They recognize Harris's power to draw them out of that region. Although the instructor–students relationship is a hierarchical one, they transfer themselves to the sphere where Harris is and presides. Thus, with a very careful air of self-restraint, this letter in fact asserts a confidence in their standpoint as conscious agents able to regulate their language. Always respecting Harris as an authority in philology, they show a justifiable pride developed through their studies.

The scarcity of the extant letters and the polite reserve which characterizes most of them prevent Sarah Fielding from being classified as a prominent writer of familiar letters. As we can see from the extant letters, unlike Catherine Talbot (1721–70) and Elizabeth Carter, who enjoyed a mutually beneficial epistolary relationship, she did not have any equals with whom she could freely exchange ideas and enjoy mutual intellectual cultivation. Thus, her situation does not appear to have given her many opportunities to use her epistolary talents in intellectual discourse. How then did she manage them in her fictional world?

Sarah Fielding adopted epistles primarily in her *Familiar Letters*, which was a kind of sequel to her *David Simple*.[17] She may have paid a compliment to Richardson in calling her work *Familiar Letters*, though Richardson's was not

---

[15] Thus Jane Collier and Sarah Fielding thought that they were benefited by *Hermes*, while, in an interesting contrast, Richardson admitted he was not learned enough to reap benefits: 'I pretend not to be Scholar enough (Hence my Grief!) to be benefited by the Learning, with which it abounds' (quoted in Clive T. Probyn, *The Sociable Humanist: The Life and Works of James Harris 1709–1780* (Oxford: Clarendon Press, 1991), pp. 172–73).

[16] For discussion of such stereotypes, see, for example, *Writing the Female Voice*, 4, 28–30, 41, 68.

[17] *Familiar Letters between the Principal Characters in David Simple, and Some Others, to which is added A Vision*, 2 vols (London: for the Author, 1747) was published by subscription. Further references to this work are given after quotations in the text. The delay in publication may confirm the difficulty Battestin suggests that Sarah Fielding found in 'drawing out her story to a length sufficient to fill the two volumes her subscribers had paid for' (Martin C. Battestin and Ruth R. Battestin, *Henry Fielding: A Life* (London: Routledge, 1989), p. 414).

the only precedent.[18] Richardson, in turn, subscribed to her work, and some years later it was these two volumes that induced him to write to her in flattering terms:

I [. . .] have re-perused them with great pleasure, and found many beauties in them. What a knowledge of the human heart! Well might a critical judge of writing say, as he did to me, that your late brother's knowledge of it was not (fine writer as he was) comparable to your's. His was but as the knowledge of the outside of a clock-work machine, while your's was that of all the finer springs and movements of the inside.

(*Correspondence*, p. 132)

The comparison invites us to identify the merits of Sarah Fielding with those of Richardson because of the similar comparison between Henry Fielding and Richardson by Samuel Johnson.[19] Richardson, in making this comparison, seems to be projecting a version of his writing onto hers.[20] However, drawing Sarah Fielding too close to Richardson does not help an understanding of this work of hers. It seems that she was more influenced by social values and literary traditions other than those Richardson represents. She depended on a fundamentally different notion of familiarity. Here I focus on the differences between Sarah Fielding and Richardson, before proceeding to seek for the meaning of 'familiarity' in her use of the term. Here the issue of gender is intricate. I shall argue that her conception of familiar letters or familiarity was different from the one assumed by the fashion of 'feminine' familiar letters epitomized by Richardson. I shall examine this apparently minor work of Sarah Fielding with an attention to her ideas about the letter form, and also with a view to connecting her attitude in writing fictional letters with her standpoint in her genuine letters.

The most noticeable characteristic of Richardson's practical letter-writing manual is its display of model behaviour to be adopted in daily life. In these letters the freedom and spontaneity associated with familiar letters are suppressed and discipline is imposed. Control over life is reinforced by claiming the power of fixed and written words in letters. The epistle is endowed with more power than words spoken face-to-face (p. 71). Writing a letter itself is considered valuable, and neglecting it is almost a crime. By inculcating the importance of letter-writing, Richardson was able to bring the reader within his ethical control. Thus, in his *Familiar Letters*, letters are used in order to regulate the reader's mind. Rather than asking for the

---

[18] Richardson's letter manual was: *Letters Written to And for Particular Friends, on The Most Important Occasions. Directing Not Only the Requisite Style and Forms to Be observed in Writing Familiar Letters; But How To Think And Act Justly And Prudently, in The Common Concerns of Human Life* (London, 1741). For detailed study of letter-writing manuals, see Katherine Gee Hornbeak, *The Complete Letter Writer in English 1568–1800*, Smith College Studies in Modern Languages, 15 (Northampton, MA, 1934), p. viii, Chapter 4.

[19] Boswell records Johnson's remark as mentioned in conversation in 1768: 'There was as great a difference between them as between a man who knew how a watch was made, and a man who could tell the hour by looking on the dial-plate' (*James Boswell's Life of Samuel Johnson*, ed. by George Birkbeck Hill, rev. by L. F. Powell, 6 vols (Oxford: Clarendon Press, 1934–50), II, 49.

[20] Battestin places Sarah Fielding in the middle of the rivalry between Henry Fielding and Richardson; he argues that *Familiar Letters* illustrates her leaning towards the side of Richardson (*Henry Fielding*, p. 415).

reader's agreement with his moral scheme, he gives instruction; the reader is taught to think and act justly and prudently, to establish a sense of morality, and sometimes, possibly, to deceive decently his or her own mind, contrary to the image of familiar letters professed by the characters in Richardson's novels.[21]

Although its title is similar to Richardson's collection of letters, Sarah Fielding's *Familiar Letters* is not intended as a model for the practical letter-writer. It does not tell how to write a letter nor how to behave as Richardson's mentors and their obedient followers show. Consequently the reader is modelled in a different manner. The reader of Sarah Fielding's *Familiar Letters* is expected to agree and sympathize with the author rather than to be taught by an imposing writer. As Henry Fielding indicates, the supposed reader is a person of the same intellectual milieu as the well-educated author, not an ignorant pupil to be taught the basic codes of society by an authoritative mentor. He underscores the subtleties to be detected by resourceful readers: 'These nice Touches will, like the Signs of Masonry, escape the Observation and Detection of all those, who are not already in the Secret' (I, xix). He also points out that it is a book 'whose Beauties (if it have any) require the same Attention to discover them, with which the Author herself hath considered that Book of Nature' (I, xii–xiii). In his opinion, therefore, the observations and sentiments are to be shared between the author and the reader who is already in possession of the same values. He compares the book to a looking-glass that enables one to reflect and judge for oneself rather than to a source that gives information and instruction (I, xx). Her reader is supposed to be more autonomous than the reader who learns from Richardson's letter-writing manual. Sarah Fielding's setting of the relationships between the addresser and the addressee within the fiction seems to be analogous to the relationship Henry Fielding points out in the preface. Each writer requires fellow-feeling from the addressed. As most of the recipients know what to grasp in the episodes and narratives addressed to them, they can reply with another story which confirms the sentiments of the first writer.

Nor is this work like Richardsonian epistolary novels. The most explicit feature that distinguishes it from the epistolary novels is that it has no coherent plot. Nor does it use the epistolary technique to establish the narrative's authenticity.[22] Moreover, *Familiar Letters* presents a lack of reciprocity and confidentiality. The letters are apparently reciprocal, but the role of recipients as internal readers is too undeveloped for the letters to be

---

[21] See for example, *Clarissa*, 4 vols (London and Melbourne: Dent, 1932), II, p. 431.
[22] For discussions of narrative's authenticity, see, for example, Ian Watt, *The Rise of the Novel: Studies in Defoe, Richardson and Fielding* (London: Hogarth Press, 1987), pp. 191–96; Wayne C. Booth argues that the distinction of person is less important than it seems, in *The Rhetoric of Fiction*, 2nd edn (Harmondsworth: Penguin, 1987), Chapter 6; see also Michael McKeon, *The Origins of the English Novel 1600–1740* (Baltimore, MD: Johns Hopkins University Press, 1987), pp. 39–64, 357–58, 414.

regarded as truly reciprocal.[23] This lack of reciprocity is related to the absence of confidentiality. Although the letters in Sarah Fielding's *Familiar Letters* are addressed to specific persons who have specific names, they lack the Richardsonian method of creating familiarity by pinpointing a confidante who is allowed to know what the addresser does not want to reveal to others. In other words, these are not confidential communications between particular individuals. Instead, they assure each other that they share public knowledge and moral judgement. The writer's world and the recipient's are not two separate and different private spheres of individuals, but communal. Both the writer and the reader know that the domain where he or she is does not have any boundaries of peculiarity, so the observation on it automatically proves to be applicable to the sphere around the recipient of the letters and consequently the universal, even though the writer's perception is committed only to the limited area where he or she sees. Accordingly the writer does not need to invite the reader to his or her own sphere confidentially.

There is a marked reluctance in this text to enter into personal experience and feelings. The first letter from Cynthia to Camilla begins with Cynthia's telling about herself; she spent the morning very happily, conversing with her husband, but even here, though she focuses on herself, she does not go into detail of conversation. Shortly after she begins, she switches topics, because 'I need not tell [Camilla] how happily I passed the Morning' with her beloved Valentine, implying that Camilla knows not only how happy she is but also what actually makes her happy (I, 50). Conversations and events in which the letter-writer is involved are not reported with full details. What she devotes attention to is not herself but other people's behaviour. Her topics shift as her thoughts wander in sketching people's follies. The other letter writers, too, are detached from the events which they describe in their letters. Another typically disengaged writer is found in Letter xxv. The writer Clemenes reflects that he is happy to have been the only sober observer among the others' frenzy of affectation: 'I was pleased to think I was the only Person that was not acting a Part' (II, 66).

Even when the story of an individual is told in a letter, it is not the writer's own immediate experience but the story somebody else retrospectively told to the writer. The events in the story are remote; the teller calmly looks at the self in the past; the writer puts down the teller's words faithfully as they are told without any sign of being absorbed in the story. An example of this kind of detached writer is Camilla in Letters II, IV, and VI. In these letters the writer is not even an observer of the events. Camilla reports a story of Isabinda in Isabinda's first-person narrative. Camilla does not have anything to do with the events, nor does she offer any comment while the story is told. She claims that 'I took it down from her own Mouth' (I, 60). This claim

---

[23] Janet Gurkin Altman discusses works of a borderline nature which adopt the form of epistles but lack reciprocity; see *Epistolarity: Approaches to a Form* (Columbus: Ohio State University Press, 1982), pp. 87–115.

enables Camilla to recede from the story by hiding behind the narrating Isabinda. In reply to her report, Cynthia writes about events and people at some distance, repeatedly claiming that she is writing down everything, but everything that 'passed', not what is currently happening to her (1, 54). In this way these writers and their readers are not involved or kept in suspense; they always know the consequence and meaning of the events and stories.

Summing up, both in temporal and personal terms, distance dominates in Sarah Fielding's familiar letters. Her letter-writing characters sketch people's manners, and retell somebody else's story. They are not concerned with an individual's experience and feelings, but their observation consists of the description of other people's behaviour. Other people's stories are told in the form of a memoir and the teller always knows the outcome of the narrative. Several stories are told in the first person, as the letter-writers write down in the narrators' own language what the narrators have told. In this sense the letter-writer turns into a scriber rather than scribbler, losing subjectivity. Sarah Fielding's characters do not expose their own agitation of the heart, as they have little direct personal commitment to the events they tell. They are always in control of themselves either as an observer or a memoir teller. Thus she did not follow a typical strategy of epistolary literature in constructing the relationship between the letter-writer and the topic.

The product of such a relationship is different from what an emotionally committed letter-writer puts down. Here the binary model of the epistolary novel proposed by Elizabeth MacArthur helps to place Sarah Fielding in the context of literary tradition. She points out that the metonymical structure of epistles and epistolary novels has been underestimated by critics who base their formal criteria mainly on the novels of the nineteenth century. She argues that metonymy (which stands for combination, movement, instability, disorder, openness, and desire), contrasted with metaphor (which is marked by selection, stability, closure, and meaning), characterizes both genuine and fictional letters of the late seventeenth century and the eighteenth century.[24] She maintains that the metonymical openness of the epistolary form corresponds to a desire of women to question the problems of meaning and authority, relating the literary form favoured by women to socially and politically gendered power structures.[25] Richardson's principle of writing 'to the moment' can be justly fitted in the metonymical form of letters for its orientation toward openness and movement.

In contrast, the letters in Sarah Fielding's *Familiar Letters* tend to be metaphorical: their orientation is toward order, closure, and meaning. Their

---

[24] Elizabeth J. MacArthur, *Extravagant Narratives: Closure and Dynamics in the Epistolary Form* (Princeton, NJ: Princeton University Press, 1990). Developing Peter Brooks's study of narrative closure, she attempts to liberate epistolary discourse from the values constructed for the nineteenth-century novel, by challenging the view of metaphor-oriented reading which seeks closure and meaning.
[25] MacArthur, 'Devious Narratives', p. 18.

observations and reports invite the addressees to grasp the meaning of the accounts and to look for some moral interpretation. In addition, there are frequent remarks in generalized terms rather than those emphasizing the particularities of the individual experience. For example, we always encounter synthesizing comments about human beings, such as 'all Mankind can travel in [the Paths that lead to Misery] without jostling one another', and 'nothing is so common, as mens ruining themselves' (1, 200, 199). In this way *Familiar Letters* seeks for metaphor in the supposedly metonymical form of letters. It is likely that Sarah Fielding could have availed herself of Richardson's conception of the epistolary novel, of epistolary discourse as the topos of the intimate, private, and confessional. However, she did not adopt the confessional method and the metonymical structure of epistolary novelists. She played a different game.

The seemingly stray work, *Familiar Letters*, suggests a need to rethink Sarah Fielding's notion of 'familiarity'. Examination of the relationships between her characters in these letters helps to construe her sense of 'familiarity'. Almost always in her literary career Sarah Fielding is concerned about negotiation and communication between the author and the reader. In this created world of familiar letters, she is again articulately attentive to the conveyance of ideas, for here she describes the importance of conversation, the mutual exchange of ideas, between her characters repeatedly. Notably their concerns in such exchanges are not private, amorous, or political, but public, moral, and social. Her idea of familiarity is not established by the standards of the epistolary novel where the author makes the characters focus on their own actions and inner conflicts by inviting the confidante into their private space. Her familiarity consists in the exchange of ideas to stimulate thinking and in assuring each other of the certainty of common values.

Her *Familiar Letters* addresses the age's epistemological question of relationships between a person and the outer world and between human beings. It expresses a consciousness of the necessity of politeness in human relationships brought about by the Enlightenment.[26] There was a proliferation of texts on conversation, politeness, and familiarity. Among them, Addison (1672–1719) and Steele (1672–1729) advocated urbanized familiar politeness, Swift wrote on conversation and good manners, and both Henry and Sarah Fielding were very interested in the notion of conversation. Sarah Fielding's conception of familiarity in *Familiar Letters* depends on her notion of conversation, and this is noteworthily social and intellectual rather than private and emotional.

---

[26] John Mullan, *Sentiment and Sociability: The Language of Feeling in the Eighteenth Century* (Oxford: Clarendon Press, 1990); Peter Borsay, *The English Urban Renaissance: Culture and Society in the Provincial Town 1660–1770* (Oxford: Clarendon Press, 1989), pp. 257–83; Lawrence E. Klein, 'Liberty, Manners, and Politeness in early Eighteenth-Century England', *The Historical Journal* 32 (1989), 583–605.

In his contributory letters as well as in his preface to her *Familiar Letters* Henry Fielding presents his conception of familiar letters. Of course, it does not indicate all models of Sarah Fielding's 'familiar letters', but his models are suggestive in examining hers. In one of his letters (Letter XLI) his exemplars are those who are celebrated for their sophisticated elaboration of an easy style along with satirical hints; the title of the letter is: 'A Letter from a French Gentleman to his Friend at Paris; an imitation of Horace, Addison, and all other Writers of Travelling Letters'. The chief feature that he considers epistolary writers should achieve is an easy, familiar style, adopted in the discourse of fairly serious subjects.[27] One of Henry Fielding's avowed models was Horace (65–8 BC).[28] What he highlights in Horace is his polished elegant style and refined conversation just as Dudley Ryder (16??–1756), who was a very eager student of styles in writing and conversation, admiringly remarked: 'One cannot read any book I believe more fit to learn one the polite way of writing and conversing than Horace.'[29] Addison, another of Henry Fielding's models, epitomized good writing in the familiar style. According to Johnson: 'Whoever wishes to attain an English style, familiar but not coarse, and elegant but not ostentatious, must give his days and nights to the volumes of Addison.'[30] This kind of 'masculine' familiarity was available to Sarah Fielding as well as an Ovidian 'feminine' intimacy.

A discussion of epistolary writing in verse in *The Spectator* throws light on Sarah Fielding's method in *Familiar Letters*. The writer classifies letters into two main groups: Ovidian love letters, and Horatian 'Familiar, Critical, and Moral' letters. According to the writer, the qualifications required to follow Horace are 'a good Fund of strong Masculine Sense' with 'a thorough Knowledge of Mankind' and mastery of language 'with an easie and concise manner of expression'.[31] As if he had these requirements in mind and wanted to defend Sarah Fielding's collection of letters with compensating qualities, Henry Fielding anticipates and refutes objections to the author's being a woman and not in the world of business. He defends her letters, starting with the assumption that letters in a familiar style are identified as a masculine product: 'The Objection to the Sex of the Author hardly requires an Answer', and 'as such Observations are generally supposed to be the Effects of long Experience in, and much Acquaintance with Mankind, it may perhaps surprize many, to find them in the Works of a Woman;

---

[27] See this preface to *Familiar Letters*.

[28] Howard D. Weinbrot argues that though Horace was powerfully influential for his sophisticated art in the eighteenth century, there was also mistrust of his political stance and personality, and Pope, usually thought to be Horatian, also had anti-Horatian qualities. See *Eighteenth-Century Satire: Essays on Text and Context from Dryden to Peter Pindar* (Cambridge: Cambridge University Press, 1988), pp. 21–33, 186–203; Weinbrot, *Alexander Pope and the Traditions of Formal Verse Satire* (Princeton, NJ: Princeton University Press, 1982).

[29] *The Diary of Dudley Ryder 1715–1716*, ed. by William Matthews (London: Methuen, 1939), p. 78.

[30] Johnson, *Lives of the English Poets*, II, 150.

[31] *Spectator*, no. 618, *The Spectator*, ed. by Donald F. Bond, 5 vols (Oxford: Clarendon Press, 1965), V, 113.

especially of one, who, to use the common Phrase, hath *seen so little of the World*' (I, xv, xiv).[32] He praises her achievement in such a genre, although with a hint of condescension.

In the text of *Familiar Letters* Horatian refinement is referred to with ambiguity. Cynthia enjoys conversation with Valentine's visitors very much because of their politeness and sociability. She appreciates their urbane relaxed conversation (I, 95–96). Especially, one of the gentlemen is endowed with the congenial characteristics *The Spectator* demanded of those wishing to follow Horace. He has 'a Fund of Wit and Entertainment' and his conversation is 'at once so lively, one can hardly imagine he has time to think, and yet so solid and judicious, it is almost impossible to conceive but every Thought must arise from the most deliberate Reflection'. In short, he is furnished with the best praises an elegant conversationalist can be given. Nevertheless, Cynthia cannot but recognize a problem. It is his Horatian sneer that annoys her; he sneers when he talks of others. The sneer reminds Cynthia of the description of Horace in Persius's (AD 34–62) satire, which she quotes in the letter: 'The Croud he sneer'd, but sneer'd with such a Grace, | It pass'd for downright Innocence of Face' (I, 96). His sneer causes disconcertion in her, not simply because it shows displeasing disdain, but all the more because she makes much of his otherwise entertaining conversation which gives her pleasant intellectual stimuli.

Sarah Fielding shared an interest in these lines with Henry Fielding, and quoted the same verses by the same translator that Henry Fielding cited in his 'Essay on Conversation'. He quotes first in Latin, followed by an English translation by Thomas Ewster.[33] Yet, the purposes of their quotation are different. Henry Fielding quotes the verses in the course of defending raillery: 'I shall recommend to my well-bred Man, who aims at Raillery, the excellent Character given of Horace by Persius.' In the essay he proceeds from a consideration of good behaviour to that of conversation, reaching at the end a vindication of raillery. He recommends Horatian raillery as a means to enliven conversation, because 'in skilful and wittty [*sic*] Hands, I have known Raillery, thus confined, afford a very diverting, as well as inoffensive Entertainment to the whole Company' (I, 150, 152)

Cynthia's perplexity about the gentleman proclaims that Sarah Fielding is less in favour of Horatian sophistication. Even if it is a sneer made with grace, she perceives an intolerable tincture of contempt rather than sheer refinement, and feels ill at ease with 'a Delight in a low Ridicule'. Her attitude represents both a willingness and a reluctance to admire Horatian sophistication. So, compared with Henry Fielding's acceptance, Sarah

---

[32] For analysis that regards familiar letters as fundamentally feminine, see for example, Salmon, esp. pp. 37–81.
[33] *Miscellanies by Henry Fielding, Esq.* ed. by Henry Knight Miller and others, 2 vols (Oxford: Clarendon Press, 1972–93), I, 150.

Fielding at least throws doubt on ridicule, raillery, and satire; her ambivalent feelings about Horace suggest that she is seeking a different style.

Although her characters cannot but point out the ridiculous behaviour of people and be satiric for the same reason that makes the gentleman sneer, they attempt to achieve a critical viewpoint not through sarcasm but through an appeal to a sympathetic agreement based on mutual understanding and shared moral values. Such an agreement is achieved by the four main characters, Cynthia, Camilla, Valentine, and David. *Familiar Letters* gives an impression that truly enjoyable conversation takes place among them. One of the probable direct sources of her notion of conversation is Henry Fielding. He defines conversation as 'reciprocal Interchange of Ideas', an essential part of the human activities through which human beings learn truth. What conversation enables people to develop is, importantly, insight and participation in the construction of shared knowledge rather than subjective perception: 'Things are, in a manner, *turned round*, and sifted, and all our Knowledge communicated to each other.'[34] Following him, Sarah Fielding moulds the image of conversation, focusing on exchanges of ideas and mental exercise rather than emotion and the heart. Cynthia and Valentine spend hours 'in great pleasure, reciprocally conveying our Ideas to each other, without any Disguise or artful Concealment of our Thoughts' (1, 54).

She contrasts such an ideal relationship between the main characters with the dismal state of other people. Those who have experienced blissful mutual understanding notice other people's inability to communicate. People flock together, talking loudly, but utterance is in one direction only. This is an illustration of the complete lack of conversation, defined as the 'reciprocal Interchange of Ideas'. In the Pump Room in Bath, people are eagerly talking to such a degree that the music played there is not to be heard. What they are uttering so enthusiastically is nothing more than comments on the weather (1, 82–88). On another occasion Cynthia is in a company, every member of which seems determined to make others unhappy, for each thinks selfishly that there is nobody worth paying attention to: 'Every one affects to confine all the Senses to herself, and will not allow her Companions even to hear or see but in the same manner and degree, as she herself does' (1, 175).

They live surrounded by a complete illusion of conversing with another person, but in fact their utterance is directed only to themselves and they live in a self-contained world of illusion. In this world of self-deceiving people love is all illusion; lovers' tenderness and affectionate speeches are not directed to the seemingly beloved ones, but are for the sake of the satisfaction of the lovers themselves. In the analyses offered by the awakened retrospective life-story-tellers and by the keen observers, such love consists of

---

[34] *Miscellanies*, 1, 120.

imposition on both sides; the loved one 'looked on her Lovers but as so many Looking-Glasses, which were to keep up her Good-humour, by letting her view her own Charms in the fairest Light', and the lovers are intoxicated in pleasing themselves by playing the role of passionate lovers. Even when Corydon pays compliments to Elmira, Cynthia 'thought it was easily to be perceived, that he was much more pleased with his own Speeches, than with the Object to whom he addressed them' (I, 92).

Self-deception can be a source of pleasure and complacency, but it is only a temporary happiness or vain contentment from the viewpoint of shrewd observers:

For, whatever is the most predominant Passion of Mind, is apt to prevail over our Senses, so far as to make us easily believe, we have found an Object to gratify it. And we feel such a Happiness in thus imposing on ourselves, as makes it hard for us to endeavour to find out the Truth. (I, 171)

Sarah Fielding marks the folly and falsity of this complacency by emphasizing the existence of perceptive observers who can look through the fallacy. She presents the main characters as observers of this kind, distinguishing them from those who are deluded. However, the dividing line between the two groups becomes less clear when Cynthia thinks of the general susceptibility to illusion, comparing this imposition sympathetically with Don Quixote's fancy;

If Mankind were all fairly to examine themselves, I question much, whether they would think Don Quixote's fancying a Country Girl to be a great Princess, and insisting, that she was stringing Pearl, instead of winnowing Corn, was so extraordinary an Effect of the human Imagination, as it appears at first sight. (I, 171)

People's vulnerability to such fancy is repeatedly described with an emphasis on its seizing power. Although we are always reminded of its weakness by the existence of the narrators who know the difference between deceit and truth, the danger of self-deception is ubiquitous.

Indeed, the sircle of the main characters, a group of perfect understanding, is also immersed in the same system of communication as those who practise one-way utterance. Mutual understanding is idealized to such a degree that actual communication becomes unnecessary in this ideal circle of friends. Cynthia and Camilla are apart, one in London and the other in Bath, but Cynthia feels as though Camilla were with her, not by correspondence as letter writers often feel that letters are a substitute for the real presence of friends and lovers, but by imaginary communication:

As it is one of the great Pleasures of Friendship, reciprocally to communicate our Thoughts to each other; [. . .] I doubly enjoy every new Idea, every fresh Subject of Observation, by reflecting on what you will think or say upon it.

Thus in my Closet, at a hundred Miles distance, I converse with you, previously form in my Mind what will be your Answers; and I am so well acquainted with your way of thinking, that I flatter myself, that, was you present, you would generally speak the Words I in fancy say for you. Thus I contrive all the Methods I can, to make myself some amends for our Separation. (II, 94–95)

Reciprocal understanding is so heightened as to become possible even in the other's absence or before writing a letter. When Cynthia describes a pleasant conversation with her husband, she assumes that Camilla and David can share their view without being told the details of their conversation (1, 54). The problem lies in that the reader is not allowed to know what they actually talk about. The description of their conversation ends without any concrete topics or dialogues. It seems insufficient, but it is the very feature of familiarity in *Familiar Letters*; significantly, such tacit concurrence of thoughts constructs familiarity here.

The same logic works when David Simple omits the conversation between him, his father, and Camilla: 'Now Cynthia, I have related to you every thing I have heard, *except* what is uttered by my Father and Camilla, that has given me pleasure ever since I saw you.' Not only does David withhold his own opinion (because he pays attention only to what he heard other people say), but also the remarks of his father and Camilla are excluded from the letter because he assumes Cynthia knows what his father, Camilla, and David himself think of and say about the events and people's behaviour. He takes it for granted that perfect sympathy and agreement reign between them, as real friends, and there is no need to express them in words. He knows 'you partake of all the Sensations of your Friends' and that it is naturally possible that 'I guess your Heart by my own' (1, 190). His contentment could be the same as that felt by the one-way utterers in that it does not require a reply. The only difference between the one-way utterers and the main characters is that the latter people can be confident in communication and agreement with each other.

This assumption of tacit understanding within a close circle of friends is an idealization of communication. Indeed, the relationship of Camilla and Cynthia is most familiar and ideal. They are like an internalized friend or an external self to each other. While their complacency ironically precludes conversibility between persons, they can feel assured in comprehending the sentiments of each other. Mutual understanding is in the air, rather than kept in the hearts of the people. In consequence, they do not feel any need to reveal feelings in epistles. Instead of being caught by scepticism and solipsism, assuming that other people are 'mere delusive figments of the solitary mind', Cynthia can imagine a friend's thought without feeling the threat and fear of isolation.[35] The father of Jane Collier, Sarah Fielding's intimate friend, was a sceptic.[36] To what degree he directly influenced Sarah Fielding is not known, but this almost excessive emphasis on the hope of silent understanding is her defensive answer to the question of human

---

[35] See William C. Dowling, *The Epistolary Moment: The Poetics of the Eighteenth-Century Verse Epistle* (Princeton, NJ: Princeton University Press, 1991). He argues that the eighteenth-century verse epistle is 'an attempt to solve in literary terms the philosophical problem of solipsism' (p. 22).
[36] Her father was Arthur Collier (1680–1732), a metaphysician.

perception. She clings to the belief in the certainty of existence and the possibility of perfect communication.

The assumption of perfect mutual understanding also shows Sarah Fielding's supposition of an understanding and partaking reader. It is in order to secure and confirm a circle of judicious people separated from the mass of absurd people that she shows how people are driven by selfishness, pride, and folly, how meaningless are the words they utter, and how people make themselves miserable. She anticipates a reader who can nod approval at her moral values without being told how to behave; moral values are shared beforehand and what the author is showing is her acuteness in observation, how well she can examine and demonstrate subtleties of the labyrinthine minds of people who are outside the circle. She writes her text, talking to an internalized friend who is in exact agreement with her, and expects the sentiments of an external reader to be in harmony with hers.

The society of Sarah Fielding's main characters is a world of perfect communication and familiarity where every moral value is shared. They do not feel the need to confess their emotions as they can correctly anticipate the others' reactions. They only exchange ideas about the world seen from the spectator's viewpoint, so as to confirm their moral ideas and beliefs. In terms of the gender categories of the time, Sarah Fielding adjusted the masculine tradition of satire in her gentler, say, feminine style, instead of taking advantage of the vogue of feminine familiar letters. 'True Love ever hesitates' and a true affectionate relationship does not therefore consist in forwardness, in pouring out one's own sentiments and emotions, but in the exchange of thoughts and ideas in order to enhance understanding without a breach of modesty. Just like her 'genuine' letters, her fictional letters consist of sober analysis and intellectual observation. As a writer active at the time of 'the rise of the novel' and 'the rise of the woman novelist', she attempted to fashion her own original style beyond the gendered stereotypes of writing. Her endeavours show one pattern of female authorship in the mid-eighteenth-century literary milieu. Not overtly authoritative and rebellious, it is a locus of subtle complexities of anxiety, reserve, ambition, assertiveness, and manipulation. Thus she tried to control and give order to her language and narrative, making her text 'cultivated Plains' rather than releasing 'spontaneity' or 'the barren Desarts of arbitrary words'.

'Arts of Appropriation':
Language, Circulation, and Appropriation in the Work of Maria Edgeworth

JACQUELINE PEARSON

University of Manchester

In Maria Edgeworth's last novel, *Helen*, the vain literary dilettante Horace Churchill impresses the heroine with a witty saying, but it is soon discovered to be plagiarized when she finds it 'word for word in a book from which Churchill's card fell as she opened it'.[1] This is not, apparently, his first use of 'arts of appropriation' (p. 170) which are already suspected by Helen's more experienced mentor, Lady Davenant. The act of verbal, and especially textual, appropriation is central to this novel, in both comic and serious registers, but this motif is also important elsewhere in Edgeworth's tales, novels, and autobiographical writings. The circulation of spoken words and written texts is a vital mechanism of operation for language and for culture itself, but it also generates a high degree of ambivalence centred on the vulnerability of language to appropriation.

In this essay I shall begin with an examination of verbal appropriation and related themes in a range of Edgeworth's work, including her tales for children and young people, before finally focusing on two of her most effective and underrated novels, *Helen* (1834) and *Patronage* (1813). My argument will be not only formal, that appropriation provides an organizing metaphor for two long and complex works: I shall also examine this theme in the context of some eighteenth-century discussions about language. Edgeworth was keenly interested in, and influenced by, contemporary debates on language: her letters, and the education works she wrote with her father, show an awareness of a number of works on language by authors including Bacon, Rousseau, Lord Monboddo, Dugald Stewart, John Horne Tooke, Mrs Piozzi, Dr Johnson, Prevost, Sir William Jones, and John Wilkins.[2] She was interested in arguments about the relationship between words and ideas (Horne Tooke's view that 'language is thought' versus the

---

[1] *Helen*, ed. by Maggie Gee (London: Pandora, 1987), p. 170. Further references to this edition are given after quotations in the text.
[2] See Maria and Richard Lovell Edgeworth, *Practical Education* (London: Johnson, 1798), pp. 63–64, 80; Olivia Smith, *The Politics of Language (1791–1819)* (Oxford: Clarendon Press, 1984), p. 147; *Practical Education*, pp. 701, 76, 376; Maria Edgeworth, *Leonora* (1806), in *The Novels of Maria Edgeworth in 12 Volumes* (London: Dent, 1893), III, 16; *Maria Edgeworth in France and Switzerland: Selections from the Edgeworth Family Letters*, ed. by Christina Colvin (Oxford: Clarendon Press, 1979), p. 80; *The Life and Letters of Maria Edgeworth*, ed. by Augustus J. C. Hare, 2 vols (London: Arnold, 1894), I, 146, 38; Edgeworth, *Patronage*, ed. by Eva Figes (London: Pandora, 1986), p. 295.

view that, as her father expressed it, 'words' do not create thought but are created by it, and merely 'represent ideas')[3] and in the idea of a universal language, the impact of class on language, and the significance of the ability of some birds to speak for formulating a definition of civilization based on language use (all these will be further discussed below). Finally, I shall speculate on the reasons why Edgeworth as a woman writer was so preoccupied by ideas of verbal and textual circulation and appropriation.

In *Practical Education* (1798), which he wrote with his daughter, Richard Lovell Edgeworth describes effective language in an elaborate economic metaphor as 'current' and 'sterling', and with words able to 'increase our wealth by keeping it in continual circulation' (p. 64), exactly as, in *Conversations on Political Economy* by Maria's friend Jane Marcet, 'capital is [. . .] constantly circulating' and so increasing the wealth of the whole of society.[4] Maria Edgeworth's children's stories show both wealth and language in circulation. They approvingly depict a healthy market economy inhabited by 'characters who are producers and consumers', so that the 'currency' of society, whether in the form of money or of 'tokens of love or status', circulates freely,[5] and the same is true of language: the circulation of books and the growth of literacy in particular are shown to bring not only intellectual but literal profit to her young characters.[6] (Marcet even uses some of Edgeworth's children's fiction to illustrate principles of political economy under discussion (p. 11)).

Language, then, is a form of capital which functions through efficient circulation. Edgeworth, influenced by her father who was a pioneer of the telegraph and had experimented with other coded languages, was fascinated by the technology of communication in all its aspects.[7] Ways of increasing the speed, efficiency, and confidentiality of communications feature repeatedly in her work. Like her father, she was interested in codes (ciphers and decipherment are thematically important in *Patronage* and elsewhere) and other forms of secure communication. In 'Manoeuvring' a young woman, imprisoned in a Spanish convent, succeeds in procuring help to escape by conveying secret messages in nosegays of flowers which she throws over the

---

[3] Hans Aarsleff, *The Study of Language in England, 1780–1860* (Princeton, NJ: Princeton University Press, 1967), p. 53; *Practical Education*, p. 64.

[4] Jane Marcet, *Conversations on Political Economy*, 2nd edn (London: Longman, Hurst, Rees, Orme and Brown, 1817), p. 107.

[5] Marilyn Butler, 'Edgeworth's Stern Father: Escaping Thomas Day, 1795–1801', in *Tradition in Transition: Women Writers, Marginal Texts, and the Eighteenth-Century Canon*, ed. by Alvaro Ribeiro and James G. Basker (Oxford: Clarendon Press, 1996), pp. 85, 89.

[6] See, for example (as well as stories cited later in the text), 'The Orphans' (where a girl's knowledge of a history book enables her to identify valuable coins), and 'Eton Montes' (where the child Violetta amuses herself by reading a story by Edgeworth herself), both from *The Parent's Assistant* (1796, 1800), new edn (London: Routledge: [n.d.]), pp. 11, 170.

[7] R. L. and Maria Edgeworth, *Memoirs of Richard Lovell Edgeworth* (1820), 2 vols (Shannon: Irish University Press, 1969), II, 162–63, 167–69.

wall, with 'a stone tied to a string, and to the stone a letter';[8] Archer, in 'The Barring Out', practises a 'method of holding secret correspondence' through the whistling of tunes which he has learned from reading the history of Richard I.[9] 'The White Pigeon' (1796) illustrates both Edgeworth's interest in the circulation of information and her optimism about literacy. The poor Irish boy Brian O'Neill learns, by 'reading his book very attentively', about the use of 'pigeons who carried notes and letters', and by experimenting with carrier pigeons he not only improves communications and earns money for his impoverished parents, but is also able to prevent a robbery by intercepting a note sent by thieves using a stolen pigeon.[10]

The circulation of information and texts fascinated Edgeworth. It was her 'practice to circulate her manuscripts among her relatives', thereby creating a space for publication which was still properly private and domestic. She also notes how effectively information is disseminated through the 'circulation of newspapers', and is impressed by the speed with which English books circulate in Europe and America. Rowland Hill and post-office reform also interest her, and in a letter she tells the story of a Mr Talbot who 'received safely a letter', although the only address it bore was 'London', through the methodical work of 'the letter carriers'.[11] Edgeworth is excited and optimistic about the technologies of the word, this early nineteenth-century information superhighway. The 'greatest wonder of all', the 'real magic' in our prosaic lives, is the power of those 'little black marks' that compose 'printed letters and words'.[12]

Yet this optimism about the technologizing of textuality and the circulation of language exists in tension with a constant anxiety about communication, for language, spoken and written, has a special vulnerability to inadvertent or malicious misinterpretation or appropriation, and circulation may proliferate disinformation instead of universalizing information. If maintaining the confidentiality of communication is good, its dark double, 'secret correspondence', is bad, and attacking it is, as we shall see, a central aim in both *Patronage* and *Helen*. '*Lettres de cachet*', written authorization used by the *ancien régime* to allow imprisonment without trial, 'Dangerous instruments in bad hands!', are an extreme form of the sinister potential of written language,[13] but forgery, treason, smuggling, and perjury as well as tyranny become important metaphors. In 'Manoeuvring' Mrs Beaumont reveals her duplicity by giving Sir John Hunter a '*written assurance*' (p. 64) of her permission to marry her daughter, although they both know Amelia will

---

[8] *Tales of Fashionable Life* (1809), in *Tales and Novels by Maria Edgeworth*, 10 vols (London: Bohn and Simpkin, Marshall, 1870), v, 18.
[9] *The Parent's Assistant*, p. 272.
[10] *The Parent's Assistant*, p. 118.
[11] *Maria Edgeworth: Letters from England 1813–1834*, ed. by Christina Colvin (Oxford: Clarendon Press, 1971), pp. 4, 41, 341, 353.
[12] *Orlandino* (Edinburgh: Chambers, 1848), p. 108.
[13] *Patronage*, pp. 11, 516.

never agree, and in *Harrington*, the imposter Psalmanazar's 'pretended Dictionary of the Formosan language' becomes a metaphor for the hero's seduction by the falsifying stereotypes of antisemitism.[14] Forgery and 'false letters' form a recurrent motif,[15] and flawed, lost, or dubious wills or leases are important not only in a number of fictional works, such as 'Almeria', *Patronage*, 'Simple Susan', and 'The Contrast', but also in Edgeworth family history.[16]

If written language is perilously likely to gain associations with crime and falsehood, spoken language raises equal dangers of misinterpretation, misunderstanding, and conflict. The quarrelsome wife in 'The Modern Griselda' regards literacy as 'a glorious field of battle', and argues fiercely with her husband over the pronunciation of the word 'wind' (a trivial episode, but a symptom of the combativeness that will lead to the breakdown of the marriage).[17] Not only pronunciation but also homophones, metaphorical usages, and double meanings may cause confusion. The *Memoirs of Richard Lovell Edgeworth* quotes the actor Macklin's homophonic tongue-twisters (I, 126–27), and Maria Edgeworth in *Practical Education* warns about the 'defects of language' and the problems of teaching children a language where there are 'ten meanings for *sweet*, ten for *open*, twenty-two for *upon*, and sixty-three for *to fall*': unscrupulous people 'who want to puzzle and to deceive' take advantage of these defects and use as many 'unmeaning, or [. . .] ambiguous words' as they can.[18] Small wonder that in *Harry and Lucy Concluded* Harry dislikes similes for not being 'exact', and is confused 'when a word is used that has two senses'.[19] However, even apparently simple and unambiguous language cannot be taken at face value, for when dealing with some people one has to recognize 'even when they said "No" that they meant "Yes"': women in particular allegedly '*say* one thing [when] we *mean* quite another'.[20]

Eighteenth-century theories of language 'were centrally and explicitly concerned with class division' with language 'an integral part of the class structure',[21] and in Edgeworth's fiction, communication might be impeded because the languages of the classes are different, with 'workman's language' incomprehensible to a middle-class listener, as Harry and Lucy fail to understand the 'terms [. . .] familiar to shipwrights' used by the boat-builder they visit (III, 55). Characters of lower-class origins who try to emulate their

[14] *Harrington and Ormond*, in *Tales*, 2nd edn, 2 vols (London, 1817), I, 17.
[15] See Hare, *Life and Letters*, I, 82, 261, 279; 'Out of Debt, Out of Danger', in *Popular Tales* (1804), repr. in *Tales and Novels*, II, 148.
[16] *Tales of Fashionable Life*, V, 167–69; *Patronage*, pp. 608–13; *The Parent's Assistant*, pp. 78–108; *Popular Tales*, II, 323–76; *Memoirs of Richard Lovell Edgeworth*, I, 17–18 (an episode which feeds directly into *Patronage*).
[17] 'The Modern Griselda' (1805), repr. in *Tales and Novels*, VI, 417, 450.
[18] *Practical Education*, pp. 76–77 (and see also p. 139).
[19] *Harry and Lucy Concluded*, 4 vols (London: Hunter and Baldwin, Cradock and Joy, 1825), I, 65, IV, 138.
[20] *Helen*, pp. 250, 247.
[21] Smith, *Politics of Language*, pp. viii, 1.

new higher-status friends will misuse their language, in the form, for instance, of '*mal-apropisms*', as Lady Masham accuses Lady Bearcroft in *Helen* (though her story may itself be a forgery since it seems to have been appropriated from an account featuring quite a different person (p. 230)). Class interests more generally may contribute to the degeneration of the language, as the 'language of the market' corrupts love and marriage, and modish pseudo-genteel '*slang*' conversely adds a deceptive dignity to low-status things: 'there are no such things as *attorneys* now in England, they are all turned into solicitors and agents, just as every *shop* is become a *warehouse*, and every *service* a *situation*'.[22]

Gendered differences in language usage might also impede communication, or at least, as with class differences, suggest a hierarchy of linguistic practices, in this case with women at the bottom. Some words, especially hyperbolic expressions or words dealing with the emotions — 'prodigiously', 'interesting', 'romantic', or 'unkind', for instance — are marked as specifically feminine usages or as having specifically feminine meanings, creating 'namby-pamby little missy phrases'.[23] Other high-status words and kinds of language are firmly marked as 'masculine, not [. . .] feminine'.[24]

The language of science, of particular interest to Edgeworth, is one such gendered language. Harry expresses a growing orthodoxy when he tells his sister that it is 'not necessary for a woman to know' a 'scientific expression' (III, 27): Londa Schiebinger has pointed out how in this period science was preoccupied with 'purging the feminine' from its language.[25] Lucy, like Edgeworth herself, rejects this gendering of scientific language: 'I do not see why a woman should not know scientific expressions, as well as men'. If Lucy fails to understand the technical masculine language Harry is so proud of learning, however, he equally fails to understand hers, for feminine arts also have their own equally technical vocabulary and he does not understand her allusion to a 'minnikin pin' (II, 179). Indeed, in *Harry and Lucy Concluded*, girls are consistently 'quicker [. . .] about words' (III, 29) and more informed about language, literature, and history, than boys (I, 23–24; II, 211; III, 223). Lucy identifies a quotation from 'Il Penseroso' from 'two words', while Harry cannot 'decipher' it, and he cannot understand verbal ambiguity while she is adept at punning (III, 223; I, 65). In terms of linguistic gifts, the sexes (at least in this book) are different but equal.

Different languages and dialects, languages of the classes or the sexes or regional dialects, or technical vocabularies of one kind or another, may, then, be mutually incomprehensible, or may set up oppressive hierarchies. They may indeed be deliberately or accidentally obfuscating, like the private

[22] *Patronage*, pp. 154, 29, 266.
[23] *Patronage*, pp. 601, 222; *Helen*, pp. 58, 253, 120.
[24] *Patronage*, p. 213.
[25] *The Mind Has No Sex? Women in the Origins of Modern Science* (Cambridge, MA: Harvard University Press, 1989), p. 233.

language of euphemism used by thieves which constitutes a kind of circulating 'false money', or the sign-language allegedly used by Dervishes who 'pretended to understand one another', only to discover themselves to 'mean different things, or to mean nothing at all'.[26] Edgeworth repeatedly comments on the difficulty of understanding some kinds of non-standard English, such as the 'foreign dialect and pronunciation' of European Jews or Frenchmen, or Welsh, Irish, or Liverpudlian English.[27] Ormond ponders on the difference between the French *'aimable'* and the English 'amiable' and the dangers of confusion their similar form but different connotations risk.[28] Even an intelligent foreigner will fail to grasp nuances or be misled by metaphorical usages: in *Practical Education* a Chinese mandarin visiting Paris takes literally an injunction to consider his host's house his own, and in *Patronage* Buckhurst Falconer tells a funny story which turns on an Italian's failure to understand the colloquial force of the English word 'assurance'. (In the same novel, however, we learn that there may be advantages in claiming linguistic ignorance: Godfrey resists seduction by Miss Hauton by showing that he 'could not, or would not, understand the Italian' of an opera libretto in which she is trying to interest him.)[29]

Confusion is especially dangerous when the parties involved imagine that they share a common language. In 'The Limerick Gloves' English Phoebe Hill breaks with Irish Brian O'Neill because although she loves him she fails to understand the nuances of his Irish dialect: when he says he 'expects' her to accept him she is repelled by what she reads as complacence and presumption, ignorant that 'to expect, in Ireland, is the same thing as to hope in England'.[30] Similarly in 'Forgive and Forget' a message miscarries. Mr Grant sends a 'soft word' to placate his bad-tempered neighbour, but he 'gave his answer to his wife; she to a Welsh servant-girl, who did not perfectly comprehened her mistress's broad Scotch; and she in her turn could not make herself intelligible to Mrs Oakley, who hated the Welsh accent': as a result of regional differences in English, and the prejudices these differences inspire, the quarrel between the neighbours risks becoming worse rather than better.[31]

In the children's stories Edgeworth offers an allegory of British nationhood, suggesting optimistically that, despite temporary set-backs, harmony between England and her neighbours (or between the classes or the sexes) will ultimately prove possible in spite of linguistic differences. In both stories linguistic misunderstandings are eventually happily resolved. In 'Forgive and Forget' Mr Grant's son placates his neighbours with a gift of raspberries and the loan of a book about their cultivation (as in 'The White

---

[26] *Practical Education*, p. 247; *Harry and Lucy Concluded*, III, 236.
[27] *Harrington*, p. 31; *Patronage*, p. 10; Colvin, *Letters from England*, pp. 7, 10; *Helen*, p. 405.
[28] *Ormond* (1817; repr. Gloucester: Alan Sutton, 1990), p. 337.
[29] *Practical Education*, p. 195; *Patronage*, pp. 37, 88.
[30] *Popular Tales*, p. 105.
[31] *The Parent's Assistant*, p. 179.

Pigeon', Edgeworth argues that there is hardly anything that reading cannot do), and in 'The Limerick Gloves' the Irishman and the English family will 'live in union' (a significantly political noun granted the passage of the Act of Union in 1800).[32]

Edgeworth examines the view prevalent in contemporary conservative language studies that some kinds of English are inherently 'better' than others, with the 'refined' language of the educated upper classes self-evidently superior to the 'vulgar' language of the lower orders: 'The basic vocabulary of language study [. . .] conveyed the assumption that correct usage belonged to the upper classes'.[33] In *Practical Education*, for example, Edgeworth seems to take a conservative position, accepting that the language of non-hegemonic groups is inherently inferior: she describes, for instance, the English spoken by Irish peasants as characterized by 'evasion', and that of African plantation slaves by a 'propensity to falsehood'. But she takes a significant step in the direction of a more progressive attitude to language by arguing that these qualities are not innate but the result of social and political circumstance: 'Oppression and terror necessarily produce meanness and deceit' (pp. 208–09, 211–12). In fact, although her work shows how the rich varieties of English can lead to dangerous linguistic misunderstandings, Edgeworth offers a simple recommendation of neither a 'refined' nor a 'vulgar' language: indeed, although she does not advocate the use of 'vulgar' language (as her treatment of Lady Bearcroft demonstrates), she was attacked by the 'refined' lobby for her use of vulgarisms, most notoriously the word 'spittle' in *Patronage*. Perhaps, indeed, she embodies by example the ideal of 'an intellectual vernacular language' so rarely acknowledged in contemporary language theory.[34]

Edgeworth certainly does not recommend a blandly middle-of-the-road language without eccentricity and individuality. Her surviving notebooks show that the germ of a situation or character was frequently rooted in 'oddities of speech', for she kept a 'record of conversational styles'.[35] While for her an ideal English would be purged of the corruptions of courtly language, obfuscating jargon of all kinds, and the purely local elements of common language, Edgeworth also, as we might expect from the author of *Castle Rackrent* (1800), whose use of Irish dialect taught Scott important lessons for his Scottish novels, celebrates linguistic pluralism. Although the preface to this novel anticipates the union of Ireland and Great Britain, in which Irish 'identity', and perhaps language, will be lost, this lies in a dim future, and the author is meanwhile happy to celebrate the diversity of the languages of sexes, classes, and nations.[36] While linguistic difference can

[32] *The Parent's Assistant*, p. 180; *Popular Tales*, p. 105.
[33] Smith, *Politics of Language*, pp. 4, 35, 9.
[34] Marilyn Butler, *Maria Edgeworth: A Literary Biography* (Oxford: Clarendon Press, 1972), p. 498; Smith, *Politics of Language*, p. x.
[35] Butler, *Maria Edgeworth*, pp. 239, 571.
[36] *Castle Rackrent*, ed. by George Watson (Oxford: Oxford University Press, 1980), p. 5.

lead to confusion and misunderstanding, the answer is not for everyone to speak a standard refined English. It is significant that the critics of non-refined speakers, such as Buckhurst Fuller in *Patronage*, Lady Masham in *Helen*, or Mrs Oakley in 'Forgive and Forget', tend themselves to be criticized for their own failures to use language accurately. Lady Bearcroft and Brian O'Neill, the girl Lucy, the boat-builder and the Welsh maidservant, may continue to use their own idiolects as long as speakers of other Englishes will view them tolerantly and learn to understand their languages. 'Prejudice' is repeatedly warned against in Edgeworth's education works: the real linguistic dangers are not mutually opaque dialects but prejudice, ignorance, and the readiness to use spoken language to construct oppressive hierarchies.[37]

The differences in the languages of the classes, sexes, and nations may, then, be confusingly diffferent, and even standard English's very richness in homophones, double meanings, and metaphorical usages may also disrupt communication and impede the free circulation of language. In particular, communication becomes fraught with difficulties of either misattribution, where an innocent party is falsely accused of some verbal act, or appropriation, where one character wilfully takes over the words of another. In 'The Prussian Vase' treasonable graffiti on a piece of china are falsely attributed to its young painter and put her in danger of arrest and imprisonment,[38] and in a number of stories the appropriation of letters forms an important motif. Harrington's mother burns his letter of introduction to Mr Montenero to prevent her son socializing with Jews (p. 104), and in *Helen* the whole plot turns on the appropriation of letters. If to appropriate letters is a mark of folly or villainy, to resist such appropriation reveals virtue: in 'Mademoiselle Panache' Lady Augusta becomes terrified when she realizes she has left indiscreet letters where they might be found, but another heroic Helen returns them unread, and comments moralistically on the tacit 'reproof' offered by Alexander the Great to Hephaestion, 'whom he detected reading a letter over his shoulder'.[39] Not reading and not writing become disturbingly synonymous with female virtue.

Edgeworth's anxieties about the appropriation of private correspondence and 'private conversation' are marked.[40] Both conversation and correspondence mark the threshold between public and private discourses, a liminal area perhaps especially disturbing to the woman writer who transgresses received ideologies of feminine privacy and domesticity by entering the world of literary publication. Here the technologies which allow the free circulation of written texts and spoken language, elsewhere so optimistically celebrated, might seem dangerous, even transgressive. Her squeamishness

[37] *Practical Education*, e.g. pp. 248, 351, 630; *The Parent's Assistant*, p. 179.
[38] *Moral Tales* (1801), *Tales and Novels by Maria Edgeworth*, I, 111.
[39] *Moral Tales*, pp. 404–05.
[40] *Patronage*, p. 81.

about using her father's private correspondence in her biography of him seems exaggerated to a modern reader, especially since in her age the letters of distinguished men and women constituted a popular and commercially significant genre. Although private letters, she writes, 'afford the best means of obtaining an insight into [the] character' of her subject, she acknowledges that 'most honourable minds' will 'recoil at the idea of publishing letters', and that her father had a positive 'horror' of such a breach of 'private confidence'.[41] Even so innocent an act of textual appropriation, for the purpose of a filial celebration of her father's life, seems morally dubious: being involved in her father's memoirs both privately, as a daughter, and publicly, as a professional writer, seems painfully problematic.

An early version of these anxieties about correspondence and textual appropriation can be seen in *Leonora* (1806), a novel cast, unusually for Edgeworth, in epistolary form, so that form as well as theme and image draws attention to the letter and to the idea of (textual and other) appropriation. The anti-heroine Olivia has appropriated immoral French and German novels and philosophy, especially Rousseau and Goethe, which have corrupted her by teaching her to consider passion self-justifying: consequently she embarks on an adulterous affair with the husband of her friend Leonora. Her acts of textual (and sexual) appropriation seem poised to triumph, but they can be countered by an equal but opposite act of textual appropriation: her letters to her French confidante are 'found in a French frigate' and taken by an English cruiser to be examined as '*intercepted correspondences*' possibly containing 'state secrets' (pp. 221–22). A friend then sends these letters to Leonora, and when her husband reads them he discovers Olivia's true nature and returns to his modest, long-suffering wife. Olivia flees to the continent. Her acts of appropriation have connected her in the most literal way with both transgressive sexuality and French revolutionary politics.

Leonora seems a simple moralizing attack on Romantic fiction, revolutionary politics, and female sexual assertiveness, which provide reciprocal metaphors. And yet the history of its reception suggests that Edgeworth was right to be anxious about the possibilities of textual appropriation. Readers could, and did, resist the conservative tenor of the story and use it for their own, different, agendas. The young P. B. Shelley, for instance, sent a copy to his cousin and first love Harriet Grove as part of an attempt to indoctrinate her into his radical sexual and social politics, presumably encouraging an identification against the grain of the text with the glamorous villainess rather than the meek heroine.[42] There is no evidence that Edgeworth knew this, but she was certainly aware of a similar act of misreading or rebellious reading on the part of that 'horrible woman' Anna Seward, who was initially

---

[41] *Memoirs of Richard Lovell Edgeworth*, ii, 68.
[42] *The Letters of Percy Bysshe Shelley*, ed. by Frederick L. Jones, 2 vols (Oxford: Clarendon Press, 1964), i, 13.

'charmed' with the character of Olivia which she found 'so eloquent! so feeling! so delightful!', but when she 'found that Lady Olivia is ridiculed *she was enraged [. . .] beyond measure*' with the author.[43] Edgeworth's concern about the ambiguities of language and the dangers of appropriation of words and meanings may spring partly from the writer's dread of being read rebelliously, of readerly resistance to the authority of the author; or perhaps, even more painfully, that readers may identify latent meanings and prioritize them, forcing the author to confront unacknowledged possible meanings in her own creation.

Some critics of *Patronage* have seen it as 'over-elaborate', moralistic, 'contrived', and poorly structured.[44] However, an examination of its motifs of language, circulation, and appropriation reveals it as a novel meticulously and sometimes wittily structured around these key themes and images and, while it will not deny that the novel's basic aim is a moral one, will clarify the nature of its morality. As previously cited examples imply, *Patronage* is a novel acutely aware both of differences of language on the basis of nationality, class, gender, and idiolect and of consequent dangers of misunderstanding, and of the riskiness of the public circulation of 'private conversation' and private correspondence.[45]

In particular, the motif of verbal and textual appropriation is central. The novel begins with the loss of two important documents, one public, one private: a letter in cipher used by French spies which identifies the enemies of leading English statesman Lord Oldborough, and a lease demonstrating the virtuous Percy family's right to the estate from which, in its absence, they are evicted. It ends with the finding of two important documents, again one private and one public, the Percies' missing lease, and the evidence which reveals that an incriminating letter apparently by Lord Oldborough is actually a forgery. Motifs of the loss and finding, misappropriation and reappropriation of documents, of encoding and decoding, distinguishing between authentic and forged texts, discovering the true authorship of problematic texts, recur repeatedly. The novel contrasts the unprincipled Falconer family, who live through self-interest and 'patronage' and are associated with immoral uses of language, with the idealized Percies who succeed through family values and hard work and who are committed to moral linguistic practices. The superiority of a middle-class professional ethos, and its language, is asserted over a selfish desire to emulate a corrupt courtly ethos and its language.

The morally slippery Falconers succeed through much of the novel by acts of appropriation. M. de Tourville's 'important packet of papers' (p. 12) is found and pocketed by Mr Falconer, who hands them over to Lord

[43] Colvin, *Letters from England*, p. 23.
[44] Butler, *Maria Edgeworth*, p. 276; O. Elizabeth McWhorter Harden, *Maria Edgeworth's Art of Prose Fiction* (The Hague: Mouton, 1971), pp. 187–89, 198.
[45] See, for example, pp. 81, 70.

Oldborough and so gains his patronage and advancement for his son. Cunningham Falconer, though, lacks his father's ability, and his status can be maintained only by constant further acts of appropriation, until he becomes wholly reliant on the appropriation of texts authored by his hidden 'genius in the garret', to whose work he falsely assumes a 'just title' (p. 111). To competent readers Cunningham's claim to authorship is transparently false, since he proves to be ignorant of the literary allusions (the culturally acceptable face of textual appropriation) in the works he claims to have written (p. 167). For much of the novel the Falconers apparently rise by the appropriation of texts, while the Percies fall by losing them: a fire apparently destroys the 'valuable deed' by which Percy 'held [his] whole [. . .] estate' (p. 66), leaving them with only a 'copy' (p. 69), and allowing the appropriation of their property by an unscrupulous relative.

As the plot contrasts the moral, document-losing Percies with the immoral, document-finding (and later document-creating) Falconers, it also divides itself into male plots (which centre on work, professional success, and 'patronage' accepted or rejected as a means to success) and female plots (which centre on relationships and social success, and 'the patronage of fashion' (p. 147) accepted or rejected). In the female world as in the male apparent worldly success may be achieved through acts of appropriation: Lady Angelica has 'picked up shining scraps' of literature which she displays ostentatiously but with no real understanding (p. 182), and as a patron she attempts to appropriate the credit of the writers whom she displays at reading parties (p. 194). Like the Falconers', these acts of appropriation indicate vanity, selfishness, and the lack of a steady moral code. Like the male worlds of politics and the professions, the female world of fashion works through hidden struggles for power and prestige, to appropriate the credit of the really gifted, and for Edgeworth written and spoken language serve as metaphors for such credit: 'all the female amateurs' copy out Alfred Percy's poem, and Lady Georgiana Falconer, exactly the moral equivalent of her male relatives, 'appropriated to herself' a compliment really intended for Caroline Percy (p. 370). The appropriation of written texts and spoken language is, then, associated with a corrupt system of courtly patronage, vanity, the shady worlds of politics or fashion, and a lack of moral values.

This identification of appropriation with falsehood and corruption is re-emphasized in the case of the novel's hero, the German Count Albert Altenberg. Altenberg is placed in opposition to an inhumane and corrupt culture of appropriation right from the start, as he is first seen trying to rescue a footman who has been taken by the press gang, an act he sees as equivalent to that of 'an African slave merchant'. (This episode offended Edgeworth's more jingoistic readers and in later editions she cut some words which had been especially objected to).[46] So honourable is Altenberg in his

---

[46] Butler, *Maria Edgeworth*, p. 497.

resistance to appropriation that he even apologizes to Alfred Percy for borrowing and 'repeating [his] word', the word 'Duty', which seems to Altenberg hollow in the context of the press-gang (p. 286). He has first been heard of as a young man who risks his chances for advancement by honourably alerting the boy's father to the existence of 'secret correspondence' (p. 11) between the Prince of his minor German state and an actress. Throughout the novel he is associated with free and frank communications which contrast with the forgeries, ciphers, and secret, intercepted and appropriated correspondences elsewhere: because he speaks openly and honestly with both Countess Christina and the Prince he learns that they love each other and is able to evade an unwelcome dynastic marriage to the lady (p. 565). He is thus fit to become a member of the language community of the Percy family as Caroline's husband.

The tide begins to turn in the novel at the point at which the coded letters appropriated from the French spy are finally deciphered: that this takes place only ten pages after the description of Altenberg's opposition to pressing draws the symbolic connection between the two different acts of appropriation. The Falconers have interpreted most of the ciphers except for the key word 'Gassoc', which obviously represents an enemy of Lord Oldborough who plans to bring about his downfall, which would not be in the national interest. Mr Percy, although he rejects the corrupt world of politics in favour of private life and domestic values, is not naïve, and he is able to use his experience of 'the art of deciphering' to break the code: indeed, it becomes clear that 'it was from Mr Percy that Commissioner Falconer learnt all he knew on this subject' (p. 295).

Percy's ability to decode the secret, appropriated document indicates not only intellectual but also moral substance. In a novel where secret modes of communication are important and linguistic fragmentation and the consequent failures of speakers and writers to understand each other is so prominent, Percy, who stands like Altenberg for open and effective communication, is an important moral counter. Not only is Percy committed to decoding and thus making open secret communication: he has also, we learn, studied 'Wilkins and Leibnitz's scheme of a universal language' (p. 295).[47] Eighteenth- and nineteenth-century scholars were fascinated by the notion of a 'universal language' in the sense both of a primordial pan-human tongue and of an invented language which all human speakers could learn in order to be mutually comprehensible. In the 1790s in particular it was hoped that a 'new rational language would heal the long-standing divisions between the men of different nations and creeds', would provide, indeed, 'an instrument of peaceful revolution'.[48]

---

[47] Edgeworth records having read Wilkins's *Real Character; or, an Essay towards a Universal Philosophical Language* in a letter of 1795 (Hare, *Life and Letters*, I, 38).
[48] James Knowlson, *Universal Language Schemes in England and France 1600–1800* (Toronto: University of Toronto Press, 1975), pp. 161–62.

What exactly was that instrument to be? In the eighteenth century French had become 'the virtually international language of Europe', and Edgeworth herself had travelled in France and moved in French literary circles and had a good understanding of French: between 1803 and 1808, when she was already composing *Patronage*, about a third of the books she read were French.[49] But, perhaps inevitably for a novel of 1813, *Patronage* takes an anti-French line which is incompatible with the acceptance of French as a universal tongue: indeed it tends to associate the French language with secrecy, vanity, and falsehood, with the corrupt courtly culture, embodied by the Falconers' ally 'French' Clay, which the moral Percies oppose. Nor is Latin acceptable as a *lingua franca*: its centrality in the education of élite-class males was under fire, and if the classics 'marked out [. . .] the gentleman', asserting privilege in terms of both class and gender, new readers from the sub-genteel classes, and women of every class, might well find it in their interest to resist the power of Latin.[50] In *Harry and Lucy Concluded*, Edgeworth praised scientific Latin as a 'universal language', but it was universal only in the sense of allowing 'persons of science' from different nations to communicate (II, 123), not in the sense that all members of a speech community have equal access to it: and indeed Edgeworth elsewhere criticizes science specifically for the 'unintelligible jargon' of its 'technical language' which works against the interest of 'female' participation.[51]

Edgeworth, then, resists French and Latin for the role of universal language, and also German. Altenberg's nationality is important: his respect for 'English law, and [. . .] English liberty' immediately reveals to Alfred Percy on their first meeting that he 'is not a Frenchman' (p. 286). Germans were English allies against Napoleon, and English Romanticism showed a growing respect for German culture, but Edgeworth gives Altenberg no obvious German culture or language: indeed he speaks perfect English and respects British rather than European literature, admires Scott and is critical of French (pp. 377–78). Edgeworth's idea of a universal language seems in this case to be little more than a diffusion of English language and culture and its acceptance by well-disposed Europeans, with the addition of 'the universal language of the eye' (p. 370), what she elsewhere calls the 'universal language of action',[52] a non-verbal and hence apparently non-culture specific language, at which Altenberg is adept. The association of both Altenberg and Percy with the idea of a 'universal language' connects both

---

[49] Knowlson, *Universal Language Schemes*, p. 140; Butler, *Maria Edgeworth*, p. 200.

[50] Penelope Wilson, 'Classical Poetry and the 18th-century Reader', in *Books and their Readers in 18th-century England*, ed. by Isobel Rivers (Leicester: Leicester University Press, 1982), p. 72: for the controversy about Latin see also Smith, *Politics of Language*, esp. p. 13. The Edgeworths' work on education implicitly challenges the primacy of Latin by privileging 'modern' subjects: though Richard Lovell Edgeworth, apparently with some reluctance, accepts that as long as Latin remains the key to numerous professions it must be learned by boys (*Practical Education*, p. 387).

[51] *Letters for Literary Ladies* (1795; repr. London: Dent, 1993), p. 20.

[52] Hare, *Life and Letters*, II, 6.

with open rather than secret communication, which is equivalent to virtue rather than vice.

The pivotal episodes marking the end of the Falconers' success and the Percies' failure are, in the male/political story, Percy's decipherment of the appropriated document and in the female/personal story, the amateur performance of Voltaire's *Zaïre*. This play is performed in English, although 'French' Clay, who foolishly idolizes anything French, objects to this transposition, for unlike Altenberg and Percy he fails to see that the 'language' of 'true feeling' is the only authentically 'universal' language (p. 369). The performance of a foreign play is thematically relevant, since it opens up discussion of translation and circulation and of different kinds of language, restricted versus 'universal', élite (French, only understood by upper-class English speakers) versus popular, secret versus open. But *Zaïre* also has a more specific relevance: since its tragic catastrophe is brought about by the appropriation, and misinterpretation, of a letter, it also furthers Edgeworth's theme of textual appropriation, and warns of the tragic possibilities which textual appropriation might still threaten the protagonists.[53]

At this performance Altenberg falls in love with Caroline Percy because of her modesty and unselfishness. From this point in the novel the Falconers' acts of appropriation begin more and more to recoil upon themselves, while the Percies' commitment to open rather than coded, popular rather than élite, 'universal' rather than secret, languages begins, with some hitches, to work towards the happy ending. In one minor but thematically perfectly integrated episode, Buckhurst Falconer amuses the company by mimicking the Colonel, appropriating his speech and mannerisms, but so offends his model that he is punished by losing a living in the Colonel's gift (p. 422), the first serious challenge to the Falconer family's rise to worldly success.

In the climatic episode 'letters' apparently revealing his corruption have been 'forged in [Lord Oldborough's] name' and the virtuous characters need to 'discover the authors of this forgery' (p. 531). Mr Temple, friend of the Percies and the genius in the garret whose work Cunningham Falconer had appropriated, is, ironically, the one who tracks down the evidence which points to the real culprit. Recognizing the handwriting on a scrap of paper on which a lady has done a sketch, he is able to acquire this incriminating document: 'This hand, that seized it, long shall hold the prize' (p. 536). Temple here (mis)quotes the Baron in Pope's *Rape of the Lock*:[54] an act of literary appropriation, of a text itself about an act of appropriation, wittily frames the appropriation of a text by which Temple punishes original textual crimes of appropriation and misattribution. It is also appropriate that the

[53] 'Cette lettre [. . .] | Par vos gardes saisie', Voltaire, *Zaïre* (Paris: Librairie Larousse, 1972), lines 1239–40.
[54] *Pope: Poetical Works*, ed. by Herbert Davis (Oxford: Oxford University Press, 1978); Temple conflates p. 104, line 138 and p. 93, line 44.

guilty party is revealed as Mrs Falconer, who is compelled to make 'an avowal in writing of this whole transaction' (p. 545). The Falconers are justly punished for their unscrupulous quest for advancement at all cost by its logical development, the descent into outright crime of their matriarch, and for their self-serving textual appropriation by its turning against themselves.

Finally, Mr Percy is rescued from a debtors' prison and the family regain their estate by the discovery of the 'lost conveyance' (p. 607), which is found among the Falconers' papers: so strong is the novel's association of that family with textual appropriation that even in this instance, when they have not deliberately acquired and concealed this vital document, the association continues to function. Even now all is not settled, for a wicked kinsman counters it with a 'forged deed' (p. 613), though the Percies are ultimately able to prove the inauthenticity of this text: interestingly the proof does not lie in language, which has proved so slippery throughout the novel, but in the more concrete power of things, for a sixpence sealed into the document proves that it cannot have the date alleged and thus lacks the authority claimed for it. At last the Percies are able to return to their estate, and Lord Oldborough too retires to 'domestic life' (p. 631) with his long-lost son. Written language has had a malign power throughout this novel, operating as dangerous ciphers, forgeries, and secret correspondence, but it has also power to figure domesticity and renewal: Lord Oldborough has concentrated so much on furthering his political career that he has missed acquiring 'the vast resource of literature' (p. 621), an important aid to the domestic harmony of the highly literate Percies. By the end of the novel forged deeds, ciphers, secret correspondences, mutually opaque dialects, and dishonest acts of verbal misattribution and appropriation are put aside in favour of openness: it is an important symbolic detail that Mr Percy is now allowed to read Lord Oldborough's letters (p. 622). Virtue, a domesticity supported by shared literacy, and the optimistic hope of a 'universal language' of sincere shared feeling, are finally able to defeat the 'defects' and misuses of language.

Like *Patronage*, *Helen* uses this theme of textual appropriation both to establish the moral nature of its characters and to draw firm parallels between apparently only loosely connected episodes. In the central action, Helen's friend Cecilia fails in 'moral courage' (p. 37) by concealing from her severe husband the fact that before their marriage she had had a 'clandestine correspondence' (p. 281) with the rakish Colonel D'Aubigny, and that these indiscreet letters have now been appropriated by booksellers and are about to be published. Cecilia, inspired by the fact that there is 'a great resemblance' between her handwriting and Helen's (p. 274), allows her husband to believe that Helen is the true author: her only defence against textual appropriation is an act of textual misattribution which is not only dishonest and hurtful to her friend but in the long term actually makes her position more precarious rather than more secure. The innocent Helen becomes trapped in a suffocating web of appropriated and misattributed textuality, forced to choose between supporting her friend or saving her own reputation and her growing love for Granville Beauclerc. Finally, however, acts of counter-appropriation succeed in regaining and destroying the incriminating documents, and Helen is cleared, but only after a series of increasingly painful misunderstandings. These tend to focus on the slipperiness of language and the fallibility of the technology of communication: Lady Davenant, for instance, sends Helen a letter which hurtfully addresses her as Mrs Granville Beauclerc, not knowing that the marriage has not taken place, because a 'vessel [. . .] containing letters from England had been lost' (p. 413).

This potentially tragic plot based on textual misattribution and appropriation is underpinned by a number of sub-plots which deal with the same themes and images parodically. Horace Churchill's 'arts of appropriation' gain him an unjustified literary reputation: sometimes he 'quote[s]', sometimes he steals, sometimes he camouflages as 'his own' a passage he has read (pp. 170, 152–53). Everyone in this highly literate world quotes (the novel is full of references to books and reading) but other characters, such as Beauclerc or Lady Davenant, admit it when their apparent cleverness arises from 'recollection' rather than invention (p. 144). As in *Patronage*, appropriation becomes an important marker of the selfish, the shallow, and the wicked. While Churchill's plagiarisms are trivial in themselves, they imply a fundamentally unprincipled character, and it is not surprising to discover that he is also implicated in the much more serious plot of the appropriated letters.

Even apparently trivial episodes and images tie in wittily and effectively with the novel's central theme of 'arts of [verbal] appropriation'. In one episode Lady Castlefort is self-dramatizingly describing her depression and claiming that it results from 'too much mind', but this claim is instantly rendered 'risible' when 'a green parrot [. . .] awoke on Lady Castlefort's pronouncing, in an elevated tone, "All, all!", and conceiving himself in some way called upon, answered, "Poll! Poll!"' (p. 346), appropriating and travestying her words. Such a trivial episode gains significance in the light not only of the central theme of appropriation, but also of 'the contested space occupied by parrots in contemporary philosophy, anthropology and natural history'.[55] Speaking animals problematized the whole issue of language and what it meant to be civilized or even human, revealing that human language is a system of words which have no inevitable natural relationship with things but are only '*arbitrary* signs' that '*represent*' ideas.[56] Edgeworth knew that in some circumstances 'words [. . .] have power' to generate ideas, but also that words too often do not 'really represent ideas' at all but are simply a meaningless noise, like that of the parrot.[57] The parrot

[55] Markman Ellis, *The Politics of Sensibility: Race, Gender and Commerce in the Sentimental Novel* (Cambridge: Cambridge University Press, 1996), p. 75.
[56] Charles Bonnet, *The Contemplation of Nature* (1766), cited in Ellis, *The Politics of Sensibility*, p. 75.
[57] *Practical Education*, pp. 247, 64 (the latter is by Richard Lovell Edgeworth).

in *Helen* serves as a 'circulatory metaphor',[58] demonstrating the entirely hollow, meaningless circulation of language and allusion by characters such as the plagiarist Horace Churchill and the trivial hypochondriacal Lady Castlefort, whose literacy is confined to scandal and dubious romantic novels (pp. 173, 178).

In another subplot circulation, appropriation, and misattribution of texts again provide a vital theme. Lady Davenant falls under suspicion of an unprincipled act of appropriation and circulation in which public and private discourses become blurred: she has allegedly 'revealed a secret of state that had been confided to her husband' and 'suffered a letter from an illustrious personage to be handed about and read by several people' (p. 255). Like Helen, or like Lord Oldborough in *Patronage*, Lady Davenant is innocent: the document in question has been removed from a locked desk by the Spanish page, Carlos. Lady Davenant trusts the boy, convinced of his sincerity by 'the universal language of the eyes' (p. 258). However, while in *Patronage* a 'universal language' of gesture and feeling is seriously entertained as an alternative to coded, secret, easily misunderstood or class-specific verbal languages, in *Helen*, despite the dangers of words, a non-verbal language lacks specific and reliable power to communicate: as Richard Lovell Edgeworth wrote in *Practical Education*, the 'language of action [. . .] is expressive, but inadequate' (p. 60), and such a language is as vulnerable to misinterpretation as other languages in this novel. Lady Davenant has certainly misread the allegedly universal language, for Carlos in fact understands English, and uses this hidden linguistic knowledge to learn of the hiding place of the vital text, which he can then appropriate, bribed by a rival diplomat.

Lady Davenant emerges unscathed from this episode, for although allegations about her misuse of 'private letters' (p. 264) have been in 'private circulation', she is vindicated before 'private reports' can reach the 'public prints' (p. 265): in a world where women's influence 'should always be domestic, not public' (p. 254), to emerge from private life into the glare of publication would be disastrous. Cecilia also avoids the ultimate danger of publication, she and her husband succeeding in counter-appropriating the texts before full public circulation through 'scandalous papers' (p. 334) can take place. As in *Patronage*, but to an even more disturbing degree, that circulation which sometimes embodied for Edgeworth an optimistically open, enlarged field for communication also presents terrifying dangers.

However, while in *Patronage* such dangers menaced both sexes — Lord Oldborough and Mrs Percy are equally in danger from forged and appropriated documents — in *Helen* these dangers are gender-specific, threatening women, who 'cannot, like men, make their characters known by

---

[58] Ellis, *The Politics of Sensibility*, p. 77. The phrase is useful, though I do not use it in quite the same sense as Ellis.

public actions' (p. 259), with exposure to a public world outside the protection of home, family and reputation. *Helen* is after all a novel of 1834, influenced by the increasing acceptance of what were to become known as Victorian values. To a more explicit degree than *Patronage*, it is very alert and emphatic about socially-validated gendered differences in speaking, writing and reading practices.[59] For instance, 'such reading as ladies read' is emphatically contrasted with the more solid education of men (p. 76). One of the textual crimes of Lady Davenant's unregenerate youth was ignoring these differences (a symptom is her appropriation and regendering of a line of Pope).[60] Even virtues and vices are gendered, with 'self-love' being unsuited to the 'manly character' (p. 144), and with 'constancy, fidelity, fortitude, magnanimity' labelled as 'masculine' (p. 26), although Lady Davenant doubts the reality of such 'grammatical' distinctions (p. 37). The novel also draws firm distinctions between good and bad reading, though apparently only in the case of women readers: good reading means factual works, especially science and history (the innocent Helen is very knowledge-able about history, unlike the guilty Cecilia and the trivial Churchill), while bad reading means scandal-sheets and 'high-flown poetry and sentimental novels': the novel repeatedly emphasizes the dark side of the circulation of printed as well as written texts.[61]

Despite her own youthful temptations to transgress prescribed gender roles, especially through acts of textual (and other) appropriation, and despite her resistance to some of the most blatant signs of sexist language use, the mature matriarch Lady Davenant now accepts that women ought not to have 'ambition' beyond the 'domestic' sphere, though within that sphere they can still wield a political influence (pp. 68, 253). In a world where women's language, reading, and education are so different from men's, and where women's place was held to be a private, domestic sphere decisively different from the public sphere of men of the same class, the novel's themes of textual appropriation and publication are especially terrifying to the novel's female characters.

Behind the motifs of appropriation, misattribution, and dangerous circulation, the novel's central moral concept becomes truth. Lady Davenant insists that no 'virtue [. . .] can long exist without truth' (p. 37), and the novel's characters are judged in terms of their relation to truth and appropriation. Even the reading of history is seen as a commitment to truth: Lady Davenant enjoys reading when she can be confident of the author's 'character for truth', while Churchill dislikes 'grim, rigid truth' and prefers 'graceful fiction' (p. 170), and the weak Beauclerc, who proves unable to

---

[59] See above, notes 20, 23.
[60] *Helen*, p. 71. She applies to herself the lines 'By flatterers besieged, | And so obliging that she ne'er obliged', believing they were from 'the Characters of Women' (actually they are from the 'Epistle to Dr Arbuthnot', *Poetical Works*, p. 333).
[61] *Helen*, pp. 135, 94–95, 170, 176.

protect Helen, also reveals his moral character by his belief that the 'real happiness of life' consists not in truth but in 'blessed illusions' (p. 122). Churchill is not only an appropriator of the words of others, he is also a smuggler of verbal 'contraband' as he makes Helen uncomfortable with his whispered criticism of the company (p. 178). 'Smuggling' (p. 232) and 'forgery' (pp. 284, 352) subsequently become significant metaphors for the verbal acts that endanger truth and define the moral worlds of the novel's characters.

In *Patronage* the distinctions between truth and falsehood, open and secret languages, originality and appropriation, are clear-cut, and to a large extent the characters are developed only enough to embody a position in this scheme of oppositions. The scheme of truth and falsehood in *Helen* is as simple, indeed as simple as the very similar scheme in Edgeworth's most didactic work for very young children, 'The Little Dog Trusty', where Robert's fear of punishment leads him to evade the truth and so incur worse punishment, whereas the symbolically-named Frank speaks the truth and is rewarded.[62] In *Helen*, however, the characters are much more developed and internalized so that they embody the novel's moral polarities in a much more complex, humanly believable, and even ambiguous way: even Horace Churchill is not simply a figure of fun but is allowed to explain himself (p. 165).

Cecilia, who loves her husband and friend but hurts and endangers both because she believes she can survive only through deception, is drawn with conviction and a plausible ambiguity. Edgeworth probably derives the name from *Cecilia* (1782) by Frances Burney, an author and novel she admired, and Burney's Cecilia, manipulated into lies and secrecy in order to keep the man she loves, may have suggested the ambivalence of Edgeworth's.[63] (Edgeworth's demotion of Burney's heroine to anti-heroine suggests a critical, resistant reading of Burney's novel, convicting of weakness the heroine who agrees to a morally dubious secret marriage and then gives up her fortune rather than compel her husband to take her name as a condition of inheritance.) In *Helen*, Cecilia's relationship to truth and falsehood is more complex than any character in *Patronage*. At one point, for instance, she pressurizes Helen into spending more than she can afford on jewellery because she does not want her to be 'detected in passing off counterfeits' (p. 210). Here she seems to advocate truth rather than falsehood, but a trivial kind of truth that by involving Helen (like Burney's Cecilia) in debt becomes more dangerous than an innocent counterfeit. As the situation with

[62] *Early Lessons* (1801), 12th edn, 4 vols (London: Baldwin and Cradock, 1833), I, 1–15.
[63] Edgeworth recalls family readings of Burney, praises the novels, views places she visits in the light of Burney's novels, and often relies on allusions to Burney's characters to describe real and fictional people. See Colvin, *Letters from England*, pp. 169, 525; Hare, *Life and Letters*, I, 142, 212, 225; *Harrington*, p. 118; *Patronage*, pp. 58, 201, and so on. *Cecilia* is a special favourite: see Butler, *Maria Edgeworth*, p. 449; Colvin, *Letters from England*, pp. 45, 277, and *Maria Edgeworth in France and Switzerland*, p. 188. Another flawed Edgeworthian Cecilia is found in 'The Bracelets' (in *The Parent's Assistant*), while a more affirmatively presented one is the idealized heroine of *Ennui* (1809).

the letters becomes desperate, Cecilia becomes ever more trapped in lies and half-truths. The manuscript that is to be published is not even a just transcript of the letters, but a sinister 'confusion' of 'truth and falsehood', real letters rendered more saleable by the addition of 'forgeries', 'interpolations', and misinterpretations (pp. 358, 353, 365), which provide a powerful image for Cecilia's moral nature.

The novel's most complex figure is Lady Davenant, Cecilia's mother and Helen's beloved foster-mother. For much of the novel, she is associated with truth and cleared of charges of appropriation: she is not only innocent of having stolen and circulated her husband's letter but she also refuses a bribe from Lady Bearcroft, returning her diamond in an envelope marked '*Missent*', as her own 'handwriting' demonstrates (p. 236). However, her relation to truth and appropriation is more complex than this implies. In earlier life she had certainly tried to appropriate the power of her diplomat husband and gain favours for the husbands of friends through the unfortunate influence of her reading of Madame de Staël (p. 67), which almost imperils her marriage. If she gives up such desire to appropriate (inappropriate) power, however, she still remains guilty of minor acts of appropriation: on one occasion, for instance, she interrupts Beauclerc because she believes he is about to utter a cliché (p. 117), and so performs an act of verbal appropriation which is 'unjust [...] and unkind' (p. 120). Still more seriously, her attempts to appropriate political influence have caused her to 'neglect' (p. 444) her daughter, which is partly responsible for the way Cecilia grows up to recapitulate her mother's appetite for appropriation and the near-collapse of her marriage.

Patronage and *Helen*, then, create and organize complex structures through ideas of language, secret correspondences, and especially textual (and other) misattribution and appropriation. In both, the circulation of texts has a marked dark side: in both, the analysis of handwriting and other ways of establishing the authenticity of texts are important. Both signpost the centrality of these motifs in wittily miniaturized versions of the main theme, like the parrot in *Helen* and, more seriously, the press-gang in *Patronage*. In both, images of forgery, smuggling, plagiarism, and treason figure the dangerous ambiguities of language. *Patronage*, in some respects the more optimistic, imagines a cure for the ills of textuality through a 'universal language' of sincere feeling, but *Helen* doubts the transparency even of this alleged universal language and creates a world of intensely realized emotions and moral confusions without the support of such a language. In *Patronage*, writing, and in the darker *Helen*, both reading and writing, are dangerous and, while in the earlier novel this is equally true of both sexes, *Helen* emphasizes the vulnerability of women in its textual world.

The idea of coded language and an anxiety about secret correspondence, whether personal or political, was of course not unique to Edgeworth. The period of the French Revolution, the Napoleonic Wars, the disorders in

Ireland, and their aftermath, produced a preoccupation with these motifs in the real world as well as in fiction.[64] But Edgeworth uses them constantly and with a particular intensity, and the ambivalence of language is a constantly recurring theme. I shall end by considering why these motifs of appropriation had so much meaning for her. Perhaps, as I have already argued, Edgeworth as a writer fears, and punishes, the reader's capacity to appropriate and rewrite her texts for their own purposes. It is also possible that her Irish background sensitized her to issues of cultural appropriation: one of her most famous novels, *The Absentee* (1812), deals after all with the vexed issue of absentee landlords.

She is also, perhaps, guilty, evasive and even self-punishing about her own acts of appropriation. Both *Patronage* and *Helen* are highly allusive novels, and it may be that the 'anxiety of influence' in her case takes the form of attacking the very acts of allusion and appropriation in which she is herself involved. *Patronage*, as I have demonstrated, uses a number of intertexts, such as *The Rape of the Lock* and Voltaire's *Zaïre*, which are themselves about acts of appropriation, and otherwise draws from a number of other texts, including *The Vicar of Wakefield. Helen* engages in dialogue with earlier female novelists, critiquing Burney's *Cecilia* and giving Helen the surname Stanley, which is probably appropriated from the idealized family at the centre of Hannah More's *Coelebs in Search of a Wife*: it also draws on, but in some ways significantly reverses, Crabbe's verse tale 'The Confidant'.[65] In engaging herself in such acts of appropriation, which are sometimes signposted but sometimes not, Edgeworth perhaps fears that her own textual practices are more like those of Horace Churchill, or of Mrs Falconer, than of Helen or the Percies. As a result she draws attention to other acts of textual appropriation as a way, perhaps, of diverting attention from her own.

Moreover, for these two novels Edgeworth appropriates not only from the fund of literary allusion open to any educated person, but also, perhaps more disturbingly to her, from other private sources which she is involved in making public (rather as Lady Davenant is accused of doing her husband's confidential document). Despite Edgeworth's apparent nervousness about dragging private texts into the public world, she does so throughout her career, from her first publication, *Letters for Literary Ladies* (1795), in which she appropriates letters between her father and his friend Thomas Day to *Patronage*, which uses episodes from Edgeworth family history,[66] and, in all probability, beyond.

---

[64] See Mary A. Favret, *Romantic Correspondence: Women, Politics, and the Fiction of Letters* (Cambridge: Cambridge University Press, 1993) and Nicola J. Watson, *Revolution and the Form of the English Novel* (Oxford: Clarendon Press, 1994).

[65] Harold Bloom, *The Anxiety of Influence* (New York: Oxford University Press, 1973); Elizabeth Kowaleski-Wallace, *Their Fathers' Daughters: Hannah More, Maria Edgeworth and Patriarchal Complicity* (New York and Oxford: Oxford Univesity Press, 1991), p. 187; Butler, *Maria Edgeworth*, p. 458.

[66] Butler, *Maria Edgeworth*, p. 149; *Memoirs of Richard Lovell Edgeworth*, II, 342–43; *Patronage*, pp. 608–13; *Memoirs of Richard Lovell Edgeworth*, I, 17–18.

These tensions are particularly marked in *Patronage*, which not only appropriates the professional experience of her brothers in law and medicine to add conviction to the masculine plot, but is also based on an original whose appropriation might have caused particular guilt and anxiety, for the novel began as a series of stories of the Freeman family devised by Richard Lovell Edgeworth in 1788 or 1789.[67] That she was working on the novel at least from 1793 until its publication in late 1813 suggests that it was a difficult, even a painful, project.[68] Richard Lovell Edgeworth encouraged a 'literary partnership' with his daughter in which he corrected and edited her work, they engaged in full-scale collaboration on such works as *Practical Education*, and she completed some of his projects (finishing his memoirs and adding further volumes to his stories of Harry and Lucy). Maria Edgeworth claimed to regard this partnership as the 'pride and joy of my life',[69] but her constant role as compliant, even hagiographical, junior partner might well have created or fed both fear and desire to trespass on the preserve of the Father. Maria constantly sought her father's approval, even showing, in Elizabeth Kowaleski-Wallace's word, 'complicity' with the patriarch and the project of patriarchy: but at the same time her literary relationship with her father was, like that with her foster-father Thomas Day, 'personal, emotional, and conflicted'.[70] Maria's major admitted addition to *Patronage* is the character of Lord Oldborough, who moves in the course of the novel from a politician willing to use corrupt networks of patronage to a benevolent domestic patriarch,[71] and the portrait may reflect a degree of unacknow-ledged ambivalence about her father and their writing relationship. Appro-priating the work and patriarchal authority of her literal father as well as various literary parents seems to have caused Edgeworth both pleasure and the anxious, guilty need to exorcize the act of appropriation in the novel itself.

Finally, the idea of appropriation may have seemed particularly sinister to Edgeworth as a woman writer. It may be that the prospect of a transgressive crossing of the threshold between private and public life is the repressed term that returns, half-articulated, in the theme of appropriation in her fiction. An anxiety or, at best, ambivalence about the whole notion of authorship is implicit in two anecdotes in which Edgeworth concealed her authorship of a printed text from a close family member in order afterwards to surprise them with her achievement, simultaneously concealing and drawing attention to her identity as author. While her father was 'amused at the trick' of being given a special edition of 'The Modern Griselda' with the authorship concealed, her use of a similar trick on her

[67] Butler, *Maria Edgeworth*, pp. 246, 155–56; *Memoirs of Richard Lovell Edgeworth*, II, 363–64.
[68] Hare, *Life and Letters*, I, 31; Butler, *Maria Edgeworth*, p. 233.
[69] *Memoirs of Richard Lovell Edgeworth*, II, 190.
[70] Kowaleski-Wallace, *Their Fathers' Daughters*; Butler, 'Edgeworth's Stern Father', p. 80.
[71] *Memoirs of Richard Lovell Edgeworth*, II, 344.

aunt misfired, with her aunt believing Maria's criticism of her own *Belinda* springs from envy of a 'rival author', causing Maria to 'burst into tears'.[72] Even the appropriation of her own texts may prove disturbing in a world where female authorship is still potentially problematic.

That gender is implicated in themes of appropriation is clear from the fact that, although men are also guilty of language crimes of appropriation and misattribution, it is the revelation of the guilt of female characters that provides the climax of both *Patronage*, where Mrs Falconer is found guilty of forgery, and *Helen*, where Lady Katrine and her maid are revealed to have appropriated for the press letters which Cecilia has so unwisely written. *Helen*, which has been called Edgeworth's most personal novel, 'the tale which expressed herself', in particular 'reverberates with tensions generated by the act of writing itself', and '*writing itself has become the monster*' that menaces the woman writer.[73] Writing as a woman, both as mother (*Patronage*) and as daughter (*Helen*), is dangerous, associated with forgery, illicit publication, and other language crimes. Cecilia 'is a figure for the woman writer', a dark '*double*' of Edgeworth herself who embodies all her buried anxieties about writing and publication as a transgression of woman's private, domestic sphere.[74] By punishing her, or Mrs Falconer or Lady Katrine, for acts of appropriation, forgery, or misattribution, Edgeworth in effect punishes herself. By associating virtue with the loss or refusal of texts and vice with their appropriation or generation, Edgeworth reveals deep anxieties about the whole business of writing, and women's writing in particular.

---

[72] Hare, *Life and Letters*, I, 137–38, 72–73.
[73] Butler, *Maria Edgeworth*, p. 457; Kowaleski-Wallace, *Their Fathers' Daughters*, pp. 188, 195.
[74] Kowaleski-Wallace, *Their Fathers' Daughters*, pp. 191–92.

Reconfiguring the Past:
The Eighteenth Century Confronts
Oral Culture

PAUL J. KORSHIN

University of Pennsylvania

It is fair to begin an essay on oral culture by mentioning Wolf and Parry. Friedrich August Wolf, whose *Prolegomena to Homer* (1795) revolutionized classical studies of his day, did not discover oral culture, but he was the first to have doubts about the existence of an actual person called Homer.[1] Milman W. Parry, who *did* confirm the existence of oral culture in the 1930s, owed much to Wolf and to classical studies in general, but the proof he sought came not from studying the ancient world but rather from his recordings of bardic singers in the former Yugoslavia in the 1920s. Students of the Homeric writings have always been aware of the repetitions, stock epithets, or epic clichés that occur hundreds of times in these texts, which people thought to be a failing on Homer's part. But Parry was the first to suggest, in two epochal articles in *Harvard Studies in Classical Philology* in 1930 and 1932, that these constantly repeated phrases might be oral formulae that helped explain the composition of the Homeric poems by illiterate singers or bards and which also shed light on the way the poems were presented from memory by unlettered singers for whom the oral formulae functioned as mnemonics.[2]

Eighteenth-century English writers sensed the existence of a preliterate culture, too, although they did not call it by any such name. But I want to take a different route to the eighteenth-century confrontation with the preliterate past, or whatever they thought it was. This is a journey first made possible in the early 1980s, when the Eighteenth-Century Short-Title Catalogue (what we call the ESTC), the largest humanistic research project

---

[1] *Prolegomena to Homer*, trans. and ed. by Anthony Grafton, Glenn W. Most, and James E. G. Zetzel (Princeton, NJ: Princeton University Press, 1985); see pp. 26–35, where the editors discuss the effect of Wolf's grand synthesis. Wolf himself (Part I, Chapter 49) disclaimed any parallel between the situation of Homer and later writers, including, specifically, Ossian (p. 204).

[2] Parry's essays are: 'Studies in the Epic Technique of Oral Verse-Making: I. Homer and the Homeric Style', *Harvard Studies in Classical Philology*, 41 (1930), 73–147, and 'II. The Homeric Language as the Language of Oral Poetry', 43 (1932), 1–50. Two other useful studies are Albert Lord, *The Singer of Tales* (Cambridge, MA: Harvard University Press, 1960) and Eric A. Havelock, *The Muse Learns to Write: Reflections on Orality and Literary from Antiquity to the Present* (New Haven, CT: Yale University Press, 1986). Specifically relevant to the subject of the present essay is Nicholas Hudson, '"Oral Tradition": The Evolution of an Eighteenth-Century Concept', in *Tradition in Transition: Women Writers, Marginal Texts, and the Eighteenth-Century Canon*, ed. by Alvaro Ribeiro and James G. Basker (Oxford: Clarendon Press, 1996), pp. 161–76.

of the twentieth century, had produced a large enough sample of the record of English-language printing from 1701 to 1800 to allow some grand overviews of print culture. The scholars involved in creating the ESTC expected to find evidence of an explosion of print, and we did. In the first decade of the eighteenth century, 1701–10, the average output of the presses of England (and of all other books in English) was about 1,200 items per year. In the final decade of the century, 1791–1800, the average annual output was almost 7,000 items per year, and that does not count newspapers and magazines, which had burgeoned by that time. It was easy enough to explain the growth in print culture: the country's population had more than doubled and literacy had expanded greatly. Closer analyses of print culture, by genres, revealed that pamphlet literature, sermons, and religious books such as prayerbooks, hymnals, catechisms, and bibles had expanded enormously. But there were other kinds of literature that had essentially been invented, on a mass market basis, for the first time in publishing history, such as novels, narratives of personal recollections, recipe books, and children's literature. Now, the multiplicity of literary experiences that this knowledge explosion suggests would seem to highlight the very literariness of eighteenth-century England and, indeed, that is just what this evidence does compel us to conclude.

Whenever there is an explosion of activity in a given genre, as the wishes of the readership lead to a move by writers to satisfy that demand, especially when this expansion is accompanied by a rapid growth of literacy, there is reason for us to look at the situation more closely. There are two widely known nineteenth-century examples. When the Grimm brothers collected their German folk tales, they literally transcribed them from the oral recollections of common people, most usually old women, who had heard them recited when they were children. These tales had existed in oral tradition for centuries and, although none of them possesses the oral formulae that scholars had noticed in Homeric verse, they do have familiar repeating motifs. The other example concerns the early folklorists (they considered themselves to be antiquarians, of course) who printed the first accounts of popular superstitions of the common folk of rural districts. In their collections we find the first descriptions in writing of elves, gnomes, leprechauns, and the other good and evil folk of the fairy underworld. Here, too, we can be sure that these collectors were scratching the surface of oral legend. So, if we apply these methods to eighteenth-century English culture, we can find some prominent examples of collections that draw mainly on unprinted sources, that is, on the accounts that editors gathered from an often illiterate populace. Thomas Percy's *Reliques of Ancient English Poetry* (1765), for example, drew on his own Folio MS as well as printed records, but the ballads themselves had in most cases existed in oral form before the transcription from which Percy gleaned them. It is important to note, at this point, that the transcription Percy used was made in the 1580s; thus Percy and his literary circle could see themselves as participating in an editorial process that analogized that used by Renaissance scholars dealing with classical texts. The fact that Percy had a manuscript source validated his collection for contemporary readers and scholars, since this fact provided a convincing analogy to the editorial methods of the European Renaissance.

Children's literature mushroomed as a genre in the 1760s and 1770s and, while many exemplars are obviously literary works with no preliterate past, a great many of them are clearly first-time transcriptions of tales that circulated orally. Another important example is food literature. Cookbooks had existed before the eighteenth century, but there were very few of them, perhaps a dozen in an entire century. But in the eighteenth century the English press produced hundreds of them. Since cookbooks, as everyone knows, plagiarize recipes from other cookbooks, it is impossible to explain the outpouring of such books in the mid-eighteenth century as purely original documents, since there were too few sources for cookery writers to ransack. The tens of thousands of recipes that appear in the eighteenth century must come principally from the oral recollection of cooks, most of them, like the Grimm's storytelling servants, old women.

The anthropologist Edmund Leach, who has studied reading and writing in primitive cultures, observes that the earliest written records of a society are not divine hymns, religious writings, or narratives of epic exploits; they are usually lists, the most prosaic of all documents (sometimes documents are not even 'documents' in the accepted sense: early records can be engraved on ivory, wood, metal, or stone). These lists are records of ownership, property, residence. The earliest published recipes are similar: they are lists of instructions for concocting something to be eaten, not the least systematic. Often, in the early eighteenth century, recipes are still ungrammatical, like recollections. Early recipes are little narratives; indeed, if we recall the French word for recipe, *recette*, we come even closer to the orality behind this kind of text, for the word is cognate with *récit*. An important aspect of the Homeric narratives, as mentioned above, is what Parry called the oral formula. The formulae are an integral part of their constant repetition by the bards; the formulae did not merely reinforce the bard's memory for a few passages, they seem to have assisted these primitive poets in memorizing many thousands of lines, as in *The Iliad*. In a similar way, recipes are remembered and recited, always in the same order (if one upsets the order of the instructions, the dish will not succeed), and eighteenth-century recipes still contain mnemonic, formulaic statements, too, to make them easier to recall. Before I leave early cookery books, I should say something about their taxonomy, which in some ways is similar to that of modern cookbooks. Most cookbooks seem to have naturally fallen into chapters on types of food preparations: meats, poultry, game, salads, and so on. There is one curiosity, however, which has vanished from twentieth-century compilations; this is the medical chapter, usually located at the very end of the volume, and always consisting of recipes for medicinal preparations, some of them edible, some of them rather suspicious. I have traced these medicinal food preparations across the century in a number of different books, and their formulaic quality is unmistakable.

It is not unreasonable to expect that food preparations, close as they may be to oral culture, can appear in literature and thus provide evidence of the proximity of literate culture to the preliterate culture with which it coexists. There is a famous eighteenth-century example, equally famous in world literature, which eighteenth-century specialists call 'the bread episode' in Defoe's *Robinson Crusoe*. On his uninhabited island, Crusoe gradually assembles some of the goods of civilization from the wreck of his ship and, after two years, finds a few stalks of wheat growing which must have come from seeds he accidentally planted. He propagates more and, thanks to the fecundity of the tropical climate of his island, before too long he harvests enough wheat to be able to gather, thresh, mill, and prepare it for cooking. He does not make bread as such; rather, he kneads up his coarse flour with water into cakes which he bakes in the embers of a fire, and this breadlike concoction becomes his bread for the rest of his captivity (once Crusoe makes something for the first time, he seldom tries to improve it). Since this dish is unleavened, there are obviously biblical overtones to Crusoe's food — his bread would be a species of matzoh — but it is interesting that Crusoe complains about his unrisen food; he wishes he had yeast. He does not, to be sure, although one can make a perfectly good risen biscuit with soured milk, and we know that Crusoe has milk, for he keeps a herd of goats. (Actually, he really wants yeast so that he can make beer.) In an important discussion of the bread episode, Ian Watt, in his classic *The Rise of the Novel*, says that the reason why Defoe gives so much space to this episode is simple. By the early eighteenth century, most English people no longer made bread, they bought it from a bakery.[3] In fact, one of the curiosities of the early cookery books is that almost never do we find a recipe for bread, but not because everyone went to a bakery. Rather, the recipe for bread was such an intrinsic part of the oral culture of food that no one needed to publish a recipe for it. Indeed, only as recently as 1970, in *Mastering the Art of French Cooking*, alert readers came to appreciate that a full recipe for bread could be twelve pages long.[4] We find directions for making bread in all cookery books after about 1780, but in Defoe's time the directions he gives in *Robinson Crusoe*, laborious as they are, represent an element of oral culture embedded in a novel, its source almost unnoticed there.

There has been a long-standing debate about Defoe which concerns whether he is a consummate artist or a mere journalist who carelessly

---

[3] *The Rise of the Novel: Studies in Defoe, Richardson, & Fielding* (Berkeley and Los Angeles: University of California Press, 1957), p. 72.

[4] Simone Beck, Louisette Bertholle, and Julia Child, *Mastering the Art of French Cooking*, 2 vols (New York: Knopf, 1961), II, 55–67.

cobbled together artless works that he never revised.[5] I am not going to take sides in this debate; instead, I will suggest another approach to the topic. Readers of Defoe's recollection narratives, such as *Robinson Crusoe* and *A Journal of the Plague Year*, have noted and often complained about the fact that Defoe repeats himself a good deal in works of this kind. '[The] maddening repetition creates serious attention-deficit problems for the reader', writes a recent critic of the *Plague Year*. 'Much of *A Journal of the Plague Year* is little more interesting than a 1927 Sears Roebuck catalogue altered to offer the same articles for sale again and again and again.'[6] But these irksome repetitions are characteristic of texts that have just taken the first step from oral tradition. *Robinson Crusoe* comprises the recollections of just one man; its repetitions are fewer, but they have never been adequately explained. Defoe's narrative on the year of the great plague is ostensibly the story of one person, too, a saddler who signs himself simply with the initials 'H.F.'. However, we cannot explain the artlessness of the saddler's narrative by any conventional means: Defoe probably did collect his stories about the plague from oral tradition. This circumstance explains another curious quality of *A Journal of the Plague Year* — there is almost no chronology. The lack of a sense of chronology within the printed work itself is typical of texts that derive closely from oral tradition, which almost always lacks this one of the three unities. The genre of the personal recollection, which is new to the eighteenth century, probably contains many similar examples of oral accounts still recently transferred from non-literate culture to the world of print.

Defoe had close associations with different sects of the Puritan movement, where the personal spiritual recollection flourished. It seems reasonable that we should find, among the less learned, *autodidacte* representatives of this movement, evidence of the proximity of oral culture. There is no better example than John Bunyan. Bunyan was considerably influenced by what William Haller, in the 1930s, called 'spiritual gossip'; indeed, personal spiritual recollections, delivered orally and without notes before an assembly, were the *sine qua non* of the conversion experience in the 'gathered' churches. Bunyan himself, in the words of Kathleen Swaim, acknowledges that 'his conversion began when he heard four poor Bedford women exchanging their stories and "talking about the things of God" with an understanding and vision that far exceeded his own'.[7] In his account of this moment, in *Grace Abounding to the Chief of Sinners*, Bunyan makes it clear that the four women were talking to each other and that they were not reading from their own writings. (I might note, parenthetically, that the primacy of women's

---

[5] G. A. Starr was the first, to my knowledge, to discuss whether Defoe's inconsistencies are artful or accidental; see 'Sympathy v. Judgment in Roxana's First Liaison', in *The Augustan Milieu: Essays Presented to Louis A. Landa*, ed. by Henry Knight Miller and others (Oxford: Clarendon Press, 1970), p. 71.

[6] Frank H. Ellis, 'Review Article: Defoe's *Journal of the Plague Year*', *Review of English Studies*, 45 (1994), 76–82 (p. 80).

[7] Kathleen M. Swaim, *Puritan's Progress, Pilgrim's Progress: Discourses and Contexts* (Urbana: University of Illinois Press, 1993), p. 136.

narratives in Bunyan's conversion had no lasting effect in making him an advocate for women, for when, twenty years later, a group of women in Bedford suggested a separate women's prayer group, he was resolutely opposed (Swaim, pp. 227–28).) Christian, in *The Pilgrim's Progress*, Part 1, repeatedly retells the story of his conversion and the providences surrounding it to the people he meets; students of Bunyan have always assumed that these repetitions are there for emphasis. In fact, repetitions, even in a written work, sometimes also point to the recent oral nature of such portions of the text. The final form of *The Pilgrim's Progress* is therefore a palimpsest indicating, for those who are sensitive to the descriptors of orality, that portions of Bunyan's narrative had a recent oral existence.

There are relevant examples in two well-established genres that also mushroomed in eighteenth-century England, the fable and the character. Each of these derives from a Grecian source of relatively early origin. The parent of all fables is Aesop, while collections of characters date from Theophrastus. Both these writers come into European culture in the sixteenth century, early in the age of print, in spare collections. The original Aesop consisted of several dozen Grecian fables; the *editio princeps* of Theophrastus has fewer than thirty characters. But by the late seventeenth century, collections of Aesop's fables often contained four hundred individual fables in addition to the canonical few, while books of characters grow to include hundreds as well. It is difficult to trace the origin of these augmentations to established genres. Some, perhaps many of them are the inventions of contemporary authors, but others, especially those in cheaper, less polished collections, appear to be original relations of stories or descriptions of people that derive from everyday life. What I find interesting about this possibility is that the fable was one of the genres which eighteenth-century scholars considered to be among the first kinds of literature and therefore, although none of them knew this, closer to oral tradition than the more 'literary' genres. Eighteenth-century English writers had not read Vico's *Scienza nuova* (1727) either, so they were unaware of his discussion of the origin of human society and the invention of arts and sciences: Vico surmises that civil societies, their customs, and their arts gradually coalesced from the age of fable and the myths which sprang from the fabulous past. Just as the fables of antiquity derive from oral culture, so the efflorescence of fables in the late seventeenth and early eighteenth centuries must have had a similar impetus.[8] With the character book, which consists of sketches of different kinds of people collected with no internal unity or linkage among the individual sketches, we find that the earliest collections, like the one by Bishop Joseph Hall (1606), parallel Theophrastus most closely and have the most literary qualities. But the more modest collections of the later

---

[8] See Jayne Elizabeth Lewis, *The English Fable: Aesop and Literary Culture, 1651–1740* (Cambridge: Cambridge University Press, 1996), for a discussion of the eighteenth-century belief that fables were the first writings to make the transition from oral tradition to literature (pp. 48–70).

seventeenth century, especially those that appeared first in pamphlet form or in the periodical press, have many, sometimes all of the qualities of preliterate culture. Samuel Butler's collection (published a century after his death) exemplifies the colloquial character, witty and scurrilous, with repetitious phrases, like oral formulae of a sort, often appearing.

Children's literature is a genre without classical antecedents that undoubtedly started as a component of oral culture; early forms sometimes even contain the familiar oral formulae of the storyteller such as small rhymes, reduplicative phrases ('toc! toc!'), adjurations to pay attention, and other elements of local colour ('There runs a mouse! Whoever catches it can make a big cap of its fur!'). As with all genres that have a recent preliterate past, children's stories rapidly acquire a rich overlayering of moralizing from their transcribers who, after 1760, when contributions start to multiply, are often dissenting clergymen or the wives or daughters of dissenting clergymen. *Little Goody Two-Shoes* (1762), whether it is by Oliver Goldsmith or John Newbury, already is tinted with didactic commentary meant to socialize children to what existing authority considered proper behaviour.

The evidence for oral culture in eighteenth-century England is only partly to be found in traditional narrative and, so far as I can determine, the practitioners who adapted orality to literature often did not understand or value oral culture as such. There is another rich source for studying preliterate culture in this period, however, one that is more difficult to follow within the usual parameters of orality. Before grammatology, obviously, all human communication was oral, for there was no writing. This subject fascinated people in the European Enlightenment and, in the 1720s, both Vico and Swift approached preliteracy from different directions. Vico proposes a 'Search for the true Homer', impelled by his sense that evidence of refinement in Homer's writings suggested that 'the [Homeric] poems were composed and compiled by various hands through successive ages'.[9]

The narrator of Swift's *Gulliver's Travels* (1726) proceeds backward in literate time in each of his four voyages until finally, in Houyhnhnmland, he encounters beings who 'have no letters, [. . .] consequently their knowledge is all traditional'. Yet the Houyhnhnms do have bards, although Swift does not call them by this name: 'In poetry they must be allowed to excel all other mortals; wherein the justness of their similes, and the minuteness, as well as exactness of their descriptions, are indeed inimitable.'[10] In all European societies during this period, we can detect an interest in pre-alphabetic times, when communication was symbolic, in the form of signs or glyphs. Since the meaning of the Egyptian hieroglyphics was not understood until 1820, most writers who deal with this subject consider the glyphs to be signs that represented concepts (they are nothing of the kind). The popular

[9] *The New Science of Giambattista Vico*, trans. by Thomas Goddard Bergin and Max Harrold Fisch (Ithaca, NY: Cornell University Press, 1948), p. 275.
[10] *Gulliver's Travels*, Part IV, Chapter 9.

imagination in western Europe went further, of course; we will find popular writers who uncovered glyphic symbolism in artefacts that are not verbal at all; there is a cult of natural hieroglyphics in the eighteenth century. And, if one could identify pregrammatological signs in nature, it was a relatively easy step to spot them in visible signs of antiquity such as the Druidic stone circles of rural England. Stonehenge, the most popular of these with antiquarians, at first was thought to be the remains of a Roman temple but, by the 1720s, deeper study had shown that it was a pre-Roman antiquity that long antedated letters and whose meaning (if it had a meaning) depended not upon language but upon an understanding of preliterate societies. There is a message in Stonehenge, but the message is mute. The silence of the pregrammatologic sign is a concept that we will encounter throughout the eighteenth century.[11]

Thomas Gray's *Elegy Written in a Country Church-Yard* (1751) is one of the first important works to notice the existence of preliterate society side by side with literacy. The nostalgia for a simpler past and the melancholy that we feel in contemplating the last resting place of humble folk are the two most universal themes of the *Elegy*. Yet simultaneously Gray speculates that the dead of Stoke Poges may have included people of genius:

> Perhaps in this neglected spot is laid
> Some heart once pregnant with celestial fire;
> Hands, that the rod of empire might have sway'd,
> Or wak'd to extasy the living lyre.

Why are these folk forgotten, then? Gray's answer comes at once: 'but Knowledge to their eyes her ample page | Rich with the spoils of time did ne'er unroll.' The rural muse is unlearned. 'Some mute inglorious Milton here may rest' — without writing we can leave no record of our thoughts. It is clear, I think, that Gray does not realize at this stage that oral culture is transmitted by the memory. It is no paradox that at the very time that Gray was composing his *Elegy*, Samuel Johnson was preparing the first English dictionary on historical principles, the first listing of the English language founded on the belief that language is acceptable only if we can find examples of it *in writing*. So the reading of the epitaph at the end of Gray's *Elegy* should not surprise us. Gray's 'hoary-head'd Swain' brings the visitor to the tomb of the dead melancholic and tells us, 'Approach and read (for thou canst read) the lay, | Grav'd on the stone beneath yon aged thorn.' In other words, the old man is illiterate; the visitor alone can read. The short and simple annals of the poor are not just short, they are non-existent, at least in terms of the standards by which literate eighteenth-century England considered people to exist. Mute, without literacy, preliterate England, while it coexists with literate society, seems here to have no value at all. I do not

---

[11] Barbara M. Stafford discusses the silence of the message that ancient monuments offer; see '"Illiterate Monuments": The Ruin as Dialect or Broken Classic', *The Age of Johnson: A Scholarly Annual*, 1 (1987), 1–34 (p. 16).

want to condemn Gray for insensitivity towards oral culture, that would be unfair. He may have been aware of its existence, but he was ignorant of its significance. And, in his later odes, Gray shows that he has discovered the culture of Europe's Celtic fringe, of the septentrionalian lands that had remained untouched by literary culture. Now we value that culture for its primitive and unsullied purity, but to eighteenth-century minds the Celtic lands existed only to be colonized, to be converted to Christianity, taught to read Scripture, and persuaded to forget about their pagan superstitions. Gray, his scholarly interest in the septentrionalian or northern world notwithstanding, does not appreciate oral culture; his classical training and classicizing tendencies are too strong for that. To find a literary sensibility that appreciates what remnants of oral culture still remained, we must turn to Gray's contemporary Collins.

We remember William Collins today for his Pindaric odes. They are not the only effort to revive this genre between Dryden and Wordsworth, but they are certainly the most successful. Odes in English, starting with Abraham Cowley's Pindarics in the 1650s, are always intricately wrought classical poems, rich in literary allusion (Cowley actually printed pedantic footnotes to his, often a good deal longer than his texts, to display his wealth of classical and biblical references). No one would ever dream of associating this usual literary genre with oral transmission. However, Collins has one exception, a poem that he wrote in 1749 entitled 'An Ode on the Popular Superstitions of the Highlands of Scotland, considered as the subject of poetry'. It is much longer than most other odes in English, longer even than Wordsworth's 'Immortality' ode, and it is partially fragmentary, whether because there was some defect in transmission or (more likely) because Collins deliberately left a few lacunae in his text. In this context, I would note that the Duke of Cumberland's crushing of the Stuart rebellion at Culloden in April 1746, and his subsequent destruction of Highland resistance, was a topic of much current interest when Collins was writing this ode. These acts also heralded the end of the very Highland culture that Collins presents here; hence his hints of runic bards mourning brave chieftains in stanza 3 and his 'tale of war's alarms' where 'fire and steel' play a military role that sounds more like an eighteenth-century battle than some medieval joust before the introduction of gunpowder. There is Scottish diction, too, in the 'mirk hours' of stanza 6, and the description of the murderous kelpie, one of the evil fairies of English folklore (sts 7 and 8) comes directly from oral culture. Collins knew the antiquarian literature concerning the Highlands and the Hebrides, of course, but he augments what he found in his sources with details that can come only from oral tradition. This ode, unlike Collins's earlier examplars in the genre, lacks the classicizing that we expect to find in such poetry; there is only one literary allusion, to Shakespeare (st. 11), and it is consistent with Collins's view of Shakespeare as England's Homer figure, the great natural genius. The bards and singers in the 'Ode' are unlettered ('uncouth lyres', st. 3); we hear of music and song, but there is no hint of anything written or literary. Superstitions are pre-Christian, pagan, Celtic; they were not welcome in the literary circles of Edinburgh and the Scottish universities. So Collins is courageous and innovative in the 'Popular Superstitions' ode. What he introduces here for the first time would attract considerable attention later in the century.

Less than a decade would pass before James Macpherson published his first poem about Celtic culture, a six-canto epic entitled *The Highlander* (1758). We have tended to slight Macpherson because of the contemporary controversy about the Ossianic poetry that he published, for which he claimed to be the translator and transcriber. The literary establishment of England in the 1760s and 1770s, led by Samuel Johnson himself, argued that the poems of the so-called Ossian were really Macpherson's own composition. In other words, Macpherson was a forger, not the transmitter of a nearly forgotten oral culture; the eighteenth-century literary world was satisfied that his work was an elaborate hoax. But that world had no acquaintance with or knowledge of the characteristics of oral culture; they wanted evidence of literary transmission for antique writings. The ballads in Percy's *Reliques of Ancient English Poetry* could meet with approval (Johnson himself helped Percy to prepare the work for the press) because earlier records of their transmission survived, just as similar manuscript evidence could be produced for ancient Greek and Latin poetry. Johnson, the great codifier of language from written sources, had a personal reason for showing that Macpherson's work was fraudulent, for he made his own journey to Scotland in the same year, 1773, that he published a substantial revision of his *Dictionary* buttressed by even more printed sources than the first edition had contained. His published record of that trip, *A Journey to the Western Islands of Scotland* (1775), includes a long section, the longest in the entire book, on primitive Scottish culture, wherein we find the following passage:

I suppose my opinion of the poems of Ossian is already discovered. I believe they never existed in any other form than that which we have seen. The editor, or author, never could shew the original; nor can it be shewn by any other; to revenge reasonable incredulity, by refusing evidence, is a degree of insolence, with which the world is not yet acquainted; and stubborn audacity is the last refuge of guilt. It would be easy to shew it if he had it; but whence could it be had? It is too long to be remembered, and the language formerly had nothing written. He has doubtless inserted names that circulate in popular stories, and may have translated some wandering ballads, if any can be found; and the names, and some of the images being recollected, make an inaccurate auditor imagine, by the help of Caledonian bigotry, that he has formerly heard the whole.[12]

---

[12] *The Yale Edition of the Works of Samuel Johnson*, ed. by Allen T. Hazen and others (New Haven, CT: Yale University Press, 1958–), IX: *A Journey to the Western Islands of Scotland*, ed. by Mary Lascelles (1971), p. 118.

It would be fair to describe Johnson as hostile to Macpherson, whom he does not even mention by name, and there is a good deal more in the same vein. Yet it is incorrect to suppose that Johnson and his literary contemporaries had little or no knowledge of oral culture.

We can scarcely expect any of them to know about Parry's concept of oral formulae. Macpherson had visited Ireland and the Celtic parts of Scotland as early as the late 1740s, as his defender Hugh Blair mentioned, so he knew more about the Celtic bards than Johnson did (Johnson knew nothing at all). Johnson is suspicious because no one has produced the 'original', but with oral culture there is never an original manuscript available; the first literary transcription obliterates orality by the mere fact of its existence. 'It is too long to be remembered', Johnson alleges; by 'it' he means the Ossianic epic of *Fingal*. One can see how Johnson could make such an assertion. Yet he certainly could have known that *The Iliad*, as twentieth-century scholarship has shown, was not too long to be remembered (and it is more than three times as long as *Fingal*). Macpherson did not print *Fingal* and *Temora* in verse, but rather in long prose paragraphs, so the metrical qualities of oral formulae, as the Homeric bards used them, cannot be detected. But other descriptors of orality are present in force. There are frequent, overlapping repetitions of the same or similar events; there is a total lack of chronological references; there is almost no geographical precision. Macpherson, after his initial efforts to defend himself, lapsed into silence; we have assumed ever since that it was a silence of guilt, as Johnson bluntly assures us ('stubborn audacity is the last refuge of guilt'). This is not the place to examine the Ossianic texts in detail; let me simply say that Macpherson possessed neither the tools nor the knowledge to argue against his formidable foes. Others would carry on that argument for him.

Johnson, of course, was not ignorant of the existence of oral culture, at least in the distant past. As early as 1759, in an essay in *The Idler* on translation, he notes, 'In the first ages of the world, instruction was commonly oral and learning traditional, and what was not written could not be translated'.[13] And, like most of his literary contemporaries, he must have known Robert Wood's *Essay on the Original Genius of Homer*, which comments extensively on oral tradition in the ancient world, including the question of how one person's memory could retain poems as long as the Homeric writings:

As to the difficulty of conceiving how *Homer* could acquire, retain, and communicate, all he knew, without the aid of letters; it is, I know, very striking; and yet, I think, it will not appear insurmountable, if, upon comparing the *fidelity of oral tradition*, and the *powers of memory* with the *Poet's knowledge*, we find the *two first* much *greater*, and the *latter* much *less*, than we are apt to imagine.

But the *oral traditions* of a learned and enlightened age will greatly mislead us, if from *them* we form our judgment on *those* of a period when History had no other

13 *Idler* 68, *The Yale Edition*, II: *The Idler and The Adventurer*, ed. by W. J. Bate and others (1963), p. 212.

resource [. . .] nor can we, in this age of Dictionaries, and other technical aids to memory, judge what her use and powers were, at a time, when all a man could *know* was all he could *remember*.[14]

If the key to the ability of an oral culture to sustain poems as long those attributed to Ossian is the power of the human memory, then Johnson and his contemporaries certainly express their doubts for, in a great age of what Wood calls 'technical aids to memory' like the eighteenth century, during whose span generations of scholars improved and enlarged the compilations of the European Renaissance, it is natural for learned people to turn to their libraries in lieu of their memories. Yet Johnson himself was proud of the capacity and accuracy of his memory. In his last learned work, for example, *The Lives of the English Poets* (1778–81), he frequently quotes the poetry of the subjects of his biographies from his own extraordinary recollection, and there is anecdotal evidence suggesting many similar feats.

Johnson's strongest criticism of Macpherson has to do with his failure to produce any original manuscripts of Ossian. After Macpherson's death, his advocates searched his personal archives for any notes that he might have taken during his journeys to the Highlands. There was little in his personal papers to satisfy his defenders, but the Highland Society in Edinburgh commissioned a thorough study of Scottish traditional culture and, in 1805, this group issued a *Report of the Committee of the Highland Society of Scotland appointed to Enquire into the Nature and Authenticity of the Poems of Ossian*. By this time, those interested in early Scottish literature had already published a number of collections of ballads and other verse; the Highland Society went much further. The *Report*, although it is obviously inspired by Johnson's anti-Scottish strictures in the *Journey to the Western Islands*, has never come to the attention of Johnsonians.[15] The Highland Society's Committee could find no copies of Highland originals in Macpherson's own archives, so they proceeded to argue by analogy. Tens of thousands of lines of Celtic and early Scottish poetry were known, they note, so their members compared Macpherson's results with what they presumed to be untainted. As a result, the Committee concluded that 'Ossianic' poetry did indeed exist:

Such poetry did exist, [. . .] it was common, general, and in great abundance; [. . .] it was of a most impressive and striking sort, in a high degree eloquent, tender, and sublime. How far that collection of such poetry, published by Mr James Macpherson, is genuine? [. . .] [The Committee] is inclined to believe that he was in use to supply charms, and to give connection, by inserting passages which he did not find, and to add what he conceived to be dignity and delicacy to the original composition, by striking out passages, by softening incidents, by refining the language, in short, by changing what he considered as too simple and too rude for a

---

[14] *An Essay on the Original Genius of Homer* (London, 1769), p. lxi.
[15] James L. Clifford and Donald J. Greene list the early scholia on the *Journey*; they record nothing from 1789 to 1870; see *Samuel Johnson: A Survey and Bibliography of Critical Studies* (Minneapolis: University of Minnesota Press, 1970), pp. 249–51. In fact, almost all later eighteenth-century Scottish compilations of traditional poetry owe a debt, usually specifically acknowledged, to Johnson.

modern ear and elevating what *in his opinion* was below the standard of good poetry.[16]

Macpherson, then, defaced the authenticity of his presumed originals by an effort to make the style of Ossian more attractive to a contemporary audience, similar to the way the first codifiers of the Homeric writings had shaped the two epics into twenty-four books each, making the Homeric writings consistent with Athenian taste. Wood, in fact, not only makes this point, he actually draws a parallel between ancient Athenian transcription and Macpherson's practice:

> If [Lycurgus] collected and wrote down what the Ionian rhapsodists sung to him, as some curious fragments of ancient Poetry have been collected in the Northern parts of this island, their reduction to order at Athens might still be necessary; and those great names we have mentioned [i.e., of ancient literary critics] might claim the same merit with regard to Homer, that the ingenious Editor of Fingal is entitled to from Ossian.[17]

The *Report* regards Macpherson in a way that is similar to the position of Wood on the Homeric poems. While it does not clear Macpherson of the charge of simply modernizing old texts (to which Johnson had alluded in the *Journey*), it suggests that he did not forge the Ossianic poems. The available evidence shows that a large body of writings recently transcribed from oral tradition existed in Scotland and that these writings included many that are close in spirit and subject matter to what Macpherson described as the works of Ossian.

Macpherson's defenders never evaluated the evidence of his pre-Ossianic publications. His original composition, *The Highlander: A Poem in Six Cantos* (1758), is of no interest at all from the viewpoint of oral culture; it consists entirely of hackneyed heroic couplets. But his next publication, *Fragments of Ancient Poetry, collected in the Highlands of Scotland and Translated from the Galic or Erse Language* (1760), is as close to an unvarnished version of the Ossianic poems as exists. Long overshadowed by the more impressive Ossianic collections, the *Fragments* are closer to oral culture than anything Macpherson later published. The traditional descriptors of oral poetry that Parry would later identify are all present in this small collection of brief fragments: there are frequent repetitions of names and word-clusters, similar to the Homeric oral formulae; there is no sense of time or place; literary ornament is absent. Macpherson, in a brief preface, notes that 'such poems were handed down from race to race; some in manuscript, but more by oral tradition. And tradition, in a country so free from intermixture with foreigners, and among people so strongly attached to the memory of their ancestors, has preserved many of them in great measure incorrupted to this

---

[16] [Royal Highland and Agricultural Society,] *Report of the Committee of the Highland Society of Scotland* [. . .] *into the* [. . .] *Authenticity of the Poems of Ossian*, ed. and comp. by Henry Mackenzie (Edinburgh, 1805), pp. 151–54. The italics are mine. The shelf mark of the British Library copy is 79.d.14.
[17] *An Essay on the Original Genius of Homer*, p. lxv.

day'.[18] Of course, he would make similar claims, on a more grandiose scale, in *The Works of Ossian* five years later, where he reworks and rephrases this Preface of 1760, trying to give his original discovery corroboration by comparing it with the fate of oral traditions in other cultures.[19]

But the legendary exploits of Fingal and Temora, even if we assume the orthodox view that they are products of eighteenth-century intellect, nevertheless demonstrate the heightened interest of the post-Viconian Enlightenment in the archaeology of the preliterate past. Vico undertook no study of oral tradition at all, yet he hinted correctly at the possibly oral transmission of the Homeric poems. Macpherson does not introduce oral formulae (how could he?), but he knew from Homeric verse that repetitions and incantations conveyed an air of authenticity. Indeed they did, for he persuaded the learned Scottish scholar Hugh Blair, whose dissertation on Ossian's genuineness appeared in Macpherson's edition of his bard's collected works (1765). And, even after his presumed exposure, the cult of Ossian carried on without diminution on the Continent, where the truth either mattered less or was never revealed.[20] There is a story that Napoleon carried an edition of Ossian (as he thought him to be) with him on all his campaigns and believed himself to derive much inspiration from reading it.

Not only did oral culture survive throughout the eighteenth century; it actually seems to have flourished. Contemporaries, to whom the concept of orality was unknown, were attracted by the notion of what Collins calls the 'blest [. . .] primal innocence' of primitive societies and by the belief that an untaught, unlettered rural genius might prefigure England's Homer, Shakespeare. With our modern perspective on orality, preliterate societies, and the transmission of oral materials over time, we can see much more than did Collins, Gray, and Johnson. Johnson is unwittingly, perhaps deliberately, hostile to oral culture, since his own lexicographical work, like that of George Hickes before him on the septentrionalian tongues, was founded on strictly literary evidence. It is fair to say, I think, that his own visit to the Hebrides, as we can see from his *Journal of a Tour of the Hebrides* (1775), had little sympathy with preliterate Scotland. We should also be aware that Johnson had a financial stake in denying the existence of an oral culture, since to admit its existence would undermine his own print-based *Dictionary*, whose much revised fourth edition (1773) he was eager to promote. To many eighteenth-century English writers, the 'place in the north' that Blake would describe as the abode of the dreadful Urizen, with its primitive culture, was something deserving of polish and modern improvement. Just as Victor, the wild boy of Aveyron, when civilization found him in 1808, would duly receive instruction in language skills and reading, so primitive peoples in the

---

[18] *Fragments of Ancient Poetry*, 2nd edn (Edinburgh, 1760), p. vi.
[19] See *The Works of Ossian, the Son of Fingal*, 2 vols (London, 1765). I, xix–xx.
[20] The General Catalogue of the British Library lists 134 editions of Ossian by the end of the nineteenth century.

eighteenth century undergo conversion to Christianity and are taught to read and write as soon as it is convenient for them to do so. So much damage was done to oral culture through missionary zeal that we can only assemble, in makeshift fashion, secondhand fragments of what that culture was like at its height. Perhaps it is sufficient to say that, as we continue to reconfigure the past, we may acquire tools that will permit us to learn more about the 'reliques' of preliterate English culture.

The Way to Things by Words: John Cleland, the Name of the Father, and Speculative Etymology

CAROLYN D. WILLIAMS

University of Reading

'Bette is to pyne on Coals and Chalk,
Than trust on Mon, whose yerde can *talke*.'
(Alexander Pope, 'Imitation of Chaucer' (1727), l. 25.)

The etymological investigations of John Cleland (1709–89) are often ignored or dismissed as unaccountable eccentricities. Yet this seems cavalier treatment of a subject to which he devoted so much ingenuity and passion, in *The Way to Things by Words, and by Words to Things* (1766), *Specimen of an Etimological Vocabulary; or, Essay, by Means of the Analitic Method, to Retrieve the Antient Celtic* (1768), and *Additional Articles to the Specimen of an Etimological Vocabulary* (1769). His drive to reconstruct 'Antient Celtic' language and society was not a unique obsession: for Patrice Bergheaud, it is part of the 'celtomanie' which flourished between 1760 and 1780, and which he situates 'dans le mouvement complexe de "renaissance gothique" qui [. . .] rivalise avec la référence majeure du siècle, l'Antiquité latine'.[1] Cleland, however, has seldom been brought into relationship with other eighteenth-century etymologists; Stuart Piggott typically remarks, 'It may be thought surprising to find the author of *Fanny Hill* in such company.'[2] There has also been enduring reluctance to connect Cleland's etymological work with his erotic fiction. John Nichols (1745–1826) politely mentions Cleland's 'curious tracts on the Celtic language' in his obituary, but dismisses Fanny's *Memoirs* (1748–49) as a work 'too infamous to be particularised', which 'tarnished his reputation as an author': the deceased's respectability is his top priority.[3] Peter Sabor, who has different priorities, regrets that institutionalized prudery should force 'the author of the most celebrated erotic novel in English' to 'dwindle away into an undistinguished writer of miscellaneous novels, dramas, verse, journalism, and semi-learned works.'[4] Yet Cleland's etymological speculations open up fascinating perspectives on his other

---

[1] 'Le mirage celtique: antiquaires et linguistes en Grande-Bretagne au XVIIIᵉ siècle', in *La Linguistique Fantastique*, ed. by Sylvain Auroux (Paris: Clims, 1985), pp. 51–60 (p. 51).
[2] *The Druids* (London: Thames and Hudson, 1968), p. 172.
[3] *The Gentleman's Magazine*, 59 (1789), 180.
[4] 'The Censor Censured: Expurgating *Memoirs of a Woman of Pleasure*', *Eighteenth Century Life*, 9 (1985), 192–201 (p. 199).

writings, his fellow Celtomaniacs, and the wider world of eighteenth-century scholarship.

'Speculative' is used in two main senses. The more obvious conforms with Ruthven Todd's practice in his examination of the eighteenth-century 'speculative mythological background',[5] where it implies amateurishness, lack of system, and a tendency to uninformed guesswork. A second, more literal, usage refers to the tradition of compiling schematic, non-alphabetic dictionaries, whose structure provides a mirror (*speculum*) of reality.[6] Both areas of endeavour are closely involved with the etymological theories currently under investigation. Their proponents seek to establish, or restore, hitherto neglected connections between language and reality. Some claim that words have a divinely ordained, intrinsic correspondence with things that practically makes them things in their own right; others argue that languages are arbitrary codes devised by human agency. All, however, agree that linguistic investigation confers political, historical, or religious insight.

The material under discussion has been subjected to a gender-conscious reading; references are made to twentieth-century views on the link between language learning, entrance into the symbolic order, and the development of the Œdipus complex. These are not intended to endorse the psycholinguistic theories with which these views are commonly associated: invocations of the 'name of the father' are simply responses to the generally patriarchal, and specifically phallic, implications of the subject matter. Language theory itself is examined here, and eighteenth-century speculative etymologists set in a tradition of patriarchal linguistics extending from Plato to Lacan.

'An upright, springing or living line'

Establishing the importance of Celtic culture was a high priority for many eighteenth-century Britons: even Eugene Aram (1704–59) left a manuscript specimen for a Celtic Dictionary behind him when he was hanged for murder.[7] A typical example was Henry Rowlands (1655–1723) who subscribed to the commonly held theory that Celtic language, races, and traditions originated with Gomer and Magog, sons of Noah's son Japhet

[5] *Tracks in the Snow: Studies in English Science and Art* (London: Grey Walls Press, 1946), p. 28. See the chapter on 'William Blake and the Eighteenth-Century Mythologists', pp. 28–60.

[6] Werner Hüllen, 'Speculative Lexicography: Difficulties in Following the Historical Path of a Linguistic Idea', *Studies of the History of the Language Sciences*, 38 (1987), 18–26 (p. 19). There are also echoes of the 'speculative grammar' of the medieval *modistae*: see R. H. Robins, *A Short History of Linguistics*, 3rd edn (London and New York: Longman, 1990), p. 88.

[7] See Allen Walker Read, 'Projected English Dictionaries, 1755–1828', *Journal of English and Germanic Philology*, 36 (1937), 188–205 and 347–66 (p. 191, n. 20). Two recent attempts to integrate Celtomania with mainstream eighteenth-century British literature and politics are the chapter on 'Patriot Gothic' in Christine Gerrard's *The Patriot Opposition to Walpole: Politics, Poetry, and National Myth, 1725–1742* (Oxford: Clarendon Press, 1994), pp. 108–49, and Howard D. Weinbrot, *Britannia's Issue: The Rise of British Literature from Dryden to Ossian* (Cambridge: Cambridge University Press, 1993).

(Genesis 10.9).[8] Rowlands attributed political and linguistic authority to the Druids; they were indispensable in the colonization of the earth, providing the 'Language, Laws, and Religion' necessary for this enterprise (p. 53). The languages they devised were not mere arbitrary sounds, but systems for recording and conveying knowledge about the real world: 'Their most important indefatigable endeavours *in arte signorum* — in framing, enlarging, and polishing of languages, gave them occasion to make ample discoveries into the nature, habitudes, and concatenations of things' (p. 54). The correct analysis of language could, in turn, reveal the facts that lay behind it; for example, Hercules is exposed as an invader whose true name was derived from the Welsh '*Erchyll* (horrendous) a noted tyrant and destroyer of people' (p. 43, n.). Many of these opinions reappear in the mid-century works which form the basis of this study.

Perhaps the most idiosyncratic etymologist, and certainly one of the most obviously obsessed with phallic symbolism, was Rowland Jones (1722–74). Arguing with fanatical conviction, he pronounces linguistic history 'perhaps the least understood of any branch of science. This being in a great measure owing to the present corrupt state of languages, and the wrong course and direction of lexicographers in the investigation of them'.[9] He claims that Celtic was 'the first speech of mankind',[10] evolving 'a cosy world of lunatic linguistics' to prove that words have intrinsic meaning.[11] Even Plato presents this view as controversial: in the *Cratylus* Socrates considers it, citing passages in Homer's *Iliad* where gods and men use different names for the same things; this is useful knowledge, because the gods 'call things by the names that are naturally right.'[12] But in the end, he refuses to offer a conclusion on the subject. Such theories generally met with an unenthusiastic reception in the eighteenth century. In the notes to Pope's *Iliad*, for example, Plato's idea of a divine 'original Language' is cited with cool irony as 'a Notion so uncommon, that I could not forbear to mention it.'[13] The tone was set by John Locke (1632–1704), in his influential *Essay Concerning Human Understanding* (1690–1700). He believed God had given man linguistic potential, but no particular language: 'The same Liberty also, that *Adam* had of affixing any new name to any *Idea*; the same has any one still' (III. 6. §51).[14] James Knowlson, however, draws attention to the lasting influence of 'the belief

---

[8] See Henry Rowlands, *Mona Antiqua Restaurata: An Archaeological Discourse on the Antiquities, Natural and Historical, of the Isle of Anglesey, the Ancient Seat of the British Druids*, 2nd edn (London: Knox, 1766), p. 42.

[9] Rowland Jones, *Hieroglyfic: or, A Grammatical Introduction to an Universal Hieroglyfical Language* (London: Dodsley, 1768; repr. Menston: Scolar Press, 1972), Preface, A2[r].

[10] Jones, *The Origin of Language and Nations* (London: Hughs, 1764; repr. Menston: Scolar Press, 1972), Preface, B2[v].

[11] Piggott, *The Druids*, p. 171.

[12] *Cratylus*, in *Plato's Works*, VI, trans. by H. N. Fowler, Loeb Classical Library (London: Heinemann; New York: Putnam, 1926), p. 35.

[13] *The Twickenham Edition of the Poems of Alexander Pope*, ed. by John Butt and others, 11 vols (London: Methuen, 1939–69), VIII, 179.

[14] John Locke, *An Essay Concerning Human Understanding*, ed. by Peter Nidditch (Oxford: Clarendon Press, 1987), pp. 470–71.

that there had once been a common *lingua humana*, from which all other languages had descended, and that this common language had once provided an insight into supernatural truths'.[15] Jones declares, 'Language ought not to be considered as mere arbitrary sounds, or any thing less than a part, at least, of that living soul, which God is said to have breathed into man.'[16] His attribution of mystical significance to the sounds of speech appears in his statement that

Man of all animals in the expression of joy and admiration makes use of the o, which signifies eternity; but other animals seem to sound the letter a, signifying the earth; man also is upright, with his countenance towards heaven; but beasts look downwards upon the earth, as if their utmost joy and pleasure centered there. Besides all nature, according to the psalmist, declares this handy work of providence, even the dull sheep, though perhaps insensibly, calls out ba, which signifies an earthly animal. (B2^r)

Jones found meaning not only in sounds, but in letter-shapes. He uncovered the significance of the primitive alphabet conferred upon Adam: 'Mercury, Gomer, or Hermes, and other Druids, leaders of the western colonies, were always possest of those *secret* characters' (p. 12). They were composed of 'strait lines, and circles', very like the Roman alphabet used in most western writing at the present day (p. 12). Others had noticed the simplicity of the alphabet's basic ingredients, but attributed it to human ingenuity.[17] The pictures formed by the letters are sometimes easy to spot, once Jones has explained them. In 'An Universal English Grammar' he says, 'The letter i is the element of fire and all its qualities, which by its rays, dots and lines penetrates bodies and causes the flow and spring of things and also light, and it signifies man, as a lighted candle, and an upright, springing or living line and also length, the pronoun i and the first person singular or man.'[18] *Y* 'represents man on his head, with his legs extended after his fall in Eden' (p. 4), a passage curiously reminiscent of the 'Meditation on a Broomstick' (1710; written in 1703) by Jonathan Swift (1667–1745): 'What is Man but a topsy-turvy Creature' His Animal Faculties perpetually mounted on his Rational; his Head where his Heels should be, groveling on the Earth.'[19] Like other enthusiasts, Jones could be impressively immune to humour.

[15] *Universal Language Schemes in England and France, 1600–1800* (Toronto and Buffalo: University of Toronto Press, 1975), p. 13. Eighteenth-century etymologists either had no knowledge of the most obviously cabalistic texts of the Middle Ages and the Renaissance, which Knowlson discusses in detail, or deliberately refrained from citing them. Rowland Jones, in the list of 'Authors before referred to' at the beginning of the *Origin of Language* ([C]1^r–[C]2^r), which is rich in classical and near-contemporary references, especially histories, steers clear of such compromising company as Lull and his followers, even though their theories closely resemble his own.
[16] *Hieroglyfic*, B2^r.
[17] See Sir John Chardin, *Voyages du Chevalier Chardin, en Perse, et Autres Lieux de l'Orient*, 4 vols (Amsterdam, 1735), II, 168, and Jean-Jacques Rousseau, *Essai sur l'Origine des Langues*, in *Oeuvres Complètes*, 6 vols (Paris: Hachette, 1856–57), I (1856), p. 377.
[18] 'An Universal English Grammar', in *The Circles of Gomer* (London: Crowder, 1771; repr. Menston: Scolar Press, 1970), pp. 3–4.
[19] Jonathan Swift, *Prose Works*, ed. by H. Davis, 14 vols (Oxford: Blackwell, 1939–68), I, 240.

According to Jones's system, letters had a morally ambiguous origin:

The generative powers, or certain characters or letters representing them, engraved on the *bark* of the tree of knowledge of good and evil, furnishing the first pair, in their state of innocence, with two sorts of ideas or knowledge, and the means of gratifying their lust, as well as pride or curiosity of knowing good and evil, like their superiors.[20]

To prove his point, images of human sexuality emerge from Jones's account of the alphabet, in letters such as

Epsilon and Heta, the elitoris [sic], erectors, and all the interjectory generative springs.
Phi, the penis in action and generative qualities.
Gamma, the testicles, or an action about the mother.
Pe and Psi, the penis not in action, and animal and other dead parts. (p. 13)

In Jones's last work, *The Io-Triads* (1773), the apparatus of generation tends to appear with disconcerting frequency, and little or no introduction: the information that c, f, g, ch, q, and several other letters 'are not primary symbols' is immediately followed by the intelligence that 'f and g signify the semen and its fluxion in generation, flying &c.'[21] For Jones, the phallic and the linguistic are inseparably entwined at a fundamental level.

Jones paid microscopic attention to the form of words, attributing meaning to every single letter or pair of letters. A single word could emerge as the agglutination of several primitive roots. This technique is applied throughout the *Origin of Language*'s 'Etymological and Critical Lexicon', where Jones demonstrates the kinship of European languages by giving each word in English, Welsh, Greek, and Latin before proceeding to the derivation, which is considered as equivalent to a definition. It is hard not to suspect a certain amount of circular reasoning in the following entry, which so conveniently underpins eighteenth-century attitudes to prostitution: 'WHORE; PYTAN; PORNE; MERETRIX. Pytan is from py–tan, a filthy or dirty under, or from pe–tan, an under thing; porne seems to be from p–arni, the thing upon her; or from phy–arni, the phye upon her; whore is from who–ar, all upon her, who, as in whole, here signifying all; meretrix is from merx–trix, an unfortunate woman.' There might, however, be even more grounds for feminist readers to resent Jones's treatment of respectable women: 'WOMAN or WIFE, MERX or GWRAIG; GYNE or GUNAIKOS; MULIER or UXOR. As to mulier, see Maid; uxor is from ax–wr, from man; gyne is from ag–un, from one or an offspring; wife is from w–fe, my animal; woman is from w–o–man, an animal from man; gwraig is from gwr–ag, from man; merx is from mi–wr–ax, my offspring.' Whether Jones is thinking in physical or political terms, his linguistic theory emanates from a man's world.

Similar attitudes appear in L. D. Nelme's *Essay towards an Investigation of the Origin and Elements of Language and Letters* (1772). He identifies English-Saxon

[20] *Hieroglyfic*, Preface, A3ʳ.
[21] Jones, *The Io-Triads; or, The Tenth Muse* (London: 1773), p. 10.

with the language of Japhet, whom the Europeans 'have ever acknowledged' as 'the father of speech, and of language'.[22] Like Jones, he is fascinated by letter formation. The line, as sign of supreme patriarchal power, takes precedence over the explicitly feminine circle:

This *symbol* of extent, and the badge of executive power, appears to have been received in all ages, and by (nearly) all nations: hence, probably, the universal regard shewn to *staffs* among the Druids. [. . .]

O the second *rad–ic–al* symbol, is expressed by a *rod* or *staff* bended round. We give this the second place in the table, because it is as a *matrix* to all the other symbols, whence, or rather wherein, they are formed. (p. 104; see Figure 1)

Nelme is also ready to envisage a ceremonial combination of rod with circle, and to associate this with public acknowledgement of human sexuality and fertility:

The *circle* hath already been hinted at, as the *form* wherein the primordial assemblies were held for worship, debate, consultation, and rejoicing: the latter cause of assembling may have been the origin of our May-pole and garland (a *line* and a *circle*) and the custom of *kissing the maids under the missletoe* [. . .] that was hung thereon; for, at such assemblies, the inclinations of the young people were discovered, not to be hindered, but to be promoted for the general weal. (p. 105)

'One of the most sacred and expressive of names'

Jones and Nelme could be considered obscure nonentities, but James Parsons (1705–70) is a different matter. His claim to fame, like Cleland's, was quite independent of etymology — and, some observers might think, quite foreign to it. He had a distinguished medical career; his most famous publication was *A Mechanical and Critical Enquiry into the Nature of Hermaphrodites* (1741). His contribution to the etymological debate was the massive *Remains of Japhet: Being Historical Enquiries into the Affinity and Origin of the European Languages* (1767). Although he does not introduce human reproductive apparatus into his etymological analysis, he employs the techniques of textual exegesis when establishing sexual boundaries. He considers the 'Certainty of the Existence of Hermaphrodites in Human Nature [. . .] a Scandal thrown upon the whole Race of Mankind.'[23] The scandal arises when observers ignorant of the existence of the clitoris misread the signs: 'It is therefore not much to be wonder'd at, that at the first Sight of a large Clitoris, divers odd Conjectures should arise, and supply the Fancy of those unskill'd in a due Knowledge of the Part, with Matter sufficient for the Erection of a new Doctrine' (p. 9). He appeals to the divine word's creative authority to validate the sexual identity of every human being — including, incidentally, the author: 'It is impossible that there should be the least

[22] (London: Leacroft, 1772; repr. Menston: Scolar Press, 1972), pp. 14–15.

[23] James Parsons, *A Mechanical and Critical Enquiry into the Nature of Hermaphrodites* (London: Walthoe, 1741), p. liii.

FIGURE I. 'The Chief Druid', Henry Rowlands, *Mona Antiqua Restaurata*, opposite p. 65. Reading University Library, Overstone 21 J

Reproduced by permission of Reading University Library

Imperfection in the Rudiments of any of the Ova, since they were implanted in Females from the Beginning of Time, by the Almighty *Fiat*, and were under the Restriction of that Law, that every Day's Experience confirms to us is certain; for if there was not so absolute a Law, with respect to the being of only one Sex in one Body, we might then, indeed, expect to find every Day many preposterous Digressions from our present Standard' (pp. 6–7).

The Remains of Japhet also vindicates the ways of God, in this case by demonstrating the benign efficiency with which he superintended mankind's primitive history: 'We see also in every ordination of GOD, whether physical or œconomical, the most consummate wisdom in the distribution of the necessary incidents for the progress of the divine purposes, till they are actually fulfilled.'[24] He aims to prove the primordial antiquity of the Irish and Welsh (or, as he calls them, 'Magogian' and 'Gomerian') languages. A high point for those who appreciate grand claims is his translation, and enthusiastic approval, of Colonel Grant's letter to Monsieur de Lisle. Grant describes a Tibetan medal, identifying the language of the inscription as Irish, and recognizing one of the words as the genitive case of the Irish word for *God*: 'The word DIA is one of the most sacred and expressive of names; its roots are the word, or affirmative particle, *Do*, and the five vowels *u, o, i, e, a*: these vowels are not only the elements of the *Irish* language, but also of the distinct names of GOD, forming as many names of GOD besides, as their combinations together can admit of' (Parsons, p. 190).[25] Pronouncing this name with a proper knowledge of the roots is a religious education: 'It is the property of our tongue to have all its words expressive, and all its sounds calculated to represent all the tracts, or lines, and paintings of nature' (p. 191). This name of the father is pregnant with its own meanings. Grant concludes (and Parsons agrees) that 'our common language of *Ireland*, is the sacred language of this religious sect; a knowledge that gives us a true notion of the theology of the *Lamas*' (p. 195).

'*The* standing May *of Justice*'

Compared to the foregoing speculations, Cleland's theories and methods are a triumph of moderation. Far from suggesting mystical interpretations, he adopts an aggressively secular stance: many words associated with Christian rites and doctrine are derived from Druidic legal and political institutions; *religion* itself alludes to the binding power of law.[26] He attributes no intrinsic significance to sounds or letter shapes; he has no wish to 'reduce

---

[24] Parsons, *The Remains of Japhet: Being Historical Enquiries into the Affinity and Origin of the European Languages* (London, 1767; repr. Menston: Scolar Press, 1968), p. 10.
[25] The mystic significance of vowels is not a dogma confined to Irish etymology. For Dante's use of this idea, see Albert Russell Ascoli, 'The Vowels of Authority (Dante's *Convivio* IV. vi. 3–4)', in *Discourses of Authority in Medieval and Renaissance Literature*, ed. by Kevin Brownlee and Walter Stephens (Hanover, NH and London: University Press of New England, 1989), pp. 23–46.
[26] John Cleland, *The Way to Things by Words* (London: Davis and Reymers, 1766), p. 6.

the language sought for to nothing but the vague of mere minims of speech, or sounds of vowels and consonants' (p. iii). He makes no claim to having discovered the *lingua humana*, and does not attempt to establish the superior merit or antiquity of any living language. He maintains only that an ancient Celtic language must have been the mother tongue of Europe. That is not to say that his arguments would carry conviction today. From the evidence of Homer's reference to the language of the gods, Cleland deduces that Homer was the inheritor of a culture far older than that of ancient Greece, which he only imperfectly understood (p. 1). Homer's poems were not originally composed in Greek, but translated from the 'Celto-Etruscan' (p. 70). This was one dialect of the language of the '*Gods*, or, literally speaking, the *Goths*' (p. 9, sub *styx*), which was 'a name the north-western conquerors assumed, under *Bacchus*, who is demonstrably the *Osiris* of Egypt, and the *Indathyrsus* of Strabo' (p. 1). In support of his thesis, he cites 'the assertion of the ancients, that the heathen mythology had a Celtic original' (p. v).

Cleland reconstructed ancient European languages and customs with the aid of a wide acquaintance with living languages, a smattering of historical knowledge, a flair for free association, and unbounded agility at leaping to conclusions. Strong political inferences could be drawn from his picture of an oligarchical society, where a sturdy aristocracy, guided by benevolent Druid wisdom, defended their freedom and rights to justice, participating conscientiously in the processes of government, and never knuckling under to tyranny. Cleland's chief object was 'to penetrate specifically into the state of our national antiquities, in the times prior to the Roman invasion: remote as which age may seem, most of our laws and customs, at this very moment in vigor, essentially depend on those times, and have demonstrated an unbroken connection with them.'[27] This was stirring stuff in the 1760s, when there were frequent protests at the excessive powers of the crown. Cleland recounts the penalties which he believes were paid by those who neglected their political responsibilities, under *Mallom-Mot*. This was a national assembly, where prompt attendance was, according to Cleland, encouraged by sacrificing the member who arrived last:

This severity was however, at length, softened to a defamatory punishment, which was, in the face of the assembly, to carry a dog, and to kiss his posteriors. This shame was held little inferior to death itself. Thence that low expression *lag-last*, &c. thence the Dutch term of contumely *Hound's-foot*, allusively to having been the footstool to a dog (*Hound.*) Thence the French have their word *Vergogna* (*Fer-cagna*) carrying a dog. This custom of *carrying the dog*, was especially inflicted on traitors, whose crime was not absolutely capital, and existed in Germany till very lately. There are traces of this custom, to this day, in Poland.[28]

Cleland invokes the potent patriarchal forces in support of his system. He exercises his etymological prowess on the names of the classical gods,

---

[27] Cleland, *Additional Articles to the specimen of an Etimological Vocabulary* (London: Davis, 1769), pp. viii–ix.
[28] Cleland, *The Way to Things by Words*, p. 29.

beginning with '*Jupiter*. God the Father, or rather the *Good* Father', which he annotates with the observation that 'It is very remarkable, that the attribute of *Good* for *God*, which is but a contraction of *Good*, is almost universal. Zeus, *Deus*, and *Dieu* all signify *Good*. The Egyptian *Theut* is the Good, and with the *paragoge* of *ates* Theutates is the *Good Father*, Th'eut-Dad' (p. 3). But worship of a heavenly despot does not endorse earthly monarchy. Cleland shows an ancient phallic symbol standing for the people's rights, when he describes the Druids giving judgement under a column, or *May*.[29] In Cleland's hands, the maypole becomes an implement with which to demolish the divine right of kings:

Majesty. This word is taken to come from a Latin word *Majestas*, which is so far from true, that

Majestas comes demonstrably from the Celtic *May-est*, or the *standing May* of Justice. [. . .] It was essentially peculiar to republics, the people assembling round it.[30]

Modern symbols of regal power are transformed into memorials of republican glories:

Many of our *Insignia* of authority, now in use, the Crown, the Scepter, the *Sanction* of the *Scepter*, by touching the Acts, or *Bills*, the Mace, the Sheriffs Wand, and so low as the Constable's staff, being all relicks or types of that Reign of Themis (the Wand of Justice) or *Astrea* (the May-pole) so much regretted by the Poets, and which were beyond all doubt of Druidical institution, all the symbols, all the terms of government being taken from their *Religion* of the *Grove*, and its great column the May, (by pleonasm the Maypole) for they are synonymous. (p. 33)

Cleland attributes political significance, albeit indirectly, to another distinctive aspect of male anatomy in the course of an attempt to prove that *priest* had, originally, no spiritual connotation, but was the word for a high-ranking official, charged with civil administration. He claims that '*Balac* or *Belec*, is one of the ancient words to signify a *priest* [. . .] Balac of Baron's Ley, or contractedly *Brehon Ley*, furnishes the solution of a vile vulgarism, most probably, at first, used to ridicule the ministers of the antient Laws of Britain' (p. 9). Readers who find the solution more accessible than the problem may be enlightened by consulting the *Lexicon Balatronicum* (1811), which glosses *ballocks* as 'a vulgar nick name for a parson. His brains are in his ballocks, a cant saying to designate a fool'.[31] Yet again, a glorious past is reconstructed from the fragments of an imperfect present.

Cleland and the other etymologists were not working in a cultural vacuum: contemporary reaction reflects a conscientious effort to understand whatever seems worthy of comprehension. Authors are praised in proportion to the perceived rationality of their arguments. Nelme and Jones were

---

[29] For an instance of Cleland's passion for justice, see the account of his conduct in the lawsuit between Soncurr and Lowther, in William J. Epstein, *John Cleland: Images of a Life* (New York and London: Columbia University Press, 1974), pp. 39–43.
[30] Cleland, *Additional Articles*, p. 66.
[31] [Francis Grose and others], *Lexicon Balatronicum* (London: Chappell, 1811).

ridiculed by the reviewers. Nelme's *Essay* is parodied by a 'Symbolical Investigation of the Word TIBURN': it is written in Hebrew characters; each letter is revealed as a pictorial representation of some aspect of the execution.[32] The *Critical Review* places Jones beyond the reach of conventional criticism: 'The author talks like a druid rising out of the grave after eighteen hundred years asleep. No man dares disbelieve him, and no critic can contradict him.'[33] Evan Evans (1731–88), the greatest Welsh scholar of his day, gives Jones short shrift in a letter to Thomas Percy, dated 6 September 1765: 'a shame to common sense! O fie! O fie!'[34] (The connotations of 'fie' at that period suggest that Evans is not only responding to Jones's poor logic, but rebuking perceived obscenity.) Cantankerous to the last, Jones pours contempt on Nelme and Cleland:

> Thus we see the elaborate fabric of the redoubtable Mr. Nelme, after 30 years of hard labour, sapped to the ground, like the baseless fabric of a vision, without a single prop left him for its support; and his blessed coadjutor for the Belgic Saxon, the author of the Essay upon the Way by Words to Things, ought to know how to make his own way to words before he should pretend to teach others how to make their way to things by words; for although he pretends to be perfectly convinced of the natural connection betwixt words and things, he has not been able to furnish us with a single, perfectly right definition of his own in his whole Essay.[35]

Even more temerarious is his patronizing attitude to Johnson's *Dictionary*, 'which must always stand its ground, as the doctor like others has not presumed, by any definitions, to force the English language from its true origin' (p. 47).

Where Cleland and Parsons are concerned, urbanity is the order of the day. Cleland himself, writing on *The Remains of Japhet* for the *Monthly Review*, is unconvinced by Parsons's identification of Welsh and Irish with Gomerian and Magogian, but acknowledges that 'what the Author adds of the antiquity of the Druids of both Britain and Ireland being much superior to that of the Greek mythologers, is demonstrably true.'[36] The *Critical Review* responds to Cleland's work by conceding that 'nothing can be more plain than the radical affinity between the different languages that now exist not only in Europe, but in Asia', but takes him to task for 'the confused, inconclusive, and arbitrary state in which his performance presents itself'.[37] By any standards, this is fair treatment.

Mid-century etymologists received a warning from the grave. Swift, ever alert to linguistic developments, parodied such endeavours in his post-humously published 'Discourse to prove the Antiquity of the English

---

[32] *Critical Review*, 33 (April, 1772), p. 313.
[33] *Critical Review*, 18 (October, 1764), p. 306.
[34] *The Correspondence of Thomas Percy and Evan Evans*, ed. by Aneirin Lewis (Clinton, MA: Louisiana State University Press, 1957), Letter 34, p. 115.
[35] Jones, *The Io-Triads*, p. 47.
[36] [Cleland], *Monthly Review*, 38 (June 1768), p. 477. See Epstein, *John Cleland*, p. 161.
[37] *Critical Review*, 22 (August, 1766), pp. 135–36.

Tongue' (1765); his satiric persona claims that 'our language, as we now speak it, was originally the same with those of the Jews, the Greeks, and the Romans.' In his version of events, Hercules acquired his name from his excessive devotion to the Lydian queen Omphale: because he was longer subject to her than any of her other lovers, 'he was in a particular manner called the chief of *her cullies*'.[38] Linguistic analysis is reduced to a vulgar pun, implying a more or less serious suspicion that all such studies operate at a low intellectual level. But such satire proved to be a glass in which, like other men, etymologists saw every face but their own.

'A very natural symbol'

Did Cleland and other pre-Freudian etymologists know what they were doing? There is plenty of evidence that eighteenth-century Englishmen recognized phallic symbols. The most celebrated eighteenth-century publication on the subject was *An Account of the Worship of Priapus* (1786) by Sir William Hamilton (1730–1803) and Richard Payne Knight (1750–1824). The latter's 'Discourse on the Worship of Priapus' insists that phallic images associated with religious rites, Christian or pagan, should not be viewed as simple imitations of the erect penis, but as signs of divine glory: it will 'be found to be a very natural symbol of a very natural and philosophical system of religion, if considered according to its original use and intention'.[39] Phallic worship is presented as a concomitant of the innocence and simplicity of ancient peoples:

What more just and natural image could they find, by which to express their idea of the beneficent power of the great Creator, than that organ which endowed them with the power of procreation, and made them partakers, not only of the felicity of the Deity, but of his great characteristic attribute, that of multiplying his own image, communicating his blessings, and extending them to generations yet unborn? (pp. 28–29)

The phallus as image of law, order, and the speaking voice can also be found in an engraving of 'the celebrated bronze in the VATICAN' (See Figure 2), which has

the male organs of generation placed upon the head of a Cock, the emblem of the Sun, supported by the neck and shoulders of a Man. In this composition they represented the generative power of the Ερως, the OSIRIS, MITHRAS, or BACCHUS, whose center is the sun, incarnate with man. By the inscription on the pedestal, the attribute, thus personified, is styled The Saviour of the World [. . .]; a title always venerable, under whatever image it be represented. (p. 54)

The word used for world, κόσμος, means more than just the material universe: it implies order. This phallus, placed at the customary site of

---

[38] Swift, *Prose Works*, IV, 231–39 (pp. 232, 234).
[39] William Hamilton and Richard Payne Knight, *An Account of the Remains of the Worship of Priapus, Lately Existing at Isernia, in the Kingdom of Naples [. . .] To which is added, A Discourse on the Worship of Priapus and its Connexion with the Mystic Theology of the Ancients* (London: Spilsbury, 1786), p. 24.

FIGURE 2.   Bronze in the Vatican
collection, W. Hamilton and R. P. Knight,
An Account of the Remains of the Worship of Priapus,
Plate II, Fig. 3 (p. 3). Bodleian Library,
Vet. A5.d. 1445
Reproduced by permission of the Bodleian Library, University of Oxford

speech and thought, is a powerful guarantor of universal laws endorsed by
the might of natural and supernatural patriarchy. It is not surprising that, in
a subsequent publication, Knight elaborated his discoveries into a systematic
account of a 'Symbolic Language'.[40] An even more explicit link with
speculative etymology is forged when Thomas Maurice (1754–1824)
gleefully observes that, during their dance round the maypole, 'Englishmen
unknowingly celebrate the Phallic festival of India and Egypt'.[41] Still, it
would be a mistake to leave Freud and his successors out of the frame. If the
customary angle of vision is slightly altered, their presence in the same
picture as the eightcenth-century speculative etymologists becomes very
instructive.

[40] See Knight, *An Enquiry into the Symbolic Language of Ancient Art and Mythology* (London: Valpy, 1818),
especially pp. 13–15.
[41] [Thomas Maurice], *Indian Antiquities*, 7 vols (London, 1792–1800), VI, 87.

John Forrester points out that the first psychoanalysts used the techniques of contemporary philology in their search for symbols, which are 'privileged since they refer us back to a time when the name and the thing matched each other perfectly'.[42] More sophisticated, but still recognizably similar, are the theories of Jacques Lacan. He argues that language marks the child's entrance from the imaginary into the symbolic order; it breaks up the blissful mother-child dyad which lasts from birth through the 'mirror stage', when the helpless uncoordinated baby, supported by its mother, receives a flattering image of its own power and stability:

> Cette image est fonctionnellement essentielle chez l'homme, pour autant qu'elle lui donne le complément orthopédique de cette insuffisance native, de ce déconcert, ou désaccord constitutif, lié à sa prématuration à la naissance. Son unification ne sera jamais complète parce qu'elle s'est fit précisément par une voie aliénante, sous la forme d'une image étrangère, qui constitue une fonction psychique originale.[43]

This state of affairs cannot be allowed to go on for ever: 'Mais supposons un instant, dans une sorte d'Eden à l'envers, un être humain entièrement réduit dans ses relations avec ses semblables, à cette capture assimilante et dissimilante à la fois. Qu'en résulte-t-il?' (p. 110). To avoid a disastrous collision, the name of the father must be invoked:

> Le complexe d'Œdipe veut dire que la relation imaginaire, conflictuelle, incestueuse en elle-même, est voué au conflit et à la ruine. Pour que l'être humain puisse établir la relation la plus naturelle, celle du mâle à la femelle, il faut qu'intervienne un tiers, qui soit l'image de quelque chose de réussi, le modèle d'une harmonie. Ce n'est pas assez dire — il y faut une loi, une chaine, une ordre symbolique, l'intervention de l'ordre de la parole, c'est-à-dire du père. Non pas le père naturel, mais de ce qui s'appèle le père. L'ordre qui empêche la collision et l'éclatement de la situation dans l'ensemble est fondé sur l'existence de ce nom du père. (p. 111)

The phallus plays a crucial part in these negotiations. In 'The Meaning of the Phallus' (first presented in 1958) Lacan calls it 'a privileged signifier, a signifier of that mark where the share of the logos is wedded to the advent of desire'. But 'the phallus can only play its role as veiled, that is, as in itself the sign of the latency with which everything signifiable is struck as soon as it is raised (*aufgehoben*) to the function of signifier'.[44] In Freudian doctrine, Lacan reminds us, the phallus is not 'the organ, penis or clitoris, which it symbolizes. And it is not incidental that Freud took his reference for it from the simulacrum which which it represented for the Ancients' (p. 79). Its true identity lies in its political and lingusitic functions.

---

[42] *Language and the Origins of Psychoanalysis* (London and Basingstoke: Macmillan, 1980), p. 129.
[43] *Le Séminaire de Jacques Lacan*, Texte Établie par Jacques-Alain Miller, *Livre III: Les Psychoses (1955–1956)* (Paris: Seuil, 1981), p. 110.
[44] Jacques Lacan, 'The Meaning of the Phallus', in *Feminine Sexuality: Jacques Lacan and the 'Ecole Freudienne'*, ed. by Juliet Mitchell and Jacqueline Rose, trans. by Jacqueline Rose (Basingstoke: Macmillan, 1982), pp. 74–85 (p. 82).

'A social *language!*'

Sandra Gilbert and Susan Gubar have shrewdly noted that mothers play a crucial role in teaching babies to speak, and that language acquisition precedes the Œdipus complex. Consequently, the phallus seems an inappropriate entrance cue to the linguistic symbolic order. They suggest that

the power of the father, while obviously representing the law of patriarchy, need not be inextricably bound to the power of language. Indeed, the fact that the father is a supreme fiction in this now widely disseminated French Freudian theory points, paradoxically enough, to the primordial supremacy of the mother [. . .]. If the primary moment of symbolisation occurs when the child identifies difference with distance from the mother, it is not only the presence of the mother's words that teaches the child words, but also the absence of the mother's flesh that requires the child to acquire words.[45]

This is a convincing interpretation of Sigmund Freud's famous account of the *fort-da* game, showing how speech and ritual play enabled a child to attain the 'great cultural achievement' of accepting his mother's departure without complaint.[46] More immediately interesting is their insight that men's accounts of language formation and acquisition are in themselves suitable cases for critical treatment as forms of 'male fantasy devised to soothe men's feelings of secondariness, sexual dread, womb and breast envy' (p. 97).

The founding Judæo-Christian myth of language formation reflects the emotional inadequacy of the solitary human male. Adam's first recorded words were spoken after God, deeming that it was not good that the man should be alone, decided to alleviate his solitude:

And out of the ground the Lord God formed every beast of the field, and every fowl of the air; and brought them unto Adam to see what he would call them: and whatsoever Adam called every living creature, that was the name thereof.
And Adam gave names to all cattle, and to the fowl of the air, and to every beast of the field; but for Adam there was not found an help meet for him. (Genesis 2. 9–10)

The problem is solved only when God makes Eve. Opinions vary, however, as to how closely Adam's acquisition of language was related to the search for companionship: Pierre Bayle (1647–1706) mentions, only to deny, rabbinical rumours that 'ingressus fuerat Adam super omne jumentum & feram, neque refrigerata est illius concupiscentia, quosque [sic: misprint for *quousque*] copulata est ei Eva'.[47] More decorously, Edward Davies (1756–1831) presents Adam's linguistic development as a pastoral idyll, where his knowledge of animals provides entertainment for Eve. At first,

[45] Sandra M. Gilbert and Susan Gubar, 'Sexual Linguistics: Gender, Language, Sexuality', *New Literary History*, 16 (1985), 515–16, 523–42; repr. in *The Feminist Reader: Essays in Gender and the Politics of Literary Criticism*, ed. by Catherine Belsey and Jane Moore (Basingstoke: Macmillan, 1989), pp. 91–99, 225–29 (p. 96).
[46] Sigmund Freud, 'Beyond the Pleasure Principle', Standard Edition, 24 vols (London: Hogarth, 1953–74), XVIII: *Beyond the Pleasure Principle, Group Psychology and Other Works*, p. 14.
[47] *A General Dictionary, Historical and Critical*, trans. by J. P. Bernard and others, 10 vols (London: Strahan, 1734–41), V, 123, n. *H*, sub *Eve*.

when Adam saw animals, 'the social character of his disposition prompted him to attract their attention, by visible, and audible signs,' but he soon realized none of them was his intellectual equal.[48] Eve's creation, however, put him on his conversational mettle; this is how he would set about describing the elephant (*behemoth*):

His arms would be elevated, and spread abroad — in order to intimate the comprehension of gigantic space.

This descriptive gesture would be aided by an immediate, and spontaneous inflation of his cheeks, till breath would find a passage through his nostrils. This natural description of a huge bulk would produce the sound *B*, — *M*; and that sound, rendered articulate by the intervention of a vowel, would describe bulkiness, and might be appropriated most happily, to the *elephant*, or great beast. (pp. 382–83)

Later, Adam and Eve take a walk:

The elephant presents his enormous bulk; — the horse flies over the field; the *bēm*, and the *soos* are soon, and readily distinguished. They are saluted by the *cow*, the *sheep*, and the *dove*: the *Moo*, the *Baa*, and the *Toor*, are immediately recognised. How great must have been their joy, to find themselves in possession of a *social* language! (p. 383)

This pattern fits in very well with subsequent developments in psychology and anthropology. Freud cites Hans Sperber's theory that 'the original sounds of speech served for communication, and summoned the speaker's sexual partner; the further development of linguistic roots accompanied the working activities of primal man'.[49] Charles Darwin claims that 'musical notes and rhythm were first acquired by the male or female progenitors of mankind for the sake of charming the opposite sex', and 'afforded one of the bases for the development of language'.[50] Yet, according to Lacan, such calls could never be properly answered, since the basis of romantic love is not need, which can be satisfied, but desire, which must ultimately be a state of permanent dissatisfaction, dating from the days of infancy:

The demand for love can only suffer from a desire whose signifier is alien to it. If the desire of the mother *is* the phallus, then the child wishes to be the phallus so as to satisfy this desire. Thus the division immanent to desire already makes itself felt in the desire of the Other, since it stops the subject from being satisfied with presenting to the Other anything real it might *have* which corresponds to this phallus — what he has being worth no more than what he does not have as far as his demand for love is concerned, which requires that he *be* the phallus. (p. 83)

The function of the phallus ensures that satisfaction can never be achieved: 'Let us say that these relations will revolve around a being and a having which, because they refer to a signifier, the phallus, have the contradictory effect of on the one hand lending reality to the subject in that signifier, and

---

[48] *Celtic Researches, on the Origin, Traditions & Language, of the Ancient Britons* (London, 1804), p. 376.
[49] Freud, 'Symbolism in Dreams', Standard Edition, xv: *Introductory Lectures on Psycho-Analysis (1915–1916), Parts I and II*, p. 167.
[50] *The Descent of Man, and Selection in Relation to Sex*, 2nd edn (London: Murray, 1874), p. 572, n. 39. In support of this contention, he cites the opinion of Dr Blacklock, pp. 572–73, n. 40, cited in Monboddo, *The Origin and Progress of Language* (see below, note 53), I, 469.

on the other making unreal the relations to be signified' (pp. 83–84). Lacan's account of language as an attempt to say the unsayable in order to obtain the unobtainable both describes and re-enacts fundamental frustration at the vagaries of language and women.

Where Lacan was content to observe and analyse, the speculative etymologists had rushed in, prepared for action. Their stress on the phallic element in language and civilization formed part of a wide-ranging debate, involving many early modern scholars. High on the agenda was the need to place language on a rational basis. Rowland Jones believed that the language he had reconstructed already met this requirement. It was created by God, the only being capable of inventing language; after the confusion of tongues at Babel, 'those primary signs transmitted from Adam amongst his posterity', preserved among the decendants of Shem and Japhet, eventually enabled those who had lost their language to 'recover a rational scheme of speech'.[51] This view, however, was insufficently secular to be fashionable. Margreta de Grazia observes, 'For the seventeenth century, language becomes more the slipshod invention of illiterate man than the gift of omniscient God.'[52] Eighteenth-century scholars who accepted this belief did not see how primitive language could possibly be rational. In the first volume of his *Origin and Progress of Language*, James Burnett, Lord Monboddo (1714–99) follows Horace and Lucretius in describing the gradual rise of mankind from bestial stupidity to a level of social and intellectual organization that would facilitate the formation of language.[53] At first, it would be a ramshackle affair, full of clumsy agglutinations. Monboddo finds what he considers a close analogy in 'the language of a barbarous people [. . .] upon the banks of the river Amazons', whose word for *three* is '*poetazzarorincouroac*' (I, 343) He accords little respect to the fathers of language like this.[54] Even more detrimental to paternal dignity was the theory that children invented language. The Abbé Etienne Bonnot de Condillac (1714–80) invites the reader to imagine a scenario in which a couple, separated from other humans in infancy, developed a rough-and-ready language, largely based on gesture: their baby, whose tongue was extemely pliant, 'made an extraordinary motion, and produced a new expression. [. . .] The parents, surprized, having at length guessed his meaning, gave him what he wanted, but tried as they gave it

[51] *Origin of Language*, Preface, B2ʳ.
[52] 'The Secularization of Language in the Seventeenth Century', in *Language and the History of Thought*, ed. by Nancy Streuver (New York: University of Rochester Press, 1995), pp. 16–26 (p. 23).
[53] James Burnet [sic] (Lord Monboddo), *The Origin and Progress of Language*, 6 vols (Edinburgh: Kincaid and Creech, 1773–92; repr. Menston: Scolar, 1967), I, 246. The chief classical sources on this subject are Lucretius, *De Rerum Natura*, v. 1011–90, and Horace, *Satires* I. 3. 100–04.
[54] For recent critical comment on Monboddo's assumption that 'savages' and their languages can be used as evidence of the past state of 'civilized' cultures, see Rüdiger Schreyer, 'Linguistics Meets Caliban: or the Uses of Savagery in 18th Century Theoretical History of Language', *Studies of the History of the Language Sciences*, 68 (1992), 302–14.

him, to repeat the same word. The difficulty they had to pronounce it, shewed that they were not of themselves capable of inventing it'.[55]

Such views were sometimes regarded as degrading to human nature. James Beattie (1735–1803) attacks all representations of man as a mute savage at the beginning of the world: 'surely those writings cannot be on the side of virtue'.[56] Samuel Johnson (1709–84) dismisses Monboddo's unflattering portrait of primaeval man as 'conjecture as to what it would be useless to know'.[57] He argues that originating language was not just difficult, but impossible: 'While the organs are pliable, there is not understanding enough to form a language; by the time there is understanding enough, the organs are become too stiff' (IV, 207).[58] He takes this as evidence that man must have received the concept of language by divine inspiration, thus paying proper respect to the authority of language and the dignity of his forefathers.

'A sex in words'

Whatever the history of language may be, eighteenth-century etymologists and lexicographers find it necessary to preserve an intimate connexion between linguistic and sexual discrimination. Johnson finds sexual distinctions necessary when drawing the parameters of his task: he is 'not yet so lost in lexicography, as to forget that *words are the daughters of earth, and things the sons of heaven*'.[59] It is entirely appropriate that this image should appear in the preface to a dictionary: when explaining the fundamental principles of his own linguistic analysis, Lacan uses the signs 'Hommes' and 'Dames' over lavatory doors, 'pour montrer comment le signifiant entre en fait dans le signifié'.[60] In the eighteenth century, much theory and practice was devoted to the linguistic segregation of ladies and gentlemen.

The same words might have different meanings in male and female utterance. Rowland Jones, an extreme case, conflates grammatical terminology with biblical history, identifying the first and second persons singular with Adam and Eve, thus rendering female subjectivity a grammatical impossibility. *I* is always the man, *you* the woman. His most generous concession to women occurs in *Hieroglyfics*: 'The first personal pronoun substantively, and not substitutionally signifies man as an indefinite line placed alone or by himself in the centre of things before his extension or

---

[55] *An Essay Concerning the Origin of Human Knowledge, Being a Supplement to Mr. Locke's Essay on the Human Understanding*, trans. by [Thomas] Nugent (London: Nourse, 1756; repr. Gainesville, FL: Scholars' Facsimiles and Reprints, 1971), p. 175.

[56] *The Theory of Language* (London: Strahan and Cadell; Edinburgh: Creech, 1788; repr. Menston: Scolar Press, 1968), p. 100.

[57] James Boswell, *Life of Samuel Johnson*, ed. by G. Birkbeck Hill, 6 vols (Oxford: Clarendon Press, 1887), II, 260.

[58] For another version of this argument, see Beattie, *The Theory of Language*, p. 100.

[59] Samuel Johnson, *A Dictionary of the English Language*, 4th edn (1773; repr. London: Robinson, 1828), p. ii.

[60] 'L'instance de la lettre dans l'inconscient', *Écrits*, 2 vols (Paris: Seuil, 1970–71), I, 257.

division into u the male and female spring; the 2d, the - o - u or y - o - u, *the off man* or woman' (p. 31). Yet inclusion in the first person singular of the double-sexed Adam might not satisfy a female speaker: if Jones were truly interested in sexual equality, would he refer to this ambiguous being as 'himself'? Even by eighteenth-century standards, however, this assault on female subjectivity is unusual. In contrast, Adam Smith (1723–90) scrupulously respects the sexual neutrality of *I*: 'Whatever speaks may denote itself by this personal pronoun.'[61] But Jones's etymology will always set a degree of gendered asymmetry between *you* and *I*.

Applying different words to men and women was a common method of linguistic discrimination. Hester Lynch Piozzi (1741–1821), one of the few women to publish on language in eighteenth-century Britain, recalls Johnson's dictum that there was 'a sex in words', illustrating it in her statement that women

have seldom occasion to act WISELY and JUDICIOUSLY — adverbs which imply a choice of profession or situation — seldom in their power; active principles of industry, art, or strength, with which they have seldom aught to do; although by managing PRUDENTLY and DISCREETLY those districts which fall particularly under female inspection, they may doubtless take much of the burden from their companion's shoulders, and lighten the load of life to mortal man.[62]

Jean-Jacques Rousseau (1712–78) creates a linguistic history in which there are two different sorts of language. In his *Discours sur l'Origine de l'Inégalité parmi les Hommes* (1755), Rousseau claims that the first languages emerged from the efforts of babies to communicate with their mothers:

Remarquez encore que l'enfant ayant tous ses besoins à expliquer, et par conséquent plus de choses à dire à la mère que la mère à l'enfant, c'est lui qui doit faire les plus grands frais de l'invention, et que la langue qu'il emploie doit être en grand partie son propre ouvrage; ce qui multiplie autant les langues qu'il y a d'individus à les parler.[63]

These private, domestic dialects correspond closely with Gilbert and Gubar's account of individual development, while extending it into the development of the family. By facilitating communication within the family, while preventing contacts outside it, they preserve that Edenic communion of like with like which characterizes the mirror stage. Such languages are immune

---

[61] *The Theory of Moral Sentiments, to which is added, A Dissertation on the Origin of Languages*, 6th edn, 2 vols (London: Strahan and Cadell; Edinburgh: Creech and Bell, 1790), II, 443. See also Emile Benveniste, *Problems in General Linguistics*, trans. by Mary Elizabeth Meek (Florida: University of Miami Press, 1971), pp. 224–25.

[62] *British Synonymy*, 2 vols (London: Robinson, 1794; repr. Menston: Scolar Press, 1968), II, 106, 366, 367.

[63] 'Discours sur l'Origine de l'Inégalité parmi les Hommes' (also known as the *Second Discourse*), in *Oeuvres Complètes*, I, 93. For Lacan's debt to Rousseau, see Juliet Flower MacCannell, *Figuring Lacan: Criticism and the Cultural Unconscious* (London and Sydney: Croom Helm, 1986), pp. 79–83. In its origins, this private dialect bears some resemblance to the 'Semiotic Chora' identified by Julia Kristeva in *Desire and Language* (Oxford: Blackwell, 1980), but it should be noted that the form of communication in question here is a complete and viable language, spoken by adults — though, admittedly, only by the adults in one family.

to outside interference; consequently, Rousseau finds them deeply unsatisfactory. In his *Essai sur l'Origine des Langues* (1781), he argues that the first major languages were formed when the inhabitants of hot, dry countries began to meet on a regular basis to water their flocks and refresh themselves at wells:

Là se firent premières fêtes: les pieds bondissaient de joie, le geste empressé ne suffisoit plus, la voix l'accompagnoit d'accens passionnés; le plaisir et le désir confundus ensemble, se faisoient sentir à la fois: là enfin le vrai berceau des peuples, et du pur cristal des fontaines sortirent les premiers feux d'amour.[64]

Language and society had existed before, Rousseau concedes, but this was a new sort of language, accompanied by a new pattern of society, which, in building up larger groups, would break up the family unit and, for the first time in history, outlaw the sibling incest which, up to now, had kept each family reproductively self-sufficient:

Il y avoit des familles, mais il n'y avoit point de nations; il y avoit des langues domestiques, mais il n'y avoit point de langues populaires; il y avoit des mariages, mais il n'y avoit point d'amour. Chaque famille se suffisoit à elle-même et se perpétuoit par son seul sang. (p. 392)

In nature and function, this is exactly the sort of language one would expect to be formed according to the theories of Lacan, when the symbolic phallus, representing the law of the father, splits apart the mother–child dyad and inaugurates the Œdipus complex.

Rousseau believes that, although women no longer participate in language formation, they still play too large a part in its transmission. His strictures on language training in Book 1 of *Emile* (1762) indicates his determination to free the (male) speaking subject from undue female influence, so that he can play his part in the political arena where men must be truly men: 'Un homme qui n'apprit à parler que dans les ruelles se fera mal entendre à la tête d'un bataillon, et n'en impose guère au peuple dans une émeute. Enseignez premièrement aux enfans à parler aux hommes, ils sauront bien parler aux femmes quand il faudra' (p. 450). This effort must be renewed in each generation: as Walter Ong says, 'There are no father tongues.'[65] But linguistic history is full of attempts to remedy this deficiency.

'Men of art'

In Plato's *Cratylus*, a word is defined as 'an instrument of teaching and of separating reality', it takes an expert to make them properly, and some are more expert than others. Men attribute names more skilfully than women, and among men the task should be reserved 'for him who may be called the

---

[64] *Oeuvres Complètes*, I, 392.
[65] Walter J. Ong, *Fighting for Life: Contest, Sexuality, and Consciousness* (Amherst: University of Massachusetts Press, 1989), p. 36.

name-maker (ὀνομαστής); and he, it appears, is the lawgiver (νομοθέτης), who is of all the artisans among men the rarest'.[66] The ability to write, often perceived as a male prerogative, proved extremely useful to such artisans. Johnson notes, with obvious regret, that 'as language was in its beginning merely oral, all words of necessary or common use were spoken before they were written'.[67] It was a 'wild and barbarous jargon' before literate men reduced it to orthographic order.

Eighteenth-century scholars thought most order could be found in the learned languages, which were not acquired in babyhood from mothers and nurses, but taught by masters to boys. Such languages were believed to consist of elaborate but systematic variations on a small number of roots; even those who believed that language was based on purely arbitrary signs liked to keep that arbitrariness to a minimum. Monboddo argues that Hebrew must be the result of conscious (masculine) skill: 'The roots of it consist of triads of the several consonants variously combined. This shows evidently, that the language is the work, not of savages, but of men of art' (1, 344). Another learned language was Sanskrit. In *The Way to Things by Words*, Cleland included 'A Summary Account of the Sanscort or, Learned Language of the Bramins', translated from a letter by Father Pons: 'It is surprising, that the human mind has been able to arrive at the perfection observable in these grammars. The authors have, in them, by analysis, reduced the richest language in the world to a few primitive elements, which may be looked upon as the *caput mortuum* of this language' (p. 92).[68] The fact that Sanskrit is not quite what Cleland imagined does not detract from its usefulness here as an example of the two-thousand-year campaign which men had been waging in an effort to relocate the source of language from the maternal mouth to the magisterial pen.

The most direct attempt to produce a father tongue is the creation of an artificial language. Appropriately, such enterprises link paternal with linguistic law at the highest possible level: in *A Common Writing* Francis Lodwick (fl. 1647–86) offers, as a sample of his wares, the first chapter of St John's Gospel; George Dalgarno (*c.* 1626–87) in *Ars Signorum* renders the first chapter of Genesis; in his *Essay towards a Real Character*, John Wilkins (1614–72) includes the Lord's Prayer and the Creed in his newly-invented character, as well as the Lord's Prayer in fifty-two existing languages.[69] Each of these texts focuses on the creative power or divine authority of God's word. Wilkins typically seeks to create 'a *Real universal Character*, that should not signifie *words*, but *things* and *notions*, and consequently might be legible by any Nation in their own Tongue' (p. 13). He sees no harm in reversing the

---

[66] Plato, *Cratylus*, pp. 23, 37, 25.
[67] *Dictionary*, p. [i].
[68] For further details about Father Pons's letter, see Epstein, pp. 163–64 and p. 236, n. 159.
[69] Francis Lodwick, *A Common Writing* (London, 1647), pp. 28–29; George Dalgarno, *Ars Signorum* (London: Hayes, 1661), pp. 118–19; John Wilkins, *An Essay Towards a Real Character, and a Philosophical Language* (London: Gellibrand and Martyn, 1668; repr. Menston: Scolar Press, 1968), pp. 395, 435.

normal process: 'Though it be true, that men did first *speak* before they did *write*, [. . .] *voice* and *sounds* may be as well assigned to Figure, as *Figures* may be to Sounds' (p. 385). The core of his work is a massive catalogue of all the phenomena to which he assigns characters, complete with an account of their natures and interconnexions. It is a magnificent *speculum*, whose very completeness contains the seeds of its own futility; it does not leave the gaps necessary to accommodate new knowledge. Words seldom have a stable relationship with things: the fact that there are faults on both sides brings scant consolation to the lexicographer.

Perhaps a double-sexed Adam, undivided and unfallen, would negotiate more successfully the gaps between signifier and signified, desire and attainment. One of the most notorious artificial languages to emerge from this period was that spoken by the androgynous natives of *La Terre Australe Connue* by Gabriel de Foigny (*c.* 1630–92), a logical structure whose every letter was significant: 'On devient philosophe, en apprenant les premiers éléments, et qu'on ne peut nommer aucune chose en ce pays qu'on n'explique sa nature en même temps.'[70] As Georges Benrekassa observes, 'Il n'est que trop tentant de joindre ces deux aspects, hermaphrodisme et langage originel; on se sent légitime à le faire par les conceptions des préadamites ou de l'Adam originel.'[71] But neither book nor language enjoyed official approval; they threatened too many 'preposterous Digressions from our present Standard'.

'This important language'

The Way to Things by Words was not Cleland's first deliberate engagement with linguistic issues. In *Memoirs of a Coxcomb* (1751), Cleland's narrator expresses contempt for the outdated clichés which encumber romantic courtship. When Lord Merville falls in love with Lady Gertrude Sunly, he speaks of 'my assiduity, my respect'. The hero ridicules these words: 'Assiduity, and respect too! What solemn terms are these! Have you been pillaging for them the old obsolete dictionary of the love-cant of our ancestors [. . .]?'[72] A typical 'obsolete dictionary' is *Mysteries of Love and Eloquence* (1658), compiled by John Milton's nephew, Edward Phillips (1630–?96), reprinted as *The Beau's Academy* in 1699; from this substantial tome an aspiring lover, unsure of his social or sexual standing, might learn to utter such formulas as 'Madam, the ambition which I have to wait on you in a Countrey Dance, emboldens me to invite you from your seat', and 'Lady, Who are inspir'd with all the praises that the world can bestow upon

---

[70] 'M. Sadeur' [Gabriel Foigny], *La Terre Australe Connue* ('Vannes: Jacques Verneuil' [Geneva: La Pierre], 1676), p. 170.
[71] 'La matière du language: la linguistique utopique de Gabriel de Foigny', in *La Linguistique Fantastique*, pp. 150–65 (p. 151).
[72] John Cleland, *Memoirs of a Coxcomb* (London: Compact Library, 1964), p. 167.

your sex, I am come to offer you my service, which you may at present call obedient, hoping that your better knowledge thereof will stile it faithful'.[73] The intended readers of this book might not be awe-struck courtly lovers in their thoughts: in a section entitled 'Miscelania', the question '*What differences a woman from a man?*' is answered by 'Meum & tuum' (p. 165). This bawdy Latin answer, a reminder that 'thing' often had sexual connotations, encouraged young men to concentrate their minds on anatomical issues, however flowery their speech might be. Nevertheless, it is hard to envisage mid-eighteenth-century ladies impressed by the clichés of Renaissance courtship: nobody would find the way to their things by words like these.

Cleland found a worthier target when he set about exposing language that might be all too effective. In 1753 he published *The Dictionary of Love*, based on the *Dictionnaire d'Amour* (1741) by Jean François Dreux de Radier (1714–80). In his preface, he depicts himself as a protector of innocent girls, endeavouring to save them from being ruined by accepting the corrupt coinage of modern love-talk:

Young people, and especially of the fair sex, whose mistakes are the most dangerous, may find their account in reading it. Those who have no tincture of knowledge in the terms of this important language, will be sufficiently instructed, and taught to distinguish the Birmingham-trash, so often palmed upon them, for the true lawful coin of the kingdom of Love, in which nothing is commoner than false coiners.[74]

Of course, such a work could also be used by enterprising men who wished to find out just what sort of false coinage was most likely to pass as current among innocent young girls. Cleland's gloss on *adore*, an almost literal translation of Dreux, shows his method at its plainest:

I love: love did I say? I adore you!
The true meaning of which fine speech is, 'The secret of pleasing consists in flattering your self-love, at the expence of your understanding. I am straining hard to persuade you, that you have distracted my brain; not that it is so in the least; but, whilst I laugh at you in my sleeve, for your swallowing this stuff, I may gain wherewith to laugh at you in good earnest.'

Cleland depicts a society in which relationships between language and reality, aspiration and attainment, are subject to eternal slippage. *Desires* 'are not only the life-hold of love, which is sure to die with them, but the very power of it. They mark out the lodging'. Under *love*, he notes that 'some knowing Ladies prefer by much, that Love which is a corporeal want, to that which is an imaginary one'. Romantic love must be maintained by barriers and conflicts which may be as imaginary as the wants they keep in a permanent state of frustration. *Quarrels* (*brouilleries*) 'are the zest of coquettes

[73] Edward Phillips, *The Mysteries of Love and Eloquence* (London: Brooks, 1658; repr. Menston: Scolar Press, 1972), 'The Mode of *Hide Park*', pp. 11, 17.
[74] [Cleland], *The Dictionary of Love. In Which is Contained, the Explanation of Most of the Terms Used in that Language* (London: Griffiths, 1753), pp. x–xi. (Adapted from [Jean François Dreux du Radier], *Dictionnaire d'Amour, Dans Lequel on Trouvera l'Explication des Termes les plus Usités dans cette Langue* (The Hague, 1741).)

and professed gallants. Accusing and justifying, form a necessary diversion. Take away these grand movers, and you rob the sphere of love of its greatest activity'. Lacan once noted this use of *brouiller* as one of those 'créées dans le cercle des précieuses': like Cleland, he knew that physical satisfaction could not fulfill romantic yearnings.[75]

'That peculiar sceptre-member, which commands us all'

The *Memoirs* is deeply concerned with language: a monument to Cleland's resolve to write an erotic work without using dirty words. Fanny self-consciously complains of 'the extreme difficulty of continuing so long in one strain, in a mean temper'd with taste, between the revoltingness of gross, rank, and vulgar expressions, and the ridicule of mincing metaphors and affected circumlocutions'.[76] Yet Michael Ragussis is one of the few critics to link Cleland's fiction with his etymological and lexicographical enterprises. He notes that two competing systems of naming existed side by side in the Enlightenment: 'The science of classification investigated things, and attempted to name those things through a newly fabricated, arbitrary system of signs. Etymology, on the other hand, investigated names.'[77] Ragussis sees the *Memoirs* as an exercise in classification: Cleland 'writes up a comprehens-ive science of pleasure by extending the act of naming not through breaking the ban on naming the sexual organs themselves, and not through inventing a radical new set of metaphors, but through drawing up a catalogue of erotic acts' (p. 193). He produces a *speculum*, systematically instructing readers in 'the great art and science of pleasure'.[78] By Ragussis's standards, more creative, poetic responses to language might be found in Cleland's linguistic studies: 'In etymology each name is itself an intertext, the charged locus of other names that lie buried within it' (p. 178). But has he dismissed the *Memoirs* too briskly? Philip E. Simmons explores the implications of Cleland's claim that early language was predominantly poetic and metaphorical: 'From this perspective, Cleland's avoidance of obscene language in the *Memoirs*, his use of metaphor and euphemism for sexual organs and acts, can be seen as an attempt not to conceal the referents and reduce the impact of sexually explicit scenes, but rather to increase their force.'[79]

Nancy K. Miller was among the first critics to notice the novel's obsessive focus on male genitalia, and also to recognize this as a predominantly masculine preoccupation: 'The "longitudinal fallacy," or the "phallacy" of

[75] *Le Séminaire*, III. 133.
[76] *Memoirs of a Woman of Pleasure*, ed. by Peter Sabor (Oxford and New York: Oxford University Press, 1985), p. 91.
[77] *Acts of Naming: The Family Plot in Fiction* (New York and Oxford: Oxford University Press, 1986), p. 177.
[78] Cleland, *Memoirs of a Woman of Pleasure*, p. 120.
[79] 'John Cleland's *Memoirs of a Woman of Pleasure*: Literary Voyeurism and the Techniques of Novelistic Transgression', *Eighteenth-Century Fiction*, 3 (1990), 43–63 (p. 57). His reference is to Cleland, *The Way to Things by Words*, p. 23.

reference, tells us that the "I" of narration is indeed in drag. The memoir of this woman of pleasure is the celebration of a familiar privileged signifier.'[80] The episode in the *Memoirs* where Fanny becomes the mistress to Mr H. suggests that this signifier already bears the political weight attributed to it in Cleland's later works:

his firm texture of limbs, his square shoulders, broad chest, compact hard muscles, in short a system of manliness, that might pass for no bad image of our antient sturdy barons, when they weilded the battle-ax, whose race is now so thoroughly refin'd and fritter'd away into the more delicate and modern-built frame of our pap-nerv'd softlings, who are as pale, as pretty, and almost as masculine as their sisters (p. 64).

Today's readers might be content to picture these 'antient sturdy barons' as medieval, but Cleland, in his *Specimen*, goes back much further. Under *Parliament-Robes*, he says, 'From the very antientist times of Britain and the Gauls, Peers, or Barons, were distinguished by *robes of state*.'[81] He adds that 'The *Bough, Mace*, or *Scepter*, was then one of the *Baron*'s Insignia. Another was the *Crown*', both 'taken from the *May*, or *Column* of Justice' (p. 44). Appropriately, Mr H. is equipped with a rod of office, a 'stiff staring truncheon, red-topt' (p. 63). He embodies the manly splendours of ancient Britain.

In the *Memoirs*, the penis is explicitly likened to a maypole, on occasions when an atmosphere of rustic innocence hangs about its possessor. In one case, Fanny and her colleague Louisa set about the seduction of '*Good-natur'd Dick*', an idiot boy who sells flowers for a living. Fanny, seeing Louisa's eagerness to enjoy his enormous penis, 'was content in spite of the temptation that star'd me in the face, with having rais'd a may-pole for another to hang a garland' (pp. 160, 162). Mr H.'s footman Will is 'a tenant's son, just come out of the country, a very handsome young lad, scarce turn'd of nineteen, fresh as a rose, well shap'd, and clever-limb'd' (p. 70). He sports 'a may-pole of so enormous a standard, that had proportions been observ'd, it must have belonged to a young giant' (p. 72). Fanny, offended by Mr H.'s infidelity, regards her fornication with Will as a 'worthy act of justice' (p. 70), anticipating the association of justice with phallic authority that pervades Cleland's reconstruction of Ancient British society. Charles, Fanny's future husband, wields 'that peculiar sceptre-member, which commands us all' (p. 183), but even good-natured Dick qualified for rule in this sense: 'It was full manifest that he inherited, and largely too, the prerogative of majesty, which distinguishes that otherwise most unfortunate condition' (p. 162). Is men's authority over women really based on a distinction in which any fool can be superior to an intelligent man? Cleland does not allow Fanny to interrogate this phenomenon: as she recalls her blissful reunion with Charles,

---

[80] ' "I's" in Drag: The Sex of Recollection', *The Eighteenth Century*, 22 (1981), 47–57 (p. 53).
[81] *Specimen of an Etimological Vocabulary, or, Essay, by Means of the Analitic Method, to Retrieve the Antient Celtic* (London: Davis and Reymers, 1768), p. 42.

she loses command of the linguistic situation: 'I see! I feel! the delicious velvet tip! — he enters might and main, with — oh— my pen drops from me here in that extasy now present to my faithful memory! Description too deserts me, and delivers over a task, above its strength to Wing, to the imagination' (p. 183). This is a Lacanian moment, as described by Robert Markley, when the penis becomes the veiled signifier that transcends all linguistic power: 'Cleland asserts a form of social (and sexual) hegemony by placing its symbolic origin — the phallus — beyond the ability of language to circumscribe and control it'.[82]

However eager modern critics have been to keep them asunder, there is evidence that sex, politics, and etymology came together all too closely in Cleland's personal life. In a conversation with Josiah Beckwith (b. 1734) on 27 May 1781, he complained of ministerial oppression. Given Cleland's disrespectful treatment of monarchy, and praise of the more democratic Druids, 'it is no Wonder, in this Age, that he lost his Place or Pension [. . .] — Or that he should pass under the Censure of being a Sodomite, as he now does, and in Consequence thereof Persons of Character decline visiting him, or cultivating his Acquaintance'.[83] If this account is true, Cleland's subversive manipulation of maypoles provoked accusations of another phallic misdemeanour, and left him carrying the dog.

---

[82] 'Language, Power, and Sexuality in Cleland's *Fanny Hill*', *Philological Quarterly*, 63 (1984), 343–56 (p. 347).
[83] Henry Merritt, 'A Biographical Note on John Cleland', *Notes and Queries*, n. s. 28.4 (August 1981), 306.

Thomas Chatterton Was A Forger

NICK GROOM

University of Exeter

At that point Don Giuseppe would explain to him at length how the work of the historian is all deception, all fraud; how there was more merit in inventing history than transcribing it from old maps and tablets and ancient tombs; how, therefore, in all honesty, their efforts deserved an immensely larger compensation than the work of a real historian, a historiographer who enjoyed the benefits of merit and status.

'It's all fraud. History does not exist. Perhaps you think the generations of leaves that have dropped from that tree autumn after autumn still exist? The tree exists; its new leaves exist; but these leaves will also fall; in time, the tree itself will disappear — in smoke, in ashes. [. . .] What we are making, you and I, is a little fire, a little smoke with these limbs, in order to beguile people, whole nations — every living human being . . . History!'[1] (Leonardo Sciasca, *The Council of Egypt*).

Thomas Chatterton was a forger. What does this statement, this knowledge, mean? Chatterton forged literature: he forged language, he forged scholarly credentials, he forged sources. Yet he was not a mere forger: only the works attributed to Thomas Rowley and his set are called forgeries. Chatterton's other pieces in his two-volume *Works* are literature, as opposed to literary forgeries (in a sense, they are aberrant works in the canon of a forger). This essay will focus on Rowley: is it enough to say that Thomas Chatterton forged the works attributed to Thomas Rowley?

The definition of forgery begs a thousand questions: questions of intention and reception, counterfeit and plagiarism, imitation and pastiche, mimesis and representation. In a word, it always refers to a set of conditions outside the text. It is criminal evidence of authorial intention, or (in the case of the death of the forger) it is an enigma ravelled about the discourses of scholarly opinion. The word anticipates both the problem to be solved, and the solution. But Chatterton, I will argue, produced forgeries-within-forgeries which magnify the clumsiness of attempts to explain away his work, and which radically challenged notions of history and writing in the eighteenth century.

In Chatterton's work, meaning is always escaping into the remnants of things, language bristles like a hedgehog rolled up beneath spikes, or blurs into the scorch marks of decaying manuscripts. The reader is left to puzzle over quills or cinders. Indeed in 'Clifton' (unforged), Chatterton suggests that history may appear to evade its own process by side-stepping into

---

[1] *The Council of Egypt* (1963), trans. by Adrienne Foulkes (London: Harvill, 1993), pp. 63–64.

THE ACCOUNTE OF W. CANYNGES
FEAST.

T HOROWE the halle the belle han founde;
    Byelecoyle doe the Grave befeeme;
The ealdermenne doe fytte arounde,
Ande fnoffelle oppe the cheorte fteeme.

Lyche affes wylde ynne defarte wafte
Sworelye the morneynge ayre doe tafte,

Syke keene theie ate; the minftrels plaie,
The dynne of angelles doe theie keepe;
Heie ftylle the gueftes ha ne to faie,
Butte nodde yer thankes ande falle aflape.
Thus echone daie bee I to deene,
Gyf Rowley, Ifcamm, or Tyb. Gorges be ne feene.

THE END.

A GLOS.

FIGURE I. _Poems, supposed to have been written at Bristol by Thomas Rowley and Others, in the Fifteenth Century_ (London, 1777), p. 288 and facing

language and then shrouding itself in mildew upon the worm-eaten page.
Yet the page itself is rotting away, enacting the very process of time:

> O'er the historick page my fancy runs,
> Of Britain's fortunes, of her valiant sons,
> Yon castle, erst of Saxon standards proud,
> Its neighbouring meadows dy'd with Danish bloody [. . .]
> But for its ancient use no more employ'd,
> Its walls all moulder'd and its gates destroy'd;
> In Hist'ry's roll it still a shade retains,
> Tho' of the fortress scarce a stone remains.[2]

Thus in the shade of 'Hist'ry's roll', we see only the sign of writing having
passed, not the language itself. In fact, meaning decays as inevitably as the
fragile medium of the medieval manuscript. This essay will argue that the
manuscript defied eighteenth-century literary antiquarianism. It was in
opposition to the print ideology of scholarship, and so was judged to be
fundamentally inauthentic. But the manuscript (especially in the Rowley
corpus) inevitably remained a vehicle, a mode of transference, or a
metaphor, for history — a version of history that would embarrass literary
antiquarianism. The argument draws on my own earlier work, and has been
indirectly inspired by a minor constellation of theoretical essays.[3]

On 8 February 1777, Thomas Tyrwhitt published the first volume of
Rowley poetry: *Poems, supposed to have been written at Bristol, by Thomas Rowley
and Others, in the Fifteenth Century*. The collection contained a selection of
ancient poems and dramatic verse, mainly by one Thomas Rowley. These
literary remains had been discovered in St Mary Redcliffe Church in Bristol
in the late 1760s by a teenager called Thomas Chatterton, a Colston charity
boy and an attorney's clerk. Chatterton's father had begun rifling through
the old chests in the muniment room in the 1750s, and his posthumous son
followed him in these wormy habits. Chatterton, a voracious reader and a
prolific writer, claimed in about 1768 to have discovered the works of
Thomas Rowley, a fifteenth-century priest, in an old chest in the muniment
room over the north porch of the church. The Rowley corpus was enormous,
including poems, prose, drawings, and maps, and appeared to be a major
literary find. Chatterton had produced more and more examples while living
and working in Bristol before moving to London a few months before his
death in 1770, either adolescent suicide or dreadful accident. He was only

[2] *The Complete Works of Thomas Chatterton*, ed. by Donald S. Taylor, 2 vols (Oxford: Clarendon Press, 1971). I, 343.
[3] See *Narratives of Forgery*, ed. by Nick Groom, *Angelaki*, 1.2 (1993); Nick Groom, 'Celts, Goths, and the Nature of the Literary Source', in *Tradition in Transition: Women Writers, Marginal Texts, and the Eighteenth-Century Canon*, ed, by Alvaro Ribeiro, SJ, and James G. Basker (Oxford: Clarendon Press, 1996), pp. 275–96; Jean Baudrillard, 'Gesture and Signature: Semiurgy in Contemporary Art', in *For a Critique of the Political Economy of the Sign*, trans. by Charles Levin (n.p.: Telos Press, 1981), pp. 102–11; Jacques Derrida, 'Signature Event Context', in *Margins of Philosophy*, ed. and trans. by Alan Bass (Chicago: University of Chicago Press, 1982), pp. 307–30; Michel Foucault, 'Nietzsche Genealogy History', in *The Foucault Reader*, ed. by Paul Rabinow (Harmondsworth: Penguin, 1984).

seventeen. Soon after, these 'Rowley Poems' found themselves at the centre of an argument concerning their authenticity, first in Bristol and Bath, then in London. With the 1777 edition, these sparks of doubt were blown into an inferno of controversy which raged for the next two or three decades. It was eventually concluded that the works were all forged by the boy. History was written rather than rewritten.

The proofs were (and in a sense still are) conclusive, and so the story of Chatterton is already anticipated in its telling — anticipated as a story explaining and explaining away the phenomenon of 'literary forgery'. But a doubt remains in the plausible accounts of the eighteenth-century literati, not in the Romantic mythography of Wordsworth and Coleridge and Keats, nor in the postmodern intertextuality of Peter Ackroyd. A single page from the 1777 edition of the *Rowley Poems* presents a riddle. The title-page of Tyrwhitt's *Rowley Poems* highlighted the manuscript status of Rowley: 'THE GREATEST PART NOW FIRST PUBLISHED FROM THE MOST AUTHENTIC COPIES, WITH AN ENGRAVED SPECIMEN OF ONE OF THE MSS.'[4] This engraving, 'The Accounte of W. Canynges Feast', was a startling image, displaying extravagantly archaic calligraphy, exotic Gothic lettering, and featuring illustrations of two heraldic shields. The visual impact of the document was further enhanced by its position in the volume: facing the printed transcript of 'The Accounte of W. Canynges Feast', which looked desolate in comparison (pp. 288 and facing; see Figure 1). The relationship between the typographic text and the unique engraving of a Rowley manuscript is both fascinating and bewildering.

Despite the sparse image of print compared with the magnificence of the parchments, the form of Rowley on the printed page was still grotesquely strange: Chatterton forged a pseudo-medieval language. He scavenged archaic words from the glossaries of Chaucer and Thomas Percy's *Reliques of Ancient English Poetry*, and had a Shakespearean talent for comparable neologism and coinage. And he garbed this odd pastiche in an idiosyncratic, supposedly archaic orthography. Chatterton invented a poetic Rowleyan language by doubling consonants, substitutions ('y' for 'i' and 'c' for 'k'), and (indeed like Percy in his *Reliques*) adding redundant 'e's to most words.[5] Antiquity was guaranteed by redundancy and copiousness, like Gothic architecture (indeed, very like the Gothic of St Mary Redcliffe). All these orthographic oddities were faithfully reproduced in the *Rowley Poems* and *Miscellanies in Verse and Prose* (a follow-up volume printed in 1778), and the very lines drew attention to their rough physicality:

> Geofroie makes vearse, as handycraftes theyr ware;
> Wordes wythoute sense fulle groffyngelye* he twynes,

---

[4] *Poems, supposed to have been written at Bristol, by Thomas Rowley and Others, in the Fifteenth Century*, ed. by Thomas Tyrwhitt (London, 1777), sig. a1ʳ.
[5] *The Poetical Works of Thomas Chatterton*, ed. by Walter W. Skeat, 2 vols (London: Bell & Daldy, 1872), II, xxxv–xl, 1176–80.

Cotteynge hys storie off as wythe a sheere;
*foolishly. [Chatterton's note.][6]

For the majority of readers, readers of the posthumous, printed editions, this bizarre language was the most immediately compelling aspect of Rowley. It barked and rasped with a guttural new poetic voice, echoing from the iron depths of fantastic medieval armour, even if it was easily strangled by deft wit.[7]

In his *History of English Poetry* in 1781, the pioneering literary historian and poet, Thomas Warton, modernized the 'Notbrowne Mayde' to challenge Edward Capell's dating of the poem.[8] This technique of textual analysis was based on the assumption that history was integral rather than superficial to a poem, but was ultimately simply a force acting on language, a factor of linguistic change, a structuring principle: that language is writ on the roll of history and offered the sign of times passed.

The technique was full of all the confidence of burgeoning literary history: indeed it could be seen as its whole rationale, the demonstration of historical change and literary improvement. There was none of the abysmal semantic melancholy that Chatterton suggests in 'Clifton' and elsewhere. In consequence, translation and pastiche were enthusiastically propounded by 'anti-Rowleyans' as demystifiers in the debates about the poems. William Mason deployed the device most tellingly in *An Archeological Epistle to the Reverend and Worshipful Jeremiah Milles* (1782): the 'Epistlle to Doctoure Mylles' was a piece of verse describing the controversy and its participants in Rowleyan language, and the effect was both absurd and hallucinatory. George Hardinge added a little Rowley pastiche, 'To the Dygne Reader' to his play *Rowley and Chatterton in the Shades: or, Nugæ Antiquitæ et Novæ* (1782). The Shakespearean editor Edmond Malone, too, in his pamphlet *Cursory Observations on the Poems attributed to Thomas Rowley* (1782), took delight in rewriting Chatterton's poems: 'Chatterton in Masquerade' was a translation of 'Narva and Mored' into Rowleyan, while 'Chatterton Unmasked' modernized the Rowleyan 'First Eclogue'.

Of most interest is an unsigned letter to the *Public Advertiser*, dated 19 March 1782, in homage to Mason's 'Epistlle to Doctoure Mylles' (the pastiche of a forgery). The correspondent suggests that other authors be garbed in 'Archæological Language' to affect a sort of textual alchemy: 'This, however, I would not call *Translation*, but *Transmutation*, for a very obvious Reason.' The opening of *Paradise Lost* and the famous soliloquy from *Hamlet* are offered as tongue-in-cheek examples:

Offe mannes fyrste bykrous volunde wolle I singe,
And offe the fruicte offe yatte caltyfnyd tre

---

[6] *Rowley Poems*, p. 69: *Works*, I, 176.
[7] See Richard Holmes, 'Thomas Chatterton: The Case Re-Opened', *Cornhill Magazine*, 178 (1970), 230.
[8] *The History of English Poetry*, 3 vols (London, 1774–81), III, 136.

Whose lethall taste ynto thys Worlde dydde brynge
Both mothe and tene to all posteritie.

To blynne or not to blynne the denwere is;
Gif ytte bee bette wythinne the spryte to beare
The bawsyn floes and tackels of dystresse,
Or by forloynyng amenuse them clere.

Ironically, this transmutation does dazzle us like newly-minted gold as we recognize the familiar in a new radiance. It is reminiscent of R. L. C. Lorimer's recent Scottish *Macbeth*

Whuff, cannle-dowp!
Life's nocht but a scug gangin, a bauch actor
as strunts an fykes his ae hour on the stage.[9]

The perspective of the text is strictly from the present looking to the past (sidelong, in the case of Lorimer); history is focused like a spectacle before the gaze of the present. There could be no more powerful demonstration that eighteenth-century literary antiquarianism heralded the genealogy of the perfection of the art of writing.[10] History came of age in the genius of the present.

Having proved to their satisfaction that Chatterton's Rowley language actually supported their theories of linguistic integrity, the antiquarians pursued this theme by considering each word as an object, with its own linear history. Reviewing the *Rowley Poems* in 1777, Ralph Griffiths called them '*Mock Ruins*', (although the volume contained no fragments), and in 1782, Warton observed, 'A builder of ruins is seldom exact throughout in his imitation of the old-fashioned architecture.'[11] He presented Chatterton's work as a visual pastiche: 'In dictionaries of old English, he saw words detached and separated from their context: these he seized and combined with others, without considering their relative or other accidental significa-tion.'[12] Malone too described the poems in architectural terms: 'Many of the stones which this ingenious boy employed in his building [. . .] are as old as those at Stone-henge; but the beautiful fabrick that he has raised is tied together by modern cement, and is covered by a stucco of no older date than that of Wyat and Adams.'[13] He gave several examples of Chatterton's plagiarisms from the cultural monument of the canon. Indeed, spotting Rowley's sources was a game started in the *St. James's Chronicle* in 1778 and

[9] *Times Literary Supplement*, 18 September 1992. p. 14.
[10] See David Fairer, 'Organizing Verse: Burke's *Reflections* and Eighteenth-Century English Poetry' (forthcoming, *Romanticism*).
[11] *Monthly Review*, 28 (1777), 256. After printing the 'Testimony of George Catcott' in the May issue (originally his 'Introduction' and 'Remarks'), the June *Review* concluded 'We do not hesitate to pronounce that these Poems are the original production of Rowley, with many alterations and interpolation by Chatterton' (pp. 312, 449). The sceptical *Gentleman's Magazine* printed the song of Robin and Alice from '*Ælla*', 'With some trivial Alterations': it was compeletely modernized (*Gentleman's Magazine*, 47 (1777), 275).
[12] Thomas Warton, *An Enquiry into the Authenticity of the Poems attributed to Rowley* (London, 1782), p. 43.
[13] Edmond Malone, *Cursory Observations on the Poems attributed to Thomas Rowley, A Priest of the Fifteenth Century* (London, 1782), pp. 11–12.

enthusiastically prosecuted by another Shakespearean, George Steevens. This device effectively foiled a discussion of the poetical merits of Rowley by implying that any verse could be composed in this allusive way, that it was entirely dependent on earlier writers, that it was parasitic and derivative and plagiarized.

Jacob Bryant, a fearsomely and erratically learned defender of Rowley, was scornful of Chatterton's supposed use of dictionaries and glossaries: 'We may as well suppose, that a pedlar built York cathedral by stealing a tile, or a stone, in every parish he passed through.'[14] But Vicesimus Knox was nonplussed:

Thyself thou has emblazoned; thine own monument thou hast erected. [. . .] Thou hast built an artificial ruin. The stones are mossy and old, the whole fabric appears really antique to the distant and the careless spectator; even the connoisseur, who pores with spectacles on the single stones, and inspects the mossy concretions with an antiquarian eye, boldly authenticates its antiquity; but they who examine without prejudice, and by the criterion of common sense, clearly discover the cement and the workmanship of a modern mason.[15]

Why the architectural imagery? Horace Walpole, in his *Anecdotes of Painting in England*, had famously made antiquarianism visionary, a way of feeling the 'magic hardiness' of the Gothic: 'One must have taste to be sensible of the beauties of Grecian architecture; one only wants passions to feel Gothic.'[16] He described the English Gothic past as an enormous painting or piece of architecture, both visual and tactile — 'vaults, tombs, painted windows, gloom, and perspectives' — analogous to his own medieval simulation, Strawberry Hill. Walpole's Gothic metonyms derived from the persistent use in earlier works of architectural images to describe old language. For example, Elizabeth Cooper's *The Muses Library* compared the 'Gothique Rudeness' of Chaucer and Spencer [*sic*] to the 'Monumental Statues of the Dead', and John Weever's *Ancient Funeral Monuments* (quoted by Chatterton) had an ecclesiastical Gothic atmosphere of black-letter inscriptions and crypts which is redolent of Walpole, and Rowley too.[17] Gothic was a sentimental reading of the past in which archaic language was objectified and fetishized. Moreover, as with architectural uses of porticoes or arched windows, each medieval word, even each unexpected use of a 'k' or doubled

---

[14] Jacob Bryant, *Observations upon the Poems of Thomas Rowley: in which the Authenticity of those Poems is Ascertained* (London, 1781), p. 423.

[15] 'On the Poems attributed to Rowley', in *Essays Moral and Literary*, 2 vols (London, 1782), ii, 251.

[16] *Anecdotes of Painting in England*, 3 vols (Twickenham, 1762), ii, 107–08.

[17] Elizabeth Cooper [and William Oldys], *The Muses Library; or, A Series of English Poetry, from the Saxons to the Reign of King Charles II*, 2 vols (London, 1737), i, xii[i]; John Weever, *Antient Funeral Monuments, of Great-Britain, Ireland, and the Islands Adjacent* (1631), 2nd edn (London, 1767), 'A Discourse on Funeral Monuments, &c.', p. vi. This prefatory Discourse defined monument not simply as physical testaments to human lives or achievements, but 'to speak properly of a monument [. . .] it is a receptacle or sepulchre, purposely made, erected, or built, to receive a dead corps, and to preserve the same from violation'. Chatterton claimed to have discovered the Rowley works in William Canynge's chest in the muniment room over the north porch of St Mary Redcliffe, Bristol. Chatterton referred to Weever in 'Antiquity of Christmas Games' (*Works*, i, 411) and 'Memoirs of a Sad Dog' (*Works*, i, 659).

consonant or redundant 'e', was a gesture that alluded to the whole culture and recalled history. They functioned as relics, or rather meaning was securely encased in these encrusted reliquaries. Like bits and pieces of saints (or in antiquarian cabinets of curiosities, like the remains of secular heroes and heroines) the presentation of words in this ritual way seemed to suggest that they shared in the physical reality of some event—history—but also transcended it. They were fragments of true meaning, with the authority of their own existence.

Why was this metaphor so insistent? It is not enough to state that Chatterton's art rose with the archive, was an odd contortion of a print culture which favoured ready retrieval devices such as glossaries and dictionaries. Rowley's works were discovered in a church muniment room, and Rowley was in one sense a sepulchre. But the sepulchre was empty, there was no poetry among the vellum scraps Chatterton and his father collected. Chatterton is suggesting that meaning has an origin outside of history.

This is apparent in his weaving of text and commentary: the double narratives of medieval poetry and editorial annotations. Chatterton's editorial persona provided a constant commentary and at times drowned out the poetry. Sometimes nearly every word in a line would be footnoted. The reader was prevented from reading the pieces: the poetry represented its own disappearance under the tide of the present. When the pieces were published, the reader was bullied into seeing in them merely the sign of ancient poetry: the polyvalency of archaisms and footnotes. Annotation was ostentatious: to conspicuously display erudition served to authenticate the poems within the discourses of scholarship.

Rowley was split into many voices. For the antiquarians, the question was to discover where these voices began, either in the 1760s or the 1460s, but the question of origins also carried the big cultural question, where did our history, our national past, begin? Rowley does not offer the convenient linearity of Warton's scheme, precisely because he is not part of the great tradition: he is an outsider, whether real (interred in the muniment room) or not. Rowley's history is fragmentary, a decaying palimpsest too fragile to scrape clean. In the shady muniment room, where the vellum scraps were gathered like so many sibylline leaves, the broken texts could only be a metaphor for the past. There was nothing really there.

So English literary history was no longer confined to the past in the 1760s when Rowley was emerging. The works appeared in a highly charged literary context, at the moment of the construction of the canon of English poetry in Percy's *Reliques*, and were published at the moment of literary history's being written in Warton's *History of English Poetry* (1774–81). In fact, Rowley actually featured in the second volume of Warton's *History* (1778) in a twenty-five page section, which was in press some time before Tyrwhitt's edition.

Warton had published the first volume of his authoritative *History* in 1774, in which a preliminary dissertation had stressed the importance of literacy: indeed, the essay 'On the Introduction of Learning into England' reads like a bibliolator's Grand Tour. Literacy flourished all over Gothic Europe. King Alfred promoted no illiterate priests and translated Latin authors into his native Saxon, while 'the conqueror himself patronised and loved letters' and demonstrated his power and control over his new land by outlawing the Saxon tongue.[18] In this case, literate language had created problems for the native Saxons: the Normans would not accept Saxon documents of property rights because they implied a rejection of the new ruler, and this necessitated the 'pious fraud' of forging monastic charters (reminiscent of the Donation of Constantine) (I, 3 n.). Moreover, forgery was an inevitable part of medieval manuscript culture: copying and plagiarizing from manuscripts were the only way of disseminating and circulating texts. But precisely because of this, it became a characteristic against which eighteenth-century print culture and scholarship defined itself.

Warton's *History* did raise concern about the status of sources. Although his first volume was derived from manuscripts, Warton made no mention of the uniqueness of his texts, nor the nature of chirographic culture: he was wary of mentioning the word 'manuscript' at all. One of the aims of the *History* seems to have been to create an anthology or 'general repository of our antient poetry', although Warton explicitly denied this (I, 208). Because so much of Warton's material had not previously been published he quoted his illustrations at length, reprinting the earliest extant manuscript of a poem under the assumption that it provided the most reliable text (I, 101).

In the second volume of his *History of English Poetry*, Warton encountered Caxton, and very briefly described the impact of moveable type: it played a vital part in disseminating literature, 'contributed to sow the seeds of a national erudition, and to form a popular taste'; and 'multiplied English readers, and these again produced new vernacular writers' (II, 122, 124 n.). But because Warton had treated the chirographic texts of pre-Caxton verse as if they had the authority of typographic texts, he did not suggest that Caxton's innovation in any way revolutionized the word on the page. The transition between manuscript and print culture was elided. Eighteenth-century scholarship was grounded in print and printed books, which itself implied a linear history. Literature, the object of antiquarian study, necessarily predated it, but scholarship had the capaciousness enabled by print to comprehend it. English verse did not arrive with Caxton's press; its origins had to be presented as lost in the mists and myths of time (and as competitors with the Celts and other northern pretenders), but also recoverable through historical theory and research. Warton was writing a

---

[18] Warton, I, sig. f.1ᵛ.

teleological history of English poetry; he only stressed that print provided the instruments of modern scholarship.

Warton devoted a whole section of his second volume to Rowley. For this chapter, he quoted long passages of Rowley as part of his larger argument of literary progress. The technique enabled him to juxtapose Rowley with the fifteenth-century verse that supported his argument, and so to deny the incongruous Rowley a place in the system he was perfecting. Although the Rowley remains were constantly invoked and scrutinized by Warton, no referent such as 'The Accounte of W. Canynges Feast' was provided. And although Warton described his analyses of calligraphy, ink, and parchment, this forensic account had to be taken on trust because these very features were not reproducible in a printed book.

Rowley appeared then at the moment the canon became an issue: who was to be included or excluded from Warton's epoch-making work? The work of Percy and Warton, not to mention Samuel Johnson in the *Dictionary* and the *Lives*, was about uncovering the printable manuscript: recognizing the manuscripts in which inherent typography was most lucidly articulated. Print was the yardstick of antiquarian evidence. The cause and consequence of the canon, formulated in the eighteenth century, was that typographic structures were perceived to be inherent in manuscripts. And it was this print-determined selectivity that literary forgery exposed.

Rowley attempted to find or construct a place outside the all-pervasive culture of typography, and therefore insisted on all the untypographic elements of the medium: calligraphy, ink, paper or parchment, as well as provenance, damage, and supplementarity. They forced print to insist and re-insist upon its totalitarianism, because these untranslatable aspects of the manuscript exposed the absolutist assumptions of typography. To establish that Rowley was spurious, Warton did not in fact visit Bristol, or even handle a Rowleian manuscript: they were described to him in correspondence which, being ideally suited to printing, he of course published. The manuscript was treated as an entirely inauthentic document, because it was unsuited to being printed — though it was never declared to be inauthentic, except in cases such as the Rowley controversy.

So the actual conceptual problem that Rowley's manuscript posed the eighteenth-century literary antiquarians — is there anything more to letters than typography? — was never actually answered. The works of Chatterton were declared 'forgeries' by Warton, and others, and dismissed to an incoherent twilight, because if this work, called forgery, did find a place outside typography, it could, like Archimedes and his place to stand on, move the world. All literature might be forged.

This is the challenge posed by the manuscript, the crux of Chatterton–Rowley so dramatically played out in the two (printed) pages of 'The Accounte of W. Canynges Feast'. The whole dreadful significance of the Rowley hoard lay in Chatterton's use of the found manuscript. Manuscripts subverted print: the *manuscrit trouvé*, complete with lacunae and illegible letters, could not be adequately reproduced on the printed page of eighteenth-century literary histories. While exposing the profound limitations of print, the page exercised an extraordinary fascination upon contemporaries. It was reproduced in all the editions of Rowley and in commentaries as late as 1809, and was discussed, almost without exception, in Rowley Controversy books, pamphlets, and magazine articles.[19] This was a tantalizing glimpse of the real thing, the supposed manuscript, although it was, of course, just a particularly well-disguised printed page.

The page collapses definitions of forgery and originality. This manuscript is supposedly original (and yet in an important sense it is still a copy). It is a forgery of a work which is original, yet which (it is claimed by detractors) has no original. It exposes a contradiction, or paradox, in the very definition of forgery: while an economic forger, a counterfeiter, is able to forge a bank note (that is, make an exact copy of something which already exists), such as a £5 note, the same forger is not able to pass of an original forgery, such as a £3 note. But art and literary forgers do forge works that might never have previously existed. So, strangely, the text is sign and proof of both authenticity and fraudulence. It is both true and untrue (and was employed as evidence on both sides of the authenticity debate). So it seems that the whole idea of forgery becomes impossibly refracted. The word loses its authority to present and solve a problem, because Chatterton has produced, (posthumously) on this page, and more radically in his vellum Rowley manuscripts, forgeries-within-forgeries. They secrete the odour of an intricate textual problem, but the secret they reveal is that there is no secret, and no basis for literary antiquarian criticism. We see a printed skeleton, clothed (on the right) with the flesh of chirography. But it is, at its core, for Tyrwhitt and Warton and Walpole, a printed artefact. The manuscript, within the metaphysics of typography, is simply a corruption of print, a deviation from it. All manuscripts are already typographic on these terms, but still the manuscript is more: it has an excess, a capacity uncontained by the typeface and engraving.

For this reason, the manuscript *per se* was not part of published literary antiquarianism: it was an image rather than an object, a shadow cast upon the screen of print. Of course Percy, Warton, Capell, and Walpole all used manuscripts, but they did not publish engravings of manuscripts as textual artefacts, nor did they clearly acknowledge their indebtedness to manuscript sources. The jockeying for ancient sources between Percy and James

---

[19] In 1809 John Sherwen tried to resume the defence of Rowley, but despite the passage of a quarter of a century, could offer no new angle on the question. He resorted to 'The Accounte of W. Canynges Feast' in order to solve two textual cruces and thereby authenticate the poems. He suggested 'hath' for 'han' and 'Yche corse' for 'Syke keene' (*Introduction to an Examination of Some Part of the Internal Evidence, respecting the Antiquity and Authenticity of Certain Publications, said to have been found in Manuscripts at Bristol, Written by a Learned Priest and Others, in the Fifteenth Century; but generally considered as the Supposititious Productions of an Ingenious Youth of the Present Age* (Bath, 1809), p. 130).

Macpherson in *Five Pieces of Runic Poetry* (1763) and the *Reliques*, and the collected *Ossian* (1765) respectively, demonstrated that not just the emergent canon but cultural identity was at stake. But evidently there was a great deal of confusion about the status afforded to literary-antiquarian evidence. The over-scrupulous editing of Edward Capell and 'Don' Bowle was contrasted with the sentimental panache of Richard Hurd and Walpole; and both Macpherson and Percy ran into difficulties when they tried to present manuscripts.

Because Chatterton produced manuscripts that could be circulated, rather than transcriptions or proofsheets, there are enormous differences between his work and that of Macpherson and Percy and other antiquarians. Editors with ambitions to publish experienced great difficulties expressing themselves on the printed page, but Chatterton side-stepped these problems by concentrating on the manuscripts, leaving others to plan the publication.[20] Although Chatterton verified his source as Macpherson and Percy had verified theirs, by local testimonial, internal proofs, and supporting argument, he alone introduced forensic evidence. It was the latter that precipitated the Rowley controversy: the existence of palpable objects was missing from *Ossian* and the *Reliques*. No matter how hard the antiquarians tried in claiming that old Gothic words had the 'magic hardiness' of old Gothic buildings, it was clear that they did not have the ephemeral precision of a manuscript. Chatterton slotted Rowley between Macpherson's late recognition of the necessity of manuscripts and Percy's mirage of the source (his jealously guarded folio manuscript). Critics and scholars alike were able to exercise their wit and erudition on their impression of one of these actual documents. Indeed, because only two Rowley pieces were published in Chatterton's lifetime (the 'Bridge Narrative' in *Felix Farley's Bristol Journal*, 1 October 1768, and 'Elinoure and Juga' in the *Town and Country Magazine*, May 1769), we are left with a body of material which created a controversy motivated in part by the problems in printing it.

Chatterton cheerfully embraced the protean nature of manuscript culture. A lengthy closing footnote to the 'Bristowe Tragedy' stressed the importance of this context. After verifying the beheading of Bawdin with reference to the historian John Stow, Chatterton wrote asking for more evidence:

[20] Ian Haywood, 'Chatterton's Plans for the Publication of the Forgery', *RES*, 36 (1985), 58–68 (reprinted in *The Making of History: A Study of the Literary Forgeries of James Macpherson and Thomas Chatterton in relation to Eighteenth-Century Ideas of History and Fiction* (London: Associated University Press, 1986), pp. 175–84). See also Michael F. Suarez, 'What Thomas Knew: Chatterton and the Business of getting into Print', in *Angelaki*, 1.2 (1993), 83–94; Jonathan Barry, 'The History and Antiquities of the City of Bristol: Chatterton in Bristol', in *Angelaki*, 1.2 (1993), 55–58; Jonathan Barry, 'Provincial Town Culture, 1640–1789: Urbane or Civic?', in *Interpretation and Cultural History*, ed. by Joan H. Pittock and Andrew Wear (London: Macmillan, 1991), 198–223, p. 219); Jonathan Barry, 'Representations of the Past in Bristol: 1625–1789' (unpublished typescript, pp. 26–27). I am grateful to Dr Barry for making this research available to me.

But a more Authentick Evidence of this Fact I met with in an old Parchment Roll, in which among other Curiosities preserv'd in the Cabinet of Mr Canynge, is mentioned [. . .].

I shall conclude this with remarking, that if Gentlemen of Fortune wou'd take the trouble of looking over the Manuscripts in their Possession, which are only valued for their Antiquity, it might possibly throw Light upon many obscure Passages in and help to establish a more Concise History of our Native Country, than even *Cambden's Britannia*. (*Works*, 1, 20 n.)

Chatterton's reinvention of manuscript sources received its fullest exposition in 'A Brief Account of William Cannings from the Life of Thomas Rowlie Preeste'. This short prose piece explained how Canynge ordered Rowley to 'goe to all the Abbies and Pryoryes, and gather together auncient drawynges, if of any Account; at any Price' (1, 51). The Wapolean Canynge was interested in old English painters, but the Chattertonian Rowley was more concerned with manuscripts, and discovered a Saxon parchment at the 'Minster of oure Ladie and Saincte Godwyne', which he bought and set 'diligentlie to translate and worde it in Englishe Metre' (1, 52, 54). A year later he had the 'Battle of Hastynges'. Over eight hundred years, the poem had been transmitted from Turgotus to Rowley to Chatterton. The nature of the source affected the poem and its presentation, and the uniqueness of the source was stressed because it determined the text. In this case, Chatterton complained in his editorial introduction that the poem was incomplete:

AN Ancient poem called the Battle of Hastynges written by Turgot a Saxon Monk in the *Tenth* Century and translated by Thomas Ronlie [*sic*: a deliberate error by Chatterton's editorial persona] the remaynyng Part of this Poem I have not been happy enough to meet with – (1, 26–27)

which was hardly surprising after eight centuries. But the transmission of the poem did more than reinscribe, did more than record the impact of history upon the text. The silence of the absent part is not Chatterton's suppressed rejoicing at having found an excuse not to finish the piece, but the resounding silence of history. Language has passed without a trace, only the rump of the poem remains.

The manuscript as a metaphor for history, a vehicle for the liquidation of language, was reflected in Rowley's other activities. Canynge employed Rowley to compile lists of inscriptions, recording relics of antique text on a parchment which Chatterton reduced to a hopeless fragment itself (1, 117–18, facing p. 116). Fragmentation verified the manuscript source in the act of destroying it, and the inevitable attempts of readers to fill in the gaps with conjectural emendations was cruelly satirized by Chatterton. In the effervescent prose skit 'Memoirs of a Sad Dog', he had Baron Otranto misread a broken and eroded gravestone, 'James Hicks lieth here, with Hester his wife', as '*Hic jacet corpus Kenelmæ Sancto Legero. Requiescat*' (1, 659).

The fragmentary stone was a memorial to lost languages rather than a testament to antiquarian genius.

The shift of focus, from writing to history, from print to manuscript, from language to silence, that Rowley precipitated created a contagious game of Chinese whispers, or rather, a wild paper chase. If ancient manuscripts spoke most eloquently of their silence and meaninglessness, modern manuscripts (in the guise of transcripts) larded this profound silence with the clamour of voices, all saying the same thing but every one speaking in a different tongue. Tyrwhitt had provided the *Rowley Poems* with an 'Introductory Account of the Several Pieces contained in this Volume', which detailed provenance, textual variants, historical background, references, and sources (pp. xv–xxv). George Catcott and William Barrett, original Bristol supporters of Rowley, had gradually disseminated transcripts to trusted allies, who in turn had copied the texts to enlist supporters, and so on. This had been going on for seven years, so the Rowley texts existed in countless variants. They had spawned a subculture of migratory and self-duplicating manuscripts that further upset the authority of print and actually mirrored the clamorous manuscript culture of Rowley. If a manuscript copy of a genuine ancient manuscript could be made by Chatterton or Catcott, a facsimile (or counterfeit) manuscript copy could also be made: a forgery of a forgery. This copy would not necessarily invalidate the original document, but as the 'original forgery' needed not exist anyway, it made the concept of the original superfluous. Transcripts were marauders: wonderfully ambiguous signs which harried the unanimous uniformity of print with ever-mutating texts, so they too became engaged in another ceaseless Chattertonian attack upon the assumption that typography was the fundamental medium of literature and the empirical unit of literary history.

This sort of argument was elaborated by pro-Rowleians such as Henry Dampier, who responded to Warton with *Remarks upon the Eighth Section of the Second Volume of Mr. Warton's History of English Poetry*.[21] Dampier answered some of Warton's points — the staining of the paper, the colour of the ink — while at the same time denying that the extant manuscripts represented any definite grounds for refutation anyway: 'The proofs that even this manuscript is a forgery, are by no means incontestable; nor if they were, would it follow the course, that all or any of the other manuscripts must necessarily be so too' (p. 30). If the parchments were fakes, it meant that they could be Chatterton's counterfeits of genuine documents, and another link in the chain of transmission from the fifteenth century to the eighteenth. (Dampier also criticized Warton's instinctive citation of Percy's glossary to the *Reliques* as a Rowley source. It simply showed the literati closing ranks.)

---

[21] (London, [1780(?)]). This has also been attributed to Francis Woodward. See E. H. W. Meyerstein, *A Life of Thomas Chatterton* (London: Ingpen & Grant, 1930), p. 470 n.

Rayner Hickford argued with most awareness on the issue of sources, in *Observations on the Poems attributed to Rowley*. Hickford was not afraid to argue that sources, and therefore meaning, were endlessly deferred: for example, he brilliantly demonstrated that the provenance of 'Verses to Johne Ladgate, with Johne Ladgate's Answer' was a maze of chirographic transmission.[22] Hickford also pointed out that Rowley himself was not unlike certain eighteenth-century editors, and was prepared to rewrite ancient history, to '*clean it from it's rust*' (p. 13).

But the most obsessive defence came from the grinding pen of Jacob Bryant. Bryant's doorstop of a book, *Observations upon the Poems of Thomas Rowley* (1781), was an unstable juggernaut pulled along by sheer erudition. Writing as if through gritted teeth, he insisted that the lexical peculiarities of Rowley were caused by the influence of oral dialects on chirographic culture:

Before the art of printing became of general use, it is scarcely possible to conceive, but that people must have written in dialects: for they had no standard, by which they could be regulated; and if there had existed any thing of this nature in any particular place, it could not have been universally kept up, for want of that intercourse and correspondence, which are so essential to its influence and authority. (p. 8)

Bryant's whole method was based on what he perceived to be the shortcomings of scribal culture, and it was the scholar's unflinching duty to scrape away these transcriptural mistakes. Bryant attempted to reconstitute the archetypal manuscripts from which Chatterton had worked. His scholarship was visionary: an absolute recovery and reconstitution of what was incoherently expressed:

Whether the Mss. was at all impaired, and the words in some degree effaced: or whether it were owing to his ignorance, and carelessness, I know not: but thus much is certain, that the terms are sadly transposed, and changed, to the ruin of the context. (p. 95)

Bryant brought his etymological researches to Rowley: as John Cleland had suggested a few years earlier (1768), 'The antientest way of spelling a word is ever the best guide to the decomposition of it'.[23] No letter or word was secure from interrogation and revision, no phrase or meaning was contained, but seeped hermetic inference, enabling Bryant to rewrite Rowley. He queried whether it was possible for the Bristol youth to be familiar with as much arcane lore as he was himself:

There are many dark hints and intimations, with which he [Chatterton] was totally unacquainted. From these secret allusions I have been induced to think, that some of these poems were not even of the age of Rowley, but far antecedent: being composed by some person, or persons, who were not far removed from the times and events, which they celebrate [e.g. 'Hastings']. (p. 206)

[22] *Observations on the Poems attributed to Rowley* (London, 1782), pp. 11–12.
[23] John Cleland, *The Way to Things by Words, and to Words by Things, being a Sketch of an Attempt at the Retrieval of the Antient Celtic, or, Primitive Language of Europe* (London, 1768), p. 83.

Bryant therefore interpreted literature as a semiotic medium: cultural significance was only conducted to those familiar with a structure underlying everyday language. In this way Bryant extended his notion of language to the whole system of signs — Chatterton's biography, manuscript provenance, etymology, aesthetics, intertextuality — which constituted the reception of Rowley. The distinction between text and context was entirely dissolved. Ultimately, texts for Bryant were only part of a large cultural code; they did not constitute it: in fact they constituted a celebration of his own abstruse learning.

Bryant's work reads like a crusade down the road of history, a road littered with manuscripts, with ashes, indeed with cinders. Derrida has proposed the metaphor of the cinder to describe the trace, and we may perceive in the manuscript, read 'In Hist'ry's roll' (itself subject to reduction by tearing, mildew, and cinders), what is left after language has been exhausted.[24] Crumbling manuscripts are both fragile and tenacious, they are on the border between things and words, and they may carry us down the path that leads to origins. But they testify to the passing of language, not to language itself; the manuscript is always already too late, it is record of something done and gone. Chatterton aged a manuscript by holding it over a flame and thereby fading the words to leave 'the mellow vestiges of evanescent ink'.[25] If the manuscript carries us down the path that leads to origins, there are only cinders there.

'The Accounte of W. Canynges Feast' is now in the British Library.[26] It is a tiny document (the 1777 facsimile is full size). The text runs to all edges of the parchment; there is a complete absence of margins, whitespace, titles, and in these versions, notes. And it is black as soot.

On 9 March 1784, William Jessop wrote to Thomas Percy on the subject of the *Reliques of Ancient English Poetry*:

Oh for a ray of Chatterton's genius. Had I this, I should soon send you a roll ten yards long of wormeaten vellum, which should, here and there, amidst undecypherable hieroglyphics, exhibit to you a legible distambour upon the miserable substratum with silk and gold of your own property.[27]

The manuscript source was acknowledged 'undecypherable'; it stretched like a canvas for the editor to embroider. Antiquarian literary history spun its loquacious myths out of the indecipherable, incomprehensible silence of history. The most poignant Rowley manuscripts that remain are those that Taylor lists as 'illegible antiqued parchments': unreadable manuscripts that gave up their secrets when no one was reading. Writing has passed 'O'er the historick page', and passed away.

---

[24] Jaques Derrida, *Cinders*, trans. by Ned Lukacher (Lincoln and London: University of Nebraska Press, 1991).
[25] Warton, *An Enquiry*, p. 3.
[26] London, British Library, Add. MS 5766A, fol. 6.
[27] Oxford, Bodleian Library, MS Percy b. 1, fol. 3r.

Reviews

Strange Attractors: Literature, Culture, and Chaos Theory. By HARRIETT HAWKINS. New York, London, and Sydney: Prentice Hall; Harvester Wheatsheaf. 1995. xiv + 180 pp. £11.95.

In this lucid and provocative book, Harriett Hawkins champions chaos theory as a critical approach to literary texts. In good introductory fashion, she acquaints us with the principles of chaos and its illustration in an astonishing range of texts, both canonical and popular: from *Paradise Lost* to *Jurassic Park*, and from *The Tempest* to *Star Trek*. Part polemic against cultural relativism, part exercise in protracted analogy, and part theoretical model, Hawkins's book makes large critical claims for the theories of chaos that have emerged from studies of the natural world.

Among the most controversial of the book's statements is the author's insistence on the universality of chaos, its applicability to literature of all periods and to the reality of life in the world. Hawkins argues that we are all alike in our human incapacity to predict the future and to calculate the potentially massive repercussions of small events. Thus, 'chaos theory provides the basis for a cosmopolitan human commonality based on a common humility and mutual dependency stemming from our universal ignorance concerning what is going to happen next' (p. 40). Thanks to its universal relevance, chaos theory, unlike the science of other periods, shares concepts not only with literature of its own time, but with the art of all times, pre-modern and post-modern alike. Accordingly, Hawkins reads the conflict between chaos and order in *Paradise Lost* as a realist picture of life in the world: 'Why', she asks, '*is* there so much chaos, so much turbulence in *art* unless art reflects cognate mysteries in life?' (p. 47).

The evidence for the universality of chaos is, not surprisingly, insufficient; but Hawkins builds this argument into a critique of other modes of criticism, particularly those concerned with politics and ideology. Ideological readings, she argues, impose artificial order on complex works of art, which necessarily spawn numerous, even competing, interpretations. But Hawkins's critique, here, is not quite fair: few political critics have insisted on the impossibility of multiple readings, and, if they have imposed 'order', have done so in the interests of investigating significant links between culture and power. This question may not be Hawkins's prime concern, but surely it deserves recognition on its own terms.

The stronger claims of this book include the application of fractal geometry to the complexity of literary language, an intriguing, chaotic way of conceptualizing the links between high and popular culture; a turbulent look at cross-dressing in Shakespeare; and even a realist reading of the pathetic fallacy. As a remarkably fruitful exercise in analogy, the book urges us to compare science to art, Shakespeare's 'Dark Lady' to nature's so-called 'strange attractors', *Star Trek* and *Jurassic Park* to *Paradise Lost*, traditional criticism to Newtonian physics, *The Tempest* to *The Forbidden Planet*, Shakespearean drama to the fractal geometry of nature, *Antony and Cleopatra* to William Sleator's teen novel, *The Strange Attractors*.

Finally, Hawkins offers us chaos as an overarching, all-encompassing theory, one which emphasizes complexity, turbulence, unpredictability, and even beauty.

BIRKBECK COLLEGE, LONDON   CAROLINE LEVINE

Ordinary Heroines: Transforming the Male Myth. By NADYA AISENBERG. New York:
Continuum. 1994. x + 240 pp. $22.95.

Nadya Aisenberg advances here a broad, ambitious argument. The myth of the
hero that has long prevailed in our culture must give way, she argues, to a new
paradigm. A new heroine is emerging who will lead us toward a 'more humane
society'. The heroics of violence and predestination must yield to a model in which
the 'ordinary heroine' assumes a new importance. Her book attempts to define such
a new heroine as she appears in a range of cultural artefacts.

A prologue and an introductory chapter outline her project and set up a working
opposition between the old hero, and the new heroine. Three succeeding chapters,
'Woman/Space', 'Woman/Sight', and 'Woman/Speech' rehearse familiar arguments about femininity in Western culture: tradition, still dominant in many
contemporary works, has associated women with domestic space; the male gaze
alienates women from their experience of themselves; powerful stereotypes undermine women's speech. In works ranging from Marilynne Robinson's *Housekeeping*
and May Sarton's 'The Muse as Medusa' to Doris Lessing's *The Diaries of Jane
Somers*, Aisenberg charts the development of a new attitude toward space, a new
subjectivity and voice. Although she refers to Freud, Lacan, Cixous, Kristeva, and
other theorists, she does so rapidly and superficially.

In a fifth chapter, 'Spirit, Sorority, Sense', Aisenberg identifies three foci within
feminism of 'efforts to project female authenticity and self-transcendence': spiritual-
ity, sisterhood, and the female body. Each, she argues, contributes only partially to
the project. To each of these major subjects she devotes a handful of pages. Two
succeeding chapters identify several popular literary genres as the arenas in which,
Aisenberg suggests, the New Heroine makes her most promising appearances: the
New Romance, the crime novel, science fiction, and the feminist utopia. Again
devoting just a few pages to each genre, Aisenberg makes a rapid survey. An
epilogue offers an encomium to the new heroine.

From this summary, the book's major flaw should be clear: its very scope leads
the author repeatedly to oversimplify complex matters. Scholars who have followed
debates of these issues in recent years are likely to find her summaries unsatisfying.
Since she attempts so much, it is not surprising that she often neglects important
sources. (To name just two examples, her section on the romance makes no
mention of Janice Radway, and her bibliography on feminist utopia is missing the
prominent study by Marlene Barr, *Feminist Fabulation*. These examples are not
exceptional.) Perhaps a general reader will find her book a useful introduction, but
it is not clear she has the general reader in mind. Nor is this a work that is likely to
convert the unconverted. Repeatedly, Aisenberg distorts as she oversimplifies.
Does she really want to imply that 'the hero' of western tradition (as though only
one such being existed) is, unlike the heroine, *not* 'deeply committed to a more
humane society' (p. 13)? (Dante? Wordsworth?) Does the hero never 'remain [. . .]
responsive leader of the society from which [he] has emerged, an ordinary [man]
endeavoring, nevertheless, to tackle extraordinary problems', as she discribes the
new heroine in an ostensible contrast to the hero? Aisenberg argues that the
heroine 'substitutes moral courage and a moral voice for the hero's physical
courage and sense of predestination'. Does the hero *not* possess moral courage and
a moral voice? Do all important heroes in the western tradition possess physical
courage? Such sweeping treatment is, unfortunately, the rule rather than the
exception in this book. However much we may sympathize with the impulses

behind it, we contribute more to the state of feminist criticism if we insist on more accountability.

SKIDMORE COLLEGE, SARATOGA SPRINGS,   SARAH WEBSTER GOODWIN
NEW YORK

Women, the Book and the Godly: Selected Proceedings of the St Hilda's Conference, 1993. Vol. I.
    Ed. by LESLEY SMITH and JANE H. M. TAYLOR. Cambridge: Brewer. 1995.
    xiii + 191 pp. £29.50; $51.
Women, the Book and the Worldly: Selected Proceedings of the St Hilda's Conference, 1993.
    Vol. II. Ed. by LESLEY SMITH and JANE H. M. TAYLOR. Cambridge: Brewer.
    1995. xiv + 193 pp. £29.50; $53.

In the 1993 St Hilda's centenary conference on women and the book, an institution of female learning of some longevity and, in spite of all difficulties, continuing survival, gave intellectual hospitality to a broadly-conceived tradition in women's history. From the sixth century AD to the late fifteenth century, nearly a millennium of women's reading and composition is selectively exemplified in the thirty papers from the conference gathered in these two volumes (a third on women and art is to follow). Their collective impact gives a vivid sense both of systematic exclusions and depreciations and of opportunities and enterprise in the experience of early women readers, writers, and patrons. In their lucid and witty introductions, the editors point to the huge range of materials and methods involved. They are well aware of the relative arbitrariness of the volumes' 'godly' and 'worldly' categories: their organization of the volumes represents not only a practical decision, but a (still necessary) reminder of the primacy of devotional literacies and composition in women's relations with the book (still undervalued in a century whose canonical literary history has been so largely male and secular).

Volume I begins with Alcuin Blamires discussing Henry of Ghent's *Quaestio* on who may study scripture, a key example of women's exclusion and the clerical anxieties which promote and sustain it. Jacqueline Murray follows on thirteenth-century penitential manuals and their attitudes to female penitents. Women's books and other documents are considered in Wybren Schepsma's survey of the collective biographies, 'sister-books', from Low Countries convents and in Anne Dutton's investigation of women's book bequests in late medieval England; Rosalynn Voaden examines the convention of enlisting God's authority among women mystical writers; Grace Jantzen contrasts Bernard and Hildegard's authorizing strategies and later medieval male strategies (in Eckhardt, Ruysbroek, and the *Cloud of Unknowing*) for excluding women from mystic authority; Elizabeth A. Andersen surveys Mechthild of Magdeburg's audience and creativity, and Thomas Luongo discusses Catherine of Siena's extraordinary account of her relationship with the young Perugian nobleman Niccolò di Toldo, a dead man walking, in this case, to the fourteenth-century Sienese scaffold. The relations of learned men with women are considered in Sr Benedicta Ward's argument that Bede did not so much ignore the learning of Anglo-Saxon women as encourage the valuing of wisdom over learning; and in two articles (by Gopa Roy and Georges Whalen) on Goscelin of St Bertin, an eleventh-century cleric whose relations with, and writings for, women are, if less influential, of a richness to rival those of Jerome. A famous English guide for anchoresses, *Ancrene Wisse*, is defended by Catherine Innes Parker from recent charges of simple misogyny, while a subtle reading of contemporary French literature by Helen Phillips suggests some new contexts for Julian of Norwich and the materials of her thought. Two powerful studies of female literacy, in Lollard communities by Shannon McSheffrey, and in the heretical communities of Languedoc Catharism by Peter Biller, conclude the volume. McSheffrey argues that evidence to be gathered from addressing the question not of who owns books but of who learns to read produces a less optimistic view than studies of book ownership have done: Biller shows North–South regional variations in literacy and argues too that the question of who reads a Cathar text may depend not just on degrees of literacy but on assumptions about readers' roles and ascribed authority. Both studies have important implications for current work in the history of women's reading.

Volume II opens with secular female literacy in Southern Italy AD 900–1200, valiantly surveyed by Patrica Skinner. Female readers are studied in and for Froissart (Philip E. Bennett) and Dante (Mark Balfour, focusing on Francesca da Rimini) in two solid and sensitive accounts, while Margaret Beaufort and Elizabeth Woodville co-opting chivalric romance in the marriage of their children and St Teresa of Avila's imitation of her mother's reading of chivalric romance as studied by Jennifer R. Goodman add new dimensions to medieval women's romance reading. A study by Anne Birrell of medieval Chinese women's love-poetry is of interest in itself and usefully points up the existence of other middle ages beyond the Western Eurocentric focus of this collection.

Two studies trace the effects of interventions argued to be misogynistic in textual transmission: convincingly so in Karen Jambek's thoughful and informed discussion of Marie de France's *Fables*, less so in Beverley Kennedy's account of the transmission of Chaucer's *Wife of Bath's Prologue*, where the argument depends on an assumed and external set of moral standards for this text. Women's writing is addressed in two studies of Christine de Pisan's bold and original appropriations of textual authority in her translation of Vegetius (Charity Cannon Willard) and her re-writing of Boethius in *Lavision Christine* (Benjamin Semple). Jeannette Beer studies an early *querelle des dames* generated by Richard Fournival's thirteenth-century *Bestiaire d'Amour* (given the high interest of the case, a summary of the reasons for female attribution rather than a direction to Beer's longer study would be welcome). Carol J. Harvey, looks at a courtly heroine of Griselda-like aspect in the thirteenth-century verse romance *Mankine*, and Heather Arden examines Ami and La Vielle in discussing women as readers and as text in the *Roman de la Rose*. Caxton is the key figure of the fifteenth-century studies in the book. In addition to Goodman's article, he features in the final trio of powerful studies: Julia Boffey's lucid and suggestive discussion of Lydgate's lyrics and women readers, Jennifer Summit's account of Caxton's relations with his patron Margaret Beaufort, and Margarita Stocker's more speculative but densely-argued case for Caxton's political partisanship in the Woodville marriage as revealed in his textual interventions in the *Golden Legend*.

While there is inevitable fluctuation in the quality of individual studies, the volumes are more than the sum of their parts. The editors point out the persistence and homogeneity of certain problems for women in their relations with the book and the academy in a way that could usefully inform post-medieval study of women's literary culture. This is engaged but non-polemical scholarship, where the most important activities are sometimes not the most exciting ones: where the building-up and nuancing of detail towards a broad picture is critical. Few overviews of this territory exist: these volumes promote awareness of that absence and of why detailed work with primary sources has still much to offer in writing the history of women and the book.

University of Liverpool   Jocelyn Wogan-Browne

'The Sins of Madame Eglentyne' and Other Essays on Chaucer. By RICHARD REX. Cranbury, NJ: University of Delaware Press; London: Associated University Presses. 1995. 201 pp. £27.

This book consists of a series of essays all of which, with one exception, relate to aspects (sometimes points of linguistic detail) of the presentation of, and cultural contextualizations for, Chaucer's Prioress and the nature of her Tale. The general concern appears to be to reinforce the argument that Chaucer is primarily concerned with exposing the Prioress's hypocrisy, and in pursuing this line Richard Rex tends to consolidate and refine other modern commentators' discussions of the issues rather than break new ground in Chaucer criticism.

The first chapter sets a general context for the Prioress and the Tale, with a welcome garnering of further evidence, from medieval sources, in favour of Richard Schoeck's argument that anti-Semitism is not necessarily at the heart of Middle English writing on the Jews, and that Chaucer's attitude is an enlightened one. This chapter which, according to the acknowledgements, is a revision of a piece originally published in 1984, also sets the book's conservative scholarly tone, as it does not engage with the wealth of more recent theoretical and inter-disciplinary work concerning the nature of, and attitudes to, Jewishness in the Middle Ages.

This is also a curiously assembled set of essays, however, for a piece on the possible authorship by Chaucer of two obscene poems, the substance of the brief Chapter 2, disrupts the flow of the argument about the Prioress and strikes one as bizarre, not only in its positioning but also in its omissions: there is a cursory survey of earlier editors' far-from-objective practices in determining the Chaucer canon, but the poems are neither adequately summarized nor reproduced, and they receive virtually no analysis, where one might have expected some kind of link here between the subjects of decorum, modes of representation, and the ostensible main subject of the book, if only as a means of justifying the piece's inclusion in the collection.

Subsequent chapters work rather better together in their presentation of a series of mutually-informing perspectives on the Prioress's Tale. Rex considers the text as a pastiche of a saint's life, the ironies of which are best appreciated as relating directly to the personality of the Tale's narrator; he shows how the details of justice in the Tale expose the Prioress's vindictiveness, and suggests that what other commentators might consider harmless or even endearing affectations on the character's part, such as singing through her nose, or being tender-hearted towards animals, are indicative, if one looks at their incidence in contemporaneous and earlier religious and devotional literature, of rather more serious sins. There is an intriguing essay also on the link between property owned by St Leonard's priory and the maintenance of brothels on Bankside, which serves as further evidence for Chaucer's indictment of the Prioress's moral corruption.

These essays bring together a wealth of detail, but their organization makes for a fragmentary rather than a cumulatively powerful argument, and much of the material would perhaps be better suited to explication in publications such as *Notes and Queries*, rather than in book form; one feels this especially in the essays regarding what it means to have 'grey' eyes (which Rex concludes must mean 'lively' rather than indicating a specific colour), and on the ambivalence of the medieval colour symbolism of which Chaucer makes use. In sum, this is a useful book to dip into for evidence in support of an argument that Chaucer is condemnatory of, rather than ambivalent about, his Prioress, but its format leaves one feeling dissatisfied that the material was not worked into a more cohesive study.

UNIVERSITY OF LEEDS   CATHERINE BATT

Chaucer on Love, Knowledge and Sight. By NORMAN KLASSEN. (Chaucer Studies, XXI)
   Cambridge: Brewer. 1995. xi + 225 pp. £29.50; $53.

This is a revised version of the author's doctoral thesis, submitted at the University
of Oxford under the same title in 1993. While there is much in Klassen's study to
recommend publication, his work would have benefited from a more sustained
period of reflection and reconsideration, when its driving ideas might have been
distilled, clarified, and allowed to mature.

The book is useful as a survey in which to find summaries of the interconnections
of light, vision, and knowledge in a wide range of medieval writings in both Western
and Arabic traditions, from Plotinus to Aquinas and Dante, from Alhazen to
Grosseteste, Rolle, and Ockham, from natural philosophy and metaphysics to
sermons and lyrics. Furthermore, Klassen has an enviable facility to précis complex
material in ways that are both succinct and attractive. His steady, methodical
account of Augustine, his conclusions about the spiritually positive and destructive
effects of the eye, his stress on the importance and significance of optical science to
cognitive questions, his sensitive evaluation of light imagery in the *Book of the Duchess*
and *Troilus and Criseyde*, his lucid version of Alhazen's theory of vision, all of these are
persuasively written.

Klassen's engaging enthusiasm results in a book where plenitude yields its own
problems. First, the depth of reference to primary and secondary contexts is
sometimes quite shallow. For example, there is nothing on Basil's *Hexaemeron,* nor
mention of Reames's important and relevant work on the Second Nun's Tale.
Secondly, Klassen's compendious approach tends to produce a Monk's Tale of an
argument. By the time one reaches Chaucer it is sometimes with the sense that there
is little left to say other than by way of illustrating points already made. His analysis
of the Merchant's Tale, for instance, adds nothing to existing commentaries.
Thirdly, the evidence for his argument is not always evaluated with sufficient care.
Klassen states that rationalism is a response which the convention of love at first
sight 'strictly forbids' (p. ix). This might describe the involuntary, intuitive moment
itself, but it could be said with greater conviction that love at first sight actually
enables and stimulates rationalism, as the case of Troilus demonstrates.

Fourthly, Klassen introduces into the argument an element of theory, that of
parasitisme, as developed by Serres, which is out of kilter with the kinds of relationship
among love, vision, and sight which he is actually trying to identify. *Parasitisme* has
no basis as a descriptive term in Chaucer's conceptual world and tends towards
obfuscation because it is never clear precisely how the idea works in a literary
setting. Which is the parasite and which is the host? It appears at first that,
punningly, the parasite is sight, feeding off love and knowledge. As the term recurs,
it applies to the other two components as well, so that all three seem to become
mutually parasitic, a 'parasitic system' (p. 12), involved in a kind of troilism Troilus
never imagined (though perhaps Pandarus did). Various permutations thus become
possible: knowledge as the parasite of love, love as the parasite of sight. It is not
finally clear which model Klassen wants us to adopt. Better to have omitted the
term altogether; it distracts and jars and is inappropriate since Chaucer, as Klassen
reminds us, represents sight as something primal, initiatory, and fundamentally
healthy.

Finally, two quibbles of detail and emphasis. Commenting on part of Troilus's
Boethian reverie (*TC*, IV, 957–63 and 1023–29) Klassen observes that 'Until now
he has responded intuitively and been able to exist on a bare minimum of
ratiocination' (p. 134). This is hardly true. From the outset, Troilus's vision of
Criseyde has provoked introspective analysis which becomes ever more complex

until, at this stage of the narrative, it takes a metaphysical turn. Secondly, Klassen claims that the motif of vision does not enter into the Wife of Bath's Prologue. It does, but in disguised, if crucial, form, when Alisoun relates how she fell for the clerk Jankyn at the funeral of her fourth husband 'whan that I saugh hym go | After the beere' (596–97). Is this a new motif to be added to Klassen's compendium, 'love of legs at first sight'?

UNIVERSITY OF KENT AT CANTERBURY   PETER BROWN

From Pearl to Gawain: Forme to Fynisment.   By ROBERT J. BLANCH and JULIAN N.
    WASSERMAN. Gainesville, Tallahassee, and Tampa: University Press of Florida.
    1995. v + 207 pp. £36.

To judge by the style of this study of aspects of the Cotton Nero manuscript poems, Blanch and Wasserman had a good time collaborating on the project. The tone of the writing is of a kind to attract, in the first instance, lively student response and engagement, as there is some exploration of how these texts work in classroom discussion, and occasional use of pedagogy as a reference-point, as when the Green Knight is likened to a 'world-weary teacher' (p. 20). Jaunty, idiomatic chapter headings, such as that to Chapter 5, 'Quicker than the "I": The Hand of the Poet and the Pronouns of Narrative', seem designed to reassure the student of the accessibility of apparently difficult concepts and material, and both argument proper and footnotes convey the same impression (an example is the treatment of the work of Derrida in Chapter 5).

The book sets out to examine the *Gawain*-Poet's attitude to history, noting that taken as a whole the poems cover human history from Creation to Apocalyse (and in passing, the authors wittily observe how the positioning of *Pearl* at the beginning of the manuscript fulfils the poem's stated theme that 'the last shall be first' (pp. 6–7)), but the individual chapters concentrate on salient aspects of the interrelation of human and divine in this context, rather than attempt an exhaustive overview of medieval historiography. Chapter 1 concentrates on how the poet's interest in society as speech community links with an interest in history as process, but where one might consider, for example, *Sir Gawain* as a poem concerned with the provisionality of signs and their interpretation, the authors here prefer a judgemental analysis whereby Arthur's rule is a failure of stewardship of the word, a failure of 'correct' reading. Chapter 2 interestingly sets the covenants of *Sir Gawain and the Green Knight* and (briefly) of the other Nero poems in the context of a fourteenth-century legal emphasis on the importance of 'good will' in human transactions, and again judges Camelot and Gawain negatively, though one might also want to counter that surely the shape-shifting Bertilak is himself no model of good will.

Chapter 3 is rather more wide-ranging, however, in its consideration of miracles in the poems as interventions in, and even suspensions of, the covenantal history that characterizes the human/divine relation: the strength of this reading lies in the flexibility and sophistication that the operation of miracles as 'transrational signs' suggests for the models of human perception and routes to knowledge the *Gawain*-poet sets up and explores. Chapter 4 draws on a wealth of fascinating iconographic detail for its central argument that human hands are associated in the poems with human volition (a connection other medieval literature supports), while the hand of God indicates His presence and His sanctioning of events. But in the assertion that the human hand is in general emblematic of sin, the authors present us with certain interpretative difficulties: are we, for example, to understand cynically the mention of Gawain's 'fyue fyngres' (l. 641) in the description of the pentangle, or his blessing himself 'with hande' (l. 1203)? Similarly, Chapter 5, which considers God and the Poet as 'makers', is extremely thought-provoking, both in the way it shows how pronominal use determines communities, but also traces their shifting and exclusive natures, and in its suggestive notes on the relation between cognition and the anthropomorphization of God; but while there is some nuanced treatment of the narrators of *Pearl* and *Sir Gawain*, the presentation of the narrators of *Patience* and *Cleanness* as 'strongly-centred' closes down investigation of how these poems might in fact differ markedly from other homiletic literature in respect of their narrators.

The authors modestly present their work as 'a premise to be extended and explored rather than a thesis to be proven' (p. 1), and certainly both their material and their approach invite further discussion: one hopes that, in pursuing the lines of inquiry Blanch and Wasserman indicate, students and scholars will also engage in vigorous debate over some of the authors' conclusions, for a generalizing and judgemental tendency occasionally obscures the argument's exciting and innovative dimensions.

UNIVERSITY OF LEEDS   CATHERINE BATT

The French Tradition and the Literature of Medieval England. By WILLIAM CALIN. Toronto,
   Buffalo, NY, and London: University of Toronto Press. 1994. xvi + 587 pp.
   £48 (paperbound £19.50).

Fifty years ago it was still common to find, in books on English romance, crude and nationalistic assertions on the nature of French and English writing. The English romances were 'less lascivious' than their French counterparts, more restrained, sober, primitive, and unsophisticated, and therefore good; the French were artificial, conventionalized, verbose, sophisticated, and therefore bad. It would be pleasant to believe such nonsense had entirely disappeared from contemporary criticism, but its by-products are still with us, in the continuing marginalization of the Anglo-Norman and French fiction that exerted a profound influence on Middle English literature.

William Calin's large book has a large aim: to redress this neglect by an extended coverage of literature in French, both insular and Continental, which was seminal for the development of literature in English and of some of our greatest medieval writers: Chaucer, Gower, and Malory. He draws together the work of many different critics (Crane, Wimsatt, Muscatine, to name only a few) who have already shown the way. In his discussion of both Anglo-Norman romances and Continental French texts there are new and interesting ideas. I particularly appreciated the pages on *Ipomedon* and *Amadas et Ydoine*, but no less welcome were sections on French texts, some undeservedly neglected: the *Roman de la Rose*, Guillaume de Digulleville's *Pélerinage de la Vie Humaine*, Machaut, Froissart, Chartier, and the Vulgate Cycle, (somewhat confusingly called the *Prose Lancelot*).

Calin insists that all these texts should be considered as 'part of our common cultural heritage'. He deplores what Ian Short saw as Middle English scholars' inability to 'break free from an unproductive and misleading bipolarity inherited from the past: a polarity between French speakers and Middle English speakers' ('Patrons and Polyglots', *Anglo-Norman Studies*, 14 (1991), 246). Both scholars remind us of the rich symbiosis of cultures in medieval England: not English vs French, but English *and* French (and Latin). One cannot claim originality for Middle English texts by wilfully ignoring what insular and Continental French had already achieved, the rich substratum on which Middle English creatively builds.

Calin contests, in particular, the view that Chaucer used French poets in his early works, but outgrew and surpassed them in his maturity. A large part of his book is devoted to proving that Chaucer continued throughout his career to make creative use of prior French texts. Calin persuasively argues that Chaucer's interest in metatextuality, and his characteristic persona, were derived from thirteenth-century and fourteenth-century French poetry, but it is debatable whether the 'Chaucerian vision of life' in the Merchant's Tale is to be found 'in the French tradition'. Nor are attempts to derive Chaucer's stylistic features from French romance especially satisfactory.

This section illustrates what is characteristic of the book as a whole: while the overall aim is admirable, it can be taken to extremes, and vitiated by weak or unproven claims. Despite Calin's generous praise of English authors, it frequently seems his insistent subtext is that they invented nothing of significance. He denies the existence of all English material about native heroes: Anglo-Norman poets 'invented them'. But Gaimar surely found his Havelok story in Lincolnshire, when he accompanied his patroness there, and some of the narrative motifs in *Horn* suggest a decidedly English origin. Nor can the references to stories in English about Aalof (in *Horn* and *Waldef*) all be dismissed as spurious.

Other surprising statements are the claims that tail-rhyme metre is probably of French origin (p. 438), and that English alliterative romance is the 'logical sequel' to Anglo-Norman romance, though why, for example, the non-alliterative *Beues of Hamtoun* and *Guy of Warwick*, often closely imitating their predecessors, cannot be their logical sequels is unclear. The positive side of this part of the book, however, is the way Calin draws attention to the infinite variety of means by which Middle English romance poets adapted their French originals.

The organization of this book allows for too much later repetition of what has already been fully discussed. In places, the commentary reads as if directed at students newly discovering medieval literature: too many *Canterbury Tales* plot summaries and quotations. Yet the clear and informative coverage of lesser-known authors is a boon. All in all, this is an impressive book: to disagree with parts of it is not to detract from its substantial achievement.

ROBINSON COLLEGE, CAMBRIDGE   JUDITH WEISS

The Two Versions of Malory's 'Morte Darthur': Multiple Negation and the Editing of the Text.
    By INGRID TIEKEN-BOON VAN OSTADE. (Arthurian Studies, XXXV) Cambridge:
    Brewer. 1995. ix + 169 pp. £29.50; $53.

This detailed comparison of multiple negation in the Winchester MS (W) and Caxton's text (C) offers no support for any theory concerning the relationship of the two texts of Malory's *Morte Darthur*. The editor of C seems to have worked in a contradictory fashion, both following instructions to modernize W by removing examples of multiple negation (sixty-five are missing from C), while at the same time introducing 'archaic features' 'subconsciously'; 'the use of old-fashioned language may well have seemed appropriate' for 'the history of King Arthur' (p. 121). There are sixty-eight examples in C which are absent from W. Since C contains marginally more double negations than W, one may be somewhat uneasy with the conclusion that the 'disappearing process, with multiple negation clearly on its way out [. . .] has actually been shown in progress in the *Morte Darthur*' (p. 131).

The book's most important objective, to provide evidence for the theory that C descends linearly from W, suffers from the fact that Ingrid Tieken-Boon Van Ostade spends too much time demolishing Vinaver's arguments and not enough laying the foundations for her own. Vinaver jusitified his stemma by taking three examples. The first is not difficult to dismiss: C could well be a correction of W itself (pp. 88–89). The argument against Vinaver's second example (pp. 89–90) is convincing enough, but anyone not setting out (as this book does) to prove the linear descent theory might find Vinaver's explanation equally convincing. The case against Vinaver's third example seems extremely contrived (pp. 90–92). What troubles me most is that Vinaver's examples were merely a sample of hundreds that he might have chosen, examples that this book never examines. C may well edit W, may well clarify and modernize in a way that does not necessarily restore Malory's original text, but there are times when C's variants cannot possibly be his own unless we accept the theory, which the book, rightly, I think, rejects (p. 133), that C's editor/reviser consulted Malory's sources. There are passages where W makes perfect sense but where C's changes coincide with Malory's French book. A few of these may be coincidental (p. 95), but coincidence has its limits. When the copyist of C added 'in the midst of his forehead' (XVI. 17) after W's 'made a signe of the crosse' it was perhaps mere chance that Malory's source had 'en mis son front' in the corresponding place (*La Queste del Saint Graal*, ed. by Albert Pauphilet (Paris: Honoré Champion, 1967) p. 194); when he changed W's 'swete Lorde Jesu Cryst whos creature I am' into 'Fair sweet Lord Jesu Christ, whose liege man I am' (XVI. 9), it is tempting to suggest that inspiration guided him, for the French source says 'Biax douz perez Jhesucriz, cui hons liges je sui' (p. 175); but when the dully repetitive 'Sir Galahad [. . .] dud so mervaylously that they had mervayle of him' (W f. 397ᵛ), becomes in C 'did such marvels that there was none that saw him that wened he had been none earthly man, but a monster' (XVII. 10), it is extremely difficult to accept the idea that this is no more than the contribution of 'an ambitious young man' eager 'to demonstrate to Caxton his skills as an editor' (p. 121) for it is almost a word for word translation from the French 'et fex tiex merveilles qu'il n'est hons qui le veist qui cuidast qu'il fut hons terriens, mes aucuns monstres' (p. 235). The linear descent theory cannot afford to overlook examples such as these.

The most valuable chapters of this book are those which concentrate on multiple negation as such. Elsewhere, the results are less satisfactory and, perhaps, not always clear. Unless I have misunderstood, the author at two points claims the opposite of what she (presumably) intended: in 'Hellinga's hypothesis that W might be based on C' (p. 132) and 'there is no reason to interpret this passage as evidence that W contains a reading closer to the original than the one in C' (p. 90), W and C should be inverted.

UNIVERSITY OF BURGUNDY, DIJON   TERENCE MCCARTHY

The Emperor of Men's Minds: Literature and the Renaissance Discourse of Rhetoric. By WAYNE A. REBHORN. (Rhetoric and Society) Ithaca, NY, and London: Cornell University Press. 1995. xviii + 276 pp. $35

This book is a compelling study of rhetoric as a cultural construct in Renaissance education and a marker of social hopes and anxieties for the mobile middle class. In a helpful introduction, Rebhorn establishes rhetoric as a 'growth industry' in the Renaissance, the means by which a middle-class man might aim for social mobility, the writing of rhetorics being a way to establish credentials for advancement. He positions rhetoric in dialogue with literature rather than technical subordination to it, and argues that we must historicize rhetoric, seeing it not simply as part of the classical tradition but, instead, as a reflection of its contemporary culture.

In four chapters, in each case treating first rhetorical texts and then literary ones, Rebhorn explores the central tropes that define the social possibilities for Renaissance rhetoric: orator as ruler in a hierarchical society, rhetoric as subversive rebel of emotions, hermaphroditic depictions of rhetoric signifying distrust, and bad rhetoric represented by the monstrous body. Under the orator as ruler, Rebhorn examines the associations of rhetoric and weapon, orator and warrior, orator as civilizer, and rhetoric and spectacle. Indicated by the number of treatises on rhetoric addressed to rulers, the association of rhetoric with dominance or rule (as opposed to the Roman association of rhetoric with republican democracy) accounts for the coincidence of the rise of rhetoric and that of absolutism in the Renaissance, as well as the political cast of Renaissance epideictic rhetoric. While the section on rhetoric and spectacle as tools of rule in Shakespeare's Henry plays does not add a great deal to Shakespearean criticism, Rebhorn's reading of Lady Rhetoric in her numerous early modern portraits goes brilliantly against the grain of previous analysis: she is bound by rules of rhetoric and etiquette just as much as she gains power over others through her chains. The second chapter seems too clever to be fully convincing: while Rebhorn carries us easily through his alignment of rhetoric with the unstable in Renaissance society because of its appeal to passions (a topic considered by many mid-century historians of literature and rhetoric), the links between this conception of rhetoric and subversion or rebellion are tenuous at best. Part of the problem seems to be a confusion between influence on superiors and acquiring power over them (pp. 107–08); here Rebhorn could have benefited from feminist analyses of power, such as Constance Jordan's in *Renaissance Feminism* (Ithaca, NY, and London: Cornell University Press, 1990), which nicely distinguishes between the two. However, this chapter offers a fascinating analysis of Bacon's equation of intellect with the upper classes ruling over base emotions, as well as an intriguing reading of the anonymous picaresque novel, *Lazarillo de Tormes*. In an extremely complex argument in the next chapter, Rebhorn explores representations of rhetoric as Circe's garden (of figurative language) and Mercury's rod of eloquence, and anxieties about rhetoric as dressing up or putting on cosmetics, suggesting that such representations result in associating the power of the word with lasciviousness, effeminacy, and homosexuality. Circe as a woman and the misogyny of the presentation of rhetoric as ravishment disappears in this reading: this is feminism without women. But still, by means of the route Rebhorn takes through the rhetorical texts, he also achieves wonderful readings of Carew's elegy for Donne, and of Don Juan in Tirso de Molina's *El burlador de Sevilla*. In a final chapter, Rebhorn analyses the associations of rhetoric with monstrosity, through the Socratean comparison to cookery, the fable of the belly, the alignment of oratory with the monstrous body, and the equation of orator with trickster and deceiver. In this chapter, there are very fine readings of both rhetorical texts (especially of Antoine Furetière's *Nouvelle allégorique ou Histoire [. . .] d'Eloquence*) and of literary texts (Machiavelli's *Mandragola*, Jonson's *Alchemist*, and Molière's *Tartuffe*). Rebhorn ends his book with this analysis of the progressive containment of the power of rhetoric to promote social mobility, since Machiavelli's trickster-orators successfully take over power while leaving the nominal head of household in charge, Jonson's tricksters are returned to their former status, and Tartuffe is expelled and punished. With the rise of absolutism, the energy and power of rhetoric is seen with increasing distrust.

Pursuing the topoi of rhetoric as ruler, rebel, hermaphrodite, and monster through five European languages, Rebhorn is superb in his primary research. In comparison to this virtuosity, his secondary research covers little before 1985; I missed the conversation he might have had with a whole generation of critics who introduced Renaissance rhetoric and literature to each other (Madeleine Doran and Ruth Wallerstein, for example), as well as a second generation of metadramatic critics who deconstructed Shakespearean conceptions of language before the deconstructionists (Sigurd Burckhardt and James Calderwood, for example). Nevertheless, this book is a success: quirky, insightful, impressively researched, provocative.

UNIVERSITY OF MARYLAND   JANE DONAWERTH

Echoes of Desire: English Petrarchism and Its Counterdiscourses. By HEATHER DUBROW. Ithaca, NY, and London: Cornell University Press. 1995. xi + 295 pp. £35.50.

Petrarchan poetry has found a highly suitable critic in Heather Dubrow, whose trenchant prose, scrupulous analysis, and tightly constructed arguments share some of the qualities of the sonnet form. She aims to demonstrate the inadequacy of critical clichés, especially any simple binary opposition between Petrarchism and a later anti-Petrarchism. Instead, she shows how, even from its origins in Petrarch's own work, this was always a self-questioning and self-inverting mode of writing.

The echo-poem is used as a paradigm for this: an echo can provide various responses, ranging from replication to parody to contradiction, and similarly, Petrarchan poetry in general is shown to be diversely self-reflexive; hence Dubrow's preference for the term 'counterdiscourses', with its implications of plurality and integrality. She also coins the phrase 'diacritical desire' to describe how Petrarchism operates through distinctions (between the present poet and his predecessors, his contemporaries, his mistress) while simultaneously complicating and blurring these distinctions. Again, one Petrarchan trope, the evocation of passion through oxymorons of freezing fire and burning ice, is used as a paradigm for the whole genre: 'As in the oxymoron [. . .] difference and sameness collide and elide' (p. 81).

Conversely, or accordingly, Dubrow shows how the work of apparent anti-Petrarchans is profoundly rooted in Petrarchism, giving readings of Sidney, Shakespeare, Donne, Mary Wroth, and authors of 'ugly beauty' anti-blazons such as the little-known John Collop. Thus this is a book which deals in paradoxes, and its chapters, after meticulously tracing problems and ambiguities in poetic texts and in prior readings of them, frequently end with an antithetical punchline which is almost too neat, not unlike the concluding couplet of an Elizabethan sonnet.

Mary Wroth features as a supposed anti-Petrarchan largely because of her gender. One of the critical clichés which Dubrow reassesses is that Petrarchism always entails the objectification and silencing of a woman by a male poet, who, while appearing to write about and to a mistress, in fact writes about himself and addresses an admiring male audience. Instead, Dubrow argues, the Petrarchan poet often occupies a feminized position; and the sonnet mistress is often given voice, or indeed exercises a silence which is itself a powerful utterance. Thus terms such as 'voice', 'silence' and 'power' break down under Dubrow's intensive scrutiny into a complex gradation of meanings. Dubrow also challenges the recent critical orthodoxy that Petrarchan writing, while appearing to be about love and the pursuit of a mistress, is in fact about court hierarchy and the pursuit of political ambition, proposing a more flexible reading which recognizes that both surface and metaphor have significance.

Dubrow interestingly traces parallels between Petrarchism and the contemporary literary academy; in both, she remarks, identities and careers are constructed upon the often exaggerated assertion of difference from predecessors and rivals. She is therefore highly self-conscious about her own methodology, which adeptly reconciles close reading and genre-study with New Historicism and feminism. She also broaches a historicized psychoanalysis in her suggestion that the diacritical desire of Elizabethan and Jacobean writers might be attributable to the fractured familial structures of the period, in which early mortality and re-marriage made common the positions of displaced stepchild and competitive stepsibling. Dubrow advances this tentatively, sensibly cautioning against assumptions based on attitudes to 'blended families' in our own era, but further exploration of this intriguing idea would have been welcome. Unfortunately her usual precision slips a little here: not all Tudor and Stuart writers lost a parent in childhood, and the assertion that 'to Sidney and other members of his generation, who had witnessed the loss and replacement of mothers in the wake of the mortality crisis of 1557–1559, [. . .] references to stepmothers must have been especially resonant' (p. 105) needs qualification by recognition that Sidney's own mother, although she withdrew from society after her scarring by smallpox in 1562, lived until the year of his own death, 1586. But this moment is unusual in a study which is otherwise tenacious in its probing of texts and interpretations, and should rapidly become one of the standard works on its subject.

UNIVERSITY COLLEGE LONDON   HELEN HACKETT

Spenser's Allegory of Love: Social Vision in Books III, IV, and V of 'The Faerie Queene'. By JAMES W. BROADDUS. Cranbury, NJ: Fairleigh Dickinson University Press; London: Associated University Presses. 1995. 185 pp. £23.

James W. Broaddus treats *The Faerie Queene* by quest (pp. 13, 17, 20, et passim), 'episodes' and 'stories' being inserted into 'the quests of which they are a part' (p. 103). Thus Britomart's quest for Artegall, occurring across Books III, IV, and V, unifies Spenser's allegory of love. Other trans-book quests are interwoven: Timias for the love of Belphoebe, Florimell for love of Marinell, Scudamore for that of Amoret. This emphasis on overriding rigid book divisions is all to the good.

    Spenser's allegory of love could be called 'Spenser's allegory of seed' (p. 15) and the defining element of Broaddus's study is his 'Renaissance Psychophysiological approach' (p. 9, et passim). Everyone and everything is moved by self-love to conserve itself (Thomas Wright, *The Passions of the Minde* (1621), cited pp. 14 and 15, 22–23, 37, and so on), this taking the form of procreation in humans; sexual desire can breed love of honour and good deeds or their opposites (*The Faerie Queene*, III.i.49 and 50, iii.1–2). According to 'Galenic sexual physiology' the testicles, including the ovaries, 'are the source of dynamic life, augmenting the heart in supplying the body with vital heat' (Helkiah Crooke, *Microcosmographia*, 2nd edn (1631); Broaddus, pp. 163–64, n.7). The seed is thus the ultimate source of energy 'necessary for a healthy commonwealth' (p. 15). Broaddus suggests that characters (a deliberate word) in *The Faerie Queene* function quite exactly according to this psychophysiology which is crucial to Spenser's representations of sexuality and social vision (p. 15); for, as we are often reminded, the love that moves the stars moves also the commonwealth and the human psychophysiological system. This energetic self-love must be subordinated hierarchically in certain ways: lust to chaste love, woman to husband — ultimately to the state. Naturally chaotic, rebellious energy must be suppressed (not repressed) 'bound to the larger order' (p. 154). There are other ways of expressing the same point: 'the theme of Spenser's allegory of love: the control of fortune through love' (pp. 107 and 162–63, n. 12; the voluminous literature on this is not mentioned). Marinell is initially unsubordinated to his natural role as lover (p. 59 and chapter 2, passim); Busyrane would force Amoret to a love insubordinate to marriage (pp. 60 ff.); Radigund is insubordinate to the proper hierarchical roles of courtship becoming thereby politically insubordinate (a 'form of insanity' (p. 137)).

Broaddus is an avowedly 'innocent' reader (pp. 22 and 162–63, n. 12), which may devalue his work for some, though an innocent reading is not bad by virtue of its innocence. But 'innocent' should not mean 'simplistic', and there is unfortunately an aura of incompleteness about the book. This reveals itself in remarks which are inadequate to the point of being false ('the reluctance natural [. . .] to a virtuous female on the way to leaving the virgin state' (p. 83) — compare Juliet?), or careless to the point of being unintentionally offensive (an awkward confusion occurs between sex and gender (pp. 138–40)). More generally, analyses are not pressed far enough (for example, on story-telling (p. 41), on power (p. 132)), and there is a damaging separation between the medical evidence and the conclusions (for example, Britomart's imagination (p. 29), on Busyrane (pp. 86–87), and the threat he poses (p. 90)). The framework of quotations from the Galenic psychophysiologists does not generate, nor always support, the conclusions. Chapter 4, on Belphoebe, makes more use of the Queen's two bodies nexus and the Letter to Raleigh than Galen, while Chapters 5 and 6, on Artegall, make more use of some quotations from the homilies on obedience. It is one thing to note that certain limited aspects of Renaissance psychophysiology initially suggested readings, eventually developed by other means, and quite another to present them as evidence for an historical reading, innocent or not. Broaddus attempts the latter but achieves only the former.

UNIVERSITY OF TUBINGEN   J. B. LETHBRIDGE

Shakespeare at Work. By JOHN JONES. Oxford: Clarendon Press. 1995. vii + 293 pp. £35.

In *Shakespeare at Work* John Jones discusses the variations between the Quartos and Folio as evidence for a process of authorial revision in ways that address all those concerned with how textual transmission impacts upon literary interpretation. It is now a critical commonplace that Renaissance drama is the result not of the singular endeavours of authorial genius but rather of a collaborative process in which numerous hands intervene to compose the text. In some quarters this has led to the abandonment of concepts of authorship and authoritative editions. Acknowledging but largely side-stepping this debate, Jones prefers a narrative in which the revisions reveal Shakespeare as a meticulous and careful author facilitating the emergence of what he calls the play's 'personality' in the enlargement of its dramatic possibilities. Recognizing that textual criticism is based not on proof but 'probability maturing towards a certainty beyond reasonable doubt' (p. 2), Jones's claims are self-consciously not matters of fact but of critical and aesthetic judgement and his method depends primarily upon his forensic skills. It is therefore fortunate that he proves to be a judicious commentator on textual and dramatic nuance.

The book's opening chapter is a lucid exposition of evidence of Shakespeare's method of revision in the autograph pages of *Sir Thomas More*, while the chapter on the history plays and *Troilus and Cressida* yields fascinating observations about the revision process. However, in so far as these chapters accumulate examples rather than lead to firm conclusions, they remain preparatory to the book's main concern: the three great tragedies *Hamlet*, *King Lear*, and *Othello*. Jones finds these of special interest because they 'are the only cases of work begun and declared finished that was thought about again and thought about as a whole' (p. 51).

In an extended chapter on *Hamlet* he accepts the critical consensus that the 'good' Quarto (1604/5) is an acting text anticipating the Folio; but, while affirming that the 'bad' Quarto is an actor's memorial reconstruction, he nevertheless regards it as valuable, if indirect, evidence of how the play was being revised at that time. Jones painstakingly examines the variants, discovering in them evidence of an emergent 'rhetoric of the hidden' to explore a world in which a 'secret evil committed and laid bare forms the robust front of the story' (p. 108). He also sanctions the excision of two soliloquies ('O what a rogue and peasant slave' and 'How all occasions') on the grounds that they reiterate earlier passages and that 'reduced to one delay soliloquy, *Hamlet* is still a play about procrastination' (p. 136). For Jones, continued editorial commitment to these soliloquies perpetuates an inappropriate eighteenth-century critical sensibility in which character is more important than dramatic integrity.

Jones again acknowledges prevailing opinion when discussing *King Lear*, accepting that the 1608 Quarto is not a working draft of the play but a distinct version with a 'personality' of its own. The specific, and potentially contentious, twist he offers is that he regards the earlier version (*The History*) as a proto-romance. His discussion of the alterations in the staging of the scene in which Lear awakens from the deep slumber following his ordeal (*History*, sc. 21; *Tragedy*, IV, 6) is connected with the removal from the Folio of the scene describing Cordelia's response to the news of her father's plight (*History*, sc. 17; IV, 3 in conflated editions). This argument provides enough evidence to raise reasonable doubt about more conventional readings but, while suggestive, it can only indicate the presence of romance motifs, because the ending (implicit from the opening scene) remains supremely, even cruelly, tragic whichever version is preferred.

The discussion of *Othello*, exploring the assumption that Quarto and Folio are two acting texts of that one play and bear more evidence of careful revision, focuses on the augmentation of Emilia's role and the related introduction of the Willow Song. These observations are somewhat truncated but provide useful material for comparative analysis.

Jones's basic assumptions and his critical vocabulary will not square with the more partisan literary theorist. Nevertheless, this book is compelling and learned, seamlessly blending textual and literary criticism. His book should provide thought for anyone concerned with the textual history of these plays and its implications for interpretation.

STAFFORDSHIRE UNIVERSITY   DARRELL HINCHLIFFE

Sudden Shakespeare: The Shaping of Shakespeare's Creative Thought. By PHILIP DAVIS. London: Athlone. 1996. viii + 259 pp. £45.

'How did Shakespeare think?' is the question which opens *Sudden Shakespeare: The Shaping of Shakespeare's Creative Thought.* Philip Davis argues for 'a technical language which would be capable of responding suddenly — at a level prior to the settlement of definite human opinion — to the speed, transforming shape and even violence of Shakespeare's way of thinking as it comes *into* meaning' (Davis's emphasis, p. 6). It is a laudable aim, but unless you are Seamus Heaney with critical judgement and creative expression seamlessly fused, the result is repetitious phrases and a fatal reliance on the italicised exclamatory style: 'For what is "character" in Shakespeare? — it is in the first instance simply somebody occupying a place *and* being aware *of* it *in* it' (Davis's emphases, p. 38). The book has a considerable number of statements like this one which unwittingly demonstrate that any attempt on the part of criticism to imitate the creative process of its subject is almost always incapable of conveying the dynamics of creativity. When Davis rightly draws attention to Shakespearean performance as a 'sheer renewed coming-to-life' in 'attempts to re-perform him on the page' (p. 190), or when he provides the insight that 'there is a built-in evanescence to Shakespeare's curving sentences', and tries to convey that such sentences have a 'being-in-time' (p. 78), the approach would have benefited from a more precise analysis of how the language is made to work: the many and varied ways in which subtle syntactical touches at line breaks create meaning, for example, and the wonderfully inventive variety of uses he makes of shared lines. Indeed, throughout the book a rather more delineated examination of how time and process make meaning on Shakespeare's stage in the voice and body of his actors would have greatly helped to substantiate the discussions.

Interestingly, the book is at its best on Shakespeare's exploration of character. Arguing that a reading of Montaigne is 'crucial to a study of Hamlet', Davis provides a suggestive discussion of how the emergence of the individual con-sciousness 'no longer at home in the world, and equally ill at ease with itself [. . .] disturbs the shape of the plays accordingly' (pp. 68, 64). But at other times the book makes less helpful generalizations: 'Shakespeare thinks quickly and powerfully and intuitively because he thinks in terms of spaces and places and shapes, long before he thinks of humans or morals or principles' (p. 1). Such a statement, for me, is hard to reconcile with Lear's unbearably human crying-out against a justice which allows a rat life and his daughter no breath at all; or even with Orlando's solicitous care of Adam shown to us immediately after Jaques has reduced human life to a meaningless itinerary.

Davis examines the late plays as 'alternative metaphysical histories' and argues that 'the history play needed to become a tragedy' (pp. 155, 143), and takes issue with recent critics for separating out Shakespeare's 'political interests' to make the important point that this emphasis on the political is bound to predominate 'when critics associate role-playing in the theatre with role-playing in the world of kingship and power politics' (pp. 142–43).

One aspect of the book which would try the patience of the most interested reader is the sudden intrusions of unidentified quotations: Kierkegaard, Montaigne, Bruno, Augustine, and numerous others are called up throughout but seem insufficiently anchored to the Shakespearean texts to make connections meaningful. The absence of identifications in the main body of the text made for a particularly irksome read because the notes are printed at the end of the book with no page numbers or even chapter headings identified on the running titles.

UNIVERSITY OF READING   PAULINE KIERNAN

Shakespeare and the Theatre of Wonder. By T. G. BISHOP. (Cambridge Studies in Renaissance Literature and Culture) Cambridge, New York, and Melbourne: Cambridge University Press. 1996. xiii + 222 pp. £30.

That a book with such a title should appear under the Cambridge Studies in Renaissance Literature and Culture imprint, if not itself a wonder, is at least at first sight a surprise. That we need a book which seeks to account for the emotional charge created between an actor and a text and between both of these and the audience, is not in doubt. But T. G. Bishop's thesis that 'wonder provides a turbulent space, rich at once in emotion and self-consciousness, where the nature and value of knowing is brought into question' (p. i), is a mystery born of tautology, still begging the question of how it is that the sense of wonder is created in the first place.

The book reaches the conclusion that Shakespeare, unlike the 'dramatic theorists or the more avant-garde practitioners of his day' creates 'evocations of wonder' that are 'profoundly transactional, delicate, and full of difficult turbulences' (p. 176). But Bishop's comparison is not between Shakespeare and other writers of plays, but between Shakespeare and Jonson as a writer of court masques. This is not comparing like with like, nor does it do justice to other contemporary playwrights (including Jonson) whose dramatic treatments of contemporary issues are often at least as questioning, and just as much spectacles to wonder about, if different in tone from Shakespeare's. The masque, as Bishop rightly observes, uses miraculous spectacle for political coercion, and the book never grapples with the problem that in the past, those most likely to use the term 'wonder' when talking about Shakespeare were least likely to find the plays 'transactional'.

The rest of the book is a curious mixture of often quite persuasive close reading with sweeping, unproved, and unhelpful generalization: 'Of all Shakespeare's young women, save perhaps Juliet, [Perdita] is the most open in welcoming the biological life of the sexual body' (p. 154). Open to whom? We see Desdemona entertaining bawdy jokes from Iago and later going happily to bed with Othello twice in the same scene (he, of course, through Iago's language later sees her in bed with Cassio), while Viola necessarily disguising her desires in front of Orsino, thereby makes them quite apparent to us the lookers-on. But these are part of the careful and complex structures of their respective plays in which our understanding of character is created as much by the juxtaposition of situation and the play on words sometimes unintended by the character concerned, as by what they say about themselves. Bishop, however, does not always clearly distinguish between desires and feelings expressed by individual characters and the complex mix of emotional and intellectual responses that might be engendered in audiences exposed to the unfolding patterns of a play.

It is certain both that as human beings we have an insatiable psychological need for dramatic fiction and that in the modern age we are exposed to a greater quantity of such fiction than ever before. As always when fictional forms become genuinely popular, doubts are raised about their effect on the moral health of the nation. We all, therefore, need to wonder about the ways in which a theatrical (or indeed, filmed) experience moves and engages us, and critics of the drama must consider precisely how such effects are created. The obfuscatory language in which this book is couched will ensure that it does not get read beyond the realms of academe.

QUEEN MARY AND WESTFIELD COLLEGE, LONDON   ROSALIND KING

The Shapes of Revenge: Victimization, Vengeance, and Vindictiveness in Shakespeare. By HARRY KEYISHIAN. New Jersey: Humanities Press. 1995. ix + 182 pp. £27.50; $39.95.

We all have what seem to be crackpot theories that we hardly dare to bring to the light of day until there is a glimmer of support from some other source. One of my own is that the Massacre of St Bartholomew's Day, which occurred in Paris on 24 August 1572, haunted late-sixteenth-century England as the holocaust has haunted the late-twentieth century, and that Shakespeare in particular obliquely reveals its significance in his plays. The slaughter of innocent Huguenots, witnessed and reported by people as influential as Sir Philip Sidney, must have sent shock waves through all Protestant countries, and England is geographically so close, and politically so entwined, that the event must have been particularly disquieting.

There are many oblique snippets of evidence one could adduce, but more pervasive in Shakespeare is the motif of the slaughtered innocent, the death in each tragedy of women and children who are caught up in a larger political conflict. Complicated feelings of outrage, desire for revenge, and the potential for forgiveness are voiced in the plays after the deaths of characters such as Lavinia, Ophelia, Desdemona, and Cordelia, to the point that the motif is a Shakespearean signature denoting his transferred response to injustice. Behind his insistence on the theme, one feels, is some great cultural injustice which could well be a folk memory of St Bartholomew's Day, and behind this, of course, lies the even more potent paradigm of the crucifixion of Jesus Christ.

Harry Keyishian, in *The Shapes of Revenge*, although he does not mention St Bartholomew, gives me the glimmer of support for the theory which enables me to pursue it as more than a wild and unsubstantiated hunch. Whereas the modern orthodoxy has been that revenge in Elizabethan plays is a Senecan inheritance, milked for its dramatically fertile conflict between Christian forgiveness and pagan vindictiveness, Keyishian argues for a much more complex and rich amalgam of motives which essentially include victimization as part of the equation. Parallels with cultural and political responses to the Jewish holocaust, while again not invoked, become quite insistent. The pagan associations of revenge, and the Christian prohibitions against it, argues Keyishian, become less than relevant when some great wrong has been committed and has led to the death of innocent people, especially when public channels for justice are closed off through corrupt authority. In these cases 'anger hath a privilege', and audiences would inescapably have a sense of profound, secular injustice, which provokes an outraged desire for vengeance. Revenge here can 'restore personal integrity', allowing recovery from 'feelings of powerlessness, violation, and injustice' (p. 9).

Keyishian's book is suggestive rather than systematic, as he deals briefly with a surprising range of plays: revenge has rarely, for example, been analysed in *A Midsummer Night's Dream*, the first history tetralogy, and *The Winter's Tale*. The nexus between victimization and revenge is located in *The Spanish Tragedy* and in characters such as Ophelia, Desdemona, and Hermione. Other plays exemplify different contexts for revenge. *Titus Andronicus* and *The Rape of Lucrece* show 'redemptive revenge', utterly sane reactions to insane situations, as Keyishian puts it; 'destructive revenge' marks *Julius Caesar* and *Othello*; while justified revenge is distinguished from the simple vindictiveness that the writer finds in Shylock, Malvolio, and Coriolanus. Given the broad definition of revenge, the book does not prioritize *Hamlet*, which is linked with *King Lear*, both plays depicting 'problematic revenge', where justice is achieved only at the risk of the revenger's incrimination. *The Tempest* shows a way of 'solving the problem' by allowing 'nobler reason', a philosophical vindication, to overcome fury.

In the final analysis, Harry Keyishian's book has a strong and interesting thesis, but the applications are too brief to make them fully convincing, and the Elizabethan psychology which, it is argued, is the source for the idea of the victim's revenge is thinly researched and perfunctory. There is more than enough evidence to fuel another book. It is not only because the St Bartholomew's Massacre is not mentioned, that I found the book, although potentially exciting, a missed opportunity.

UNIVERSITY OF WESTERN AUSTRALIA   R. S. WHITE

Middleton's 'Vulgar Pasquin': Essays on 'A Game at Chess'. By T. H. HOWARD-HILL.
   Cranbury, NJ: University of Delaware Press; London and Toronto: Associated
   University Presses. 1995. 341 pp. £34.50.

No one knows more about Middleton's *A Game at Chess* than Trevor Howard-Hill.
That is a large claim to make in any field of scholarship, but in this case I think it is
irrefutable. He has produced a steady stream of articles on the play, and on one of
its scribes, Ralph Crane, since the mid-1980s. In 1900 he edited the holograph
Trinity College manuscript of the play for Malone Society Reprints (old spelling);
in 1993 he completed the monumental task of producing a modern-spelling edition
of the play for the Revels Plays, based on an exhaustive study of all the early
versions.
   The magnitude of the latter task can hardly be exaggerated, since the play
survives in six early manuscript and two printed versions, all quite significantly
different from each other. So, as he put it in the preface to the edition: 'Even as
scholarly an edition as the Revels cannot accommodate all the materials relative to
A Game at Chess, so besides the edition I have written studies of the more complex
and problematic elements of the play for separate publication. [. . .] These essays
will justify the conclusions that have been presented here more succinctly —
especially on the text and political auspices — as well as setting out in tables the
information essential for a thorough understanding of the textual situation' (p. ix).
The volume reviewed here is those essays and tables. And very simply, all future
scholarship on the play starts here.
   That is another large claim to make, but again easy to substantiate, since the
book does not only unravel the complex relationship between the eight early
versions of the play (building, as Howard-Hill readily acknowledges, on the work of
Susan Zimmerman Nascimento, but going well beyond it); it also painstakingly
examines the political situation which first made the play possible, and then so
successful. The two matters, of course, go hand in hand. If the play had not been as
politically sensitive as it was, it is unlikely that it would have been as scandalously
successful as it was, running an unprecedented nine consecutive performances in a
packed Globe; and without that scandal it is unlikely that so many versions would
have been produced, bequeathing us these embarrassing editorial riches. It is the
particular combination of scandal and textual complexity which gives the play such
a special place in the scholarship of early modern drama, and never more so than in
the re-historicization of that drama that has occurred over the last twenty years.
   The key question has always been: to what extent is the play exemplary of the
conditions of the drama (both in performance and for a readership) of the era as a
whole. Annabel Patterson, for example, dubbed the play one of 'those famous
puzzling incidents of *noncensorship*' (*Censorship and Interpretation* (Madison: University
of Wisconsin Press, 1984), p. 17), indicating its status as an unusual test case.
Howard-Hill's essays here, each in its different way, unravel and attempt to
demystify one aspect of that peculiar status. To take the editorial issues first: he
demonstrates — to my mind beyond contravention — a sequence of relationships
between the surviving versions in which Middleton was solely responsible for the
Trinity College manuscript (which, however, does not entirely reflect the play as it
was finally staged), in which the scribe Ralph Crane was a key mediating figure for
the early, short Archdale-Folger manuscript, the later of the two printed quarto
versions, and the Lansdowne and Malone manuscripts (these together representing
a separate and distinct line of transmission), and in which other, less expert scribes
were responsible for the Bridgewater–Huntingdon, Rosenbach-Folger and first
quarto versions, sometimes with Middleton's own assistance, and drawing on other

Middleton and Crane versions. It is apparent, in fact, that there were many more manuscript copies of the play than have survived, and that the differences between those that have survived must be ascribed to a variety of factors, including relatively late rewriting by Middleton, possibly to accommodate changes required by the actors (either with or without the knowledge of the Master of the Revels); widely differing scribal practices; the pressure to produce large numbers of copies quickly, without regard to consistency or a single, definitive authorial or playhouse copy.

As I say, to have produced the Revels edition from that chaos is a major achievement. To have documented the process of editorial discrimination that made it possible is little short of a miracle, but this is one of the things this book does, and in this sense all future editorial work on the play clearly has to start here. Given his own demonstration of the extent to which Middleton's personal interventions in the text were driven by a variety of different motivations, it is not impossible to query Howard-Hill's conclusion that a text closest to Middleton is the most desirable for a modern edition. He also demonstrates just how good Ralph Crane was at reducing Middleton's often chaotic copy to readable form, and it might be argued that we should let a highly professional contemporary witness, who actually collaborated with Middleton, do some of that work for us. But any such debate about a choice of copy-text will incontrovertibly have to be made against Howard-Hill's analysis of the options.

Much more controversial are likely to be Howard-Hill's assessments of the political context within which the play was written, and the extent to which it could be seen as 'dangerous matter'. He is particularly at pains to establish that 'in the upshot, *A Game at Chess* conspicuously fails to deal with a topical political issue' (p. 106). That is, he insists on being strict in his definitions of 'topical'. Count Gondomar and Archbishop De Dominis, who are the figures most strongly attacked in the play's allegorical satire, were no longer in the country or active in relation to English politics and religion. Everybody, including the King, Buckingham, and Prince Charles, had turned against a Spanish marriage and alliance, and the country was preparing for war with the old enemy; Buckingham had forged an alliance with Pembroke, formerly one of the few men powerful enough to resist him in the Council. In such a context, he argues, the play was not 'dangerous' in the way that, for example, Margot Heinemann has argued that it was. He sees no need to imagine special conspiracies by Buckingham, Pembroke, or anyone else to get it staged. In a painstaking dissection of the many contemporary accounts of performance (he is most acute in pointing out how few of these are genuine eye-witness accounts, as distinct from hearsay) he suggests that true impersonation by the actors was reserved for Gondomar and De Dominis. If the roles of the King, the Prince, and so on were readily decodable within the allegory, it need not follow that they were disrespectfully guyed on stage (as some accounts have too easily assumed). On the contrary, he argues that the play offers something more like a 'carnivalistic celebration of national deliverance [. . .]. Issuing from a halcyon period of national unity, the play embodies the spirit of the times and provided occasion for local celebration. Middleton's play is too comprehensive to be diminished by narrow political readings' (p. 226).

This is unlikely to be the last word on the politics of the play, but the argument is conducted far too scrupulously simply to be dismissed as revisionist discontent with Marxist agendas. Running through much of what Howard-Hill says is a conviction that *A Game at Chess* is a very fine play, the qualities of which have been obscured by its political notoriety. He sees it as primarily a moral allegory, the emphases of which were perhaps skewed by the determination of the actors to make it more comic and sensational than Middleton had originally intended. It is an argument that will have to be taken seriously. One lingering doubt I am left with myself derives from looking at Howard-Hill's editorial and contextual arguments in conjunction. He shows that Middleton had begun what amounted to a production line for manuscripts even before the play was staged. That is, he anticipated unusual success even before impersonations and other bits of business by the actors (including bringing Gondomar's own 'chair of ease' on stage) had had their effect. Moreover, there is no evidence that the manuscripts took particular pains to capture the effects of the staging, which they would surely have done if that was the true source of notoriety; on the contrary, the Archdale-Folger copy was transcribed on one of the actual days of performance but is actually from a very early version, entirely without De Dominis and the sensational ending. This leaves open the possibility that there was something more 'dangerous' in the play that Middleton actually wrote (as distinct from the version the actors staged) than Howard-Hill allows for, something that called in its own right for a production line of scribes.

LANCASTER UNIVERSITY   RICHARD DUTTON

The Works of John Webster: An Old-Spelling Critical Edition. Vol. 1. *The White Devil, The Duchess of Malfi.* Ed. by DAVID GUNBY, DAVID CARNEGIE, and ANTONY HAMMOND. Cambridge, New York, and Melbourne: Cambridge University Press. 1995. xxxiv + 803 pp. £90; $135.

This is the first volume of a projected two-volume old-spelling edition of Webster's works, following on in the series of Cambridge University Press editions of Dekker, Marlowe, and Beaumont and Fletcher. The two volumes are likely to become the standard critical edition, though their price may well limit buyers mainly to libraries. This first volume contains the texts of Webster's two best-known plays; but the precise contents of the projected second volume are less easy to establish. These are not, unfortunately, listed with the contents of the first volume, and the reader has to compare the General Preface with the outline of the Webster canon (a useful checklist in its own right) in order to work out what the plans for the second volume seem to be. The most notable exclusion is of those collaborative plays written with Dekker and Fletcher, already published in the Cambridge editions of these authors; while the most significant inclusion is of the Melbourne manuscript.

Textual apparatus broadly follows the format of earlier editions, except that the collation appears at the foot of the relevant page rather than at the end of the text. The textual editors, however, abandon the traditional distinction between 'substantives' and 'accidentals' in favour of a distinction between 'signal' and 'noise', which effectively brings far more changes to the reader's attention as significant. Though this decision inevitably swells the extra-textual material on the page, clarity of typeface and layout prevent the page from becoming dominated by the collation, so that the dramatic text is still uncluttered and easy to read. The textual editors are admirably open and clear about their procedures, and their account of their own 'silent emendation' (pp. 42–48) is particularly to be applauded as a way of ensuring that the reader is aware of where this critical edition differs from other editions and from a facsimile text in its aims and practices.

This edition goes beyond the other Cambridge editions in the range of secondary materials it provides. Where they typically include only textual apparatus, this offers critical and theatrical introductions and, most usefully, full texts of Webster's source documents as well as discussions of how Webster used them. In fact the blurb advertises the particular features of this new edition fairly for the most part, except that the book in fact offers little on 'new critical methods' and its claim to integrate theatrical, bibliographical, and literary features 'in a way not previously attempted in a scholarly edition of a Jacobean dramatist' somewhat disingenuously fails to acknowledge the work of Wells and Taylor on the Oxford Shakespeare, despite their influence on editorial practice here.

On the other hand, this is a more conservative and less theatrically driven edition than the Oxford Shakespeare. Though the textual editors, Antony Hammond and Doreen DelVecchio, take stage directions more seriously than Bowers did in earlier Cambridge editions, they also write about 'theatre people' (no scare-quotes in the original) in a way that underlines the alien status of such beings and castigates their 'disappointing' tendency to make textual choices on a purely pragmatic basis (p. 39). Nevertheless, the attention paid to stage directions, and in particular to the presence in early printed texts of *The White Devil* of marginal stage directions in addition to those included in the main body of the text, leads into an interesting thesis concerning Webster's particular conception of the printed text. Unlike many of his contemporaries, the editors argue, 'Webster was actively interested in the way his play would make an impression upon readers who had not seen it in performance, and were therefore dependent upon the printed "Poem" for their impressions' (p. 128). This argument, however, as the quotation above illustrates, is constructed via a choice of terminology that sits uneasily, I think, in any modern edition of a printed dramatic text. Taking Webster's dedication of *The Duchess of Malfi* to Lord Berkeley ('*I offer this Poem to your Patronage*') as their starting point, the editors go on to distinguish his conception of the play as printed from the play as performed using the terms 'Poem' and 'Play' respectively (p. 35). The distinction is a necessary one, but the terms distracting, especially as the argument partly relies on a very dubious interpretation of the word 'play' on the title-page of the first Quarto, which is advertised as containing '*diverse things Printed, that the length of the Play would not beare in the Presentment*'. The reading is dubious in two respects: first, it assumes that the title-page represents Webster's own voice (however 'authorized' the text, this is an extreme position); and secondly, it supposes that Webster was using 'Play' as related or equivalent to 'Presentment' (performance), when the phrasing seems to me to be equally open to precisely the opposite reading, namely, that 'Play' is to be aligned with the full, unperformed version.

Yet I would not wish to close this review on a negative note. A good new edition of a Jacobean dramatist is a welcome addition to Renaissance scholarship. My only reservation is that there are several Renaissance dramatists whose works are more desperately in need of a new edition, and it is to be hoped that Cambridge is also commissioning some of these.

University of Nottingham Janette Dillon

Henry Vaughan. By Stevie Davies. (Border Lines) Bridgend: Seren (Poetry Wales Press). 1995. 213 pp. £12.95 (paperbound £6.95).

In a critical biography published to coincide with the tercentenary of Henry Vaughan's death in 1695, Stevie Davies makes perceptive use of the sparse documentary evidence of letters, litigation, and local records, but it is mainly from their own writings and from the landscapes of the Usk Valley and the Brecon Beacons that she seeks to evoke both the poet and his twin brother, Thomas, 'as real and breathing persons' (p. 7). Indeed, the fact of his twinship is central to her reading of Henry's life and work. Identifying Thomas as 'the centrifugal twin', making a place for himself in the outside world, and Henry as 'the centripetal twin', drawn back to the 'home-world' of his happy childhood after a brief sojourn in Oxford and London, she attributes to the prodigy of their double birth the brothers' 'individual and joint interest in the secret and arcane' (p. 35) and the insecurity and volatility of their temperaments. She also sees their separation in the early 1640s as the cause of Henry's profound need, at critical junctures in his life, 'to twin to another identity in order to be himself' (p. 65). After abortive attempts to find an individual voice by imitating Donne and the Cavaliers, Vaughan turned to 'the language of union and affinity offered by Hermeticism' in that search for a lost other self which 'threads the poetry' (p. 75). It was in the political and personal disasters that befell him at the close of the 1640s that his personality underwent the decisive crisis of disintegration and renewal which informs the religious poems collected in the two editions of *Silex Scintillans* in 1650 and 1655. The death of his younger brother, William, upon whom he may have 'projected his identity' (p. 82) in the absence of Thomas, not only generated some of the elegies in which Vaughan 'writes unsurpassedly about loss' (p. 83), but also prepared him for the spiritual rebirth and the remaking of his expressive idiom that was effected by his surrender to the transforming influence of the poetry of George Herbert.

From the evidence of the poetry itself, since there is little else to go on for this period of his life, Davies surmises that Vaughan had not yet taken up the profession of homeopathic physician during the years of his poetic flowering (*c.* 1647–55) and that his activities were essentially 'solitary and ascetic' (p. 113). Some of the poems that are most characteristic of his religious sensibility seem to be 'the testaments of a person in a state of self-induced sleep-starvation' (p. 107) and in the contemporary prose work, *The Mount of Olives* (1652), he appears to manifest 'a chronic case of the separation-anxiety which can accompany belief' (p. 109). The nostalgia for the visionary intuitions of the Creator in early childhood, the Blakean 'freshness and conscious naivete' (p. 114) with which he reads the Scriptures, the combination of tenderness and awe he brings to his contemplation of the creatures and plants of the natural world, and the urgency of his longing for the Second Coming of Christ: all can be interpreted as compensatory strategies for the failure to experience 'the fulfilment of the mystic's quest in full union with the Deity' (p. 119).

Although her primary emphases are on Vaughan's elusive search for origins and for a stabilizing relationship with another, and on the complementary experiences of loss, dispossession, and absence, Stevie Davies also calls attention to the strain of anti-Commonwealth satire in his work and acknowledges that even 'the most spiritual and inward poems in *Silex Scintillans* are charged with counter-revolutionary energy' (p. 156). The execution of his king and the suppression of his church combined with the death of William to produce the identity crisis and the need to live intensely within himself which gave birth to a unique body of poetry. His biographer speculates that with the passing of this peculiar set of circumstances, the meditations of the poet gave way to the 'creative and secret' (p. 190) work of the self-taught Hermetic doctor, concocting his own herbal medicines in a chemical laboratory in the paternal house at Newton which he eventually inherited in 1658. The rest is more or less silence, for the last thirty years of a long life, broken regrettably by the bitter legal wrangling between Vaughan and the children borne by the two sisters he had married successively.

Stevie Davies communicates a genuine sense of discovery and delight as she undertakes her own journey through the Welsh landscapes known to the Vaughan brothers and into the hidden recesses of their poetry and prose, which she reads with great sensitivity and with a lively awareness of historical and geographical contexts. For the beginner there could be no better introduction to the work of a

major seventeenth-century writer and for the initiated there are many new insights
to provoke and stimulate.

UNIVERSITY OF BIRMINGHAM   ROBERT WILCHER

Reading Rochester. Ed. by EDWARD BURNS. (Liverpool English Texts and Studies)
Liverpool: Liverpool University Press. 1995. viii + 232 pp. £30 (paperbound £11.75).

The title of this collection suggests that the book purports to supply guidance for the
Rochester student, in a wide sense of the word, but its usefulness in that respect is
limited. For one thing, it devotes very little space to Rochester's best-known and
most complex work, the *Satyr against Reason and Mankind*. Two of the eleven
contributions, while valuable in themselves and welcome in print, do not provide
much in the way of assistance to readers grappling with the texts, being more
informative on Oldham than on Rochester (Raman Selden's comparative essay on
the two poets) and on publishing history (Jim McGhee on 'The Imperfect
Enjoyment'). One factor that reduces the serviceability of the volume as an
academic textbook is its scholarly deficiencies: while some of the authors are
thoroughly acquainted with previous work on Rochester, others (for example,
Helen Wilcox and Simon Dentith) appear unaware that several of the main points
made in their analyses have long been familiar to Rochester critics. The potential
usefulness of the volume as a handbook for Rochester students is further diminished
by the fact that the notes, which contain such scholarly materials as there are, are
not indexed and there is no bibliography.

Even so, the strengths of the book are not inconsiderable. It starts off in a highly
auspicious way with a concise and well-written introduction in which the editor,
Edward Burns, pinpoints those aspects of Rochester's work that are most apt to
engage a present-day audience. Helen Wilcox's essay on 'Song of a Young Lady to
Her Ancient Lover' is an attentive exploration of the significance of 'art' in
Rochester's poetry and of the paradoxes inherent in a male poet's adoption of a
female persona. In his commitment to 'fine writing', Stephen Clark almost loses
sight of his ostensible subject, Rochester and misogyny, but every now and then a
lucid and insightful remark puts him and the reader back on course. Edward Burns
himself is particularly good on problems of identity in a Rochester context. Simon
Dentith moves on well-charted territory but formulates some striking observations,
and Tony Barley examines *Upon Nothing* with a fine sense of its essential absurdity.
In fact, *Upon Nothing* receives a disproportionate amount of attention in the volume.
One of the writers concerned with it is the author of the weightiest (in more than
one sense) contribution, Paul Baines; his excellent discussion contemplates Roches-
ter's 'Nothing' in conjunction with Pope's 'Silence'. Both Brean S. Hammond and
Bernard Beatty have important things to say about Rochester in relation to Dryden.

With his shifting poses, linguistic subtleties, and insistent physicality, Rochester
should be *gefundenes Fressen* for critics with affiliations to various current theoretical
approaches, but the attempts made along such lines in this book are not encouraging.
To quote a single instance, Nick Davis's essay begins with a most interesting premise
(Rochester's involvement with intellectual politics, with special reference to the
Latitudinarians) but goes on to puzzle the reader with sentences such as the
following one, on 'Artemiza to Chloe': 'The poem is structured as a sequence of
disappearances [. . .] into ego's compelling counterpart to ego, on the principle that
social desire (we might say "socialized" desire, which for the Freudian tradition
desire always already is) consists of accession to the desire of the other; this calls into

play a relationship of aggressivity towards an other whose attitude to "self" one has somehow to take on without having the remotest chance of displacing it — "it" is where "you" find yourself having to be' (p. 130). Now what was that Rochester said about bladders of philosophy?

LUND UNIVERSITY   MARIANNE THORMÄHLEN

Restoration Politics and Drama: The Plays of Thomas Otway, 1675–1683. By JESSICA MUNNS. Cranbury, NJ: University of Delaware Press; London: Associated University Presses. 1995. 269 pp. £32.50.

The title implies a broader and more historical book than the one Jessica Munns has written. What we have here is basically a close reading of Otway's ten plays in chronological order with the comedies pulled out into a chapter of their own. *Caius Marius* (1679), *The Orphan* (1680), and *Venice Preserv'd* (1682) receive chapter-length discussion; the other plays get more summary treatment. Munns provides a conscientious and generally accurate survey of pertinent primary and secondary material, and she is commendably sceptical about the late and sentimental biographical anecdotes that have long polluted Otway criticism. She is sufficiently uncontentious towards her predecessors that her interpretations sometimes verge on pastiche. She agrees here, borrows a bit there, conflates and synthesizes, the results being generally unobjectionable if not terribly exciting readings. This is the first full-length study of Otway's plays, and if it does not greatly change our sense of them, it has the virtue of pulling the subject together in a brisk and tidy way. Beyond that, I have two significant reservations about this book.

First, there are too many howlers and minor errors. 'Jeremy' Sandford (p. 29), 'Mille. de Scudery' (p. 34), 'Theoderet' for Theodoret fully a dozen times (e.g., p. 79), 'Odly' for Oldys (p. 214), Dryden's *Limberham* dated '1670' instead of 1678 (p. 222), Nicoll's *History* reduced to two volumes (p. 257), Patricia A. Parker's *Inescapable Romance: Studies in the Poetics of a Mode* (1979) attributed to Otway in the bibliography, *'Huntingdon' Library Quarterly* (p. 260); the list could go on. Names, dates, and transcriptions are usually right, but are wrong just often enough to undermine the reader's confidence.

Secondly, and far more important, the book suffers from kitchen sink methodology. Munns makes virtually no effort to see these works as plays, to consider their impact in performance, or (for example) to use cast information to help determine how they appeared to the original audiences. This is a defensible choice. Less satisfactory is her failure to decide whether she is trying (a) to set Otway's work in its historical context, or (b) to reconstruct Otway's personal, social, and political views from his texts, or (c) to analyse those texts in light of twentieth-century theory and paradigms. All of these are valid methodologies, but the combination here does not strike me as felicitous or convincing. Such account of 1670s and 1680s history and politics as Munns offers does not connect in much detail with her textual analysis of the plays, which is distinctly skewed towards psycho-methods. So we are given Freud and Lacan and Cixous (among others). Nothing is wrong with this in itself, but it sits oddly with the announced aim of situating Otway in a period of what is said to be critical 'transition' in its social philosophy and politics. The effect, ultimately, is of a jumble of historical and modern critical methods, with the latter providing more top-dressing than real substance.

Munns is best when least pretentious. When she describes the plays she is straightforward and assured. When she strains after grander things, she stumbles. The broader statements rarely strike me as happy: 'Restoration literature was engaged in mediating the transition to a new form of rule' (p. 14). Consciously? On whose part? When? How? Is this what Otway thought he was trying to do? Was his work understood in this way by his contemporaries? Or, to take a much smaller kind of example, we are told that *The Cheats of Scapin* offers commentary on 'freedom of marriage choice and the rebellion of sons against paternal sexual regulation' (p. 54). True enough, but so do at least three hundred other plays of the time: is this 'serious' commentary? In sum, this is a book with both virtues and limitations.

PENNSYLVANIA STATE UNIVERSITY, UNIVERSITY PARK   ROBERT D. HUME

The Margins of Orthodoxy: Heterodox Writing and Cultural Response, 1660–1750. Ed. by ROGER D. LUND. Cambridge, New York, and Melbourne: Cambridge University Press. 1995. xiv + 298 pp. £35; $59.95.

The editor of this collection, Roger Lund, is an eighteenth-century scholar's eighteenth-century scholar. He would be very high on my top ten list of scholars who have never published a monograph but whose exquisite articles are far more valuable than the monographs of many others. He is, in short, the kind of scholar who reduces to absurdity our Great British Research Assessment Exercise. The present book of essays is the fruit of a conference, glittering with big names, that Lund staged in Le Moyne College, Syracuse in 1991. It concentrates on writers who took up or (in the cases of Richard Ashcraft's essay on John Locke and Ronald Paulson's on Henry Fielding) can be argued to have taken up, a position of religious heterodoxy in the post-Restoration period: figures usually considered 'marginal' such as Tindal, Toland, Woolston, Shaftesbury, and Blount. It also covers the backlash to deist, Socinian, and other heterodoxies to be found in places as diverse as the pro-persecution tracts of Samuel Parker, the preachers who provided the ideological fuel for the Societies for the Reformation of Manners, the Bishops who arraigned Thomas Woolston, and (perhaps the most unexpected quarter) those Moderns such as Bentley and Wotton whom Joseph Levine argues were taking on the Ancients because they could perceive a deist threat in their arguments. Even Latitudinarian churchmen developed clear limits to their toleration, as Jeffrey S. Chamberlain shows in his case-study of one such, Thomas Curteis. Chamberlain's conclusion, that the only real difference between High and Low churchmen was that they had 'different boiling points', epitomizes this book's struggle to distinguish clearly between orthodoxy and heterodoxy in the period, which dialectical process is the volume's main interest and value.

J. G. A. Pocock's essay, 'Within the Margins: The Definitions of Orthodoxy' tackles this head-on in a complex argument that requires us at all times to exercise our historical imaginations in recreating a period in which 'orthodoxy' meant the simultaneous subscription to two potentially conflicting views of the Church of England: that it was the church by law established, and that it was the body of Christ in the world. Shelley Burtt's piece on the Societies for the Reformation of Manners tries to advance our thinking on the meaning of 'orthodoxy' by arguing that it was not an ossified, reactionary body of thought. The Societies are themselves an example not so much of an old orthodoxy battling with a new but of 'transformation from within' orthodoxy itself. The argument seems to me to assume what it should prove, however. If we consider the conflict between Jeremy Collier and William Congreve for example (which Burtt does not), how do we determine whether Collier represents an old orthodoxy transforming itself from within or, as I would see it, a new bourgeois movement pitting itself against the vestigially aristocratic codes assumed by the dramatist?

Both Christopher Hill and Richard Ashcraft stress the importance of seventeenth-century radicalism on the free-thinking, libertine, and anti-clerical strands of thinking in the eighteenth, in Ashcraft's case specifically on John Locke. Both reiterate positions familiar from the main body of their writings; but what is fascinating about Ashcraft's essay is its contention, made almost as an appendix, that although Max Weber has long been credited with the argument that radical Protestantism is the seed bed of capitalism, there exist writings in which Weber might easily have directed his thinking down the opposite path. The seventeenth-century sectaries and radicals espoused Protestant forms of religiosity that could have sponsored collectivist forms of political action. G. A. J. Rogers's essay on Locke treads a more cautious line, however. His conviction is that Locke's theological views were always submitted to the scrutiny of a strong rationalism that derived from his epistemological premises. Faith was always subordinate to reason for Locke. Clearly, this could be read as a quasi-deist position, and there are other heterodoxies such as anti-Trinitarianism to which it could lead; but Rogers emphasizes that Locke remained an orthodox communicant, did not himself tease out the consequences of his own thinking, and adopted a view very close to Swift's: that there is a distinction between what we can think and what it is prudent to express in public. Finally, Locke might have been shocked by the constructions made of his writing. Perhaps he will be shocked by Richard Ashcraft when they meet in the next world.

From some of the most unpromising characters, we learn a great deal in this volume. Gordon Schochet's piece on Samuel Parker permits him to make very valuable distinctions between different species of early nonconformism and to recreate very painstakingly the various degrees of toleration that contemporaries believed could be extended to them. Roger Lund's own contribution to the volume is another gem. He shows that Woolston's prosecution for exposing Christ's miracles to ridicule was part of a wider cultural tendency to regard witty style, more than blasphemous content, as the real danger to established orthodoxy. How I wish his argument had embraced the most vexed case, that of Jonathan Swift. Swift, after all, employed wit and ridicule to ridicule those who employed wit and ridicule, such as Anthony Collins and Woolston himself. Indeed, Collins's *Discourse of Irony and Wit in Writing* (1729) makes the plaintive accusation that, while his own style is being criminalized, Jonathan Swift has been getting away with it for years. It is not fair. Doubtless, Lund will devote attention to Swift in the longer work he is writing on this topic. Woolston also looms large in the final and, to my mind, least convincing essay in the volume. Occam's Razor can seldom have been blunted more often on any writer than on Henry Fielding. Byzantine explanations have been given of his political loyalties (or lack of them) and in Ronald Paulson's contribution to this volume, the argument is made that although he became more orthodox and reactionary later, Fielding's early plays exhibit deist influence. It is asserted that Woolston's *Discourses*, like Fielding's plays, 'are really about the bad critics and exegetes, often associated with clergymen', and that assertion is about as much evidence as we get. I seriously doubt if a reading of Woolston's *Six Discourses of the Miracles of Our Saviour* (1727–30) could have impressed Fielding other than by its appalling vulgarity and lack of any vestige of respect. And that is my view, even though (unlike the Anglican apologist Martin Battestin whom Paulson is challenging in this essay) I have no religious affiliation whatsoever.

All in all, though, this is a collection of high quality which, if as Pocock himself points out, it is not quite as 'marginal' as it claims to be (no Scots, Irish, Americans or women of any nationality in sight) deserves to be read by all those who want to improve their understanding of the precise nature of post-Reformation religious conflict.

UNIVERSITY OF WALES, ABERYSTWYTH   BREAN S. HAMMOND

James Boswell's 'Life of Johnson': An Edition of the Original Manuscript, In Four Volumes. Ed. by CLAUDE RAWSON. Vol. 1. *1709–1765.* Ed. by MARSHALL WAINGROW. (Yale Editions of the Private Papers of James Boswell) Edinburgh: Edinburgh University Press; New Haven, CT, and London: Yale University Press. 1995. xxxix + 518 pp. £75.

This is to me a memorable year for in [this year I was happy enough to obtain the acquaintance of /Dr. Samuel/Johnson∫ Dr. Johnson's aquaintance, which I shall ever reckon∫ esteem as one of the most fortunate∫ valuable circumstances∫ events >] it I had the happiness of obtaining the acquaintance of that extraordinary man whose memoirs I am now writing. [. . .] I found that I had a very [perfect∫ exact >] perfect idea of Johnson's [appearance∫ figure >] figure, from a picture of him by [/Sir Joshua/ >] Sir Joshua Reynolds in the attitude of sitting in his easy = chair /MS 208/ in deep meditation ⅄ soon after he had published his Dictionary λ which [I believe *del*] was the first picture his friend did [of >] for him ⅄ of which Sir Joshua has been so very good as to make me a present λ ⅄ and from which an engraving has been made for this work λ. [It has never been finished∫ produced, though I cannot but think∫ help thinking it a striking likeness. *del*] (pp. 264, 269)

Boswell's first meeting with the man who was to ensure his lasting literary reputation was not easily accomplished, though with patience and doggedness Boswell at last achieved the now celebrated introduction in Davies's bookshop. This has always been well known because Boswell told us so himself. What is now also apparent is how far that telling was itself accomplished with a patience and doggedness if anything exceeding that of the original event. Partly, this was in the interests of decorum. As Marshall Waingrow reminds us in a footnote, Johnson's 'figure' was described with much greater immediacy in Boswell's journal entry for the day of the meeting: 'Mr. Johnson is a Man of most dreadful appearance. He is a very big Man is troubled with sore eyes, the Palsy & the King's evil. He is very slovenly in his dress & speaks with a most uncouth voice' (p. 269 n. 3). But it was also the consequence of Boswell's method of composition, which involved less the writing of a continuous narrative than, for large stretches at least, the weaving together of disparate materials, including his own journal entries, letters between Johnson and a range of correspondents, and other people's accounts and anecdotes supplied at Boswell's request. All of these Boswell felt free to edit, censor, amplify, and rewrite as part of a coherent presentation of Johnson, certainly, but also of himself. The endless alternating between words and phrasings is often quite inconsequential as far as Johnson is concerned but plays a part, nevertheless, in sustaining the personality and authority of the 'memoirist', narrator, editor, and friend.

Again, this has been well known, but this edition allows us to see in full the painstaking methods of Boswell's work, painstaking and painful, given Boswell's desperate frame of mind at this final period of his life. His reworking, at different times, in different inks, on different parts of the manuscript, on the 'Papers Apart', his directions to the compositor, his queries to Edmond Malone (the mainstay of his support during much of the time) and Malone's to him, are recorded and rendered as coherent as possible in Waingrow's own painstaking editorial apparatus. Quite apart from the representations within the text, as in the example above, there are two layers of footnotes dealing with different sets of issues, and over a hundred pages of endnotes giving explanation of further textual items. This labour of love has produced a work that with the three volumes yet to come, will provide an indispensable research tool, and also ensure Marshall Waingrow's own place amongst the heroes of Boswellian studies.

University of Northumbria at Newcastle   Allan Ingram

Rural Life in Eighteenth-Century English Poetry. By John Goodridge. (Cambridge
    Studies in Eighteenth-Century English Literature and Thought) Cambridge,
    New York, and Melbourne: Cambridge University Press. 1996. xiv + 227 pp.
    £35.

It is possible to write a sentence like 'As usual Dyer's observation of sheep is keen' (p. 153) and still come up with an interesting book, but clearly the odds are stacked heavily against it. John Goodridge does so, partly because his subject, despite the work of John Barrell and others, is still suffering from a lack of attention, and partly because of his own keen observation of texture and intertextuality in the writing of Thomson, Duck, and Collier. There is also useful restorative work on John Dyer, a writer so remote from critical familiarity that the 1989 reprint of his work carried a portrait of Samuel Dyer, 'a member of Johnson's Literary Club, and no relation' (p. 92). With such errors to be set right, there is clearly much to do. Yet there are problems. Goodridge's own style is sometimes awkward, or prone to make self-conscious fun, as when Thomson's description in 'Summer' of sheep-shearing is said to conclude 'by giving the beast an account of the "borrowing" of its fleece that is, to say the least, economical with the truth' (p. 56). He also has an irritating tendency to litter his writing with promises of what is to be delivered later. More seriously, while rightly anxious to discuss the status of the 'poetic' view of rural life in Thomson, as against the 'down-to-earth' view of Duck and Collier, and to consider critical responses to those status, he finds himself needing to discriminate positively in favour of all three. He does not wish, for example, to downgrade Thomson for being 'unrealistic', but when it comes to praising Mary Collier for, basically, saying what it was really like, he is reduced to calling it 'an illuminating alternative' (p. 43). This is particularly troublesome when he has Collier galloping in at the end of several sections to put the men 'right'. Again, he cannot quite bring himself to censure Duck for expressing misogynistic sentiments, preferring parodic paraphrase ('for him the hayfield and the harvest are places where the fittest survive, and women are a damned nuisance' (p. 42)) to direct confrontation, but at the same time he is over-anxious to present his own credentials, firmly (though parenthetically): '(This of course in no sense excuses his attitude, either for her [Collier] or for the modern reader.)' (p. 20). Clearly Goodridge finds not offending anyone something of a minefield.

Nevertheless, the textual discussion is impressive, with useful comparison, for example, between the 1730 and 1736 editions of Duck's *Poems*, and careful contextualizing of all three poets in terms of each other, of conventional forms and set scenes, and of contemporary events and attitudes. 'A nuanced reading', he summarizes, 'reveals many areas in which eighteenth-century rural poetry can describe and express the experience of labour, and can tell us much about the ideologies that inform the construction of labour' (p. 91). This is a fair judgement of the first half of Goodridge's book. I suspect, though, that readers might have more doubts about the second half, which is devoted to John Dyer, and specifically to *The Fleece*, 1, on 'The Care of Sheep'. A truly impressive amount of research has gone into these chapters, with authoritative information on landscape, soils, breeds and their characteristics, the diseases of sheep and their cure, as well as the needs of the herd throughout the changing year. Some sections, that on 'Climate and National Identity', for example, with Dyer's contempt for the 'trifling Gaul, Effeminate' who cannot tolerate our robust British fogs (pp. 122–23), are fascinating, and capable of generalization to wider issues. Others perhaps will be found too narrowly focused for readers who do not go to poetry to learn the difference between the Ryelands and the South-Western Horn (p. 139).

University of Northumbria at Newcastle   Allan Ingram

Models of Value: Eighteenth-Century Political Economy and the Novel. By James Thompson. Durham, NC, and London: Duke University Press. 1996. viii + 270 pp. £43.95 (paperbound £15.95).

James Thompson's ambitious book seeks to synthesize several on-going discussions in eighteenth-century English studies: the rise of the novel, the rise of political economy, and the emergence of the doctrine of separate spheres. Thompson contends that eighteenth-century England experienced a 'crisis of value' occasioned by 'the early modern reconceptualization of money from treasure to capital and the consequent refiguration of money from specie to paper' (p. 2). As precious metals gave way to paper money, nominalist conceptions of value destabilized the meaning of wealth. Two new literary discourses, the novel and political economy, emerged as a means 'to manage this crisis'. Following Bourdieu, Thompson sees 'symbolic capital' as a disguised form of economic capital, which enables him to read the novel as a disguised form of political economy. Finance and romance are dialectically related in a manner obscured by the 'doctrine of separate spheres', which keeps economic men distinct from domestic women, financial transactions separate from emotional exchange, and the public realm of political economy apart from the private worlds of novelistic fiction. The apparently opposed discourses of business and literature are actually related features of the larger capitalist process of cultural transformation.

The book begins with a discussion of monetary theory through Locke, Adam Smith, and Sir James Steuart, tracing the discursive separation of finance and romance as it emerged from this 'new language of money'. Three chapters then focus sequentially on Defoe, Henry Fielding, and Burney, offering some provocative contrasts: for Defoe, value is always in danger of being lost; for Fielding, value can never really be lost; for Burney, male financial debt parallels female emotional excess. Concluding, via Austen's novels, that the 'cultural work of the novel' is to 'suture a historically specific [. . .] wholeness' out of the 'fragmentation, isolation, and alienation' of capitalism (p. 194), Thompson sees the early novel as 'a promise of freedom from a realm of purely financial and instrumental social relations' (p. 198).

Marx looms like a crumbling colossus over *Models of Value*, at once both overwhelming and insufficient. Thompson implicitly asks a fascinating and timely question about the relation between literature and economics: why are literary studies and contemporary (non-Marxist) economics regarded as opposite lines of work today, when each engages in establishing and assessing social value, including the value of academic disciplines in this world of corporate-style university administrations? In responding, however, Thompson, does not add much to Marx's insight into the historical specificity of capitalism, an insight that carries curiously little weight in contemporary economics. Thompson's analysis tries to update Marxism by reconciling it to feminism, but despite his efforts (Thompson's citation of other scholars is profuse, with his notes and bibliography taking up twenty-five per cent of the book's length) he never manages to free himself from Marx's confining shadow. As a result, the argument appears to break little new ground, instead wandering over its vast erudition, never threatening to challenge its sources. It can be repetitive (a straightforward question about nominal versus real value on p. 51 is repeated twice on p. 53, rephrased four times on p. 54, then asked again on p. 59); unfocused (the chapter on Fielding digresses to discuss some legal decisions of Lord Mansfield, though Thompson himself admits that he does 'not think that these decision of Mansfield prove anything about Fielding's text or motives'); yet feels constrained by the predetermined conclusion that novels (and, by implication, literary studies) represent a possible escape from the oppression of capitalist social relations. However reassuring for literary critics, this predictable conclusion does not escape the finance/romance dichotomy that Thompson sets out to explain.

HARVARD UNIVERSITY   WENDY MOTOOKA

The Beautiful, Novel, and Strange: Aesthetics and Heterodoxy. By RONALD PAULSON. Baltimore, MD, and London: Johns Hopkins University Press. 1996. xix + 369 pp. £33.

In *Breaking and Remaking: Aesthetic Practice in England, 1700–1820* (New Brunswick, NJ: Rutgers University Press, 1989), Ronald Paulson argued that certain eighteenth-century poets, in an aesthetic practice that was fundamentally iconoclastic, reshaped the classical and Christian models of their predecessors to reflect the truths of history. In a review of that book, Dabney Townsend proposed that the novel, rather than poetry, was a more promising genre in which to look for innovation in eighteenth-century aesthetics: poets simply had too much tradition to answer to. Paulson's latest effort can be read as taking Townsend up on his suggestion. What is most valuable about *The Beautiful, Novel, and Strange* is the connection that it draws between certain eighteenth-century aesthetic theories and the practice of the novel.

The connection between theory and practice is the heterodox ideology of deism, defined by Mandeville as the loss of faith 'in anything reveal'd to us'. Paulson contends that deists such as John Toland gave artists such as Hogarth the impetus to construct an alternative aesthetics to the civic humanism of Shaftesbury and Reynolds. Instead of basing his art on the disinterested contemplation of beauty, Hogarth makes pictures depicting the interested pursuit of pleasure, often embodied in a beautiful woman. In both deist theology and Hogarthian aesthetics, the emphasis is on demystifying what had been seen as remote and mysterious: deists revealed how a belief in miracles kept a priestly caste in power, and Hogarth exposed the desire behind every claim to spiritual and temporal authority. Paulson links this demystified aesthetics to narrative through Addison's category, midway between the Beautiful and the Sublime, of the Novel (or Strange), which Addison associated with the qualities of 'surprise', 'the pursuit of knowledge', 'curiosity', and 'variety'. When Paulson finds these qualities, and the demystifying impulse, in the comic epics of Fielding, the erotic and sentimental fiction of Cleland and Sterne, and children's books, he extends the theory of the Novel to actual narratives.

Paulson's thesis pays its greatest dividends in the chapter on Fielding which, despite the ubiquitous presence of Hogarth, strikes this reader as the heart of the book. Without claiming that Fielding, usually regarded as a champion of Anglican orthodoxy, was himself a deist, Paulson shows how he accepts 'the consequences of deism', namely that it had rendered 'the providential order [. . .] no longer valid except as a fiction' (p. 107). At least in his first two novels, Fielding did not as much reject the 'fiction' of a providential order as substitute for it the more reliable one of the novelist, where rewards and punishments can be distributed through a strict sense of poetic justice. In a postscript, Paulson uses his subversive reading of Fielding's heterodox side to make new the old contrast with Richardson. While Fielding (and Hogarth) demystify the enchantments of everyday life, Richardson spiritualizes them.

The problem with Paulson's thesis is that he tends to find deism everywhere. It is one thing to say that Fielding heightens the fictionality of his providential order the better to inculcate belief in the doctrine of rewards and punishments; it is another to say that Goldsmith's Vicar of Wakefield knows that the same doctrine is a 'harmless delusion' when he preaches it to his fellow prisoners in order to encourage their happiness, especially when the harmless delusion, according to the Vicar himself (and undocumented as so by Paulson), is his wife's vanity. But Paulson's juxtaposition of familiar texts with the unfamiliar, and the visual with the verbal, coupled with his vast knowledge of the eighteenth century, almost always produces insights that are as persuasive as they are provocative.

AUBURN UNIVERSITY   TIMOTHY DYKSTAL

Wordsworth's Pope: A Study in Literary Historiography. By ROBERT J. GRIFFIN. (Cambridge Studies in Romanticism) Cambridge, New York, and Melbourne: Cambridge University Press. 1995. xii + 190 pp. £30; $49.95.

That Wordsworth translated the first three books of Virgil's *Æneid* into heroic couplets is a fact many scholars will have suppressed, if they ever knew it, such is the disparity between that seemingly Augustan exercise and Wordsworth's reputation as the poet of originality, feeling, and nature. But it is such suppressions as this, in the service of the convenient and powerful period opposition between Augustans and Romantics, which Robert J. Griffin targets in his largely convincing attempt to redraw the literary-historical map of writing between 1740 and 1830. Griffin argues that the 'master narrative of literary history' (p. 18), by which Romanticism figures as a revolutionary rejection of an Augustan poetics of rationality and polish, is a fiction constructed by Wordsworth, and that such a view of Augustan practice is itself based on a misprision practised by mid-century poets in order to free imaginative space for themselves against the fatal dominance of Pope. Thomas and Joseph Warton construct a new poetic ideology by suppressing aspects of Pope with which they strongly identify (the poet as prophet, or Gothic Melancholy) and shaping a 'selected' Pope as an alien, negative poet of didactic reason. The traces of this act of suppression are deftly located in close readings of the Wartons' poetry and criticism, with similar evidence from the writings of Edward Young, and the obsessive Pope-hater William Cowper. Similarly, Wordsworth himself, actually a much less culturally pervasive figure than Pope in the early nineteenth century, seeks to displace Pope (not, as in Bloom, Milton) with a vehemence which is symptomatic of an internal repression; sensing in Wordsworth's constructed naturalism what he felicitously calls 'the still, sad music of textuality' (p. 99), Griffin discerns the transformed presence of Pope, the ousted, negated poetical father, in tiny echoes in Wordsworth's writing, mostly linked to tropes of separation and maturation. A wider narrative considers the role of institutional criticism (the *Edinburgh Review*, and latterly Abrams's *The Mirror and the Lamp*) in disseminating Romanticism's self-privileging (if untenable) opposition between mimesis and expression.

Griffin's exact, nuanced historiography of textual relations is irreproachably lucid, despite its (disarmingly open) theoretical grounding in deconstruction; and the 'oedipal dynamics' (p. 53) of Harold Bloom's 'Anxiety of Influence' is here stripped of its own mystifying Romanticism and idiosyncratic tropical categories. (If any theorist is transcendent, it is the only-too-lucid Freud, whose 'family romance' is rather too briefly defended as the appropriate model for the male rivalries under discussion.) This blend of eighteenth-century virtues (one wants to call the book 'candid' and 'ingenious') with a critical practice more commonly found in Romantic criticism is perhaps part of the book's educative design. Much of what Griffin says will receive ready assent from eighteenth-century scholars, but he may well be right to be pessimistic about his chances of dislodging the deep-seated hegemony Romantic literary history continues to award itself. Wordsworthians might rechristen the book *Pope's Wordsworth*, since it disclaims any need to explore 'positive' manifestations of Romanticism, concentrating solely on Romanticism's negative construction of Pope and the unacknowledged continuities of practice (good sense, refinement) which subvert that model; one is left to consider what actually is different about the writing we call 'Romantic'. There is perhaps a slightly light-weight feel to the overall account of Wordsworth's literary practice, the local brilliance of particular analyses notwithstanding; an extended comparison between the card game passages in *The Prelude*, Book I and *The Rape of the Lock*, Canto III would have been especially apposite. Griffin also denies the need to explore the reaction of other canonical Romantic poets to Pope, which in a relatively short book is surely a pity; a further chapter exploring other aspects of Pope in the Romantic age might have added much cogent, and pleasing, material.

UNIVERSITY OF LIVERPOOL   PAUL BAINES

Romantic Vagrancy: Wordsworth and the Simulation of Freedom. By CELESTE LANGAN. (Cambridge Studies in Romanticism) Cambridge, New York, and Melbourne: Cambridge University Press. 1995. x + 304 pp. £35; $54.95.

Unlike the work of John Barrell and, more recently, that of Gary Harrison, *Romantic Vagrancy* is not a study either of the condition of actual vagrants during the romantic period or, more generally, of the romantic response to the actual phenomenon of vagrancy. Rather, it is a book about Wordsworth or, more specifically, aspects of Wordsworth, out of which Celeste Langan fashions what can perhaps be termed an archaeology of liberalism. Nor is it merely incidental that a study of this one thing, liberalism, would be so titled or so cryptically subtitled. For it is very much to Langan's purpose not just to mislead her reader but to make us realize that this misleading is really the result of a deficit in understanding. That is, *Romantic Vagrancy* assumes a conception of liberalism on the reader's part that, however chastened or sophisticated by a theoretical knowledge (which Langan, somewhat paradoxically, too often takes for granted), is basically wrong: namely, that 'liberalism is [. . .] a plan of social action that *responds* to perceived conditions of distress or inequity' through institutions such as 'a democracy populated by sovereign subjects, a system of "liberal" education that increases social mobility', and '*laissez-faire* capitalism' (pp. 229–30). These, Langan argues, are not the features of liberalism so much as the means by which liberalism has effectively concealed and mystified what Langan claims as its material or discursive base. This base turns out to be nothing less than capital itself, whose circulation in an increasingly commodity-based economy is figured by an 'endless mobility and identity shorn of all contingent properties'

(p. 12) which is in turn the subject-position in its most unadulterated form of the liberal individual.

However, it is also, as Langan maintains, the position of the vagrant, whose prevalence in Wordsworth's poetry is less a measure therefore of the poet's concern for the disenfranchised — an otherwise liberal concern — than an unconscious register of the desire for the ultimate 'freedom of speech and freedom of movement' (p. 17) that doubles in Wordsworth as both the vagrant's condition and the subject's prerogative. Readers familiar with this sort of criticism will immediately recognize the move by which an honourable, if obviously flawed, institution is cleverly deconstructed and by which a poet (not infrequently Wordsworth) becomes a symptom of something much larger, over and against which he can exert no control and of which he has no conscious understanding. Thus, they may also feel that the materialist intervention most relevant to *Romantic Vagrancy* is less the rise of capital and its psychological fallout than the insuperably tight market conditions, institutional and intellectual, that have compelled Langan to a study that, to follow her own subscription to the writings of Marx, is rather alienated. Removed not just from its audience for whom little patience is afforded, or its ostensible subject whose works are selectively marshalled sometimes beyond recognition (for example, see the treatment of 'The Brothers'), *Romantic Vagrancy* is also alienated from, and unsympathetic to, the very culture of which it claims some profoundly structural knowledge.

Langan's most aggressive intervention, her dislodgment of liberty from its structural base in ownership or property by way of reconceiving it as a highly sublimated reaction-formation to a mercantile or market-based economy, allows her to do some provocative things with the 'free' agents who circulate in Wordsworth's poetry. This is especially true of her treatment of the Pedlar/ Wanderer in the various drafts of what became Book 1 of *The Excursion*. But it necessarily prevents her from appreciating or allowing the reader to appreciate the dilemma that arguably informs Wordsworth's writing and with which he wrestles often with a good deal of circumspection. I am speaking, then, of the contradiction inherent in the revolutionary programme that imagines 'a democracy populated by sovereign subjects'. Wordsworth's poetry is continually vexed by, but also mindful of, the structural slippage in an ideology that juxtaposes freedom and equality, privileging and demonizing the very hierarchy without which liberty and plenitude would be inconceivable. This subtle reckoning on his part issues in a different and seemingly more naïve story than the one Langan tells, and tells, it should be added, with a good deal of verve and intelligence. But this alternative to Langan also has the advantage, following the work of Anthony Giddens and others, in allowing both the individual and culture an agency in their respective and mutual constitution(s).

RUTGERS UNIVERSITY   WILLIAM GALPERIN

The 'Lucy Poems': A Case Study in Literary Knowledge. By MARK JONES. Toronto, Buffalo, NY, and London: University of Toronto Press. 1995. xv + 337 pp. £35.75; $55.

In his concluding chapter, Mark Jones acknowledges that he redefined his project over the decade of its composition; mirroring the shifting preoccupations of North American criticism, his own work evolved from being a 'reception-study' into 'a case-study in the emergence of English as a "discipline"' (p. 231). Although his scholarship is consistently impressive, his argument still bears traces of that change in direction. As a result, readers may find individual chapters of *The 'Lucy Poems'* more rewarding than the work as a whole.

Jones begins by painstakingly tracing the ways in which Wordsworth suggested but never substantiated the grouping of the lyrics later known as the 'Lucy Poems'. Uneasy with their interpretative uncertainty, Victorian readers sought to contain the poems' ambiguity by formulating them into a group that converted lyric indeterminacy into biographical narrative. At the same time various Victorian parodists undercut the scholars' closural strategies with works which seem to subvert critical readings of the poems more than the poems themselves.

If Victorian parodists destabilized scholarly certainty by playing with the generic boundaries of literary discourse itself, Jones finds no such respect for indeterminacy in the responses to E. D. Hirsch, Jr's effort to establish the disciplinarity of English studies through 'objective interpretation'. Jones organizes his account of the debate between objectivists and relativists and their common desire for disciplinary authority around the readings of one of the 'Lucy Poems', 'A slumber did my spirit seal'. The final chapter of *The 'Lucy Poems'* compares the deconstructive readings of Paul de Man with Geoffrey Hartman's dialectical openness in reading the poems.

Although its strengths are many, *The 'Lucy Poems'* struggles at times to sustain an argument. Ultimately, Wordsworth's poems are the McGuffin for Jones's various discussions of theoretical problems and practices in English studies over a period of almost a hundred and fifty years. The constraints of using the 'Lucy Poems' as a 'case-study' are evident in the chapter on Hirsch and the relativists. Instead of moving swiftly to the larger disciplinary consequences of the debate between the objectivists and the relativists, Jones analyses in exhaustive, and at times exhausting, detail the local interpretative moves of critics whose work he holds in no high esteem. Even in the earlier chapter on Victorian parody, the 'Lucy Poems' are more of an occasion (and, in the cases of the novels which he discusses, perhaps not the best occasion) for developing a subtle and powerful theory of parody as a culturally subversive 'anti-genre'.

After reading *The 'Lucy Poems'*, it is not clear whether a history of the discipline of English studies can be culled exclusively from its various interpretative strategies. For example, in reserving high praise for Geoffrey Hartman, Jones singles out a critic whom Marjorie Levinson attacks (along with the rest of the 'Yale School') in *Wordsworth's Great Period Poems: Four Essays* (Cambridge: Cambridge University Press, 1986) for stifling political and cultural readings of the Romantics. Whether or not Levinson's critique of Hartman is valid, it is none the less clear that he serves her as a figure for the narrow, apolitical formalism of English studies. Jones's intelligent evaluation of Hartman's work suggests that he might have a compelling reply to Levinson and similar critiques of the discipline's politics; we will have to wait for it, though, in his future work.

PRINCETON UNIVERSITY   ADRIENNE DONALD

Keats and History. Ed. by NICHOLAS ROE. Cambridge, New York and Melbourne: Cambridge University Press. 1995. xviii + 320 pp. £37.50; $59.95.

The strength of this collection of essays by various hands is that it places Keats at the centre of one of the most lively debates in contemporary criticism: the debate provoked by Jerome J. McGann's contention that Romanticism constitutes a reactionary ideology. McGann argued that Keats, like Wordsworth, treated poetry as a discourse in which writer and reader could escape from, rather than confront, social and political conflicts.

Most of the contributors to the volume take issue with McGann. Their counter-arguments take two forms: several suggest that social and political conflicts are in fact addressed in Keats's poems, at the levels of allusion, symbolism, and imagery if not of subject-matter. Others argue that the poems are indeed largely free of reference to such conflicts, but should not therefore be seen as escapist. For Michael O'Neill, discussing the Hyperion poems, and for Vincent Newey, discussing 'To Autumn', Keats's importance lies in his ability to transcend the 'tensions of which experience of historical and social circumstance is a major — though not the only — source' (p. 190). From their essays emerges a subtler and more complex understanding of poetry and its relationship with the historical than McGann's escapist/confrontational polarity allows for.

If O'Neill's and Newey's essays stand out for their sensitivity to the complex self-consciousness encoded in great verse, a sensitivity they show to be lacking in McGann's criticism of Keats's poetry, Nicholas Roe demonstrates that the history of Keats's time can also be understood in a more sophisticated way than it is by McGann. The natural images and mythological figures of Keats's Odes had a political currency in the radical discourse of 1819–21; parts of 'To Autumn', indeed, were published by Leigh Hunt in his 'Calendar of Nature' showing, Roe argues, that the radical journalist explicitly associated the poem with his own attempts to draw political and moral analogies from the changing seasons.

More than any of the other Romantics — perhaps more than any other poet in the language — Keats has been the creation of the mythologizing processes of literary history. Susan J. Wolfson, in the essay which begins the volume, examines these processes at work in the years immediately following his death. Wolfson traces the influence of Shelley's *Adonais* in changing Keats's critical reputation. He became in death a 'young flower [. . .] blighted in the bud' by the cold winds of critical reviews: 'If it is bad medical pathology and a distortion of Keats to say that he was snuffed out by an article, in terms of cultural discourse it was a truth universally acknowledged' (p. 27). Yet he had not been viewed in this way in his own lifetime; as Martin Aske shows in his discussion of the 'politics of envy', contemporary hostility to his poetry stemmed from class resentment: middle-class reviewers disliked the assumption of a working-class poet that it was in his poetry and not in the language of wealthy gentlemen of commerce that emotional sincerity and aesthetic value inhered.

Both Kelvin Everest and Terence Allan Hoagwood investigate Keats's discussions of aesthetic value, Everest in a reading of 'Isabella', Hoagwood in an examination of the symbolism of money in the letters and poems. Daniel P. Watkins, similarly, shows the portrayal of self and gender in the 'Ode to Psyche' to be conditioned by the historical context in which value was defined largely in terms of 'getting and spending'. And this theme is developed in an essay by Theresa M. Kelley showing the ekphrasis of the 'Ode on a Grecian Urn' to contain a debate about the merits of aesthetic values which seem to transcend history. With further contributions from John Barnard, Greg Kucich, Nicola Trott, and John Kerrigan examining Keats's reading of other writers and theirs of him, the volume has variety as well as coherence, leaving one with an enriched sense of the many ways in which Keats and history can be seen to engage with each other.

Nottingham Trent University   Tim Fulford

Pleasures and Pains: Opium and the Orient in Nineteenth-Century British Culture. By BARRY
    MILLIGAN. (Victorian Literature and Culture) Charlottesville and London:
    University Press of Virginia. 1995. xii + 156 pp. $29.50.

In 1968 Alethea Hayter's book *Opium and the Romantic Imagination* (London: Faber)
posed the question: 'Does opium affect the creative processes of writers who use it?'
(p. 12). Now Barry Milligan explores 'the cultural dynamics of opium in nineteenth-
century England' (p. 4) and what those dynamics reveal of attitudes towards the
East. Hayter was interested in the possibility that distinctive qualities in the works of
addict writers such as Coleridge and De Quincey might be due to the effects of
opium. Milligan traces the tension between attraction and repulsion, pleasure and
pain in English cultural responses to opium and the Orient, particularly in relation
to the disruption of notions of national and individual identity.

These differences of approach are striking and not merely because they reflect
shifts in critical fashions between the late 1960s and the mid-1990s. Nearly thirty
years of escalating recreational drug use also separate the two books. Hayter's faith
in the Romantic imagination and her interest in the creative potential of opium now
seem dated in both these contexts. Milligan, by contrast, retreats into a cocoon of
metaphorical substitutions. He explores 'the ways in which perceptions of the
responses to the Orient [. . .] are paralleled, mediated, and represented metaphoric-
ally by attitudes toward opium' (p. 7). This approach bears many similarities to
recent work on De Quincey, opium, and the East by John Barrell and Nigel Leask,
but it may also be seen in part as a product of currently repressive attitudes towards
the pleasures of recreational drug use. Hayter's bold and wide-eyed account of
opium, on the brink of the drugs crisis, gives way to Milligan's sophisticated evasions
in the midst of it.

Pleasures and Pains provides detailed readings of work by a range of writers, from
Coleridge and De Quincey to Dickens and Conan Doyle, in order to expose
ambiguous responses toward the Orient. He argues that opium provides a focal
point in this writing for a seductive and fearful vision of the East burrowing away
within the English body and culture. For Coleridge, the ingestion of opium lays the
self and the nation open to a 'retributive Oriental infection-invasion' (p. 12),
whereas De Quincey's *Confessions of an English Opium-Eater*, 'The English Mail-
Coach', and 'Suspiria de Profundis' suggest that the Orient has always been a
potentially disruptive presence within English culture. For De Quincey, opium
does not introduce a foreign infection so much as it uncovers one already lurking
there. Milligan goes on to show how, in varying combinations, both Coleridge's
and De Quincey's perceptions continue to be a significant presence in later
nineteenth-century writing about opium and the East, from Collins's *The Moonstone*
onwards.

Milligan has found a fascinating subject and has argued his case scrupulously and
for the most part persuasively. He is happiest working on a small canvas, teasing out
the implications of textual details and these parts of his argument can be very
effective. There is some uncertainty in the balance he achieves in the book between
literary criticism, cultural studies, and social history, all of which he claims to
encompass. Despite these claims and as he himself admits, *Pleasures and Pains* is
predominantly a literary critical study of canonical authors. This is a pity since the
chapters which begin to go beyond the canonical material, namely those on
representations of London opium dens, are the liveliest sections of the book. Again,
Milligan sometimes uses social history to good effect, but does not go far enough
along this path. He acknowledges the excellent work of Virginia Berridge and
Griffiths Edwards on the social history of opium in nineteenth-century Britain, but

he might have done more to situate his material in relation to their analysis of the important changes in perceptions of the drug during the period.

Considered as a literary study, *Pleasures and Pains* is generally a fine piece of work, painstaking and subtle, although some of the readings seem stretched. I remain unconvinced that Princess Puffer in *The Mystery of Edwin Drood* is 'a synecdoche for a feminized Britain' (p. 98). Her links with the character of Ezra Jennings in *The Moonstone* seem more significant and are strangely overlooked by Milligan, given their relevance to his argument. Both characters are compounds of the Oriental and the English and both, in their rôle as amateur detective/psychoanalyst, use opium to uncover the hidden crimes of English gentlemen. Milligan writes interestingly about Jennings and the disruptions of national identity in *The Moonstone* and might have brought this discussion to bear more powerfully on his reading of *Edwin Drood*.

A more serious oversight occurs in Milligan's introduction where he sets out the limits of his study. He justifies his exclusive concentration on white male writers by arguing that this reflects

an interesting feature of nineteenth-century British writing about opium and the Orient: all of it seems to have been produced by white men. Although women did write about opium, the nexus of opium and the Orient that otherwise so often dominated the discourse about the drug seems to have been absent from their work. (p. 10)

His neat excuse is rather spoilt by the case of Charlotte Brontë's *Villette*, in which Lucy Snowe, under the influence of laudanum, wanders through an orientalized city-scape at once paradisical and nightmarish. Milligan seems to have overlooked this well-known novel completely, although there is enough in it on the Orient, opium, and gender to have made for a whole chapter in his book. I suspect that a little more research might uncover other examples of women who wrote about the 'nexus' between opium and the Orient that Milligan identifies as an exclusively male preserve.

Milligan makes some interesting, though brief, remarks on the continuities between nineteenth and twentieth-century drug culture in relation to racial stereotyping: 'Even the 1920s Detroit opium-smoking party described by jazz musician Mezz Mezzrow is peopled with "borscht-guzzling Oriental potentates" and "looked like a scene straight out of the Arabian Nights"' (p. 8). He suggests that by exploring the nineteenth-century relationship between opium and the East we might come to a better understanding of some of the attitudes towards drugs in Britain and America today. As with much else in the book, this part of the argument could have been given more rein, but Milligan tends to pull back when things are getting a little too real. Despite these limitations, *Pleasures and Pains* is a stimulating read and certainly the major book to date on nineteenth-century writing about opium. However, it may well be that students will still gravitate towards Hayter's book by preference since, in my experience at least, the question of opium's creative potential is what holds their interest, rather than more academically respectable issues of what the drug might have represented.

DE MONTFORT UNIVERSITY   JULIAN NORTH

Two Poets of the Oxford Movement: John Keble and John Henry Newman. By RODNEY
STENNING EDGECOMBE. Cranbury, NJ: Fairleigh Dickinson University Press;
London: Associated University Presses. 1996. 296 pp. £32.50.

Making a Social Body: British Cultural Formation, 1830–1864. By MARY POOVEY.
Chicago and London: University of Chicago Press. 1996. x + 255 pp. £27.50;
$34 (paperbound £10.25, $12.95).

Never was there such a century as the nineteenth for formulae and systems. But the
nineteenth was also the century of the novel and of lyrical verse. How to marry the
formula to the fable, how to express the system in the simile, were the literary
challenges of the age.

The Oxford Movement began with college dons studying church history and
systematic theology. It ended with schism, ecclesiastical renewal, with incense and,
as Geoffrey Faber's classic study *Oxford Apostles* famously showed, with strife. Its
great organs of dissemination were the sermon and the tract. The movement also,
however, coincided with the development of the hymn as a vehicle of Anglican
worship, borrowed with due acknowledgement from the nonconformists. Several of
the better known lyrics of Newman and Keble are still sung as hymns. Newman's
'Lead, kindly Light' (1833) is the best known example, a good one since it shows the
two directions between which Tractarian hymnology, and Tractarian verse in
general, were torn. All religious verse is inevitably a public declaration of doctrine,
especially when set to music and sung by a congregation. It is also both prayer and
meditation: the soul talking to God and the soul envisaging God's call. To maintain
the public frame, yet retain the Ignatian inwardness, is the salient challenge of all
religious verse.

Rodney Stenning Edgecombe brings to the analysis of Tractarian poetry a mind
trained on the subtleties of Herbert's 'The Temple'. He is steeped in the logistics of
contemplative poetry. His problem is this: never has Keble's reputation been lower.
Edgecombe says that he approached *The Christian Year* (1827) in a mood of 'modified
boredom'. He had been looking for the numinous simplicity of Wordsworth, but
found instead the sententious evasiveness of the Age of Sentiment. His task has been
to rescue Keble from the dust of the antiquarian book shop and to set him up as at
least a minor devotional poet. He has not entirely succeeded.

He does a better job with Newman. This would not be difficult since Newman is
the better writer. Edgecombe, however, would have done an even better job had he
not decided arbitrarily to foreclose Newman's poetic career with his conversion to
Rome in 1845. There are in this book only a couple of fleeting references to 'The
Dream of Gerontius' (1866), a poem which possesses all the drama lacked by
Newman's contributions to *Lyra Apostolica*, written with R. H. Froude in Rome
during 1836 and first published in *The British Magazine*. He would also have done
better had he spent more time on Newman's prose writings, since these illuminate
the verse more than one would think. The *Apologia pro Vita Sua* (1864) and *The
Grammar of Assent* (1870) are not as irrelevant to Newman's earlier Anglo-Catholic
poetry as Edgecombe appears to make them, especially since he indulges in
sweeping comments on Newman's politics. I would advise him to look again at the
famous passage in the *Lectures on Anglican Difficulties* about the beggar woman and the
moral advantages that she shares over the 'state's pattern man'. The sentiments are
at least as strong as those in Wordsworth's 'Old Cumberland Beggar'. Newman was
no radical, but his social compassion was patent. Ethically, he was a leveller.

Social compassion is at least partly Mary Poovey's theme. She has courageously
decided to outwit and outface the current scholarly mania for fragmentation with a
thoroughly holistic study of the early Victorian age. She reminds us of the

Victorians' own passion for wholeness, for integration, their determination against all the odds to view society as a body. We are reminded how obsessed they all were with statistics and numbers, the 'facts' that Dickens pilloried in Gradgrind but which resembled none the less the care of a doctor taking the social pulse. To transform society, the Victorians believed, you needed to understand it first. Complementary drives towards tabulation and practical charity impelled the careers of philanthropists such as Thomas Chalmers, Edwin Chadwick, and Ellen Raynard, with all of whom Poovey deals at some length.

She is less at ease with imaginative writers. As Jenny Uglow's biography, *Elizabeth Gaskell: A Habit of Stories* (London: Faber, 1993) has shown, Gaskell, a Unitarian minister's wife, was inspired by missionary zeal of a sort. Her main impulse, however, was to tell tales. For Poovey this simply will not do. Discussing *Mary Barton*, she revealingly remarks that John and Mary Barton are both 'cursed with (what we would call) psychological complexity' (p. 147), as if this was some kind of impediment to the plot and to the clarity of social perception. She earlier remarks that Gaskell 'explores issues that we (like the Victorians) call private' (p. 144). What else, pray, do novelists do, even if their name is Tolstoy?

Stylistically both these books have contracted vices from their subject matter. Poovey is a little dry and matter of fact; Edgecombe a little sententious. He is also an accomplished practitioner of the mixed metaphor, who speaks at one point of eyebrows being raised within the mainstream of Anglicanism. I hope that this is a reference to Kingsley's *The Water Babies*; otherwise it is metaphorical gobbledegook. Poovey could have learned from Edgecombe's subtlety, and Edgecombe from Poovey's directness. But that two such different books faithfully mirror aspects of the same period is a heartening reminder of just how versatile, despite or because of its wholeness, the Victorian age was. I am relieved that neither author calls it 'post-modern'.

ROYAL HOLLOWAY, LONDON   ROBERT FRASER

Walking the Victorian Streets: Women, Representation, and the City. By DEBORAH EPSTEIN NORD. Ithaca, NY, and London: Cornell University Press. 1995. xiii + 270 pp. $39.95; £30.95 (paperbound $16.95; £13.50).

The male stroller and observer of urban life is a significant figure in nineteenth- and twentieth-century literature. Critics working on modernist texts have pointed out that he has no straightforward female equivalent, even at a time when women begin to gain their independence. The terms 'street walker' and 'woman of the streets' define the woman 'freely' traversing the city as a sexual commodity rather than as an autonomous viewer, and women wishing to be urban spectators must battle against this definition which robs them of anonymity by turning them into objects of male sexual interest. Deborah Epstein Nord's new study offers an interesting survey of the female stroller as represented both by men and women in a range of texts from De Quincey to Virginia Woolf, and provides a thought-provoking commentary on the ambiguities of these representations.

Epstein Nord divides her book into three parts. The first deals with the male stroller and men's representations of women on the streets. Here she shows how in the 1820s the city is seen through ideal panoramic surveys inherited from romanticism, but by the 1850s becomes all encompassing, immersing its inhabitants in an environment of social crisis. Likewise, the prostitute changes from being the romanticized double of the male walker to a figure of potential threat and contamination. Fear of epidemic infection which is also a fear of social breakdown demonizes the woman of the streets or the sexually suspect 'respectable' woman who may invade and contaminate the middle-class home. Epstein Nord ends this section with pertinent readings of female sexuality in *Bleak House* and *Dombey and Son* which throw into question the apparent clear distinction between 'the woman of the hearth' and the 'woman of the streets'.

Part II looks at the experience of a female spectator as presented by Flora Tristan as foreign observer of London and by Elizabeth Gaskell as social mediator. Tristan inventively adopts a number of disguises to aid her observations. Her wary textual and literal distance from the figure of the prostitute is punctuated by moments of realization that the fallen woman might be her own 'debased double' (p. 134). Epstein Nord suggests that Gaskell's experience of 'being jostled or scrutinized by those she wished to observe' (p. 177) is transformed in her novels into moments of exposure and engagement with the crowd in which her heroines 'bear witness' and run the risk of public disgrace (p. 178).

Part III examines the various writings of single middle-class women living in the city in the 1880s and 1890s as 'they rewrote London out of a new relationship to its dangers, fascinations, and pleasures' (p. 14). As many of these women take on the new role of social investigator 'visiting' the urban poor, they experience a tension between their advocacy of an ideal domesticity and their own professional aspirations towards the public sphere of work outside the home. On a different tack, Mary Higgs's investigation of female vagrancy, *Glimpses into the Abyss* (1906), shows how the disguise she adopted when 'on the tramp' rendered her even more vulnerable to male sexual aggression.

This collection of writings about women and the city is, in many ways, somewhat disparate, although linked by some suggestive thematic concerns. A comparatively small amount of material deals with women's direct experiences of the streets, apparently because 'it remains difficult to track the street lives of women in the 1840s, 1850s, and 1860s' (p. 3). None the less this well-written study makes a useful starting-place and should provide some invaluable background to current discussions on the 'impossibility' of the *flâneuse*.

QUEEN MARY AND WESTFIELD COLLEGE, LONDON   CATHERINE MAXWELL

Novels Behind Glass: Commodity Culture and Victorian Narrative. By ANDREW H. MILLER. (Literature, Culture, Theory, 17) Cambridge, New York, and Melbourne: Cambridge University Press. 1995. xi + 242 pp. £32.50; $54.95.

Novels Behind Glass works within terms by now well known in discussions of the nineteenth century: the commodity; fetishism; consumption; the Great Exhibition as inaugurating commodity culture; possessive individualism. Such ways of thinking derived from Marx, Freud, Lukács, and Benjamin have been in circulation for some time, and Andrew H. Miller's book is not especially original in explaining them as he does, or in devoting the space he gives to the 1851 Exhibition. These Marxist concepts are given non-Marxist emphases in this account of certain classic Victorian texts: *Vanity Fair, Cranford, Our Mutual Friend, The Eustace Diamonds,* Trollope's *Autobiography,* and *Middlemarch.* A familiar emphasis on woman as the chief commodity bought, sold, or looked at, resonates through the readings, especially of Thackeray and Trollope. In a move which owes a little to new historicism, the author tries to pick on a telling anecdote by which to open the readings of the texts. The study questions the reaction of the writers to material culture: according to the afterword, 'each of these novelists (Trollope partially excepted) attempted to construct an alternative understanding of goods, to organize narrative structures in such a fashion that more flexible and generous ways of forming their "external custom" would be possible: *Cranford* turned to the routines of everyday life; *Our Mutual Friend* attempted to integrate play with work; and *Middlemarch* translated economic into aesthetic value' (p. 219).

Having described the book and indicated its familiar provenance, I should add my scepticism. I think Miller overplays his reading of the Swiss chalet at Gad's Hill (not set up till 1865) and implies that 'Catherine' as he calls Dickens's wife, suffered her oppression there at that house (see p. 137). There is much to be said about the importance of Gad's Hill to Dickens's re-creation of himself, and it would have much to do with commodity culture, but the details in such a reading (the thick description) are missing here, rendered anecdotal, symptomatic of an approach that wears theory awkwardly, overplays its sense of history to make large theses out of small suggestions and complicates its otherwise interesting (but basically new-critical) readings of canonical texts. One can appreciate his interest in writing about them, but their subject-matter gets cramped as much as the reading of them does. Miller's sense that Rosamond Vincey is a Thackerayan character (p. 198) is more interesting (partly because a revaluation of Thackeray's importance in the period is long overdue) than his comment that 'a domestic economy of commodities interpellate[s] Rosamond Vincy as a good herself, turning her into a cold and repellent figure, an object amid the goods she possesses' (p. 220). The point may be valid, but it is not interesting as a way of differentiating Rosamond, and how would it work against Eliot's own Comtian sense of Rosamond as born in moral stupidity (as 'we are all of us') and not emergent from it? The study of *Our Mutual Friend* is fine in, for instance, its account of atomized thinking, but it is less satisfactory in eliding Dickens's industry with Podsnap's mechanical sense of the arts as ideally like a bourgeois businessman (pp. 127–28), or in assuming the voice of the Uncommercial Traveller fits unproblematically with a truth about Dickens. Here, jumps in the argument insist on making one thing into another in the interest of a relatively unoriginal thesis. If it is said of Lydgate that 'it was to be feared that neither biology nor schemes of reform would lift him above the vulgarity of feeling that there would be an incompatibility in his furniture not being of the best', does that authorize the comment 'Lygate assumes material culture is beneath his notice, unconnected with his wider thoughts and cares' (p. 207), in a move assimilating him in this to Eliot? Is it not a more materialistic viewpoint? The moves in the argument may convince some; their tendentiousness justifies going back to the readings of the text, but they leave for this reader the sense of an inadequate thesis whose main components are already in the market-place, and already rummaged over by critical theory.

University of Hong Kong   Jeremy Tambling

Dickens, Violence and the Modern State: Dreams of the Scaffold. By Jeremy Tambling. Basingstoke: Macmillan; New York: St Martin's Press. 1995. x + 237 pp. £35.

After an introductory chapter, Jeremy Tambling's book deals mainly with *Great Expectations, Dombey and Son, Bleak House, Little Dorrit, Barnaby Rudge* and *A Tale of Two Cities, Oliver Twist* and *Edwin Drood*, and *Our Mutual Friend* in the combinations and order indicated.

A summary of his commentary on *Great Expectations* will indicate the nature of his approach. This is initially based on Foucault, from whom Tambling takes two different things. The first is an historical thesis that Enlightenment rationalism supplied the liberal bourgeois state with techniques of surveillance, notably the

Panopticon; the second is a theory that language is organized in discourses and that these function as categories in the sense that people cannot think beyond them. Tambling does not examine these propositions critically but applies them axiomatically to *Great Expectations* in the following chain of argument. The novel is presented as Pip's autobiography; but autobiographies merely 'reproduce the discourse the Panopticon society promotes' (p. 37); so the book cannot be usefully approached through Pip's character, however ironized. Rather, since all identities are merely instances of social control exerted through the nominating power of the panoptical discourse, the useful way to read the book is in terms of its charting of the 'production, and reproduction, of oppression' (p. 36). Up to this point the argument points to a conclusion in cultural materialism, but Tambling sidesteps this dead end for the literary by changing his own discourse from the historical to the psychoanalytic and then proceeds as follows. Shame is what a masculinized male feels when looked at, since this makes him feel feminized, and Pip is often looked at. To be looked at is also to be under panoptical surveillance. The person made to feel shame must take one of two options, the first classically Freudian, the second a revision of Freud by Deleuze. Either the shame is converted into guilt, in which case the ego aligns itself with the patriarchal super-ego and thereby with masculinity and the bourgeois liberal state. Or the shame is accepted, even cultivated, in masochism, a feminization of the male in which the paternal super-ego is punished. Both choices entail violence, one in support of the state, the other in revolt against it. Pip and the text in which we find him exhibit both choices and the book can therefore be read both with and against the grain of its overt intentions and that is what makes it considerable as literature.

Such is the logic of the main part of the chapter on *Great Expectations*. Those attracted by that kind of analysis will know what to expect and will find it extended to include 'the other scene' of imperialism in the later chapters. They should be warned that to extract the logic will require some effort, since logic is not allowed to control the exposition, which appears to be modelled more on the elliptical impulses of a talking cure than on academic prose. Take, for instance of a style relaxed to the point of incoherence, the following: 'If the orthopaedics of modernity shape Dickens's own attitudes, the last three chapters of the book (Chapters 5–7) form a unity, where the focus is on Dickens's complex reactionary stance towards violence and the state, resistant to dispersal, antagonistic also to the orthodoxies of the modern state and colluding with them which in its own way is repressive, violent, even proto-fascist' (p. 15). In this reviewer's opinion, that style is symptomatic of an irresponsible and jejune licentiousness of thinking yet more deeply betrayed by the uncritical use of Foucault and unnegotiated transition to psychoanalysis already indicated. Let the reader choose.

Churchill College, Cambridge   T. J. Cribb

Wilkie Collins to the Forefront: Some Reassessments. Ed. by Nelson Smith and R. C. Terry. (AMS Studies in Nineteenth-Century Literature and Culture, 1) New York: AMS Press. 1995. xiv + 273 pp. $55.

The fifteen essays collected together in this volume do indeed bring Wilkie Collins 'to the forefront', a project that was crucial in 1989, when the Wilkie Collins Centennial Conference was held at the University of Victoria. Most of these papers originated in that conference, and their shared goal of taking Collins seriously as an artist is apparent. Since that time, however, a number of new books on Collins, and articles on aspects of his work, have appeared, making some of what appears in this volume seem redundant or outdated. That caveat aside, the volume comprises a thoughtful and intriguing reassessment of one of the period's most misunderstood and misread writers, one whom I am happy to see taken seriously and valued so highly.

The first four essays, by R. C. Terry, Catherine Peters, William M. Clarke, and Sue Lonoff, are primarily biographical, shedding light on Collins's relationships with women, especially, and with other writers and artists. Peters and Clarke have both written biographies of Collins, and Lonoff's book on Collins appeared in 1982; all four shed light on Collins's enigmatic private life, and they make interesting connections between Collins's life and work, especially as regards Collins's own need for privacy and concealment, and his repeated explorations in fiction of the threats to identity arising from such practices.

The essays by William M. Burgan (originally published in *Dickens Studies Annual* in 1987), Peter L. Caracciolo, and Barbara Fass Leavy all take up the question of allusions in and sources for specific Collins novels. Burgan and Caracciolo find, in Masonic symbolism and allusion to the *Arabian Nights*, respectively, evidence of a private 'erotic code' (p. 170) between Dickens and Collins embedded in Collins's novels. Leavy's article uncovers folkloric motifs in *The New Magdalen*; her argument, that Collins inverts certain familiar paradigms for his own ends, is particularly interesting and well-developed.

Essays focusing on specific issues raised in Collins's fiction include those by Barbara T. Gates (on suicide, originally published in *Dickens Studies Annual* in 1983), C. S. Wiesenthal (on hysteria in *Heart and Science*) and Kathleen O'Fallon (on gender roles). Wiesenthal's essay seems particularly subtle in its attention to Collins's problematic concerns with and for women; pre-Victorian conceptions of hysteria are central, she argues, to an understanding of 'science' and women in *Heart and Science*.

The remaining five essays share a concern with narrative and the narratological in Collins's fiction, from Ira B. Nadel's discussion of the interplay between text and illustration in several novels, to John R. Reed's new reading of *The Moonstone*. Nadel's reading of the frontispiece to *No Name* is particularly relevant to an understanding of Collins's deployment of suspense in the novel. Reed, whose 1973 essay on *The Moonstone* is a landmark of Collins criticism, deepens our understanding of the novel again in his essay 'The Stories of *The Moonstone*', which focuses on the interplay between Western 'love' and Eastern 'religious zeal' as two types of obsession. John Sutherland's essay is a sharp and thoughtful analysis of the relationship between sensation fiction (particularly in Collins's use of multiple narrators) and the legal uses of circumstantial evidence; these connections have recently been explored by Alexander Welsh in *Strong Representations: Narrative and Circumstantial Evidence in England* (Baltimore, MD: Johns Hopkins University Press, 1992) and one wishes that Sutherland's piece, like the rest of the volume, could have been available sooner after its conception. Peter Thoms's essay, an explication of plot and story as thematic as well as structural components of *The Woman in White*, nicely complements Christopher Kent's outstanding contribution to the collection; both are concerned with questions of freedom and truth in the novels. Kent's more unified argument perceptively argues for a thematics of contingency in Collins's work. His reading of Collins's understanding of contingency opens up for us the recognition that our Victorian ancestors were no less perceptive than we are in their understanding of the constructed nature of so much that goes by the name of 'reality'.

UNIVERSITY OF RICHMOND   ELISABETH ROSE GRUNER

The Ethnography of Manners: Hawthorne, James, Wharton. By NANCY BENTLEY. (Cambridge Studies in American Literature and Culture) Cambridge, New York, and Melbourne: Cambridge University Press. 1995. x + 242 pp. £35; $49.95.

Nancy Bentley's study of the subject of manners is concerned to reorientate our understanding of the novels of Hawthorne, James, and Wharton within a cultural nexus of interdependent disciplines and discourses designed to display the writers' 'enhanced authority over a bounded sphere of culture, an aesthetic and intellectual "ownership" of manners intended to surpass coarser forms of cultural possession' (p. 1). The texts which inform her literary as well as cultural critique are a range of works by Bronislaw Malinowski, Marcel Mauss, Thorstein Veblen, and Emile Durkheim, as well as E. B. Tylor's *Primitive Culture*, Matthew Arnold's *Culture and Anarchy*, and Charlotte Perkins Gilman's *Women and Economics* amongst others. The vexed question of the 'culture concept' (p. 3) is at the heart of the convergences traced between novel and ethnography; with the intercourse between fictional and non-fictional genres scrutinized as shaping and reflecting as well as encompassing the contradictions inherent in the idea of culture as anything other than 'an enabling myth' (p. 5).

Bentley's introductory chapter familiarizes us with the pleasures to be gained from the intersections of genre, many of which are illustrated through James's 1901 novel, *The Sacred Fount*, read as a scientific romance which is poised in an ambiguity designed to incorporate both decadence of style and of subject. Bentley constructs this novel as paradigmatic of the revision of manners in the fictional enterprises of all three writers whereby 'importing a figural primitivism from ethnography, the literature of manners serves to domesticate the forms of otherness that were increasingly difficult to shut out from view' (p. 20). The superficiality of the well-mannered restraint which distinguishes their work in the drawing room is exposed felicitously by a number of direct comparisons of ceremony and ritual between fiction and anthropology. The scene in Wharton's 1905 novel, *The House of Mirth*, where Bertha Dorset dismisses Lily Bart from her yacht becomes the 'chasing away' (p. 94) ceremony which Bronislaw Malinowski describes in *Crime and Punishment in Savage Society* (1926) as cleansing by expulsion; in *The Spoils of Poynton* 'James presents Fleda as a *tonga*, a piece of "feminine property," that creates the desired alliances' (p. 150); and, building on the anthropological language and tropes proffered explicitly by Wharton, the final dinner party in *The Age of Innocence* is examined in the light of Malinowski's formulation of the 'conditional curse', here invoked to warn Newland Archer of the fate of those who break tribal law. The 'euphemised violence' (p. 110) which Bentley locates in many of these scenes is explicated both as the 'curse' and the prohibition against overt resistance built into the silent regulations of tribal discipline; thus, the forms of social coercion which are invoked against offenders can only ever be implicit and inadmissable as provocation.

The individual texts which are the chief locations for Bentley's exhaustive negotiations between literary and cultural criticisms are Hawthorne's *The Marble Faun*, where the discussion focuses on anxieties surrounding postbellum conceptualizations of race in the culture, James's *The Spoils of Poynton*, viewed through property and exchange media, and Wharton's *The Custom of the Country*, considered in the context of the anthropology of womanhood where Undine Spragg's divorces are seen to 'signify only a surface temporizing within an emerging modern polyandry' (p. 207). In her chapter, 'Nathaniel Hawthorne and the Fetish of Race' Bentley advances the figure of the faun as precipitate between two worlds, intersecting the divide between romance and realism, with the capacity to express something of the vexed cultural complexities of matters of race in nineteenth-century America as an 'an entity poised "between the Real and the Fantastic"' (p. 25). It is perhaps in discussion of James, however, that Bentley's thesis comes most incisively to life as she anatomizes forms of violence in the Jamesian text, comparing the writing in *The Golden Bowl*, in a glancing reference which leaves one wishing for more, to the tone of 'lurid composure that characterizes ethnographies' (p. 92). Her analysis of *The Spoils of Poynton* is capacious, allusive, and enlightening, drawing the widest possible anthropological range of reference around the text in order to illustrate the means by which James estranges both aesthetics and manners in the construction of 'the war of property' (p. 135). Bentley's study is ambitious and complex but serves its subjects as well in close reading as in the range of reference to discourses and institutional models which are invoked as expressive of the conditions of cultural production in the late nineteenth century.

ROEHAMPTON INSTITUTE LONDON   JANET BEER

Mark Twain on the Loose: A Comic Writer and the American Self. By BRUCE MICHELSON. Amherst: University of Massachusetts Press. 1995. ix + 269 pp. £42.50 (paperbound £16.15).

'A foolish consistency is the hobgoblin of little minds', Emerson famously decreed, and the remark might well serve as the motto for Bruce Michelson's critical project here. His tone overall is modest and mannerly, yet he declares at the outset 'I have heresies to suggest about Mark Twain' (p. 3); and his principal heresy is the claim that Twain was throughout his writing life so continuously, carelessly, incurably inconsistent that the academic attempt to classify him, as other writers more readily may be classified, constitutes an essential misreading of the person who was Samuel Clemens and the body of work that was Mark Twain's. For Twain, as Michelson's title has it, was 'on the loose', a creature of the wild, obedient to no literary or intellectual or ethical authority; he was, in a fine concluding phrase, 'the best escape artist in the American canon' (p. 227), a loose cannon, indeed, forever threatening the composure of all and sundry categorizers.

Caught and tamed by twentieth-century schoolmen, how has Twain been presented to their students? As a humorist of course, a folk-tale-teller, an iconoclast, a satirist, a moralist, a humanist, a realist, and in old age a nihilist in sincere existential or metaphysical despair. Conducting his case by means of an orderly examination of virtually all Twain's principal writings, including works published posthumously, Michelson argues not that all or any of the above descriptions of him are wrong, but that they are right only if it is recognized that any one or other of them tells only part of the truth for only part of the time. Yes, sometimes Twain may have had a moral purpose, but often not; yes, he may often have had a realist literary programme, but sometimes not; yes, he was sincere, sometimes, or iconoclastic, but by no means always. Thus, with respect to Twain's greatest achievement, 'to sidestep the romantic anarchy of *Huckleberry Finn* is to enjoy only a part of the novel' (p. 97); thus, with regard to literary realism, 'if liberation from the thrall of romance proves a powerful strain in Mark Twain's work', just as strong is the desire to liberate 'the narrative from every doctrinal hold' (p. 113); thus, in the context of some well considered later writings, 'these far-fetched yarns we dignify as novels may be only yarns after all', without 'claim to moral authority' (p. 202). At the same time Michelson will not settle in any postmodernist language-based camp, for, differing from a fellow critic's view of *Huckleberry Finn*, he insists that 'the novel's anarchic resistance to categories extends even to the categorical definition of the self as a linguistic construct' (p. 250).

Occasionally espied as a protodadaist, occasionally glimpsed in the company of absurdist dramatists, Michelson's Twain is first and last a polymorphous platform comedian, whose 'penchant for anarchic humour' defies systematic analysis and whose work should be allowed to stay 'inherently wild' (p. 227), but not just a platform comedian, of course, for sometimes solemnly motivated, and wild, of course, only until labelled 'wild'. The 'phunny phellow' of the untutored public; Tom Sawyer's Island in Disneyland; 'America's greatest writer' of the popular press: all these are Mark Twain, as much as is the Twain of the academies who in turn — moralist, satirist, humanist — is every bit as real as the 'phunny phellow'. He is like America, so Michelson exults in a somewhat triumphalist finale; America and Twain as one, 'loud, crude, violent, chaotic, greedy, tormented [...] out to beat everything [...] incessantly reinventing [themselves], and trusting in headlong, vibrant improvisation to keep the darkness away' (p. 227).

University of Essex   R. W. (Herbie) Butterfield

The Family Saga in the South: Generations and Destinies. By Robert O. Stephens. (Southern Literary Studies) Baton Rouge and London: Louisiana State University Press. 1995. xii + 233 pp. £28.50.

Robert O. Stephens's account of the family saga novel in the South opens with Andrew Lytle's definition of the particular nature of the family as '*the* institution of Southern life' (p. 2) and, having once enumerated the generic features of the saga, the rest of this study is absorbed by the rehearsal of the plots of a number of different texts which demonstrate it to be 'a prototypal story with clearly recognized marking points and expectations' (p. 4). The defining features of the genre, as derived from the Book of Genesis, are outlined in the opening chapter and Stephens then proceeds to parade their manifestations in a range of Southern literary texts.

The work of the first author discussed, George Washington Cable, is capable of yielding most interest when considered in generic terms and Stephens examines the literary antecedents of his 1879 novel, *The Grandissimes*, in order to make a case for the uniquely Southern nature of the opportunity which presented itself to the novelist: to take up the family story and make it his own. The connection between the country estate and the pastoral tradition, the pre-eminent position in the neighbourhood of one family, the ties between lord, land, and people celebrated, for example, in the 'Country-House' poems of Jonson and Marvell — these were mediated to the Southern States via Washington Irving and William Alexander Caruthers, the last-named a practitioner in the Sir Walter Scott mode. In Stephens's estimation, however, it is Cable who brought the saga as genre to full fruition and, whilst his account of the plot of *The Grandissimes* gives full credit to Cable's attempt to face 'up to that significant fact about many southern families that made them different: there is also a black line running with the white, and the family saga has to recognise them both' (p. 28), there is very little by way of analysis of the narrative strategies Cable used to incorporate the 'black line' or of the response of the contemporary audience to this aspect of his work.

Stephens does include some useful observations on the practice of their craft by the novelists he chooses to discuss, Caroline Gordon, Allen Tate, William Faulkner, and Eudora Welty among them, and delineates the work of the otherwise forgotten T. S. Stribling as consolidating the work Cable had begun. Stephens makes connections between Stribling's work in the saga and that of Faulkner, to whom he

gives credit for reinventing the 'narrator-historian'; (p. 52) in *Absalom, Absalom!*
published in 1936, and also for exposing the indelibility of the 'black line'. A
separate chapter is devoted to 'The Black Family Saga in the South' and the
conditions of its coming of age in the mid-twentieth century are given a brief outline.
The novelists under consideration are Margaret Walker, Alex Haley, Ernest Gaines,
and Toni Morrison but the discussion fails to appraise the questions raised here and
elsewhere about the essential differences between white and black family sagas
rather than their contiguities; indeed, what might be considered as the inimicable
nature of the saga, as formulated here, to the story of the Southern black family is
not allowed to surface as a complicating issue. The route taken by Morrison into
'magical realism' (p. 163) in order to locate a position from which to communicate
a lineage for the black family is too briefly touched upon; the variations possible
within the genre are always given short shrift compared to the recurrence of
particular motifs or plots in the work of different writers. The version of the South
with which Stephens begins: 'It was family as institution which best expressed its
culture', is not one which is forced to reveal dysfunction.

ROEHAMPTON INSTITUTE LONDON   JANET BEER

Henry James and the Art of Nonfiction. By TONY TANNER. (Georgia Southern
    University, Jack N. and Addie D. Averitt Lecture Series, 4) Athens and
    London: University of Georgia Press. 1995. xiii + 92 pp. £19.95.

Published lectures generally come in solitary splendour or by the half dozen: three
make a slender gathering, modest in demeanour yet considerable in scope. The
negative 'Nonfiction' rebuffs easy acceptance, but Travel Writing, Criticism,
Autobiography urge fascination beyond the novels. Hearing two of these papers
before reading the volume sharpened the intrigue for me. The prose is composed
for voice and ear, dancing and crammed with figurative teasing (luscious, erotic,
preposterous) to tickle an audience; but the phrasing, the sentences, the span of the
argument demand sustained attention and repay study. For James, *pace* Barthes, 'in
literature assuredly criticism *is* the critic, just as art is the artist' (Tanner p. 27).
Tanner's practice is infected or in homage to that assurance (his book is dedicated
to two fellow-Jamesians, Agostino Lombardo and Sergio Perosa, who would
endorse the allegiance); in summary: 'Criticism is not, and cannot be, a theory. It is
an art' (p. 41).

    How then can criticism work, how reconcile basic curiosity with 'that respect for
the subject which [James] would be willing to name as *the* great sign of a painter of
the first order' (p. 53)? Asking questions, some rhetorical (p. 45), is one way:
demonstrably affirming and thus delimiting inquisitiveness. Allowing the subject his
own voice, in copious quotation, is another; attending both to what and how James
speaks or writes; noticing shifts or contradictions over time in the author's
assessment of other novelists as his own affiliation moved from realism beyond
romance towards what Tanner recognizes as a vision that is essentially modernist.
Yet another way is discriminating carefully between James's degrees of 'vagueness'
(p. 14) to show, from the travel writings for example, how the danger of 'omissions,
and ignorings, and avoidances' (p. 17) may be transmuted into a 'larger apprehension of the uniqueness of the place' (p. 16); scanning rich surfaces, whether
topographical, critical, or from the family history and that of *The American Scene*, but
with an eye to what lies beneath.

    It is this 'amusement, of social and sensual margin, overflow and by-play' (p. 18)
that Tanner's generous tribute to James permits him to explore: 'something behind

and beneath' which it would be a travesty to reduce to 'the sexual'. The comic, the entertaining, the cultural as well as the 'sensual' aspects of this underground and irregular torrent attract his attention. Power, pleasure, and patterns of repression contribute to the fullness of experience. Tanner spends a paragraph on James's appreciation of 'mist [. . .] fog [. . .] smoke' (p. 14) but two pages on the syntactically and semantically labile 'flush' (pp. 74–75), which as adjective, noun, transitive or intransitive verb, can burst from colour to form, 'the glowing and the flowing, with the rushing and the blushing, the flashing and the filling' (p. 75), finally 'to fit perfectly together, on the same metal plane, level with each other. Flush' (p. 75). It is a fertile term, not only for erotic suggestion but containment too: the tension of dramatic expression.

'Look for your pleasure in the differences' (pp. 3, 24) acts critically for Tanner as more than a procedural imperative: it is alluring and corrective. Though slim, this book is wonderfully inviting and encouraging.

University of Reading   Nicola Bradbury

Fictions of Power in English Literature: 1900–1950. By Lee Horsley. (Studies in Twentieth-Century Literature) London and New York: Longman. 1995. x + 300 pp. £40 (paperbound £15.99).

The idea of literature as autonomous misrepresents both the nature of culture and the ambition of many writers. This study engages with a range of modern British fiction-writers who, in the author's view, have directed their attention to issues of political power. Those discussed in some detail are Conrad, Chesterton, and Shaw (under the heading 'Narratives of Imperialism'); Buchan, Shaw, and D. H. Lawrence ('Narratives of Nationalistic Faith'); E. M. Hull, Lawrence, Huxley, Lewis, and Woolf ('Leaders and Lovers'); Household, Ambler, and Greene ('The Thirties Thriller'); Forster, Greene, Spender, and Koestler ('The Liberal Critique and the Totalitarian Nightmare'); Zamyatin, Wells, Huxley, and Orwell ('Dystopian Science Fiction'). This is an interesting range, including three plays, *The Man of Destiny, St. Joan,* and *Trial of a Judge,* among the novels which constitute the main material for discussion. The texts are generally well selected. Hull's *The Sheik* finds itself in exalted company, but in view of its popularity (as well as its disturbing sexual politics), it is appropriate to a consideration of images of male/female power relations in the fiction of the period; Horsley also makes the interesting point that although Lawrence gives a highly acute critical judgement on *The Sheik* in 'Surgery for the Novel — or a Bomb?' he 'uses many of the same fictional ingredients as the sensationalist romance' (p. 121) in later stories such as *The Plumed Serpent.* In contrast, we are given an account of the anti-patriarchal argument of *Three Guineas.*

A neat encompassing antithesis which Horsley recognizes as over-simplified but which remains useful, is given at the beginning of the introductory chapter, 'The Cult of Power'. Here we find Leonard Woolf in *Quack, Quack* in 1936 attacking Fascism as representative of an atavistic attitude to life based on 'superstition and magic' and appealing to 'primitive tribal instincts, fear, hatred' set against Lawrence in 'Reflections on the Death of a Porcupine' in 1925 asserting: 'Better to be a Russian and shoot oneself out of sheer terror of Peter the Great's displeasure, than to live like a well-to-do American and never know the mystery of Power at all.' The rest of this interesting book looks at some of the ways in which writers located themselves in relation to these attitudes, particularly after the First World War when the British Empire was ceasing to offer the outlets for masculine enterprise that it had done for the 'energetic and worthy men' summoned by Ruskin in his 1870

lecture. The discussion is organized chronologically, and ends neatly with Orwell in
The Road to Wigan Pier in 1937 pondering the paradox that 'all progress is seen to be
a struggle towards an objective which you hope and pray will never be achieved'
because its mechanical/bureaucratic nature will leave no room for adventure or
achievement. These issues do not lend themselves to simple conclusions, and
Horsley is content to leave the reader to relate her discussion to the world today in
which the attitudes deplored by Leonard Woolf are no less powerful and disturbing.

This is a clearly written and illuminating survey of the area, which shows a range
of mostly British writers engaging with material coming within the author's
definition of relevance. Horsley has some good discussions of specific texts, including
some neglected by other critics, but seems less interested in what might be thought
of as the unavoidable question: what implications are there for our view of writers
such as Joyce, or Woolf outside *Three Guineas*, if they are rightly omitted from a book
dealing with questions of power in twentieth-century writing? Finally, I have to
record my regret that the publishers have adopted the convention by which the
bibliography (though fortunately not the text) deprives titles of their capital letters,
and articles of their usual indicators.

UNIVERSITY OF EXETER   PETER FAULKNER

Women Editing Modernism: 'Little' Magazines & Literary History. By JAYNE E. MAREK.
   Lexington: University Press of Kentucky.   1996.   xi + 252 pp. $34.95
   (paperbound $14.95).

If one thing has marked the recent study of literary modernism it is the growing
awareness of gender as a determining force within it. Jayne E. Marek's book on
little magazines gives that awareness a distinctive edge, attending to the role of
women as editorial shapers of the new writing. Marek's chapters cover the most
important of these editors — Harriet Monroe and Alice Corbin Henderson (*Poetry*),
Margaret Anderson and Jane Heap (the *Little Review*), H. D. and Bryher (*Close Up*),
Marianne Moore (the *Dial*) — though, as she notes at the beginning of the book,
there are many others equally deserving of recognition: Kay Boyle, Emily Clark,
Caresse Crosby, Nancy Cunard, Jessie Fauset, Florence Gilliam, Maria Jolas, Amy
Lowell, Katherine Mansfield, Lola Ridge, Laura Riding, May Sinclair, Rebecca
West, Virginia Woolf. It is, to say the least, an impressive list, and one which
certainly undermines the conventional view of women's literary magazines as
merely targets for takeovers by the male writers who would then go on to produce
what we now think of as modernism. Pound, of course, is the swashbuckling hero or
villain of that particular narrative, and Marek devotes a chapter to his opportunism
and self-promotion. Perhaps significantly, this is not the best part of her book,
offering a rather one-dimensional view of Pound as egotist and authoritarian
(p. 182), riding roughshod over the intentions and feelings of his female editors.
That Pound frequently behaved in a cavalier and macho way is hardly news, and
one wishes that Marek had followed through the logic of her description to a deeper
level, telling us more about the gendered nature of the poetics Pound was advocating
in the pages of these magazines.

Marek is more original, because less simply polemical, in her account of Alice
Corbin Henderson's contribution to *Poetry*. Here the tensions and differences
between Henderson, Monroe, and Pound yield a lively sense of working relationships and of the competing forces of regionalism and cosmopolitanism that gave
Poetry its distinctive feel. So too, Marek's chapter on the *Little Review* gives us a timely
reminder of Jane Heap's formative involvement in the editorial policy of that

magazine and particularly of her influential promotion of avant-garde visual arts. While the discussion of H. D. and film seems a trifle thin and dependent on other critical accounts, Marek's exploration of Marianne Moore's critical diplomacy at the *Dial* stresses not only Moore's editorial achievements but also the characteristic sophistication of her manoeuvering. Here, as elsewhere, one may be reminded of the sheer difficulty of evaluating the work of an editor, so much of it behind the scenes, so little of it now preserved (Marek notes, for example, that only a few of Monroe's letters to Pound survive; while recipients tended to save his letters, 'Pound rarely returned the favor'). *Women Editing Modernism* does not solve all those problems but it does make a very effective case both for the shaping influence of these women and for continued study of the little magazine as a forcefield of literary modernism rather than merely its polemical vehicle.

UNIVERSITY OF SUSSEX

PETER NICHOLLS